KEEPING INDONESIA SAFE FROM THE COVID-19 PANDEMIC

The **Ministry of Finance of the Republic of Indonesia (MoF RI)** is the ministry responsible for Indonesia's finance and state assets. MoF RI is strongly committed to adopt sustainable and disciplined fiscal policy with three major functions for the economy: Growth & Distribution, Allocation and Stabilization. Amidst the pandemic, the latter function, with the expansion of the Indonesia's Government Annual Budget Deficit for countercyclical purposes had proven to be effective to return the economy back to the positive growth in 2021 without overheating inflation.

The **ISEAS – Yusof Ishak Institute** (formerly Institute of Southeast Asian Studies) is an autonomous organization established in 1968. It is a regional centre dedicated to the study of socio-political, security, and economic trends and developments in Southeast Asia and its wider geostrategic and economic environment. The Institute's research programmes are grouped under Regional Economic Studies (RES), Regional Strategic and Political Studies (RSPS), and Regional Social and Cultural Studies (RSCS). The Institute is also home to the ASEAN Studies Centre (ASC), the Singapore APEC Study Centre and the Temasek History Research Centre (THRC).

ISEAS Publishing, an established academic press, has issued more than 2,000 books and journals. It is the largest scholarly publisher of research about Southeast Asia from within the region. ISEAS Publishing works with many other academic and trade publishers and distributors to disseminate important research and analyses from and about Southeast Asia to the rest of the world.

KEEPING INDONESIA SAFE FROM THE COVID-19 PANDEMIC

Lessons Learnt from the National Economic Recovery Programme

Editors:
Sri Mulyani Indrawati
Suahasil Nazara
Titik Anas
Candra Fajri Ananda
Kiki Verico

NAGARA DANA RAKSA
MINISTRY OF FINANCE
REPUBLIC OF INDONESIA

ISEAS YUSOF ISHAK INSTITUTE

First published jointly in Singapore in 2022 by
ISEAS Publishing
30 Heng Mui Keng Terrace
Singapore 119614
E-mail: publish@iseas.edu.sg
Website: http://bookshop.iseas.edu.sg

and

Ministry of Finance of the Republic of Indonesia
Pusat Kontak Layanan Kemenkeu PRIME 134
Gedung Djuanda I
Jl. Dr. Wahidin Raya No. 1
Jakarta Pusat, DKI Jakarta 10710
Indonesia

ISEAS Library Cataloguing-in-Publication Data

Name(s): Indrawati, Sri Mulyani, 1962–, editor. | Nazara, Suahasil, editor. | Anas, Titik, editor. | Ananda, Candra Fajri, 1964–, editor. | Verico, Kiki, editor.
Title: Keeping Indonesia safe from the COVID-19 pandemic: lessons learnt from the National Economic Recovery Programme / editors, Sri Mulyani Indrawati, Suahasil Nazara, Titik Anas, Candra Fajri Ananda, Kiki Verico.
Description: Singapore : ISEAS-Yusof Ishak Institute, 2022. | Includes bibliographical references and index.
Identifiers: ISBN 9789815011609 (soft cover) | ISBN 9789815011623 (ebook PDF)
Subjects: LCSH: COVID-19 Pandemic, 2020-—Government policy—Indonesia. | COVID-19 Pandemic, 2020-—Economic aspects—Indonesia. | COVID-19 Pandemic, 2020-—Social aspects—Indonesia.
Classification: LCC HC450 H43K26

Book cover designed by Ministry of Finance of the Republic of Indonesia—Putri Indra Permatahati and Aditya Wirananda
Typeset by Superskill Graphics Pte Ltd
Indexed by Raffaie Nahar
Printed in Singapore by Mainland Press Pte Ltd

Contents

List of Figures

List of Tables

List of Boxes, Annexes and Appendixes

Acknowledgements

This book documents how Indonesia managed the economy during the COVID-19 pandemic. The book is written by policymakers and analysts involved in policy formulation during the pandemic, in collaboration with reputable non-government experts who closely follow the pandemic and its impacts. We would like to extend our highest appreciation to the contributors.

The book also benefits from extensive reviews provided by a distinguished panel of experts: Professor Budy P. Resosudarmo and Dr Arianto Patunru from the Australian National University; His Excellency Dr M. Chatib Basri, former Minister of Finance of Indonesia; Professor Arief Anshory Yusuf from Padjadjaran University; Dr David Nellor, Dr Rubino Sugana, Ms Roksana Khan and Dr Rullan Rinaldi from PROSPERA; Dr Reza Siregar, Senior Executive Vice President of the IFG Progress; Dr Daniel Suryadarma, Research Fellow at the Asian Development Bank Institute; Mr I Gede Putra Arsana, Senior Financial Sector Specialist of the World Bank; Dr Vivi Alatas, CEO of Asakreativita; Dr Yanuar Nugroho, Senior Adviser at the Center for Innovation Policy Governance; Dr Ariane Utomo from the University of Melbourne; Dr Pandu Riono from the University of Indonesia; Dr Risky Kusuma Hartono from STIKES Indonesia Maju; Mr Helmi Arman, Chief Economist of Citibank; Mr Astera Primanto Bhakti, Director General for Fiscal Balance of the Ministry of Finance; and Dr Andin Hadiyanto, Head of Financial Education and Training of the Ministry of Finance.

The book is edited and obtained direct supervision by Her Excellency Sri Mulyani Indrawati, PhD, Minister of Finance, and Professor Suahasil Nazara, Vice Minister of Finance, and received full administrative support from Mr Heru Pambudi, Secretary General of the Ministry of Finance.

We also would like to extend our gratitude to PROSPERA (Australia Indonesia Partnership for Economic Development) for its support.

Last but not least, we also would like to extend our appreciation to the technical support team: Mr Sugeng Wardoyo, Mr Abdul Aziz, Mr Anton Nugraha Sudarto, Mr Rangga Satya Negara, Mr Adry Dharmawan, Ms Bunga and Ms Nadia Febriana Muhidin.

Glossary

ABW	Activity-Based Workplace
ADB	Asian Development Bank
AFC	Asian Financial Crisis
AIDRAN	Australia-Indonesia Disability Research and Advocacy Network
ALZI	Alzheimer Indonesia
AMMS	Acceptability of Mental Health Mobile App Survey
APBD	Anggaran Pendapatan dan Belanja Daerah (Regional Budget)
APBN	Anggaran Pendapatan dan Belanja Negara (State Budget)
ARG	Anggaran Responsif Gender (Gender-Responsive Budget)
ASPD	Asistensi Sosial Penyandang Disabilitas (Social Assistance for People with Disability)
BAPPENAS	Badan Perencanaan dan Pembangunan Nasional (National Development Planning Agency)
BCP	Business Continuity Plan
BI	Bank Indonesia (Indonesia's Central Bank)
BLT Desa	Bantuan Langsung Tunai Dana Desa (Village Fund Direct Cash Assistance)
BNPB	Badan Nasional Penanggulangan Bencana (National Disaster Management Authority)
BOK	Bantuan Operasional Kesehatan (Health Operational Assistance)
BP	Bukan Pekerja (Non-Wage Worker)

BPJS Kesehatan	Badan Penyelenggara Jaminan Sosial Kesehatan (Social Security Agency for Health)
BPJS Ketenagakerjaan/ BPJAMSOSTEK	Badan Penyelenggara Jaminan Sosial Ketenagakerjaan (Social Security Agency for Employment
BPK	Badan Pemeriksa Keuangan (Audit Board of Indonesia)
BPKP	Badan Pengawasan Keuangan dan Pembangunan (Indonesia's National Government Internal Auditor)
BPNT	Bantuan Pangan Non Tunai (Non-Cash Food Assistance)
BPS	Badan Pusat Statistik (Statistics Indonesia)
BPTKLW	Bantuan Tunai untuk Pedagang Kaki Lima dan Warung (Cash Assistance for Street Vendors and Stall Owners)
BPUM	Bantuan Produktif Usaha Mikro (Productive Presidential Assistance for Micro Businesses)
BST	Bantuan Sosial Tunai (Cash Social Assistance)
BUKU	Bank Umum Kegiatan Usaha (Commercial Banks Classification Based on Business Activities)
C&E	Customs & Excise
CAD	Current Account Deficit
CBT	Climate Change Budget Tagging
CEISA	Customs and Excise Information System and Automation
CIO	Chief Information Officer
CIT	Corporate Income Tax
COVID-19	Coronavirus 2019
DAK	Dana Alokasi Khusus (Specific Allocation Fund)
DALY	Disability Adjusted Life Years
DAU	Dana Alokasi Umum (General Allocation Fund)
DBH	Dana Bagi Hasil (Revenue Sharing Fund)
DID	Dana Insentif Daerah (Regional Incentives Fund)
Dit P2MKJN	Direktorat Pencegahan dan Pengendalian Masalah Kesehatan Jiwa dan Napza (Directorate of Mental Health and Drugs Problem Prevention and Control)

DJBC	Direktorat Jenderal Bea & Cukai (Directorate General Customs & Excise)
DJP	Direktorat Jenderal Pajak (Directorate General of Taxes)
DPD	Dewan Perwakilan Daerah (The Regional Representative Council)
DPR	Dewan Perwakilan Rakyat (The People's Representative Council/Parliament)
DRM	Domestic Resources Mobilization
EA	Enterprise Architecture
ECEC	Pendidikan dan Pengasuhan Anak Usia Dini (Early Childhood Education and Care)
EoDB	Ease of Doing Business
EU	European Union
EUA	Emergency Use of Authorization
FAS	Free Alongside Ship
FGD	Focus Group Discussion
FWA	Flexible Working Arrangement
FWH	Flexible Working Hour
FWS	Flexible Working Space
G20	Group of Twenty
G2B	Government to Business
G2C	Government to Citizen
G2E	Government to Employee
G2G	Government to Government
GBD	Global Burden Disease
GDP	Gross Domestic Product
GDS	Government Debt Securities
GFC	Global Financial Crisis
GGGI	Indeks Kesenjangan Gender Global (Global Gender Gap Index)
GOI	Government of Indonesia
GRDP	Gross Regional Domestic Product
GS	Government Securities
GSO	Green Shoe Option
HCW	Health Care Worker
HI	Herfindahl Index
HIMPSI	Himpunan Psikologi Indonesia (The Association of Indonesian Psychology)

HKPD	Hubungan Keuangan antara Pemerintah Pusat dan Pemerintahan Daerah (Intergovernmental Fiscal Relation)
HPP	Harmonisasi Peraturan Perpajakan (Harmonized Tax Regulation)
HPV	Human Papilloma Virus
HSBC	Hongkong and Shanghai Banking Corporation
ICD	International Statistical Classification of Diseases and Related Health Problems
ICMA	The International Capital Market Association
ICT	Information and Communication Technology
IDR	Indonesia Rupiah
IIGF	Indonesia Infrastructure Guarantee Fund
IJP	Imbal Jasa Penjaminan (Guarantee Fee)
ILO	International Labor Organisation
IMF	International Monetary Fund
ISIC	International Standard Industrial Classification of All Economic Activities
IT	Information Technology
JKN	Jaminan Kesehatan Nasional (National Health Insurance; NHI)
J-PAL	The Abdul Latif Jameel Poverty Action Lab
JPY	Japanese Yen
KITE	Kemudahan Impor Tujuan Ekspor (Ease of Import for Export)
KLC2	Kemenkeu Learning Centre 2
Komnas Perempuan	Komisi Nasional Anti Kekerasan Terhadap Perempuan (National Commission on Violence Against Women)
KPPN	Kantor Pelayanan Perbendaraan Negara (State Treasury Payment Office)
KPR	Kredit Kepemilikan Rumah (House Ownership Loan)
KPSI	Komunitas Peduli Skizofrenia Indonesia (Indonesian Schizophrenia Care Community)
KSSK	Komite Stabilitas Sistem Keuangan (Financial System Stability Committee)
KUR	Kredit Usaha Rakyat (People's Business Credit; The Low Interest Rate Credit Programme)

LD UI	Lembaga Demografi (Demographic Institute), University of Indonesia
LEs	Large-sized Enterprises
LGST	Luxury Goods Sales Tax
LKPP	Laporan Keuangan Pemerintah Pusat (Central Government Financial Report)
LM	Liability Management
LPDB	Lembaga Pengelola Dana Bergulir (Revolving Fund Management Agency)
LPEM UI	Lembaga Penyelidikan Ekonomi dan Masyarakat, Universitas of Indonesia (Institute for Economic and Social Research–Faculty of Economics and Business, University of Indonesia)
LPS	Lembaga Penjamin Simpanan (Indonesia Deposit Insurance Corporation)
LS	Laporan Surveyor (Surveyor Reports)
MAHKOTA	Program Menuju Masyarakat Indonesia yang Kokoh dan Sejahtera (Towards a Strong and Prosperous Indonesian Society Programme)
MENA	Middle East and North Africa
MEs	Medium-sized Enterprises
MiEs	Micro-sized Enterprises
MoECRT	Ministry of Education and Culture, and Research and Technology
MoF	Ministry of Finance
MoH	Ministry of Health
MoM	Ministry of Manpower
MSMEs	Micro, Small and Medium-sized Enterprises
NIM	Net Interest Margin
NLE	National Logistics Ecosystems
NPL	Non-Performing Loan
NTT	Nusa Tenggara Timur (East Nusa Tenggara)
NWOW	New Ways of Working
OECD	Organisation for Economic Co-operation and Development
OJK	Otoritas Jasa Keuangan (Financial Services Authority)
P3B	Perjanjian Penghindaran Pajak Berganda (Tax Treaty)

PAD	Pendapatan Asli Daerah (Own Source Revenue)
PBPU	Pekerja Bukan Penerima Upah (Non-wage recipients)
PBS	Project-Based Sukuk
PCR	Polymerase Chain Reaction
PCV	Pneumococcal Conjugate Vaccine
PCPEN	Penananganan COVID-19 dan Pemulihan Ekonomi Nasional (COVID-19 Responses and National Economic Recovery Programme)
PEN	Pemulihan Ekonomi Nasional (National Economic Recovery Programme)
PERPPU	Peraturan Pemerintah Pengganti Undang-Undang (Government Regulation in lieu of Law)
PFM	Public Financial Management
PIT	Personal Income Tax
PKH	Program Keluarga Harapan (Family Hope Programme)
PKL	Pedagang Kaki Lima (Street Vendors)
PLM	Penyangga Likuiditas Makroprudensial (Macroprudential Liquidity Buffer)
PLN	Perusahaan Listrik Negara (State Electricity Company)
PMK	Peraturan Menteri Keuangan (Ministry of Finance Regulation)
PMN	Penyertaan Modal Negara (State Equity Participation)
PNM Mekaar	Program Permodalan Nasional Madani Membina Ekonomi Keluarga Sejahtera (Fostering a Prosperous Family Economy Programme)
PP	Peraturan Pemerintah (Government Regulation)
PPE	Personal Protective Equipment
PPh	Pajak Penghasilan (Income Tax)
PPKM	Pemberlakuan Pembatasan Kegiatan Masyarakat (Community Activities Restriction Enforcement)
PPP	Public-Private Partnership
PPP	Purchasing Power Parity
PROSPERA	Program Kemitraan Indonesia Australia untuk

	Perekonomian (Australia Indonesia Partnership for Economic Development)
PSBB	Pembatasan Sosial Berskala Besar (Large Scale Sosial Restrictions)
PSLD	Pusat Studi Layanan Disabilitas Universitas Brawijaya (Centre for Studies on Disability Services)
Puskesmas	Pusat Kesehatan Masyarakat (Public Healthcare)
QE	Quantitative Easing
RBTK	Reformasi Birokrasi & Transformasi Kelembagaan (Bureaucracy Reform and Institutional Transformation)
RT/RW	Rukun Tetangga/Rukun Warga (Community Group)
SAKTI	Sistem Aplikasi Keuangan Tingkat Instansi (Financial Application System for Agency)
SARS	Severe Acute Respiratory Syndrome
SAS	Special Access Scheme
SBN	Surat Berharga Negara (Government Securities)
SBSN	Surat Berharga Syariah Negara (Sharia Government Securities)
SDGs	Sustainable Development Goals
SEC	Securities and Exchange Commission
SEJIWA	Kesehatan Jiwa (Mental Health)
SEs	Small-sized Enterprises
SID	Single Investor Identification
SKB	Surat Keputusan Bersama (Joint Decree)
SMEs	Small and Medium-sized Enterprises
SOEs	State-owned Enterprises
SOP	Standard Operating Procedures
SPAN	Sistem Perbendaharaan & Anggaran Negara (State Budget & Treasury System)
SPBE	Sistem Pemerintahan Berbasis Elektronis (e-Government)
SSA	Sovereign, Supranational and Agency
SUN	Surat Utang Negara (Government Debt Securities)
SWR	Sukuk Waqaf Retail (Sukuk Waqf Retail)
TKDD	Transfer ke Daerah dan Dana Desa (Intergovernmental Transfer)

TNP2K	TNP2K (Tim Nasional Percepatan Penanggulangan Kemiskinan / National Team for Acceleration of Poverty Reduction)
Umi	Pembiayaan Ultra Mikro (Ultra-Micro Financing Program)
UNDP	United Nations Development Programme
UNESCAP	United Nations Economic and Social Commission for Asia and the Pacific
UNICEF	United Nations International Children's Emergency Fund
UU	Undang-Undang (Law)
UU HPP	Undang-Undang Harmonisasi Peraturan Perpajakan (Harmonized Tax Law)
VAT	Value Added Tax
WFH	Working From Home
YLD	Years Lived in Disability
YoY	Year on year

The Contributors

Editors

Sri Mulyani Indrawati, Minister of Finance of the Republic of Indonesia. She was awarded Finance Minister of the Year for East Asia Pacific from *Global Markets* magazine in recognition of her efforts in handling the COVID-19 pandemic in Indonesia. She earned a PhD in Economics, University of Illinois at Urbana-Champaign, USA, in 1992.

Suahasil Nazara, Vice Minister of Finance of the Republic Indonesia. He earned a Doctor of Philosophy (PhD) from the University of Illinois at Urbana-Champaign, USA. Professor Nazara has also been given a mandate by the President as Chair of the National Economic Recovery Task Force since March 2021 and is also trusted to be Deputy Chairperson of the Job Creation Law Task Force since May 2021.

Titik Anas, Special Adviser to the Minister of Finance of the Republic of Indonesia and Lecturer at Padjajaran University, Indonesia. Dr Anas holds a Doctoral degree from the Australian National University, Canberra.

Candra Fajri Ananda, Special Adviser to the Minister of Finance of the Republic of Indonesia in the field of Regional Fiscal Policy Formulation. He obtained a Doctoral degree from the Institute of Rural Development University of Göttingen, Germany.

Kiki Verico, Advisor for International Trade and Industry for the Finance Minister of the Republic of Indonesia, Senior Lecturer of International Economics in the Faculty of Economics and Business, University of Indonesia (FEB UI). He received a PhD in International Studies (International Economics) from Waseda University, Tokyo.

Chapter Contributors

Abdurohman, Head of Center for Macroeconomic Policy, Fiscal Policy Agency. He received the Australian Leadership Award (ALA) scholarship from the Government of Australia for his Doctoral degree and successfully completed his PhD degree from the Arndt-Corden Department of Economics, Australian National University, Canberra in 2013.

Latif Adam, Researcher at the Research Center for Macroeconomics and Finance, National Research and Innovation Agency (BRIN). He earned his PhD in Economics from the University of Queensland, Australia in 2007.

Mirza Adityaswara was an Expert of the Minister of Finance in the Financial Services Sector from January 2020 to May 2022. He earned a Bachelor of Economics from the University of Indonesia and Master of Applied Finance from Macquarie University, Sydney, Australia.

Rythia Afkar, Education Economist of the East Asia Pacific, World Bank, since 2016. She previously worked on research on poverty and social assistance with the Poverty Team in Indonesia. Rythia holds a Doctoral degree in Economics from the University of Bonn, Germany.

Luky Alfirman, Director General of Budget Financing and Risk Management. He earned a Doctor of Philosophy (PhD) in Economics from the University of Colorado, Boulder, USA, in 2004.

Riko Amir, Director of Strategy and Financing Portfolio, Ministry of Finance. He holds a Double Master's degree in 2005 at Bandung Institute of Technology (ITB) for the Urban and Regional Planning Programme and at Rijksuniversiteit Groningen, The Netherlands for the Environmental and Infrastructure Planning Programme.

Devina Anindita, Research Assistant at LPEM FEB UI. She completed her Bachelor's degree majoring in Economics with two concentrations: Public Sector Economics and Human Resource Economics at the Faculty of Economics, University of Indonesia.

Bondi Arifin, Policy Analyst at the Fiscal Policy Agency of the Ministry of Finance. He obtained a Master of Science (MSc) from Gadjah Mada

University and a Master of Arts (MA) and Doctor of Philosophy (PhD) in Economics from Georgia State University, Atlanta, USA.

Yon Arsal, Assistant to the Minister of Finance for Tax Compliance Affairs. He completed his PhD in Economics at Kobe University, Japan in 2007.

I Kadek Dian Sutrisna Artha, Chief Economist at PT Sarana Multi Infrastruktur (SMI). He received his PhD in Economics from Groningen University and wrote a dissertation on "Financial Crises: Impact on Central Bank Independence, Output, and Inflation".

Andry Asmoro, Chief Economist of Bank Mandiri since March 2019. Andry holds a Master's degree in Economics from Georgia State University, Atlanta, USA.

Bimbika Sijapati Basnett, Senior Adviser – Gender and Social Inclusion at PROSPERA (Australia Indonesia Partnership for Economic Development). She holds a PhD in Development Studies from the London School of Economics and Political Science, UK.

Masyita Crystallin, Special Adviser to the Minister of Finance for Fiscal Policy Formulation and Macroeconomics, with various experiences prior to joining the Ministry of Finance. Masyita earned a Doctorate in Economics from Claremont Graduate University, USA, with a specialization in International Monetary and Finance in 2015.

Calista Endrina Dewi, Researcher at LPEM FEB UI. She obtained a Bachelor's degree in Economics at the Department of Economics, Faculty of Economics and Business, Universitas Indonesia (FEB UI) in 2020.

Prasetya Dwicahya is working at GovTech Edu, where he led the launching of *Rapor Pendidikan* (education outcome monitoring platform) and SDS (*Sumber Daya Sekolah*, school financial management platform). He is also currently assuming COO role at Think Policy, a social enterprise that aims to nurture public leaders who champion evidence-based and empathy-driven policymaking.

Anton Gunawan, Lead Adviser on Economics, Finance, and Inclusion division at PROSPERA (Australia Indonesia Partnership for Economic

Development). He was also appointed a member of the Taxation Oversight Committee by the Minister of Finance of the Republic of Indonesia in December 2019.

Yadi Hadian, Head of Section of Disbursement and Reporting Village Fund Policy Formulation at the Directorate General of Fiscal Balance, Ministry of Finance of the Republic of Indonesia. He earned a PhD in Social Sciences from Flinders University, Australia in 2019.

Aktiva Primananda Hadiarta, Head of Instructional Activity Improvement and Development Unit, STAN Polytechnic of State Finance, Ministry of Finance. She earned a Master's degree in Economic Science at the Postgraduate Programme in Economics, University of Indonesia, in 2013.

R. Wiwin Istanti, Head of the Planning and Finance Bureau at the Secretariat General of the Ministry of Finance of the Republic of Indonesia. She earned a Master of Laws degree from Kyushu University, Japan in 2008.

Febrio Nathan Kacaribu, Head of the Fiscal Policy Agency. In 2014, he obtained a PhD from the University of Kansas, USA. His areas of expertise include Business Economics and Projection, Economic Models, Financial Economics, Monetary Economics, and Public Policy Analysis.

Nugraheni Kusumaningsih, Policy Analyst at National Budget Policy Center, Fiscal Policy Agency. She obtained a Master of Science and Master of Arts in Economics from Gadjah Mada University and the Andrew Young School of Policy Studies, Georgia State University, USA in 2013.

Irma Marlina, Policy Analyst at the Center for Budget Policy, Fiscal Policy Agency of the Ministry of Finance. She earned a Master of Science in Applied Mathematics (concentration in Actuarial Science) from University of Illinois at Urbana-Champaign, USA.

Irsyan Maududy, Analyst at the Centre for Budget Policy, Fiscal Policy Agency, Indonesia's Ministry of Finance. He holds a Bachelor in Economics from the University of Indonesia with a focus in Public Economics. During the COVID-19 pandemic, he joined the task force for COVID-19 Handling and National Economic Recovery in the Ministry of Finance.

Bobby A.A. Nazief, Special Adviser to the Minister at the Ministry of Finance of the Republic of Indonesia. He is also active as Senior Lecturer and Researcher at the Faculty of Computer Science, University of Indonesia. He holds a Doctoral degree in computer science from the University of Illinois at Urbana-Champaign, USA.

Yustinus Prastowo, Special Adviser to the Minister of Finance for Strategic Communication. Previously he was active as Executive Director of the Center for Indonesia Taxation Analysis (CITA), an independent tax study institution dedicated to mainstreaming issues related to tax policy.

Denni Puspa Purbasari, Executive Director at PMO Pra-Kerja. She earned her Bachelor's degree from Gadjah Mada University in 1997, Master's degree at the University of Illinois Urbana, USA in 2000, and PhD at the University of Colorado, Boulder, USA in 2006.

Raden Muhamad Purnagunawan, Lecturer in the Department of Economics, Padjadjaran University in West Java, Indonesia, and Researcher at the Center for Economics and Development Studies (CEDS), Padjadjaran University. He is also the Economic Capacity Improvement Policy Team Leader in the Secretariat of the National Team for the Acceleration of Poverty Reduction.

Ririn Salwa Purnamasari, Senior Economist with the World Bank's East Asia and Pacific Poverty and Equity Global Practice. She also serves as a Diversity, Equity, and Inclusion representative for the World Bank Indonesia Country Office. She holds a PhD in Economics from University of Melbourne, Australia.

Sri Kusumastuti Rahayu, Chief of the Social Protection Policy Team, Secretariat of Indonesia National Team for Acceleration of Poverty Reduction. She obtained her Master's degree in economics from North Carolina State University (NCSU), Raleigh, USA in 1993.

Mohamad Dian Revindo, Senior Research Associate at the Institute for Economic and Social Research, Faculty of Economics and Business, University of Indonesia (LPEM FEB UI) and Lecturer at the Graduate School of Strategic and Global Studies, University of Indonesia. He earned his PhD from Lincoln University, New Zealand.

Jahen Fachrul Rezki, Head of Macroeconomics and Political Economy Research Group at the Institute for Economic and Social Research, Faculty of Economics and Business, University of Indonesia (LPEM FEB UI) and Lecturer at the Faculty of Economics and Business, Universitas Indonesia. He received his PhD in Economics from the University of York, UK in 2019.

Deni Ridwan, Director of Government Debt Securities at the Directorate General of Financing and Risk Management, Ministry of Finance. He earned a Doctor of Philosophy (PhD) from Victoria University, Australia in 2014.

Usha Adelina Riyanto, Research Analyst for Gender and Social Inclusion at PROSPERA (Australia Indonesia Partnership for Economic Development). She holds a Master's degree in Development Economics and Policy from the University of Manchester, UK.

Arifin Rosid, Section Chief of Tax Policy Impact at the Directorate of Tax Potential, Compliance, and Revenue, Directorate General of Taxes. He is also Lecturer at the Faculty of Economics and Business, University of Indonesia. He completed his PhD in Taxation from School of Taxation and Business Law at the University of New South Wales, Sydney, Australia in 2017.

Elan Satriawan, Associate Professor in the Department of Economics, Universitas Gadjah Mada at Yogyakarta, Indonesia. He is also Chief of Policy Team, a high-profile policy think-tank under the National Team for the Acceleration of Poverty Reduction. He obtained his PhD from Michigan State University, USA in 2009.

Putut Hari Satyaka, Director of Budget for Human Development and Culture, Directorate General of Budget, Ministry of Finance. Prior to this position, he was the Director for Specific Transfer Fund, Directorate General of Fiscal Balance, Ministry of Finance. He also serves at Supervisory Board of Government Investment Center (PIP). He holds a Master's degree in Public Policy from the Australia National University, Canberra.

Chairina Hanum Siregar, Researcher at the Institute for Economic and Community Research, Faculty of Economics and Business, University of Indonesia (LPEM FEB UI). She earned a Bachelor's degree in Economics from Parahyangan Catholic University Bandung in 2007 and a Master's degree from the University of Indonesia in 2010.

Adiatma Y.M. Siregar, Director of the Center for Economics and Development Studies (CEDS), Lecturer and Researcher at the Department of Economics, Faculty of Economics and Business, Universitas Padjadjaran. He obtained his PhD in Health Economics from Radboud University Nijmegen, The Netherlands in 2014.

Romora Edward Sitorus, Head of Evaluation and Research at Project Management Office (PMO) of Kartu Prakerja, the Indonesian Coordinating Ministry for Economic Affairs. He received his PhD in Finance from Michael F. Price College of Business, University of Oklahoma, USA.

Suharti, Secretary General of Ministry of Education, Culture, Research, and Technology. She earned her Doctoral degree majoring in Demographic and Social Research Institute from the Australian National University, Canberra in 2013.

Yusuf A. M. Sujono, Private Sector Development Advisor at PROSPERA (Australia Indonesia Partnership for Economic Development). He earned his Master of Business Administration from Kellogg-HKUST Executive MBA Programme in 2019.

Sukaryo, Policy Analyst at the Directorate General of Taxes, Ministry of Finance Indonesia. He completed his Master of Public Policy degree from the London School of Economics and Political Science in 2020.

Sudarno Sumarto, Policy Adviser at the National Team for the Acceleration of Poverty Reduction (TNP2K), Office of the Vice President of the Republic of Indonesia. He holds an MA and a PhD, both in economics, from Vanderbilt University, USA.

Dewinta Illiana Sumartono, Economist in the Economic Research Division at PT Sarana Multi Infrastruktur. She received her Master's degree in Health Economics at Erasmus University in Rotterdam.

Suminto Sastrosuwito, Assistant Finance Minister for Financial Sector Policy and acting as Secretary of Financial System Stability Committee. He holds a Master's degree in Development Finance from Hiroshima

University, and a PhD degree in Economic Development from Ritsumeikan Asia Pacific University, Japan.

Sumiyati, Commissioner at Indonesia Financial Group and former Inspector General of the Ministry of Finance of the Republic of Indonesia.

Della Temenggung, Deputy Director for Advisory and Policy at PROSPERA (Australia Indonesia Partnership for Economic Development). She holds a PhD in Economics from the Australian National University. Della has been working in the areas of economic policy, private sector development, and international and development economics.

Florischa Ayu Tresnatri, Research Analyst for the Budget Policy Team at PROSPERA (Australia Indonesia Partnership for Economic Development). She holds a Master's degree in International and Development Economics from the Australian National University, and a Bachelor's degree in Industrial Engineering from Bandung Institute of Technology.

Wahyu Utomo, Head of the Center for State Revenue and Expenditure Policy. He earned his Bachelor of Social Sciences and Master of Development Economics from Gadjah Mada University in 2005.

Matthew Wai-Poi, Lead Economist for the Poverty and Equity Global Practice of the World Bank, Global Lead for the Distributional Impacts of Fiscal and Social Policies and co-editor of a recent flagship report updating two decades of experience in targeting social assistance to the poor and vulnerable. He has a PhD in Economics from Columbia University and degrees in Law and Business.

Eko Wicaksono, Policy Analyst at the Center for Macroeconomic Policy, Fiscal Policy Agency. He holds Master of Arts in Economics from Georgia State University, USA and Master of Science in Economics from Gadjah Mada University.

Dian Ayu Yustina, Department Head of Macroeconomics and Financial Market Research in Bank Mandiri since August 2020. Dian Ayu's expertise are macroeconomics, currency and bond analysis, and policy formulation. She holds a postgraduate degree in Economics and Finance from University of Queensland, Australia.

Foreword

Keeping Indonesia Safe from the COVID-19 Pandemic

Lessons Learnt from the National Economic Recovery Programme

Sri Mulyani Indrawati, PhD,
Minister of Finance of the Republic of Indonesia

> *"If the past is cut off, the future does not exist"* (Alexander Lowen). *This book shows us that past experiences were the best teacher to face the unprecedented global COVID-19 pandemic. We are trying to record every single step we took to absorb any economic impacts of the pandemic for the lessons learned to the next generations.*

1. BACKGROUND

The unprecedented COVID-19 virus became a global pandemic in 2020. Indonesia's first case of COVID-19 was found on 2 March 2020. The pandemic dramatically changed human life as all public places such as airports, seaports, train stations, bus stations, malls, shopping centres, roads, railways, restaurants, hotels, and movie theatres were suddenly closed. People work and pray from home, and students, teachers, and lecturers study from home. There were only essential activities that are exempted from mobility restrictions.

Changi Airport in Singapore, one of the busiest airports in the world, was suddenly empty. Jakarta, like other big cities in the world, suddenly changed from a high-density and traffic-jam metropolitan to an empty city with empty roads. The public crowd suddenly disappeared, and economic activities were just stopped and hibernated.

People have no memories of the global pandemic as the latest one was around one century ago, from 1918 to 1920, when the world faced a global pandemic of the H1N1 virus, well known as the Spanish flu, infecting around one-third of the world population. No prior reference can be used on how the COVID-19 pandemic will end. The only vivid figures that people can imagine about the end of the pandemic were taken from the movies that displayed the global pandemic, such as *Outbreak* (1995), *Quarantine* (2008), *Black Death* (2010), *Contagion* (2011), *Flu* (2013), and *Infection* (2019). At the very least, these movies gave optimism that the pandemic is bearable and can be cured.

The real game changer in the global COVID-19 pandemic is vaccine production that can be publicly available within one year. It is an extra-ordinary outcome as it usually takes more than five years to make the vaccine available for public use.

2. IMMEDIATE GOVERNMENT RESPONSE

The COVID-19 global pandemic that has changed human life dramatically made governments all around the world alter existing policies to combat the pandemic. Some governments decided on hard-core lockdown. Some others applied the so-called 3T of Tracing, Tracking, and Treatment, while others implemented conditional people mobility by region based on positivity rates. Indonesia adopted conditional people mobility complemented with 3T policies.

The impact of the COVID-19 global pandemic on the economy is similar to the impact of the Spanish flu one hundred years ago. The pandemic resulted in lower aggregate demand from consumption and investment. With the contraction in consumption and investment, the government must come to the rescue to compensate for the decline. However, the pandemic also hit the government revenue from taxes and non-tax as economic activities slowed. With the government expenditure expected to increase to cushion the economy from the shock, given the decline in revenue, the government budget deficit is expected to soar.

Allowing the deficit beyond the mandated threshold can be dangerous for the economy. A prudent and accountable fiscal management needs to be established. Empirical evidence in this book showed that the increased budget deficit was effective as the fiscal discipline was already established for several years before the government budget deficit expanded above 3 per cent of the GDP. The fiscal discipline has generated positive outcomes on the output gap that economic growth is consistently higher than the inflation rate with a continuous decrease in the open unemployment rate, poverty rate, and income inequality.

3. FUNDAMENTAL FISCAL POLICY RESPONSE: PRUDENT COUNTERCYCLICAL

Indonesian fiscal policy follows the principle: *during positive economic growth, it is maintained to be not crowding out, while during negative economic growth, it must be countercyclical*. The latter is temporary and depends on the economic recovery cycle. Therefore, in the policy responses designed to handle the COVID-19 pandemic and its impact, as outlined in Law No. 2/2020, the Government of Indonesia adopted a countercyclical fiscal policy for a limited period only, designed for three years, from 2020 to 2022.

Political economic theory explains that whenever a government faces a crisis, it might have to make emergency and extraordinary policies that can swing between discretion and rule-based ones. When the global pandemic of COVID-19 finally hit Indonesia in March 2020, the Government of Indonesia had to make quick yet effective policy responses, which can be discretionary but also has to be rule-based at the same time.

The government, after evaluating the situation and the pandemic's possible impact, made a fundamental decision to expand the annual budget deficit above 3 per cent of GDP for three years before returning to below 3 per cent of GDP in 2023. This three-year time frame had been chosen based on at least three considerations: a lesson from the Spanish flu time frame, the trust in technological advancement to produce the vaccine or medicine within three years, and the political-economic outlook before the next presidential election in 2024. Allowing an annual budget deficit above 3 per cent is discretionary in nature but framed under the rule of law—Law No. 2/2020.

The unprecedented COVID-19 pandemic had also changed Indonesia's established institutional, political and economic arrangement into a totally different one that can be labelled an "extraordinary" process, mostly against existing practice. The pandemic required changing political relations within government institutions, across government institutions, and with the parliament. As a democratic country, the process of enacting legislation is complex that the government has to obtain legal approval from the parliament, be supervised by the Audit Board of Indonesia (*Badan Pemeriksa Keuangan*), General Attorney (*Kejaksaan Agung*), and the Corruption Eradication Commission (*Komisi Pemberantasan Korupsi*). This book discusses the dynamics on the ground when the government seeks political and legal support for enlarging the annual budget deficit for countercyclical.

In handling the pandemic, Indonesia's government aimed to keep the COVID-19 pandemic contained so it did not become economic and financial problems. We consider the best panacea to cure the health and low-demand problems is activating the role of countercyclical fiscal policy. Unlike the shock in aggregate supply, indicated by negative economic growth and hyperinflation, the global pandemic also hit aggregate demand. It then created a significant distinctiveness of a low inflation rate with negative economic growth. The first involves a moral hazard that requires structural reform, while the latter is a kind of liquidity trap that needs a countercyclical government budget deficit.

This countercyclical fiscal requires a healthy fiscal condition because the budget must be enlarged and the budget deficit exceeding the 3 per cent cap. The budget deficit reached –6.34 per cent in 2020, –5.7 per cent in 2021 and –4.85 per cent in 2022. The increasing budget deficit will need financing in the near future. The source of financing requires mixed macroeconomic policies, one of which comes from the central bank's support. From the regional perspective, the local government is also expected to be able to move quickly and act out of the box in the midst of a pandemic. For this reason, the central government encourages the reallocation and refocusing of the budget from Transfers to Regions and Village Funds (TKDD) as an effort to support healthcare, social safety nets, and economic recovery as well as for COVID-19 vaccinations and incentives for health workers from the budget perspective. In addition, through the Special Mission Vehicle (SMV) of the Ministry of Finance, the Government prepared a loan scheme for local governments as part of the National Economic Recovery (PEN) Programme to anticipate regional government budget limitations.

4. MIX MACROECONOMIC POLICIES: FISCAL AND MONETARY COLLABORATION

When designing the macroeconomic policy mix to respond to the pandemic, the policymakers benefited from the playbooks that Indonesia had from the previous crises: the 1998 Asian Financial Crises (AFC) and the 2008 Global Financial Crisis (GFC). The first crisis left Playbook One as its footprint, and the second left Playbook Two as legacies. Playbook One gave significant reforms to the independence of the central bank (Bank Indonesia, BI) and the establishment of the Deposit Insurance Corporation (*Lembaga Penjamin Simpanan,* LPS).

Fast forward to designing the pandemic policy response, policymakers faced a dilemma of soaring financing needs to finance the budget deficit and the less favourable sovereign bonds market. To finance the deficit, the government asked for the central bank's support to share the burden of the financing cost. The framework was reflected in the SKB (*Surat Keputusan Bersama*) I on 16 April 2020, as the first joint decree between the Ministry of Finance and BI, in which BI acted as a "standby buyer" of the government bonds, SKB II and SKB III for the burden sharing.

Reflecting on Playbook Two from the 2008 GFC which gave birth to the Financial Services Authority (*Otoritas Jasa Keuangan,* OJK), it is important to note that the policy responses during the pandemic were made possible by the existence of the authority. During the pandemic, OJK closely monitored the condition of financial institutions. Prudent, calculated measures and close collaboration between BI, OJK, and LPS under the Financial Sector Stability Committee (*Komite Stabilitas Sektor Keuangan,* KSSK) chaired by the Minister of Finance prevented LPS and OJK from utilizing their economic crisis protocol in 2020 and 2021. The government's ability to isolate the COVID-19 global pandemic as public health crisis with prudent countercyclical policy protected Indonesia's economy from stagflation and financial crises.

In turn, this global COVID-19 pandemic provided Indonesia with Playbook Three outlining policy responses to contain the pandemic and guide the economy out of the crisis, which will be very important for Indonesia and other countries to face future pandemics. Amidst the global pandemic, in 2020 and 2021, Indonesia's economy successfully returned to the pre-pandemic level and entered positive economic growth with annual growth with a relatively low inflation rate. Both indicators generated a stable nominal exchange rate which is important for BI. These achievements would not be there without solid cooperation between the Ministry of Finance and BI and strong support from the OJK and LPS.

5. CONCLUSION

The global pandemic hit Indonesia in early 2020, decreasing its annual economic growth from 2.97 per cent in the first quarter to –5.3 per cent in the second quarter and increasing open unemployment from around 5 per cent to 7 per cent in the second quarter within only six months. The poverty rate increased to more than 10 per cent and the inequality increased as indicated by the increase in the Gini ratio, from 0.380 to 0.385.

Nevertheless, with relentless efforts and appropriate required policies, the Government of Indonesia's countercyclical fiscal policy, with support from the central bank, rode the wave and returned to positive economic growth with a stable annual inflation rate in 2021. The outcomes were back to the pre-pandemic level with a non-inflationary growth pattern. Indonesia had returned to the upper middle-income country status as of the pre-pandemic level of 2019.

The annual economic growth has recovered from –2.1 per cent (2020) to 3.7 per cent (2021), while the annual inflation rate (CPI) was stable, increased stable, and low from 1.7 per cent to 1.9 per cent. This magnificent achievement is consistent with other outcome indicators. The open unemployment rate decreased from 7.1 per cent in August 2020 to 6.5 per cent in August 2021. The Gini ratio in 2021 was 0.381, which returned very close to the 2019 level at 0.380. The 2021 poverty rate had returned to below 10 per cent of the population, that is, 9.7 per cent.

In addition to government efforts like aggregate supply side problems in the AFC 1998 and GFC 2008, at any time Indonesia's economy faced economic crises, including the aggregate demand challenges, Indonesia's Current Account somehow turned to a surplus and compensated for other macroeconomic variables. These experiences humbly reminded us of *Ora et*

Labora (Pray and Work). We indeed understand that economic equilibrium is arranged by the Invisible Hand and not over human efforts per se.

Finally, this book is about something worth reading—the effective policy known as the National Economic Recovery Programme (*Program Pemulihan Ekonomi Nasional*, or PEN), which the Government of Indonesia did something worth writing. This book records and provides readers with various lessons learnt on how Indonesia navigated the first two years of the global COVID-19 pandemic.

PART I

Health Shock

1

Keeping Indonesia Safe during the Pandemic 2020–21

Sri Mulyani Indrawati, Suahasil Nazara, Titik Anas, Candra Fajri Ananda and Kiki Verico

"Either write something worth reading or do something worth writing (Benjamin Franklin)"

This book is writing something worth reading about the effective policy known as Program Pemulihan Ekonomi (PEN) of Indonesia in 2020 and 2021

1.1 SETTING THE SCENE

The World Health Organization (WHO) detected cases of "viral pneumonia" in Wuhan city in the People's Republic of China on 31 December 2019. The virus was later named COVID-19 (World Health Organization 2022). In January 2020, several countries reported their first cases of COVID-19, including Thailand on 13 January 2020, Japan on 15 January 2020, France on 21 January 2020, and the United States on 24 January 2020. At that time, Indonesia had not yet found any cases although the screening and preparedness to detect the virus had been in place, including the installation of thermal scanners at major airports and the appointment of more than a hundred COVID-19 hospitals. Indonesia had also imposed international travel restrictions from 1 January 2020, temporarily suspended all flights connecting Indonesia and China and imports of live animal products from China. The first cases of COVID-19 in Indonesia were detected and reported on 2 March 2020.

WHO and the Chinese health authorities closely studied the virus from its first discovery. On 24 February 2020, the WHO-China mission on COVID-19 reported the main findings of their mission and highlighted the importance of large-scale implementation of non-pharmaceutical public health measures, COVID-19 case detection and isolation, contact tracing and monitoring/quarantining as well as community engagement to control the COVID-19 transmission and reduce illness and death resulting from the COVID-19 infection (World Health Organization 2022). WHO declared COVID-19 as a pandemic on 11 March 2020 and regularly updated the COVID-19 situation and recommended measures to address the pandemic and mobilized resources on a global scale to handle the pandemic.

Many countries began to close their borders and implemented the measures recommended by WHO, including lockdowns. China took more extreme measures than what was recommended by WHO, locking down the city of Wuhan and other cities in Hubei province on 23 January 2020, to quarantine the centre of the COVID-19 outbreak. Indonesia introduced social distancing, namely the Work, Study, and Worship at Home policy, on 16 March 2020, and implemented large-scale social restrictions (*Pembatasan Sosial Berskala Besar*, or PSBB) on 10 April 2020 in Jakarta Province, the epicentre of COVID-19 in Indonesia. The social distancing measures continued with many different names and different stringency levels following the increase in case numbers.

Figure 1.1 shows the timeline of the escalation of the COVID-19 cases since December 2020. With vaccination not yet developed, the combination of speed of the transmission and mutation of the virus and unpreparedness of the society resulted in an increasing number of cases and fatalities during 2020 and early 2021. With vaccination, the fatality rate significantly subsided in the later period of 2021. Although the highest transmission rate occurred due to the Omicron variant of COVID-19 at the end of 2021, the fatality rate was very low.

The COVID-19 pandemic was not only about health issues. The catastrophic economic and social crisis worldwide has also changed the

FIGURE 1.1
COVID-19 Pandemic, 2020–21

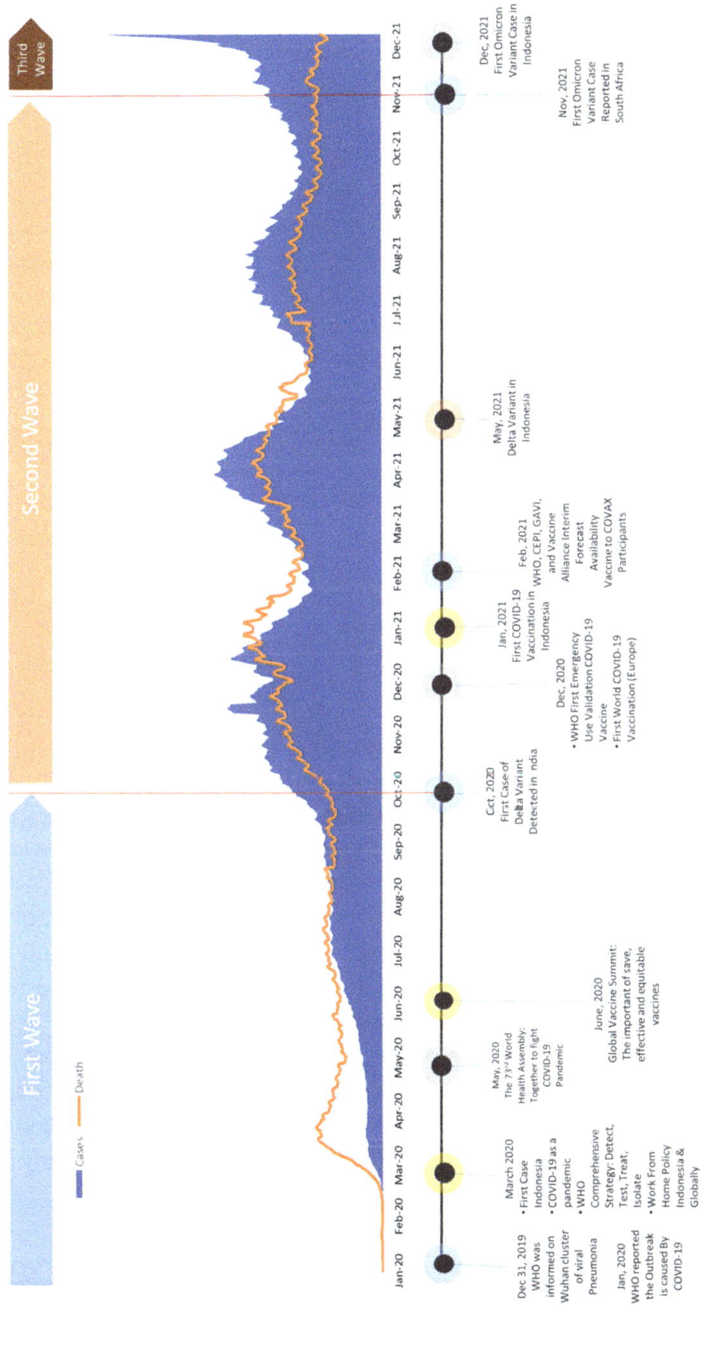

way people live in a significant way. The outbreak and the implementation of social restrictions worldwide resulted in a reduction in economic activity by many consumers and producers, including corporate and banking stress (Siregar, Gunawan, and Saputro 2021), massive unemployment (Petrosky-Nadeau and Valletta 2020; Şahin, Tasci, and Yan 2020), global supply chain disruption (Deconinck, Avery, and Jackson 2020), and learning loss due to disruption of the education system (Donnelly and Patrinos 2021). This unprecedented combination of adverse shocks caused deep recessions in economies worldwide (World Bank 2020), including Indonesia (Gibson and Olivia 2020; Suryahadi, Al Izzati, and Yumna 2021). Global economies contracted by 3.1 per cent in 2020 in contrast to earlier growth forecasts of 3.3 per cent (IMF 2020, 2022). Indonesia experienced an economic contraction of 2.07 per cent in 2020 in contrast to the 5.3 per cent target in the 2020 budget (MoF 2020) and increased open unemployment from around 5 per cent to 7.07 per cent or about 9.77 million in 2020. The poverty rate also increased to more than 10 per cent, the Gini ratio rose from 0.380 to 0.385 (BPS 2021).

Countries around the world provided sizeable fiscal support in response to the pandemic. Indonesia's fiscal response to COVID-19 was modified according to developments at both global and national levels. In January 2020, the fiscal policy adopted was in response to COVID-19 and refocused and reallocated government spending to handle COVID-19 with modest stimulus of IDR8.5 trillion (Stimulus I) to protect the poor and vulnerable and to support the negatively impacted sectors followed by another stimulus of IDR22.5 trillion (Stimulus II) for business support including fiscal incentives and trade facilitation (MoF 2021).

In line with central government's budget policy, the intergovernmental transfer (*Transfer ke Daerah dan Dana Desa*, or TKDD) and regional budget policy were also modified. During the pandemic, the TKDD and regional budget policy focused and reallocated on handling the health and economic impacts of the COVID-19 pandemic. For instance, the requirements for the distribution and use of some TKDD funds, such as the Revenue Sharing Fund (*Dana Bagi Hasil*, or DBH), the General Allocation Fund (*Dana Alokasi Umum*, or DAU), and the Regional Incentive Fund (*Dana Insentif Daerah*, or DID) have been simplified since the pandemic began in Indonesia. It aims to ease the handling of the pandemic in the regional.

As soon as the first case of COVID-19 was declared in Indonesia, the Indonesian Financial System Stability Committee (*Komite Stabilitas Sistem Keuangan*, or KSSK)—comprising of the Ministry of Finance, the Indonesian

Central Bank (Bank Indonesia, or BI), the Indonesian Financial Sector Authority (*Otoritas Jasa Keuangan*, or OJK), and the Indonesian Deposit Insurance Corporation (*Lembaga Penjaminan Simpanan*, or LPS)—started to seek projections about what is going to happen with the economy. The global pandemic hit Indonesia in early 2020, decreasing its annual economic growth from 2.97 per cent in the first quarter to –5.3 per cent in the second quarter (BPS 2021).

A pressing issue at that time was the fact that there are no economic models to use, as COVID-19 was unprecedented. There is no relationship that can be established from past data, for example, number of infections and people's mobility and economic activity. Nevertheless, on one afternoon in March 2020, the above four agencies sat and discussed the projection, which was a bit closer to (educated) guesses.

With the worsening global and domestic economic indicators posing a risk to the financial system stability, the KSSK, chaired by the Minister of Finance, drafted a more comprehensive intervention package, a combination of fiscal, monetary and financial sector policy interventions which was later on 31 March 2020 enacted as Government Regulation Number 1 Year 2020 in Lieu of Law of the Republic of Indonesia Concerning State Financial Policy and Financial System Stability to Control Corona Virus Disease 2019 (COVID-19) Pandemic and/or in Response to Dangerous Threats to the National Economy and/or the Stability of the Financial System (referred to as PERPU 1/2020 in this book).

PERPU 1/2020 provided the legal basis for the National Economic Recovery Programme (*Program Pemulihan Ekonomi Nasional*, or PEN). PEN contained the essence of a stability function that was temporary or ad hoc where the programme being trimmed and finished once the economy recovered, the market and real sector returned to normal.

One of the important results of the solid synergy between the government and the agencies mentioned above is the implementation of the burden-sharing programme. This programme was implemented between the Ministry of Finance and BI due to the drastically increasing budget deficit for handling the pandemic and economic recovery. Based on PERPU 1/2020, Bank Indonesia is allowed to buy government bonds (*Surat Utang Negara*, or SUN, and *Surat Berharga Syariah Negara*, or SBSN) in the primary market. This is very important in providing financial certainty at low costs for the government in the midst of high volatility in the financial market at that time.

1.2 THE NATIONAL ECONOMIC RECOVERY PROGRAMME (PEN) POLICY FRAMEWORK

Before the pandemic, the Government of Indonesia adopted regularity in its planning process, with the five-year medium-term plan set within the long-term twenty-five-year plan. The fiscal policy followed the regularity of the national planning process. The annual government budget was designed and implemented in accordance with the medium- and long-term plans.

The 2020 government budget was already designed and approved by the Parliament in 2019. According to the law, changes to the approved budget require the Parliament's approval. The fiscal policy before the pandemic was disciplined within the mandatory fiscal deficit below 3 per cent of GDP. In 2019, the budget deficit was as low as 1.84 per cent of GDP, the lowest since 2013 (MoF 2019). The 2020 fiscal deficit was planned to be at 1.76 per cent of GDP (MoF 2020).

The uncertainties resulting from the COVID-19 pandemic require new way of governance as the regularity is no longer compatible to the new circumstances. With the projected extraordinary socio-economic impact of the COVID-19, the Ministry of Finance understood that the role of government is pivotal in the economics of the pandemic. When the consumption, investment and export (and import) were paralysed, the government expenditure becomes the only game in town. The government budget serves as cushions for not allowing the national output to slide down even further. The new circumstances require the fiscal policy to be flexible, responsive and adaptive at the same time.

Fiscal policy has three main functions: allocation, distribution, and stabilization. Each part may be mixed to achieve the primary objective of accelerating economic growth while keeping the inflation rate stable or simply, a stable economic growth. In normal situation, fiscal policy should keep market mechanisms properly working to avoid the so-called "crowding-out". This is known as fiscal discipline. The Government of Indonesia's budgetary disciplines before the arrival of the global pandemic were Indonesia's most advantageous factors supporting the government's budget deficit expansion above 3 per cent of GDP from 2020 to 2022.

PERPU 1/2020 provides flexibility for the fiscal authority to tackle the pandemic and its subsequent impact, and together with the OJK's financial sector relaxation, served as the basis for managing the economy, protecting the people towards economic recovery. The critical economic situation, as projected by KSSK at that time, provided justification for the government to issue the PERPU which was later legislated as Law Number 2, 2020 by the Parliament on 1 May 2020.

With PERPU 1/2020 as a legal basis, the government could quickly revise the 2020 budget to allow fiscal supports for the pandemic management, larger social protection to the poor and vulnerable, and greater supports to micro and small enterprises. In 2020, the budget was revised twice to allow budget reallocation and automatic adjustment without going through the parliamentary approval process which takes time. Nevertheless, the government always kept the Parliament informed of the planned budget revisions. With PERPU 1/2020, the OJK was also allowed to undertake necessary policies to support loan restructuring, and BI was allowed to purchase government bonds in the primary market. It is indeed a breakthrough in the fiscal-monetary policy coordination in Indonesia.

1.3 ABOUT THIS BOOK

The stabilization function of the fiscal policy is super relevant and vital when the economy is facing an economic crisis at the time when economic growth is negative, regardless of whether the inflation rate is skyrocketing (hyperinflation or stagflation) or plunging (low inflation rate or liquidity trap alike). In any economic crisis, the most dominant function is stabilization. This book assesses the impact of the pandemic and evaluates the effectiveness of fiscal stabilization in Indonesia amidst the global pandemic in 2020 and 2021.

It assesses the impact of the pandemic and evaluates the effectiveness of PEN, a countercyclical fiscal policy implemented in Indonesia during 2020–21. The challenge for fiscal policymakers during the pandemic was the need to design appropriate, agile and effective fiscal policies to support the economy that was projected to be very turbulent, leading to stagnation in the real sector and market mechanisms. Both the effectiveness of fiscal allocations and distribution function reform would affect the success of the fiscal stabilization function. This book is unique as it was jointly written by policymakers involved in the decision-making process and policy implementation, and independent analysts who evaluated the impact of the programmes.

The book discusses policy impacts and outcomes as revealed by several independent surveys and studies. The book begins with a chapter discussing the health aspect of COVID-19 and how the government, through the PEN programme addressed the health crisis. It is followed by four chapters in Part II addressing macroeconomic, monetary and financial sector developments as well as the institutional challenges faced in order to achieve a more flexible fiscal policy. Part III continues with the discussion on the revenue side challenges of the fiscal policy, followed by discussions on debt financing of the increased fiscal deficit. The next 2 parts discuss the expenditure side of the fiscal policy, with Part IV covering expenditure to protect people, and Part V on expenditure to support businesses. The regional dimension of the pandemic, how local governments handled the health crisis and its impact are discussed in Part VI as decentralization is an important element of economic development in Indonesia. As the pandemic triggered a new way of working, the final Part VII discusses the pandemic-induced bureaucratic reform.

The chapters in this book discuss the lessons learnt and include discussions about the challenges such as lack of data and inclusion-exclusion error, policy scenarios, the chosen policy, and its output details, as well as the timeline explanation. The book then concludes with a self-critique, discussing the pros and cons of actions taken, factual-counterfactual approach, and study limitation description.

We argue that there are no perfect policies. Even if the best policies are implemented, there must be side effects. This book explains the side effects of the policies based on field research findings. It applies a post-factum perspective to assess the effectiveness of the related response policies made during the early pandemic, known as ex-ante policies.

In the long run, it shows that industrialization remains the game-changer, which explains why in 2021, the GDP per capita in US dollar, poverty rate and the Gini ratio returned to the pre-pandemic trajectory. In the short run, the PMI index (manufacture) as the aggregate supply-side proxy, in the third quarter of 2021 (Year-on-Year) has had a quicker recovery than consumption (CC Index) as the aggregate demand proxy. Thus, significantly improving the manufacturing sector with significant economic growth is vital. However, investigating this transformation is beyond the scope of this book.

In the short run, as shown in Figure 1.2, annual economic growth (AG) has recovered from –2.1 per cent (2020) to 3.7 per cent (2021), while

FIGURE 1.2
Indonesia's Economic Recovery Pattern (Total Real Growth, Inflation Rate and Real Manufacturing Growth)

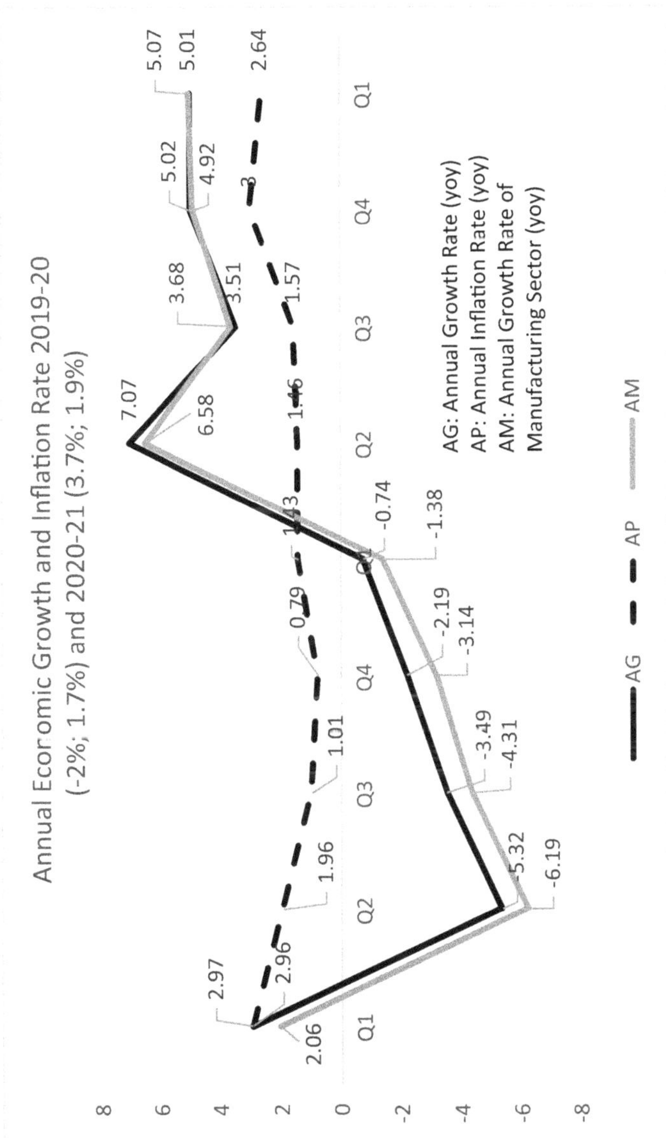

Source: Authors' own illustration, BRS BPS (2022).

the annual inflation rate (AP) remained between 1.7 per cent (2020) and 1.9 per cent (2021). This pattern indicated that actual output had returned to levels attained in the last five years. The open unemployment rate has decreased from 7.1 per cent in August 2020 to 6.5 per cent in August 2021. The Gini ratio in 2021 was 0.381 and has very nearly returned to the 2019 level of 0.380. The poverty rate has returned to below 10 per cent of the population at 9.7 per cent. Indonesia's economic status has returned to the classification of upper-middle income country with higher than US$4,046 in contrast to its 2020 classification as lower middle-income level because of the global pandemic.

Indonesia's achievement during the pandemic was relatively better than most countries as it avoided stagflation and took only one year to recover. However, Indonesia continues to face structural and long-term manufacturing sector issues that were confirmed not only during normal times but also during the pandemic. The sector recovery was already falling behind other sectors, as seen from the lower level of the grey line which represents manufacturing growth compared to the black line of total economic growth in Figure 1.2. As argued, manufacturing remains a game-changer in Indonesia's economy as it connects both sources of economic growth of foreign direct investment (FDI) inflows and net export as well as short-run investments.

1.4 CHAPTER SYNTHESIS

Chapter 2: Ensuring Indonesians Are Safe from COVID-19

This chapter assesses the health aspects of COVID-19 in Indonesia. The authors analyse the strengths, innovations and limitations of the government interventions for the containment and mitigation of COVID-19. It discusses the measures adopted, the social distancing measures and the correlation with a case number. The authors found that the measures and the level of stringency are correlated with the case number.

The authors also discuss the medical supply chain disruption and how the PEN programme for the health sector is designed and addresses the issue. The authors also discuss the additional incentives provided to health workers, additional funding for diagnostic and patient treatment, vaccines, medicine and JKN (*Jaminan Kesehatan Nasional*) contribution support, and the tax incentives for imported health equipment and devices, medicines and COVID-19 vaccine.

The authors show that the COVID-19 vaccine is very crucial for Indonesia that the government of Indonesia intensified the vaccination programme using different channels and incentives which resulted in a significant increase in the number of beneficiaries.

The authors concluded the chapter with the lessons learnt from the global pandemic that there is a need to improve the public health sector. As a response, the government designed six transformation pillars for the future of the Indonesian health sector: primary care transformation, secondary care transformation, healthcare resilience transformation, health financing transformation, health talent transformation, and technology transformation.

Chapter 3: Maintaining Macroeconomic Stability during the Pandemic

This chapter focuses on how the government of Indonesia maintained macroeconomic stability during the COVID-19 pandemic. The global financial sector experienced one of the biggest shocks in history: stock markets collapsed, developing country exchange rates fell sharply, and there was the biggest sell-off in history. It did not stop there, the real sector also experienced great pressure due to restrictions on market activities throughout the world. Macroeconomic indicators reflected a severe contraction. This, in the end, also had an impact on the stability of the financial sector, where financial service institutions were under pressure from risks, such as credit risk.

Amidst the current health and economic crisis, a dilemma arose regarding what should be prioritized: health or the economy? Despite the risks associated with being forced to trade off health and economic activities, the Indonesian government chose to save both. The authors described how the Indonesian government quickly began to discuss the possibility of budget flexibility to deal with the unprecedented situation, through PERPU 1/2020. Despite taking extraordinary measures, the government has been maintaining measured and prudent fiscal policies.

The authors conclude the chapter with a medium-term reflection on the need for the government to implement fiscal consolidation by returning the budget deficit to a maximum of 3 per cent of the budget deficit in 2023 while continuing to strengthen fiscal measures for the COVID-19 pandemic handling and economic recovery as well as structural reforms.

Chapter 4: Financial Sector and Monetary Policy during the Pandemic

This chapter elaborates on the response of the financial sector and monetary policy to the need for keeping the Indonesian economy safe. During the COVID-19 pandemic, keeping the real and financial sectors active was very important, restricting people's activities could create a contraction of economic and business activities.

Increased credit risk, if it is not managed properly, would lead to a decline in consumer confidence in the banking system. Therefore, the government and the authorities (Indonesia's Central Bank and Financial Services Authority) immediately coordinated and arranged policy support to minimize the impact of the pandemic on the economy and the financial sectors.

The government and authorities maintained the banking industry's stability, supporting the postponement of principal payments, relaxing credit policies, and ensuring there was enough liquidity in the banking system. These policies were translated into several programmes as follows: direct placement of funds in the banking system, credit restructuring, interest subsidy programmes and credit guarantees.

The burden-sharing scheme, a monetary policy option that had never been included in textbooks, has proven to be able to bring a credible source of financing for the government to withstand the impact of the pandemic. In this scheme, BI participates in financing the ballooning fiscal deficit through the purchase of government bonds in the primary market. The first Joint Decree, commonly referred to as SKB I (*Surat Keputusan Bersama I*) was signed on 16 April 2020. This agreement ruled that BI could act as a backstop buyer in the primary market. Then, on 7 July 2020, SKB II (further amended on 20 July 2020) regulated the distribution of the burden of issuing government securities for public goods and non-public goods. And lastly, SKB III, initiated by BI, aimed to respond to the significant spread of the COVID-19 Delta variant and it required a large amount of funding for health and humanity.

Chapter 5: Financing to Save Indonesia

This chapter focuses on the discussion of how the government financed the fiscal stimulus when state revenues were declining. Facing the pandemic, the State Budget deficit was expected to surpass the maximum limit of 3 per cent of GDP. It raised the question of how the government could meet the debt financing targets. Amidst global debt market pressures, the government was also facing challenges in the depth of domestic financial markets, including the government bond market. Simultaneously, there was an outflow of foreign capital as reflected in the sharp decline in foreign ownership.

This phenomenon forced the government to analyse all available policy options amidst low demand from investors while maintaining prudent debt management. In this case, the government has to come up with a breakthrough strategy to meet the financing needs amid low demand from investors. The synergy of fiscal and monetary policies through the burden-sharing scheme was a very important milestone during the unfavourable financing market conditions at that time. The government launched SBN (*Surat Berharga Negara*) online to induce higher demand for retail investors. The government also relaxed the tax burden on bonds holding to a single rate of 10 per cent. These breakthroughs boosted the positive performance of SBN so that the Indonesian government still achieved its issuance target.

Chapter 6: Turning Bottlenecks into Breakthroughs

This chapter explores how the government responded to the pandemic quickly through institutional breakthroughs, even though they had no experience with the impact of pandemics. The government had to take emergency steps and extraordinary measures; there was stuttering and indecision because there was no legal basis for taking steps, no budget had been prepared, and there were no rules for implementing the budget in an emergency. The authors elaborate on how the government made a fundamental decision to address multiple crises by stipulating PERPU 1, 2020. The authors also emphasize the importance of engaging in communication with stakeholders in a transparent, routine and sustainable manner to gain support and build public confidence and trust. The authors argue that good communications, followed by high commitment and close cooperation were proven to be very important in overcoming deadlocks in the implementation of programmes or policies. In this case, Indonesia has also learned that the courage of leaders in making breakthroughs can make a very positive contribution to the handling of crises. On the other hand, governance, risk and control must be strictly maintained so that people who dare to take action can be held accountable in a good and transparent manner.

Chapter 7: Balancing the Scale: Providing Tax Incentives and Collecting Revenue

This chapter discusses Indonesia's responses to the global pandemic from the revenue side of the government budget. The Ministry of Finance (MoF) rearranges the annual budget with several scenarios taking into account various economic forecasts. This changing scenario includes the role of tax and collecting revenue as well as the provision of tax incentives. The MoF has provided information on fiscal incentives as part of the tax expenditure report since 2018. The increasing economic challenges due to the pandemic required more extensive fiscal support, including tax stimulus. Therefore, the MoF had launched a wave of financial support for tax and duties relief, deductions, and relaxation.

The global pandemic made the MoF adopt and apply a countercyclical fiscal policy with tax revenue dwindling as further fiscal intervention was necessary to boost the economy. The MoF designed the fiscal frameworks considering the avoidance of the "wasteful spending" principle and following the general directions of stimulus programmes. There are three general principles in designing a fiscal framework during a crisis: timely, targeted and temporary (Summers 2008).

This chapter shows the lessons learnt from the global pandemic during the implementation of the Indonesian tax incentives, which include a need for collaboration with external stakeholders such as the businesses to strengthen the government's understanding of the taxpayers' actual situation. This chapter also explains that the MoF had applied primary data collection through field surveys and secondary data analysis based on the administrative data. Both methods had equipped the MoF with comprehensive information on what had happened on the ground, which was essential for designing and implementing the right policies for the accurately targeted impacts.

This chapter shows that technology-led tax incentives administration impacts are vital because they significantly reduce the paperwork for the taxpayers and provide an effective monitoring method for the government of Indonesia. In the long run, the pandemic motivated the government to adopt, adapt and apply related fiscal reforms from domestic resources (Domestic Resource Mobilization, or DRM) and international taxation reforms (Pillar I and Pillar II).

Chapter 8: Protecting the People

This chapter elaborates on how social protection was provided during the pandemic. It begins with a brief elaboration on the existing social safety net programme and links the discussion to the necessary adjustments to effectively cushion the impact on poor and vulnerable households. Although immediately existing programmes such as conditional cash transfers to the poorest households, the family hope programme (*Program Keluarga Harapan*, or PKH) and the electronic food voucher (*Kartu Sembako*) were expanded, it appeared that more support was needed, due to exclusion errors encountered within the existing social assistance beneficiary database and the potential impact of the pandemic on vulnerable middle-income households.

The authors discuss elaborately and provide evidence from several surveys on how the government expanded the safety net in 2020 and 2021 to cover the poor and vulnerable families. It also discusses the challenges the government faced in expanding a programme, which did not happen smoothly at the beginning but covered most of the vulnerable groups in the end. The new social assistance programmes designed or adjusted from the existing non-social assistance programmes such as the Village Fund and Pre-employment Card programme successfully captured and protected the impacted households which were not already in the established database of social assistance beneficiaries. The authors also discuss the importance of monitoring and evaluating the safety net programme and how the government worked closely with universities and research institutes to monitor and evaluate the safety net programme during the pandemic.

The authors conclude with a reflection on the need for a robust social protection system in the future to protect Indonesians both in normal conditions and during crisis times throughout their life cycle. It will include a social registry, on-demand applications and increased levels of investment.

Chapter 9: *Kartu Prakerja*: A Breakthrough for Boosting Labour Market Productivity and Social Assistance Inclusiveness

President Joko Widodo's second term in government put human capital development as one of his main priorities. With the low quality of the workforce and limited skill upgrading programme, the Pre-employment Card Programme (*Kartu Prakerja*) was designed as a labour market instrument for skill upgrading. The programme was designed for implementation in 2020 for those at least 18 years old, who had graduated from school and/or were unemployed to get free training according to their preferences and receive some allowance after finishing the training. However, because of the pandemic and based on the review of the impact of the pandemic on households and the ability of existing available programmes to respond to the pandemic in early 2020, *Kartu Prakerja* was transformed into a programme with a double mission: skill upgrading and social assistance. The authors discuss the transformation of *Kartu Prakerja* from purely skill upgrading to an on-demand application social safety net which rode on the online skill-upgrading programme. The redesigned *Kartu Prakerja* was intended to allow the selected participants to take an online course and receive social assistance upon finishing the training.

This chapter begins with a discussion about the labour market in Indonesia and the original design of *Kartu Prakerja* and its strategy to fill the gap in the labour market. The authors follow with a discussion about the implementation of the redesigned *Kartu Prakerja* during the pandemic and the challenges encountered. The authors also presented an evaluation of the impact of the *Kartu Prakerja* as a social assistance and skill upgrading programme. The authors conclude the chapter with a reflection on the innovations in the *Kartu Prakerja* programme and the possible replication and expansion of the programme.

Chapter 10: Mental Health during the COVID-19 Pandemic: An Issue Less Visited

This chapter evaluates the impact of the global pandemic on mental health, which had negatively affected socio-economic life. From a public health perspective, government intervention during a pandemic not only focuses on physical health but also on mental health. The government of Indonesia, in mitigating the socio-economic impact of the pandemic, adopts several measures. One of the examples was the shifting role of *Kartu Prakerja* as both a reskilling and upskilling tool for the working labour force and to play a role as a scholarship for "discouraged workers", i.e., those who previously worked but lost their jobs because of the pandemic and were unable to obtain jobs but did not want to be unemployed. They decided to be a non-labour force. The *Kartu Prakerja* has provided beneficiaries with monetary benefits and new skills. The well-managed targeting and disbursement mechanism helped encourage workers to avoid mental health disorders, such as anger and anxiety. This chapter found that *Kartu Prakerja* had successfully acted as a scholarship to improve the beneficiaries' mental health during the pandemic.

This chapter analysed the results of a field survey covering 4,000 respondents in Indonesia nationwide on several mental health indicators such as happiness, anxiety, sadness and anger in this field survey. This survey found that people became less happy and felt pressure and sadness due to the pandemic. The problematic situation developed as a result of the existence of the direct physical threat encountered whilst facing a virus pandemic without available vaccines combined with other unforeseen experiences which caused more anxiety and, in the end, mental illness. The survey found that 50 per cent of the male respondents experienced deprivation of happiness, which was very slightly higher than female respondents. Respondents started to experience declining happiness in March 2020 when the Indonesian government announced its first pandemic patient and applied people mobility with a social restriction policy. This study found that in the job sector, around 60 per cent of the respondents had been severely impacted by the pandemic, particularly those working in the accommodation and restaurant sector. They also experienced the most severe deprivation of happiness. It found that the more the pandemic affected the industry, the higher the negative effect on its workers' mental health.

Chapter 11: COVID-19 and Education in Indonesia: When School Reopening Is Not Enough to Avert Losing a Generation

The COVID-19 pandemic and school policies gave students, teachers and parents huge challenges. Not every teacher and student had equal quality computers or smartphones. The quality of the connections was also not equal at home. To add to those issues, there was competition for the Internet reception at home. Another important issue was the education curriculum that need to be adjusted for a virtual meeting mode.

The pandemic added to the already existing learning gap and disparities in learning outcomes. The authors discuss the impact of COVID-19 on the education sector in greater detail benefiting from the World Bank High Frequency Household Survey. To begin the discussion, the authors highlight the importance of quality education for Indonesian growth. The authors continue the discussion with an elaboration on how the COVID-19 pandemic exacerbated the pre-existing challenges in the Indonesian education system—the learning gap and outcome disparities.

To mitigate the impact of the pandemic on education, the government implemented several interventions including the emergency curriculum, different modes of distance learning, and hybrid learning. However, significant variation remained in terms of access across students and variations in school readiness to deliver quality education. On the fiscal side, the government increased the budget allocation for education and changed the guidelines regarding the utilization of DAK (*Dana Alokasi Khusus*, or Special Allocation Fund) funding. The authors examined the effectiveness of government intervention during the pandemic. The authors conclude with forward-looking policy suggestions on how Indonesia should address these growing challenges to help drive the country's transition to a high-income country, from the education policy standpoint as well as budget policy.

Chapter 12: Towards an Inclusive Response to Combat COVID-19 Impacts on Women and People with Disabilities: Lessons from Indonesia for Peer Countries

Globally, the pandemic and its economic fallout were found to have had a regressive effect on the goals of gender equality and disability inclusion. Was Indonesia any different? This chapter looks at the pandemic from a gender and disability inclusion perspective. The authors discuss how gender and disability were impacted differently by the effects of the COVID-19 pandemic in Indonesia and how different it was from global trends.

The discussion in this chapter begins with the pre-pandemic state of the gender gap and disability inclusion in Indonesia followed by a discussion on the different impacts of the pandemic on women and people with disability. The authors contrast the impact of the pandemic on female-headed households with male-headed households as well as women-led businesses with male-led businesses. On the government response to the COVID-19 pandemic, the authors again apply gender and disability inclusion to the issue. The authors discuss in detail each of the government interventions during the pandemic and their effects on women and people with disability. The authors argue that although most policy responses were not designed specifically to address gender and disability inclusion, women and people with disability were covered by government intervention, through social assistance and business financial relief.

The authors conclude the chapter with a reflection on the long term and sustainable reform needed to address the gender gap and disability inclusion including consensus building on the importance of gender equality and disability inclusion, better investment in education, skills training, affordable childcare and aged care, provision of flexible working arrangement and investment in adaptive and inclusive social protection.

Chapter 13: Weathering and Recovering from the Pandemic: Lessons Learnt from MSMEs in Indonesia

This chapter discusses the impact of the global pandemic of COVID-19 on Indonesian Micro Small and Medium Enterprises (MSMEs) across sectors with the pattern of impacts as a result of the pandemic depending on when the infection numbers increased or decreased. The authors highlight that nine out of ten MSMEs experienced decreasing demand and revenue during the pandemic. Almost two-thirds of MSMEs experienced decreasing revenue and around 53 per cent of MSMEs experienced a decrease in asset value.

Under the PEN programme, the government of Indonesia had implemented policies for business sectors such as loan interest subsidies, deferred principal and interest loan payments, working capital loan guarantees, tax incentives and regional incentive funds. This chapter explains the impact of the pandemic on MSMEs with a discussion of the results of several previous surveys before the global pandemic came. It concluded that different kinds of strategies were adopted by MSMEs to contain the crisis. It identified appropriate strategy options to accelerate recovery progress for Indonesia and MSMEs around the world. It gives details of the policy's effectiveness and lessons learnt for the future.

This chapter elaborates that PEN has assisted MSMEs, but there was still room for improvement. Further extensive evaluation and refinement are needed to complete Indonesia's PEN to enable it to assist MSMEs with their recovery from any pandemic or aggregate demand pressure.

Chapter 14: Financial Inclusion and Economic Recovery Programme: From Limiting Factor to Opportunity

Financial inclusion is a key enabler to reducing poverty and boosting prosperity. Indonesia together with more than fifty-five other countries has adopted and implemented a national financial inclusion strategy. In the G20, Indonesia also promotes financial inclusion through a Global Programme for Financial Inclusion (GPFI) with the mandate to have tangible outcomes during Indonesia's current President's term in 2022. This chapter begins with a discussion on the essence of financial inclusion and why it is important for Indonesia. The authors provide a brief overview of Indonesia's National Strategy on Financial Inclusion.

The effect of the COVID-19 pandemic on society exposed the crucial role of financial inclusion. The authors discuss how the state of financial inclusion affected economic activities during the pandemic and the speed of delivery of government policy intervention. Interestingly, the authors discuss how the government, through its economic recovery programme, contributed to financial inclusion. The expansion of social protection programmes to families and financial support to micro-businesses during the pandemic is among the contributors to financial inclusion. The new beneficiaries are registered collectively by the government with financial institutions to receive financial support. The authors argued that the state of financial inclusion at the beginning was the limiting factor for the delivery of significant government support. Nevertheless, the authors provided evidence that the national economic recovery programme designed to mitigate the negative impact of COVID-19 helped improve financial inclusion. The chapter concludes with a reflection on the need to accelerate financial inclusion and the way to achieve it.

Chapter 15: Corporate Sector Performance during the COVID-19 Pandemic

With sales across sectors dropping significantly but financial commitments concerning workers, suppliers and lenders remaining, financial losses in most businesses were inevitable. Liquidity shortages in the corporate sector were foreseen which in turn could have potentially affected the stability of the financial system. The authors elaborate on the impact of COVID-19 on corporations in greater detail using multi-dimensional indicators developed from the performance of companies. The authors discuss the channels for relaying data on the effects of COVID-19 on the corporate sector and show the different effects on various sectors. Stringent social restrictions to contain the spread of the virus affected services involving direct contact between buyers and sellers, activities which resulted in people gathering in public places, travelling as well as non-essential sectors involving physical contact among employees. Business activities that could be undertaken remotely and those related to medical and pharmaceutical industries remained resilient.

The authors also evaluate the emergency lifeline that the government provided to support corporations, from loan restructuring, tax incentives and subsidies as well as the Financial System Stability Committee (*Komite Stabilitas Sistem Keuangan*, or KSSK) coordinated policy support, from macro to micro-prudential intervention, fiscal supports, and business facilitation. Two case studies of specific pandemic-related fiscal incentives add to the discussion. The authors conclude the discussion with an acknowledgement that the different measures undertaken resulted in different outcomes for corporations. Using two case studies of fiscal support to the automobile and real estate sectors, the authors showed that consumption stimulating fiscal incentives supported the faster recovery in some sectors.

Chapter 16: Regional Dynamics during the COVID-19 Pandemic in Indonesia

How the local government responded to the national policy for handling the pandemic and implementing PEN at the local level is explored in this chapter. In the midst of the pandemic, during which mobility restrictions were imposed, regions experienced a decline in income and economic activities.

Bali, for example, experienced a large increase in the unemployment rate and poverty. Bali is one of ten provinces with the highest increase in poverty during the pandemic. The central government issued policies regarding the distribution and use of Transfer Funds to Regions and Village Funds (*Transfer ke Daerah dan Dana Desa*, or TKDD) which were more focused on handling health and the recovery in economic conditions.

The government also directed the reallocation and refocusing of budget spending towards regional economic recovery. The central government also issued village cash assistance (*Bantuan Langsung Tunai Dana Desa*, or BLT Desa) and additional regional incentive funds (*Dana Insentif Daerah*, or DID) to accelerate economic recovery. Additional DID was allocated to local governments based on their performance and their innovations in preventing and managing the pandemic in their regions.

In 2021, it became evident that Indonesia had performed very well in limiting the spread of the virus, managing public health, providing social protection and promoting economic recovery.

From the pandemic, we learned that apart from being affected by sectoral factors, regional resilience to shocks is also influenced by the fiscal structure, especially in terms of balancing funds and regional original revenues (*Pendapatan Asli Daerah*, or PAD). For this reason, the government is using the lessons learnt during this pandemic to improve the quality of the central-regional financial relationship and the quality of fiscal decentralization by the ratification of Law No. 1 of 2022 concerning the relationship between central and regional finance or the fiscal decentralization law (UU HKPD).

Chapter 17: New Ways of Working: Bureaucracy Reforms

This chapter refers to the four factors known as the VUCA (Volatility, Uncertainty, Complexity, and Ambiguity) which have moved the world into new dimensions and challenges. Many governments have faced similar challenges in adjusting to the progress in fast information and digital technologies, given the VUCA. The global pandemic has significantly affected global health and the health system, education and social activities in general. This chapter analyses the challenges faced when adjusting to the fast information and communications technology (ICT) and ICT's role in cushioning the impact of the global pandemic.

This chapter has a disclaimer that focuses on the government's ICT development, particularly the Republic of Indonesia's Ministry of Finance (MoF). The analysis period is seven consecutive years which means before and during the pandemic. The MoF began applying the digital transformation as part of the MoF RBTK (Bureaucracy Reform and Institutional Transformation). This programme was launched in 2016 with four central pillars—Revenue, Budget, Treasury and Cross-Cutting (Corporate), and the so-called New Ways of Working (NWOW). The latter becomes more important as part of the response to the pandemic situation.

NWOW has become much more relevant but applicable because of the solid sponsorship and commitment from the top leaders. NWOW becomes vital as most MoF staff must adopt Work from Home (WFH).

This chapter also provides an explanation based on the internal survey in the MoF. The survey found that more than 88 per cent of the respondents have already used e-MoF since the beginning of WFH. Nevertheless, there is still room for improvements to make it close to 100 per cent. The MoF consistently focuses on upskilling and reskilling its existing digital talent using a strategic combination proportion of 70:20:10 for learning, development, and proper reward and incentive.

References

Badan Pusat Statistik (BPS). 2020a. "Pertumbuhan Ekonomi Indonesia Triwulan II-2020". www.bps.go.id, (17/02/Th. XXIV), pp. 1–12. https://www.bps.go.id/pressrelease/2020/02/05/1755/ekonomi-indonesia-2019-tumbuh-5-02-persen.html

———. 2020b. "Pertumbuhan Ekonomi Indonesia Triwulan I-2020". https://www.bps.go.id/pressrelease/2020/02/05/1755/ekonomi-indonesia-2019-tumbuh-5-02-persen.html

———. 2021. "Berita Resmi Statistik Februari, Mei, Agustus dan November". BPS.

Deconinck, K., E. Avery, and L.A. Jackson. 2020. "Food Supply Chains and COVID-19: Impacts and policy Lessons". *EuroChoices* 19, no. 3: 34–39.

Donnelly, R., and H.A. Patrinos. 2021. "Learning Loss during COVID-19: An Early Systematic Review". *Prospects*, pp. 1–9.

Gibson, J., and S. Olivia. 2020. "Direct and Indirect Effects of COVID-19 on Life Expectancy and Poverty in Indonesia". *Bulletin of Indonesian Economic Studies* 56, no. 3: 325–44.

International Monetary Fund (IMF). 2020. "Tentative Stabilization, Sluggish Recovery?". *World Economic Outlook Update*, January.

———. 2022. "War Sets Back the Global Recovery". *World Economic Outlook*, April.

Ministry of Finance. 2019. "Informasi APBN 2019: APBN untuk Mendorong Investasi dan Daya Saing Melalui Pembangunan Sumber Daya Manusia". https://www.kemenkeu.go.id/media/11213/buku-informasi-apbn-2019.pdf

———. 2020. "APBN, 2020: Akselerasi Daya Saing Melalui Inovasi dan Penguatan Sumber Daya Manusia". https://www.kemenkeu.go.id/media/13339/apbn-2020-bahan-final.pdf

———. 2021. *Mengawal Akuntabilitas Penanganan COVID-19 dan Pemulihan Ekonomi Nasional Tahun 2020*. Jakarta: Ministry of Finance.

Petrosky-Nadeau, N., and R.G. Valletta. 2020. "An Unemployment Crisis after the Onset of COVID-19". *FRBSF Economic Letter* 12: 1–5.

Şahin, A., M. Tasci, and J. Yan. 2020. "The Unemployment Cost of COVID-19: How High and How Long?". *Economic Commentary* (2020–09).

Siregar, R.Y., A.H. Gunawan, and A.N. Saputro. 2021. "Impact of the COVID-19 Shock on Banking and Corporate Sector Vulnerabilities in Indonesia". *Bulletin of Indonesian Economic Studies*, 57, no. 2: 147–73.

Summers, L. 2008."Fiscal Stimulus Issue: Testimony before the Joint Economic Committee". 2008. http://larrysummers.com/wp-content/uploads/2012/10/1-16-08_Fiscal_Stimulus_Issues.pdf

Suryahadi, A., R. Al Izzati, and A. Yumna. 2021. "The Impact of COVID-19 and Social Protection Programs on Poverty in Indonesia". *Bulletin of Indonesian Economic Studies* 57, no. 3: 267–96.

Verico, K. 2021. "The Usage of Economic Position in Understanding Indonesia's Economy and the Pandemic Effects". *Jurnal Ekonomi Indonesia* 10, no. 2: 91–105. https://doi.org/10.52813/jei.v10i2.152

———, and Y. Natanael. 2018. "Let's Talk about the FTA: The Five ASEAN Members Highlighting Indonesia". *LPEM FEB UI Working Paper No. 23*, 13 July 2018. http://www.lpem.org/let's-talk-about-the-free-trade-agreement-fta-the-five-asean-members-highlighting-indonesia/

World Bank. 2020. *Global Outlook: Pandemic, Recession: The Global Economy in Crisis.* https://doi.org/10.1596/978-1-4648-1553-9_ch1

World Health Organization. 2020. "Listings of WHO's Response to COVID-19".

2

Ensuring Indonesians Are Safe from COVID-19

Bondi Arifin, Titik Anas, Eko Wicaksono, Irsyan Maududy and Nugraheni Kusumaningsih

2.1 INTRODUCTION

The novel coronavirus 2019 (COVID-19) outbreak has devastating public health consequences and poses a major economic threat. The ongoing pandemic continues to chart the path for global public health and economic activities. The Johns Hopkins University Coronavirus Resource Center reported more than 470 million total confirmed cases worldwide in March 2022. Global economic growth shrank by 3.5 per cent in 2020 (Weiss et al. 2020; World Bank 2021), with a recovery projected to happen in 2021 and 2022. Globally, countries implemented various responses to COVID-19 which can be classified into four key areas: saving lives; protecting the purchasing power of the poor and vulnerable; saving jobs and businesses; restoring countries to become more resilient (World Bank 2020).

The first two confirmed COVID-19 cases in Indonesia emerged on 2 March 2020 and spread exponentially within a short time. By January 2022, the Indonesian National Disaster Management Authority (*Badan*

Nasional Penanggulangan Bencana, or BNPB) reported more than 4.2 million cases. Indonesia had already faced three large waves of COVID-19 cases between 2020 and early 2022: the original Wuhan coronavirus variant in 2020, the Delta variant in mid-2021, and the Omicron variant in early 2022. The Indonesian government took various significant steps to reduce the spread of the virus and protect the poor and vulnerable families, jobs and businesses, and maintain economic recovery.

To reduce the spread of COVID-19 in the early days of the pandemic, Indonesia introduced international travel restrictions on 1 January 2020 before the first COVID-19 cases were detected in the country. The government introduced the Work, Study, and Worship at Home policy on 16 March 2020 and implemented large-scale social restrictions (*Pembatasan Sosial Berskala Besar*, or PSBB) on 31 March 2020 as recommended by many studies and international organizations (Glass et al. 2006; Gottlieb et al. 2020; Maharaj and Kleczkowski 2012; Reluga 2020).

Later, on 11 May 2020, Indonesia launched comprehensive health, economic and social containment measures, the National Economic Recovery (*Pemulihan Ekonomi Nasional*, or PEN) programme. It covers public health support, social protection for the poor and vulnerable, fiscal incentives and financial support for businesses. The government spent IDR575.9 trillion in 2020 and IDR657.1 trillion in 2021 for the PEN programme. In 2022, the government continued the programme by allocating IDR455.62 trillion.

The most striking feature of the COVID-19 pandemic and the associated government responses was the social and ecological complexity (Wernli et al. 2021). Governance, control strategies, interventions (Jung et al. 2021), as well as the dynamic COVID-19 environment (Wernli et al. 2021), have affected the country's ability to provide effective measures. This chapter discusses Indonesia's intervention experiences with COVID-19 containment in 2020–21.

This chapter begins with the empirical analysis of the correlation between the adopted social distancing policy and the COVID-19 cases followed with the discussion on the health challenges that Indonesia faced during the pandemic and the strategies adopted.

2.2 DATA AND METHODOLOGY

This study closely looks at the measures undertaken by the Indonesian government to contain the COVID-19 pandemic using qualitative and quantitative analysis. We utilized the Synthetic Control method to estimate the relationship of the PSBB on people's mobility and the Event-Study-Style model to estimate the relationship between mobility and COVID-19 confirmed cases.

The Synthetic Control method is developed from the standard difference-in-difference method and matching technique employing the weighted average of the control units using explicit relative contribution of each unit which provides transparency and safeguards (Abadie, Diamond, and Hainmueller 2010, 2015). Following Abadie, Diamond, and Hainmueller (2010, 2015), if there are J+1 provinces, with only j=1 province is exposed to the intervention (treated unit), then j=2 to j=J+1 provinces are the "donor pool" units for the Synthetic Control.

In the model, DKI Jakarta which implemented PSBB is the treated unit. This study excludes West Sumatra and Gorontalo in the "donor pools" because these two provinces were conducting PSBB in the same sample period, leaving thirty-one other provinces as donor pools. We also use Google Mobility Reports from 16 February 2020, the first day the mobility data was publicly available for Indonesia, with the COVID-19 sample period starting from 1 March 2020, one day before the first COVID-19 case was announced.

To estimate the relationship between mobility and COVID-19 confirmed cases we use the modified Event-Study-Style model as in Courtemanche et al. (2020). The model is a generalization of a standard difference-in-difference model which provides more flexible timing of impacts than difference-in-difference models by interacting treatment with several indicators of time. This model is suitable for the study as the impact of social distancing restriction is more likely to be gradual over time due to several factors, including delays in getting a test and medical care, and waiting time for the test results (Courtemanche et al. 2020; Lauer et al. 2020). We modify the Event-Study-Style model by including mobility variation across provinces. Using this model, there is supposed to be a similar trend of confirmed cases if there is no intervention.

In the estimation, we use official case counts of thirty-four provinces in Indonesia from the BNPB. We identify the level of mobility restriction applied in each of the thirty-four provinces from the regulation enacted at the provincial level. Google Mobility Index is utilized as the interaction variable for mobility restriction.

To evaluate multiple measures of the PEN programme, we use surveys, descriptive statistics and qualitative methods. The government expenditure data for PEN was obtained from the 2020–21 Ministry of Finance COVID-19 and National Economic Recovery Handling Monitoring and Evaluation Report (Ministry of Finance 2020a, 2021). The government spending on COVID-19 test kits was obtained from the 2020 Ministry of Health expenditure report comprising national and regional expenditures for antigen and polymerase chain reaction (PCR) test kits. The daily COVID-19 cases, PCR tests, and positivity rates in 2020–21 were obtained from the kawalcovid19.id website. Vaccination data were obtained from the Ministry of Health vaccination dashboard. We aggregated the information at the provincial level.

2.3 COVID-19 EARLY GOVERNMENT INTERVENTION

Figure 2.1 shows important COVID-19 containment measures and the timeline from 1 January 2020 to March 2022. It shows that the Indonesian government undertook important steps to reduce the spread of the virus in the early period of 2020 even before the PEN programme was formally launched. International travel restriction has been in place since 1 January 2020. One hundred hospitals were transformed into dedicated COVID-19 hospitals on 23 January 2020, before the first cases were detected in the country.

Indonesia introduced social distancing, namely the Work, Study, and Worship at Home policy, on 16 March 2020 and implemented large-scale social restrictions (PSBB) on 10 April 2020 in Jakarta province to limit the spread of the virus. The social distancing measures continued with many different names and stringency levels following the increase in case numbers. For example, Emergency Community Activities Restriction Enforcement (*Pemberlakuan Pembatasan Kegiatan Masyarakat Darurat*, or Emergency PPKM) was introduced in July 2021 when the Delta variant surged.

The PEN programme, a comprehensive COVID-19 policy response programme, was launched on 11 May 2020. The vaccination programme started on 13 January 2021 and vaccination boosters were made available in January 2022 for free to all Indonesian citizens and residents.

2.3.1 Work from Home, Social Distancing and Social Mobility

To flatten the epidemic curve, researchers and international organizations recommend social distancing measures (Glass et al. 2006; Gottlieb et al.

FIGURE 2.1
Indonesia COVID-19 Policy Timeline

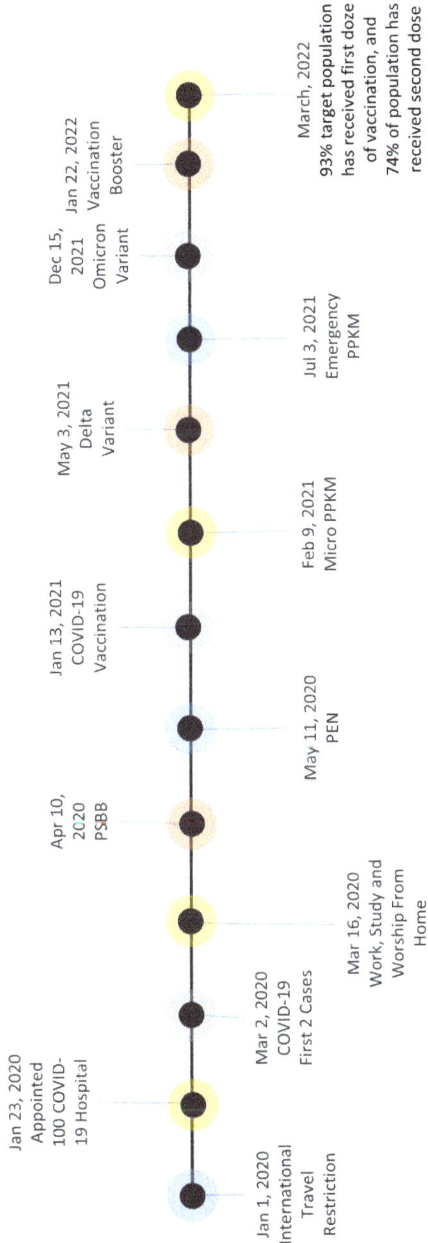

Source: Authors' compilation.

2020; Maharaj and Kleczkowski 2012; Reluga 2020). Although a majority of countries applied social distancing intervention, the implementation and stringency varied across countries depending on their public health, culture and socio-economic condition. Indonesia implemented social distancing measures less stringent than a complete lockdown. A complete lockdown policy was considered to be costly as it would completely close economic activities. For example, lockdowns are considered to cause a bigger income gap between the upper-middle class and lower-middle class (Elena 2021). Therefore, the government chose social distancing to overcome the health crisis but did not forget the handling of the economy (Laoli 2021). Indonesian policymakers considered social distancing combined with societal discipline, testing, tracing and treatment suit Indonesia's conditions (Intan 2020).

The government imposed two substantial social distancing measures in the early pandemic period. First, the Work, Study, and Worship at Home policy that required all business offices, schools and places of worship to close their doors from 16 March 2020. Employees, students and worshippers began to do their activities from home. The government also adopted the large-scale social restrictions policy on 31 March 2020. The policy was first implemented in Jakarta on 10 April 2020. The PSBB required schools and offices to close and limited activities in places of worship and public facilities. Figure 2.2 displays workplace mobility from Google Mobility Reports from February 2020 to May 2020 with the orange solid line for Indonesia, the black dashed line for the world average and the solid grey lines for the rest of the world. It suggests that workplace mobility in Indonesia follows the world trend until 10 March 2020; from then on, the lines started to diverge later on. While most countries had already implemented social distancing measures on 11 March 2020, Indonesia only started on 16 March 2020. The restriction reduced the average workplace mobility to around 30 per cent compared to a normal period.

2.3.2 PSBB and Social Mobility

In evaluating the impact of PSBB on workplace mobility, the main question is how the workplace mobility would have developed in the absence of PSBB? To answer the question, we use the Synthetic Control model on DKI Jakarta province, the first to apply mobility restriction. A synthetic (counterfactual) Jakarta, a combination of provinces in Indonesia within the "donor" pool, which are a close resemblance in terms of the level of

FIGURE 2.2
Indonesia and World Workplace Mobility

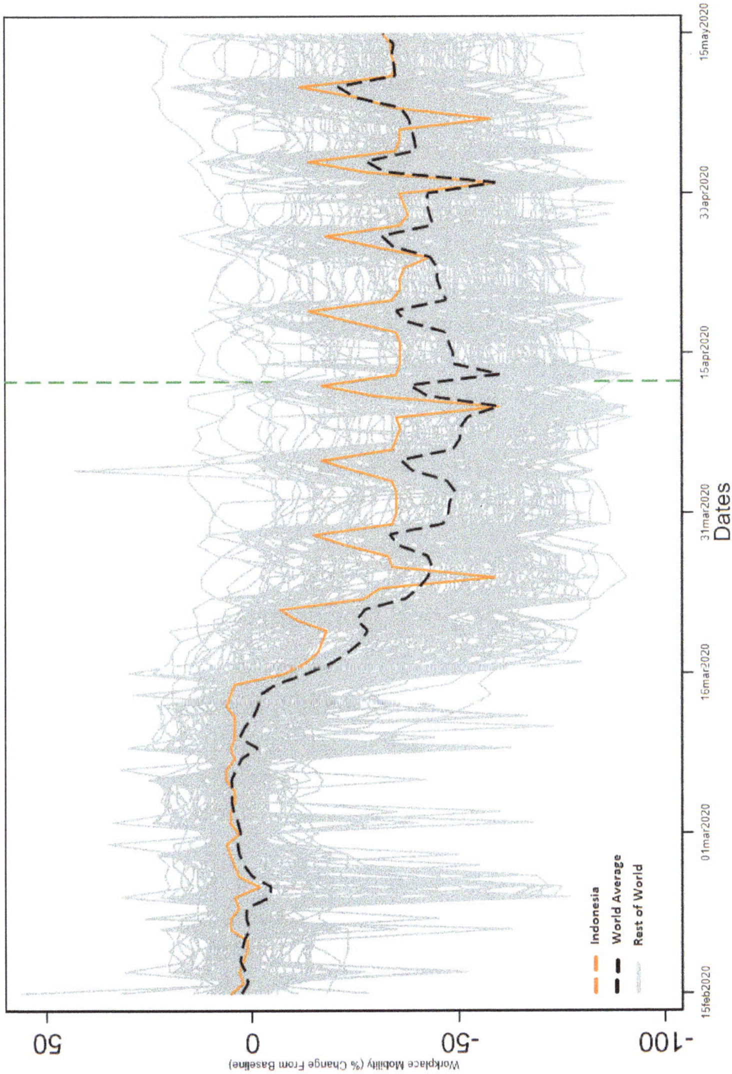

Source: Authors' calculation.

mobility in the pre-PSBB period. Figure 2.3 highlights the actual workplace mobility in DKI Jakarta and the synthetic DKI Jakarta during the pre-PSBB period, 15 February to 9 April 2020. Workplace mobility in the synthetic DKI Jakarta very closely tracked the path of DKI Jakarta for the whole pre-PSBB period. It indicates that the synthetic DKI Jakarta provides a sound approximation of workplace mobility in the two provinces in the absence of PSBB.

In contrast, soon after the enactment of PSBB, the two lines between the treatment province and its synthetic counterparts started to diverge and create wider gaps. The disparity between the two lines suggests a significant negative effect of PSBB on workplace mobility. The results suggest that during the period of 10 April to 2 May 2020, PSBB in Jakarta reduced workplace mobility by 9.52 per cent. In constructing the synthetic controls, we include several additional predictors of workplace mobility prevalence to assess the robustness of our results. These predictors are mobility to places other than workplaces which include retail and recreation, grocery and pharmacy, parks as well as transit stations. The results remain stable regardless of the various combination of predictors used.

2.3.3 Social Distancing and Confirmed COVID-19 Cases Development

The relationship between social distancing measures and the COVID-19 growth rate is evaluated using the accumulated case growth before and after the issuance of government intervention. The growth rate is measured as differences in the log of daily cases; Thus, it can be interpreted as daily cases percentage growth.

Figure 2.4 shows that social distancing is more likely to reduce the COVID-19 growth rate. There is no significant impact of social distancing on the COVID-19 transmission growth rate in the first seven days of the social distancing enforcement. Yet, after fifteen days of enforcement, increases in the residential activities significantly reduced the growth rate of COVID-19 cases. It is important to note that the impact of social distancing is quite stable after three weeks of enforcement. The estimates also suggest that a 1 per cent increase in residential activity reduced cases growth by 1.15 to 1.48 per cent.

The government scaled up the level of stringency after three weeks of implementation that the province and municipal governments can propose

FIGURE 2.3
PSBB and Workplace Mobility in DKI Jakarta (Synthetic Control)

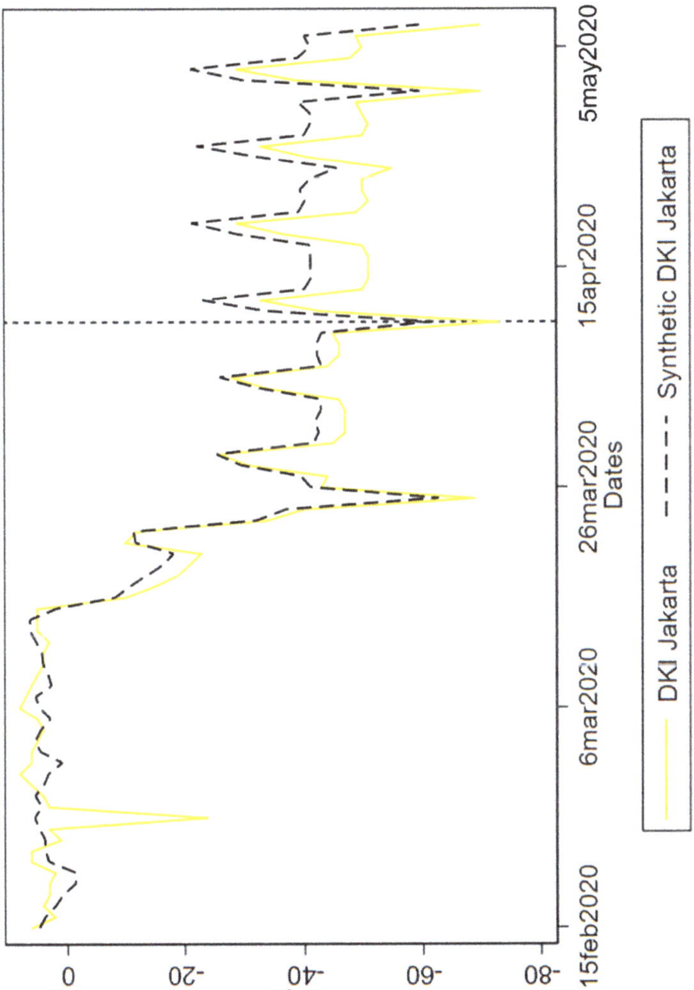

Source: Authors' calculation.

FIGURE 2.4
Social Distancing Measures and COVID-19 Growth

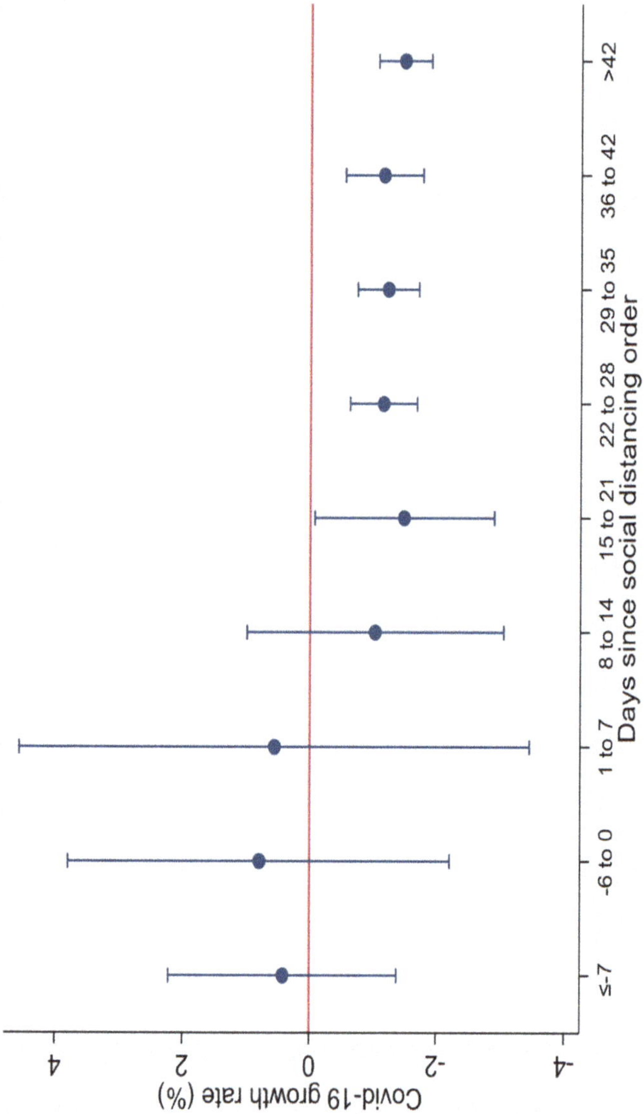

Source: Authors' calculation.

tighter social distancing policies. West Sumatra and Gorontalo provinces followed DKI Jakarta to implement PSBB. Tighter measures resulted in an estimated additional 0.22 per cent reduction in case growth. Based on these results, we estimated how the COVID-19 would have evolved if there were no social distancing measures at all. We constructed a counterfactual scenario by setting residential activity to the level observed before the first COVID-19 case was confirmed. This predicts what the growth rate would have been if there are no social distancing measures.

Figure 2.5 illustrates the comparison between predicted counterfactual cases and observed cases. At the beginning of the social distancing period, there is no noticeable difference between predicted cases and observed cases which implies that the model fits the observed cases. By the third week of March 2020, the predicted counterfactual started to create its own trend above the trend of the observed cases. According to our estimation, without distancing policies, COVID-19 cases would be around 37 per cent higher by 7 May 2020. Given the limited capacity of the healthcare system, the flattening of the curve of the COVID-19 cases prevented the collapse of the healthcare system. Indonesia continued to implement social distancing measures during the pandemic under different names and stringency levels following the development of COVID-19 cases.

2.3.4 Medical Supplies Disruption and Policy

The global outbreak of the COVID-19 resulted in global supply chain disruption which in turn affected production, processing, transport, logistics and final demand (Deconinck, Avery, and Jackson 2020). Increased world demand for medical supplies created huge global shortage. In March 2020, the World Health Organization (WHO) estimated that frontline health workers around the world required 89 million masks, 30 million gowns, 1.59 million goggles, 76 million gloves, and 2.9 million litres of hand sanitizer each month (Al-Mansour and Al-Ajmi 2020).

Although the social distancing policy exempted mobility restrictions in business related to basic needs provisions such as food and medical supplies transportation, the measures did affect the distribution capabilities. For instance, the social distancing policy made cargo officers work in shifts resulting in a longer time for cargo transportation of goods. As a result, the logistic cost also increased. The implementation of PSBB in several areas in Eastern Indonesia also disrupted the distribution of goods to the areas.

FIGURE 2.5
Predicted Cases under No Measures vs. Observed Cases

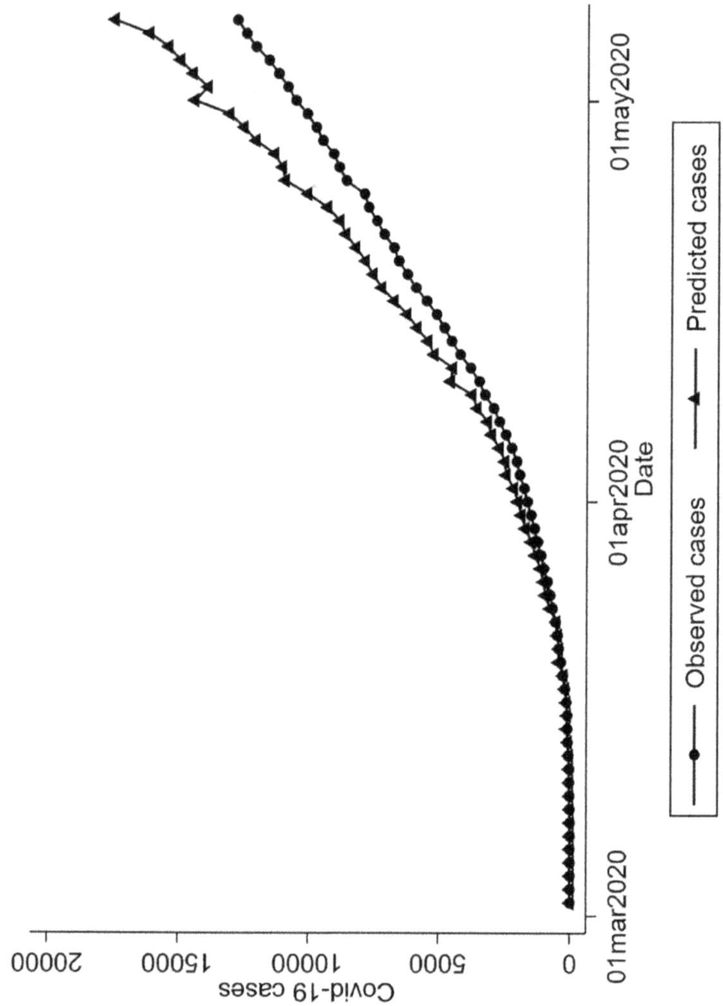

Source: Authors' calculation.

Figure 2.6 provides an estimate of the COVID-19-induced demand for medical supplies for 2020, based on calculated hospital needs in April 2020. This estimate does not include public healthcare (*Puskesmas*) and private healthcare institutions. The estimates suggest large amounts of medical supplies are required to support frontline health workers in Indonesia. For example, they need 5.5 million gowns, 58,000 ventilators, and 129.1 million surgical masks. Despite the increasing demand for medical supplies, there was a shortage of medical supplies delivered to medical care facilities. As of the end of April 2020, the estimated realization of PPE distribution to the regions was in the range of 0–28 per cent of total needs with a larger gap existing in outer Java islands (Ministry of Finance 2020d).

The Indonesian government has taken some notable measures to improve the availability of medical supplies. Fiscal incentives, relaxation of import permits for medical devices, excise exemption for alcohol use in COVID-19 handling, relaxation of import income taxes paid for small and medium exporters with export facility status (*Kemudahan Impor untuk Tujuan Ekspor*, or KITE), acceleration of online custom and trade facilitation services for COVID-19 handling, acceleration of logistics services with the National Logistics Ecosystems (NLE) system, and relaxation of local sales for exporters in the bonded zones and exporters with KITE facility and procedures for Free Alongside Ship (FAS) imports (Ministry of Finance 2020b). Due to the high domestic demand, the government temporarily limited the export of antiseptic products, mask raw materials, PPE, masks final products and ethyl alcohol (Ministry of Trade 2020). Minister of Trade Regulation No. 28/2020 temporarily exempted surveyor reports (LS) for the import of masks and PPE products, as well as medical equipment needs and equipment until 30 June 2020 to improve import speeds (Ministry of Trade 2020). Minister of Health Regulation No. 7/2020 and Decree of the Minister of Health No. HK.01.07/2020 relaxed the special access scheme (SAS) authorization to ease the import of medical devices such as in-vitro diagnostic medical devices, and household health supplies used for handling COVID-19 (Wildan 2020). Over time, the availability of medical devices for COVID-19 increased.

2.4 THE NATIONAL ECONOMIC RECOVERY PROGRAMME

Non-pharmaceutical interventions such as social distancing measures, although successfully reduced the COVID-19 cases growth, had caused

FIGURE 2.6
Indonesia Medical Supplies Demand Estimates for the Year 2020

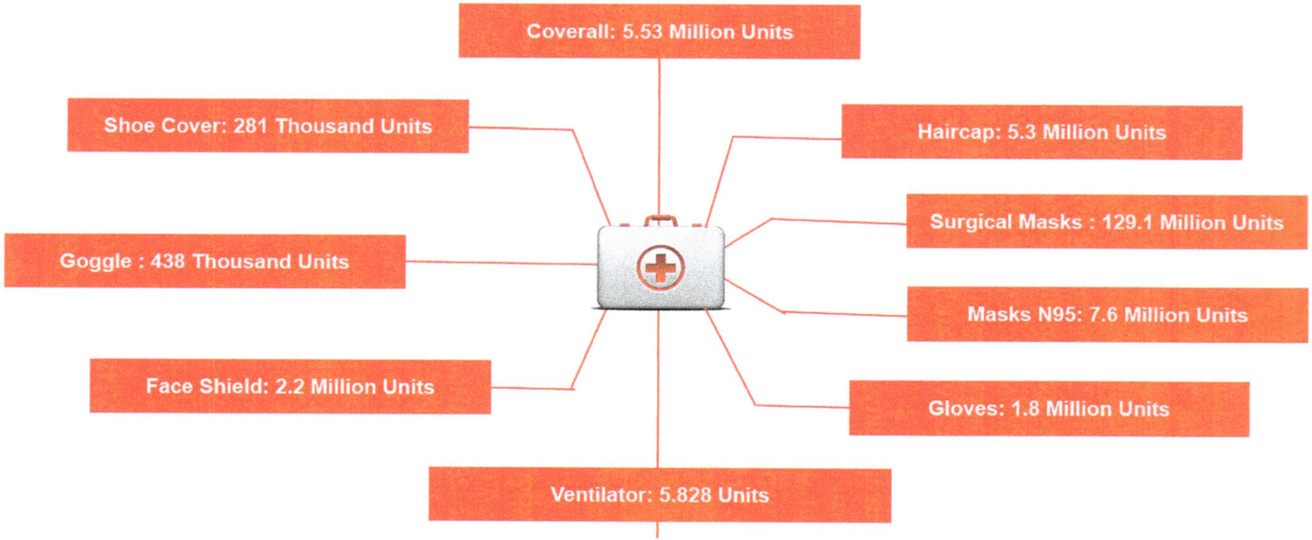

Source: Authors' calculation from National Disaster Management Authority Information (2020).

adverse impacts on the socio-economic condition. At the same time, it had a negative impact on demand and supply. The negative effect was reflected in the GDP contraction of 5.32 per cent (year-on-year) in the second quarter of 2020 and higher unemployment of 7.07 per cent in August 2020. Amidst the decline in economic activities, countercyclical fiscal policy played an important role in containing the negative effect. The National Economic Recovery Programme (*Program Pemulihan Ekonomi Nasional*, or PEN) was designed to provide support to those negatively affected by COVID-19. This programme covered many aspects which include social protection, health intervention and business support. The handling of COVID-19 in the health sector is one of the main focuses of the national economic recovery which amounted to IDR62.67 trillion in 2020 and IDR199.68 trillion in 2021. The health spending includes the provision of diagnostic and patient treatment, health worker incentives and bereavement support payment for families of health workers, medicine, vaccines, the National Health Insurance (*Jaminan Kesehatan Nasional*, or JKN) contribution assistance, and tax incentives for the health sector. This chapter primarily focuses on health intervention. The evaluation of social protection programmes is discussed in Utomo et al. (2022), Purbasari, Satriawan, and Sitorus (2022) and Basnett et al. (2022). Meanwhile, Sastrosuwito et al. (2022) and Revindo et al. (2022) elaborate on business support programme.

2.4.1 Testing and Tracing

Indonesia, similar to other 104 countries, applied measures to handle the pandemic including the containment of the COVID-19 transmission, adequate healthcare service, testing, treatment, and vaccination (World Bank 2020). Multiple interventions are required to prevent the transmission of COVID-19 as each intervention is not perfect at stopping transmission as described in the "Swiss cheese model" with holes on every layer as depicted in Figure 2.7 (Bode and Vraga 2021; Kompas 2020; Noh et al. 2020; Sarin et al. 2020).

Testing is one of the key elements to handling the spread of COVID-19 (Beeching, Fletcher, and Beadsworth 2020; Bossuyt 2020; Gollier and Gossner 2020). Government policy interventions are important in ensuring the successful implementation of COVID-19 testing in Indonesia. Figure 2.8 details the government's COVID-19 test kit procurement and

FIGURE 2.7
The Swiss Cheese Model

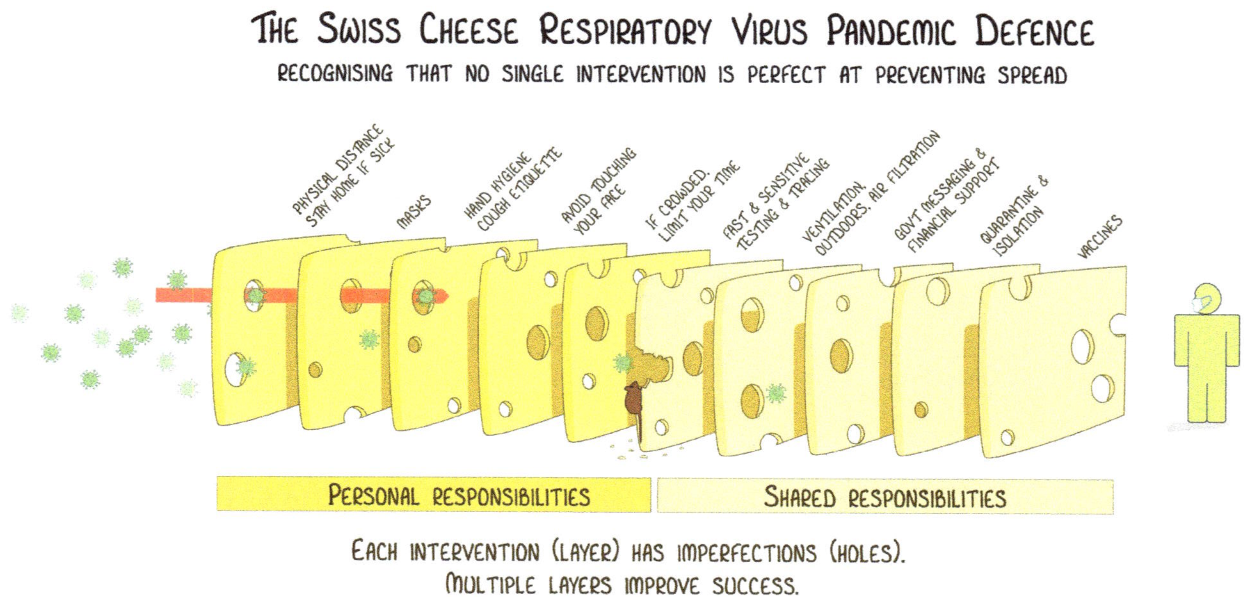

Source: Mackay (2020).

FIGURE 2.8
COVID-19 Test Kit Procurement and Distribution, 2020

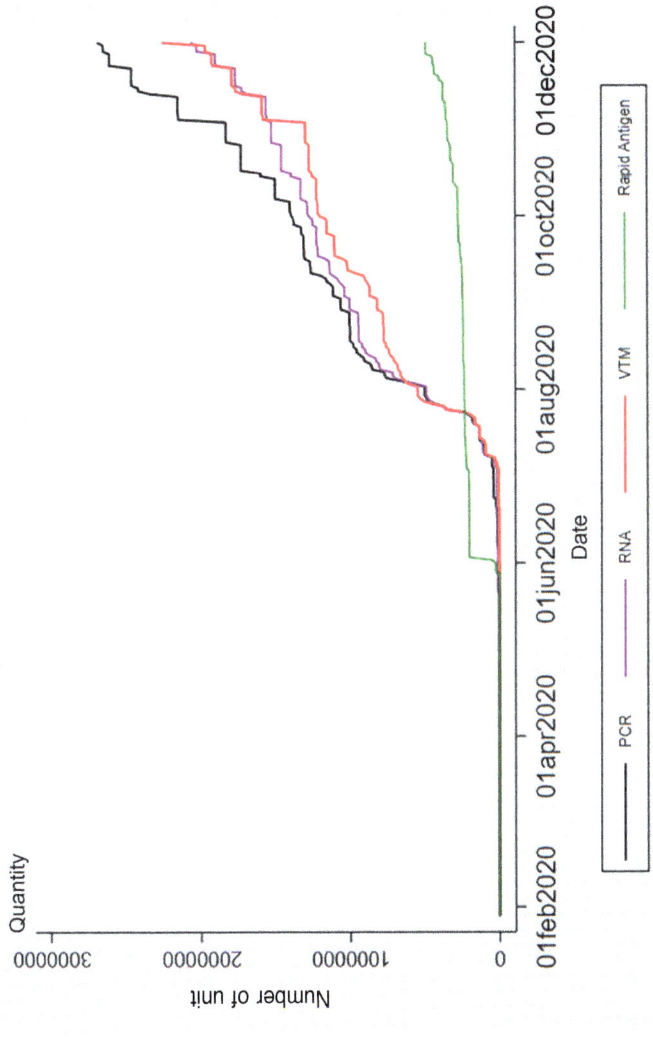

Source: Authors' calculation.

distribution (accumulation) from the early pandemic up to 1 December 2020. The figure suggests that at the beginning of the pandemic period, there were very limited test kits available in Indonesia and mostly were rapid antigen test kits. The procurement and the distribution of test kits, including the golden standard PCR test kit, increased substantially after PEN was launched.

Figure 2.9 shows the relationship between daily confirmed cases and daily PCR test rates in Indonesia for 2020. It suggests that the number of PCR tests per day is closely related to the number of confirmed COVID-19 cases. For the first 100 days of the COVID-19 period, the daily PCR tests were less than 10,000 and confirmed COVID-19 cases were less than 1,000 cases per day. The daily PCR testing capacity was increased to 30,000 tests per day with more than 4,000 confirmed cases per day in November 2020. The Ministry of Health increased testing capacity over time. Isolation, treatment and tracing of the closest contacts were immediately carried out when the COVID-19 was detected in the community to contain the transmission.

The tests were not only conducted by the government, but also by the private healthcare facilities. In 2020, there were more than 7.3 million PCR test specimens collected to test more than 4.9 million people, equivalent to 1.8 per cent of the population, relatively small compared to the world average. The impediments to massive testing included limited availability of laboratories, different levels of readiness and capacity between labs and regions, limited numbers of swab collection officers, limited numbers of reagents in the labs, and limited transportation (Sucahya 2020).

The government targeted 25 million test specimens in 2021 with an allocated budget for testing and tracing of IDR3.81 trillion. Figure 2.10 shows COVID-19 testing and positivity rate for 2020–21. It suggests that the testing capacity improved to more than 200,000 tests per day by the end of 2021. Meanwhile, the positivity rate fluctuated over time. In 2020, the positivity rate tends to increase over time between 10 per cent and 35 per cent. After reaching a peak of about 35 per cent, positivity rates started to decline from March–June 2021. From June to August 2021, the positivity rate increased steeply, mostly due to Delta variants. The positivity rate decreased after September 2021.

FIGURE 2.9
Relationship Between Daily Cases and Daily PCR Test in Indonesia

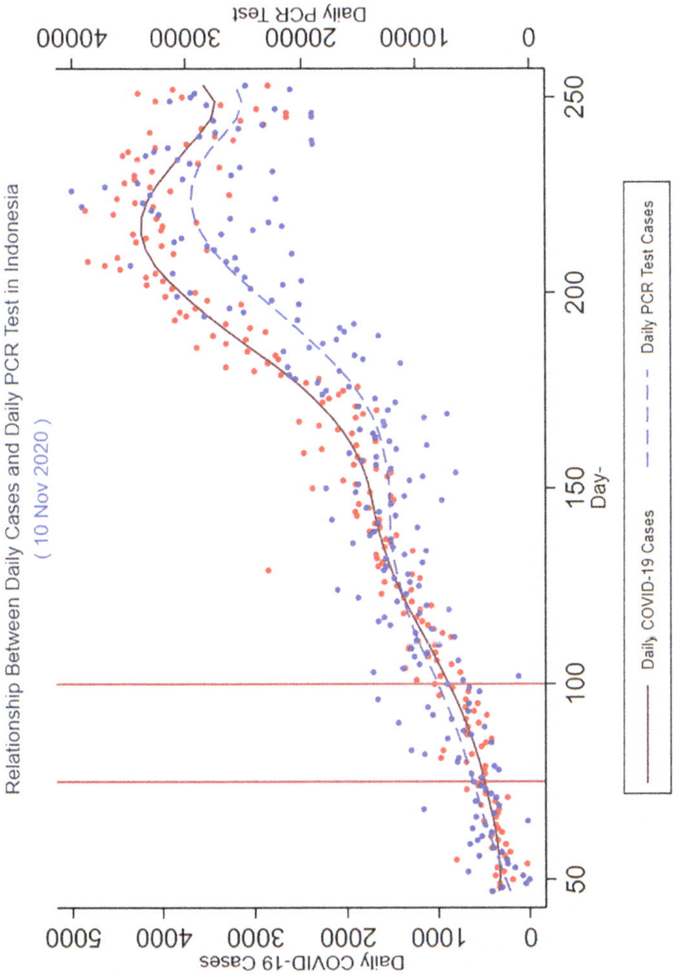

Source: Authors' calculation.

FIGURE 2.10
COVID-19 Test and Positivity Rate, 2020–21

Source: kawalcovid (2021).

2.4.2 COVID-19 Patient Treatment

The widespread occurrence of COVID-19, the high cost of COVID-19 patient treatment, and the sharp decline in economic condition occurred at the same time. The government decided to bear the cost of COVID-19 treatment for all Indonesian citizens which covers all treatment activities, from administration fees, room charges, doctors' services, personal protective equipment, and medicines, to the relocation of the dead bodies of the COVID-19 non-surviving patients.

The reimbursement process of the claims for patient treatment, however, was a big challenge, particularly at the beginning of the pandemic. A large number of claims for patient treatments with small numbers of verification personnel created a huge burden for the hospital reimbursement process. Many hospitals found it difficult to submit the claims because of the overwhelmingly large number of patients and the reduction of human resources in the hospital due to COVID-19 infection (Hamdhi 2022). Furthermore, there were high numbers of disputed claims due to different interpretations of applicable regulations, incomplete documentation, the unpreparedness of application tools and a limited number of dispute verifiers to conduct the re-verification process (Ambarwati 2021). For example, in August 2020, the verified reimbursement claims for patient treatment were only 18 per cent of the total patients on average.

To reduce the financial burden on hospitals, the Ministry of Health provided hospitals with down payments of up to 50 per cent of claims while they are waiting for their reimbursement payment. The Ministry of Health also increased the number of staff to do the verification, simplified the claim procedure and improved the E-claim system (digital submission reimbursement payment system). In 2020, with more than 743,000 COVID-19 cases, both outpatients and inpatients, the Ministry of Health received claims for more than 183,000 patients from 1,577 hospitals. It is reported that the government disbursed IDR83.26 trillion for 1.4 million patients' claims in 2021 (which also included claim reimbursements from the end of 2020).

2.4.3 Frontline Health Workers' Incentives and Benefits

Health workers are at the forefront of COVID-19 handling. A survey conducted by the Ministry of Finance (2020a) at the beginning of the pandemic among more than 5,000 health workers revealed that each health worker handled more than 200 patients with COVID-19 indications per day. The load put them at high risk of being exposed to COVID-19 even though they used complete personal protective equipment (PPE). The survey also indicated that during the pandemic, their expenditure including for PPE increased. The government provided incentives and benefits for health workers involved in COVID-19 handling, both at the central and regional levels as well as compensation to families of health workers who passed away whilst handling COVID-19. The maximum value of the monthly incentive that each health worker received varied according to the level and type of work performed as shown in Table 2.1.

The disbursement of the incentive, however, was very challenging at the beginning of the pandemic. It was difficult for the health workers to comply with the administrative requirements to receive the incentives as they were overwhelmed with a large number of patients. On the government side, as the verification was performed at the central government, the limited number and capacity of verification officers at the central government level and the lengthy reporting procedure from local to central government caused substantial delays in incentive disbursements at the beginning of the pandemic. After a careful assessment of the impediments, the government revised the technical instructions to accelerate the disbursement process.[1] The verification process moved from the central to the local government and the number of verifiers increased. The change increased the disbursement substantially, from only 32,000 or about 12 per cent of health workers who received the benefits on 29 June 2020, before the implementation of the new decree, to 207,000 workers who received the benefit one month

TABLE 2.1
Frontline Health Workers' Incentives

Description	*Value (IDR)*
Specialist	15,000,000
PPDS	12,000,000
General practitioner	10,000,000
Nurses	7,500,000
Other health workers	5,000,000

Source: Ministry of Finance.

after the changes were made effective, an increase of more than 500 per cent (Figure 2.11).

The government also provided compensation of IDR300 million to each of the 194 family descendants of health workers who passed away while performing their duties. In total, the government disbursed IDR8.83 trillion of health worker incentives and compensation in 2020 and IDR18.04 trillion in 2021.

2.4.4 National Health Insurance (JKN)

Studies show the benefits of the Indonesian National Health Insurance (JKN) include increased life expectancy, decreased infant mortality, and a substantial reduction in out-of-pocket costs (Agustina et al. 2019; Aizawa 2019). During the COVID-19 pandemic, JKN provided additional benefits so that JKN participants are covered for COVID-19 treatment otherwise not covered by the government, such as comorbidities. PEN includes contributions to the JKN programme for non-wage recipients (*Pekerja Bukan Penerima Upah*, or PBPU) and non-wage workers (*Bukan Pekerja*, or BP) class III with a benefit value of IDR16,500 per person per month for 53.87 million JKN participants with a total budget of IDR4.12 trillion in 2020 and IDR2.43 trillion for 42.02 million JKN participants in 2021.

2.4.5 Vaccination

Although the COVID-19 vaccine was not yet available in the first year of the pandemic, past experiences with vaccines demonstrated that vaccines are effective means to control various infectious diseases (Kochhar et al. 2013), including tuberculosis (Michelsen et al. 2014) and influenza (Jackson et al. 2017; Sano et al. 2017). Vaccines generate virus-neutralizing antibodies that optimally prevent infection and unfavourable effects from infectious diseases.

To contain COVID-19 transmission, the government secured vaccines in 2020 even before the vaccine manufacturers declared their clinical trial results. The decision was made in anticipation of the high global demand for COVID-19 vaccines. Presidential Decree No. 9/2020 enacted on 5 October 2020 provides a legal basis for COVID-19 procurement and vaccination implementation. The Ministry of Health secured more than 426 million doses from Sinovac Biotech, Pfizer, Novavax, AstraZeneca

FIGURE 2.11
Health Worker Incentive Recipients

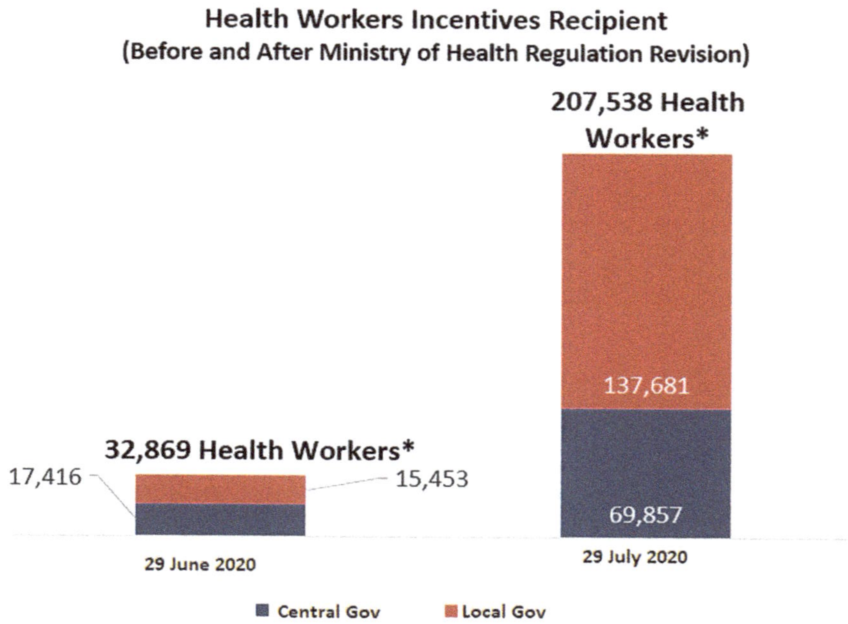

Source: Ministry of Finance (2020).

and other providers through COVAX/GAVI facilities before the first vaccine, Sinovac, was declared safe (Salma 2021) and Emergency Use of Authorization (EUA) issued on 11 January 2021. Indonesia took part in the Sinovac COVID-19 Phase 3 Global Clinical Trial for the COVID-19 vaccine (Voi 2020). A total of 1,620 of 1,866 registered volunteers for the phase 3 clinical trials in Indonesia received the complete doses on 16 August 2020 (Biofarma 2021). By the end of 2020, the government had already purchased 3 million Sinovac vaccines that cost IDR630 billion. In 2021, the government spent IDR33.27 trillion to purchase 310.9 million doses of the Sinovac vaccine.

A real-time centralized vaccination information system was prepared in 2020 to improve the vaccination infrastructure. There are five main stages of establishing the COVID-19 vaccine information system: (1) integrating data from various sources; (2) filtering the priority vaccine recipients, (3) establishing digital vaccine registration, (4) mapping the supply and distribution of vaccines, and (5) monitoring the implementation of the vaccination programme (PCPEN 2020). In its next development stage, the system integrates three applications, namely *Peduli Lindungi*, Primary Care, and Smile. *Peduli Lindungi* is used for registering people for vaccination, testing and tracking people's daily activities. Primary Care records vaccination results, and Smile monitors vaccine distribution (Agustini 2021).

Table 2.2 details the initial COVID-19 vaccination targets and timeline in Indonesia. The plan was to vaccinate 181 million people aged 18 and above. The first wave of the vaccination programme was for health

TABLE 2.2
Vaccination Target and Wave in Indonesia

Period	*Period I*	*Period II*	*Period III*	*Period IV*
Vaccination targets	Health workers	Elderly and public service workers	Communities in high-risk areas	General population
Estimated population	1.46 million	38.4 million	63.9 million	77.7 million
Estimated time	January–June 2021	January–June 2021	June 2021 – March 2022	June 2021 – March 2022

Source: Ministry of Health (2021); Arifin and Anas (2022).

workers. The next wave was for the elderly and public service workers, followed by people living in the high-risk areas, and then the remaining general population. The vaccination plan was adjusted following the latest update from the vaccine clinical trial. For example, following the result of the latest clinical trial, the government allowed pregnant women and children aged 12–18 years old to be vaccinated beginning on 29 June 2021. Children 6–11 years old can also be vaccinated from 14 December 2021. The adjustment increases Indonesia's target population to 208 million, a 15 per cent increase from the initial plan.

Figure 2.12 shows Indonesia's vaccination rate from January 2021 to March 2022. The vaccination programme started on 13 January 2021 with low uptake in the first stage of the programme due to the limited vaccine supply from the manufacturers. As more vaccine supply became available, vaccination rates accelerated substantially. By March 2022, 93 per cent of the target population had received their first dose and 74 per cent of the population had received their second dose. Vaccination was accelerated by utilizing strategic public places, public and private offices and engaging the private sector to implement the vaccination programme. Drive-through and walk-in vaccinations were also provided at particular venues. The government also engaged public transportation companies to provide transportation to vaccination sites (Arifin and Anas 2021) and mobilized the army and police to organize vaccination programmes.

Although there has been substantial progress in vaccination rates in Indonesia, there are many individuals who have not been vaccinated as shown in Figure 2.13. Noting that the level of population immunity is important for further decision-making, the Ministry of Health, supported by the Faculty of Public Health of the University of Indonesia conducted a SARS Cov-2 serology survey during the period November–December 2021 in nine provinces in agglomeration areas with 9,541 samples and twenty-five provinces in non-agglomeration areas with 10,969 samples. The targeted respondents were people older than 1 year old.[2]

Figure 2.13 depicts the result of the survey that the SARS Cov-2 antibodies were found in 86.6 per cent of the Indonesian population. Surprisingly, 73.9 per cent of the unvaccinated population already had SARS Cov-2 antibodies. This implies that a very significant portion of the population has been exposed to SARS Cov-2. The survey also reveals that antibodies were much higher in the vaccinated population. This finding implies that there are already high levels of natural immunity

FIGURE 2.12
COVID-19 Vaccination in Indonesia

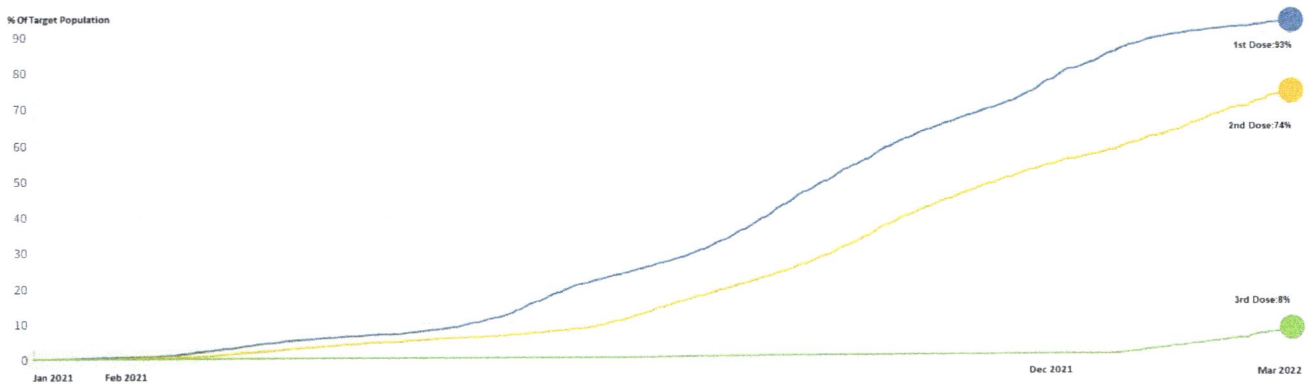

Source: COVID-19 and National Economic Recovery Committee (2022).

FIGURE 2.13
Proportion of Population with SARS Cov-2 Antibodies

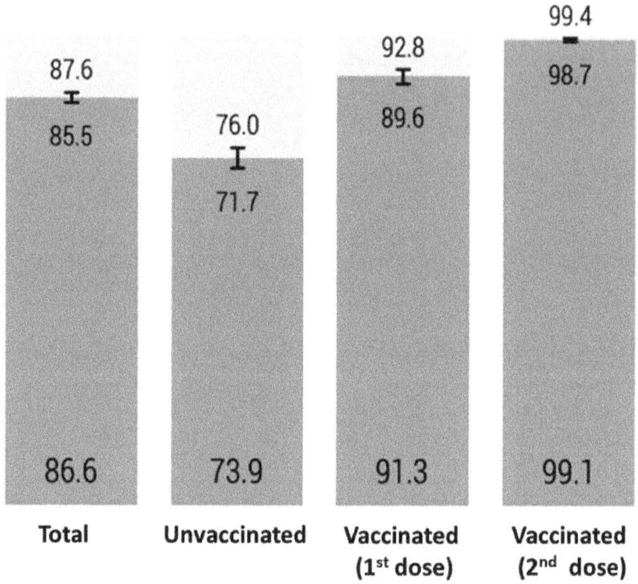

Source: Pandemic Team, Faculty of Public Health UI (2021).

from SARS COV-2 among the Indonesian population. Vaccination is still required despite the presence of high protection from natural immunity to ensure sufficient protection at all times so that people are more confident to engage in economic activities and leisure which are important for economic recovery. The presence of SARS COV-2 antibodies is an important consideration in formulating relevant strategies for a seamless transition from the pandemic phase into an endemic phase in the future.

2.4.6 Tax Incentives

The government provided various incentives for imports related to the COVID-19 pandemic handling, including medical devices, to prevent supply constraints. The incentives provided in 2020 reached IDR4.05 trillion, comprise of:

i. VAT incentives for imported medical equipment, vaccines and vaccine raw materials and drugs;
ii. Import Income Tax facility;
iii. Exemption from withholding Income Tax Article 21;
iv. Exemption from withholding Income Tax Article 23;
v. Customs handling facilitation for COVID-19-related medical equipment and devices imported by the central and regional government, public service agencies and foundations/non-profits.

In 2021, when the implementation of vaccination began, the government also provided VAT exemption for the COVID-19 vaccine. The facility was not only intended for the government vaccination programme but also for privately arranged vaccination programmes. In 2021, the realization of tax incentives and import duty for COVID-19-related in the PEN programme was IDR14.53 trillion.

2.4.7 Additional Health Spending and Intervention

Local governments also mobilized their regional budget (*Anggaran Pendapatan dan Belanja Daerah*, or APBD) for COVID-19 containment and support to their residents as the central government instructed local governments (provincial or municipality) to allocate a minimum of 8 per cent of the General Allocation Fund (*Dana Alokasi Umum*, or DAU) and Revenue Sharing Fund (*Dana Bagi Hasil*, or DBH) for COVID-19 handling. The allocation is used for incentives for health workers, the implementation of COVID-19 vaccinations in the regions (logistics, distribution and transportation), and support for the government at the subdistrict level. Regional Incentive Funds (*Dana Insentif Daerah*, or DID) and Health Operational Assistance (*Bantuan Operasional Kesehatan*, or BOK) are also used for handling COVID-19 in the regions, such as for contact tracing at the regional level.

At the village level, the central government also required the village governments to allocate a minimum of 8 per cent of the Village Funds for handling COVID-19. The allocation is used for self-isolation and health protocol interventions at the village level. The total of earmarked regional expenditures (DAU/DBH, DID, BOK, and Village Fund) in 2021 reached IDR41.85 trillion, equivalent to 21 per cent of the total budget for handling COVID-19 in the PEN programme.

During the containment of the Delta variant of COVID-19, the government increased the allocation for healthcare from IDR193.93 trillion to IDR214.95 trillion. The government distributes COVID-19 drugs for free and tightens mobility with the military and police at a budgeted cost of IDR1.63 trillion. The government also established Emergency Hospitals and turned the haj guesthouses into COVID-19 facilities. Additional allocation was also provided for oxygen supply and additional patient treatment claims following the increased number of hospitalized patients.

2.5 COVID-19 EXIT STRATEGIES AND MOVING FORWARD

The COVID-19 outbreak has devastating public health consequences and poses a major economic threat. The government undertook various measures to handle COVID-19 and its impacts. International travel restrictions have been in effect since 1 January 2020. Work, Study, and Worship from Home and PSBB measures have been implemented to reduce the outbreak in the early pandemic periods and resumed during the pandemic period with different names and stringency levels. Multiple fiscal incentives and facilitation have been applied to relieve unprecedented strain on medical supply chains in the early pandemic periods. Government Regulation Number 23/2020 which took effect on 11 May 2020 officially launched the National Economic Recovery (PEN) Programme, a series of programmes to accelerate the COVID-19 pandemic handling and economic recovery.

The lessons learnt from the pandemic, its health, social and economic impacts, and the implementation of the PEN programme is the importance of flexible fiscal policies when uncertainties arose. During the COVID-19 pandemic, government spending needed to be reallocated to the health sector, social protection and business support. The adoption of Government Regulation in Substitute for Legislation (*Peraturan Pemerintah Pengganti Undang-Undang*, or Perpu) Number 1, 2020 on Public Finance Policy and Financial System Stability to Manage the COVID-19 pandemic, which was later legislated as Law No. 2, 2020, granted fiscal flexibility to the government. Based on Law No. 2, 2020, the government can change the budget allocation without going through the normal parliamentary approval process which will be more time-consuming.

The pandemic also highlights the timing for reopening the economy needs to be evaluated by considering health, social and economic aspects.

The American Enterprise Institute (2020) provided guidelines for four phases of economic reopening. The first phase requires community-level physical distancing to slow down the containment of the virus, expansion of public healthcare facilities, and thorough diagnostic and testing. The second phase allows several business sectors to resume their activities with various social restrictions, that is, when conditions have met four criteria, namely, the number of new cases has declined for at least fourteen consecutive days, rapid diagnostic testing is sufficient, the healthcare system is adequate, and public healthcare has the capacity to carry out contact tracing effectively. The third phase begins when the COVID-19 vaccine programme is already effectively implemented. The final phase is carried out after the society and government are ready to face the next health crisis.

During the pandemic period in 2020–21, the implementation of the above guidelines was very challenging due to the emergence of new COVID-19 variants, such as the Delta and Omicron variants which have different levels of severity. Donsimoni et al. (2020) suggested that the reopening policy could be carried out reversibly. If the reproduction number increased, the lockdown should be reimposed. To reopen, the government needs to have a pilot policy for about four to eight weeks before all social restrictions are lifted. Indonesia evaluated the combination of positivity, hospitalization, death and vaccination rates when relaxing social restrictions.

Going forward, the pandemic revealed the limitations in Indonesia's health facilities, health-related technology, health workers and low testing rates and capacity which urgently needed to be addressed. This calls for the substantial transformation of the health sector. The Indonesian government has designed six transformation pillars to strengthen the health sector, namely the transformation of primary and secondary healthcare, healthcare resilience, health financing, health talents, and health-related technology.

Primary care transformation is needed to shift healthcare focus from curative measures to preventive measures. Increased routine immunization and expansion of early detection in primary healthcare are important elements of the transformation. For secondary care transformation, the focus on the development of secondary care networks, laboratories and health personnel for catastrophic diseases is important. For more healthcare resilience, the transformation of pharmaceutical, medical devices and equipment manufacturers towards more competitive industries is needed. The transformation of health financing will be mainly the transformation of JKN benefits.

To enhance the health talent pool, a higher number of doctors and better-designed incentives to promote more equal health worker distribution are needed. The number of doctors can be increased through improving scholarship schemes and health education centres. Technological transformation and digitalization on the other hand have proven to be the important elements of the success of the COVID-19 vaccination programme. Technological transformation will play an important role in shaping the future healthcare sector, including the development of big data, artificial intelligence, integrated health facility system, and the health technology ecosystem. The technological advancement will improve detection capacity which will in turn prevent the severity of diseases and transmission of infectious diseases.

Notes

1. From the Decree of the Minister of Health of the Republic of Indonesia Number HK.01.07/MENKES/278/2020 to the Decree of the Minister of Health of the Republic of Indonesia Number HK.01.07/MENKES/392/2020.
2. Sehat Negeri Ku, "Hasil Sero Survey: 86,6% Penduduk Indonesia Memiliki Antibodi terhadap COVID-19", 18 March 2022, https://sehatnegeriku.kemkes.go.id/baca/rilis-media/penelitian-dan-pengembangan-kesehatan/20220318/3139545/hasil-sero-survey-866-penduduk-indonesia-memiliki-antibodi-terhadap-covid-19/

References

Abadie, A., A. Diamond, and J. Hainmueller, 2010. "Synthetic Control Methods for Comparative Case Studies: Estimating the Effect of California's Tobacco Control Program". *Journal of the American Statistical Association* 105, no. 490: 493–505.

———, A. Diamond, and J. Hainmueller. 2015. "Comparative Politics and the Synthetic Control Method." *American Journal of Political Science* 59, no. 2: 495–510.

Agustina, R., T. Dartanto, R. Sitompul, K.A. Susiloretni, E.L. Achadi et al. "Universal Health Coverage in Indonesia: Concept, Progress, and Challenges". *Lancet*. 393: 75–102.

Agustini, P. 2021. "Tiga Aplikasi Integrasikan Satu Data Vaksinasi COVID-19". Kementerian Komunikasi dan Informatika RI. 13 January 2021. https://

aptika.kominfo.go.id/2021/01/tiga-aplikasi-integrasikan-satu-data-vaksinasi-COVID-19/

Aizawa, T. 2019. "The Impact of Health Insurance on Out-of-Pocket Expenditure on Delivery in Indonesia". *Health Care for Women International* 40, issue 12: 1374–95.

Al-Mansour, J.F., and S.A. Al-Ajmi. 2020. "Coronavirus 'COVID-19': Supply Chain Disruption and Implications for Strategy, Economy, and Management". *Journal of Asian Finance, Economics, and Business* 7, no. 9: 659–72.

Ambarwati, W. 2021. "Pembiayaan Pasien COVID-19 dan Dampak Keuangan terhadap Rumah Sakit yang Melayani Pasien COVID-19 di Indonesia Analisis Periode Maret 2020–Desember 2020". *Jurnal Ekonomi Kesehatan Indonesia* 6, no. 1.

American Enterprise Institute. 2020. "National Coronavirus Response: A Road Map to Reopening". 29 March 2020. https://www.aei.org/research-products/report/national-coronavirus-response-a-road-map-to-reopening/

Arifin, B., and T. Anas. 2021. "Lessons Learned from COVID-19 Vaccination in Indonesia: Experiences, Challenges, and Opportunities". *Human Vaccines and Immunotherapeutics* 17, issue 11: 3898–906.

Basnett, B.S., U.A. Riyanto, A.P. Hadiarta, and R.W. Istanti. 2022. "Towards an Inclusive Response to Combat COVID-19 Impacts on Women and People with Disabilities: Lessons from Indonesia for Peer Countries". In *Keeping Indonesia Safe from the COVID-19 Pandemic: Lessons Learnt from the National Economic Recovery Programme*, edited by S.M. Indrawati, S. Nazara, T. Anas, C.F. Ananda and K. Verico. Singapore: ISEAS – Yusof Ishak Institute.

Beeching, N.J., T.E. Fletcher, and M.B.J. Beadsworth. 2020. "COVID-19: Testing Times". *British Medical Journal* 369.

Biofarma. 2021. "The COVID-19 Vaccine Can Be Used in Indonesia". 11 January 2021. https://www.biofarma.co.id/en/latest-news/detail/the-covid19-vaccine-can-be-used-in-indonesia

Bode, L., and E. Vraga. 2021. "The Swiss Cheese Model for Mitigating Online Misinformation". *Bulletin of the Atomic Scientists* 77, no. 3: 129–33.

Bossuyt, P.M. 2020. "Testing COVID-19 Tests Faces Methodological Challenges". *Journal of Clinical Epidemiology* 126: 172–76.

Bursztyn, L., A. Rao, C. Roth, and D. Yanagizawa-Drott. 2020. "Misinformation During a Pandemic". Becker Friedman Institute for Economics at the University of Chicago, Working Paper No. 2020–44.

CNN Indonesia. 2020. "Kemendag Klaim 283 Ribu Ton Gula Impor Sudah Masuk RI". 24 April 2020. https://www.cnnindonesia.com/ekonomi/20200424092604-92-496811/kemendag-klaim-283-ribu-ton-gula-impor-sudah-masuk-ri

Courtemanche, C.J., J. Garuccio, A. Le, J.C. Pinkston, and A. Yelowitz. 2020. "Did Social-Distancing Measures in Kentucky Help to Flatten the COVID-19 Curve?". *Health Affairs*. https://doi.org/10.1377/hlthaff.2020.00608

Deconinck, K., E. Avery, and L.A. Jackson. 2020. "Food Supply Chains and COVID-19: Impacts and Policy Lessons". *EuroChoices* 19, no. 3: 34–39.

Diao, X., and A. Kennedy. 2016. "Economywide Impact of Maize Export Bans on Agricultural Growth and Household Welfare in Tanzania: A Dynamic Computable General Equilibrium Model Analysis". *Development Policy Review* 34, no. 1: 101–34.

Donsimoni J.R., R. Glawion, B. Plachter, K. Wälde, and C. Weiser. 2020. "Should Contact Bans Have Been Lifted More in Germany?". *CESifo Econ Studies* 66: 115–33.

Elena, M. 2021. "Indonesia Tak Bisa Terapkan Lockdown, Ini Kata Chatib Basri". *Bisnis.com*. https://ekonomi.bisnis.com/read/20210703/9/1413274/indonesia-tak-bisa-terapkan-lockdown-ini-kata-chatib-basri

Glass, R.J., L.M. Glass, W.E. Beyeler, and H.J. Min. 2006. "Targeted Social Distancing Designs for Pandemic Influenza". *Emerging Infectious Diseases* 12, no. 11: 1671.

Gollier, C., and O. Gossner. 2020. "Group Testing Against COVID-19". *EconPol Policy Brief* 24 (April).

Gottlieb, S., C. Rivers, M. McClellan, L. Silvis, and C. Watson. 2020. "National Coronavirus Response: A Road Map to Reopening". American Enterprise Institute, 29 March 2020.

Hamdhi, A. 2022. "ARSSI Perjuangkan Klaim Biaya Penangangan COVID-19 yang Dianggap Tidak Valid". *Kontan.co.id*, 16 February 2022. https://nasional.kontan.co.id/news/arssi-perjuangkan-klaim-biaya-penangangan-COVID-19-yang-dianggap-tidak-valid

Intan, G. 2020. "Kenapa Indonesia Tidak 'Lockdown'? Ini Jawaban Jokowi". VOA Indonesia, 24 March 2020. https://www.voaindonesia.com/a/kenapa-indonesia-tidak-lockdown-ini-jawaban-jokowi/5343239.html

Jackson, M.L., J.R. Chung, L.A. Jackson, C.H. Phillips, J. Benoit, A.S. Monto, … Gaglani, M. 2017. "Influenza Vaccine Effectiveness in the United States during the 2015–2016 Season". *New England Journal of Medicine* 377, no. 6: 534–43.

Jung, A.-S., V. Haldane, R. Neill, S. Wu, M. Jamieson, M. Verma, M., … P. Shrestha. 2021. "National Responses to COVID-19: Drivers, Complexities, and Uncertainties in the First Year of the Pandemic". *BMJ*, 375. https://doi.org/10.1136/bmj-2021-068954

kawalcovid19 website. https://kawalcovid19.id/

Kerr, W.A. 2020. "The COVID-19 Pandemic and Agriculture: Short- and Long-Run Implications for International Trade Relations". *Canadian Journal of Agricultural Economics/Revue Canadienne d'agroeconomie* 68, no. 2: 225–29.

King, G., and L. Zeng. 2006. "The Dangers of Extreme Counterfactuals". *Political Analysis* 14, no. 2: 131–59. https://doi.org/10.1093/pan/mpj004

Kochhar, S., B. Rath, L.D. Seeber, G. Rundblad, A. Khamesipour, M. Ali, and the

Vienna Vaccine Safety Initiative. 2013. "Introducing New Vaccines in Developing Countries". *Expert Review of Vaccines* 12, no. 12: 1465–78.

Kompas. 2020. "Apa Itu 'Swiss Cheese Model' dan Bagaimana Bisa Cegah Penyebaran COVID-19?". 26 October 2020. https://www.kompas.com/tren/read/2020/10/26/101100165/apa-itu-swiss-cheese-model-dan-bagaimana-bisa-cegah-penyebaran-COVID-19?page=all

Kontan. 2020. "Ada Relaksasi Impor Bawang Putih dan Bombai, Kementan Tetap Catat RIPH Importir". 29 March 2020. https://industri.kontan.co.id/news/ada-relaksasi-impor-bawang-putih-dan-bombai-kementan-tetap-catat-riph-importir

Koppenberg, M., M. Bozzola, T. Dalhaus, and S. Hirsch. 2021. "Mapping Potential Implications of Temporary COVID-19 Export Bans for the Food Supply in Importing Countries Using Precrisis Trade Flows". *Agribusiness* 37, no. 1: 25–43.

Laoli, N. 2021. "Ini Alasan Jokowi Kenapa Tidak Memilih Lockdown untuk Cegah Penyebaran COVID-19". *Kontan.co.id*, 30 July 2021. https://nasional.kontan.co.id/news/ini-alasan-jokowi-kenapa-tidak-memilih-lockdown-untuk-cegah-penyebaran-COVID-19

Larue, B., and A. Ker. 1993. "World Price Variability Versus Protectionism in Agriculture: A Causality Analysis". *Review of Economics and Statistics* 75, no. 2: 342–46.

Lauer, S.A., K.H. Grantz, Q. Bi, F.K. Jones, Q. Zheng, H.R. Meredith, … J. Lessler. 2020. "The Incubation Period of Coronavirus Disease 2019 (COVID-19) from Publicly Reported Confirmed Cases: Estimation and Application". *Annals of Internal Medicine*, 172, no. 9 (5 May 2020): 577–82. https://doi.org/10.7326/M20-0504

Mackay, I.M. 2020. "The Swiss Cheese Respiratory Virus Defence", figshare. Figure. https://doi.org/10.6084/m9.figshare.13082618.v24

Maharaj, S., and A. Kleczkowski. 2012. "Controlling Epidemic Spread by Social Distancing: Do It Well or Not at All". *BMC Public Health* 12, no. 1: 679.

Michelsen, S.W., B. Soborg, A. Koch, L. Carstensen, S.T. Hoff, E.M. Agger, … M. Melbye. 2014. "The Effectiveness of BCG Vaccination in Preventing Mycobacterium Tuberculosis Infection and Disease in Greenland". *Thorax* 69, no. 9: 851–56.

Ministry of Finance, Republic of Indonesia. 2020a. "Realisasi PEN Sementara". https://pen.kemenkeu.go.id/in/page/data-realisasi

———. 2020b. "Government Alerts to the Impact of the COVID-19 Pandemic on the Indonesian Economy". 17 April 2020. https://www.kemenkeu.go.id/publikasi/siaran-pers/siaran-pers-pemerintah-waspada-dampak-pandemi-COVID-19-terhadap-ekonomi-indonesia/

———. 2020c. "Preventing the Spread of COVID-19, Customs Gives Ethyl Alcohol Excise Exemption for Social Purposes and Manufactures Hand Sanitizer, Surface Sanitizer, and Antiseptic". 19 March 2020. https://www.kemenkeu.

go.id/publikasi/berita/cegah-penyebaran-COVID-19-bea-cukai-berikan-pembebasan-cukai-etil-alkohol-untuk-tujuan-sosial-dan-pembuatan-hand-sanitizer-surface-sanitizer-dan-antiseptik/

———. 2020d."Analisis Ketersediaan Bahan Pokok dan Alat Kesehatan Pandemi COVID-19".

———. 2021. "Laporan Mingguan Tahun 2021". https://pen.kemenkeu.go.id/in/page/laporan-mingguan-2021

Ministry of Trade. 2020. "Fighting COVID-19: Ministry of Trade Relaxes Export and Import Regulations to Fulfil Medical Devices and Personal Protective Equipment". 6 April 2020. https://www.kemendag.go.id/id/pers/lawan-COVID-19-kemendag-relaksasi-regulasi-ekspor-dan-impor-untuk-pemenuhan-alat-kesehatan-dan-apd-1

National Disaster Management Authority Information. 2020. "Bersatu Lawan COVID-19". https://bnpb.go.id/covid-19/

Noh, J.Y., J.Y. Song, J.G. Yoon, H. Seong, H.J. Cheong, and W.J. Kim. 2020. "Safe Hospital Preparedness in the Era of COVID-19: The Swiss Cheese Model". *International Journal of Infectious Diseases* 98: 294–96.

PCPEN. 2020. "Pemerintah Telah Siapkan Sistem Satu Data Vaksinasi COVID-19". https://covid19.go.id/p/berita/pemerintah-telah-siapkan-sistem-satu-data-vaksinasi-COVID-19

Purbasari, D.P., E. Satriawan, and R.E. Sitorus. 2022. "*Kartu Prakerja*: A Breakthrough for Boosting Labour Market Productivity and Social Assistance Inclusiveness". In *Keeping Indonesia Safe from the COVID-19 Pandemic: Lessons Learnt from the National Economic Recovery Programme,* edited by S.M. Indrawati, S. Nazara, T. Anas, C.F. Ananda and K. Verico. Singapore: ISEAS – Yusof Ishak Institute.

Reluga, T.C. 2020. "Social Distancing. Definition". https://doi.org/10.32388/q7f4ke

Revindo, M.D., J.F. Rezki, D. Anindita, and C.E. Dewi. 2022. "Weathering and Recovering from the Pandemic: Lessons Learnt from MSMEs in Indonesia". In *Keeping Indonesia Safe from the COVID-19 Pandemic: Lessons Learnt from the National Economic Recovery Programme,* edited by S.M. Indrawati, S. Nazara, T. Anas, C.F. Ananda and K. Verico. Singapore: ISEAS – Yusof Ishak Institute.

Salma. 2021. "The Sinovac Vaccine, Which Showed an Efficacy of 65.3 per cent, Is Declared Safe". Universiti Gadjah Mada, 12 January 2021. https://www.ugm.ac.id/en/news/20611-ugm-expert-having-an-efficacy-rate-of-65-3-per cent-sinovac-vaccine-remains-safe

Sano, K., A. Ainai, T. Suzuki, and H. Hasegawa. 2017. "The Road to a More Effective Influenza Vaccine: Up to Date Studies and Future Prospects". *Vaccine* 35, no. 40: 5388–95.

Sarin, A., V. Bhatnagar, A. Neelakantan, and M. Khandare. 2020. "Best Practices with Optimal Outcomes during COVID-19 Pandemic: A Swiss Cheese Model

Experiment in the Naval Training Command". *Journal of Marine Medical Society* 22, no. 2: 266.

Sastrosuwito, S., Abdurohman, A. Gunawan, and Y.A.M. Sujono. 2022. "Corporate Sector Performance during the COVID-19 Pandemic". In *Keeping Indonesia Safe from the COVID-19 Pandemic: Lessons Learnt from the National Economic Recovery Programme,* edited by S.M. Indrawati, S. Nazara, T. Anas, C.F. Ananda and K. Verico. Singapore: ISEAS – Yusof Ishak Institute.

Sucahya, P.K. 2020. "Barriers to COVID-19 RT-PCR Testing in Indonesia: A Health Policy Perspective". *Journal of Indonesian Health Policy and Administration* 5, no. 2: 36–42.

Utomo, W., S.K. Rahway, I. Marlina, and S. Sumarto. 2022. "Protecting the People". In *Keeping Indonesia Safe from the COVID-19 Pandemic: Lessons Learnt from the National Economic Recovery Programme,* edited by S.M. Indrawati, S. Nazara, T. Anas, C.F. Ananda and K. Verico. Singapore: ISEAS – Yusof Ishak Institute.

VOI. 2020. "Clinical Trials Of COVID-19 Vaccine in Indonesia Enter the Monitoring Period". 12 November 2020. https://voi.id/en/news/19637/clinical-trials-of-COVID-19-vaccine-in-indonesia-enter-the-monitoring-period

Weiss, M., A. Schwarzenberg, R. Nelson, K.M. Sutter, and M.D. Sutherland. 2020. "Global economic effects of COVID-19". Congressional Research Service, 5 November 2020. https://crsreports.congress.gov/product/pdf/R/R46270/53

Wernli, D., F. Tediosi, K. Blanchet, K. Lee, C. Morel, D. Pittet, … O. Young. 2021. "A Complexity Lens on the COVID-19 Pandemic". *International Journal of Health Policy and Management*, pp. 1–4.

Wildan, M. 2020. "The Government Relaxes the Trading System for Importing Medical Devices, Here Are the Details of the Rules". *Bisnis.com,* 2 April 2020. https://ekonomi.bisnis.com/read/20200402/12/1221554/pemerintah-relaksasi-tata-niaga-impor-alkes-ini-rincian-aturannya

Workie, E., J. Mackolil, J. Nyika, and S. Ramadas. 2020. "Deciphering the Impact of COVID-19 Pandemic on Food Security, Agriculture, and Livelihoods: A Review of the Evidence from Developing Countries". *Current Research in Environmental Sustainability* 2 (December): 100014.

World Bank. 2020. "Saving Lives, Scaling-up Impact and Getting Back on Track". World Bank Group COV1D-19 Crisis Response Approach Paper, Washington, DC.

———. 2021. *Global Economic Prospect: June 2021*. Washington, DC: World Bank. https://doi.org/10.1596/978-1-4648-1665-9

PART II

Economic Shock: The Framework

3

Maintaining Macroeconomic Stability during the Pandemic

Febrio Nathan Kacaribu and Masyita Crystallin

3.1 INTRODUCTION[1]

Indonesia was on a growth trajectory between 2010 and 2019 with annual growth rates averaging 5.4 per cent and was hopeful of achieving the high-income country status by 2045. In 2019 Indonesia managed to show a healthy macroeconomic status—growth reached 5.02 per cent, the inflation rate was manageable at 2.78 per cent, the Gini ratio was at 0.39, the rupiah appreciated by 5 per cent, and there was a 138-basis point decrease in Indonesia's ten-year government bond yield in the second half of the year.

In 2020, the World Bank classified Indonesia as an upper-middle-income country. Later, due to the COVID-19 pandemic, Indonesia was then reclassified as a lower-middle-income country. The unprecedented Wuhan outbreak surprisingly shook the global economy to its core in a manner we had never seen before, except perhaps during the Spanish flu pandemic in the early 1900s. At about the time the first COVID-19 cases began to appear, the world was under a cloud due to the US-China trade war which had caused a long period of economic uncertainty and increased geopolitical tension resulting in surging commodity prices. In Q4 2019, the global economy looked set to rebound. Capital flows started returning to emerging markets assets, including Indonesia. The rupiah appreciated by 5 per cent between 31 May 2019 and 31 January 2020, and the ten-year yield went down by 138 basis points during the same period.

COVID-19 first emerged in late December 2019 in Wuhan, China (WHO 2020) and was thought to be a pneumonia disease. By mid-February 2020, positive cases had reached close to 50,000 and spread across twenty-seven countries. By this time, the global market was still in its bullish tendency, with capital flows still flowing into the emerging markets. However, the disease spread fast, pushing the World Health Organization (WHO) to announce a pandemic status on 11 March 2020. At that time, the financial market was still unaware of what was coming but there were already more than 118,000 COVID-19 cases in over 110 countries.

The global financial market was priced in less than ten days after the WHO declared the pandemic. On 20 March 2020, there was a freeze in the global financial market. The Volatility Index (VIX) hit an all-time high of 53.54. This indicates heightened volatility in the equity market, a marker for global volatility. Indonesia also felt the heat. Capital outflows reached IDR124.9 trillion in March (2020) and IDR158.3 trillion in September 2020, more profound than outflows during the 2013 taper tantrum and 2009 Global Financial Crisis (GFC). Emerging market currencies depreciated, including the rupiah which weakened by 16 per cent from February to IDR16,575 per US dollar on 23 March 2020, the lowest level since the Asian Financial Crisis.

Despite the lag in the global market's reaction, the government quickly started considering the possibility of introducing measures to make the budget more flexible whilst facing unprecedented circumstances in Lieu of Law Number 1 of 2020 (Emergency Law). Indonesia's budget has a cap of a maximum deficit of 3 per cent of GDP, and reallocation of budgets between and within ministries requires parliamentary approval. The Emergency Law provided the government room to introduce policies in response to the pandemic and its domino effects, focusing on three areas: health, social safety nets for vulnerable households, and support for the real sector, especially for the medium and small-sized enterprises (MSEs).

As a result, the law stipulated that the budget was allowed to exceed the maximum threshold of 3 per cent of GDP before going back to normal.

The Economic Recovery Programme was launched through Presidential Decree No. 72/2020, worth IDR695.2 trillion or 6.34 per cent of GDP in 2020 and another 5.7 per cent of GDP in 2021. The stimulus packages helped 5.5 million Indonesians vulnerable to poverty, which was at an all-time low of 9.78 per cent before the pandemic.

This chapter describes the policy reaction and the policy environment in a timeline to give readers an overview of how the government dealt with the pandemic under high uncertainty, volatility and tremendous pressure.

3.2 THE DAWN OF THE PANDEMIC

During the dawn of the pandemic, the first policy responses to the impact of the COVID-19 contagion could be considered forward-looking interventions. One of the responses was Financial Services Authority (FSA) Regulation Number 11/POJK.03/2020 concerning National Economic Stimulus as a Countercyclical Policy for the Impact of the Spread of Coronavirus Disease 2019. This regulation was dated 13 March 2020 and was valid until 31 March 2021. The main policy consideration behind the regulation was that the spread of COVID-19 might potentially affect debtors' performance and capacity, thus increasing credit risk and potentially disrupting the banking sector performance and even Indonesia's financial system stability.

The FSA intervention was mainly intended to prevent a further economic slowdown. In addition, it aimed to prudently optimize banking performance (i.e., intermediary function) and maintain domestic financial system stability, while minimizing moral hazard. According to the regulations, the banking industry should implement a countercyclical policy to support all debtors affected by COVID-19, including those in micro, small and medium business. This countercyclical policy has been undertaken through two channels: (1) asset quality determination; and (2) credit or financing restructuring.

First, as per the regulations, banks needed to ease the asset quality determination for debtors affected by COVID-19, especially those whose loans were up to IDR10 billion. That is to say, credit quality for those particular loans could be assessed based only on the debtors' compliance with their loan payments schedule. Therefore, other parameters of credit quality assessment, such as business prospects and debtor financial performance were deliberately relieved until 31 March 2021.

Secondly, the countercyclical policy was undertaken through credit restructuring facilities. Banks were permitted to restructure all debtors' loans whose businesses were affected by COVID-19, including loans by MSMEs, regardless of their credit ceiling limit. Moreover, as per the regulation, banks were allowed to recategorize those restructured loans into performing loans. Technically, this intervention could be carried out by lowering interest rates, extending the instalment periods, reducing principal or interest arrears, adding credit facilities, or converting loans into Temporary Equity Participation.

3.2.1 Incentivize Foreign Domestic Tourists

As mentioned earlier, "unprecedented" really does sum up all the bizarre conditions caused by the Wuhan outbreak in December 2019. Normal life was literally going to stop soon. On 30 January 2020, seven days after Wuhan started its quarantine, the WHO held an Emergency Committee meeting regarding the Wuhan outbreak. From this meeting, the committee declared the outbreak was a novel coronavirus, but they decided not to recommend any travel or trade restrictions to all countries yet. Then, on 11 March 2020, the WHO belatedly declared the outbreak a COVID-19 pandemic, and at that time, more than 118,000 cases were reported in more than 110 countries.

The vagueness of the pandemic's early stage made it difficult for governments worldwide, including in China, to make firm decisions regarding travel. While the local government in Wuhan and Beijing implemented very strict domestic quarantines and lockdowns, China's central government was strongly against international restrictions even after the WHO's pandemic declaration. Then a phone call on 27 March 2020 between US President Donald Trump and the Chinese President resulted in Xi Jinping concurring and curbing international flights from China.

Despite Chinese authorities' loose international flight policy, Indonesia recorded a major decline in tourism, significantly from China. Statistics Indonesia reported a 93.5 per cent year-on-year (YoY) decline in Chinese tourist visits in February 2020 (11,780 tourists); previously there were 181,281 visits. In total, foreign tourist visits declined by 28.85 per cent YoY in February 2020 compared to February 2019.

Little did we know that the pneumonia-like disease was soon to be a global pandemic claiming millions of lives, and that limiting movements should have been a top priority in formulating policies. But with very limited knowledge and information at that time, seeing the dramatic decline in tourism, the government of Indonesia tried to stimulate tourism activity to save the sector through countercyclical fiscal policy. The declining tourism activity was even looked at as an opportunity to accelerate the promotion of national strategic tourism areas (*Kawasan Strategis Pariwisata Nasional,* or KSPN) as a part of the national strategic projects (*Proyek Strategis Nasional,* or PSN).

That fiscal policy was then translated into various incentives to attract both foreign and domestic tourists. First, a budget amounting to IDR298.5 billion was allocated to incentivize airlines, travel agents, and Indonesian tourism representatives around the world. Then IDR147.7 billion worth of grants were allocated for the regional tourism programme, and another IDR3.3 trillion was allocated for tax compensation for hotels and restaurants. On top of that, the government allocated IDR443.3 billion for transportation incentives, IDR265.6 billion compensation for aviation fuel prices, and IDR99.8 billion compensation for aviation service tariffs.

3.2.2 Emergency Law

With the magnitude of the crisis still unknown, the government immediately intervened with fiscal policy. The first intervention was a state budget refocusing and reallocation per Presidential Instruction Number 4 of 2020, dated 20 March 2020, a week after the WHO officially announced the pandemic. The President instructed government agencies to re-evaluate spending priorities for programmes or activities that could effectively offset the COVID-19 spillovers.

In addition, three stimulus packages were launched by President Jokowi's administration. The first stimulus package was launched in February 2020, when the spread of the virus was still centred in China. Stimulus Package I, worth IDR8.5 trillion, included policies such as accelerated disbursements and labour-intensive stimulus for vulnerable groups and sectors affected by the outbreak.

Stimulus Package II, worth IDR22.5 trillion, was launched the following month, consisting of tax reductions and incentives for exports and imports of particular commodities, including sectoral support for manufacturing, food, and health services whose business operations were considered relevant to COVID-19 pandemic handling. Export-import processes for

Reputable Traders were also eased. The government also supported the most affected debtors through credit payment relaxation and credit restructuring, especially MSMEs. In addition, the government also relaxed the *BP Jamsostek* social security contribution for businesses and employers affected by the economic slowdown.

Anticipating more profound pandemic impacts, Stimulus Package III was launched on 31 March 2020. Amounting to IDR405 trillion, the stimulus was intended to support the health sector, social safety net, the real economy, and the financial sector. However, COVID-19 spillovers seemed to expand and threaten beyond just livelihoods and needed extraordinary policies.

Therefore, a breakthrough policy was undertaken by the Jokowi administration. Emergency Law, the so-called Government Regulation in Lieu of Law Number 1 of 2020, was then ratified to provide a legal basis for the government to take extraordinary steps in minimizing the brutal pandemic's direct and indirect impacts while maintaining domestic stability and national resilience. In addition, the Emergency Law provided flexibility to expand a fiscal deficit to go beyond 3 per cent of GDP. The stimulus was then expanded from IDR405 trillion to IDR695.2 trillion, later known as the National Economic Recovery Programme (*Program Pemulihan Ekonomi Nasional*, or PEN).

3.3 THE NATIONAL ECONOMIC RECOVERY PROGRAMME

The COVID-19 pandemic shows that interconnectivity can be both a blessing and a curse. A blessing as it unveils endless possibilities for humankind to thrive. In contrast, with rapid virus transmission, interconnectivity could mean doomsday has arrived. Humans had never been more connected than ever before, thus enabling the coronavirus to move from Wuhan to every corner of every country across the globe. A few days after being declared a pandemic on 11 March 2020, COVID-19 moved the world into a bleak, bizarre reality: recession.

The global economy slowed down immensely. Indonesia suffered a contraction of 5.32 per cent in Q2 2020. The mobility restrictions resulted in a major shock to domestic demand and short-term supply, crashing the manufacturing Purchasing Managers Index (PMI) to 27.5. In May 2020, more than 1.7 million formal and informal workers lost their jobs.[2] Income inequality worsened, shown by the increase in the Gini ratio to

0.393; and the poverty rate increased 37 percentage points the same month the pandemic hit. In only six months, job loss in the formal sector grew from over 1.7 million to 5.62 million, in which 81 per cent switched to the informal sector.

While the economy contracted, the death toll kept eerily increasing. The government needed to be present with responsive policies enabling people to make ends meet while battling for life. One of the monumental policies undertaken was the economic recovery programme. The programme covers broad areas, with health issues as the top priority.

On 18 May 2020, the Parliament passed the Emergency Law in Law Number 2 of 2020. The law added more certainty for the government to take extraordinary, forward-looking, and anticipative strategies as significant uncertainty existed. As a result, the deficit could go beyond its upper limit of 3 per cent of GDP. The 2020 deficit widened to 6.34 per cent of GDP and added IDR695.2 trillion (4.2 per cent of GDP) spending for the economic recovery programme according to Presidential Regulation No. 72/2020, as seen in Figure 3.1.

As a countercyclical strategy, deficit widening aimed to support the demand-side (e.g., social protection expansion), increase sectoral and regional government support, supply-side support for SMEs, and corporate financing, including tax incentives and facilities. In addition, to maintain household consumption, the social protection programme was expanded. Amongst these were the Family Hope Programme, food assistance, cash transfers, electricity bill discounts, and the Pre-employment Card Programme. At the end of 2020, the budget was realized at 83.4 per cent or IDR579.78 trillion.

With the pandemic still very much a threat to the country, the economic recovery programme was extended for 2021. The programme prioritized five areas: the health sector, social protection, priority programmes, firms and MSMEs support, and business incentives. A budget of IDR744.77 trillion was allocated and the realization reached IDR658.6 trillion or 88.4 per cent of the budget.

One of the defining programmes within the economic recovery programme was social protection. Having been undertaken since 1998, social protection during the pandemic—amounting to IDR203.9 trillion in 2020—became the mechanism most closely matching the immediate needs of households (Table 3.1).

FIGURE 3.1
Indonesia's Economic Recovery Programme, 2020–22

Source: Indonesia's Ministry of Finance, 2021.

TABLE 3.1
Social Protection Expansion

	Conditional Cash Transfer Program or *PKH*	Basic Food Voucher or *Kartu Sembako*	Electricity Subsidy	Cash Transfer for outer Jabodetabek Region	Basic Food Social Assistance for Jabodetabek Region	Village Fund Cash Transfer or *BLT Dana Desa*	Pre-employment Card or *Kartu Prakerja*	Internet Quota
Decile of Income (6, 5, 4, 3, 2, 1)	10 million households (HH) Index per component rises by 25%	20 million HH (2020) 18.8 million HH (2021) IDR 200 K/month	450 VA: 24 million HH 900 VA: 7.2 million HH 450 VA→free 900 VA→50% discount	9 million HH (2020) 10 millions HH (2021) Apr – Jun: IDR 600K/month Jul – Sept: IDR 300K/month 2021: IDR 300K/month *2020: Excluding PKH & Food Voucher recipients.*	1.3 million HH 600.000 HH Apr – Jun: IDR 600K/month Jul – Sept: IDR 300K/month 2021: IDR 300K/month *2020: Excluding PKH & Food Voucher recipients.* *2021: 2020's criteria plus excluding Cash Transfer and Pre-employment recipients*	11 million HH (2020) 8 millions HH (2021) Apr – Jun: IDR 600K/month Jul – Sept: IDR 300K/month ***Excluding PKH & Food Voucher recipients***	5.6 million HH **Training** IDR 1 million/month **Incentive** IDR 600K/month **Survey (3x)** IDR 50K/month	41.8 million recipients Early Childhood (20 GB), Elementary - SHS (35 GB), University (50 GB), Teacher/lecturer (42 GB), at price of 1 GB of IDR 1 K Students and teachers
Time Frame	montlhy, for 12 months	monthly, for 12 months	6 months	9 months (2020) 4 months (2021)	9 months	6 months	Incentive for 4 months	5 months

Fiscal Year	Additional Budget (trillion)	Total Budget (trillion) FY 2020: IDR 220.39 FY 2021: IDR 157.41
PKH 2020	8.3	37.4
PKH 2021	-	28.71
Kartu Sembako 2020	15.5	43.6
Kartu Sembako 2021	-	45.12
Electricity Subsidy Apr - Sept 2020	6.9	6.9
Electricity Subsidy Jan – Jun 2021	-	5.64
Cash Transfer Apr – Dec 2020	32.4	32.4
Cash Transfer Jan – Apr 2021	-	12
Basic Food Social Assistance Apr – Dec 2020	6.8	6.8
Basic Food Social Assistance 2021	-	-
BLT Dana Desa Apr - Sept 2020	31.8	31.8
BLT Dana Desa Jan – Jun 2021	-	14.4
Kartu Prakerja Apr - Nov 2020	10.0	20.0
Kartu Prakerja 2021	-	20.0
Internet Quota 2020	-	
Internet Quota Jan - May 2021	-	4.98

Notes: BLT = Village Fund cash transfer programme (*Bantuan Langsung Tunai*), GB = gigabyte, HH = household, PKH = cash transfer programme known as Family Hope Programme (*Program Keluarga Harapan*), SHS = senior high school, VA = volt-ampere.
Source: Indonesia's Ministry of Social Affairs (2021) and Indonesia's Ministry of Finance (2021b).

The other major components within the economic recovery programme were sectoral and regional stimulus amounting to IDR66.59 trillion. This budget was fully disbursed by the end of 2020 and was essential to support frontline institutions such as local governments in assisting labour-intensive sectors, which were hit hard. This also included regional incentive funds to enhance innovation and special allocation funds to support infrastructure development. This stimulus was extended in the following year. The focus included food security, job creation, information and communications technology (ICT) development, industrial development, loans to the regions, and tourism.

The economic recovery programme was a response to both the demand- and supply-side shocks. In response to the supply-side shock, the policy set focused on MSMEs, strategic sectors, and subnational and state-owned enterprises (SOEs). The relief was given through interest rate subsidies, tax relief, working capital access, state equity participation for SOEs, cash transfer for MSMEs, and loan restructuring. In addition, incentives and compensation for MSMEs in several strategic tourism spots were there, as well.

The intervention was also in labour-intensive sectors, as informality covers 57 per cent of Indonesia's economy. The top three GDP contributors which employed many informal workers are agriculture, manufacturing, wholesale and retail. With these settings, fiscal relief will be more effective if directly focused on industrial-labour relations. Direct fiscal relief through social protection expansion in the agriculture and wholesale and retail sectors should be more effective than tax incentives, working capital access, and debt restructuring.

Meanwhile, fiscal relief delivery will be more effective for sectors with low informality such as manufacturing, if provided to both employers and employees through tax incentives, working capital access via state guarantee provisions and credit restructuring. Capital structure strengthening was also encouraged through capital injections and compensation.

3.4 INDONESIAN ECONOMY 2020

3.4.1 The Rebound Moment

After experiencing reasonably high growth in 2019, Indonesia was under pressure in 2020 due to the COVID-19 pandemic. The economic slowdown began in Q1 2020 when the economy grew by just 2.97 per cent (YoY). The downturn occurred in almost all components of expenditure; public consumption and investment slowed sharply. Weakening global economic conditions are reflected in the decline of exports and imports.

As seen in Figure 3.2 and Table 3.2, in Q2 2020, the economy experienced a contraction of –5.3 per cent (YoY). Mobility restriction policy somehow reduced economic activity as reflected in the Google Mobility report, i.e., declining by 24.1 per cent compared to normal conditions (January–February 2020). The decline led to a contraction in household spending, such as for clothes, transportation and communications, and leisure, e.g., hotels and restaurants. Growth in government consumption also contracted by 6.9 per cent (YoY). In terms of investment, government capital spending

FIGURE 3.2
Indonesia's Economic Growth, 2019–21

Source: Indonesia's Ministry of Finance, 2021.

TABLE 3.2
Indonesia's Expenditure Growth by Components, 2020 (%, YoY)

	Q1	*Q2*	*Q3*	*Q4*
Consumption	2.65	–5.58	–4.00	–3.58
Government	3.80	–6.92	9.79	1.79
Investment	1.70	–8.61	–6.52	–6.17
Export	0.17	–12.43	–13.04	–6.89
Import	–5.44	–20.74	–24.49	–15.83
Total GDP	2.97	–5.32	–3.49	–2.17

Source: Indonesia's Ministry of Finance, 2021.

and private investment also declined. In addition, indirect investment, both foreign and domestic, diminished.

The global trade shock also put pressure on the country's exports and imports. Indonesia's exports recorded negative growth of 11.7 per cent (YoY), while imports declined by –17 per cent (YoY). In terms of goods, non-oil and gas were still primary. Meanwhile, service exports experienced a significant drop due to a sharp decline in foreign tourist arrivals. The domestic slowdown also pressured imports of all types of goods. The decline in imports of raw materials and capital goods indicated a slowdown in manufacturing productivity. The PMI manufacturing index fell considerably to 31.7 (average) in Q2 2020, as seen on the right side of Figure 3.3.

In Q3 2020, the economy improved, though it still contracted by –3.49 per cent (YoY). Mobility relaxation and various fiscal stimuli helped relieve the pressure. For example, social protection expansion helped to maintain the purchasing power of vulnerable groups. In addition, relaxing mobility restrictions (Figure 3.3, left) also encouraged consumption although the impact was limited. This progress has prompted an improvement in sectors such as transportation, restaurants and hotels.

Government consumption grew quite a lot at 9.8 per cent (YoY) amid the pandemic, acting as a countercyclical instrument to help economic recovery. The increase was mainly due to the PEN programme, including incentives for medical personnel, expenditure on goods, and social assistance. Investment in Q3 2020 signalled a recovery trajectory, in which its YoY growth improved from –8.61 per cent to –6.52 per cent, showing a slight recovery in the construction sector.

FIGURE 3.3
Mobility Index and PMI Manufacture

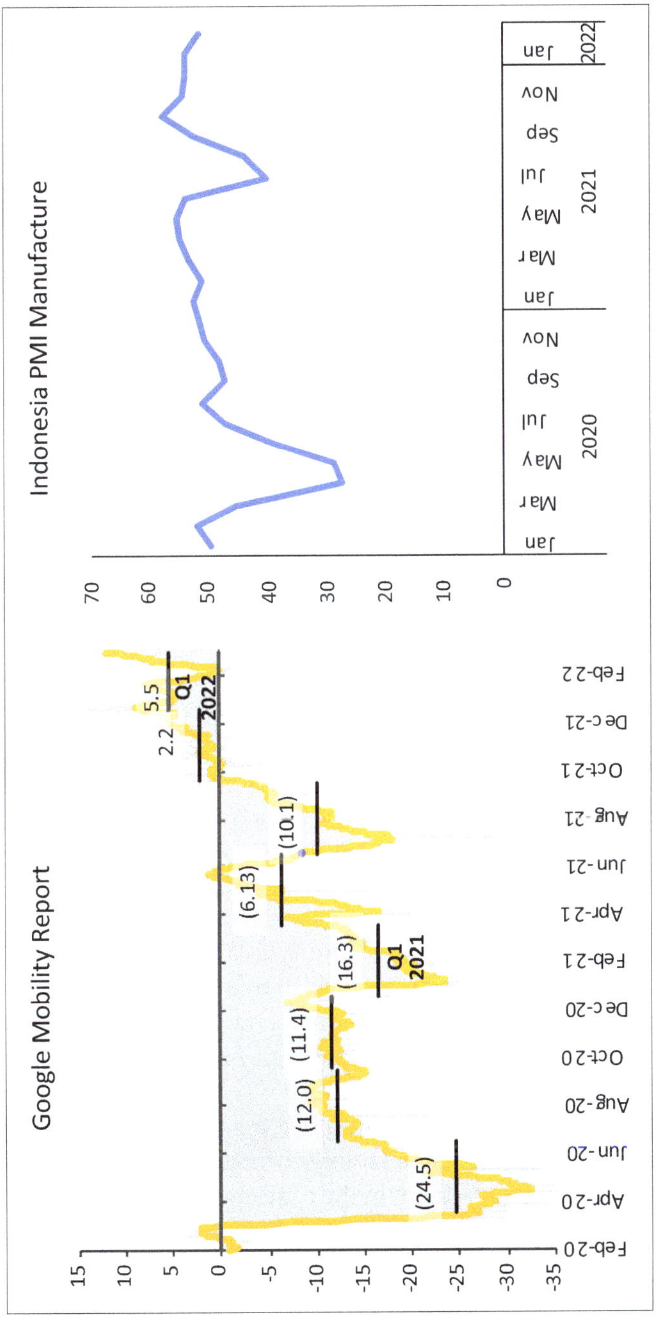

Source: Indonesia's Ministry of Finance, 2021.

Exports in Q3 2020 grew by –10.8 per cent (YoY), while imports were still under pressure with a larger contraction (–21.9 per cent YoY). This led to a higher trade balance surplus. Although imports remained depressed, PMI manufacturing significantly improved. This pointed to a better direction for the recovery trend.

In Q4 2020, growth was recorded at –2.19 per cent (YoY). The smaller contraction indicated continuous recovery. Consumption trends continue to increase as social assistance programmes maintained purchasing power stability and the public was getting more confident. Fiscal expansion supported vulnerable groups and private businesses through PEN.

In addition, in Q4 government capital expenditure helped improve investment amidst a private sector freeze. On the external side, exports of goods improved as the global economy, especially Indonesia's major trading partner countries, recovered. Exports of services had not yet recovered. Import contraction began to slow down as raw materials and capital goods imports improved.

3.4.2 Fiscal Consolidation

Indonesia's fiscal policy struck the right balance between countercyclical and prudence measures during the pandemic. Extraordinary stimulus cushioned the most vulnerable groups via various social assistance. Further, extensive support to the business sector helped sustain business resilience during the economic hardship.

Since the effect of the COVID-19 pandemic was more than just economic hardship, i.e., it was a health crisis as well, financing for strengthening the health system and virus containment was always at the heart of the fiscal policy. Consequently, fiscal deficits widened. Fortunately, Indonesia had adequate fiscal room to manoeuvre. The country has long been noted for prudent fiscal management, including its discipline in keeping fiscal deficits below 3 per cent of GDP with one of the lowest debt levels among its peers.

Despite extraordinary stimulus, prudent fiscal policy preserved medium- or long-run sustainability through gradual consolidation. This was taken into consideration in the drafting of the Emergency Law, which outlined the obligation for the fiscal deficit to return to a maximum of 3 per cent of GDP in 2023.

In the first year of the pandemic, the fiscal deficit jumped to 6.14 per cent of GDP. Revenue performance was hit by slowing economic activities while spending needed to increase to prevent further slowdown. The following year, the fiscal deficit improved to 4.65 per cent of GDP, creating a favourable basis for further consolidation. The recovery in economic activities in 2021 was one of the most critical factors, as state revenue was boosted by more than 21 per cent. Now, the state budget in 2022 aims to smoothen and sustain this improvement towards budget discipline in 2023. The budget's central policy is strengthening COVID-19 handling and economic recovery while promoting structural reforms.

3.5 LIQUIDITY TRAP

Excess liquidity occurred in the financial sector. Deposits experienced high positive growth, the highest since 2017. In contrast, credit growth contracted for the first time in two decades. When COVID-19 hit, uncertainty lingered, and mobility was limited—people tended to save their funds. Credit contraction occurred for eight consecutive months from October 2020 to May 2021 (Figure 3.4) while the contraction in investments and working capital loans lasted longer than for consumption loans (Figure 3.5).

The excess was also shown by a declining trend in the loan-to-deposit ratio (LDR) (Figure 3.6). Experiencing a credit crunch, Indonesia's monetary policy transmission was asymmetric when compared to interest rates. The commercial banks' lending rate declined slower than BI's 7 Days Reverse Repo Rate (BI 7 DRR) although BI 7 DRR reached a historical record low, falling by 150 bps from early 2020 to December 2021, reaching 3.5 per cent. Moreover, the commercial banks' lending rate which was still high, showed a significant spread with Indonesia's benchmark rate (Figure 3.7). This combined situation was an early indication of the liquidity trap.

High savings rates and low credit at a time when the benchmark interest rate was at lower levels could be considered a threat to the economy. A liquidity trap can be triggered by several conditions: zero lower bound benchmark rate, deflation, stagnant wages, and low credit (Amadeo 2021). Once the interest rate is at zero lower bound and cannot fall any further, Bank Indonesia (BI, or Indonesia's Central Bank) has no tools left to stimulate consumption and lending in times of excess liquidity. In other words, conventional monetary policy becomes powerless in increasing aggregate demand.

In theory, monetary expansion during a recession (by lowering the benchmark rate) is expected to spur consumption and investment,

FIGURE 3.4
Deposit and Credit Growth (%, YoY)

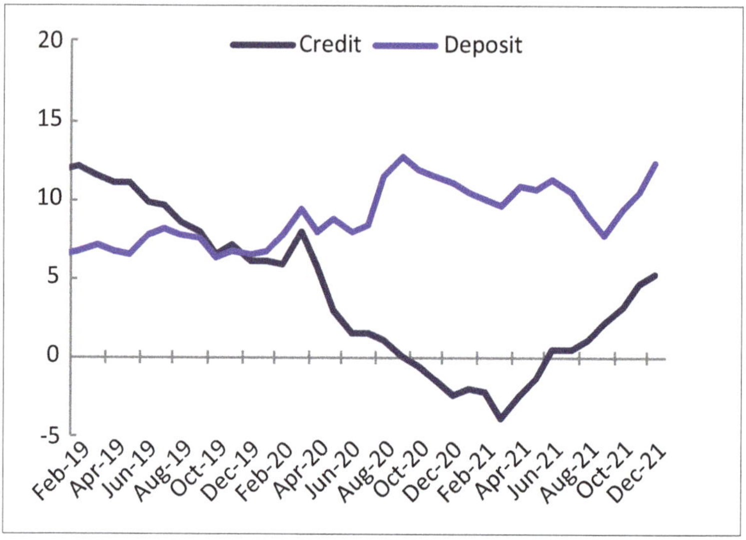

Source: BI, OJK, CEIC.

FIGURE 3.5
Credit Growth by Type (%, YoY)

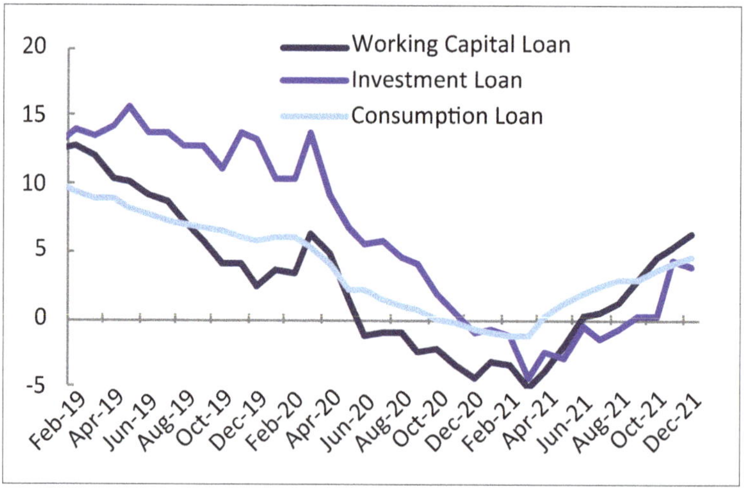

Source: BI, OJK, CEIC.

FIGURE 3.6
Loan to Deposit Ratio

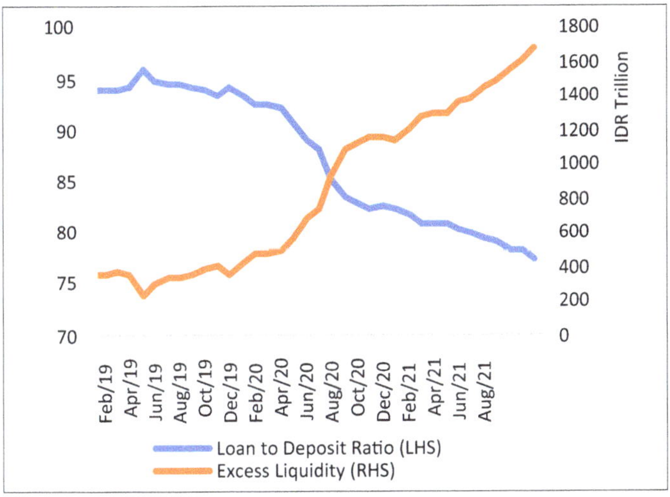

Source: BI, OJK, CEIC.

FIGURE 3.7
Interest Rate

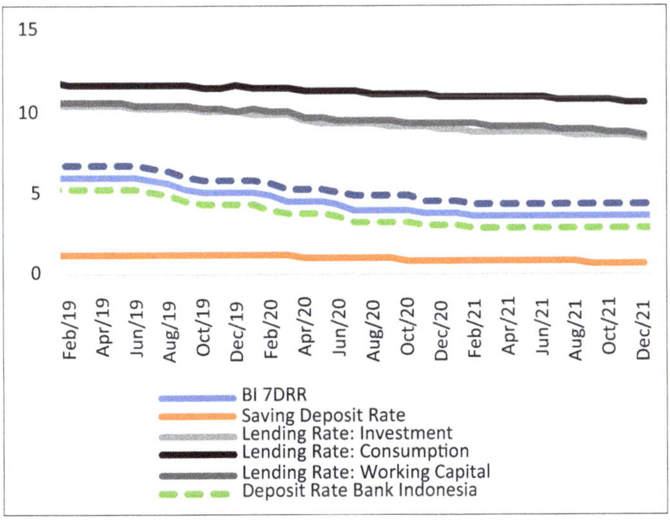

Source: BI, OJK, CEIC.

eventually growing inflation. However, in a liquidity trap situation, the money supply increase drives people to hoard cash, instead of spending or investing (Arias and Wen 2014). This is because the opportunity cost of holding cash is practically zero. After all, interest rates are very low.

In this situation, the increase in liquidity cannot be translated into consumption or investment to drive the economy. The worst-case scenario is that persistent liquidity traps lead the economy into low inflation (even trapped in a deflationary vortex) and weak aggregate demand. Consequently, the situation hampers economic growth, as has been the case in Japan over the last three decades.

Several things characterize the liquidity trap in Japan. *First*, the accommodative monetary policy by the Japanese Central Bank keeps interest rates low, yet has not been able to revive the economy since the early 1990s. *Second*, wages and price levels that have tended to weaken over the last decades have not been able to encourage the labour sector and real per capita income growth. *Third*, business confidence appears to be waning, and Japanese private companies were reluctant to increase spending and investment (Akram 2016).

During the first year and a half of the pandemic, Indonesia seemed at risk of being trapped in a liquidity trap. Inflation was at the lowest rate throughout 2020 reaching 1.68 per cent (a historic low) and in 2021 reaching 1.87 per cent, reflecting low aggregate demand. Meanwhile, monetary policy lagged in spurring credit that has been contracting for eight consecutive months. Anyway, Indonesia has not yet entered the liquidity trap phase (Verico 2021). As the credit crunch and low inflation occurred in a low-interest rate regime, fortunately, Indonesia still has room to lower its interest rate.

3.5.1 Debt Monetization (Helicopter Money)

Due to weak demand and disrupted supply chains in the real economy, the countries' production declined. This situation disrupted companies' and MSMEs' liquidity, which if left unchecked could lead to solvency issues. Monetary easing could not be entirely helpful as demand was weak, and banks became increasingly cautious about lending. In addition, capital owners might become highly risk-averse, thus preferring to hold cash or release financial assets, causing stock and bond prices to fall freely.

Debt monetization often appears as an alternative response. It works via "helicopter money". The term was first introduced by the American economist Milton Friedman in 1969 the core of which is government spending monetization, meaning the Central Bank prints new money. Helicopter money is less popular among economists because it might cause stagflation. Nonetheless, when there are not many conventional policy options are on the table, non-conventional policies such as helicopter money can be an alternative.

Several countries had started considering helicopter money to help the economy stay intact. Additional funds from the policy can be used to provide pandemic relief, e.g., direct transfers and/or liquidity assistance for both the real economy and financial sector. This could help avoid a massive credit crunch and bankruptcy.

3.5.2 The Pandemic Bonds

In early April 2020, the Indonesian government planned to issue thematic bonds called pandemic bonds. Yet, a month later, the plan was cancelled. State financing was then more focused on *above-the-line* and *below-the-line* schemes via a regular series of auctions in the primary market with BI as a last resort. In other words, what will be offered to BI was the existing series of debt securities, not the issuance of new series, if later the central bank had to purchase government debt securities (*Surat Utang Negara*, or SUN) and sharia government securities (*Surat Berharga Syariah Negara*, or SBSN).

The above-the-line mechanism was carried out by BI purchasing SUN/SBSN in the primary market. BI acted as a non-competitive bidder, green shoe option (GSO), and private placement option. Meanwhile, below-the-line was carried out via BI providing liquidity for banks through the purchase of SBN. The scheme aims to finance credit restructuring and provide fiscal space for national economic recovery.

Indonesia carried out several SBN auctions during 2020 and 2021. In early April 2020, it was the first Asian country to issue sovereign bonds. Indonesia issued the longest tenor global bonds with a fifty-year trance (RI0470) and a 4.5 per cent yield rate worth US$1 billion, the longest global bond ever issued by an Asian nation.

In total, US$4.3 billion of global bonds was issued during that period. Moreover, Indonesia's government bond market also experienced high demand from institutional and retail investors. This occurred when Indonesia had just passed the Delta wave in August 2021. Income bids from investors at the SBN auction on 31 August and 3 August 2021, achieved the second-highest and third-highest records in the history of SBN issuance, reaching IDR116.1 trillion and IDR107.6 trillion, respectively (Figure 3.8).

SBN investors almost doubled in number between the end of 2019 and 2021. However, in December 2021, the numbers reflected a slowdown, only increasing by 32.7 per cent from 460,372 to 611,143 investors. In 2020, it managed to shoot up 45.57 per cent from 2019, equaling 316,263 investors. Retail SBN issuance realization also increased, with the realization in 2020 of IDR76.81 trillion, and in 2021 of IDR90 trillion, much higher than the 2019 realization of IDR49.89 trillion. This shows investor confidence in robust macroeconomic conditions and prudent management of state finances in Indonesia.

3.5.3 Policy Mix (*Surat Keputusan Bersama* or Joint Decree)

The implementation of the burden-sharing programme, a kind of debt monetization policy, has raised concerns by investors, global media and multilateral institutions' regarding the Central Bank's independence. Addressing the concerns, both the government and BI ensure that the Government Bond Purchase Agreement is implemented by maintaining market integrity. This burden-sharing policy commenced in April 2020 and was extended twice with *Surat Keputusan Bersama* (SKB) II in July 2020 and SKB III in August 2021. BI has been committed to ending the burden-sharing programme at the end of the SKB III in late 2022. In January 2022, BI delivered a signal it intended to sell the owned government bonds through reverse repurchase arrangements in 2023.

The burden-sharing scheme is categorized by the use of financing groups for both public goods and non-public goods. The financing for public goods, i.e., IDR397.6 trillion, can be broken down into health (IDR87.55 trillion), social protection (IDR203.9 trillion), as well as ministries/agencies and local governments (IDR106.11 trillion). This financing burden will be entirely borne by BI through the purchase of SBN via a private placement mechanism with a coupon rate equal to the BI 3-months reverse repo rate.

Meanwhile, non-public goods financing supports the economy via microfinance for MSMEs, corporations and others. In financing non-public goods for MSMEs and non-MSME corporations, BI acts as a standby buyer. It buys SBN according to the market mechanism. See Table 3.3.

FIGURE 3.8
Government Bonds Bid to Cover Ratio (%)

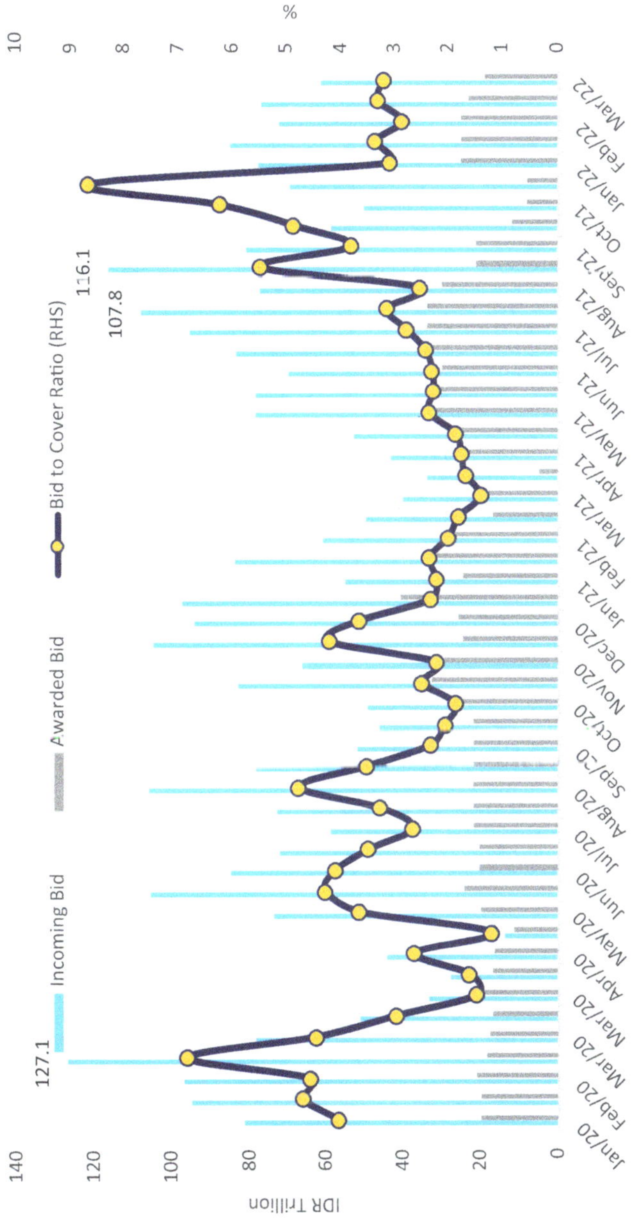

Source: Indonesia's Ministry of Finance (2022).

TABLE 3.3
Government Bond Purchase Agreement Scheme

	Amount (IDR trillion)	*Coupon Rate*	*Type*
SKB I	*IDR 218.4 trillion* 2020: IDR75 trillion 2021: IDR143 trillion	Market rate	Fixed
SKB II – Public Goods	IDR397.6 trillion	3-month reverse repo rate	Floating
Non-Public Goods	MSMEs and non-MSME corporation: *IDR177 trillion* • MSMEs: IDR123.4 trillion • Non-MSME: IDR53.6 trillion • Other: IDR328.9 trillion	Market rate	Fixed
SKB III – Public Goods	*IDR341.0 trillion* 2021: IDR157 trillion 2022: IDR184 trillion	3-month reverse repo rate	Floating
Non-Public Goods	*IDR98.0 trillion* 2021: IDR58 trillion 2022: IDR40 trillion	3-month reverse repo rate	Floating

Source: IMF Country Report, March 2022.

3.6 EXPANDING RECOVERY PROGRESS IN 2022

3.6.1 Facing Omicron Wave

The WHO and its networks have been classifying SARS-Cov-2 variants since late 2020. The variants are categorized into three groups based on their risk to global public health. From the consequences point of view, the variants are grouped by the monitoring and research depth and response urgencies.

Variants whose genetic changes are predictable and whose transmissibility, disease severity, immune escape, diagnostics, and therapeutics are known are identified as variants of interest (VOI). While those that meet the VOI definition and reduce the effectiveness of public health and social measures, change the epidemiology detrimentally or increase the disease presentation are designated as variants of concern (VOC). Among all variants, those whose genetic mutations are suspected of posing future risks and thus need more assessment to collect new evidence are categorized as variants under monitoring (VUM), according to the WHO.

Among the variants mentioned above, Alpha, Beta, Delta and Omicron have already entered and been disrupting Indonesia's public health and economy for almost two years. As of May 2021, the Indonesian Ministry of Health recorded the former three variants, and then Omicron came later in December 2021. According to the WHO, all four are identified as VOCs (Table 3.4).

Omicron's transmissibility is the fastest one up until now. The variant spreads 500 per cent faster than Delta variants. Not surprisingly, therefore, because 100,000 cases were confirmed in Indonesia, the Omicron's case surge experienced its fastest increase from February 2022, as can be seen in the fourth red triangle in Figure 3.9. However, this may not be the last slope we will face because in January 2022 a new variant under the Pango lineage named "XD" was already found in France by WHO monitors on 9 March 2022.

Daily Omicron transmission in Indonesia reached 64,718 cases in mid-February 2022, or almost 8,000 more cases than at the peak of Delta

TABLE 3.4
SARS-Cov-2 Variants Grouping

WHO Labels/ Pango Lineage	*Earliest Samples*	*VOC*	*VOI*	*VUM*
Omicron	Multiple countries, Nov 21	26 Nov 21	–	24 Nov 21
Delta	India, Oct 20	11 May 21	4 Apr 21	–
Alpha	UK, Sep 20	18 Dec 20	–	–
Beta	South Africa, May 20	18 Dec 20	–	–
Gamma	Brazil, Nov 20	11 Jan 21	–	–
Epsilon	USA, Mar 20	–	5 Mar 21	–
Zeta	Brazil, Apr 20	–	17 Mar 21	–
Eta	Multiple countries, Dec 20	–	17 Mar 21	–
Theta	Philippines, Jan 21	–	24 Mar 21	–
Iota	USA, Nov 20	–	24 Mar 21	–
Kappa	India, Oct 20	–	4 Apr 21	–
Lambda	Peru, Dec 20	–	14 Jun 21	–
Mu	Colombia, Jan 21	–	30 Aug 21	–
B.1.640	Multiple countries, Sep 21	–	–	22 Nov 21
XD	France, Jan 22	–	–	9 Mar 22

Source: WHO, March 2022.

FIGURE 3.9
SARS-Cov-2 Transmission Dynamic in Indonesia (Sept 2020–March 2022)

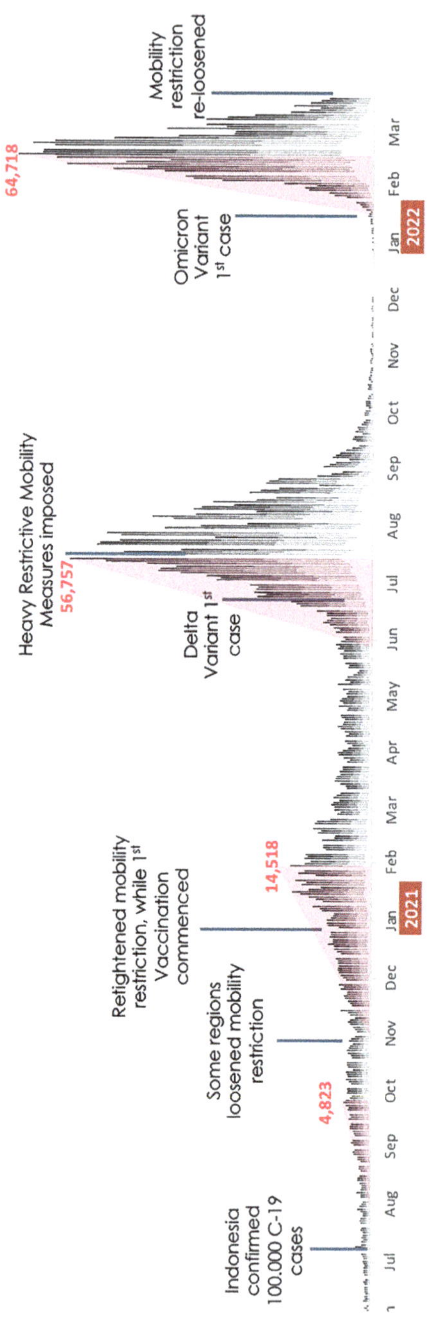

Source: Indonesian MoF and MoH, March 2022.

which was in mid-July 2021 of 56,757 daily cases. In terms of death rate, the mortality rate of the Omicron variant is seemingly converse to Delta's. The Omicron's death rate reached 122 daily fatalities, while the Delta fatality rate was seventeen times higher, i.e., 2,069 deaths.

As seen in Figure 3.10, COVID-19 the transmission and death level in Indonesia is much lower than in the rest of the world. Its cumulative COVID-19 case numbers account for only 2.2 per cent of the population, equivalent to 5.98 million people (ranked 155 out of 225). Meanwhile, its mortality rate count reached about 154,300 lives or 0.06 per cent of the population (ranked 123 of 225).

3.6.2 The Vaccination Rate

Whether the COVID-19 statistics will peak, decline, or stop, the pattern is still considered fuzzy. It is unclear whether the low Omicron case numbers in March 2022 can be regarded as "post-pandemic" or merely the calm before the storm. The generally accepted term "post-pandemic" often misled people. Some perceive it as the end of all pandemic uncertainties or even the demise of the pandemic itself. On the flip side, others define post-pandemic as the arrival at the endemic phase of particular Coronavirus variants.

That is to say, for planning circumstances and crisis prevention, the question of whether the pandemic has been over or not should be considered irrelevant. Laypeople with no expertise in immunology and virology can even sense that the series of COVID-19 waves will continue to circulate for the foreseeable future. Therefore, if SARS-Cov-2 continues evolving and escaping the immune pressure at a rate faster than the vaccination rate, then herd immunity can wane.

The larger the number of susceptible individuals to infection and the bigger the transmission opportunity, the bigger the risks and chance we will face the vicious cycle of COVID-19 surge shortly. Furthermore, the more relevant question is whether or not we are ready to face the storm. The main objective function is thus to keep the death rate low enough so that the society and economy can tolerate or bear it.

Learning from past pandemics and health measures for infectious diseases, there are at least two parameters needed to be considered essential for death minimization. The first parameter is vaccination level, and the second is the provision of (antiviral) therapies by health facilities. Both

FIGURE 3.10
Cross-Countries Cumulative COVID-19

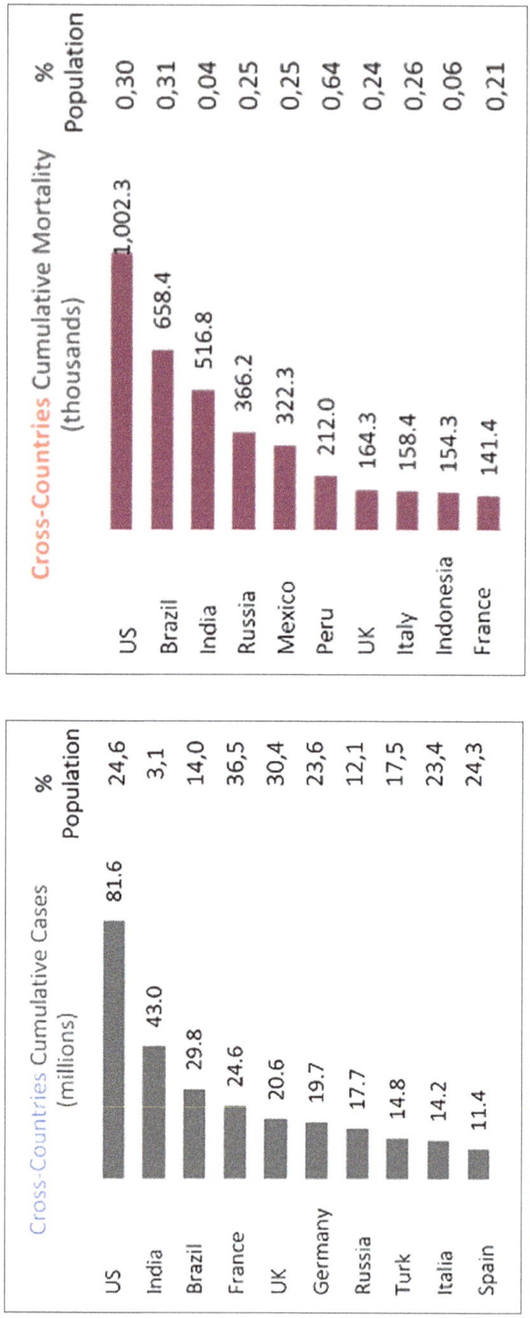

Source: Worldmeters.info, ourworldindata, 23 March 2022.

parameters are directly interlinked with COVID-19 mortality statistics during the pandemic. Moreover, other parameters such as zoonosis prevention, ecological preservation, and climate action have several indirect transmissions to death prevention from infectious disease in the short run.

Until 22 April 2022, more than 396.73 million vaccines have been administered, covering more than 70 per cent of the Indonesian population. The first shots covered almost 74 per cent of the population, and the second shot coverage already reached nearly 61 per cent during the month of Ramadan in the last week of April. The third shot covered almost 13 per cent of Indonesian residents in less than eight months. Thus, vaccine booster coverage has been growing with a daily moving average of 2.1 per cent since 1 September 2021.

The occupancy of public facilities for self-isolation and treatment (ICU) by the end of March 2022 is quite low at the national level—only 11 per cent. On the other hand, hospital bed occupancy rates reached 38 per cent during the peak period of Omicron infection in mid-February 2022. Comparing it with the Delta peak at June–July 2021, in which the occupancy rate skyrocketed to 75 per cent, Omicron was relatively much more controllable. Moreover, with a significant decline in positivity rate of more than three times, from 18.2 per cent in February to 6 per cent in March 2022, this circumstance nudged authorities to loosen the mobility restriction post-Omicron crisis.

3.6.3 Asia's Supply Chain Disruption

The pandemic has caused severe disruption to the supply chain in the global economy. With the pandemic still in the picture and the geopolitical tension caused by the war between Russia and Ukraine, supply chain disruptions appear to be a challenge that will need to be dealt with over the long term. Figure 3.11 is a dashboard showing the factors impacting manufacturers' logistics and production processes, both from the perspective of price and activity.

The pressure coming from the pandemic and global tension make both the delivery of parts to factories and goods to market costly and slow. The Baltic Dry Index is used to show price indicators for commodity shipments. It started increasing from July 2021, and then it reached its peak in October 2021 before decreasing. The World Container Freight Rate

FIGURE 3.11
Asia Supply Chain Indices

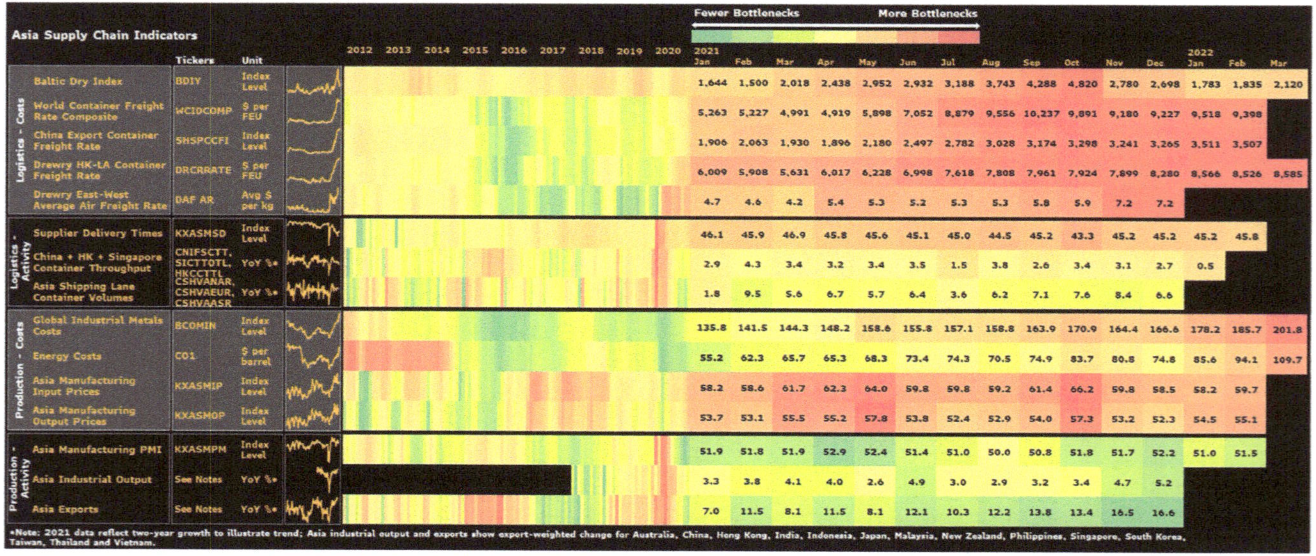

Source: Bloomberg (2022).

Composite is used as an indicator for more general shipments, and it has shown a high rate from July 2021 to the present. Meanwhile, the China Export Container Freight Rate and Drewry HK-LA Container Freight Rate indicate shipments from greater China. Similar to the composite world container freight index, shipments from greater China have also struggled with high costs. The increasing cost also happened in air freight, as shown by the Drewry East-West Average Air Freight Rate.

Supplier Delivery Times in the dashboard is a sub-index in Markit's Asia manufacturing PMI. An index above 50 signals an improvement in delivery times and vice versa. It had been below the 50-mark since before the pandemic, but conditions worsened in 2021 and showed little recovery. Port throughput reflects the YoY change in the movement of shipping containers through Asia's biggest ports (mainland China, Hong Kong and Singapore). It bounced back last year from 2020's depressed level but is still below the average over the previous decade, with port congestion likely playing a large part. Asia Shipping Lane Container Volume shows the year-on-year change in container volumes through major shipping lanes between Asia and North America, Europe, and intra-Asia.

To measure production costs, the dashboard uses Bloomberg's composite index for global industrial metals costs, Brent crude oil, and the input and output price sub-indexes from Markit's Asia manufacturing PMI, and all show increasing trend. Then higher input costs are putting pressure on profits and driving global inflation.

3.6.4 Economic Rebound

With Omicron management in place, economic recovery followed. Among the few countries that successfully managed their economic indicators to their pre-pandemic levels, Indonesia stood out as better than India and Brazil in terms of real GDP. Emerging countries in Asia, such as Turkey, China and Vietnam, are the top three global performers with a Real GDP index of 113, 108.1, and 105.5, respectively.

With real GDP 2019 as a baseline, several G-20 and ASEAN-6 members had not yet signalled a rebound stage by 14 March 2022. As seen in Figure 3.12, the radar map signalled our country's rebound juncture. Indonesia's RGDP index reached 101.6 in mid-March 2022.

This recovery trajectory improvement continues with the positive movement of leading indicators. For example, Indonesia's PMI manu-

FIGURE 3.12
Cross-Countries Rebound Stage (RGDP 2019 = 100)

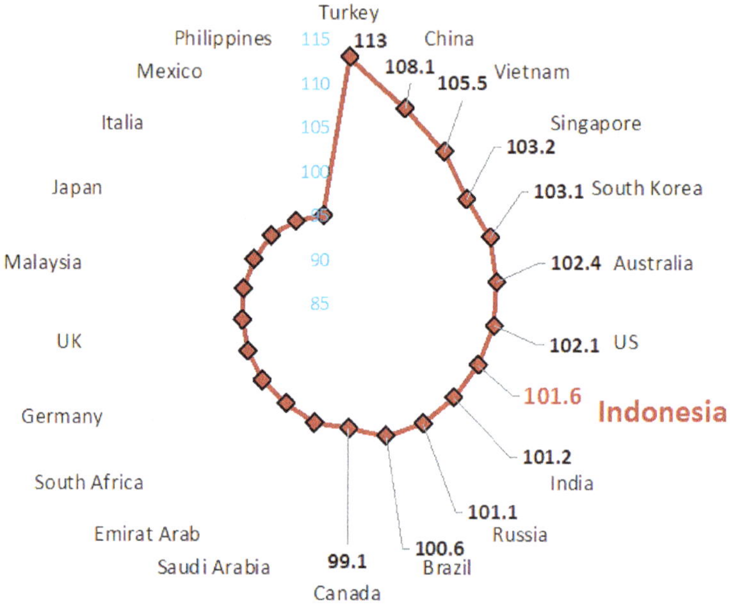

Source: CEIC and Bloomberg, as of 14 March 2022, calculated.

facturing index inched up and has been in the expansive zone for six months. In addition, electricity consumption was highly positive, while material goods imports recorded remarkable growth.

Private consumption indicators also conveyed an upward trend. For example, Google's Mobility Indicator (GMI) has slightly improved to the pre-pandemic level, indicating people are resuming activities despite the moderation in mid-February. Meanwhile, household consumption improved robustly, as reflected in the recent Retail Sales Index (RSI), Consumer Confidence Index (CCI), and Mandiri Spending Index (MSI). The household consumption significantly improved from –2.63 per cent (last year) to 2.02 per cent in 2021. Yet Indonesia's inflation is still benign relative to the rest of the world.

Consumption's leading indicators (e.g., GMI, RSI, CCI) were improved for almost a semester after the Delta variant storm in July–August 2021. It marked the longest improvement since the dawn of the COVID-19 pandemic. Moreover, pent-up demand was unleashed in the household sector post-Delta storm. As a result, HH consumption in Q4 2021 grew by 3.55 per cent YoY, improving the RGDP Index from the HH-Consumption component by 101.79 and RGDP itself by 103.97 (Figure 3.13).

Investment in 2021 improved significantly from –5.0 (last year) to 3.8 per cent. It was mainly contributed by the public (through PSN [*Proyek Strategis Nasional*] or National Strategic Projects) and private investments, mostly from base metal and its derivatives industries (14.4 per cent), real estate and business district developers (11.8 per cent), and the mining sector (11.6 per cent). In addition, export activities ballooned by 29.83 per cent (YoY) in Q4 or 24.04 per cent annually—as global demand surged for processed palm oil, automotive/machinery, stainless steel, and pig-iron nickel.

Economic growth is predicted to reach 4.8–5.5 per cent in 2022, as seen in Figure 3.14. Domestic inflation is still manageable at 2.1 per cent (YoY), in line with production surpluses in some food commodities and the price ceiling for cooking oil. Given the risk of imported inflation transmission, high global prices, and recovery on the demand side, the

FIGURE 3.13
Indonesia's RGDP Pre and Post-Pandemic

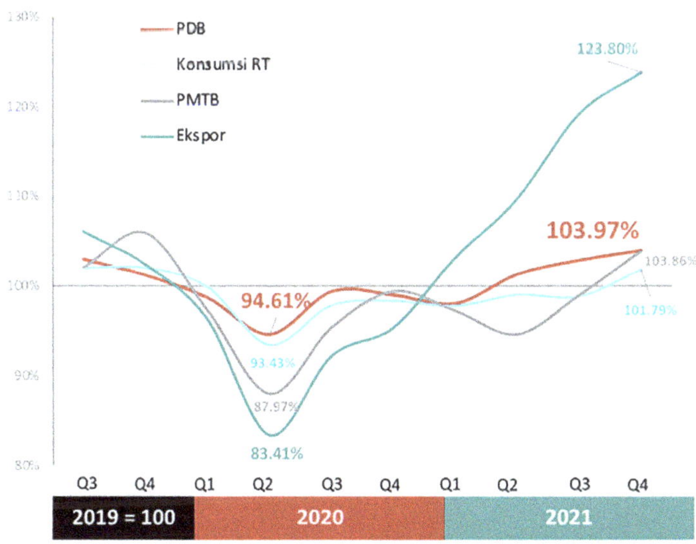

Source: Statistics Indonesia, 2022, processed.

FIGURE 3.14
Growth Outlook

Source: IMF, WEO & Bloomberg Forecast (25 February 2022), processed.

government anticipates stabilizing prices while spurring recovery with the policy mix. On the external balance side, the trade balance recorded a surplus for twenty-two consecutive months. Exports improvement in early 2022 was driven mainly by the price factor, that is to say, by the rise in leading non-oil and gas exports. Meanwhile, Indonesia's import growth is still dominated by intermediate goods, both raw materials and capital goods.

This economic improvement trajectory is channelled into public finance through government revenue. By 31 January 2022, revenue collection posted a remarkable growth of 54.9 per cent YoY or about IDR156 trillion. The revenue upturn was mainly supported by an increase in tax and customs revenues, reaching more than 65 per cent YoY basis on the back of economic recovery, rising commodity prices, and well-performing international trade. Meanwhile, non-tax revenue also rose well by a double-digit 11.4 per cent.

This auspicious performance signals a strong economic recovery at the beginning of the year. However, the effect of the Omicron variant is likely to weaken the revenue performance in February and March. Hoping that that will be temporary, we expect the recovery path will continue right after. In addition, monetary policy tightening and the Russia-Ukraine conflict spillover effects on both the global and the domestic economy need our attention. The potential propagation impact, both in the financial and trading channels, must be intelligibly scrutinized. Therefore, continuous monitoring and anticipating the spillover of domestic inflation and economic growth need to be undertaken to ensure that the domestic recovery is maintained.

3.6.5 Reiterating Policy Design

During the pandemic, the policy responses to the crisis were made with no pandemic crisis management precedents which could be used as a reference for policymaking. However, public finance and crisis management policymaking in Indonesia—after the WHO announcement regarding the pandemic status in March 2020— went beyond merely a relief fund distribution. Policymakers seemed to sense the possibility of the COVID-19 pandemic's domino effect on the real sector, financial sector, and even further on financial system stability and the economic structure.

As seen in Figure 3.15, among the top five keywords mentioned or those that were the subject of the high-level meeting are PEN (economic recovery programme), MSMEs, PEN monitoring and evaluation, sectoral supports and health. Hence, after the Emergency Bill was ratified into Emergency Law on 31 March 2020, the snowball rolled out, and the economic recovery programme (PEN) acted as its nexus.

Since then, policymaking was adapted to the new strategic environment. That is to say, domestic revenue mobilization to particular socio-economic layers was eased, spending was reallocated and refocused on essential services for pandemic measures, the social safety net was expanded and employment programmes were modified. In the monetary and financial markets, the policy mix for fiscal and monetary transmission was quite radically tweaked to anticipate recession and economic paralysis. Policymakers even discussed further structural reform from March until

FIGURE 3.15
Keywords Cloud during Pandemic Policymaking

Note: The bigger the word/phrase, the more the words are mentioned or become subjects of the high-level meeting. Words such as "PEN" (i.e., Economic Recovery Programme in Indonesia), MSMEs, and Monev (monitoring and evaluation), sectoral support, and health are the top five keywords of the Finance Minister Meeting.
Source: Office of Finance Minister & Vice Minister (processed), 2022.

September 2020, learning from Indonesia's experiences in the previous series of crises, whether the Asian Financial Crisis, the Global Financial Crisis, or even oil shocks in the 1970s and 1980s.

3.6.6 Further Reforms

The Pandemic Crisis urges further reform. Moreover, reforms are much needed to offset the COVID-19 scarring effects. The scarring effects will prolong the job search period in the labour market, reduce the youth workforce's employment and income, and lead to poor mental health. Combined with learning loss, Indonesian youth skills and productivity might depreciate in the long run due to the pandemic. This, in turn, will exacerbate the social mobility decline.

A shift towards informality might also happen. Larger informality means a potential loss to the economy because it offers lower wages and workers' protection and low tax compliance. Moreover, the crisis pushed workers aged 55 and above to exit the labour force. In the feminized sector, female labour participation declined, the gender pay gap widened, and violence against women increased. Widened financial distress will lead to greater long-run inequality. Youth from the poorest families are prone to job and earning loss, thus higher debt. In contrast, the wealthier family whose spending is reigned in are most likely to increase their savings.

The series of crises that hit our society has opened a window for us to continue the progress of development with ongoing economic reforms (ADB and Indrawati 2020). Indonesia aspires to become a high-income country by a century post-independence day. Therefore, productivity and economic growth above their potential, i.e., around 5 per cent of pre-pandemic era growth, is greatly needed for long-run development goals.

Yet, the recovery progress will be subject to the COVID-19 dynamic and our ability to prevent further pandemic waves. Thus, supports for vulnerable households and businesses are a profound response while at the same time necessary, considering fiscal sustainability in the medium term. However, the temporary breach of the maximum 3 per cent fiscal deficit stipulated by law could be unsustainable for the whole economy. Therefore, short-run fiscal and monetary stimulus and changing strategic environment need eminent response such as structural reform for Indonesia to succeed in unlocking its growth potential.

FIGURE 3.16
Indonesia's Series of Pandemic Reliefs and Progress of Reforms

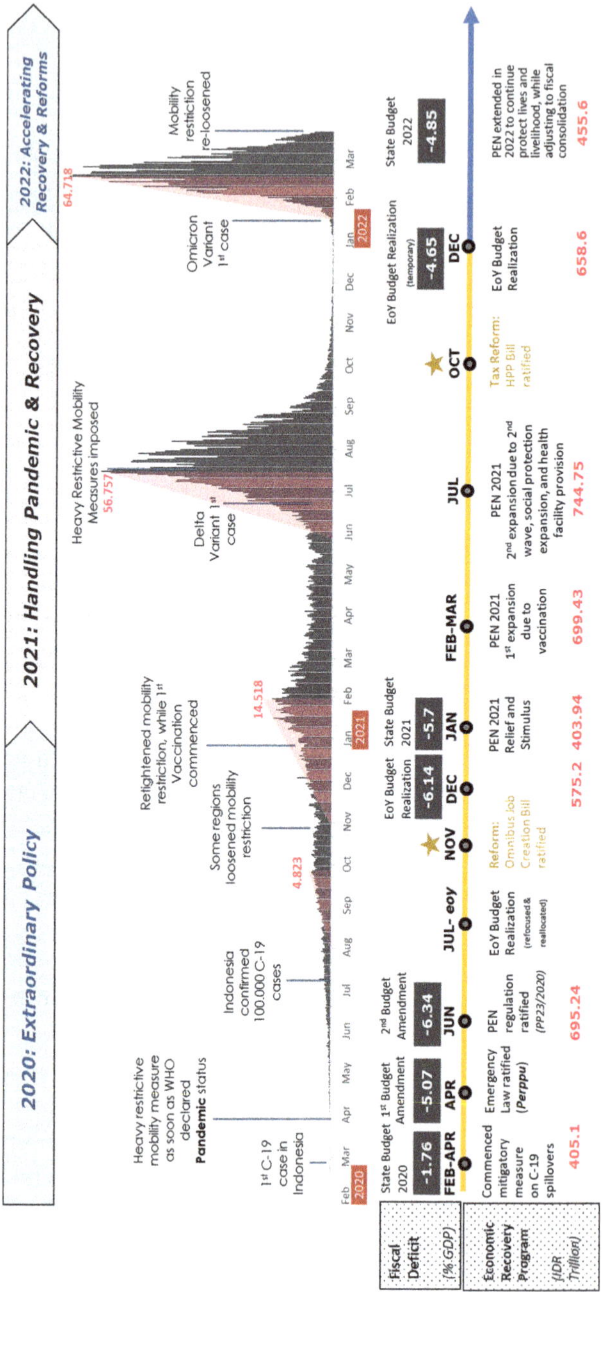

Source: MoF, March 2022.

Several reforms are currently underway in the public finance areas, such as taxation and expenditure, including but not limited to social safety nets, education, health, as well as data integration for better policymaking and productivity and competitiveness improvement. As seen in Figure 3.16 (the starred timeline), while the countercyclical policy mix aimed to help relieve the pandemic spillovers, "Omnibus Bill" on Job Creation (*UU Cipta Kerja*) and Tax Reform were ratified in November 2021 and October 2022, respectively.

Omnibus Job Creation, Tax Reform, UU HKPD, and the incoming financial sectoral reforms hopefully could keep "Vision 2045" on track and offset the scarring effects and global anxiety over fragmented recovery and widening inequality. Structural reform is vital and thus expected to enhance Indonesia's long-run productivity, growth and inclusiveness.

Notes

1. The authors wish to acknowledge Andi Nugroho Suryo Kuncoro, Muhammad Fajar Nugraha and Indrie Yuli Pratiwi for their valuable input.
2. Indonesia's Ministry of Labour, 2020.

References

ADB, and Sri Mulyani Indrawati. 2020. *53rd Annual Meeting of the Board of Governors (2nd Stage)* 17 September 2020. https://www.adb.org/sites/default/files/annual-meeting/2015/statements/INO-AM2020-Governor-statement.pdf?1600266283=

Akram, Tanweer. 2016. "Japan's Liquidity Trap". *SSRN Electronic Journal*. https://doi.org/10.2139/ssrn.2753107

Amadeo, Kimberly. 2021. "Liquidity Trap with Causes, Signs, and Cures: Why the Fed Must Raise Interest Rates". *The Balance*, 4 March 2021, https://www.thebalance.com/liquidity-trap-examples-with-5-signs-and-5-cures-3306141

Arias, Maria A., and Yi Wen. 2014. "The Liquidity Trap: A Reason for Today's Low Inflation". Federal Reserve Bank of St Louis, 1 April 2014. https://www.stlouisfed.org/publications/regional-economist/april-2014/the-liquidity-trap-an-alternative-explanation-for-todays-low-inflation

Bloomberg. 2022. "Bloomberg Markets Full Show (02/25/2022)", 25 February 2022. https://www.bloomberg.com/news/videos/2022-02-25/bloomberg-markets-full-show-02-25-2022-video

Center for Disease Control and Prevention (CDC). 2020. "Coronavirus Disease

2019 (COVID-19)". 11 February 2020. https://www.cdc.gov/coronavirus/2019-ncov/variants/about-variants.html

CEIC, and Bloomberg. 2022. "Countries Real GDP 1994–2022". 14 March 2022, https://www.ceicdata.com/en/indicator/indonesia/real-gdp-growth

Financial Services Authority, Indonesia. 2020. "POJK Number 11/POJK.3/2020 on National Economic Stimulus as A Countercyclical Policy on the Impact of Coronavirus Disease 2019". 13 March 2020.

Harvard T.H. Chan School of Public Health. 2022. "As Omicron Wanes, What Is the State of the Pandemic?". 1 March 2022. https://www.hsph.harvard.edu/news/features/as-omicron-wanes-what-is-the-state-of-the-pandemic/

International Monetary Fund (IMF). 2022a. "World Economic Outlook Update, January 2022: Rising Caseloads, A Disrupted Recovery, and Higher Inflation". January 2022. https://www.imf.org/en/Publications/WEO/Issues/2022/01/25/world-economic-outlook-update-january-2022

———. 2022b. "Indonesia: 2022 Article IV Consultation-Press Release; Staff Report; Staff Statement; and Statement by the Executive Director for Indonesia". Country Report No. 2022/084, 22 March 2022. https://www.imf.org/en/Publications/CR/Issues/2022/03/22/Indonesia-2022-Article-IV-Consultation-Press-Release-Staff-Report-Staff-Statement-and-515612

Jimenez, Justin. "Asia Insight: Brittle Supply Chains Bracing for Ukraine Impact". April 2022, p. 3.

Ministry of Finance, Indonesia. "Economic and Fiscal Updates, Minister's Material for Finance Fitch on Indonesia Conference". Jakarta.

Ministry of Health, Indonesia, and Ministry of Finance, Indonesia. 2022."Situasi COVID-19." Tableau Software, March 2022.

Ministry of Social Affairs, Indonesia, and Ministry of Finance, Indonesia. "Data Terpadu Kesejahteran Sosial". https://dtks.kemensos.go.id/

New York Times. 2020. "The New COVID Strain in the UK: Questions and Answers". 21 December 2020. https://archive.is/dMEdJ

Office of Finance Minister and Vice Minister. 2022. "Indonesia's Finance Minister & Vice Minister Minutes of Meeting 2020". 2022.

Office of Governor of Jakarta. 2022. "What Is the Difference between COVID-19 Variants?". 19 January 2022. https://corona.jakarta.go.id/en/artikel/varian-varian-COVID-19-apa-perbedaannya

President of the Republic of Indonesia. 2020. "Presidential Decree Number 72 Year 2020". 25 June 2020. https://peraturan.go.id/common/dokumen/ln/2020/ps72-2020.pdf

Verico, Kiki. 2021. "The Usage of Economic Position in Understanding Indonesia's Economy and the Pandemic Effects". Aug. 2021, https://doi.org/10.52813/jei.v10i2.152

World Health Organization (WHO). 2020. "Origin of SARS-CoV-2". 26 March 2020.

https://apps.who.int/iris/bitstream/handle/10665/332197/WHO-2019-nCoV-FAQ-Virus_origin-2020.1-eng.pdf

———. 2022. "Tracking SARS-CoV-2 Variants". 22 March 2022. https://www.who.int/en/activities/tracking-SARS-CoV-2-variants/

Worldometer. 2022. "COVID Live—Coronavirus Statistics". 23 March 2022. https://www.worldometers.info/coronavirus/

4

Financial Sector and Monetary Policy during the Pandemic

Mirza Adityaswara, Andry Asmoro and Dian Ayu Yustina

4.1 PRE-PANDEMIC INDONESIAN BANKING SECTOR: STRONG CAPITAL AND LOW RISK

Before the pandemic, Indonesia's banking sector performed positively, in line with the economic growth in the past few years. Having been through a few big economic crises, i.e., the Asian Financial Crisis (1997–98) and the Global Financial Crisis (2008), Indonesia's banking sector has come a long way and has continued to implement good governance and prudent risk management practices. Up to this day, the banking sector remains the most regulated industry in Indonesia as it is the backbone of the financial sector.

Over the years leading to the pandemic-led crisis, Indonesia's banking sector proved to be resilient and withstood episodes of economic slowdown with strong capital, sufficient liquidity and low credit risk. The banking sector's capital adequacy ratio was relatively stable at 23 per cent by the end of 2019 (Table 4.1). Credit risk was relatively low, as the non-performing loans (NPLs) remained below 3 per cent in the pre-pandemic years. Yet, credit growth had started a notable slowdown. By the end of 2019, credit recorded 6 per cent growth, declining from as high as 13 per cent in 2018 (Figure 4.1). Furthermore, banks' liquidity was slightly tighter, as the loan-to-deposit ratio was at 93.6 per cent by the end of 2019.

Credit growth generally moves in line with the pace of economic growth. During the commodity boom, the banking sector recorded strong growth. Credit disbursement managed to reach double-digit growth due to rising economic activities related to and/or derived from the commodity sectors. In 2010–13, credit growth recorded 20–25 per cent growth. Unfortunately, following the slowdown of China's economy, commodity prices started declining, which soon marked the end of Indonesia's commodity boom.

Since 2016, credit growth has continued to decelerate to <10 per cent, which gives an indication of the significance of commodity sectors to the economy. The unfavourable global environment at the time—with rising geopolitical tensions between the US and China, which led to a trade war—had brought negative effects on global growth and then reduced global demand for commodities. The slowdown in credit was also shown by a continuously lowering loan growth to nominal GDP growth ratio in the last four to five years. Anecdotally, the high-end property prices (as one of the leading indicators) have not improved since 2016, demonstrating the low appetite of medium-to-high-income earners for investing in this sector. It is worth noting that the property sector is backward- and forward-linked to >160 subsectors.

During 2014–19, credit growth was boosted by expansions in government projects. The newly elected government focused on building

TABLE 4.1
Capital Adequacy Ratio, 2016–November 2019 (%)

Category	*2016*	*2017*	*2018*	*2019*	*2020*	*Aug-21*	*Sep-21*	*Oct-21*	*Nov-21*
SOE Bank	21.5	21.1	20.9	21.2	18.8	19.1	21.0	21.2	21.4
Regional Dev't Bank	21.7	21.7	22.1	21.2	22.1	22.1	22.2	22.6	22.8
Domestic Private Bank	18.1	18.8	19.0	20.1	23.4	26.1	26.0	26.1	26.6
Foreign Bank	48.9	53.1	47.9	50.4	54.6	60.1	60.1	60.5	59.2
Banking Industry	22.9	23.2	23.0	23.4	23.9	24.4	25.2	25.3	25.6

Source: Financial Service Authority.

FIGURE 4.1
Credit and Deposit Growth (%)

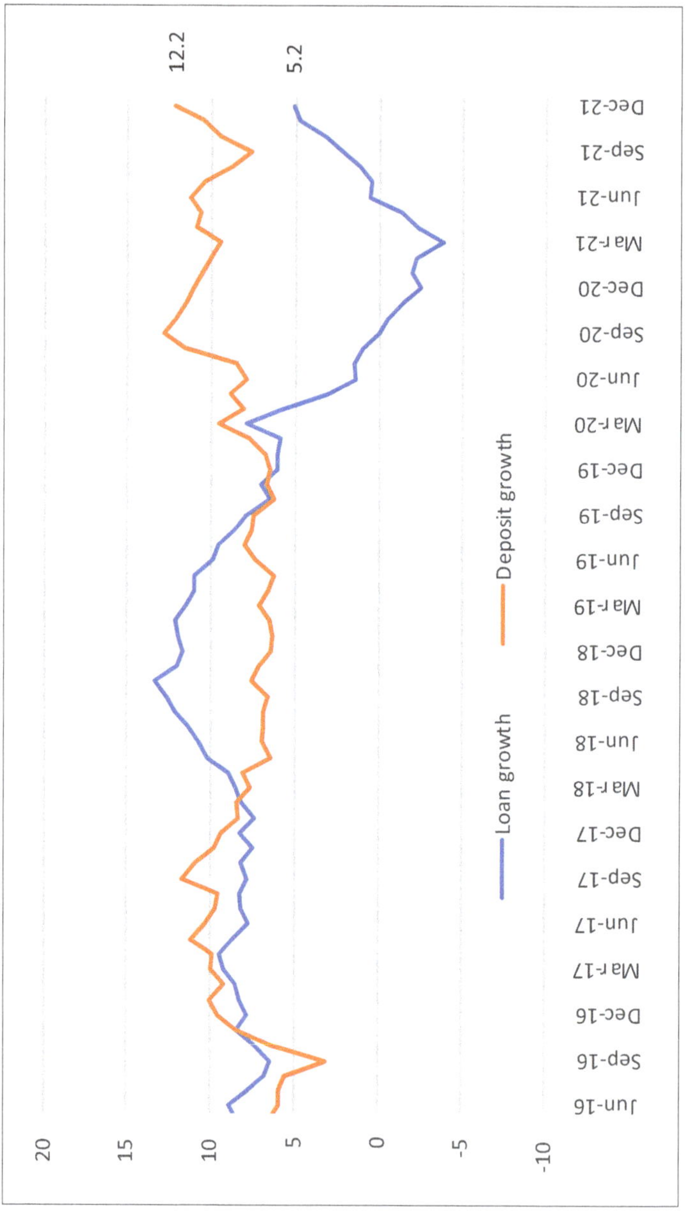

Source: Financial Service Authority.

massive infrastructure to raise competitiveness and fix the structural issues that have long plagued Indonesia's economy. Therefore, infrastructure financing at some point helped credit grow amid the weak global economic sentiment. Nonetheless, the push from infrastructure development to credit growth was not as strong as from the commodity boom. In the meantime, the global sentiment continued to worsen with the escalation of the US-China trade war, which affected both countries' economies, and both are Indonesia's main trading partners. This caused further downside to the domestic economy as demand slowed down, especially for commodity-related sectors. Just before the pandemic, credit only recorded 6.1 per cent growth at the end of December 2019.

Based on our historical analysis, the ratio between loans and GDP has continued to decline. During the commodity boom, the ratio of credit growth to GDP growth was as high as fourfold. This meant that when the economy grew by 5 per cent, credit growth recorded a 20 per cent growth. Now, the ratio of credit growth to GDP growth is roughly 1.1 times, indicating that when GDP grew by 5 per cent, credit growth was only at 6 per cent (2019). This declining ratio implied that the growth source was not centred on commodities anymore, which, at the time, had a multiplier effect on other sectors, hence generating larger growth. From 2014 onward, the growth was propped up by government spending, especially on infrastructure projects. However, infrastructure is a long-term investment that may take longer to have a multiplier effect on the economy.

4.1.1 Inefficiency and Segmented Banking Sector Persist

The banking sector's positive performance was not without flaws. During 2010–19, Indonesian banks were well known among their peers for their high net interest margin (NIM), making them attractive to foreign investors. Compared to other Asian countries, Indonesia had one of the highest NIMs, which was partly due to the relatively high interest rates (Figure 4.2). Despite being some of the most profitable banks, Indonesian banks' high NIMs also reflected their high operational costs. Their cost-to-income ratio reached 56 per cent, reflecting the high cost of banking operations, as Indonesia is a vast economy with many remote regions that have not had access to financial services yet (Figure 4.3). The banks compensated for their high operational costs by charging relatively high

FIGURE 4.2
NIM Comparison in Asia

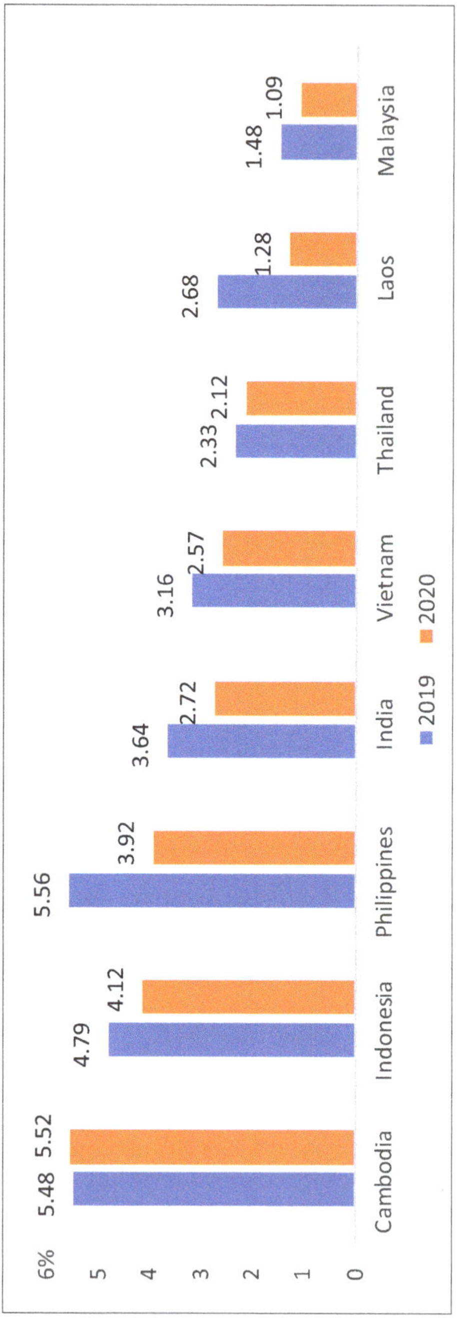

Source: theglobaleconomy.com

FIGURE 4.3
Cost-to-Income Ratio Comparison in Asia

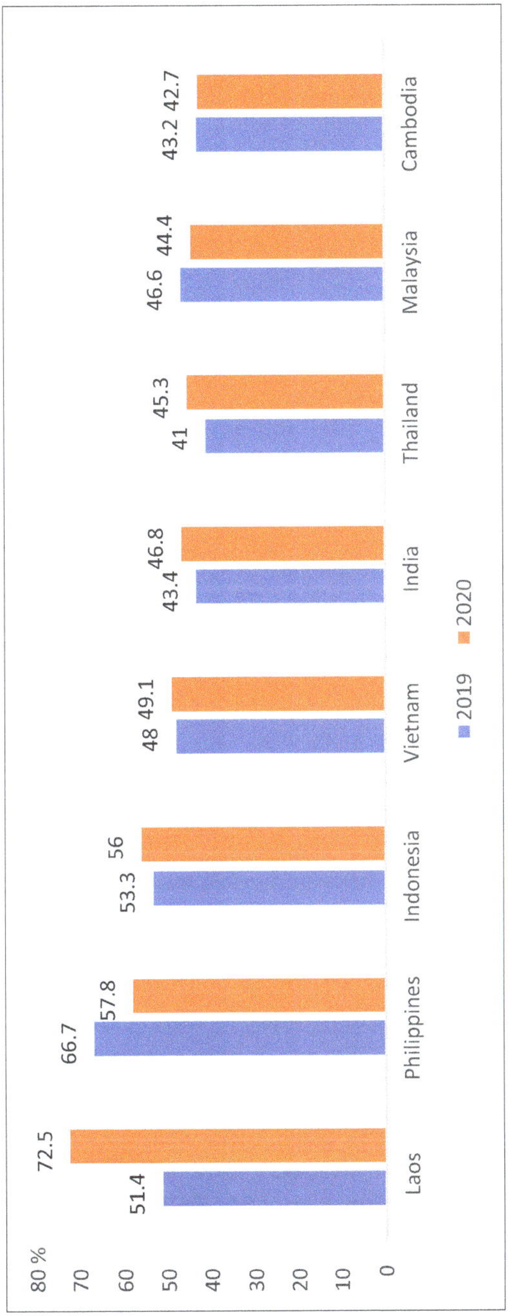

Source: theglobaleconomy.com

interest rates compared to their foreign peers. High interest rates have long been a problem for Indonesia since it has stunted access, especially for the lower-income classes to the acquisition of credit or for those in the middle, small, and micro businesses.

Another source of inefficiency in the Indonesian banking system is the large number of banks. The number of banks in Indonesia once reached 200 banks, but that number had declined to 107 by July 2021. During the economic boom, when credit grew strongly and liquidity was limited, the banks competed fiercely to acquire funding or deposits. The tight competition in funding led these banks to offer special deposit rates—obviously higher than the market rate. This phenomenon resulted in the rising cost of funds, which in turn raised credit rates.

Issues of inefficiency, high interest rates, limited financial access, and low financial inclusion have long been structural issues in Indonesia's banking sector. There have been many policies directed to improve efficiency in the banking system. For example, the Financial Services Authority (*Otoritas Jasa Keuangan*, or OJK) has capped the deposit rates to prevent them from sharply rising. The OJK implements tiered deposit rate caps for banks according to their BUKU[1] levels. Banks with lower BUKU levels can charge deposit rates slightly higher than those with higher BUKU levels. These caps on deposit rates are to keep the rise in interest rates at bay. From the monetary management side, Bank Indonesia keeps the liquidity in the banking system sufficient to avoid any tight funding competition among banks. Other policies include banking consolidations, in which the OJK pushes for more mergers and acquisitions to trim the number of banks in Indonesia and eventually improve the banking sector's efficiency.

The structurally high interest rates have reduced financial accessibility, especially for micro businesses. To increase the financial access for MSMEs, the government uses fiscal policies, as well as the low interest rate credit programme (*Kredit Usaha Rakyat*, or KUR) by cooperating with state banks to channel the programme to MSMEs.

4.2 PANDEMIC IMPACT ON THE ECONOMY AND FINANCIAL SECTOR

The global economy had just come out from a trade war during 2018–19. The negative sentiment on the global economy due to the trade war had caused Indonesia's economic growth to slow from 5.17 per cent to 5.02 per cent in 2019. By the end of 2019, the world was rattled by the emergence of the first COVID-19 cases in Wuhan, China.

In 2020, the COVID-19 cases spread fast worldwide and caused an unprecedented impact on the financial market, weakening the sentiment in the global economy. The first COVID-19 case in Indonesia was found in March 2020, which immediately brought negative sentiment, i.e., a sharp weakening of the rupiah reached IDR16,000 per US dollar, a level not seen since the Asian Financial Crisis.

Throughout 2020, the spread of the virus caused a broad decline across asset classes, while people reverted to safe-haven assets, i.e., gold. The stock index declined across the globe. Massive foreign capital outflows, both from bonds and equities, caused a sharp rupiah depreciation. In 2020, the foreign ownership ratio of total outstanding government bonds dropped from 38 per cent to 25 per cent (around US$9.4 billion of foreign capital outflows).

The pandemic also affected many aspects of life. Social distancing reduced people's mobility, thus constraining economic activities and transactions. The impact was especially felt in Indonesia, where there is a relative abundance of workers and businesses in the informal sectors that generally need close-contact interactions. The sudden loss in demand and falling revenues reduced the liquidity of those businesses, thus restricting them from operating normally.

Since the start of the pandemic, Indonesia has gone through three waves of COVID-19 outbreaks. The first was the Alpha variant in 2020, which was handled with very tight restrictions that consequently caused a contraction in the economy. In mid-2021, the outbreak of the Delta variant brought the heaviest blow to the health sector as we saw hospitals flooded with COVID-19 patients. Yet, the economy was still able to grow modestly by 3.69 per cent year-on-year (YoY) in 2021, as the restrictions were not as strict as in 2020, and most people have already adjusted to the situation. At the beginning of 2022, the new Omicron variant hit, but the economy was in a better position, with better handling of the pandemic and higher and wider vaccinations across the country.

Overall, there are significant differences between the impacts of the COVID-19-driven crisis and several previous crises. The unprecedented pandemic crisis saw people's health issues become the main driver of the global crisis, which has affected more countries than the previous 1998

Asian Financial Crisis and the 2008 Global Financial Crisis (Figure 4.4). In the 1998 and 2008 crises, large and middle-sized corporations suffered due to external volatility within the capital market, currencies and debt mismatch. SMEs were relatively more resilient due to lower exposures to those factors. This year, the limited mobility and transactions (due to lockdowns and "new normal") have severely hit SMEs' cashflows more than large companies' cashflows.

Some sectors have suffered losses while others have gained from the crises. Mobility-related sectors, i.e., transportation, real estate and automotive, have been hit the hardest. Sectors that require close interactions have also suffered, i.e., tourism, hotels, manufacturing and financial services. Other sectors have fared much better after adjusting to the mobility restriction. On the other hand, sectors related to daily necessities, health and medicine, and information and communication have been resilient as people adjusted to doing economic activities online. In 2020, almost all sectors experienced contractions except for a few utility sectors, i.e., IT and health and social activities. The largest sectors, i.e., manufacturing, transportation and storage, and accommodation, food and beverages, suffered contractions in 2020 (Figure 4.5).

The sectors recover in stages. The more resilient sectors (basic-needs products, such as food and drinks and supplements), with limited restaurant deliveries and micro retailers, should rebound faster once they have adjusted to the restrictions. In the next stage, once confidence improves, along with better handling of the pandemic, consumers will start purchasing durable goods, such as clothes, shoes, electronics and automobiles. In the last stage, when the pandemic can be fully contained or the economy transitions from pandemic to endemic, sectors that need mobility and direct interactions the most (transportation, tourism, hotels, property) will recover. See Figure 4.6.

The pandemic has created tremendous pressure on the business sectors, on both sides of supply and demand. The supply side has been disrupted because mobility restrictions have reduced the number of workers that operate the businesses. Lockdowns and quarantines have caused operational shutdowns. And lastly, the global spread of COVID-19 has disrupted supply chains, leading to shortages of parts and intermediate/ input goods.

FIGURE 4.4
Comparison of the Impacts of Several Crises in Indonesia

	COVID-19 CRISIS 2020	GLOBAL FINANCIAL CRISIS 2008	ASIA FINANCIAL CRISIS 1998
Scope of Crisis	• The COVID-19 Pandemic happens in 200 countries. • Global economy is in recession. Global growth contracted by -3 3% in 2020. • Indonesia economy significantly affected.	• The center of the crisis was in the US and other advanced countries (esp. Europe) • Developing countries still managed to record high growth, i.e. China grew by 9.4% • Indonesia economy grew moderately at 4,6%.	• The center of the crisis was in Asia, more specifically Thailand, South Korea and Indonesia. • Indonesia economy contracted sharply by -13%.
Indonesia External Position	CAD : **-2.7% of GDP**(2019) Forex Reserve: **USD 130.5bn** (May 2020)	CAD : **0.02% to GDP** Forex Reserve: **USD 51.6bn**	CAD : **-2.27% to GDP** Forex Reserve: **USD 17.5bn**
Crisis Impact	• All sectors and lines of business were impacted, **including retail**, *consumer*, **MSME** (including MSME *value chain*), and had also impacted corporate • Impacted sectors: **Tourism, Hotel, Trade, Manufacture and Finance**	• Crisis only impacted large corporates • Most impacted sectors are financial sectors, especially **banking** and *capital market*.	• Crisis impacted large companies, specifically the ones with large foreign liabilities. • Most impacted sector are the **banking sector**, as many corporates defaulted.

Source: CEIC and Bloomberg.

FIGURE 4.5
Sectoral Growth

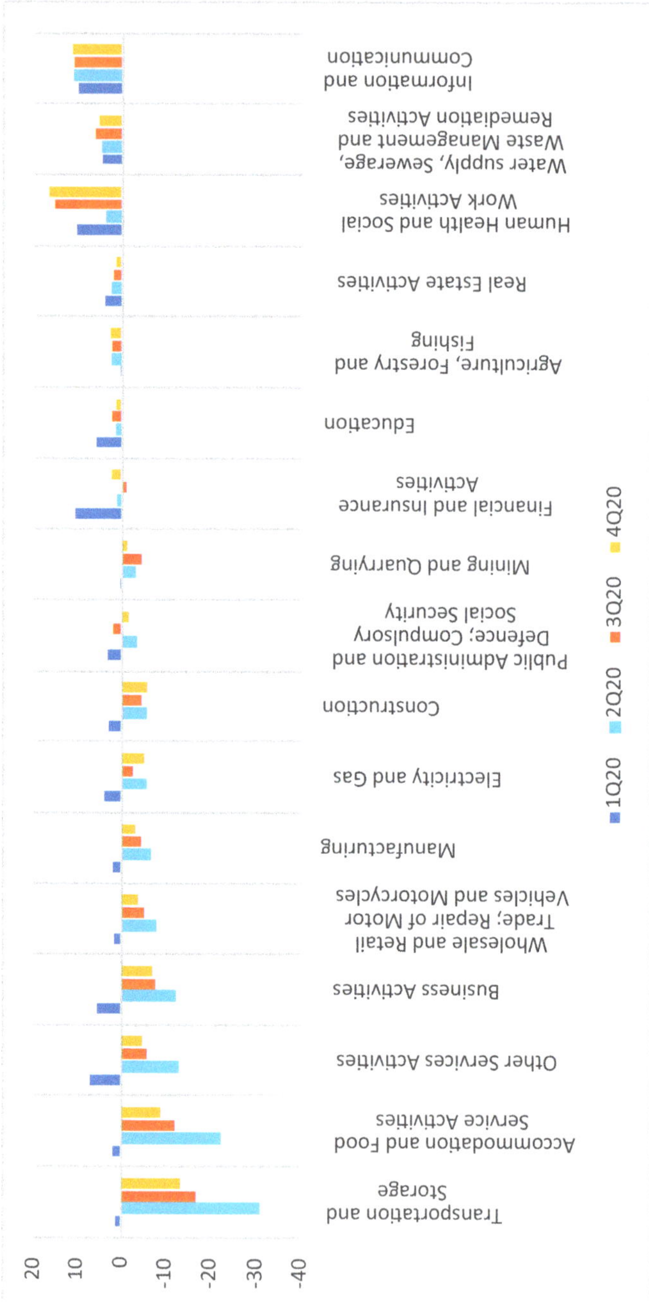

Source: CEIC.

FIGURE 4.6
Stages of Recovery

Source: CEIC and team analysis.

4.2.1 Specific Impact on Banks: Declining Demand for Credit; Selective Credit Disbursement

The declining business operations, combined with a dimming prospect of economic recovery, have discouraged companies and business owners from expanding their businesses. Hence, banks are facing declining demand for credit, given most business owners prefer to save money and adjust production with the falling domestic demand (Figure 4.7). Some business owners even chose to take the opportunity to pay off their existing loans to reduce the burden of debt servicing.

From the banking sector's perspective, the dimming outlook for the economy has led banks to become more selective in disbursing credit. As a result, the overall credit growth contracted by –2.4 per cent YoY by the end of 2020, which was the first contraction in credit growth since the Asian Financial Crisis. The deceleration on both sides will eventually decrease banks' interest revenue and profit. Banks would have to make up for the declining interest income from other sources of income, i.e., fee-based income or revenue from bond transactions.

In short, Indonesian banks are affected by six main factors:

(a) lower demand for loans;
(b) rising NPLs;
(c) increasing needs for liquidity, especially for smaller banks;
(d) lower interest income;
(e) rising operating costs; and
(f) potentially lower capital adequacy ratio.

Similar factors apply to non-banking financial institutions, such as multifinance, insurance, and venture capital. Multifinance companies face lower loan demand, rising NPL, and tighter liquidity due to payment postponements, whereas insurance companies face higher risks on asset prices and lower insurance premiums. The bottom line was that the pandemic was unprecedented in scale and impact; none of us was prepared for a double whammy of health and economic crises. See Figure 4.8.

During the pandemic, banks must be adaptive and more flexible in adjusting to the shift in daily activity patterns, as most activities are now done remotely through various online platforms. Banks can take the opportunity to generate higher fee-based income by shifting to and investing more in digital platforms, for example. Around the same time,

FIGURE 4.7
Impact of COVID-19 Crisis on Indonesian Banks

1 . Uncertainty of duration and severity of the COVID-19 Pandemi

Uncertainty on the COVID-19 pandemic remains high due to:

- The emergence of new variants
- The disparity of COVID-19 handling (tests, vaccinations, etc) across the world continue to be a threat going forward.

2. Global economic recession and its impact to Indonesia economy

- The global economy contracted in 2020 by -3.3%. Indonesia economy also impacted and record contraction of -2%.
- The weak demand causes credit growth to decline and will in turn lower the interest income

3. Commodity prices declining due to global economic slowdown

- During the pandemic, global growth slowdown causes significant decline in fuel demand. Oil price decline to as low as USD37,6 in 2020.
- Declining commodity prices also affect credit growth slowdown.

4. Weakening consumers purchasing power as economy slowing down.

- Growth slowdown led to massive employment layoffs. Rising unemployment will significantly affect the consumers purchasing power.
- Banks become more selective in channeling credit

5. Liquidity tightening in the banking system, especially the small banks

- Amid uncertainties, appetite for investment shifted from high risk assets to safer assets i.e. Banks deposit. Further, consumers tend to prefer large banks which considered to be safer. The phenomenon could disrupt the liquidity of the smaller banks
- The policy of postponement in loan repayment can also reduce banking liquidity

6. Declining asset quality, higher provision cost, and higher operational cost for health protocol implementation

- Weak global and domestic economy significantly impact many industries and sectors. This in turn will also affect the asset quality in various sectors esp. Services industry and MSMEs.
- Declining profit due to rising provision cost may potentially lower the capital (CAR)

Source: Various sources and team analysis.

FIGURE 4.8
Summary of Impact of Pandemic Crisis on Indonesian Non-banking Financial Institutions

Multifinance	• Vehicle and motorcycle leasing is one of the most impacted sector from the debtor's default risk, especially for the productive segment (i.e. online presentation) due to the declining social activities with the implementation of social restriction.
Insurance	• COVID-19 and social restriction that ensued may cause increasing **claims ratio** and declining **gross written premium (GWP)** in insurance industry. • Fluctuation in the capital market will affect insurance companies who are heavily exposed to bundling product (unit link), yet the impact should be limited to conventional insurance companies who manage their assets conservatively (i.e. deposit, *hold to maturity* government bond)
Investment & venture capital	• High market volatility is one of the causes of declining business and transaction activities in investment industry (brokerage income, underwriting and advisory). • Further, declining market valuation can impact the fee income (AUM) and more or less the trading/proprietary position (even when the position is not significant).

Source: Various sources and team analysis.

digital banks are emerging, creating competition by aiming to capture the market niche of customers who prefer fully online banking transactions.

As the pandemic continues, another serious concern is the credit risk, which is reflected in the NPL ratio. Note that NPL indicates a debtor's ability to service their debt. Weakening debtor revenue will eventually affect their ability to pay back their liabilities. The pandemic and the restrictions that followed have negatively impacted the economy. Domestic demand declined, transaction numbers declined, and revenues for most sectors also declined. This raised concerns about rising NPLs amid the already deteriorated banking performance. During the 1997 Asian Financial Crisis, the NPL climbed to as high as 48.6 per cent, causing liquidity problems in the banking sector. The condition was aggravated by declining confidence and the distrust that swept through the whole economy. Many large banks experienced a "bank rush", which threatened to collapse the banking system at the time.

At the early onset of the pandemic, the banking indicators were healthy and stable. Credit grew modestly at 6 per cent by the end of 2019, whereas NPL remained low at 2.5 per cent. When the pandemic hit—and mobility restrictions followed—concerns over the declining ability of debtors to service their loans were rising, as reflected in the rising NPL ratio. NPL climbed to >3 per cent in 2020 and reached as high as 3.4 per cent in August 2021.

During times of crises, the government, the financial authority, and the central bank believe that the most important thing to do is to keep the pressure of bad debts contained and not cause a negative spiralling effect on the economy. Some of the important policies taken during the pandemic were the credit relaxation and loan restructuring policies. By the end of 2021, the NPL ratio had declined to 3.2 per cent, though still relatively higher than the pre-pandemic level. Yet, it should be noted that the number of special mention loans (loans with collectability category 2) increased, reflecting the notable impact of the pandemic on the debtors (Figure 4.9). Nonetheless, overall, the banking system remained stable with ample liquidity.

From a liquidity perspective, fortunately, the banking sector was relatively safe. Unlike any other crisis, while credits declined, deposits grew as people were more comfortable saving than spending or investing amid an unfavourable economy. Thus, the banking liquidity was relatively high, as reflected in the loan-to-deposit ratio, which fell from 90 per cent before

FIGURE 4.9
NPL and Special Mention Loan (SML)

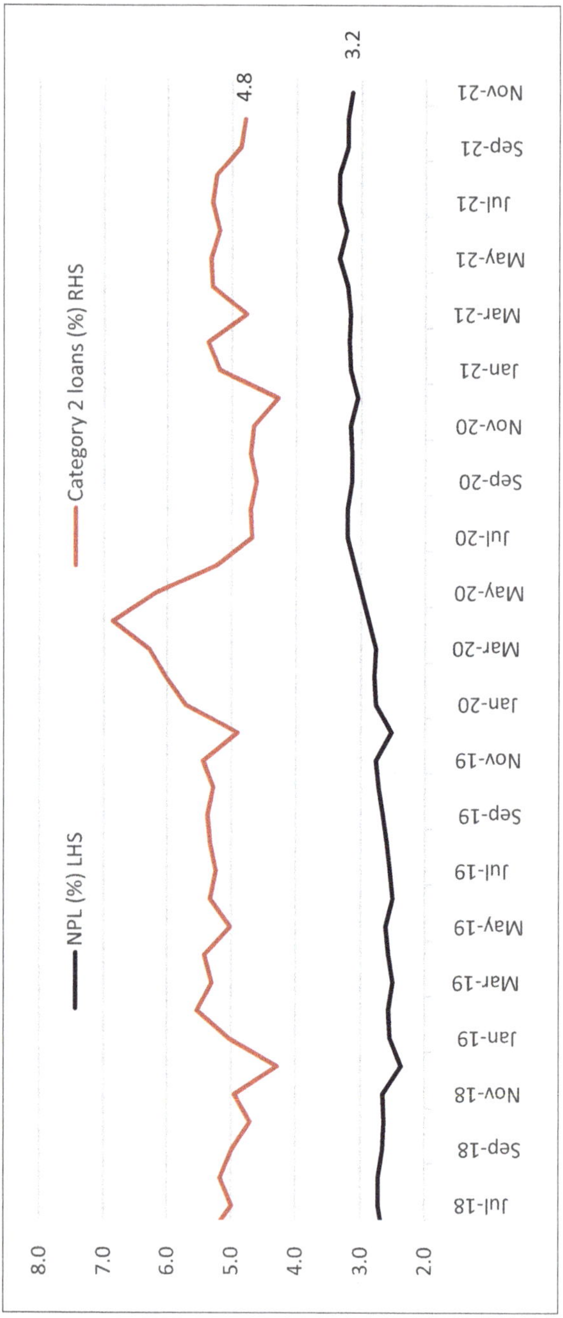

Source: FSA.

the pandemic to the current 77 per cent (end of 2021). Bank Indonesia, as the monetary authority, has also pledged to continue to maintain ample liquidity.

As the pandemic impact was felt across the board, people tended to save more and avoid spending and investing. Declining confidence in the economy led to large depositors shifting their deposits to large banks, a phenomenon called "flight to quality". The situation benefited the large banks, as they could lower their cost of funds. However, the monetary and financial authorities have raised concerns over the state of the smaller banks. See Figure 4.10.

Another aspect of the pandemic is that mobility restrictions have changed people's behaviour and their ways of doing daily activities. People have become more concerned about their well-being, and they pay more attention to cleanliness and social distancing in their daily activities, including banking activities. Even though the government still allows banks (as one of the vital public services) to operate normally, the government requires banks to apply strict health protocols and social distancing. Therefore, banks must endure additional costs to implement these protocols. Adjusting to the pandemic, most consumers have also preferred to do online banking transactions. Thus, banks must reinvent their ways of doing business according to these changes, including some immediate investment allocations into information and technology (IT).

4.3 POLICY SUPPORT TO AVOID A SYSTEMIC IMPACT

The government introduced several economic stimuli at the start of 2020 amid rising concerns over the rapid spread of COVID-19 cases in China. One of the stimuli was to encourage visits to tourist sites through travel discounts amid a sharp decline of foreign tourists due to the early COVID-19 spread in some countries. The government also expanded the coverage of several social security programs, i.e., staple food card and pre-employment card. The rationale of the early-stage stimuli was clear: to support domestic demand and specific sectors that were heavily affected by the mobility restriction amid the rising COVID-19 case.

Yet, the stimulus programmes were redesigned and refocused a couple of months later when the cases started rising further, and the government initiated social restrictions to limit the spread of the virus.

FIGURE 4.10
Deposit Growth Based on Nominal Tiering (% YoY)

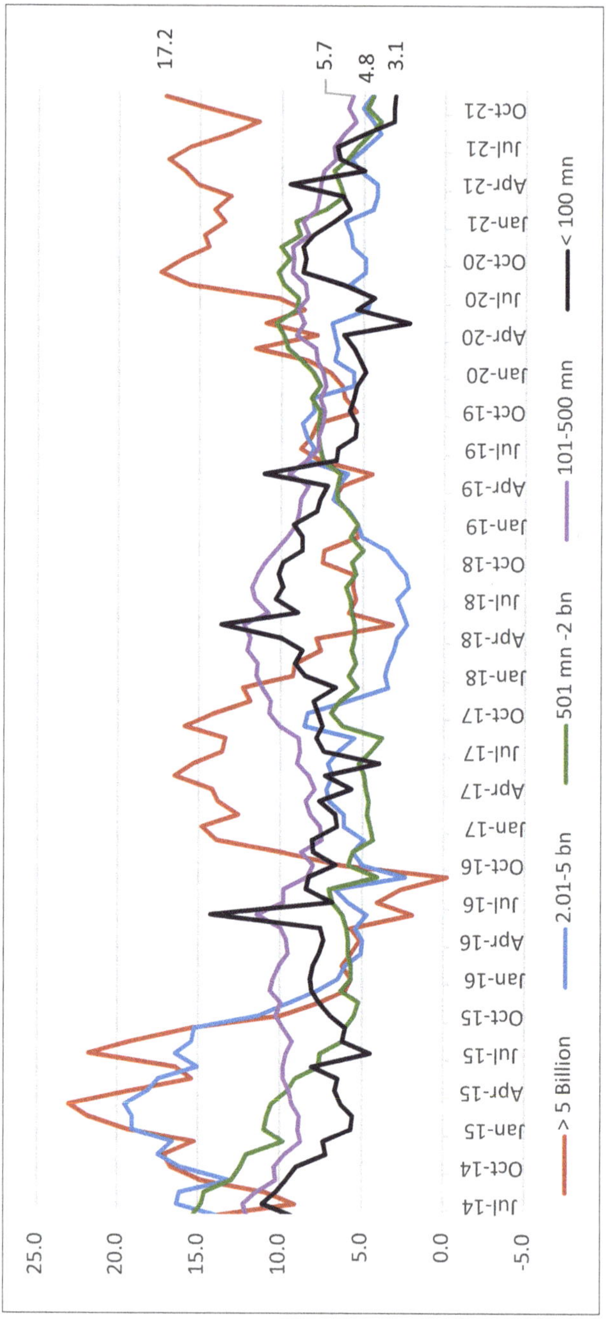

Source: Indonesian Deposit Insurance Corporation.

In the first half of 2020, the government announced the National Economic Recovery Programme, allocating IDR695 trillion for programmes such as social security, healthcare, and business incentives to reduce the impacts of the pandemic and the social/activity restrictions that followed. The government, in coordination with the monetary and financial authorities, also applied several policies in the financial sector. At the time, the rising NPL was the main concern, as there were debtors (corporate, MSMEs, retail, and individuals) heavily hit by social restrictions and thus were at risk of default. Rising credit risk will eventually affect banks' liquidity. Debtors not able to service their debts would mean lower revenue for banks and rising NPLs. Banks would have to set aside provisions for the NPLs, eventually reducing their profit. Yet, not all banks had the ability to set aside large provisions. Smaller banks with lower profit and capital would have to find a way to set aside larger provisions without sacrificing profit. Hence, small banks might be more prone to this NPL pressure.

We have learned from past events that banks of any size can pose a systemic risk in times of crisis. Banking is about trust. During the Asian Financial Crisis, a collapse in one bank triggered widespread panic that eventually led to a "bank rush" and dragged down the whole banking system. Thus, the risk could escalate to a bigger perspective: the banking system's stability.

There was a targeted series of policy responses during the early COVID-19 period (1–3 months) and afterwards. At first, the government, Bank Indonesia (BI) and the Financial Services Authority (FSA) were more concerned about supporting the real sectors (especially MSMEs and ultra-micro players) and the banks by ensuring enough liquidity in the banking system. Therefore, the government, BI and the FSA immediately coordinated and arranged a set of stimuli to minimize the impact of the pandemic on the economy and the financial sectors. We can summarize the policies in the early COVID-19 timeframe as below:

- Policy measures to maintain the banking industry's stability. These policies by the FSA and BI focus on maintaining stable asset quality and sufficient liquidity in the banking sector. Through POJK No. 11/POJK.03/2020, the FSA has allowed a relaxation for banks to assess loan quality only based on one pillar: the ability of debtors to fulfil their liabilities on time for loans up to IDR10 billion, whereas loans of more than IDR10 billion are still required to include the other two pillars in assessing loan quality, i.e., financial condition and business prospects. Furthermore, the regulation also relaxed the loan restructuring for all segments.

- Policy to support postponement of principal payments. The government also provided relaxation through the postponement of principal payments for six months for small/micro and medium enterprises and ultra-micro businesses that have been hit by the pandemic. The relaxation value amounted to IDR271 trillion, including interest subsidies for those loan segments. With all those relaxations, banks conducted massive restructuring afterwards. As a result, NPL was under control, and the restructuring strategies generally included interest rate adjustments, loan period extensions, and loan/financing conversions to temporary equity participations. With bank debtors delaying their payments, the restructuring affected banks' cash flows, especially small banks' cash flows. Hence, at that time, liquidity in the banking industry was a major concern for the regulators. At the same time, banks had to prepare their liquidity ahead of the Ramadan festivity.
- Policy to ensure enough liquidity in the banking system. BI conducted a quantitative easing (QE) policy. Before April 2020, the total liquidity from the QE reached IDR386 trillion, which includes bond-buying in the secondary market and through term repo instruments, thus lowering the IDR reserve requirement ratio and foreign exchange swap instrument. In May 2020, there was IDR117 trillion of additional liquidity injection from the further cut in the IDR reserve requirement and from the relaxation in the additional demand deposit obligation to meet the macroprudential intermediation ratio (MIR). In total, the additional liquidity from BI's QE in January–May 2020 was IDR503.8 trillion. Furthermore, the government also prepared liquidity support by placements of government funds in banks that were conducting loan restructuring (Figure 4.11).

4.3.1 The Financial Services Authority Policy: Credit Relaxation Policy

Rising credit risk, if not managed, can lead to reputation risk affecting consumer confidence and trust in the banking system. Therefore, there

FIGURE 4.11
Restructured Loans (IDR trillion)

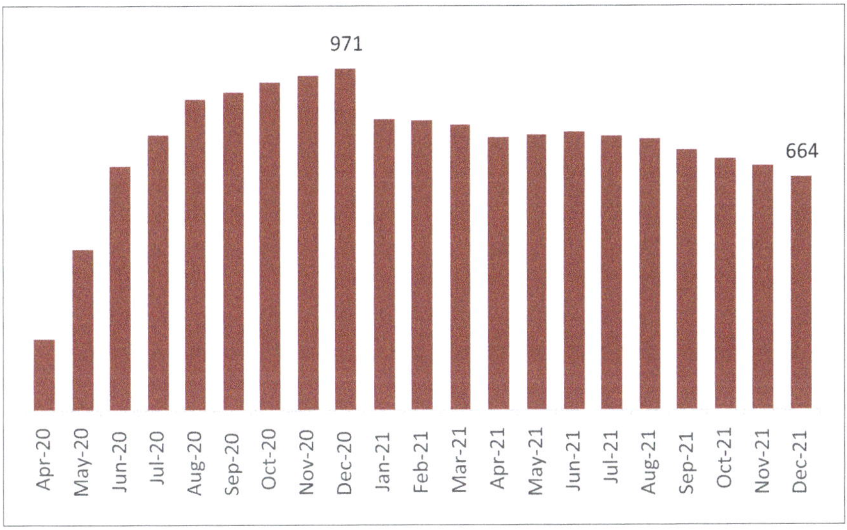

Source: FSA.

must be coordinated countercyclical policies to avoid the worst possible outcome, which is the systemic risk that can endanger the financial sector's stability.

In the years leading up to the 1997 Asian Financial Crisis, Indonesia's banks grew rapidly due to the deregulation of the banking sector in 1988. Yet, the banking sector's condition was not strong enough; it had inadequate capital and a high proportion of lending to affiliated sectors. Additionally, the supervision over the banking sector was not adequate at the time. Following the collapse of the rupiah in mid-1997, the country's banking system was in a crisis. The NPL recorded double-digit growth at 48 per cent. Declining confidence and trust in the banking system led to episodes of bank rush, resulting in a liquidity crisis.

For Indonesia, the most important lesson from past crises is the importance of maintaining people's confidence in the banking system, hence ensuring the financial sector's stability. For this reason, banking liquidity needs to be kept high, thus enabling customers to do banking transactions without worrying that the money is not available. Therefore, maintaining ample liquidity should be the focus in preserving the financial sector's stability.

On 16 March 2020, the FSA issued Regulation No. 11/POJK.03/2020 on COVID-19 stimulus for banks. The FSA relaxed the requirements of Indonesian banks in assessing the asset quality of debtors affected by the pandemic. The policy contains relaxation in asset quality assessment, a separate assessment (no uniform classification) for new loans, and credit restructuring. The relaxation of asset quality assessment would allow banks to manage their non-performing loans better and provide some flexibility for the affected debtors, enabling them for loan restructure (Figure 4.12). This FSA regulation was initially applied until 31 March 2021, but then it was extended to March 2023, considering that the pandemic lingered longer than expected and the economy has yet to recover fully.

Under this FSA regulation, Indonesian banks can now determine the asset quality of debtors based only on the timeliness of payments by the debtor, without considering other aspects. Before the implementation of

FIGURE 4.12
Loan at Risk (% of Total Loans)

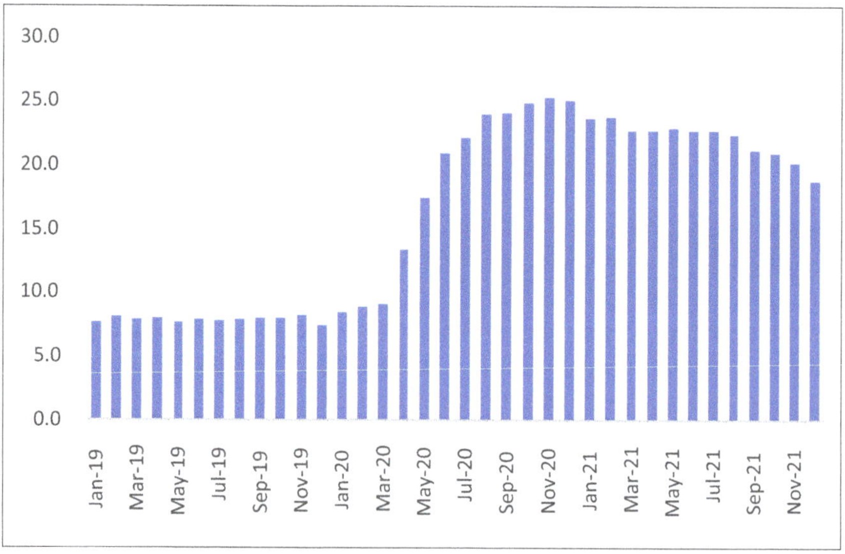

Source: FSA and team's calculation.

this FSA regulation, many aspects must be considered in the assessment of asset quality, such as the timeliness of payments, business prospects and financial condition of the debtors.

Banks may also do loan restructuring for affected debtors. The restructured loan portfolio will then be considered a performing loan. In December 2020, the relaxation policy was extended to 2023, to avoid any potential "cliff effect", which means a sharp rise in the NPL if the relaxation is lifted too soon before the economic situation improves.

4.3.2 Synergy between Government and BI in Supporting Economic Recovery

From the monetary side, BI has embarked on a monetary easing policy since the end of 2019. The benchmark rate (BI 7-Day Reverse Repo Rate) has been lowered by 150 basis points (bps) to 3.5 per cent throughout 2020–21 (Figure 4.13). BI had room to lower interest rates since the inflation rate had declined and remained in the low territory during the first two years of the pandemic as domestic demand fell due to mobility restrictions and lower consumer confidence. BI also lowered the reserve requirement ratio by around the same amount to support more liquidity in the banking system.

Having learned lessons from past crises, maintaining liquidity has become an important aspect and BI's main focus for the banking system. In the face of higher pressure on the exchange rate and heavy capital outflows from both bonds and equities, BI keeps focusing on continuing stability measures in the foreign exchange market, i.e., market sterilization and bond market stabilization by purchasing government bonds in the secondary market.

The lesson learnt: The crisis was unprecedented and required unconventional policy measures. Concerns and debates led to some policy decisions. The government faced a difficult choice between being more expansionary to support the economy and staying prudent and compliant with the law-stated fiscal deficit. The government needed to expand the fiscal spending to accommodate various programmes to counter the pandemic's impact, but the fiscal deficit at the time, by law, was not allowed to exceed the threshold of 3 per cent of GDP. Furthermore, concerns emerged over the state budget financing if the government decided to widen the fiscal deficit. The large capital outflows at the time in the bond

FIGURE 4.13
BI Rate and Inflation

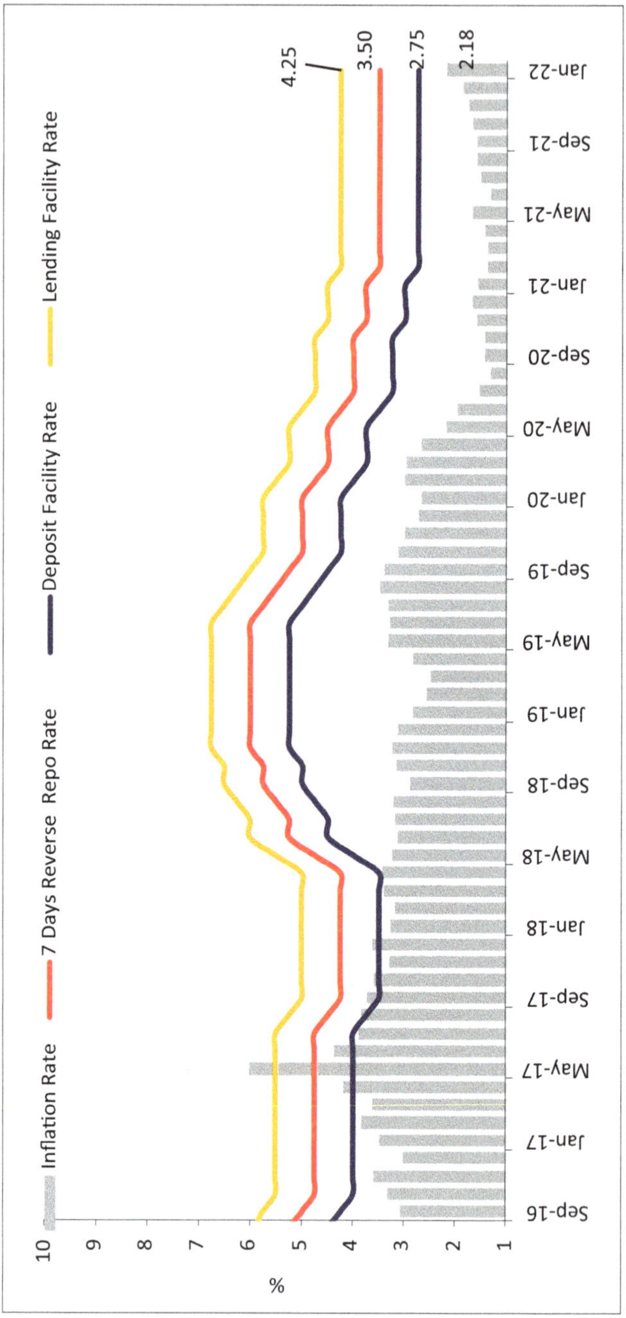

Source: BI, CEIC.

market caused the bond yield to rise sharply, which then raised concerns about the financing cost of the fiscal deficit.

A marathon of coordination meetings between the government, BI, the OJK, and the Indonesian Deposit Insurance Corporation (*Lembaga Penjamin Simpanan*, or LPS) resulted in the government issuing a government decree, Regulation in Lieu of the Law (Perppu) No. 20, which allowed the fiscal deficit to exceed the threshold of 3 per cent of GDP. The regulation was eventually approved by the parliament to become the law, UU no. 2/2020. See Figure 4.14.

The Perppu regulates two topics: the national budget (*Anggaran Pendapatan dan Belanja Negara*, or APBN) and financial sector policies during the pandemic. Regarding the national budget, the Perppu allows the fiscal deficit to exceed 3 per cent for three years. By 2023, the fiscal deficit must return to a maximum of 3 per cent. The regulation provides a base for the government to reallocate expenditures, use alternative budget sources (e.g., SAL, endowment funds, funds managed by public service agencies), do bond financing, lend to the LPS, and apply taxation policies. The Perppu also regulates the flexibility in financial sector policies by improving coordination among *Komite Stabilitas Sistem Keuangan* (KSSK, or Financial System Stability Committee) members, providing the necessary authority to four institutions in KSSK to prevent a crisis.

The regulation also aims to improve coordination in handling problematic banks. A wider scope of authority will be given to the LPS to handle problematic banks, even before a bank fails. The purpose is for the policy to be more preventive, hence avoiding any systemic impact on the financial system.

The law states that the fiscal deficit is allowed to widen to accommodate the COVID-19 stimulus, better known as the National Economic Recovery (PEN) programme. The PEN has a budget of IDR695 trillion. The stimulus recovery package covers budget allocation for health, social transfers, and business incentives, including several schemes for financial sectors, i.e., interest subsidy, credit guarantee, and direct placement for banks facilitating COVID-19 restructuring for their customers. As a result, the fiscal deficit in 2020 was enlarged to 6.3 per cent of GDP, causing the increasing budget financing to up to IDR1,039 trillion. The law stipulates that the fiscal deficit may be enlarged to >3 per cent of GDP for three years due to the unprecedented economic situation.

FIGURE 4.14
Government Regulation UU No. 2/2020, Previously Perppu No. 1/2020

Regulates two topics: (1) National Budget (APBN) and (2) Financial Sector Policy

National Budget (APBN)

1. Relaxation of fiscal deficit to exceed 3%, but starting in 2023 it returns to the maximum level of 3%.
2. Relaxation is related to the allocation/reallocation of expenditure between institutions, between functions, and between programs and mandatory spending.
3. Relaxation of allocation / reallocation of Regional Government Expenditures.
4. Lending to LPS.
5. Issuance of SUN and SBSN can be purchased by BI, BUMN, Corporate, Investors and /or retail investors.
6. Use of alternative budget sources for example SAL, education endowment funds, and funds managed by the Public Service Agency.
7. Taxation Policy: a) Decrease in Corporate Income Tax Rates gradually to 20% starting in 2022; b) Taxation Incentives in the Capital Market for public ownership <40%; c) Taxation of Electronic Transactions; d) Extension of tax administration time; e) Customs facilities in the context of COVID- 19.

Financial Sector Policy

1. Improved Coordination among KSSK members
2. Provide the necessary authority to 4 institutions to prevent a crisis (forward looking) in the KSSK forum for example to issue instruments, BI buys SUN on the primary market, lending to LPS and OJK may request a merger or consolidation of Financial Services Institutions.
3. Foreign exchange management (LLD) management for residents
4. Increase public confidence without causing moral hazard.

Source: Coordinating Ministry for Economic Affairs.

Widening budget financing then became an issue. In an environment of worsening sentiment, the bond market performance was choppy, as foreign investors unwound their position to some extent. Coordination between BI and the government becomes important to resolve the issue. An agreement between BI and the government took place, resulting in BI's role as a standby buyer for the government bond. BI acting as the standby buyer proved effective in supporting government financing, while at the same time, also stabilizing the bond market amid the rising capital outflows.

4.3.3 Burden-Sharing Scheme

At the onset of the pandemic, the financial market was heavily pressured. During March–June 2020, concerns over the pandemic drove capital outflows from both the stock and bond markets (Figure 4.15). The rupiah exchange rate weakened sharply and touched as high as IDR16,000 per US dollar. The bond yield went up from as low as 6.5 per cent in early March to 8.38 per cent at the end of March (Figure 4.16). The yield stayed high for some time. The higher yield then raised concerns over the government's capacity to finance the widening fiscal deficit, given a large stimulus programme was being designed. The fiscal deficit has been allowed by law to widen to >3 per cent of GDP, yet it raised questions on how the government could raise the financing and service debts with significantly higher yields. This shed light on the importance of the burden-sharing scheme between the central bank and the government. To ease pressure on the budget financing, as well as to keep the primary balance healthy, the central bank can contribute by taking the role of standby buyer and sharing the interest burden of the budget financing.

However, the agreement stated in the mutual agreement (SKB I) was not an easy decision. There were several concerns:

(1) Concern about inflation. BI's move to share the burden of financing through bond buying may cause inflation to rise.
(2) High monetary operation cost. There were also concerns that the BI would eventually have to sterilize the impact of the bond-buying policy in the financial market, and the sterilization cost might hurt BI's capital.
(3) The bond-buying policy is similar to quantitative easing policies (debt monetization) in other countries. If not done carefully, it

FIGURE 4.15
Net Capital Flows (IDR trillion)

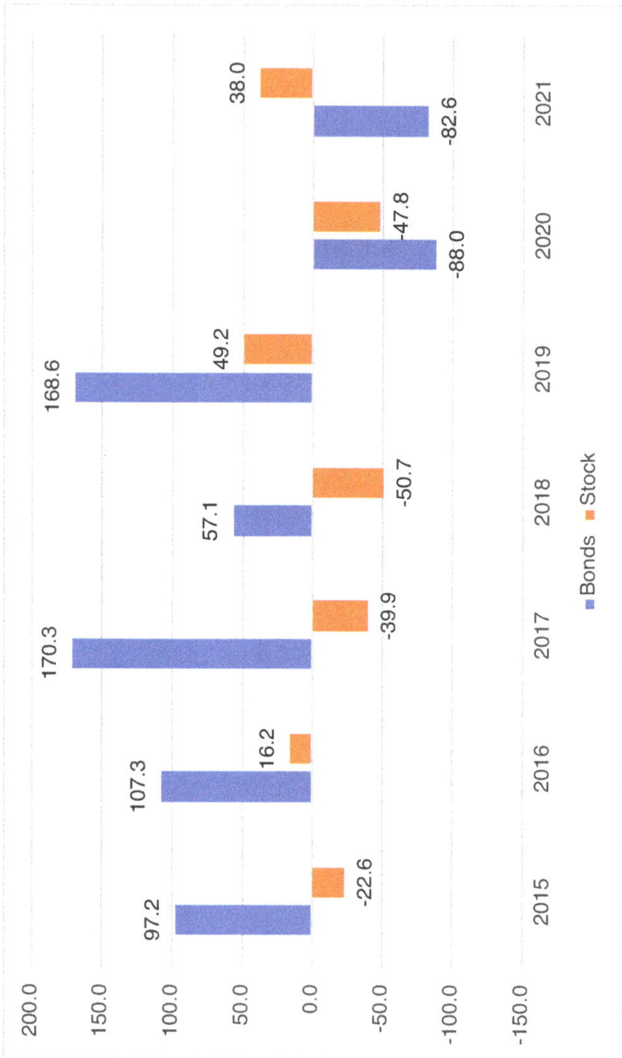

Source: Bloomberg.

FIGURE 4.16
Currency and Bond Yield

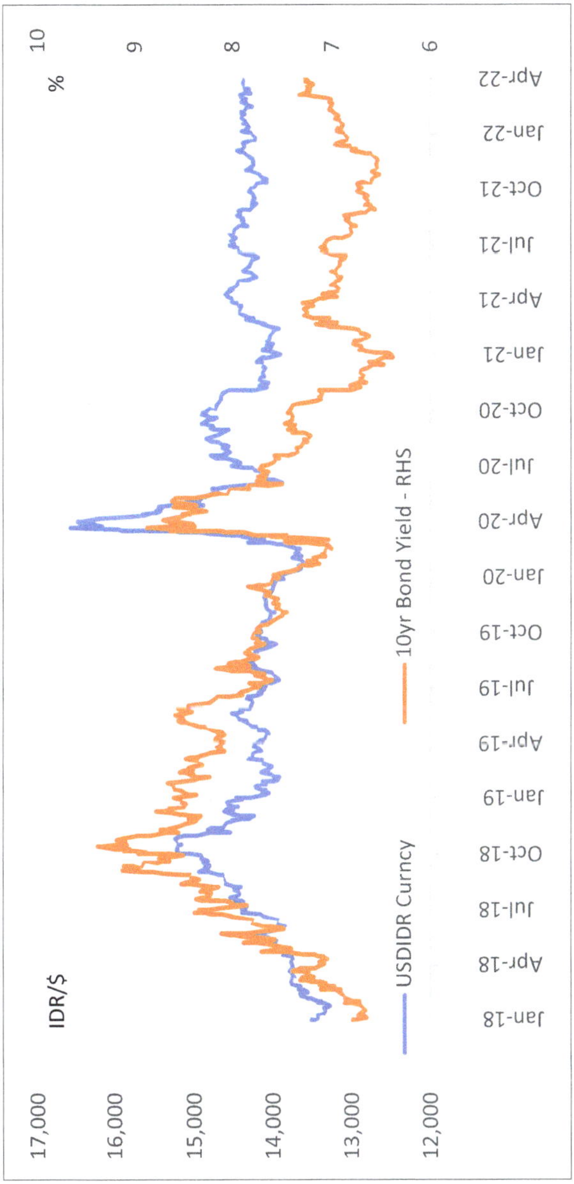

Source: Bloomberg.

might cause negative sentiment in the market and trigger massive capital outflows.

Nonetheless, none of the concerns seemed valid. The inflation rate in Indonesia was at a historic low due to a sharp decline in economic activities. Meanwhile, from the perspective of the central bank's balance sheet, the burden-sharing scheme may potentially reduce the central bank's capital ratio, but the decline will not be substantial. The BI expects the capital ratio to decline to around 4–5 per cent by the end of 2022. This figure is below their comfortable level of 10 per cent, but the capital ratio has so far remained adequate and will not disrupt BI's ability to stabilize the financial market. Furthermore, while it is true that the burden-sharing scheme is similar to the quantitative easing policies by many other countries, the scheme should not disrupt market confidence as long as it is a temporary measure and done prudently. Indonesia's fundamental economic condition is relatively strong despite the pandemic's pressure. The inflation rate reached as low as 1.2 per cent (April 2021), while the foreign exchange was also relatively stable at IDR14,300–14,400 per US dollar. This provided room for BI to conduct quantitative easing policies without hurting inflation and market confidence.

The government and BI have agreed to a burden-sharing scheme, hence coordinating the handling of the pandemic by financing the ballooning fiscal deficit to finance the nation's COVID-19 response and bolster economic recovery. The scheme involves the central bank buying government bonds for four purposes:

(1) IDR397.5 trillion to fund public goods;
(2) IDR123.46 trillion for a non-public goods programme, specifically for MSMEs;
(3) IDR53.4 trillion to finance a non-public goods programme, specifically for corporates;
(4) IDR329.03 trillion for other non-public goods purposes.

The central bank will then return the bond yield to the government in full through the so-called burden-sharing scheme. The scheme is intended to reduce the government's interest burden.

The burden-sharing scheme is an adjustment of the profit-sharing scheme between the government and BI. During better times, the financial management of BI's budget often yields a surplus, which must be returned to the government. It is estimated that the burden-sharing scheme will cost BI around IDR28 trillion, or about 80 per cent of its surplus in 2019 of IDR33 trillion. Therefore, with this burden-sharing scheme, basically, BI's surplus next year, which has to be returned to the government, will decline by the exact amount in the burden-sharing scheme.

From that perspective, the burden-sharing scheme should not disrupt the central bank's balance sheet. BI's capital reached IDR216 trillion at the end of 2019 and was sufficient. Apart from the additional burden that BI has to bear, it will not reduce its ability to maintain exchange rate stability and its mandate to keep inflation at bay.

The scheme was initially intended to be a one-off policy and implemented only in 2020. However, entering 2021, the fiscal deficit gradually lessened but remained wider than historical levels. BI and the government saw that there was still the need to maintain the bond-buying and burden-sharing scheme to maintain financial stability and ensure the government budget financing.

4.3.4 Other Stimuli for Financial Sector

For the financial sector, the government prepared several stimulus schemes designed to help buffer the economy against the pandemic's impact. The programmes included direct placements of funds in the banking system, interest subsidy, and the credit guarantee programme.

To support the loan restructuring programme and encourage more new working capital loan disbursement, the government planned to place funds directly in the banking system. The purpose was to provide liquidity support for banks by providing government-backed funding for banks that were facilitating debt restructuring or providing more working capital loans. Initially, the government had planned to disburse the funds through selected banks, called "anchor banks", which were banks that had fulfilled the government's prerequisites. The policy appeared in Government Regulation (PP) No. 23/2020 on the implementation of the PEN.

The anchor banks were supposed to be the commercial banks with the most substantial assets, which were financially healthy, based on the OJK assessments. The anchor banks could then provide liquidity buffers for other banks, called the "executing banks". Executing banks were commercial banks that facilitated credit restructuring and financing or provided additional credit or working capital to MSMEs and cooperatives; in other words, banks that might need liquidity support. However, this scheme was not implemented, as there were many concerns about additional risks borne by the potential anchor banks. There were also concerns about, among others, the reporting process, which might become overly complicated, as these anchor banks would have to assess other banks' health before providing liquidity while at the same time managing their own liquidity.

Eventually, the government went ahead with another plan, which was the direct placement of funds to domestic commercial banks, requiring them to channel funds through credit disbursement to the private sector. The regulation was laid out in PMK No. 70/PMK.05/2020. In the first stage, the government placed IDR30 trillion to state banks (BRI, Mandiri, BNI and BTN) for a period of six months maximum. In the later stage, the government continued to place funds with other banks, i.e., shariah banks and regional banks. By the end of 2021, the Minister of Finance stated that fund placement had resulted in a multiplier effect of IDR458 trillion in the form of credit disbursement for 5.49 million debtors.

Yet, many banks viewed the placement as not essential, given that banks had more than enough liquidity to channel into credit. The main problem was the very low credit demand. Furthermore, from the banks' perspective, they have also become more selective in channelling credit due to the unfavourable economic situation. Many viewed that credit guarantees and interest subsidy policies would be more effective in driving credit growth.

The government provided interest subsidies and credit guarantees for commercial banks, regional banks, and financing companies that were channelling credit for MSMEs hit by the pandemic. The credit guarantee was later expanded to include loans for companies that have a minimum of fifty employees. The policy effectively shielded against the pandemic's impact, particularly for MSMEs. As a result, credit to MSMEs rebounded to its strongest level in 2021 compared to other segments' credit. The NPL of the MSME segment remained the highest among other segments' NPLs, but so far relatively safe below the 5 per cent level.

4.4 BANKING SECTOR CONDITION AFTER COVID-19 STIMULUS

4.4.1 Stimulus Exit and Policy Normalization

As the global economy gradually improves, with increasingly better pandemic management, governments and central banks worldwide have started considering the process of normalizing their policies back to the pre-pandemic condition. This means the large stimulus measures implemented during the pandemic will be gradually withdrawn.

From the fiscal perspective, the government this year will pursue fiscal consolidation to bring the fiscal deficit back to the ratio of 3 per cent of GDP by 2023, as stipulated by the law. The budget allocation for the PEN has been gradually reduced. In 2022, the government allocated IDR455 trillion for the PEN budget, lower than the PEN realization in 2021 at IDR578 trillion. Some stimulus programmes, like social transfers, have ended, and others have been downsized or channelled with more selective requirements.

BI has also signalled to begin monetary policy normalization, citing that monetary policy will focus on maintaining market stability. The focus on financial stability becomes important because, despite the optimism of economic recovery, the global risks are also increasing along with the rising inflationary pressure. The prolonged global supply chain disruption, exacerbated by a steep rise in commodity prices due to rising geopolitical tension, has caused inflation to shoot up. Central banks worldwide have responded to the inflation pressure by tapering their quantitative easing policy or raising their interest rates. The Federal Reserve, for the first time since the pandemic, has raised its benchmark rate by 25 bps in March 2022.

At the beginning of the year, BI begins normalizing its liquidity policy by raising the reserve requirement ratio from as low as 3.5 per cent, bringing it gradually back to its pre-pandemic level at 6.5 per cent by the end of Q3 2022. The policy is expected to absorb IDR190 trillion liquidity in the banking system. Nonetheless, BI will also offer incentives for banks disbursing financing to priority sectors and inclusive financing, and for banks that have achieved the Macroprudential Inclusive Financing Ratio (*Rasio Pembiayaan Inklusif Makroprudensial*, or RPIM) target. They would be entitled to an incentive in the form of a reduction in the daily reserve requirement. The policy is projected to provide about IDR35 trillion incentive to banks; hence, this year's net liquidity absorption is expected to reach only IDR153 trillion.

The liquidity policy normalization will be done gradually and carefully as the banking liquidity is still currently very ample. The loan-to-deposit ratio currently stands at 77 per cent. The ratio of liquid assets to deposits reached 35 per cent, much higher than the pre-pandemic level of around 20 per cent. Moreover, the amount of excess liquidity placed in BI's monetary instruments is currently at a historic high at IDR800 trillion–IDR900 trillion. This means the net liquidity absorption from the normalizing reserve requirement policy will have little impact on liquidity and should not deter banks' ability to continue expanding credit growth.

Nevertheless, this is just BI's first move towards policy normalization. As the economy improves, BI will cautiously monitor the conditions, particularly the inflation number, especially considering the rising pressure of global commodity prices. A persistent rise in inflation may cause further adjustments in the monetary policy by increasing the policy rate.

The next step for a gradual policy exit should be reducing the ample market liquidity resulting from BI's quantitative easing policy before raising the policy rate. Thus far, BI still maintains policy synergy with the government, particularly in supporting the financing of the state budget through direct purchases of government bonds or the quantitative easing policy. This year, according to the third joint decree between the Minister of Finance and BI on 23 August 2021 (SKB III), BI maintains government bond purchases amounting to IDR224 trillion to support budget financing for specific government programmes, i.e., health and humanitarian assistance.

The burden-sharing scheme is expected to end in 2023, which means BI will no longer be able to directly purchase government bonds in the primary market. This is in line with the government's plan to reduce the fiscal deficit to 3 per cent of GDP by 2023, as stipulated by law. If the government can successfully reduce the fiscal deficit back to a maximum of 3 per cent of GDP, the amount of financing next year should not be as large as this year; therefore, the need for the central bank's support in budget financing should diminish.

Yet, we must note that we are currently facing increasing global inflation pressure. Domestic inflation could be affected by higher input prices (imported inflation) or higher administered prices if the government adjusted the domestic energy prices. If the inflation expectation surpasses BI's target range, BI may have to raise the policy rate before ending its quantitative easing policy.

One point of concern is how to gradually reduce the QE without causing volatility in the bond market. During the pandemic, despite the massive foreign capital outflows, the bond market remains stable with the support of domestic investors, such as the central bank, commercial banks, domestic financial institutions and retail investors. Massive capital outflows during 2020–21 have caused the share of foreign ownership in bonds to decline from its pre-pandemic level at 38 per cent to the current 18 per cent ratio of total bond ownership. Fortunately, domestic investors were able to fill in the gap left by the foreign investors, hence supporting the bond market. The muted economic activities during the pandemic drove domestic investors to look for higher yields and convert their investments into bonds. The low interest rate environment has driven financial institutions and retail investors to turn to the bond market. Low credit demand has also led banks to put their liquidity in bonds. BI's QE policy also lent material support to the bond market.

The central bank and commercial banks have remained the biggest holders in the bond market, with 15 per cent and 34.8 per cent ownership ratios, respectively. However, once the situation reverses and economic activity improves, the central bank and commercial banks may have to unwind their position. If they are not careful, this might cause volatility in the bond market, especially in an environment of negative market sentiment. The best timing to unwind their bond position is when the market sentiment improves, and capital inflows start increasing in the bond market. Yet, if the worst-case scenario were to happen and there was a prolonged negative sentiment in the global market, BI would need to think of strategies to exit without causing volatility in the bond market.

The OJK must also carefully consider the best timing for policy exit. The loan restructuring policy for COVID-19-impacted debtors is expected to end by March 2023. The OJK must carefully assess the state of improvement in the economic sectors, especially those that were badly hit by the pandemic. MSMEs, the segment that benefited the most from the loan restructuring policy, should be able to recover gradually along with the economic recovery.

Currently, the loans that are being restructured have continued to decline. Most large banks recorded a 15–30 per cent decline in their restructured loan portfolio. Yet, the constantly challenging global environment may deter the sectoral recovery, especially in manufacturing sectors, which currently face higher production costs. The OJK must carefully assess the economy and the sectoral performance to avoid any sudden rise in the NPL ratio, or the cliff effect if the loan restructuring policy is lifted in March 2023. Policy exit or the pace of normalization must also be in line with the pace of other countries. This is necessary, as we expect to maintain a positive perception and the confidence of foreign investors.

4.4.2 Banking Sector Current Development

The economy improved in Q4 2021, once the COVID-19 Delta outbreak was contained. The economic growth accelerated to 5.02 per cent in Q4 2021, back to its pre-pandemic average growth. In line with improving economic performance, the banking sector's performance also improved. The banking industry's loan growth accelerated to 5.2 per cent by the end of 2021, the fastest in nearly two years. Asset quality remained manageable, with the NPL ratio relatively stable at 3.0 per cent. Meanwhile, deposit growth stayed high at 12.2 per cent, resulting in still ample liquidity in the banking sector, reflected in the still low loan-to-deposit ratio (LDR) at 77 per cent.

All segments showed improvement. Loans to MSMEs increased significantly as the economy continued to recover with the continued support of government policies (Figure 4.17). The growth of MSME loans soared in December 2021 to 12.3 per cent YoY, which was the highest growth in MSME loans in more than two years as economic activities strengthened and people's mobility and spending rebounded. The NPL ratio finally showed a downturn by the end of 2021, declining to 3.2 per cent from as high as 3.4 per cent in November 2021, following the persistent increase in the last couple of months (Figure 4.18). As the NPL ratio decreased, wholesale and MSME loan qualities improved in December 2021 to 3.4 per cent and 3.7 per cent.

Banks have managed liquidity and operational risks quite well. Policy support from the authorities, especially the credit restructuring policy, has supported the banking sector's performance during the pandemic. Despite the good news, the government and financial authorities need to carefully consider the timing of the policy exit. The credit restructuring policy has been extended once and is supposed to end by March 2023. By that time, the economy is expected to recover, and hopefully, once the policy is lifted, banks will not have to face the cliff effect or a steep rise in the NPL ratio. Other policies that are still maintained so far are the interest rate subsidy for MSMEs and the credit guarantee scheme for MSMEs and some eligible corporations.

Further, during the period of low credit demand, several banks have boosted their digital infrastructure and taken advantage of the situation by targeting more fee-based income from rising digital transactions. Banks managed to contain their operational costs by investing and building new

FIGURE 4.17
Loan Growth by Segments (% YoY)

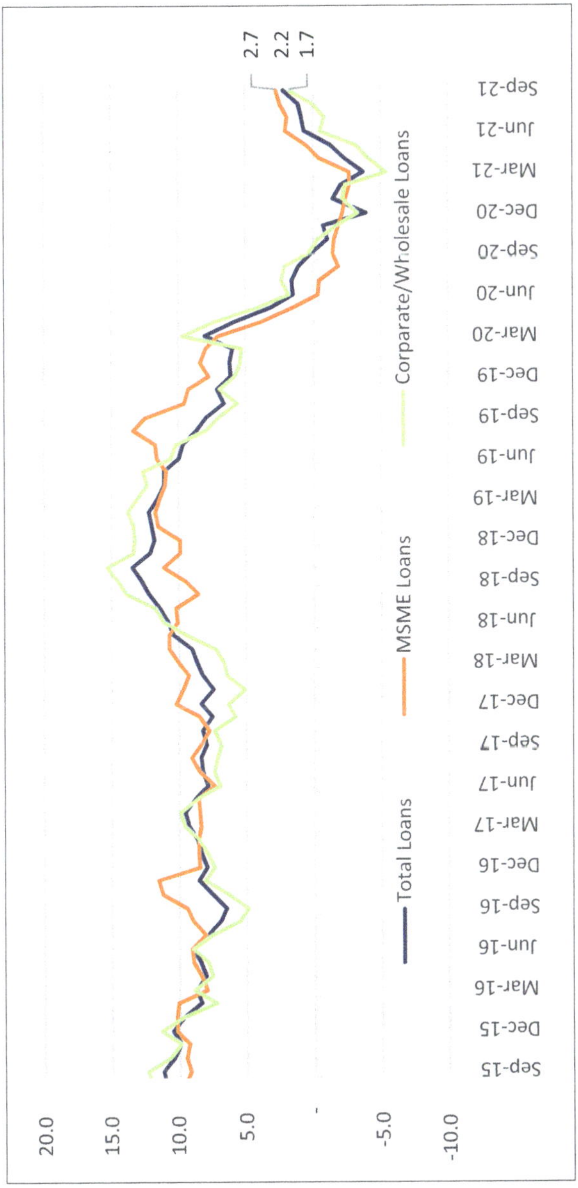

Source: FSA.

FIGURE 4.18
NPL Ratio by Segments (% of Total Loans)

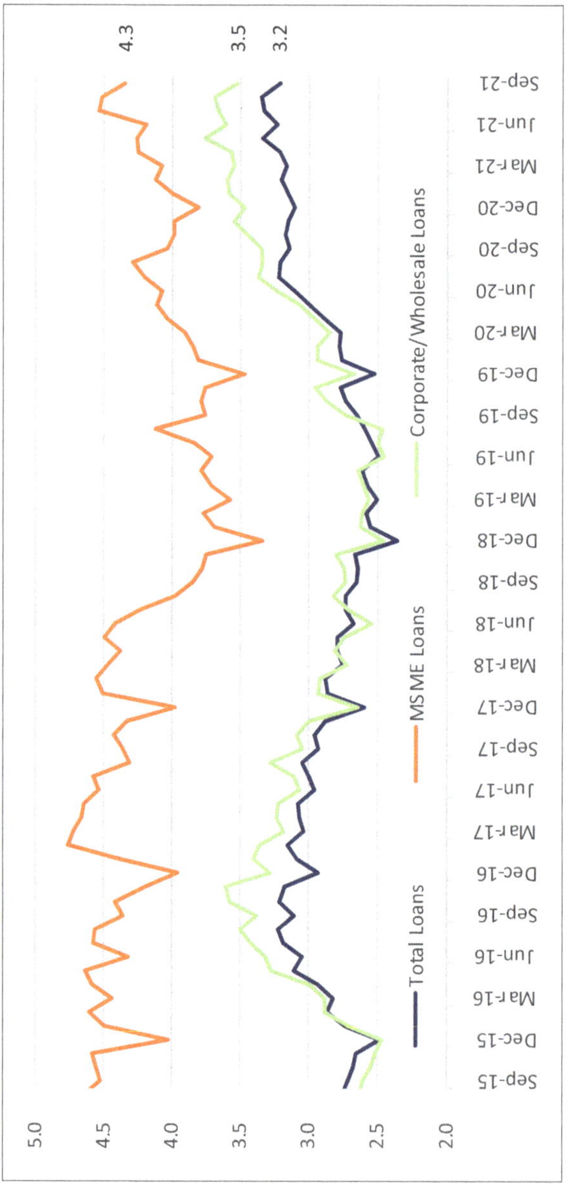

Source: FSA.

digital platforms, acquiring and building new digital banks, or basically just strengthening their existing digital platform.

4.4.3 Banking Sector Outlook

The banking sector remains strong, with sufficient capital and liquidity, as well as stable asset quality and improving confidence in the domestic economy. The condition is expected to continue in 2022, with the economy expected to continue its recovery despite several lingering risks, such as global tightening policies and geopolitical issues. Confidence will recover with better pandemic handling and wider vaccination coverage, which will support loan demand recovery. As many sectors are expected to recover, their ability to pay loan instalments will also improve. This would ease the pressure on the NPL ratio and better prepare banks for the end of the loan restructuring policy in March 2023. As confidence and economic activities recover, savers and depositors may be more confident to expand, invest, and consume, meaning that deposit growth may gradually decelerate.

Nonetheless, there are still some risks in the outlook. Liquidity in the banking sector should still be ample, though possibly not as high as in 2021, supported by recovering income, especially commodity income as commodity prices rise. BI has started its policy normalization by gradually raising the reserve requirement ratio. In the second semester of 2022, the banking sector may face a higher interest rate environment, which may slightly limit the loan acceleration pace.

In the future, banks should be able to manage and optimize their balance sheet performance in an environment of tighter liquidity. There might be a few opportunities to expand credit, for example, by targeting the prospective sectors, such as commodity-related, F&B, technology, and utility sectors. Nonetheless, banks must still carefully assess the sectors' performance to avoid rising pressure on asset quality.

Note

1. BUKU is bank size category in Indonesia by core capital.

References

Bank Indonesia. 2020. *Laporan Perekonomian Indonesia*. Jakarta: Bank Indonesia.

———. 2021. *Recent Economic Development: Strengthening the Policy Synergy to Promote Recovery and Maintaining Macroeconomic Stability.* Jakarta: Bank Indonesia.

Bank Mandiri. 2021. *Econmark: Recapturing the Growth Momentum.* Jakarta: Bank Mandiri.

BI Institute. 2018. *Pembangunan Inklusif Bagi UMKM.* Jakarta: Bank Indonesia.

Indonesian Deposit Insurance Corporation (IDIC). 2021. *Distribusi Simpanan Bank Umum.* Jakarta: Indonesia Deposit Insurance Corporation.

OJK. 2020. *Statistik Perbankan Indonesia.* April. https://www.ojk.go.id/id/kanal/perbankan/data-dan-statistik/statistik-perbankan-indonesia/Pages/Statistik-Perbankan-Indonesia---April-2020.aspx

———. 2021. *Pertemuan Tahunan Industri Jasa Keuangan.* Jakarta: OJK.

theglobaleconomy.com. 2020. "Bank Cost to Income Ratio: Country Rankings". https://www.theglobaleconomy.com/rankings/bank_cost_to_income/

World Bank. 2018. *The Little Data Book on Financial Inclusion.* https://globalfindex.worldbank.org/sites/globalfindex/files/countrybook/Indonesia.pdf

5

Financing to Save Indonesia

Luky Alfirman, Riko Amir and Deni Ridwan

5.1 INTRODUCTION

COVID-19, the virus that caused a multidimensional crisis, has impacted every economy globally, including Indonesia. Having forced mobility restriction policies to restrain the spread of the virus, many countries have experienced a great lockdown recession, referred to as a significant drop in domestic economic activity (IMF 2020). This condition led to a substantial decline in household consumption and business activities, causing state revenues, especially tax revenues, to collapse due to a sudden halt in economic activity. On the other hand, the demands for funding the health sector, social safety nets and other expenditures for handling COVID-19 were rising as well as the need to accelerate national economic recovery. Moreover, the pandemic has also threatened the financial sector with a sharp drop in the economy evoked an appetite to hold deposits and only the most liquid asset.

The pandemic crisis is also more alarming due to the uncertainty of the virus mutation and yet has massively scarring effects for people. The spread of Delta variant waves with high casualties and followed by economic pressure in mid-2021 was evidence of the uncertainty of the impact of the pandemic. Therefore, fiscal policy in Indonesia has expanded since 2020, and as a countercyclical measure, it has continuously played an essential role in protecting the poor and vulnerable until now. In a time of crisis, a fiscal response is necessary and has to be timely. However, questions arise about whether the government can prepare the financing instrument that performs yet are credible to the financial market to support the stimulus.

This chapter discusses Indonesia's experience in fulfilling financing needs during the pandemic to support the government's strategies for economic recovery. Firstly, this chapter examines the policies in responding to the unprecedented crisis, followed by the challenges and opportunities during the crisis and the strategies for utilizing financing instruments to support the budget. Lastly, this chapter ends with some lessons learnt and the way forward.

5.2 NECESSARY FISCAL RESPONSE TO STABILIZE THE ECONOMY

In the past decades, the government has utilized the State Budget (*Anggaran Pendapatan dan Belanja Negara*, or APBN) as a measure to boost economic growth through national priority programmes, which have multiplier effects, such as infrastructure provision, improving quality of health and education, as well as bureaucratic reforms. Consequently, these fiscal policies have implications for the State Budget to remain in deficit and need to be fulfilled primarily from financing sources through debt. Although there is a gradual growth in financing needs, the government still manages the debt-to-GDP ratio moderately and searches for ways to reduce the State Budget deficit. The government aims to lower the State Budget deficit from 2.15 per cent of GDP in 2015 to 1.76 per cent of GDP in the 2020 initial State Budget.

However, the COVID-19 pandemic has forcefully twisted the scheme for fiscal consolidation into an uncertain period. Learning from China's response to handling the COVID-19 outbreak where speed is everything (Cohen and Kupferschmidt 2020), almost all nations quickly responded to save their economies by carrying out fiscal expansion policies and loosening monetary policies (Guerrieri et al. 2020). The decision to relax its fiscal deficit had been the anticipatory step taken by almost all countries, including Indonesia. The policy is a necessary condition as the objective of fiscal policy is to act as a buffer during a short-term shock (Alberola et al. 2021).

In early 2020 when the pandemic started, due to a forward-looking assessment, both the Ministry of Finance and the Financial System Stability Committee (*Komite Stabilitas Sistem Keuangan*, or KSSK), revealed that it is necessary to implement an anticipatory policy immediately. It should also be noted that this was the first time that KSSK initiated a forward-looking assessment regarding financial system stability. A debate on whether to set a certain limit on the budget deficit (e.g., 5 or 7 per cent) occurred. Finally, since the impact and the period of the pandemic are still uncertain, it was agreed that certain limits were not to be applied yet. If the limit was set but the conditions worsen, then all legislation must be revised again, which may need more time and effort.

Based on the above backdrop and the huge necessity for fiscal stimulus amidst declining state revenue, the increase in the State Budget deficit surpassing the maximum limit of 3 per cent of GDP as stipulated in the State Finance Law is unavoidable. It triggered the enactment of Emergency Regulation in Lieu of Law No. 1 of 2020 (PERPU 1/2020), then specified as Law No. 2 of 2020 (UU 2/2020). In essence, the law does not solely act as a deficit fulfiller (a legal ground for generating fast and responsive decisions). However, it also served as a commitment tool to carefully measure the financing risks and committed to following fiscal discipline, reinstalling the maximum limit of 3 per cent of GDP (known as fiscal consolidation) in 2023.

The next question to be answered was how the government can fulfil the debt financing target during the pandemic, which has increased by more than three times from the pre-pandemic era (from around IDR300 trillion on a net basis to above IDR1,000 trillion) by considering adequate costs and risks. Debt financing instruments consist of the issuance of Government Securities (*Surat Berharga Negara*, or SBN) in conventional-based (*Surat Utang Negara*, or SUN) or sharia-based (*Surat Berharga Syariah Negara*, or SBSN) and also loan withdrawal from multilateral and bilateral partners.

Table 5.1 demonstrates the shift began in 2020 when the government must calibrate the State Budget portion in early 2020 due to the shock in state revenue and expenditure. It affected the financing needs as shown that the 2020 State Budget deficit was initially set at 1.76 per cent, revised to 5.07 per cent[1] and 6.34 per cent[2] but then realized at 6.14 per cent of GDP.[3]

TABLE 5.1
The State Budget Figures

Description (IDR Trillion)	2019		2020	2020			2021		2022
	Budget	Audited	Budget	Budget *	Budget **	Audited	Budget	Real. (Unaudited)	Budget
State Revenue	2,165.1	1,960.6	2,233.2	1,760.9	1,699.9	1,647.8	1,743.6	2,003.1	1,846.1
Tax Revenue	1,786.4	1,546.1	2,232.7	1.462,60	1,404.5	1,285.1	1,444.5	1,546.5	1,510.0
Non Tax Revenue	378.3	409	367.0	297.8	294.1	343,8	298.2	452.0	335,6
Government Expenditure	2,461.1	2.309,30	2,540.4	2,613.8	2,739.2	2,595.5	2,750.0	2,786.8	2,714.2
Central Government Expenditure	1,634.3	1,496.3	1,683.5	1,851.1	1,975.2	1,832.9	1,954.5	2,001.1	1,944.5
Regional Transfer and Village Funds	826.8	813.0	857.0	762.7	763.9	762.5	795.5	785.7	769.6
Primary Balance	(20.1)	(73.1)	(12.0)	(517.8)	(700.4)	(633.6)	(633.1)	(440.2)	(462.2)
Surplus (Deficit)	(296.0)	(348.7)	(307.2)	(852.9)	(1,039.2)	(947.7)	(1,006.4)	(783.7)	(868.0)
% of GDP	(1.84)	(2.20)	(1.76)	(5.07)	(6.34)	(6.14)	(5.70)	(4.65)	(4.85)
Financing*	296.0	402.1	307.2	852.9	1.039.2	1.193.3	1,006.4	868,63	868.0
SBN	389.0	446.3	389.3	549.6	1,173.7	1,177.2	1,207.3	877,5	973.6
Loan	(29.7)	(8.7)	(37.5)	6.9	46.7	52.5	(29.9)	(10.1)	(17.7)

Source: Ministry of Finance.

The financing in the 2020 State Budget increased from IDR307.2 trillion to IDR1,177.2 trillion based on Central Government Financial Report (*Laporan Keuangan Pemerintah Pusat*, or LKPP) 2020 data (audited). The deficit widening policy continued in the 2021 State Budget, with a deficit of 5.7 per cent of GDP and financing of IDR1,006.4 trillion, yet also showed the downturn of deficit realization at 4.65 per cent of GDP with the financing of IDR868.6 trillion.

The relaxation of the State Budget deficit has a consequence of increasing the outstanding debt of the government. In Figure 5.1, the debt-to-GDP ratio grew from 30.2 per cent in 2019 to 39.5 per cent at the end of 2020, which is still within the safe limit stipulated in the law (60 per cent of GDP). When compared to other countries, the difference in ratio between 2019 and 2020 is 9 per cent, below other countries experiencing above 10 per cent, such as Japan (22 per cent), Italy (21 per cent), the US (19 per cent), France (15 per cent), the UK (18 per cent), Malaysia (10 per cent), the Philippines (11 per cent), and India (16 per cent).[4] In the meantime, the ratio has been assessed to decline in 2023 following the projected performance of the fiscal consolidation strategy in 2023. Despite the current uncertainty, fiscal consolidation was enforced to deliver the economic transformation for inclusive and sustainable productivity by striving to mobilize income (i.e., the effectiveness of the Harmonized Tax Regulation [*Harmonisasi Peraturan Perpajakan*, or HPP]), spend better, and do innovative and sustainable financing.

5.3 DESPITE PANDEMIC CHALLENGES, OPPORTUNITIES ARISE

Fulfilling fiscal financing during the pandemic inevitably confronted some debt management and portfolio risks, such as refinancing risk, exchange rate risk and interest rate risk. Also, the government has intensively managed debt risk within limits set out in the State Finance Law, ruling a maximum debt ratio of 60 per cent to GDP and a debt management strategy stipulating the threshold of each risk.

Regardless of financing obstacles, the government still demonstrates manageable debt management risk as seen in Figure 5.2. First, refinancing risk can be well maintained by prioritizing the procurement of new debt with medium to long tenors. The necessity for the issuance of Treasury Bills[5] as an instrument for government cash mismatching is executed

FIGURE 5.1
The Trend of Debt Portion

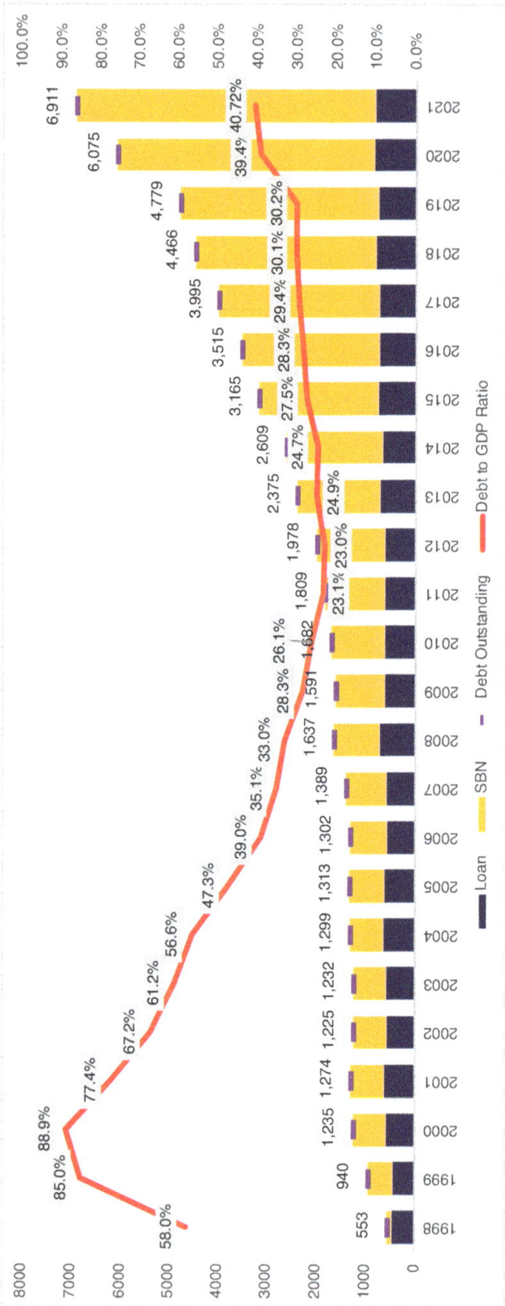

Source: Ministry of Finance.

FIGURE 5.2
Risk Indicators in Financing Strategy and Portfolio

Source: Ministry of Finance.

carefully and strictly by reckoning the financing needs and the condition of the state treasury. Second, the Average Time to Maturity is above seven years as the limit set in the medium-term debt financing strategy, stipulated in the Minister of Finance's decision.[6] Third, the exchange rate risk trend has decreased in the last two years, where the foreign currency debt ratio was 37.9 per cent in 2019 and 30 per cent at the end of 2021. The result was obtained by the optimization of domestic-sourced financing through the issuance of Government Securities (SBN[7]) and domestic loans, the growth of domestic ownership, and the synergy between the Government and the Bank of Indonesia.[8] Lastly, the government maintains a floating interest rate debt ratio below 20 per cent in the medium term to balance the government's portfolio. Following the cooperation between BI and the government, the government shared an increase in the variable debt ratio from 9.8 per cent in 2019 to 16.3 per cent in 2021. However, it should be emphasized that the variable debt ratio deriving from instruments outside the BI-government cooperation fell to 7.4 per cent in 2021.

While the debt portfolio was manageable, the government also dealt with the challenge of limited liquidity in the domestic financial market. The domestic government securities (GS) auction indicated the relatively sluggish domestic demand during the pandemic was indicated by the domestic government securities auction, where the auction performance in the 2020–21 period was quite volatile in terms of incoming bids and yield. This condition has affected the auction result. Several Green Shoe Option (GSO) auctions must be conducted to meet the indicative target that could not be fulfilled in the regular auctions.

On the other side, the same issues came from the weakened demand of foreign investors, indicated by the sharp downturn of foreign ownership of domestic GS during the pandemic period. Foreign ownership fell sharply from 38.6 per cent at the beginning of 2020 to 19.0 per cent by 2021. Foreign investors' ownership recorded a considerable decline in the domestic GS market for two straight years during the pandemic. This condition became quite critical for the performance of GS because foreign investors, historically, have played quite a critical role as the counterparts of domestic investors in the transactions of GS in the secondary market.

The phenomena forced the government to analyse and conduct every possible and available way to match the financing needs with low demand from investors. Meanwhile, the issuance cost was much higher than the issuance in normal conditions since the investors required a higher level of return to persuade them to invest in GS. However, decisions must be taken to ensure the fulfilment of budget deficit financing was timely and immediately.

Facing the uncertainty and risk-averse motive in the domestic market, the government of Indonesia still successfully achieved the issuance target in 2020 and 2021. The main reasons are, first, appropriate financing strategy, and secondly, ample liquidity in the financial market throughout the period. The significant reduction in household consumption in middle-upper-income citizens has increased a significant amount of third-party funds in the financial system, along with the decline of the loan-to-deposit ratio (Basri and Fitrania 2022). Lastly, the role of central banks in the primary market to support the economic recovery programme has reduced concerns regarding the oversupply of GS in the financial market. Arslan, Drehmann and Hofmann (2021) argue that market reaction in emerging economies was positive towards monetary participation in bond purchase during the pandemic with the decline in 10-year government bond yields on average in emerging countries around 10 bps post the bond purchase announcement and even further decline after five days.

In the first quarter of 2020, the demand from the investors was quite solid, with an average amount of IDR65.48 trillion versus the awarded bids of IDR13.9 trillion. However, the impact of the pandemic started to influence the investors' appetite. Average incoming bids dropped around 19 per cent to IDR47.65 trillion in Q2 2020. In the third quarter of 2020, the central bank (Bank Indonesia) launched a policy to reduce the reserve requirement in the banking system. The policy has injected more liquidity into the financial market, increasing the average incoming bids. Further, the increasing trend of incoming bids continued up to Q4 2020.

In 2021, the available liquidity was still ample; financial institutions were keen to invest in domestic safe-haven assets such as government bonds. It enabled the government to accomplish a smoother issuance target in 2021. On the back of the better-than-expected revenue side due to the improvement in commodity size and the optimal expenditure realization, the government issued the last securities through auction in October 2021. Figure 5.3 validates the significantly higher incoming bids than the awarded bids, specifically in Q4 2021.

FIGURE 5.3
Incoming and Awarded Bids in 2020–21

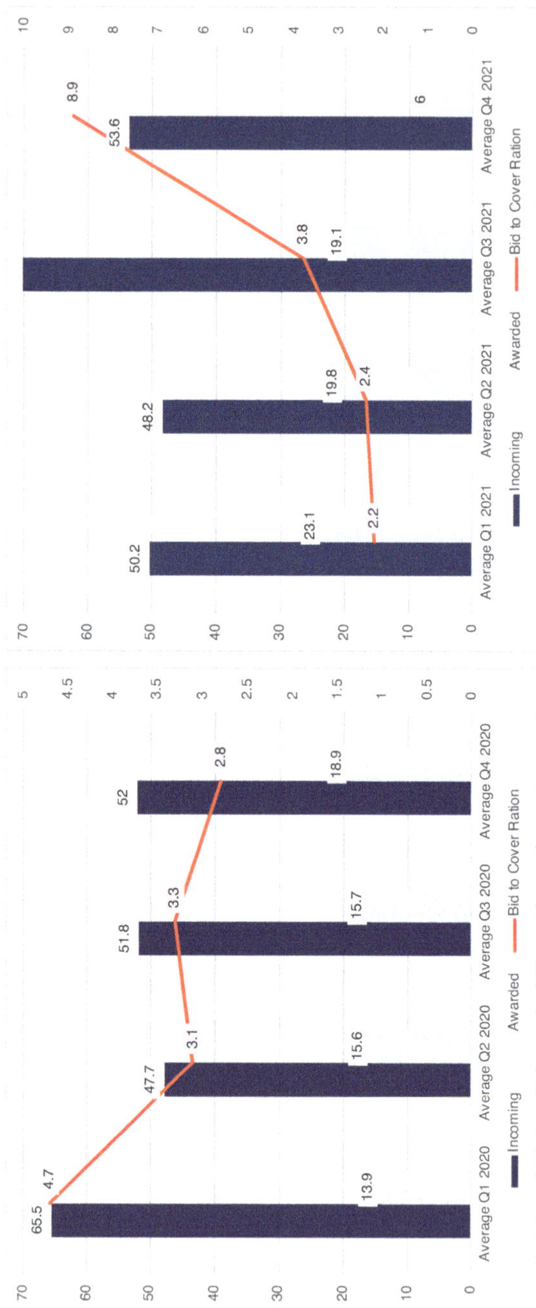

Source: Ministry of Finance.

5.3.1 Supports from Development Partners

Having a long journey in conducting prudent and sound debt management, development partners spare a strong belief and support for the government. The government utilized the pandemic-based Programme Loans to cover additional spending in response to the COVID-19 pandemic and economic recovery. The support and trust are represented in a substantial amount in the State Budget during 2020 and 2021. A further finding is due to the complexity of disbursing policy-based programme loans, and the government discovered the opportunity to reform business processes in the loan and health sector. For instance, several reforms led by the Ministry of Health have brought remarkable results. Thus, the efforts to preserve economic development and public finance have gained extensive support from development partners through the pandemic-based programme loans with favourable costs and several supplemental waivers. The cost of funds is lower than the usual loan while covering broader aspects, such as additional social assistance programmes, protecting the productive sectors, and enhancement for the response of the national health system. The detail of the Pandemic-Based Programme Loans is provided in Table 5.2.

5.4 STRATEGY ACTIONS TO MEET FINANCING NEEDS

5.4.1 Prudent, Flexible and Opportunistic Strategies

As a fundamental principle, the government utilizes debt as an instrument to support countercyclical policy in a prudent, flexible and opportunistic manner. In response to the vast need to finance the pandemic, the government must comply with the debt policy, such as maintaining the debt-to-GDP ratio within the safe limit, supporting financing flexibility on countercyclical policies, and managing the debt prudently while considering costs and risks. In practice, the government must achieve cost efficiency through market deepening, including widening the investor base and improving the funding infrastructure in the government debt securities market. Furthermore, diversifying debt instruments (i.e., setting up a new financing framework and exploring new funding schemes) and maintaining the composition of the debt portfolio to support macro-balance is also essential.

TABLE 5.2
The Pandemic-Based Programme Loans

No	Pandemic-based Program Loans	Sponsor	Objectives
1	The covid -19 Active Response and Expenditure Support (CARES)	ADB and co-financed by AIIB, JICA, the Government of Germany through KfW, and the Government of Australia	To support counter-cyclical fiscal policy through three main pillars: • delivering additional social assistance programs; • providing specific funds to prevent and control the transmission of the covid -19; • protecting the productive sector, and manufacturing workers
2	The Indonesia Emergency Response to covid -19 program	World Bank and co-financed by AIIB and KfW.	To prevent, detect, fix threats of covid -19 disease, as well as enhance the response of the national health system
3	Disaster Resilience Improvement Program	ADB	The design of this program loan was adjusted from the previous one by adding non-natural disasters such as pandemics.

Source: Ministry of Finance.

Alongside the implemented debt policy, the government has also examined several tools to diversify financing sources in responding to financing needs during the pandemic. The objectives of the tools are to accommodate long-term investors and control refinancing risk in supporting the shape of an optimal debt portfolio. For instance, the government has been studying the possibility of using perpetuity (i.e., perpetual bonds); it is still proceeding and has been a part of the current research since then. In early COVID-19 outbreaks, the government also analysed the possibility of issuing pandemic bonds. However, since the social bonds must follow a social framework and are curbed by the International Capital Market Association (ICMA) and US Securities and Exchange Commission (SEC), unsuitable with the uncertainty of COVID-19 characteristics, this option was then withdrawn. The exit strategy chosen was refining the objectives of regular GS by adding a disclaimer that allocation of GS is for handling the pandemic COVID-19 on GS prospectus. These all are to support the government focused on bringing healthy fiscal and financing performance, and keeping people safe, as well as the initial goals for accelerated development that can be achieved, particularly in the past three years.

5.4.2 Government Securities Issuance

(i) Continuing the Issuance of Foreign GS

Since 2004, Government Securities (GS/SBN) have become an essential tool to meet the financing of Indonesia's budget deficit. Initially, the portion of GS in the State Budget financing was still complementary to loans. However, with the development of the domestic financial market, the issuance of GS has become more dominant as the source of State Budget financing as shown in Figure 5.4. The increasing importance of GS in State Budget financing can be seen in the increasing target of GS issuance on a net basis from year to year. The GS has been beneficial not only for the government but also for the monetary authority and financial market players. Continuous development of the GS through the primary dealership programme, the benchmark series and issuance transparency have a positive impact on Indonesia's financial market.

However, fiscal stimulus in the pandemic period 2020 and 2021 has caused the net issuance of GS to increase significantly. This policy was deemed necessary to reduce the negative effect of the pandemic on the

FIGURE 5.4
Indonesia's Government Debt Proportion

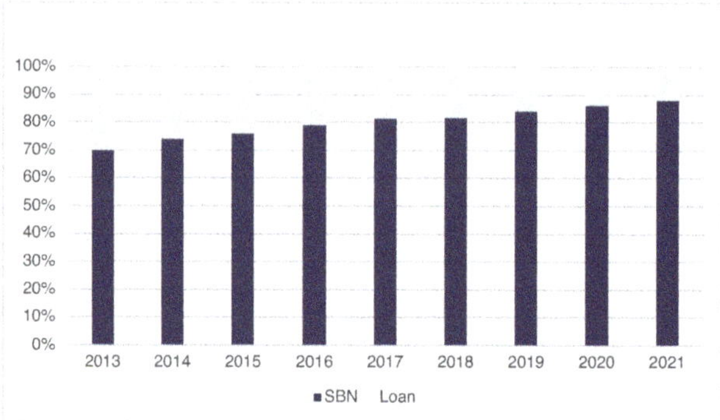

Year	SBN	Loan	Total
2013	1661	714	2375
2014	1931	678	2609
2015	2410	755	3165
2016	2781	735	3516
2017	3249	746	3995
2018	3613	806	4419
2019	4015	764	4779
2020	5232	843	6075
2021	6090	819	6909

Source: Ministry of Finance.

Indonesian economy. As depicted in Figure 5.5, the target for net issuance of GS since 2012 has been higher than the deficit target due to net issuance is also used to cover government investment financing. The sharp increase in the nominal net GS in 2020 resulted from an estimated 6.34 per cent deficit. With the higher issuance target in 2020 and 2021, the government needed to be nimble and cautious in accessing the capital market. Many argue that the Indonesian domestic market was not ready with the higher issuance amount required to finance the deficit. Previously, the domestic capital market was used to the level of a deficit below 3 per cent, thus the 6.34 per cent in 2020 was unprecedented, thus, the government needed to be careful and explore available options and combinations to cover budget financing needs (Olivia, Gibson and Nasrudin 2020). The government must rely not only on-budget funding from domestic sources, which may incur a crowding-out effect on investment in the long term (Basri and Fitrania 2022). On the flip side, excessive use of external funding may also increase domestic vulnerability through exchange rate risks and other factors (Basri 2017).

Therefore, as a complementary strategy for financing the budget in 2020, the government issued US$5 bond issuances, one-euro bond issuance, and 5 Japanese yen bond issuances. The global bonds were rated Baa2 (Stable)/BBB (Stable)/BBB (Stable), by Moody's, S&P and Fitch respectively. Capitalizing on strong investor sentiment in the new year and stable financial market conditions overnight, the government proceeded to access

FIGURE 5.5
The Trend in Fiscal Deficit and SBN Proportion, 2010–21

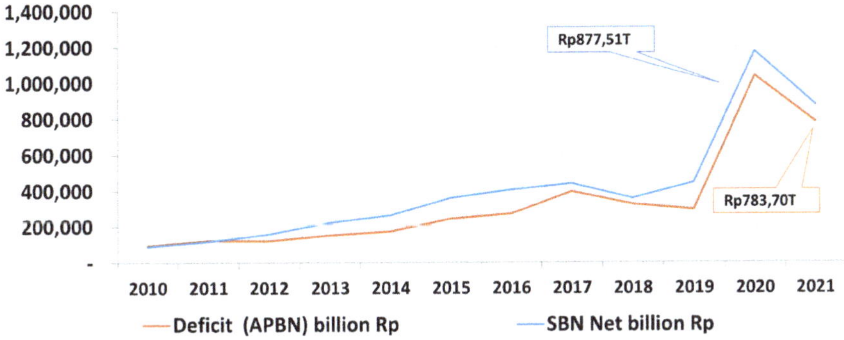

Source: Ministry of Finance.

both currency markets swiftly and opportunistically for its first issuance of the year. With the strong rally in US interest rates and credit spreads post the US-China "Phase One" trade deal announced in December, the government was able to price at the lowest-ever coupons across both US dollar and euro funding markets in January 2020.

According to the debt financing strategy, the following pipeline after January 2020 transactions was the Global Sukuk issuance. However, the Sukuk market was volatile due to the Middle Eastern countries having downturns due to the decline in oil prices. Considering this situation, the government quickly adjusted the strategy by issuing the second global bond in 2020 ahead of the global Sukuk with only one week in preparation. On 6 April 2020, the Indonesian government successfully priced a US$4.3 billion transaction. With the higher budget financing in the early stages of the pandemic, the government launched the transactions amidst volatile market conditions. The transaction marks the first Asian sovereign to issue bonds since the COVID-19 pandemic occurred. The transaction also introduces the debut 50-year offering on solid demand at the long end of the curve. The transaction is the largest global offering by the government and demonstrates the government's ability to respond swiftly to markets and capture favourable issuance windows (see Table 5.3).

After successfully launching two US dollar and euro bonds in the first half of 2020, in July 2020 the government tapped the Samurai bond

TABLE 5.3
Indonesia Global Bond Issuance in 2020

Series	Issuance Amount	*Pricing date*	*Settlement date*	Maturity date	Coupon	*Yield*	*Spread over benchmark*
RI0230	USD 1.2 bio	7 Januari 2020	14 Januari 2020	14 Februari 2030	2.850%	2.880%	105 bps
RI0250	USD 0.8 bio			14 February 2050	3.500%	3.550%	124 bps
RIEUR0227	EUR 1.0 bio			14 February 2027	0.900%	0.953%	140 bps
RI1030	USD 1.65 bio	6 April 2020	15 April 2020	15 Oktober 2030	3.850%	3.900%	232 bps
RI1050	USD 1.65 bio			15 Oktober 2050	4.200%	4.250%	297 bps
RI0470	USD 1.0 bio			15 April 2070	4.450%	4.500%	322 bps
SNI0625 (Green Sukuk)	USD 750 mio	16 Jun 2020	23 Jun 2020	23 Jun 2025	2.300%		195.3 bps
SNI0630	USD 1.0 bio			23 Jun 2030	2.800%		204.7 bps
SNI0650	USD 750 mio			23 Jun 2050	3.800%		227.7 bps
SAMURAI BONDS							
RIJPY0723	JPY 50.7 bio	2 Juli 2020	8 Juli 2020	7 Juli 2023	1.130%	1.130%	110 bps
RIJPY0725	JPY 24.3 bio			8 Juli 2025	1.350%	1.350%	130 bps
RIJPY0727	JPY 10.1 bio			8 Juli 2027	1.480%	1.480%	140 bps
RIJPY0730	JPY 13.4 bio			8 Juli 2030	1.590%	1.590%	145 bps
RIJPY0740	JPY 1.5 bio	2 Juli 2020	8 Juli 2020	6 Juli 2040	1.800%	1.800%	143 bps

Source: Ministry of Finance.

market, which has been relatively quiet due to the COVID-19 market disruption. This Samurai transaction also faced challenges due to the uncertainty of the pandemic in the global market. There is a soft-sounding activity before the official marketing period in Samurai issuance. However, during the first soft-sounding, the government did not find preferable conditions, specifically on the cost of borrowing and investor demands. The low investor demand was due to the state of emergency conditions that limited investors' business operations. After conducting two soft-sounding, the government launched transactions and became the first Sovereign JPY issuance in 2020 and the first issue from Asia after the pandemic declaration.

In January 2021, Indonesia capitalized on one of the earliest issuance windows available in the new year, maintaining its presence in the global market. It successfully captured positive investor sentiment in the markets following recent news of the roll-out of the COVID-19 vaccine and continuing robust sentiment in 2020. This transaction was not only to become the first Asian Sovereign to enter the market but also the first sovereign to price a dual-tranche US dollar/euro offering in 2021 (see Table 5.4).

On 21 May 2021, the government tapped the Samurai bond market for its second Samurai issuance since the start of the COVID-19 pandemic in July 2020. This is also the seventh consecutive year that Indonesia has accessed this market with JPY100 billion or larger-sized benchmark transactions since 2015. While Japan was in the third round of its state of emergency, the government successfully raised JPY100 billion by capturing good momentum for demand for mid to long tenors. It once again proved the government's established credit support and presence in the Samurai market. This benchmark-sized transaction has been achieved with the lowest JPY spreads and coupon levels in comparison with the government's past Samurai deals, maintaining a reasonably low premium over its US dollar secondary curves.

The government again made its annual return to the global Sukuk market and priced a total US$3 billion Sukuk offering, including Green Sukuk. The government introduced a Green format to the 30-year Sukuk for the first time, which is also the first of such issuance globally, after consistently issuing this asset class in a 5-year tenor since its debut in 2018. This issuance evidenced the government's dedication and long-term commitment to green and sustainable financing, as well as to pioneering

TABLE 5.4
Indonesia Global Bond Issuance in 2021

Series	Size	*Pricing date*	*Settlement date*	Maturity date	Coupon	Yield	*Spread over benchmark*
SEC 8							
RI0331	USD 1.25 bio	05-Jan-21	12-Jan-21	12-Mar-31	1,85%	1,900%	95.3 bps
RI0351	USD 1.25 bio			12-Mar-51	3,05%	3,100%	139.9 bps
RI0371	USD 0.50 bio			12-Mar-71	3,35%	3,400%	169.9 bps
RIEUR0333	EUR 1.00 bio			12-Mar-33	1,10%	1,174%	135 bps
Samurai Bonds							
RIJPY0524	JPY 29.0 bio	21-May-21	27-May-21	27-May-24	0,33%	0,330%	35 bps
RIJPY0526	JPY 46.8 bio			27-May-26	0,57%	0,570%	56 bps
RIJPY0528	JPY 1.2 bio			26-May-28	0,70%	0,700%	65 bps
RIJPY0531	JPY 18.2 bio			27-May-31	0,89%	0,890%	76 bps
RIJPY0536	JPY 2.5 bio			27-May-36	1,17%	1,170%	90 bps
RIJPY0541	JPY 2.3 bio			27-May-41	1,44%	1,440%	105 bps
Global Sukuk							
SNI0626	USD 1.25 bio	02-Jun-21	09-Jun-21	09-Jun-26	1,50%		70.4 bps
SNI0631	USD 1.00 bio			09-Jun-31	2,55%		95.7 bps
SNI0651 (Green Sukuk)	USD 750 mio			09-Jun-51	3,55%		125.5 bps
SEC 9							
RI0731	USD 600 mio	21-Jul-21	28-Jul-21	28-Jul-31	2,15%	2,150%	91 bps
RI0351	USD 750 mio			12-Mar-51	3,05%	3,100%	114 bps
RI0371	USD 300 mio			12-Mar-71	3,35%	3,350%	139 bps
RIEUR0729	EUR 500 mio			28-Jul-29	1,00%	1,068%	122 bps
SEC 10							
RI0731	USD 600 mio	13-Sep-21	23-Sep-21	28-Jul-31	2,15%	2,180%	86 bps
RI0961	USD 650 mio			23-Sep-61	3,20%	3,280%	138 bps
RIEUR0334	EUR 500 mio			23-Mar-34	1,30%	1,351%	118 bps

Source: Ministry of Finance.

financing methods in the effort against climate change. The 30-year tranche Green Sukuk is the fourth global Green Sukuk issued under its Green Bond and Sukuk Framework. This global Sukuk issuance was marked as the lowest ever 5-year and 10-year coupon rate achieved by the government across both conventional and Sukuk, the first-ever 30-year Global Sukuk issued and lowest ever profit rate achieved for a 30-year Sukuk issuance globally, and the largest 30-year Sukuk from Asian issuer.

(ii) Encouraging Citizens' Participation through Retail GS

Due to the COVID-19 pandemic, the uncertainty of the situation has been a wake-up call for Indonesians regarding financial awareness. Current conditions make more people understand the importance of having adequate emergency funds and investments. People are more aware of how much is allocated for current routine expenditures and how much is allocated for future needs, including preparing emergency funds and investments. Therefore, the COVID-19 pandemic in Indonesia, despite its drawbacks, may have a blessing in disguise to accelerate the transformation of Indonesia into an investment-oriented society. The reduction of household consumption due to the restrictions has raised saving levels, specifically in the middle to upper-income group. It allows the citizens to search for investment opportunities on their excess savings.

Amidst the pandemic, a breakthrough has been made in the retail SBN marketing, education, and publicity activities by switching from physical events (offline) to fully online without face-to-face interactions. The new marketing mechanism is carried out as a form of adaptation to physical and social distancing to reduce the impact of the COVID-19 pandemic. Marketing activities for retail SBN series include virtual launching, webinar events, virtual collaborating events, radio talk shows, television talk shows, and other publicity through social media.

Retail SBN demand rises significantly during this pandemic period. As a safe, easy-accessed and profitable investment product, the issuance of retail SBN reached IDR77 trillion in 2020 and IDR97 trillion in 2021. It was higher than the pre-pandemic issuance, as shown in Figure 5.6.

The government issued six retail SBN series in 2020 and 2021, respectively (Table 5.5). The difference during this pandemic period is that the government has expanded the number of tradable retail SBNs compared to the non-tradable series. This strategy aims to take advantage

FIGURE 5.6
The Trend of Retail GS Issuances

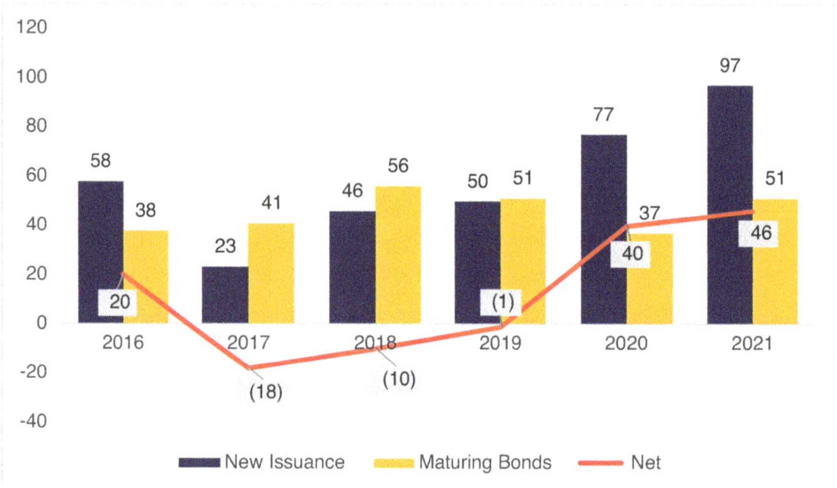

Source: Ministry of Finance.

of the ample liquidity and public interest in safe investment during the pandemic. In addition, the government continues to innovate retail SBN during the pandemic by launching Cash Waqf Linked Sukuk retail/ Sukuk Waqaf Retail (SWR) with the offline system for the first time in November 2020.

The instruments were able to attract high interest from the public, especially the millennial generation. Previously, the number of millennial investors in each Retail SBN issuance only ranged from 6 to 20 per cent since it was issued online in 2018. The number of millennial investors has jumped by an average of almost 50 per cent, and Generation Z participation was also increasing. Throughout 2020, the participation of the millennial generation dominated the purchase of retail SBN, reaching an average of 43.1 per cent of total investors for conventional bonds and an average of 38.4 per cent for retail sharia securities. In 2021, the millennial investors also dominated with a share of 39.1 per cent or equivalent to 50,917 investors from all series.

TABLE 5.5
Retail SBN Issuance during 2020–21

2020 Issuances

Series	Size	Tenor	Coupon	Issuance date	Total Investor	Tradable/ Non-tradable
SBR009	IDR 2,25T	2 years	Floating with floor at 6,30% p.a.	17 February 2020	11.247	Non-tradable
SR012	IDR 12,14T	3 years	Fixed at 6,30% p.a.	23 March 2020	23.952	Tradable
ORI017	IDR18,33T	3 years	Fixed at 6,40% p.a.	13 July 2020	42.733	Tradable
SR013	IDR 25,67T	3 years	Fixed at 6,05% p.a.	28 September 2020	44.803	Tradable
ORI018	IDR 12,97T	3 years	Fixed at 5,70% p.a.	23 October 2020	26.160	Tradable
ST007	IDR 1,46T	2 years	Floating with floor at 5,5% p.a.	2 December 2020	16.992	Non-tradable

2021 Issuances

Series	Size	Tenor	Coupon	Issuance date	Total Investor	Tradable/ Non-tradable
ORI019	IDR 26T	3 years	Fixed at 5,57% p.a.	22 February 2021	58.731	Tradable
SR014	IDR 16,7T	3 years	Fixed at 5,47% p.a.	22 March 2021	35.626	Tradable
SBR010	IDR 7,5T	2 years	Floating with floor at 5,10% p.a.	19 July 2021	23.337	Non-tradable
SR015	IDR 27T	3 years	Fixed at 5,10% p.a.	22 September 2021	49.027	Tradable
ORI020	IDR 15T	3 years	Fixed at 4,95% p.a.	25 October 2021	30.053	Tradable
ST008	IDR 5T	2 years	Floating with floor at 4,8% p.a.	24 November 2021	14.337	Non-tradable

Source: Ministry of Finance.

The success of increasing investors, particularly the millennial generation, is supported by the development of an online system called e-SBN in 2018. The government has developed e-SBN to pave an easier way for investors to invest in retail GS. People can stay at home, with no need to go to bank branches or securities companies, while investing through the e-SBN platform anytime and anywhere. The government realized that developing an online distribution platform for investments has the highest impact during this COVID-19 pandemic.

In line with implementing the digital platform e-SBN, the government also uses Single Investor Identification (SID) as the primary identifier for ordering SBN. The use of SID increases the accuracy of retail SBN investor data because of its unique nature. With the breakthrough of e-SBN and SID, the government has a better-quality database and profile of retail SBN investors. Furthermore, the government continues to improve the development of retail instruments to give broader access for citizens to invest. For instance, under the reduction of purchase policy, the minimum purchase was reduced to IDR1 million, previously IDR5 million, making retail SBN an affordable investment instrument.

(iii) Attractive Interest Income Tax on Bond Interest

The government issued Government Regulation No. 9 of 2021 and Government Regulation No. 91 of 2021 on the reduction of the income tax rate on bond interest for foreign taxpayers and domestic taxpayers to a single rate of 10 per cent. The regulation was driven by an unfavourable investment environment, such as each investor would be subject to different income tax rates. For example, the differences in tax rates occurred among foreign investors, in which investors coming from countries that have a tax cooperation agreement with Indonesia get a lower rate (0 to 15 per cent). In contrast, investors from countries without the agreement will be subject to a 20 per cent tariff. This gap in the tariff difference is allegedly used by several domestic investors to buy Indonesian bonds from abroad to gain tax benefits. Thus, some expected outputs of the *income tax policy on bond interest*[9] are boosting a deep, liquid, inclusive and efficient financial market base, especially in the bonds market, widening the investor base, increasing the participation of domestic investors in GS instruments and encouraging Indonesian citizens to take advantage of the tax treaty[10] tariff gap to invest directly in Indonesia.

5.4.3 The Institutional Synergy of Burden-Sharing

(i) The Synergy with BI through the Macroprudential Liquidity Buffer (PLM)

The monetary authority, the Bank of Indonesia (BI),[11] has been supportive in collaborating in a conducive environment in the banking sector to support economic relief. One of the means of support was adjusting statutory reserves by increasing the Macroprudential Liquidity Buffer (PLM).[12] The background of this policy was in response to restrictions on mobility and community activities that made the economy depressed, where non-performing loans (NPLs) increased due to difficulties in paying instalments and credit principals by customers. Banks have liquidity problems and could not or were reluctant to channel new loans. These conditions lead to the need for additional liquidity in the market. There was also a suggestion for BI to implement quantitative easing or printing money to increase liquidity. However, with various considerations, one of which is to maintain the stability of the rupiah exchange rate, the policy set is to reduce the Statutory Reserves and, at the same time, increase the PLM. Therefore, banks must use the additional liquidity from the PLM declining to buy SBN in the primary market through a private placement scheme. Apart from increasing liquidity in the market, this scheme also helps fund government financing needs. Transactions are carried out as much as possible using existing regulations to be executed quickly.

The two institutions worked tirelessly, ensuring smooth and successful transactions both from operational and legal aspects. It should be noted that without support from the central bank, the excess liquidity from the PLM policy may be used for other financial instruments. With the potential amount of more than IDR100 trillion over 114 banks in Indonesia, the government must act fast to deliver transactions. After a marathon series of coordination between the government and BI, it is agreed that transactions to accommodate the reduction in Statutory Reserves and PLM is carried out through a private placement through government primary dealers.

On 27 April 2020, a new landmark transaction was launched. Private placement for two fixed-rate series and one variable rate conventional bonds with a total nominal value of IDR62.62 trillion has been conducted. The transaction also included the sharia instrument, namely three series project-based Sukuk (PBS) with a total nominal value of IDR46.49 trillion. Thus, the total amount as the effect of the PLM policy of IDR109.11 trillion from 114 banks can be executed successfully.

(ii) The Synergy with BI through Joint Decrees

The collaboration scheme between the government and BI in accelerating the PEN programme is continuing through Joint Decree.[13] To maintain the credibility of BI as the monetary authority and the Ministry of Finance as the fiscal authority, the schemes in SKB I, SKB II and SKB III as the implementation of Law 2/2020 are planned very carefully. It takes enormous time and effort to finalize a credible and accountable cooperation scheme for these two agencies.

The 1st Joint Decree or SKB I, signed on 16 April 2020, is a form of coordination between the two institutions where BI acts as a backstop in fulfilling the target for SBN issuance. The government ensures to deliver SBN issuance in a fair market mechanism. The process of drafting SKB I was challenging and time-consuming. The scheme proposed did not only take a lengthy time, but it also took effort and repeated examinations. The government and BI are cautious in assuring and seizing market and investor response as well as ensuring independence, monetary policy credibility, and reputation in the financial market. Nevertheless, the SKB I became a milestone for the two institutions in implementing the State Budget financing through the issuance of SBN amidst the COVID-19 pandemic.

Based on SKB I, SBN purchases are made following the order in which the first step is through a market mechanism, namely, the regular SBN auction. BI will then enter through an additional auction mechanism or the Green Shoe Option if the market is not supportive to meet the auction target. The last order is through a private placement if the regular auction and additional auctions do not meet the government's financing needs. The SBNs used are tradable and marketable to be used for monetary operations when BI will need to absorb liquidity in the market. The tenor is 5–8 years, so the government has enough time to manage the fiscal during the pandemic.

In its development, SKB I was deemed insufficient because the need for financing was getting bigger, and the market was not expected to be able to absorb it. To reduce supply risk in the auction, the issuance of

SBN should be done through a private placement with BI. In addition, by buying SBN through an auction following SKB I, BI will also get an increased yield while the fiscal burden of paying debt interest is higher. Thus, SKB II was drafted to regulate the burden-sharing scheme between the government and BI.

The 2nd Joint Decree or SKB II was released on 7 July 2020 (further amended on 20 July 2020), and it ruled that BI contributed to the burden-sharing scheme for financing public goods and non-public goods in the field of handling the pandemic and PEN. However, SKB II is much more challenging as it underwent a process that was not as smooth as SKB I. The perception between the Ministry of Finance and BI was priorly not aligned, starting from the calculation mechanism determining the amount of BI's contribution. On the draft of SKB II, BI's contribution to the government was calculated using the interest rate/return on GS. However, it was challenging to implement, so SKB II was adjusted by agreeing to change the calculation of the amount of BI's contribution by using the yield basis of SUN. The government and BI derive a technical agreement of burden-sharing in responding to the scheme.

In 2021, the significant increasing cases prompted BI to take the first move in cooperating with the government in handling health and saving humanity due to the Delta variant. The synergy between the government and BI stated in the 3rd Joint Decree or SKB III, focused on how to finance and prioritize the health and humanitarian sector. Since the SKB III initiative originates from BI, the nominal amount and composition of SBN for health and humanity refers to the results of BI's assessment taking into account the ability of BI's balance sheet to absorb the costs. The mechanisms of SKB III consist of (i) the purchase by BI of GDS/SUN and/or Shariah Securities (SBSN) issued by the government in the primary market directly (private placement); (ii) arrangements for participation between the government and BI to reduce the burden on the state; and (iii) for funding the Health and Humanitarian Handling Budget in the context of handling the impact of COVID-19.

At first, the government received a doubtful response to this collaboration. Many parties were worried about the impact of this collaboration on BI's independence and the government's credibility. On the other side, the intensity of communicating this collaboration to the house of representatives was also a challenging process. Nevertheless, both the government and BI managed to maintain the governance aspect and have succeeded in supporting the stability of the domestic market. Also, the excellent performance of the State Budget and positive signals from the market amidst turbulence in all sectors provided evidence that all parties were focused on accelerating the nation's recovery and mitigating greater risks ahead. Furthermore, market indicators showed the reduction of market volatility after the synergy between BI and the government, such as a decrease in yield levels and an increase in incoming bids in the GS auction in the second semester of 2020.

5.4.4 Optimal Portfolio Management

In establishing innovative instruments to meet budget financing needs, the government strives to maintain efficient maturity and cost through government strategy. As part of the government's general cash management programme, particularly on its external liabilities, the government launched the first repurchase of global bonds in 2021. It became a successful completion of the inaugural Tender Offer/Liability Management (LM) Exercise launched on eight series of Notes (the Old Bonds). The LM Exercise was well received by global investors, and the total amount of tender instructions received across all series of notes reached US$2.68 billion. The government also issued a USD SEC Shelf Registered Notes Offering alongside the Tender Offer. It marks the tenth SEC-registered issuance in US dollar, demonstrates the government's commitment to enhancing the secondary liquidity pool of its tradable securities available to global investors, and is in line with the government's goals of extending its debt maturity profile and achieving cost savings by reducing interest expense.

Due to the pandemic, it is also necessary to develop business process guidelines on loan conversion, such as targeting the 0 per cent fixed rate as achieved before the pandemic. Macroeconomic policy changes also influence the interest rates that will be selected by the government. Meanwhile, strengthening currency for the Japanese yen and euro against the US dollar is one more challenging during the pandemic. On the other side, the decision for loan conversion is affected by the submission time to the World Bank headquarters. The government executes intense communication internally or with lenders to mitigate the issues and provides a strategy by setting a cap with a specific range.[14] The government has carried out five loan conversions for the ADB programme and project loans that have been fully disbursed from September 2019 to October 2020. The potential savings from the loan conversion are estimated at IDR118 billion.

The government also accelerates economic recovery through financing by implementing debt swaps. In April 2021, Germany, Indonesia and the Global Fund to Fight AIDS, Tuberculosis, and Malaria signed a new agreement on debt swap (Debt Swap VIII). It was initiated when the German embassy offered a debt swap to the government of Indonesia in the health sector (Debt2Health[15]) in 2018. Debt Swap VIII is carried out with an equal ratio scheme, the same as Debt Swap VI Climate Change, where the value of the debt written off is equal to the value of the funds distributed by the Indonesian government. Meanwhile, Debt Swap IV and VII are carried out with a ratio of 1:2 where the Government of Indonesia finances certain agreed activities with funds sourced from the State Budget at 50 per cent of the commitment allocation. Then cancellations are carried out at 100 per cent of the commitments after the programme is completed and audited by an independent auditor.

5.4.5 Utilizing Creative Financing

(i) Accelerating Infrastructure Development through PPP and Blended Financing

Public investment plays a vital role in post-COVID recovery. Global Infrastructure Hub (2020) study shows that public investment, including infrastructure, may increase GDP and have a multiplier effect of 0.98 within two to five years. With the reduced fiscal space, it is essential to explore alternative sources of funding and financing for infrastructure, one of few is through Public-Private Partnership (PPP) scheme. Through intensive collaboration with the private sector during the pandemic, the government still managed to reach financial close for four projects, while the other four projects were transacted in 2021.

Relying solely on private financing often leads to higher prices of services for users or the government, and it forced the government to rule it out, particularly during the pandemic. Therefore, combining private and government funds (blended financing) becomes an option and examines the proper financial structure for the infrastructure project. Through this scheme, funding by the government will be an important stimulus for the private sector, whereas the involvement of the private sector will be a key driver for improving the quality of service and efficiency of public investment in infrastructure. The concept of blended finance has been implemented in the Legok Nangka Waste Management Project, the Makassar-Pare Pare Railway Project and the Umbulan Water Project. Alongside the blended financing, there is also SDG Indonesia One (SIO[16]), a financing platform developed to conduct concrete, real and flexible actions in bridging public funding and private financing.

(ii) Government Guarantee, a Strong Commitment to Supporting MSMEs and SOEs

Since the business sector was the most vulnerable in responding to the pandemic, the government also interfered with recovering micro, small, and medium enterprises (MSMEs). As of July 2020, more than 80 per cent of MSMEs reported that their income had downturned. Based on several studies, fiscal support was effective in stimulating economic activities for firms (Auerbach et al. 2020; Aizenman et al. 2020).

However, forming a guarantee programme to support MSMEs was another challenging process. Through a deep, endless, and complex discussion, Minister of Finance (MoF) Regulation No. 71/2020 was thus issued in June 2020 as the legal basis of the guarantee programme for MSMEs. The supporting guidelines include loan restructuring, interest subsidy, fund placement programmes to guarantee banking liquidity, and income tax exemption for MSMEs. In a further step, MoF Regulation No. 98/2020 was issued in a short time to regulate the guarantee for corporations. The guarantee is delivered through two insurance companies, Jamkrindo and Askrindo, for the guarantee for MSMEs and through the Indonesia Eximbank and Indonesia Infrastructure Guarantee Fund (IIGF) for the guarantee for corporations. The government also developed an IT system called "eJamKU" that is expected to give confidence to the banking sector in channelling working capital loans to business actors and reducing credit risk.

Another critical piece of homework during the pandemic was on how to guarantee state-owned enterprises (SOEs) survive while at the same time encouraging SOEs' participation in implementing the PEN programme. The guarantee programme to support SOEs[17] focused not only on the affected SOEs but also on the SOEs assigned for the PEN programme. Meanwhile, the guarantee programme performance was below expectations in 2020. One of the reasons was a time lag between the issuance of the regulation (July 2020) and the first guarantee (September 2020) due to the required preparation of implementing regulations of MoF Regulation No. 98/2020.

As of December 2021, the guarantee programme has been utilized by sixty-eight companies with accumulated guaranteed capital loans since 2020 amounting to IDR5.2 trillion. The government and the guarantee companies have actively collaborated to expand dissemination to banks to optimize their performance. In April 2021, the government issued MoF Regulation No. 32/2021 to accommodate the relaxation of the criteria of corporations and guarantees to be more flexible and adjust to the risks faced by guarantors, banks, and corporations (see Table 5.6).

(iii) Green Sukuk Issuance, Strong Commitment for Climate Change Mitigation and Adaption

Corresponding to global needs, including during the pandemic, investors/financiers from developed countries/partners have changed their appetites and are committed to investing in more green, resilient and sustainable investments. However, each country has its own characteristics and conditions, resulting in the biggest challenge in implementing the commitment. In addition, the funding is undoubtedly significant. Despite this, the government consistently follows the implementation of climate change budget tagging (CBT) as a reference. CBT results have also been used to track climate change activities that are co-benefits with gender-responsive budgets, considering that climate change impacts marginalized groups, including those who are gender vulnerable during pandemics.

The government has issued Sovereign Global Green Sukuk annually from 2018 to 2021 with total financing of US$3.5 billion and issued Retail Green Sukuk in 2019–21 with a total investment of approximately US$847.24 million. This financing is allocated for the sustainable transportation sector, flood mitigation in vulnerable areas, waste management, renewable energy and energy efficiency. Since it was first published in 2018, the issuance of Green Sukuk has received fourteen international awards. The government has earned an excellent reputation internationally as the first country to issue Sovereign Green Sukuk and Sovereign Retail Green Sukuk.

TABLE 5.6
The Government Guarantee Programme

No.	*Guarantee Program*	*Guaranteed Party*	*Guaranteed Beneficiary*	*No. of Guaranteed Transaction*	*Guaranteed Tenor (year)*	*Guaranteed Working Capital Loans (billions)*	
						Original Curr.	*Eqv. IDR*
1.	Guarantees for working capital loans for Micro, Small, Medium Enterprise (MSME) entrepreneurs	MSME entrepreneurs	Banking	2,881,214	0 – 3	53,415.11	53,415.11
2.	Guarantees for working capital loans for Corporation entrepreneurs	Corporation entrepreneurs	Banking	78	0 – 1	4,713.96	4,713.96
3.	Guarantees for State-Owned Enterprise with Gov't assignment loans	SOE	Financial Institution & Trustee	1	0 – 7	9,849.46	9,849.46
	Total			2,881,294		67,978.54	67,978.54

Source: Ministry of Finance.

(iv) Indonesia's SDG Bonds Debutant

With the success story of the issuance of Green Sukuk in 2018, the government has demonstrated progress towards the 2030 Sustainable Development Goals (SDG)[18] Agenda. After a year of preparation, in September 2021, the government published the SGDs GS Framework to demonstrate how the government intends to issue Green and SDGs Securities to finance environmental and social projects. The government sought to incorporate additional aspects of SDGs into the framework to cover not only sectors or projects that contribute to climate change mitigation and adaptation efforts (green focus) but also to the advancement of the blue economy (blue focus) and positive social outcomes (social focus). In the development process, the government collaborated with the Ministry of National Development Planning (BAPPENAS) and the Coordinating Ministry of Maritime and Investments and received support from UNDP, HSBC, and Credit Agricole as joint advisers.

During the pandemic, the Indonesia SDG Bond debut issuance was released on 23 September 2021. The bond was issued in the global market amounting to €500 million, under a long twelve-year tenor, and carrying a 1.3 per cent coupon rate. This issuance marks a historic milestone for Indonesia for being the first SDG EUR bond issuance by an Asian Sovereign. On the back of solid demand from ESG-focused accounts, the government has benefited by issuing bonds without an additional New Issue Concession (NIC), which is normally applied for new bond issuances. The offering marks the tightest pricing (on a spread-basis) achieved in the twelve-year tenor for a euro-denominated issuance. The inaugural SDG bonds issuance has received two international awards for Indonesia SDG Bonds from the Asset Triple A Country Awards as Best Bond – Sustainable Finance 2021 and Best Bond and Best SSA Bond from Global Capital Asia.

5.5 GLOBAL RECOGNITION OF INDONESIA BUDGET FINANCING

5.5.1 International Awards

The pandemic is indeed a challenge for organizations in carrying out their duties and functions. However, financing service continues to be optimized despite various limitations. Several awards were received by the government in financing management during the COVID-19 pandemic as displayed in Table 5.7.

5.5.2 Indonesia Is Still Granted "Investment Grade" by Credit Rating Agencies, while Global Down Trend during the Pandemic

Based on Benmelech and Tzur-Ilan's research in 2020, a country's credit rating is the most critical indicator of its fiscal spending during the COVID-19 pandemic. Meanwhile, Indonesia managed to maintain its rating position during the 2020–21 pandemic even though the impact of COVID-19 was undoubtedly very severe, as seen in Table 5.8.

The credit rating agency's affirmation confirms that Indonesia has implemented fiscal policies on the right track. Some credit rating agencies mentioned that Indonesia's economic activity has gradually recovered, driven by solid domestic demand, controlled government debt, resilience to external shocks supported by a flexible exchange rate, and a reasonably strong monetary policy and foreign exchange reserves. It is also supported by better policies in handling the pandemic and the government's efforts to accelerate vaccination. However, weakening in Indonesia's external situation, an increase in the central government's debt, including collaboration with BI as a part of the financing scheme for the pandemic, an increase in SOEs' debts, and maintaining the fiscal discipline to achieve budget consolidation in 2023 are some of the rating agencies' concerns that the government should address.

The history of maintaining Indonesia's credit rating is not easy. To convince credit rating agencies, the government has held and recorded seventeen meetings through conference calls with the agencies during 2020–21. In order to prepare for the meeting with the credit rating agencies, internal preparations are needed by holding several meetings with relevant stakeholders.

Indonesia's success in maintaining its credit rating was one of the achievements as many countries in 2020 and 2021 experienced a change in outlook to negative or even a credit rating downgrade. More than eighty countries in 2020–21 experienced a credit rating downgrade and/or a revised outlook to negative. This indicates that although economic recovery has begun, uncertainty remains high. However, Indonesia must remain vigilant and not be careless because the challenges ahead remain, and hard work is still needed.

TABLE 5.7
International Awards

2020	International Islamic Finance Awards 2020	SNI0323 Green Sukuk	The Asset Triple-A
	3G Best Green Initiative of the Year 2020	SNI0323 Green Sukuk	Cambridge IFA
	Best Sovereign Bond	RoI USD 4.3 Billion	The Asset Triple A
	Best Sovereign, Supranational and Agencies (SSA Bond)	RoI USD 4.3 Billion	Global Capital Asia
	Cross-Border Yen Bond of the Year	RoI Japanese Yen Bonds	Deal Watch Award 2020-Refinitiy Japan
2021	Best Green Bond	SNI0625 Green Sukuk	The Asset Triple-A
	Largest Green Sukuk in 2020	SNI0625 Green Sukuk	Climate Bond Initiative (CBI)
	Best Bond and Best SSA Bond	RoI USD 1.25 Bio and SDG Bond EUR 500 Mio	Global Capital Asia
	Best Bond – Sustainable Finance.	RoI SDG Bond EUR 500 Million	The Asset Triple A

Source: Ministry of Finance.

TABLE 5.8
Development of Indonesia's Ratings during the Pandemic

	During the Pandemic	
	2020	**2021**
S&P	BBB outlook negative	BBB outlook negative
Moody's	Baa2 outlook stable	Baa2 outlook stable
Fitch	BBB outlook stable	BBB outlook stable
R&I	BBB+ outlook stable	BBB+ outlook stable
JCR	BBB+ outlook stable	BBB+ outlook stable

Source: Ministry of Finance.

5.6 LESSON LEARNT AND THE WAY FORWARD

Some key takeaways can be learnt in handling the pandemic and it is hopefully beneficial in further policy-making and research on the government's financing during the pandemic.

a. Firstly, the magnitude of deficit and uncertainty during the pandemic obliges the government to always be responsive, rapid, and willing to look for loopholes and opportunities in finding affordable financing with the acceptable cost of funds and risks. Nevertheless, at the same time, the government must manage it prudently, flexibly and opportunistically. This is quite challenging because financing management frequently revolves around many potential spillovers and challenges to the overall fiscal performance, and it must also deal with many parties with different perceptions.
b. Secondly, the positive response to the synergy scheme with BI shows confidence in the Indonesian financial market. The two institutions have a similar objective which is to save the people from the pandemic by estimating various aspects, such as global dynamics, market confidence, public expectations and political constellations in the country. Therefore, the collaboration was conducted in a careful, credible and accountable way, either in the implementation of SKB or in collaboration on PLM transactions.
c. Lastly, the commitment to fiscal consolidation is deemed necessary as an exit strategy from the pandemic crisis. The essence of the fiscal stimulus in the economic downturn is a temporary policy to maintain the sustainability of fiscal policy in the long term. If the budget deficit and public debt are unchecked, drawbacks to growth may appear as suggested by various empirical studies.[19] In light of this backdrop, the government has committed to return the budget deficit to 3 per cent of GDP in 2023. However, the task will be challenging due to many uncertainties ahead, such as the change from a pandemic to an endemic situation, the adjustment in the global interest rate due to the rise in global inflation, and heated geopolitical tension in the Russian region. Therefore, the government needs to be more focused and nimble in utilizing the budget as a tool to face many challenges ahead.

Notes

1. Revised deficit through 1st adjustment through Perpres 54/2020.
2. Revised deficit through 2nd adjustment through Perpres 72/2020.
3. Officially audited and published by Central Government Financial Report (LKPP).
4. Report of World Economic Outlook in April 2021, processed.
5. Treasury Bills, also referred to as *Surat Perbendaharaan Negara/Syariah* (SPN/S), is government securities with a period pf up to twelve months with discount-based interest payment.
6. Minister of Finance's decision here is legalized in the form of internal regulation, namely Keputusan Menteri Keuangan Number 17/KMK.08/2020 and Keputusan Menteri Keuangan 253/KMK.08/2021.
7. Government Securities, also referred to as *Surat Berharga Negara* (SBN) consists of Government Debt Securities (SUN) and Government Sharia Securities (SBSN).
8. Further details will be explored in subsection 5.4.3: The Institutional Synergy of Burden-Sharing.
9. Commonly referred to as interest income tax, withholding tax on interest, or the government bond interest tax.
10. Referred to as *Perjanjian Penghindaran Pajak Berganda* (P3B).
11. Bank of Indonesia, usually abbreviated as BI, is the central bank in Indonesia that carries three primary responsibilities as a monetary authority and the regulatory and supervisory authority for the banking system and payment system.
12. *Penyangga Likuiditas Makroprudensial*, abbreviated as PLM, is the minimum liquidity reserve in rupiah, which the banking sector must maintain in the form of securities that meet specific requirements.
13. Joint Decree, commonly referred to as *Surat Keputusan Bersama* (SKB), is an agreement between the government and BI in which BI is allowed to buy GS in the primary market.
14. For instance, set a cap with a range of 0.05 per cent to 0.22 per cent for ADB loans (if the interest rate of loan conversion beats the cap range, the government will postpone the process of loan conversion).
15. Debt2Health is an innovative financing mechanism designed to increase domestic financing in health by converting debt repayments into lifesaving investments in public health programmes.
16. SIO is an option for private foreign investors as a derisking instrument, thus attracting more private involvement. SIO is run by PT Sarana Multi Infrastruktur (a state-owned company under the Ministry of Finance), and it has attracted thirty-four commitments from development partners.

17. Issued on MoF Regulation No. 211/2020 in December 2020.
18. SDG, the abbreviation of Sustainable Development Goals, is a universal call for action to end poverty, protect the planet, and ensure that by 2030 all people enjoy peace and prosperity.
19. See, for instance, Afonso and Jalles (2013), Égert (2015), Gunarsa, Makin, and Rohde (2020), Makin (2019), Kumar and Woo (2015), and Fincke and Greiner (2015).

References

Afonso, A., and J.T. Jalles. 2013. "Growth and Productivity: The Role of Government Debt". *Int. Rev. Econ. Finance* 25: 384–407.

Aizenman et al. 2020. "Fiscal Stimulus and Commercial Bank Lending under COVID-19". NBER Working Paper Series, Cambridge.

Alberola, E., Y. Arslan, G. Cheng, and R. Moessner. 2021. "Fiscal Response to the COVID-19 Crisis in Advanced and Emerging Market Economies". *Pacific Economic Review* 26, no. 4: 459–68. https://doi.org/10.1111/1468-0106.12370

Arslan, Y., M. Drehmann, and B. Hofmann. 2020. "Central Bank Bond Purchases in Emerging Market Economies". *BIS Bulletin* no. 20. Bank for International Settlements, Basel, Switzerland.

Auerbach et al. 2020. "Inequality, Fiscal Policy and COVID-19 Restriction in a Demand-Determined Economy". NBER Working Paper Series, Cambridge.

Basri, M.C. 2017. "Twenty Years after the Asian Financial Crisis". In *Realising Indonesia's Economic Potential*, edited by L.E. Breuer, J. Gujardo, and T. Kinda, pp. 21–45. Washington, DC: International Monetary Fund.

———, and S.N. Fitrania. 2022. "The Indonesian Economy in the Time of COVID-19: Saving Lives and Likelihood?". In *COVID-19 in Indonesia: Impacts on the Economy and Ways to Recovery*, edited by L.Y. Ing and M.C. Basri, pp. 29–59. New York: Routledge.

Benmelech, E., and N. Tzur-Ilan. 2020. T*he Determinants of Fiscal and Monetary Policies During The COVID-19 Crisis*, NBER Working Paper Series, Cambridge.

Cohen, Jon, and Kai Kupferschmidt. 2020. "The Coronavirus Seems Unstoppable. What Should the World Do Now?". *Science.org*, 25 February 2020.

Directorate General of Financing and Risk Management. 2020. "Mengarungi Badai Pandemi (Kisah di Balik Layar Para Pengeloa Surat Utang Negara)". Directorate General of Financing and Risk Management, Jakarta.

Égert, B. 2015. "Public Debt, Economic Growth, and Nonlinear Effects: Myth or Reality?". *J. Macroecon* 43: 226–38.

Fincke, B., and A. Greiner. 2015. "Public Debt and Economic Growth in Emerging Market Economies". *South Afr. J. Econ.* 83, no. 3: 357–70.

Guerrieri, V., G. Lorenzoni, L. Straub, and I. Werning. 2020. "Macroeconomic Implications of COVID-19: Can Negative Supply Shocks Cause Demand Shortages?". NBER Working Paper Series, Cambridge.

Gunarsa, S., A. Makin, and N. Rohde. 2020. "Public Debt in Developing Asia: A Help or Hindrance to Growth?". *Applied Economics Letters* 27, no. 17: 1400–3.

International Monetary Fund. 2020. *World Economic Outlook*. Washington, DC: International Monetary Fund.

Kumar, M.S., and J. Woo. 2015. "Public Debt and Growth". *Economica* 82, no. 328: 705–39.

Makin, A. 2019. "Lessons for Macroeconomic Policy from the Global Financial Crisis". *Econ. Anal. Policy* 64: 13–25.

Olivia, S., J. Gibson, and R. Nasrudin. 2020. "Survey of Recent Development: Indonesia in the Time of COVID-19". *Bulletin of Indonesian Economic Studies* 56, no. 2: 143–74.

6

Turning Bottlenecks into Breakthroughs

Sumiyati and Yustinus Prastowo

6.1 INTRODUCTION

Rapid and frantic spread of the coronavirus disease at the beginning of 2020 has sent the world into chaos. Most countries were grappling with the deadly virus. Indonesia was no exception. Worse, it happened just as the government started to roll out that year's financial plans and prepare the 2019 accountability report.

Most government agencies were appalled and had no idea how to deal with the situation. Communities and business players too faltered because they had no experience in dealing with pandemics.

It was devastating, as the number of coronavirus patients continued to increase in some major cities, but government agencies could not respond immediately. One of the issues was budget constraints. The 2020 national and regional budgets were designed for a normal situation, not for the pandemic. Government officials were silent and reluctant to divert the existing budgets (APBN/APBD) to deal with the pandemic or for economic recovery. There was a growing fear that if such a condition is left unsettled, it could trigger a nationwide disaster.

The above situation indeed required the government's presence. But it failed to do so because government agencies were facing various constraints and obstacles. These include the absence of a legal framework for actions, regulations, programmes, budgets and business processes related to budget implementation in an emergency situation.

It was also not clear either which agency should be responsible for the matter. These were aggravated by invalid population data, ill-prepared human resources and inadequate digital information system, restrictions on people's movement, and the high number of employees and their family members who were exposed to COVID-19 (Chon and Kim 2022; Sundqvist-Andberg and Åkerman 2022).

The discussion also revolved around the role of Indonesia's National Disaster Management Authority (BNPB) which has mostly been dealing with natural disasters. On contrary, what the people facing was a pandemic that did not only impact health, but incurring social and economic problems. There was doubt whether BNPB is able to handle these issues. Also, existing laws only encompass natural disasters, and none are on non-natural disasters. It prompted the Indonesian government to establish a Task Force led by the BNPB chief and its membership consists of ministries and government agencies.

Other crucial issues faced by the government included people's behavioural tendencies such as negligence and disobedience. Other matters stemming from the widespread disease were employees' difficulty to meet clients, limited transportation means for passengers and cargoes, declining economic activities, scarcity of much-needed goods and services, imbalanced supply and demand, and inequality in goods distribution.

Government officials were also afraid of legal implications if there are inaccuracies in decisions or mistakes in implementing the pandemic and economic recovery programme.

Considering the tremendous challenges faced by the government in providing quick and proper response to the pandemic, it is important that the state budget (APBN) function effectively in emergencies nationwide. All programmes in the fields of health, social protection, and economic recovery must run simultaneously and be implemented quickly and appropriately, without compromising the quality of accountability (Yu, Liang, and Gao 2021).

The context above reminds us of Political Economy 101 that in times of crisis, the government must take emergency measures and extraordinary actions, even if it means swaying between discretion and rule compliance.

When the COVID-19 pandemic hit Indonesia and we stuttered and seemed hesitant to make decisions, the government was finally able to make fundamental decision, expanding the upper limit of fiscal deficit above 3 per cent of GDP through Government Regulation in Lieu of Law No. 1 of 2020 (PERPU 1/2020). This is an exercise of discretion in an emergency and eventually, through a political communication process, the People's Representative Council (DPR) ratified it into law, shifting this discretion into a positive law.

6.2 HANDLING STRATEGY

6.2.1 Legal Bases for the COVID-19 Responses and National Economic Recovery (PC-PEN) Programme

The dawn of COVID-19 which is an unprecedented crisis, coupled with the absence of implementation guide, has pushed the country into the brink of national disaster. To overcome this impasse a breakthrough was created through Government Regulation in Lieu of Law Number 1 of 2020 (PERPU 1/2020).

The regulation, in order to be implemented effectively, requires support from all stakeholders, for instance, People's Representative Council (DPR), Regional Representative Council (DPD), Attorney General, Corruption Eradication Commission (KPK), the Police Criminal Investigation Agency, and the Audit Board (BPK). Subsequently, the regulation was delivered to DPR and became Law Number 2 of 2020. It provides discretion and flexibility to the government until 2022, and in 2023 the Law on State Finance will be reinstated.

Article 27(2) of Law No. 1/2020 is provided to effectively support and encourage government officials and institutions. Further, the Financial Supervisory and Development Board (BPKP) was also appointed as the government's internal supervisory apparatus in charge of coordinating, guiding and providing assistance and consultancy to ministries, institutions and local governments.

6.2.2 Transparent Communication to Win Public Support and Trust

In turbulent times, a crisis communication is crucial. It is a strategy used to minimize uncertainty during a crisis through the dissemination and exchange of information (Collins et al. 2016). Good crisis communication is done frequently, consistently, and it involves messages of compassion delivered in an inspiring and transformational communication style.

In the face of COVID-19 pandemic, the government strives for consistent and effective communication to ensure that messages reach the people clearly and improve compliance behaviour during crisis (Rosemary, Rochimah, and Susilawati 2022). Internally, crisis communication provides clarity and guidelines for stakeholders amidst uncertainty. Externally, it helps government's performance, raising public awareness and support for the government programmes during the pandemic.

It's obvious that policy directions and programmes implemented by the government in facing COVID-19 and for national economic recovery were communicated regularly from an early stage. Political communication with relevant state institutions, intergovernmental agencies at central and regional levels, including state-owned enterprises (SOEs) or regional government-owned enterprises (ROEs) and business players. Communication with the society at large was made via various communication channels.

6.2.3 Political Communication

Since the start of the pandemic, the government has built political communication with the People's Representative Council and Regional Representative Council. Coordination among the Ministry of Finance, the Financial Services Authority (FSA), and the Indonesia Deposit Insurance Corporation (IDIC) under the Financial System Stability Committee (KSSK) was synergized for the implementation of macroprudential policies and the recovery programme in the real sector.

Consultation with the Supreme Audit Institution (BPK) was also done since the beginning. The agency mapped out the risk and finally came up with a comprehensive audit guide after going through the government programs, the situations, constraints and obstacles it faced.

In a limited circumstances due to the pandemic, transparent and ongoing communication plays an important role so that state agencies such as BPK could perform their tasks effectively. Communication with law enforcement officials has also been made at the designing stage of the programme. It was agreed that all ranks must cooperate for the success of the government's programmes for humanity.

6.2.4 Public Communication

Quidquid recipitur ad modum recipientis recipitur: whatever is received is received in the manner of the receiver. This axiom is a challenge that was felt especially at the beginning of the pandemic. The most obvious example was communication about the "new normal".

The government was trying to communicate the importance of adapting to new habits by changing pre-pandemic behaviours. As a result of persistent crisis communication, the public began to understand the significance of health protocols. Vaccine campaigns were also proven successful resulting in the declining number of COVID-19 patients.

It is just an example of challenges in communicating with the general public during a pandemic (Montes et al. 2019). The government even had difficulty communicating what it has done in dealing with the pandemic and economic recovery. To that end, several strategies were pulled together so that the message received by the public is in accordance with the aims and objectives of those programmes.

Throughout the crisis communication process, the government is required to frame the "meaning" of the crisis in order to define how the public perceives the risks, consequences and the way they respond to the actions taken (Chon and Kim 2022; Palmaccio, Schiltz, and De Witte 2022). The strategy adopted by the Indonesian government in crisis communication is strengthening the "hope" narrative to counter pessimism or fear of the future. The framework of communication strategy in times of crisis is as follows:

(a) *Ready:* Preparing to face future crisis (Yiannakoulias et al. 2020);
(b) *Respond:* Providing accurate and credible information to stakeholders, and building trust through authentic and consistent messages (Hung, Wang, and Yeh 2022; Pandey, Singh, and Kumar 2022; Tai 2021);
(c) *Recover:* Encouraging stability and recovery, as well as articulating a forward vision, while continuing to inform the public of the progress of recovery that has been achieved (Stiglitz 2021);
(d) *Restore:* Moving forward together with confidence to achieve sustainable growth and build meaningful relationships with stakeholders (Sundqvist-Andberg and Åkerman 2022).

So far, the government has done its best in preparing a communication strategy and optimizing all channels (webinars/seminars with campuses, audiences with economists/observers, talk shows, social media, audiences with NGO figures, etc.) and using Key Opinion Leaders (KOLs).

The medium or means used vary according to the intended target and type of messages to be conveyed. For example, a website is used to present actual data that can easily be accessed. Social media such as YouTube, Facebook and Twitter channels were also optimized to handle issues that require immediate response and to disseminate the National Economic Recovery programme which may be utilized by the public (Tai 2021; Yu, Liang, and Gao 2021).

The communication strategy implemented is divided into proactive and reactive or anticipatory communication. Proactive communication is used to disseminate economic recovery programmes and COVID-19 handling to raise public awareness about the endeavours made by the government. The main concern is that the public as policy targets can easily access programmes provided by the government.

An example of proactive communication is the dissemination of social protection and support for micro, small and medium enterprises (MSMEs) via various channels. It can be said that the results are effective (Ma and Yao 2022). A survey by the Ministry of Cooperatives and Small and Medium Enterprises and National Team for the Acceleration of Poverty Reduction (TNP2K) conducted on 1,261 micro enterprises and 93 other informants suggests that the respondents were aware of the PEN programme. It indicates that the outreach was going well. Out of 9,852 respondents across the archipelago, 98.9 per cent stated that the PEN funds they got—about IDR1.7 million—were used to buy raw materials, equipment rental, and paying labour debts.

Reactive or anticipatory communication style is made to clarify or explain about issues growing in society. It is applied among others on debt issue. Debt is seen as a perennial issue that continues to draw debate and politically it's effective to attract public sentiment or as a contrasting comparison tool. Debt is not just about budget or economy, but a political issue that has a strong psycho-social dimension (Montes et al. 2019).

The debt issue is classified into three. The first one is the amount. The core narrative developed is that increasing debt is a latent danger for the country, while ignoring the fact that Indonesia's economy also increases. The second one is the issue of high yields compared to other countries. However, such comparison tends to be faulty, simplistic and not "apple to apple". The third one is on debt security issue (deficit and ability to payback). Indonesia's state budget is considered in peril because we "borrow money to pay debt interest rates" and we have the potential to default. On one hand, debt is increasing, while tax revenue is stagnant.

In this case, the big narrative on debt is for productive use and presented with strong data or facts. The aspect of state revenue is elaborated. The government encourages the public to denounce the attitude of "refusing debt, but not paying taxes". Debt is an important instrument for a nation in order to seize the development momentum. Proper narrative on debt issue can improve people's understanding of state financing. In the end, they can rally behind the government in dealing with the pandemic.

6.2.5 Implementation of the Pandemic and Recovery Programme

The government's emergency response programme for COVID-19 and national economic recovery covers a period of three years (2020–22). It includes six clusters: medical expense, social protection, support for ministries or institutions and regional governments, small and medium enterprises, cooperatives, and fiscal incentives. For 2021, the National Priority Programme was added.

The COVID-19 response and national economic recovery (PC-PEN) programme was funded through a revision to the current year's budgets, (APBN/APBD) known as budget refocusing. The above programmes were prepared along with laws and regulations, including Government Regulations, Finance Ministry's regulations, and relevant regulations of other ministers, governors, regents, mayors for technical matters. Everything must be done quickly and precisely, as COVID-19 spreads quickly and forced everyone to work remotely. Commitment from all relevant parties is required. Since all decisions and regulations must be accountable, a breakthrough was needed to preserve the governance, risk and control system.

Unpreparedness in terms of regulations, business processes, data, and information systems, as well as absence of support and commitment from the parties caused reluctance on the part of government officials to respond appropriately and quickly (Yiannakoulias et al. 2020). The dissemination of various government programmes and a range of provisions was carried out massively by using all communication means at the Ministry of Finance. The ministry's technical units continue to provide assistance and consultancy to accelerate the preparation of related regulations so that they can be implemented. Congestion in technical ministries generally stems from their inability to think outside the box. They are so confined to the rules for normal situations that they do not take risk.

Another important matter is that although all the necessary provisions and various technical guidelines were completed, the preparation of budget documents was still very slow. At the initial stage, the budget ceiling was set on a top-down basis. At that time, data continued to change and the price of goods also varied greatly, but the people could not wait. Officials in charge were supposed to take bold steps.

At regional government levels, issues evolve around shortage of funding, availability of medical facilities and drugs, and the availability of goods for social protection. Regional governments were requested to refocus budgets for PC-PEN, but the progress was slow due budget constraints. The available funds were mostly used to meet mandatory costs, such as personnel expenses. It causes slow budget provision and delayed implementation of emergency and recovery programmes.

Nearly all clusters of the programme were hampered by insufficient data needed to calculate the amount of budget, data of beneficiaries, their names and address, including financial inclusion, as those who were vulnerable and in dire need of help had no bank accounts or means of communication such as a telephone, or they had moved to other location after their employment is terminated.

The implementation of such activities demanded extra effort. Despite exposure to COVID-19 was high and many employees were infected, they were required to work hard to finish given tasks. Cooperation was developed by mapping the chains of a programme from the upstream to the downstream, from planning, budgeting, activity implementation, payment, and accountability, to assistance at the time of audit by the Audit Board. High exposure to COVID-19 forced all communications and programme implementation to be carried out online.

In this difficult time, all parties must be patient, understand their co-workers and their obstacles, because everyone worked or studied from home where they shared space, facilities and time with other family members. Eventually, collaboration was developed among ministries and corporations that received government assignments, including among internal auditors (Gomes and Barros 2022; Raviglione and Rieder 2021). Each ministry or institution normally works separately, but during the pandemic, they took the initiative to support each other in order for the programmes to succeed.

Flexibility and agility are indispensable in dealing with change (Gomes and Barros 2022; Raviglione and Rieder 2021). On the other hand, government officials generally have a working culture, often rigid and may not deviate from the existing rules, and it takes time to change (Caputi et al. 2021). Changing such behaviour is not easy. The fear of being blamed in the future poses a challenge for the top management. Therefore, there is need for online meetings to invite and encourage all parties to collaborate better and remove all fears by involving leaders of law enforcement agencies, BPKP, BPK, and the Indonesian Government Internal Auditors Association (AAIPI).

But it was not easy. Moreover, the leaders or those actively and quickly responded to emergency and recovery programmes did not receive any incentives, as it was meant for low-income communities. Officials had a heavy workload and a high number of personnel worked from home. In some regions, many personnel could not even operate computers or mobile phones properly. Inadequate work equipment forced many leaders of an institution to work alone. In such situations they are required to work with all their hearts, minds and energy.

Each PC-PEN programme has its own hurdles, but the overarching challenge was outdated or invalid data. Data on population, MSMEs, low-income communities, recipients of government assistance, unemployment, bank accounts, loans, electricity accounts, social security programme for workers, taxpayer identification numbers are vital to set the target and scope of the programme.

Emergency situation demands quick response, and it cannot wait for data improvement. Invalid or outdated data can happen because of various reasons, such as inaccuracy during the process of data collection, carelessness when processing the date collected, the absence of a tiered validation process or problems with technology applications (Reggi and Dawes 2022; Rosemary, Nur Rochimah, and Susilawati 2022). Despite errors were still found, various recommendations and improvements were made and eventually it significantly eliminated inaccuracies.

In order to accelerate the emergency and recovery programmes, several facilities are provided to government agencies, such as provisions on goods and services procurement, provision of petty cash funds, and payment procedures. But it was not easy though. The National Public

Procurement Agency (NPPA) issued procurement provisions regulated in Circular Number 3 signed by the agency's chief in 2020. An e-catalogue has been published, but the necessary goods are often unavailable. Other important steps taken to support the programme include the dissemination of goods and services procurement policy in response to COVID-19 and the President's instruction that ministries, institutions and regional heads implement the emergency and recovery initiatives.

Intense communication was built among ministries, institutions, NPPA, internal auditors, producers, distributors, and transportation companies. If an indication of non-compliance or fraud is discovered, it will be submitted to competent officials for precautions or safeguard of state finance. In case a fraud still occurs, the law enforcement authority will act.

Lengthy discussion also evolved around the assistance for MSMEs, in the form of interest subsidies, whether through pawnbroker, banks, or the Ministry of Cooperatives and Small and Medium Enterprises, including the guarantee for loans extended to cooperatives. State-owned pawnbroker has a huge number of customers. Likewise, there were many banking customers for people's business credit (KUR) and MSMEs.

Corporations, such as pawnbrokers, distribute loans to customers by receiving goods as collateral. Given that the funding comes from state budget, which is subject to an audit by the audit authority (BPKP), pawnbrokers re-examined their data and provided massive training for its internal auditors. They are the ones to communicate with the audit agency and the Inspectorate General of the Ministry of Finance.

Data on pawnshops and bank customers were delivered to the Financial Services Authority (OJK) via a system. It was then submitted to the Ministry of Finance for distribution of assistance through the credit information system programme (SIKP). Many institutions were interconnected but each had different information systems. In the initial stage, although the data validation process at pawnshops or banks was implemented, the process of data delivery to the information system at OJK and SIKP was not seamless.

To help the business world or corporations emerge from the rubbles, the state budget provides support in the form of premiums for insurance guarantee contributions and fund placement with banks. Although a guarantee has been prepared and the government's funds were placed at a low interest rate, their distribution was not fast enough. Uncertainty of future business prospects became the issue. Also, some parties were reluctant to receive them for fear of investigation by BPK.

In-depth communication and discussions about the implications of policies adopted by the government must be carried out so that the programme could be implemented effectively. Everything was discussed transparently and comprehensively to prevent problems in the future. Since 2022 is the last year, relevant parties need to anticipate and prepare safeguard measures to ensure that all programmes run according to regulations and no issues are unaddressed.

Subsidy for electricity runs relatively smoothly because the data has been improved and mapped properly. Thanks to the Inspectorate General of Finance Ministry that routinely observes, monitors, and evaluates the progress report on data of electricity accounts, especially the 450 and 900-ampere households who are beneficiaries of electricity subsidy.

The incentives provided for the pre-employment cards faced another challenge. Pre-employment cards have been prepared from the beginning, but later they are used as a means to address the unemployment issue following the closure of many companies that resulted in increasing unemployment rate. The programme did not run smoothly due to inadequate human resources and technology system at the Coordinating Minister for the Economy, which is responsible to run the programme.

Business incentives provided in the form of tax relief, either through the Directorate General of Taxation and the Directorate General of Customs and Excise was implemented. However, the constraint faced by the Directorate General of Taxation is the validity of data on taxpayers entitled to the initiative. The Inspectorate General of Finance Ministry provided assistance and conducted a continuous review to ensure that the incentives go to the right persons.

The pandemic has caused revenue decline of some SOEs, particularly in the tourism sector, including the aviation industry. Some SOEs, for instance in the shipping sector, have been assigned to guarantee loans provided by the government. However, the gearing ratio of these companies needs to be observed to ensure that they have sufficient capital to facilitate government's programmes. Internal auditors from the Finance Ministry have to cooperate to audit the funds transferred from the State General Treasurer to the relevant SOEs.

The synergy of budgets, from village to national levels, is required to run the emergency and recovery programmes. Funds from regional budget (APBD) were allocated only for healthcare and social protection. The funds for physical development projects were no longer available. Programmes through ministries, especially the Ministry of Public Works and Housing, were implemented almost flawlessly because the projects have complete data and technical documents, plus the support of experts.

On the contrary, the programmes of local governments could not meet expectations due to lack of planning. The government then appointed PT Sarana Multi Infrastrukur to distribute loans to regional governments and help them throughout the implementation of the projects.

It is agreed that in an emergency situation, there is burden-sharing between the government and the central bank. The central bank supports funding for public goods expenditure, by imposing a different interest rate on the funds used to financing public goods and non-public goods. It is necessary then to have special arrangements from the time of disbursement of the loan, fund deposit, and its usage. Tracking is important so that funds are used properly.

Since the meaning of burden-sharing for PC-PEN funds is quite complex, it is important to have a common understanding among the government, Bank Indonesia, DPR and BPK as an auditor. Burden-sharing means that the government shares the interest expense or cost of money with the central bank. The impact on cash balance may be the same, but the influence on state budget would be different.

The government, Bank Indonesia and the Audit Board discussed this matter at length and eventually reached an agreement that the interest expense is shared, not Bank Indonesia depositing income. Illustration of governance in the implementation of the PC-PEN programme with various relaxations during the pandemic can be seen in Figure 6.1.

Implementation of the budget was slow at the beginning due to the issues mentioned. But in the end, it was absorbed and its amount increased significantly.

6.3 SUPERVISORY FRAMEWORK OF THE PC-PEN PROGRAMME

The pandemic and economic recovery (PC-PEN) programme is a national programme that involves national, regional and village budgets. It's designed to be implemented nationwide. But there are extremely high risks due to many unpredictable events. As a rolling budget, it may be revised at any time to respond to public needs. Accuracy and timeliness are critical in addressing health and social protection issues. They do not stand alone and their overall impacts on the economy must be taken into

FIGURE 6.1
Governance with Relaxation for the PC-PEN Programme

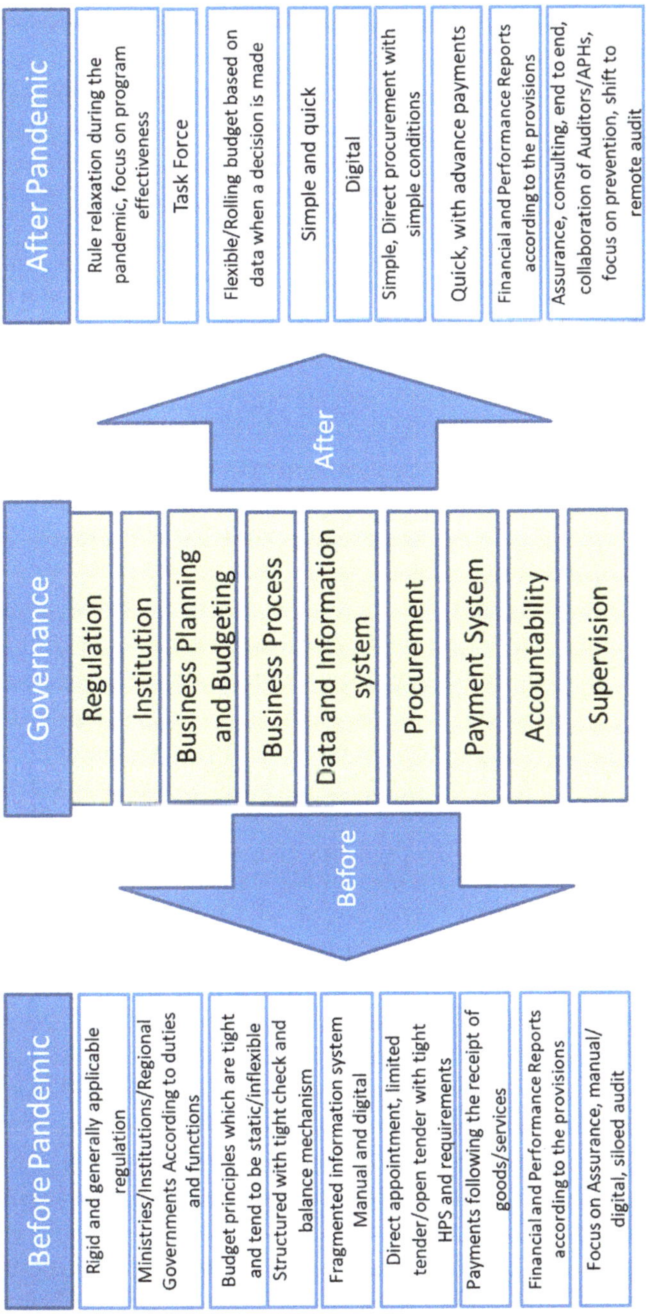

Source: PC-PEN Committee.

account collectively. It means that everyone must be in synergy with others to overcome the pandemic.

When the PC-PEN programme was designed, an audit universe can be prepared immediately along with a risk map (Le et al. 2022). Considering the difficult situation, a supervisory framework for this initiative was prepared, by mapping the types of programmes and the parties responsible for budget implementation. Internal auditors of the Finance Ministry responsible for supervising the budget cannot work alone but must coordinate with BPKP who, based on a Government Regulation, is appointed as a supervisory coordinator of the PC-PEN programme. Cooperation with internal auditors of technical ministries, regional governments and SOEs is also important. A supervisory framework for the pandemic and recovery programme was prepared (see Figure 6.2).

With a multi-layered supervision pattern, it is hoped that those in charge will be confident and fearless, so that the programme runs effectively. When problems or obstacles surface, they can be directly discussed with competent officials.

The collaboration by internal auditors is the dissemination of government policies, competency development, and sharing of experience faced by field auditors, supervision procedures during the pandemic, consultation with the relevant inspector general and law enforcement apparatus, as well as the exchange of information.

Monitoring and evaluation of the PC-PEN programme are carried out regularly. At the Ministry of Finance, the progress of each programme cluster was reported weekly. Directives from the leaders were directly followed up and monitored through the Daily Activity Monitoring Systems.

Supervision was needed to scrutinize and encourage the implementation of the PC-PEN programme. However, some activities could not run as planned. Auditors encountered several problems including budget unavailability. Local governments were instructed by the Minister of Home Affairs to allocate 1 per cent of their budgets for the supervisory programme. However, some regions were in lockdown and had no capacity to conduct digital-based audits. Such issues contributed to the delayed completion of the emergency response programme because some internal auditors were unable to carry out their duties and require assistance from the audit authority.

When the PC-PEN programme was prepared, the Annual Supervisory Work Programme (PKTP) of the Inspectorate General of Finance Ministry

FIGURE 6.2
Framework for the 2021 PC-PEN Supervision and Scrutiny

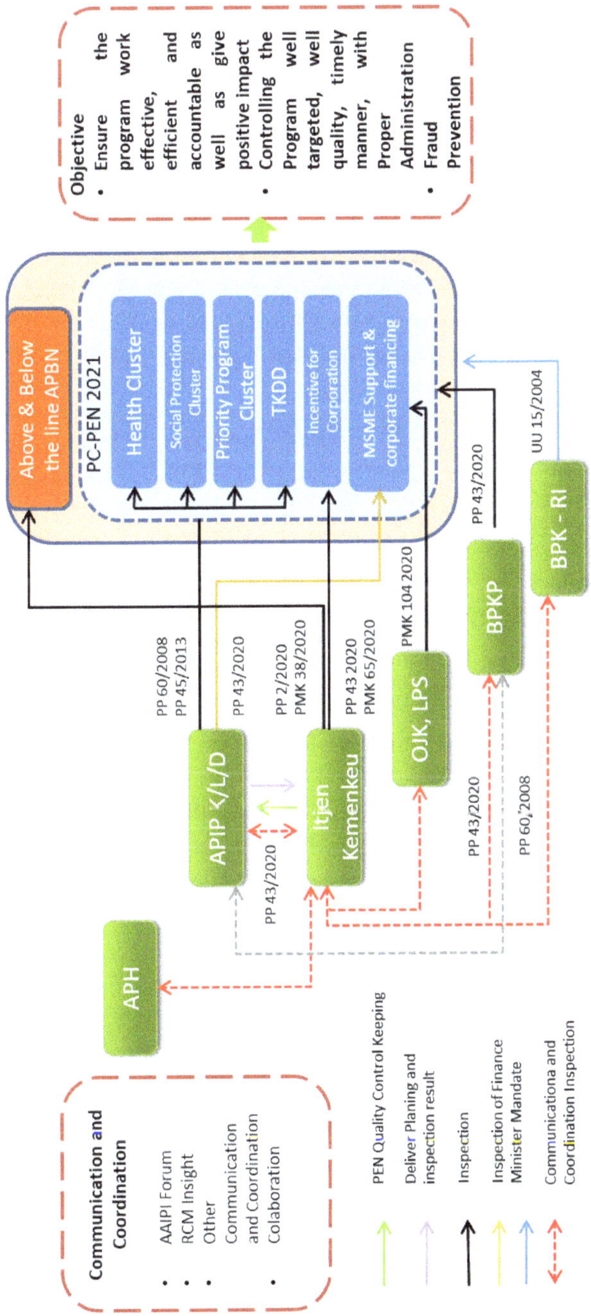

Source: PC-PEN Committee.

was just established and not prepared to supervise the emergency response programme. It triggered the several important breakthroughs in the area of internal supervision.

6.3.1 Revision to the Annual Supervisory Work Programme

If PKPT was not changed, it would be difficult for the finance ministry to oversee the PC-PEN programme. The supervisory work programme was made more flexible so that adjustments could be easily made. Internal auditors followed the minister 's directives, which usually end at 11:00 p.m., and later coordinated with internal auditors and their partner units to follow up on the minister 's directives. The next day, they would discuss provisions and business processes, anticipate risks and design a monitoring system during the implementation of activities. They must not miss any agenda because every decision could change the audit universe or risk map that has to be maintained by auditors.

6.3.2 Forming of Supervisory Task Force per Programme Cluster

The organizational structure of the Inspectorate General is structured according to the duties and functions of the Ministry of Finance. When all resources were directed to the PC-PEN initiative, the previous structure of the audit team was no longer appropriate. For audit effectiveness, a special task force was formed in 2020. The team would oversee its partners and related directorate generals, and collaborate with BPKP or internal auditors on the budget using agencies. To encourage the programme to run, this task force must often intervene and assist internal auditors from technical ministries, to become a mentor or give input for improvement.

6.3.3 Issuing Supervision Guidelines

The internal audit supervision guidelines owned by the Ministry of Finance are meant for use in normal circumstances. These guidelines are not sufficient to become the basis for auditors in conducting audits for the PC-PEN programme. In a pandemic situation, nearly all assignments are performed online and some guidelines need to be adjusted, for example, from the technical aspect of supervision. The investigative audit can be conducted online.

6.3.4 Accelerating Remote Auditing

Remote auditing is a challenge for internal auditors in Indonesia. The implementation of a digital information system, computer literacy for all personnel and security awareness are some prerequisites that must be met. Hence, along with the audit, a competency development programme to support remote auditing continued to be implemented.

During the pandemic, once people's movements were restricted or even having to work from home, remote auditing was an option. Collaboration between the auditor and the auditee or supervised clients can be a daunting task. The auditees might not be willing to submit data or allow the auditor to access data under their control. The auditor and the auditee often do not know each other, and communication by telephone has many limitations and cannot read body language. It requires them to meet in order to be able to build trust and data can be obtained accurately and quickly. The finance ministry has set up Financial Data Service System (SLDK) in order to accelerate data communication.

The implementation of audit management systems and digital-based information systems combined with sufficient data analytical capabilities at all auditing levels, and good collaboration and communication between parties, enabled audit tasks at the Ministry of Finance to be properly carried out, despite the office was empty as all staff worked remotely (Baatwah and Al-Ansi 2022; Cao et al. 2022). Remote auditing significantly cut costs and saves time. It also effectively reduced business travel and meeting costs.

6.3.5 Optimizing the Use of Audit Management System

Since all personnel worked from home, it was inevitable that all auditors must use an audit management system application. In the pre-pandemic era, this application was not fully used. But during the pandemic, all personnel used it.

6.3.6 Developing Partnership with BPKP, Internal Auditors and Law Enforcement Apparatus

Supervision of the PC-PEN programme was conducted by synergizing all resources, under the auspices of the audit authority (BPKP). Many agencies found that their internal auditors could not perform their task during the pandemic, among others, because they were working manually.

They were powerless, lacking a leadership support and the spirit to carry out duties. In such situations, in many regions, BPKP played a bigger role in supervising and assisting the government in accelerating budget implementation.

6.3.7 Strengthening the Three Lines Model

People often think that supervision is only carried out by internal auditors. In fact, there is the concept of three lines of defence. The Ministry of Finance has executed this model for several years. During the pandemic, when the Inspectorate General could not directly conduct field audit, the first and second line of defence in the system were strengthened. Collaboration and coordination became stronger. The development programme for internal compliance was enhanced and the *Irjen Menyapa* programme via a video conference was added. It enables the Inspector General to communicate and convey messages directly to auditors, remind them to be in compliance and not to commit fraud.

6.4 ACCOUNTABILITY FOR THE PC-PEN PROGRAMME

Indonesia's fiscal year spans from 1 January to 31 December of the same year. The deadlines for accountability reports vary. At the ministerial and institutional levels the due date is the end of February of the following year, and 31 March for the central government to submit its financial reports. BPK conducts an audit from February to May and the Accountability for Budget implementation bill is delivered to DPR in June of the following year.

For regional governments, financial reports must be completed in March of the following year to be audited by BPK. It is followed by the submission of the bill on accountability for regional budget implementation the Regional People's Representative Council (DPRD). It means that when the pandemic started to hit Indonesia in early 2020, the government was at the stage of preparing the 2019 financial reports. The 2019 budget was for a normal situation, but when preparing the financial reports and conducting the audit, the situation was completely different.

Financial reports were not completed as all personnel had to work remotely. The good thing is that the central government and local governments in general already use digital-based financial information systems (Huynh et al. 2021). The process of preparing financial reports is relatively safe. But the problem is that some personnel were infected with the COVID-19 virus.

These financial reports must first be reviewed by internal auditors before their submission to the President *c/q* Minister of Finance and a copy is sent to BPK. Generally there was no significant problem, as internal auditors, like the ministry's inspectorate general, were prepared for an e-review, and the existing information system was reliable. However, disturbances occurred in the initial stage, for instance, due to personnel's delay in responding important messages on their mobile phone and problems with telephones, network, laptops or computers at home, and some employees were sick.

These issues were observed and discussed in small groups until a joint agreement was made regarding the time, work method, and service level agreement for performing tasks, especially those requiring data support and approval from colleagues.

At some institutions, the review process could not be done at its best because they were not ready for an e-review or due to other constraints (Wang et al. 2022). During a webinar regarding the supervision of the PC-PEN programme, it was found that internal auditors of regional governments did not review the financial reports at all because they were incapable of doing the e-review. They were used to do it manually.

Fortunately, as the finance ministry in this case the inspectorate general has an expertise in digital-based audits, it guided relevant auditors using the data of the ministry concerned. In this way, all data could be reviewed and anomalies could be immediately identified, and corrections were made. This technique was proven effective in maintaining the reliability of financial statements.

Throughout the financial review process, internal auditors anticipated the risks arising during BPK's audit. Various issues emerged during the audit of financial statements that never happened in previous years. They include:

(a) Communication between the auditor and the auditee was entirely conducted online.
(b) Difficulty in explaining a highly technical and detailed procedure for an IT-based system in a short period of time to the auditor, even though it was necessary in the financial reports.

(c) There was no web-based application available for data exchange at the time of the audit.
(d) Data requests and submissions had not been structured. It can be one to many, many to one, or many to many.
(e) The process of acquiring and collecting necessary evidence could take longer due to disturbances, such as sick personnel, office lockdowns, limited working hours, and difficulty to visit a location.
(f) The communication process did not run smoothly because of restrictions.

In such situations, internal auditors were required to accompany the unit being audited and help them to understand better what BPK auditors seek in the reports. To ensure uncorrupted flow of data and information, a worksheet was prepared to record any progress of data requests, discussed together and agreed on to avoid misunderstanding between the auditor and the auditee.

To ensure that the agreement was implemented, the data submitted is the requested and valid, checked by internal auditors before they are given to BPK. With this system, internal auditors also monitored the adequacy and quality of data, and directly oversee follow-ups by the auditee. Discussions that were initially held weekly turned out to be a daily activity for tighter monitoring.

But problems do not stop there. Although various risks have been anticipated and closely safeguarded, there were pending technical and strategic issues. Strategic issues were then brought to high-level meetings of government leaders and BPK. Meanwhile, to address technical issues, an extension of time was agreed because there were many constraints in the field. Within an agreed timeframe, the audit process could be completed successfully and deserved unqualified opinion. It means that the accountability and transparency of state financial management should not be compromised due to the pandemic. The key here is excellent cooperation from all parties.

The accountability report for the PC-PEN budget in the 2020 fiscal year is certainly different from 2019. But auditors were already experienced in carrying out reviews and audits of financial reports. The priority for the 2020 fiscal year was the substance of the PC-PEN programme that would be reported in the financial statements.

Taking into account the provisions in Law Number 2 of 2020 and the subsequent regulations and related Presidential Regulations, it is necessary to prepare an information system can produce reliable information on the budget size, its realization, allocation, funding and achievements. Important information must be recorded for inclusion in the financial reports.

The Government Accounting Standard Committee (KSAP) then studied the PC-PEN programme to ensure that the existing Government Accounting Standard is sufficient and applicable for the programme's accountability. The committee concluded that the handling of COVID-19 pandemic remained within the budget (APBN) framework. All programmes can use the existing Government Accounting Standards. But an Accounting Guideline for each programme type was needed and prepared by the Directorate General of Treasury.

Several issues comprehensively discussed and closely monitored were the marking of the PC-PEN budget so that it can be assessed, notes on the sources and use of funds for the procurement of public goods or non-public goods, burden-sharing for debt interest with Bank Indonesia, fund placement, various subsidies, tax expenditure, and fiscal sustainability. All of these were recorded in that particular fiscal year and closely monitored, and accounted for in the 2020 financial reports, which obtained an unqualified opinion. Based on this, we can expect the PC-PEN programme of 2022 is properly concluded.

6.5 PERSONNEL PSYCHOEDUCATION DURING THE PANDEMIC

As mentioned above, the pandemic incurred a broad range of issues to employees. In such a situation, an agency needs to monitor the physical and mental health of employees. Deterioration of their physical and mental health or that of their families will have an impact on one's performance and subsequently interfere with the agency's operations. There were times when employees' works were not monitored. Or during video conferences we could hear babies crying in the background and many other disturbances took place. Those issues have to be addressed prudently by leaders to lessen the burdens on employees.

Every ministry, including the Ministry of Finance, formed a task force in charge of personnel and their families who were infected by COVID-19. Government offices provided drugs and isolation facilities for personnel infected at the state's expense. Figure 6.3 shows the pattern in managing the health of staff.

To identify the impacts of the pandemic on the employee's workload, along with their work-life balance, the Inspectorate General conducted a study on employees. The study suggests that husband or wife that work from home, while at the same time their children also study from home, faced certain issues. For instance, they must share space, equipment and time with family members. But it was agreed that their children's study was a priority. Meetings or office duties must be consulted with the superior and their team so that everything could still be in place.

The study also shows that women's workload during work from home period was heavier than the male counterparts, although men tried to help in doing household chores. The results of this survey were used to design personnel education from the aspect of psychology.

For this end, three activities were conducted: providing consulting services by assigning psychiatrists, developing good communication with

FIGURE 6.3
Personnel Health Management System

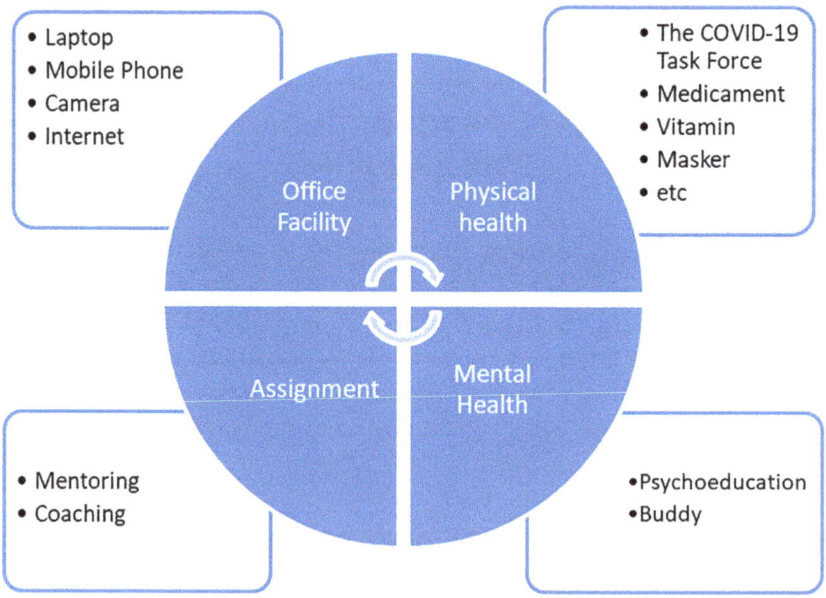

Source: PC-PEN Committee.

employees, and providing psychoeducation for employees of the Ministry of Finance, among others with topics of flexible working space for the new normal, marriage life during the pandemic, and how to be adaptive amidst the pandemic.

The goal of psychoeducation was to motivate employees to be able to cope up with issues they faced while working from home, and at the same time able to perform their tasks quickly and appropriately.

6.6 LESSON LEARNT AND RECOMMENDATIONS

The impact of the pandemic has been massive and based on working experience throughout these challenging times one can learn that broad political communication and broader public communication using various communication means are vital for conveying reliable information and to win support from political institutions and wider community.

The impasse can be settled through hard work, high level commitment, and close cooperation among stakeholders. Leaders must dare to take breakthroughs so that the initiatives can run quickly and steadily in emergency times. Governance, risk and control must be strictly maintained so that people dare to take action and is accounted for properly and transparently.

Looking at the experience in handling the COVID-19 pandemic, several matters need to be improved:

1. Regulation on emergency response and necessary guidelines (Padovani and Iacuzzi 2021; Stiglitz 2021);
2. Development of information system based on correct and up-to-date database;
3. Acceleration of government system digitization (Tai 2021);
4. Preparation of comprehensive and integrated national work plan, budget allocation with adequate data architecture and performance indicator, and supporting documents;
5. Open space work patterns by working and learning without limits;
6. Responsive, non-rigid government programme, quick and precise budget execution;
7. Developing integrated work procedure with the agreed service level agreement;
8. Eliminating a silo mentality, and replacing it with collaborative mentality and synergy;

9. Strengthening the supervision and increasing the capacity of internal auditors nationally and emphasis on the role of internal auditors as guardians of Governance, Risk, and Control (GRC) (Ferry et al. 2017; Padovani and Iacuzzi 2021).

References

Baatwah, S.R., and A.A. Al-Ansi. 2022. "Dataset for Understanding the Effort and Performance of External Auditors during the COVID-19 Crisis: A Remote Audit Analysis". *Data in Brief* 42: 108119. https://doi.org/10.1016/j.dib.2022.108119

Cao, H., L. Zhang, Y. Qi, Z. Yang, and X. Li. 2022. "Government Auditing and Environmental Governance: Evidence from China's Auditing System Reform". *Environmental Impact Assessment Review* 93 (November 2021). https://doi.org/10.1016/j.eiar.2021.106705

Caputi, N., S. de Lestang, S.J. Newman, G. Jackson, and K. Smith. 2021. "Stakeholder-Government Collaboration in Developing Cost-Effective Fishery-Independent Surveys in Rights-Based and Co-Managed Fisheries". *Marine Policy* 128 (March): 104510. https://doi.org/10.1016/j.marpol.2021.104510

Chon, M.G., and S. Kim. 2022. "Dealing with the COVID-19 Crisis: Theoretical Application of Social Media Analytics in Government Crisis Management". *Public Relations Review* 48, no. 3: 102201. https://doi.org/10.1016/j.pubrev.2022.102201

Ferry, L., Z. Zakaria, Z. Zakaria, and R. Slack. 2017. "Watchdogs, Helpers or Protectors? Internal Auditing in Malaysian Local Government". *Accounting Forum* 41, no. 4: 375–89. https://doi.org/10.1016/j.accfor.2017.10.001

Gomes, de V. L.A. and L.S. da S. Barros. 2022. "The Role of Governments in Uncertainty Orchestration in Market Formation for Sustainability Transitions". *Environmental Innovation and Societal Transitions 43* (May 2021): 127–45. https://doi.org/10.1016/j.eist.2022.03.006

Hung, L.Y., S.M. Wang, and T.K. Yeh. 2022. "Collaboration between the Government and Environmental Non-governmental Organisations for Marine Debris Policy Development: The Taiwan Experience". *Marine Policy* 135 (October 2021): 104849. https://doi.org/10.1016/j.marpol.2021.104849

Huynh, N., A. Dao, and D. Nguyen. 2021. "Openness, Economic Uncertainty, Government Responses, and International Financial Market Performance during the Coronavirus Pandemic". *Journal of Behavioral and Experimental Finance* 31 (May): 100536. https://doi.org/10.1016/j.jbef.2021.100536

Le, T.T., T.M.A. Nguyen, V.Q. Do, and T.H.C. Ngo. 2022. "Risk-based Approach and Quality of Independent Audit Using Structure Equation Modeling: Evidence from Vietnam". *European Research on Management and Business Economics* 28, no. 3. https://doi.org/10.1016/j.iedeen.2022.100196

Ma, Y., and C. Yao. 2022. "Openness and Government Size: Revisiting the Relationship Using a Large Cross-Country Panel". *International Review of Economics and Finance* 79, no. 59: 448–65. https://doi.org/10.1016/j.iref.2022.02.056

Montes, G.C., R.T. da F. Nicolay, and T. Acar. 2019. "Do Fiscal Communication and Clarity of Fiscal Announcements Affect Public Debt Uncertainty? Evidence from Brazil". *Journal of Economics and Business* 103 (December 2018): 38–60. https://doi.org/10.1016/j.jeconbus.2018.12.002

Padovani, E., and S. Iacuzzi. 2021. "Real-Time Crisis Management: Testing the Role of Accounting in Local Governments". *Journal of Accounting and Public Policy* 40, no. 3: 106854. https://doi.org/10.1016/j.jaccpubpol.2021.106854

Palmaccio, S., F. Schiltz, and K. De Witte. 2022. "Information Shocks and Parental Response in Education. A Case Study of an Open Government Initiative". *Government Information Quarterly* 39, no. 3: 101702. https://doi.org/10.1016/j.giq.2022.101702

Pandey, V., S. Singh, and D. Kumar. 2022. "COVID-19, Information Management by Local Governments, and Food Consumption". *Food Policy* 110 (September 2021): 102278. https://doi.org/10.1016/j.foodpol.2022.102278

Raviglione, M.C., and H.L. Rieder. 2021. "Synergy between Government and Non-Governmental Organizations in Health: WHO and the Union Collaboration in Tuberculosis Control". *Journal of Clinical Tuberculosis and Other Mycobacterial Diseases* 24 (June): 100251. https://doi.org/10.1016/j.jctube.2021.100251

Reggi, L., and S.S. Dawes. 2022. "Creating Open Government Data Ecosystems: Network Relations among Governments, User Communities, NGOs and the Media". *Government Information Quarterly* 39, no. 2: 101675. https://doi.org/10.1016/j.giq.2022.101675

Rosemary, R., T.H. Nur Rochimah, and N. Susilawati. 2022. "Efficacy Information in Government's Initial Responses to COVID-19 Pandemic: A Content Analysis of the Media Coverage in Indonesia". *International Journal of Disaster Risk Reduction* 77 (May): 103076. https://doi.org/10.1016/j.ijdrr.2022.103076

Stiglitz, J.E. 2021. "The Proper Role of Government in the Market Economy: The Case of the Post-COVID Recovery". *Journal of Government and Economics* 1 (May): 100004. https://doi.org/10.1016/j.jge.2021.100004

Sundqvist-Andberg, H., and M. Åkerman. 2022. "Collaborative Governance as a Means of Navigating the Uncertainties of Sustainability Transformations: The Case of Finnish Food Packaging". *Ecological Economics* 197 (November 2021): 107455. https://doi.org/10.1016/j.ecolecon.2022.107455

Tai, K.T. 2021. "Open Government Research Over a Decade: A Systematic Review". *Government Information Quarterly* 38, no. 2: 101566. https://doi.org/10.1016/j.giq.2021.101566

Wang, X., F.A.F. Ferreira, and C. Ter. Chang. 2022. "Multi-Objective Competency-Based Approach to Project Scheduling and Staff Assignment: Case Study of an Internal Audit Project". *Socio-Economic Planning Sciences* 81 (October 2021): 101182. https://doi.org/10.1016/j.seps.2021.101182

Yiannakoulias, N., C.E. Slavik, S.L. Sturrock, and J.C. Darlington. 2020. "Open Government Data, Uncertainty and Coronavirus: An Infodemiological Case Study". *Social Science and Medicine* 265: 113549. https://doi.org/10.1016/j.socscimed.2020.113549

Yu, W., P. Liang, and N. Gao. 2021. "Can Higher Levels of Disclosure Bring Greater Efficiency: Empirical Research on the Effect of Government Information Disclosure on Enterprise Investment Efficiency". *China Economic Quarterly International* 1, no. 3: 221–32. https://doi.org/10.1016/j.ceqi.2021.09.001

PART III

Revenue Shock and Response

7

Balancing the Scale
Providing Tax Incentives and Collecting Revenue

Yon Arsal, Arifin Rosid and Sukaryo

7.1 INTRODUCTION

Tax reform has been a major challenge for Indonesia which has struggled for many decades to strengthen its capacity to collect taxation revenue. The adverse impact of reduced taxation revenue has adversely impacted the Indonesian government's ability to finance needed social services.[1] This is evident in the tax-to-GDP ratio in Indonesia when compared to similar income group countries.[2] As a result, tax reform has been a continuing challenge for the government, including strengthening revenue collection capabilities.

Most recently, the Ministry of Finance (MoF) initiated tax reforms in 2017 which were a comprehensive revamp of Indonesia's current tax policy and administration landscape. Initially, the government expected to finalize the reform agenda by 2024 with the roll-out of the new core tax system. However, the pandemic hit midway through the reform and, expectedly, shifted the focus of the tax authorities to respond to the COVID-19 disruption.

The unprecedented and extraordinary challenges of the pandemic created a health and economic catastrophe on a global scale. For the government, the immediate priority was to minimize the risk of a health crisis. Nevertheless, the attempts to curb the pandemic through containment and outbreak preventative measures triggered both supply and demand shocks and created social and economic challenges. The government faced the additional challenge of cushioning and protecting impacted households and businesses.

From the perspective of an economic crisis, the COVID-19 challenge was (at a minimum) twofold: the government needed to address the immediate crisis and also provide necessary support during the post-pandemic recovery phase. As a result, the government devised a comprehensive support package through discretionary fiscal responses: additional spending and forgone revenue—to supplement and strengthen the existing automatic stabilizers. The government structured and consolidated the broad economic recovery agenda under the National Economic Recovery (*Pemulihan Ekonomi Nasional*, or PEN) Programme.

As one of the available fiscal instruments, the role of tax is to raise revenue to fund the services and income supports the community's needs and is not only about collecting revenue. The government has provided a set of fiscal incentives to support the economy and has been reporting tax expenditures since 2018. However, the widespread economic challenges of the pandemic raised a call for more extensive fiscal support, including tax stimulus. Consequently, the government launched a wave of fiscal support in the forms of tax and duties relief, deductions, and relaxation.

During economic disruption, the government plays an instrumental role in stabilizing the economy through monetary and fiscal policy. Arguably, even though countercyclical fiscal policies occur automatically as tax revenue dwindles, further fiscal intervention is necessary to boost the economy (Elmendorf and Furman 2008, p. 4). However, Taylor and Castillo (2015, pp. 5–6) suggested that the government should avoid "wasteful spending" and follow the general principles of stimulus programmes in designing a fiscal intervention.

Following the Joint Economic Committee meeting to address the Global Financial Crisis, Summers (2008) advocated for three principles of fiscal stimulus: "timely, targeted, and temporary" (also see Taylor and Castillo 2015; Elmendorf and Furman 2008). First, the stimulus policy should be timely, i.e., not ill-timed, delayed, or require a lengthy implementation period (Elmendorf and Furman 2008, p. 5). Also, the fiscal stimulus should target "those most in need" (Summers 2008) or "specific economic sectors that will yield the greatest social benefits for the resources expended" (Taylor and Castillo 2015, p. 5). Lastly, the government should ensure the stimulus spending will not burden the long-run fiscal deficit and terminate the intervention "once an economy has sufficiently recovered from recession" (Taylor and Castillo 2015, p. 6).

As a policy response to the SARS-Cov-2 outbreak, the OECD proposed four phases of tax policy sequenced with different focuses and instruments (OECD 2020, pp. 9–10). The first phase of the policy serves as the government's immediate response and focuses on income support. As the pandemic mitigation persists, the tax policy shifts to the second phase, which requires a broader tax policy response. The following phase, recovery or when the government removes mitigation measures gradually, requires expansionary fiscal policy to stimulate consumption, investment, and confidence. Lastly, after the recovery phase, the next step of tax policy is to raise revenue to "restore long-term fiscal sustainability" (OECD 2020, p. 11). See Figure 7.1.

As the global outbreak escalated, Indonesia's government swiftly responded to the COVID-19 challenges with comprehensive stimulus packages, starting with the first policy intervention in February 2020. The following month, the government declared the COVID-19 pandemic a national emergency and issued the second stimulus package, including tax incentives. As COVID-19 accelerated, the government gradually expanded the extraordinary tax intervention to support business continuity and recovery, bolster household purchasing power, and aid the pandemic countermeasure programme. Under the PEN Programme, the government continued the COVID-19 tax incentives in 2021 with a more expansive coverage to accelerate domestic economic recovery.

Nevertheless, the scale and dynamics of COVID-19 challenges required significant government intervention and, coupled with Indonesia's tight fiscal space, created a policy dilemma to formulate prompt measures without jeopardizing budget governance. Thus, this chapter attempts to capture and discuss how Indonesia, particularly the MoF, responded to and addressed the policy challenges in designing discretionary tax incentives during the pandemic.

This chapter will elaborate on the design, implementation, and impact of the government's tax stimulus during the COVID-19 pandemic. The first

FIGURE 7.1
Tax Policy Phase during the Pandemic

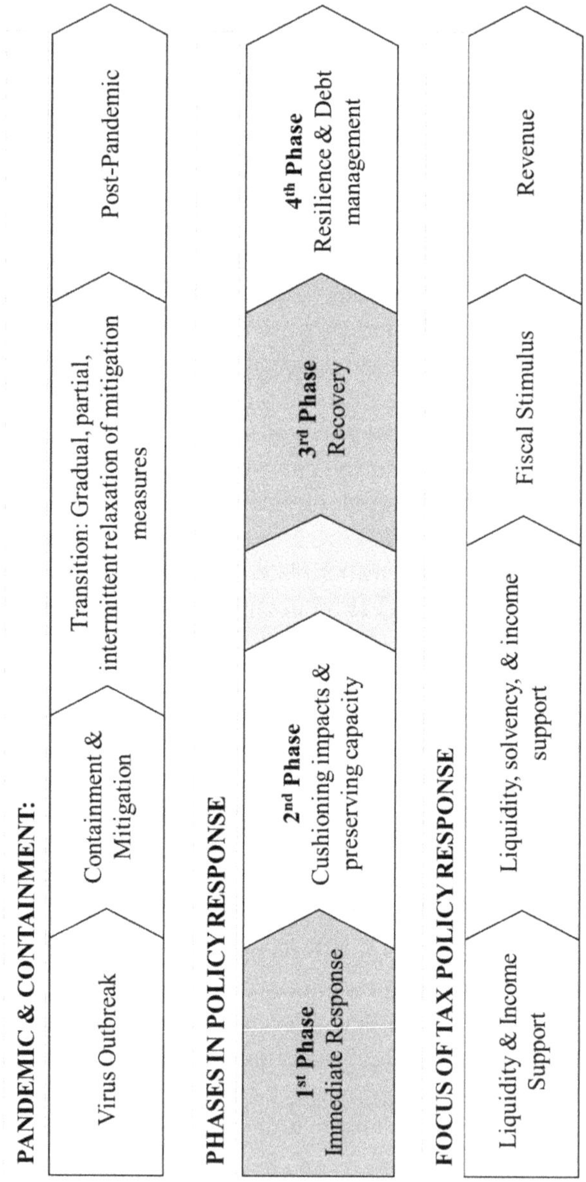

Source: OECD.

part will set the scene of this chapter, focusing on the tax revenue challenges in Indonesia before COVID-19. Subsequently, the discussion will progress with the policy design of the COVID-19 tax incentives and highlight the challenges during the initial phase. Furthermore, the discussion will continue with details on the implementation and impact of COVID-19 tax incentives, based on the evidence from the PEN Programme surveys and administrative data. Lastly, this chapter outlines the government's takeaways from the COVID-19 tax incentives implementation, enabling a robust fiscal instrument post-pandemic recovery.

7.2 PRE-PANDEMIC CHALLENGES: SUBOPTIMUM REVENUE

In Indonesia, the collection of tax revenue has been a major challenge for the government and the shortfall in revenue has limited the ability of the government to finance public goods and services provision. Averaging around 11 per cent of GDP, Indonesia's tax-to-GDP ratio ranks stands among the weakest in the similar income group and regional countries. From a growth and development perspective, the tipping point for an "adequate" revenue level is around 15 per cent of GDP to provide adequate budgetary spending (de Mooij, Nazara, and Toro 2018, p. 5). Consequently, the government's spending capacity is substantially lower than other developing and emerging economies—more than 5 percentage points lower than emerging economies' average (see Figure 7.2).

As one of the long-standing fiscal challenges in Indonesia, tax revenue collection was the subject of two significant, comprehensive policy-administration reforms in the 1980s and 2000s.[3] However, following the Global Financial Crisis in 2008 and the commodity price slump, tax revenue in Indonesia stagnated and has dwindled since 2014. Recognizing the importance of domestic resources mobilization (DRM) for the Sustainable Development Goals (SDG), the government initiated the next tax reform agenda in 2017.

Arguably, comprehensive reform that encompasses tax policy and administrative aspects would address the revenue collection challenges in Indonesia. Aside from the suboptimum revenue level, Indonesia is among the lower-ranked tax administrations based on the Paying Taxes indicator.[4] See Figure 7.3. For the headline index, Indonesia consistently scored around the 40th percentile among more than 180 economies, lower

FIGURE 7.2
Tax Revenue and Government Spending, percentage of GDP

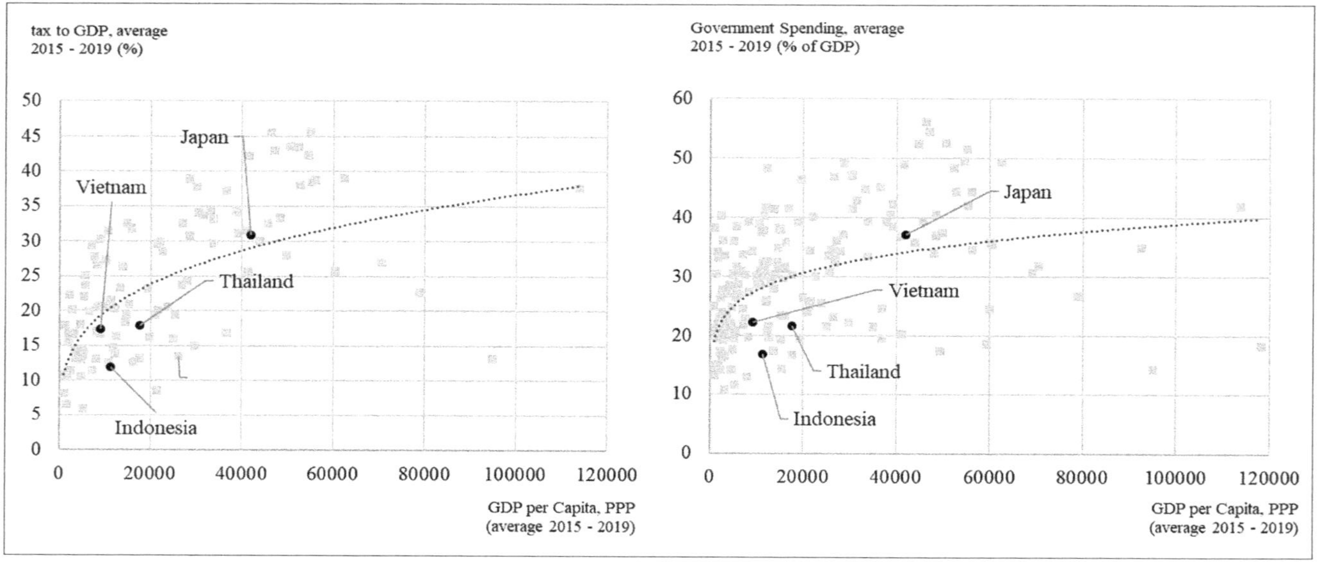

Source: Tax revenue data based on the OECD Statistics (https://stats.oecd.org/index.aspx?r=173147) while the government spending and GDP data were based on the IMF World Economic Outlook Database (https://www.imf.org/en/Publications/WEO).

FIGURE 7.3
Paying Taxes Ranking, percentile rank

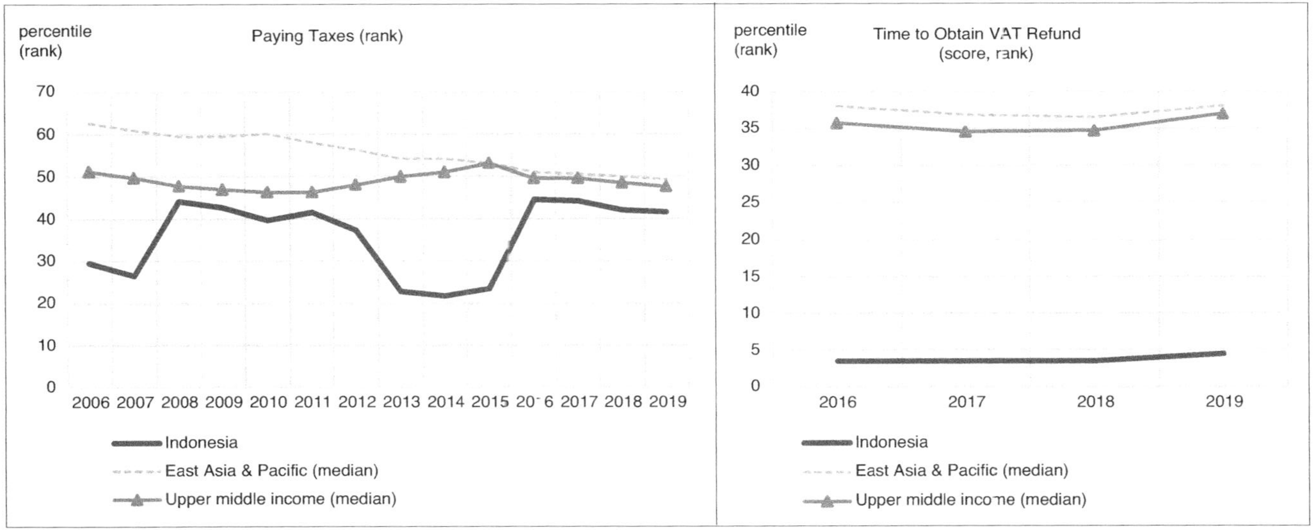

Note: Using the Paying Taxes score based on the EoDB data (https://www.worldbank.org/en/programs/business-enabling-environment/doing-business-legacy) and ranked as percentile rank (100 = highest, 0 = lowest). Regional and income-group levels were based on the classification in the EoDB dataset.
Source: www.worldbank.org

than those in the comparable income group and region. Zooming in on the Paying Taxes components, one of the weakest indicators in Indonesia was the time taken to obtain a VAT (value-added taxes) refund, which stands at around forty-seven weeks or significantly longer than other observed economies in the Paying Taxes indicators.

The MoF structured the 2017 reform agenda with five dimensions: organization, human resources, information technology, business processes, and policy/regulation. Based on the primary focus area, the government emphasized administrative reform as one of the highlights of the 2017 reform of the core tax administration system revamp. During the initial design, the government planned to finalize the reform by 2024 by implementing the new core tax system (and including other priority administrative and policy changes). However, the pandemic hit in 2020 and required comprehensive government support, with the MoF holding a crucial role in restructuring the budget and formulating discretionary fiscal intervention policy. As a result, the MoF, especially the Directorate General of Taxes (DGT), needed to refocus its resources to maintain the tax reform programme and prepare COVID-19 tax incentives.

On a more positive note, the pandemic also allowed the DGT to pilot and implement several reform strategies, which had been in the pipeline. From the policy reform, the government reduced the corporate income tax rate from 25 per cent to 22 per cent in March 2020—one of the highlights of the policy reform to improve tax competitiveness. At the same time, the DGT incorporated some administrative changes, namely, web-based services expansion and VAT refund relaxation. The restriction measures to curb virus outbreaks prevented the business-as-usual walk-in tax services and accelerated the shifts towards digital services. For the DGT, improving digital services has been a continuous agenda item, and the pandemic set the stage for a much broader digital transformation.[5] Meanwhile, the aforementioned VAT refund procedures were subject to several relaxation policies, but the COVID-19 pandemic allowed for a more progressive improvement (discussed further in the latter part).

7.2.1 Suboptimum Revenue and Pandemic

Following the escalating global cases of COVID-19 in early 2020, the government provided various initial stimulus packages in February 2020—without tax incentives. However, the emergence of COVID-19 in Indonesia called for more comprehensive measures. From an economic policy perspective, the government provided an expanded stimulus package to support businesses in March 2020, including tax incentives. Along with the existing tax expenditures, the government extended the initial COVID-19 tax stimulus during the challenging period of the pandemic.

Nevertheless, designing tax policy interventions without past analysis or experience is difficult for the government, especially the MoF. Instead of collecting historical information, the government needs to generate data and operate under various scenarios. Coupled with the challenge of limited tax collection capacity, the MoF needs to strike a balance between implementing sizeable tax incentives that will significantly support taxpayers whilst in parallel not jeopardizing the prudent fiscal management and budget structure.[6] Consequently, the policy planning was filled with dilemmas and complexity, constraining the policymaking process. Given the challenging circumstances, the government's decision on COVID-19 tax incentives was arguably the first best policy.

7.3 COVID-19 AND TAX INCENTIVE DESIGN

In March 2020, the government announced the first confirmed COVID-19 case in Indonesia and responded swiftly with various economic stimulus packages. While the government provided the first stimulus package in February 2020, it was only in March 2020 that discretionary tax incentives were introduced as part of the COVID-19 economic support measures. Following the surge in confirmed cases and the resulting stricter social containment and weakening business activities, the government structured a more comprehensive economic support initiative under the PEN Programme.

In the PEN Programme, tax incentives played an important role in supporting business and also contributed to the PEN Programme's health countermeasures and helping small-business programmes. Along with the existing tax expenditures, the MoF devised various fiscal relief, deductions, and relaxations as complementary measures, part of the "bigger picture" in the PEN Programme. However, given the unprecedented nature of the pandemic and the acute challenges of tax revenue collection in Indonesia, the policy formulation process was far from straightforward. Therefore, this part will explore the MoF's challenges and dilemmas during the tax incentives planning process, focusing on the options and policy debates preceding the "final" structure of the COVID-19 tax incentives.

7.3.1 The Initial Step: Setting up Objectives

Undeniably, the COVID-19 pandemic devastated both the demand and supply side of the global economy. Large-scale COVID-19 containment measures hampered businesses' capability to operate while, at the same time, consumption dropped due to economic and health uncertainties. Therefore, the government needed to intervene with various policies to cushion the impact of the supply and demand shocks.

In Indonesia, the government devised a comprehensive fiscal stimulus to mitigate the pandemic's impact on the domestic economy under the PEN Programme in May 2020. Nevertheless, the initial policy responses to COVID-19 started in February 2020, focusing on the expenditure side to provide income support (arguably, demand-side interventions). Subsequently, as the global disruption escalated and the first confirmed cases were reported in Indonesia, the government needed to expand support measures and structure a more comprehensive stimulus. Accordingly, the government utilized various policy tools, including tax policy, in the COVID-19 fiscal stimulus.

For the government, the primary objective of the COVID-19 fiscal stimulus was to protect people from the virus (health crisis) and the adverse economic impact of the pandemic (economic crisis). Consequently, as part of the stimulus programme, the tax stimulus measures adopted were intended to adhere to the goal of protecting people: the COVID-19 tax incentives supported the health counter-measures and cushion the economic impact of the pandemic. Nonetheless, the nature of the taxes imposed on economic activities and transactions resulted in a more significant role of the tax incentives introduced in providing business support (rather than supporting the pandemic counter-measures programme).

The primary role of tax policy to provide business support is also aligned with the OECD's policy staging (Table 7.1). The OECD suggested liquidity support as the primary objective of COVID-19 tax policy for the first two phases: immediate response and impact mitigation. Furthermore, moving towards the next juncture—recovery—the OECD suggests fiscal stimulus as a focus for the government policy response, which "supports swift recovery" (OECD 2020, p. 32) while "gradually and carefully relaxing

TABLE 7.1
Policy Considerations during Design and Planning

Topic	*Things to Consider*	*Choice(s)*
Policy Objectives	Defining the role of tax policy during the pandemic, given the history of low revenue. Also, the OECD's tax policy phases during the pandemic suggest that the government provides liquidity and income support	Tax Policy as complementary measures, part of the PEN Programme: multiple fiscal instruments are working together to cushion the impact of the pandemic.
Legal Instruments	First, there is no experience providing broad tax incentives during a crisis or disastrous events. Moreover, the "temporary" principle is less prevalent in the existing tax expenditures. Lastly, the dynamics of a pandemic crisis require a "timely" approach; thus, the government needs to consider the appropriate legal framework.	Take the existing relaxation policies of tax expenditures, enhancing the "timely" and "temporary" nuances, particularly addressing the "timely" principle by regulating the tax incentives under the MoF Regulation, instead of amending the tax law/code.
Instruments of Intervention	The primary concern is the limited relaxation policies option under the MoF Regulation. Also, echoing the objectives to provide liquidity support, the government needs to decide on tax payment relaxations that could provide adequate support without jeopardizing the budget structure.	Formulate relaxation policies mix to achieve the tax incentives' objectives.
Targeting and Delivery	The unprecedented nature of the pandemic means that there is no historical data. Meanwhile, the government needs to rely on forecasts/projections with lagging macroeconomic and administrative data. Also, the mobility restriction created administrative challenges: no walk-in services.	Collaboration with various stakeholders and provide a "blanket" approach or broad coverage, based on the industrial classification—instead of taxpayers' basis. Also, allow for higher error tolerance; thus, the government is ready for frequent amendment to address inclusion/exclusion errors.

short-term measures" (p. 31). In other words, the business support policy remained one of the primary tax policy measures throughout the pandemic. Also, the OECD (2020) reported that the main priority is "to support business cash flow" (p. 14), and deferral of tax payment is "the most common type of tax measure" (p. 15) to achieve that objective.

As part of the comprehensive stimulus package, the government implemented the COVID-19 tax incentives not as a sole policy solution but as complementary measures that supported other fiscal policy tools. In other words, the government could create fiscal policy combinations that maximize its effort to protect the people during the pandemic. As a result, the government explored the role of tax incentives to achieve other objectives, namely, supporting the health counter-measures programme and providing income support. In order to support the pandemic counter-measures, the government devised various tax relaxations and facilities to aid the provisions for medical devices, medications, protective equipment, as well as vaccines.[7] Meanwhile, the government also provided tax incentives as income support for impacted workers as a supplemental measure for household financial aid programmes. Coupled with the existing tax expenditure, the government laid out a comprehensive tax incentives programme for taxpayers during the challenging time of COVID-19.

7.3.2 Creating the Support Framework: Uptake and Enhance, Rather Than Reinvent

In general, the first role of tax support during an economic downturn is under the automatic stabilizer mechanism: reduced business activity will lower tax revenue (tax burden for the taxpayers). However, several factors impact the effectiveness of tax policy as an automatic stabilizer, such as tax revenue progressivity and tax size.[8] Echoing the previous discussion on suboptimum revenue collection in Indonesia, the automatic stabilizer would be inadequate, especially with the magnitude of the economic disruption caused by COVID-19. As a result, the discretionary measure is not complementary but a necessity.

Designing discretionary policy for an unprecedented crisis was very challenging for policymakers. From a tax policy perspective, there were no precedents where the government provided a comprehensive tax stimulus for the whole economy. Discretionary direct spending was somewhat more familiar: cash transfer, credit assistance, and subsidy. As an example, following the Asian Financial Crisis of 1997, the government opted for sector-specific tax incentives, such as the final tax regime for income from stock trading. Furthermore, under disaster events, e.g., natural disasters, the MoF relaxed the deductible grants and spending regulations, making the disaster-related expenditures eligible as deductible expenses for income tax calculation. In the new scenario, the government could not learn from previous experience to design COVID-19 tax incentives.

Meanwhile, prior to the pandemic, the government provided various tax expenditures and has officially reported the tax expenditure since 2018, covering more than 100 relaxation policies (134 in 2020). On average, the revenue forgone resulting from the tax expenditure amounted to around 1.65 per cent of GDP each year. The government classified the tax expenditure into four categories: (i) tax expenditure to support the business environment; (ii) tax expenditure to support small business; (iii) tax expenditure to support investment; and (iv) tax expenditure to support the public (welfare).

However, the current tax expenditure partially fulfils the 3T principle of tax stimulus. While we could argue about the "timely" and "targeted" nature of the tax expenditure, the "temporary" principle was hardly present in the pre-pandemic tax incentives. Most of the relaxation policies under tax expenditure came without an "expiration" period, which put the incentives under the "permanent" rather than a temporary measure category. Indeed, the government provided a limited-time tax holiday, but the temporary time frame was relatively lengthy—ten to fifteen years, not based on the economic recovery as discussed in the 3T principle. Therefore, the MoF needs to refine the current tax incentives landscape, aligning with the widescale impact of the pandemic and the 3T principle of fiscal stimulus to fulfil the objectives of the COVID-19 tax incentives (see Figure 7.4).

Also, given the dynamics and ever-changing nature of the pandemic, the government needs to provide immediate policy responses with readily available measures.[9] Rather than choosing a policy route that requires lengthy and stratified legal procedures, the government needs a policy instrument that is viable for frequent amendment and analogous to the "timely" principle of fiscal stimulus. In the pre-pandemic tax expenditure, the MoF provided relaxation policies based on multiple legislation "levels", from tax expenditures mandated by the tax law to those implemented under the MoF regulations (*Peraturan Menteri Keuangan*, or PMK), with

FIGURE 7.4
Comprehensive Tax Incentives during the Pandemic

Policy Measures

Permanent Support	Temporary Support, COVID-19 Incentives
Tax Expenditure Existing incentives prior to the pandemic: Revenue forgone resulted from "special" regulation and policy which differ from general tax regime, e.g., investment allowance, super deduction, and VAT exemptions	**Business Liquidity Support** Providing cash-flow support, helping business to stay afloat (primary objective) **Household Income Support** Providing supplemental income support through tax incentives for impacted workers (secondary) **Pandemic Countermeasure Support** Providing various tax facilities to support pandemic-related goods/services provisions, e.g., medications, vaccinee (secondary)

Administrative Measures
Additional measures to support policy relaxations, including deadlines relief (e.g., up to 3-month extension for income tax return in 2020, extended terminal operation period), digitalized services, and payment relaxation (e.g., excise).

different implications. Commonly, regulating tax relaxation under the tax law amendment allows the government to allocate a significant amount of relief, e.g., through a tax-rate cut, extensive exemptions, and changing the baseline. However, law amendments require a comprehensive legal procedure and review, which would be a digression from the "timely" principle of the fiscal stimulus.

On the other hand, while MoF regulations have limited scopes of administrative relaxation and withholding exemptions (payment deferrals), the legal procedures of amendments are relatively less stringent (only subject to legal harmonization). Also, the MoF regulations would allow the government to exercise and implement the "temporary" principle of fiscal stimulus, as it is possible to set an "expiration period". As a result, given the challenges of the pandemic, the MoF settled on channelling the COVID-19 tax incentives through MoF regulations (PMK).

7.4 NEXT CHALLENGE: SELECTING INSTRUMENTS OF INTERVENTION AND BALANCING BUDGETARY NEEDS

Once the government sets the legal procedures for the COVID-19 tax incentives, the next step is to decide on the type of incentives. From the government's perspective, there are at least two primary concerns regarding channelling the COVID-19 tax incentives: how MoF could cut the tax burden (providing cashflow support for businesses), and which type of tax payments could serve as intervention instruments.

As an automatic stabilizer, tax incidence will be parallel with the baseline, e.g., the tax burden will be lower as business activities dwindle during an economic downturn. When the businesses suffer losses, there will be no income tax due. However, in Indonesia (also in many jurisdictions[10]), taxpayers make various tax payments throughout the fiscal year, which might not necessarily reflect the final amount of tax due in the tax return. Moreover, the taxpayers in Indonesia were subject to withholding taxes for some transactions, which will serve as tax credits for end-of-fiscal-year calculations. Therefore, the government needed to provide a discretionary policy to reduce the interim tax burden, which is possible through MoF regulations.

There are several possible law-mandated discretionary tax rulings under the MoF regulations, each with different use cases and implications on the tax burden, revenue, and government spending. Under MoF regulations, there are three possible channels to reduce taxpayers' payments or burdens: deductions (*pengurangan*), exemptions from withholding taxes (*pembebasan*), and borne by the government (*ditanggung pemerintah*). For the first relaxation method, the MoF could provide a deduction or "discount" on taxpayers' tax credit payments, reducing their tax burden and lowering the tax revenue receipt for the current fiscal year. Meanwhile, for the withholding tax payments, the MoF could exempt taxpayers from withholding taxes due, which allows the taxpayers to receive the full amount of their transaction payment. However, because the taxpayers were exempt, there is no tax credit for their end-of-fiscal-year tax return calculation.[11] See Table 7.2.

Lastly, the MoF could bear the tax burden or pay the tax due (borne by the government instead of the taxpayers), which will allow the taxpayers to credit the tax payment in the end-of-fiscal-year tax return.

TABLE 7.2
Possible Discretionary Tax Rulings through MoF Regulation

Policy	*Impact on*			
	Taxpayers' Burden	*End of Fiscal Year Tax Return*	*Government Revenue*	*Government Spending*
Deduction	Lower	Neutral (no tax credit)	Lower	None
Exemption	Lower	Neutral (no tax credit)	Lower	None
Borne by the Government	Lower	Lower (taxpayers can credit in the Tax Return)	Neutral (accounted as a regular receipt)	Higher (require new allocation of spending for tax)

However, the "borne by the government" policy will require an additional spending budget to disburse the tax payment. As a result, even though the "borne by the government" incentives would provide more significant tax reductions for taxpayers, it would put considerable pressure on the budget structure.[12] The comparison for the three possible channels of tax incentives is as follows.

Along with the approaches to reduce taxpayers' burden, the MoF needs to decide on the intervention instruments, i.e., the type of payment to implement the discretionary measures. For the first objective of COVID-19 tax incentives, to provide cash flow support for businesses, two tax payments could serve as intervention instruments: income tax on imports (PPh 22 Imports) and monthly income tax payments (PPh 25).[13] In general, taxpayers are subject to PPh 22 Import Tax for import transactions, calculated as an income tax credit at the end-of-fiscal-year tax return. Also, the taxpayers are subject to PPh 25, a monthly tax credit payment for Personal Income Tax (PIT) and Corporate Income Tax (CIT), typically based on the previous fiscal year's income (see Figure 7.5).

Under normal circumstances, when taxpayers experience business losses, there will be no income tax due, and they will apply for tax refunds for their paid tax credits. However, the time gap between tax credit payments and the refund process will be very costly for taxpayers, especially during a crisis as businesses face solvency problems. Therefore, to help the taxpayers stay afloat, the government needed to relax the tax

FIGURE 7.5
Income Tax Revenue Structure in Indonesia

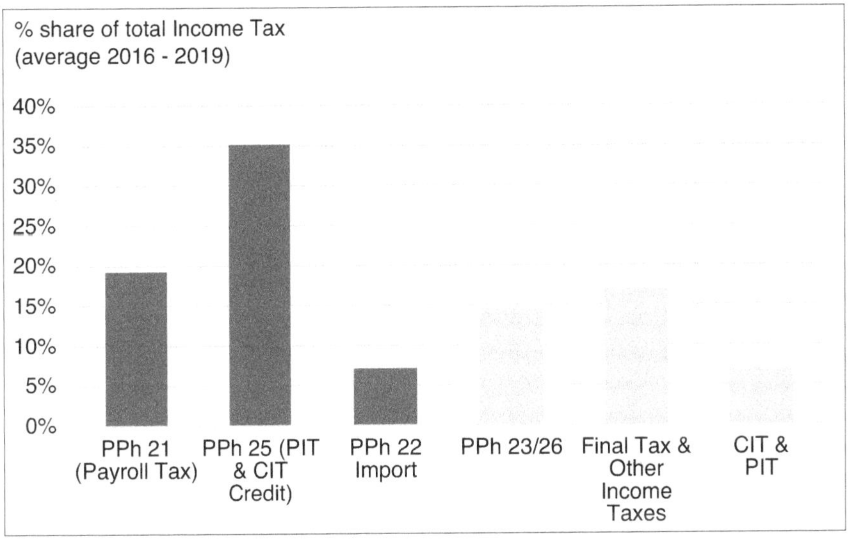

Source: Ministry of Finance and authors' calculations.

credit payment regulations, providing payment deferral through PPh 25 deductions and PPh 22 Import Tax exemptions. Nevertheless, PPh 25 remained one of the most significant sources of revenue for the government, making 100 per cent payment deductions a less viable policy option. Thus, the government settled for a 30 per cent deduction rate and subsequently expanded it to 50 per cent.

Additionally, the MoF needed to address the liquidity support policy for small businesses in Indonesia. Under the PEN Programme, the government devised various financial assistance measures, including tax incentives.[14] Prior to the pandemic, small businesses were subject to a presumptive tax regime, i.e., a 0.5 per cent final tax on turnover for taxpayers with an annual sales threshold of IDR4.8 billion (approximately US$330,000). Therefore, as part of the small business support programme, the government exempted small businesses from the 0.5 per cent final tax using the "borne by the government" measure.

Another relaxation policy that could aid the taxpayers' cash flow is the accelerated VAT refund procedures (also a common international practice during the pandemic[15]). Typically, it would take up to twelve months for taxpayers to receive their VAT refund, which has been part of the government tax reform agenda. Therefore, to alleviate taxpayers' liquidity problem and pilot the reform plan, the MoF also included the accelerated VAT refund as part of the COVID-19 tax incentives, slashing the processing time to one month.

In addition, there were two possible support channels which could be implemented in an attempt to provide additional income support for impacted households: direct tax intervention (i.e., income tax) or indirect tax facilities (i.e., tax on consumption or VAT). Arguably, the income tax approach is somewhat more straightforward and adheres to the "targeted" principle of stimulus, providing incentives based on the individual taxpayers. On the other hand, while the indirect tax policy could provide a more expansive coverage (higher forgone revenue), it would be challenging for the government to target the stimulus recipients.[16] Consequently, the government settled for the income tax intervention through payroll tax incentives[17] ("PPh 21" borne by the government) for impacted workers during the pandemic (see Figure 7.6).

Lastly, the government provided various relaxation policies that are "normally" applied to transactions as extra pandemic counter-measure activities. For procurement-related transactions, the MoF relieved importers from several levies such as VAT, "PPh 22 Imports", import duties, and excise

FIGURE 7.6
Payroll Tax as a Supplementary Income Support

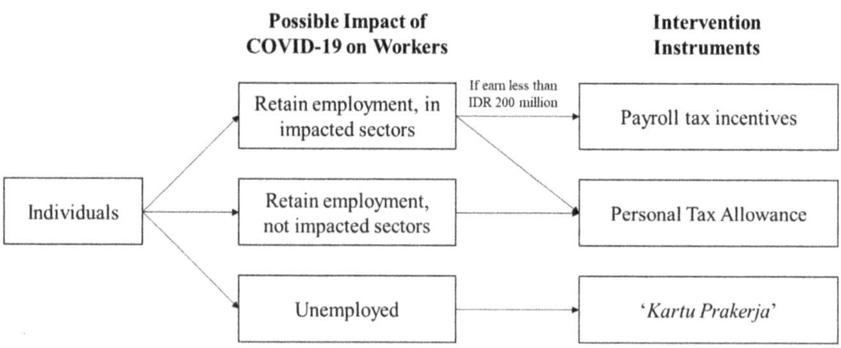

Source: Authors' calculations.

when importing hand sanitisers, testing kits, PPE, medical instruments, and related medications, including vaccines. Additionally, the government provided an additional income tax deduction for medical devices and supplies manufacturers. The MoF also provided payroll tax exemptions for healthcare workers' pandemic-related remuneration.

7.4.1 Last Identified Challenge: Targeting and Delivering

The next step in the tax incentives design process was defining the incentive recipients and the administrative procedures, especially during the COVID-19 containment phase. Following the primary objectives of the PEN Programme to protect the people, the general rule of incentives targeting would be providing incentives to impacted taxpayers. However, defining "impacted taxpayers" is a significant challenge without historical data, lead indicators, and robust projections, while the government needed to provide prompt liquidity support for the businesses. Also, identifying taxpayers would be impractical and biased given the varying impact of COVID-19 on each taxpayer, especially without timely information. Therefore, with such constraints, the MoF utilized "lagged" administrative data and collaborated with other government agencies and stakeholders to assess and define "impacted sectors"—a somewhat "blanket" approach which allowed taxpayers from listed sectors to qualify for tax incentives.

Under the coordinated action, the MoF formulated the sectoral assessment based on available administrative data and external insights from various stakeholders, made possible through the combined effort led by the Coordinating Ministry for Economic Affairs. Admittedly, the subsequent challenge to external feeding would be information filtering and calibrating for policy formulation, which is not immune to errors. Consequently, the government expects a relatively high error tolerance—inclusion and exclusion errors—for the COVID-19 tax incentives, requiring extensive monitoring and evaluation and translating into frequent regulation amendments (see Figure 7.7).

At the same time, the government formulated the stimulus for the payroll tax incentives as part of the coordinated policy action to support impacted households during the pandemic. Under the PEN Programme, the government provided financial support for lower-income households[18] and unemployment benefits (*Kartu Prakerja*[19]). Moreover, for low-income earners, the current personal income tax allowance of IDR54 million per

FIGURE 7.7
COVID-19 Tax Incentives Timeline, 2020–21

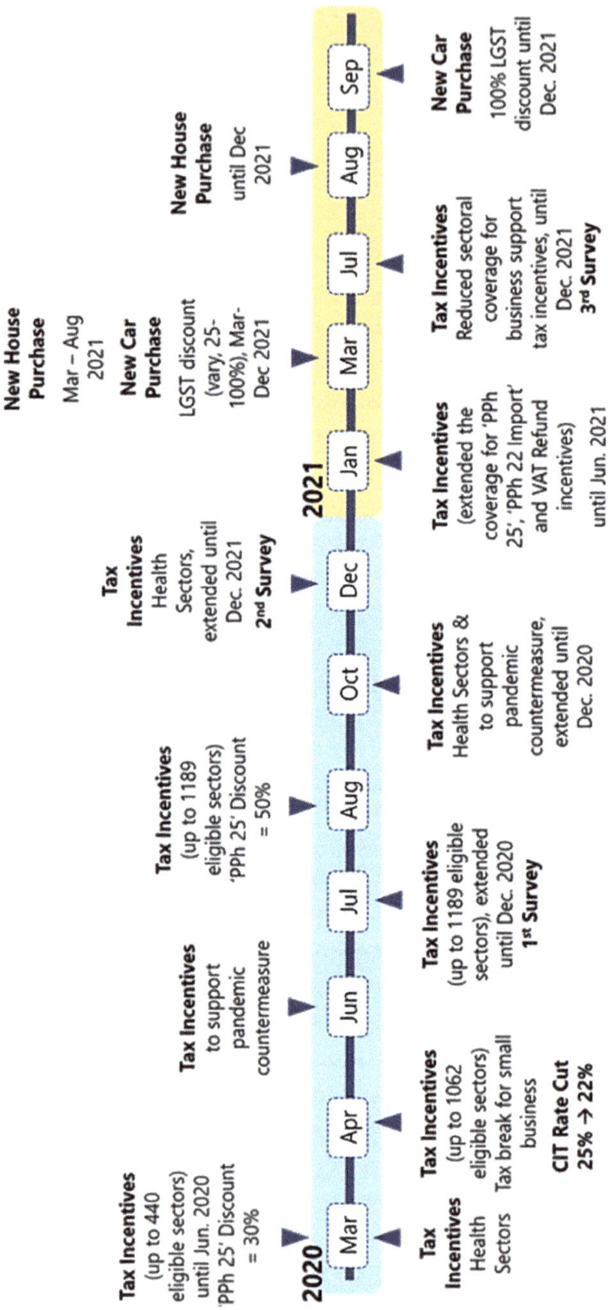

Source: Ministry of Finance and authors' calculations.

person is relatively fair,[20] i.e., there will be no income tax imposed for individuals who earn less than the annual allowance. Therefore, the payroll tax incentives will serve as policy extensions, targeting those workers who managed to retain their employment during the pandemic but facing the uncertainty of job continuity.

The next step in the payroll tax incentives planning was defining the "workers in need" or the "targeted" principle of fiscal stimulus. Following a coordinated assessment, the government decided to provide payroll tax incentives for workers from impacted sectors with qualifying annual income. While it seems "arbitrary", the government settled for an IDR200 million (around US$17,000) income threshold for workers eligible for the incentives—roughly 73 per cent of the workers based on payroll tax receipt in 2019. In other words, workers who earn no more than IDR200 million annually will be relieved from the payroll tax burden ("borne by the government").

Lastly, the challenges of incentive delivery were relatively less demanding than other policy considerations. However, without adequate planning, incentive delivery could affect the implementation of the stimulus, part of the "timely" principle. The primary concern during a pandemic is the restriction policy which disables the option for "normal" walk-in tax services. For the MoF, especially the DGT, the digitalization of tax administration has been the focal point of the current tax reform agenda. Thus, the shift towards digitalized services (web-based) was more straightforward, especially when the DGT implemented one-stop web services and digital signature technology in 2016.

Nevertheless, incentive delivery and administration require careful implementation, given the potential risk of abuse and fraud (OECD 2020, p. 29). Without an appropriate risk management system, the COVID-19 incentives would be vulnerable to fraudulent schemes, as the additional financial support might motivate struggling taxpayers to "file fraudulent claims" (OECD 2020, p. 29). Therefore, even though the primary objective of the COVID-19 tax incentives is to support the taxpayers, the MoF remains prudent in service delivery. In other words, the MoF makes it easy for taxpayers to apply for COVID-19 tax incentives while implementing periodic risk assessments and monitoring. Furthermore, the MoF established the Risk Assessment Committee to identify, monitor, and mitigate risks associated with COVID-19 tax incentives.[21] Aside from limiting non-compliance risks, another objective of the risk committee is to improve the accountability aspects, especially as the tax incentives will be subject to audit by the Audit Board of Indonesia (*Badan Pemeriksa Keuangan*, or BPK).

7.5 IMPLEMENTATION AND PROGRAMME OUTPUT

In March 2020, the government finalized the emergency legislation to allow for coordinated policy action to cushion the health and economic crisis of the pandemic (PERPU 1/2020).[22] Under the emergency legislation as a legal basis for extraordinary policies during the COVID-19 crisis, the government also implemented several tax policy reforms, with the CIT rate cut (from 25 per cent to 22 per cent) and cross-border digital services VAT collection being the two most significant changes. With the slashed CIT rate, the government's achievement is twofold: improving competitiveness[23] and alleviating the tax burden for businesses during the pandemic. Meanwhile, the legal basis for digital-service VAT collection allows the government to align with the international practice of taxing the consumption of digital goods.[24] Moreover, the digital-service VAT would serve as an additional revenue source during the pandemic, mainly from the digital and online businesses that thrive amidst mobility restrictions.

Along with the emergency legislation, the government also laid out the first pandemic-related tax incentives in March 2020—although the coverage was somewhat limited, mainly for manufacturing sectors. Arguably, the government focused the initial tax incentives package on providing fiscal intervention for supply disruption in the manufacturing sector and impacted sectors. However, as the pandemic accelerated and created vast socio-economic disruptions, the government promptly arranged a more comprehensive tax stimulus package. The MoF significantly extended the COVID-19 tax incentives coverage in the following month, coupled with the CIT rate cut and existing tax expenditures, providing an unprecedented stimulus to support taxpayers during a crisis.

The dynamics of the COVID-19 disruptions and the government's constraints in making robust assessments require continuous monitoring and evaluation to align current policy responses with the taxpayers' needs, echoing the "timely" and "targeted" principles of fiscal stimulus. As a result, the MoF made several amendments to the COVID-19 tax incentives in 2020–21, calibrating the incentives period, type of incentives, or coverage. During the initial implementation period, the government made significant revisions to extend the tax incentives support for impacted businesses. Subsequently, in mid-2021, the government began moderating the tax incentives coverage, focusing on industries with lagged recovery trends—fulfilling targeted and temporary principles of stimulus.

7.5.1 A Series of Extensions

Undeniably, due to the nature of the COVID-19 challenges that were extraordinary and uncertain, the government needed to be vigilant with its policy response. In March 2020, the government provided the initial COVID-19 tax incentives: payroll tax incentives, payment deferrals for PPh 22 Imports and PPh 25 (through deductions and exemptions), and accelerated VAT refunds. Under the first MoF regulation, the government provided six-month tax incentives for up to 440 business classifications[25] (payroll tax incentives). Nevertheless, following extensive assessments and surveys as part of the monitoring and evaluation programme, the MoF made four significant amendments to improve incentives coverage and lengthened the stimulus to the taxpayers.

Aside from improving the initial tax incentives package, the government also introduced additional facilities, namely import duties facilities (borne by the government), a tax break for small businesses, VAT relaxation on rental outlets for retailers, and industry support through big-ticket items incentives. In July 2020, the government exempted small businesses (annual turnover less than IDR4.8 billion or around US$330,000) from paying the 0.5 per cent turnover tax, which was extended until December 2021. Furthermore, in September 2020, several industries enjoyed import duties relief (duties borne by the government) which focused on manufacturing taxpayers operating within sectors selected by the Ministry of Industry. Also, as part of the small businesses support programme, the government provided VAT relaxation on rental properties for all retailers in August 2021.[26]

Lastly, in March 2021, the government decided to extend the industry support with big-ticket items incentives, automobiles and housing.[27] The objective was twofold: bolstering sectoral output and motivating consumption from higher-income earners.[28] In general, the preferred big-ticket items would satisfy several qualifications, such as significant job creation, labour absorption, high domestic inputs, and consisting of various supporting industries. For the automotive sector, the government provided a Luxury Goods Sales Tax (LGST or PPnBM) discount for the new car purchase, subject to eligibility qualifications from the Ministry of Industry. Meanwhile, the government provided a 100 per cent VAT discount for new houses and apartments with a maximum selling price of up to IDR2 billion (roughly US$139,000) and a 50 per cent discount for houses or apartments with a maximum selling price between IDR2 billion and IDR5 billion (around US$348,000)—for each taxpayer.

7.5.2 Planning the Exit Strategy

In the early months of 2021, several external indicators demonstrated positive trends, such as manufacturing activity, international trade, and social mobility. Thus, the MoF began to reassess the incentives coverage—part of the temporary principle of fiscal stimulus (see Table 7.3). For policymakers, it was challenging to provide robust sectoral assessments and projections amidst economic uncertainty. The MoF utilized various information sources: administrative data, surveys, external indicators, and, more importantly, a combined effort with external stakeholders. In collaboration with the Central Bank and Financial System Stability Committee, the MoF contributed to mapping the sectoral growth clusters during the pandemic as part of the sectoral assessment agenda (see Table 7.4).

TABLE 7.3
Changes for Initial COVID-19 Tax Incentives

Incentives	*Mar 2020*	*Apr 2020*	*Aug 2020*	*Jan 2021*
Sectoral coverage				
Payroll tax	440	1,062	1,189	1,189
"PPh 22 Import"[a]	102	431	721	721
"PPh 25"	102	846	1,013	1,013
Accelerated VAT Refund[a]	102	431	721	721
Incentives period	Until Aug 2020	Until Aug 2020	Until Dec 2020	Until Jun 2021
"PPh 25" deduction amount	30%	30%	50%	50%

Note: a. Also, includes the taxpayers registered as Perusahaan KITE (KITE Corporation, export-oriented industries).
Source: Ministry of Finance and authors' calculations.

TABLE 7.4
Sectoral Growth Cluster Analysis in Early 2021

	Classification: Resilience	*Growth Driver*	*Slow Starter*
Recovery: Fast	Food manufacturing, plantation, forestry, and ore mining	Communication, agriculture services, food, water	Coal, health, and education services
Moderate	Chemical industry	Various manufacturing, fisheries	Transportation, construction, automobile industry, trade, logistics
Slow		Real estate	Air transport, accommodation, financial sectors

Source: Ministry of Finance and authors' calculations.

In July 2021, the government revised the incentives coverage, focusing on lagged recovery industries, such as construction, accommodation, transportation, health, and education, while extending the incentives period until December 2021. Aside from payroll tax incentives, the government significantly reduced the coverage for other facilities: PPh 22 Imports (132 sectors remained), PPh 25 (216 sectors), and accelerated VAT refund (132 sectors). For the government, shrinking incentives coverage would be an instrumental part of the transition policy in the economic recovery phase (also, adhere to the "temporary" principle of fiscal stimulus).

7.5.3 Output and Implementation Gap

The government disbursed more than IDR140 trillion during the implementation period, a combination of foregone revenue and incentives expenditure ("borne by the government"). Based on the nominal, PPh 25 and PPh 22 Imports were the two most significant incentives, amounting to more than 56 per cent of the total incentives. The summary of the incentives output is shown in Table 7.5.

As previously discussed, the incentives policy design was highly challenging and prone to targeting miscalculations—both exclusions and inclusions were inevitable. The sectoral coverage extension is, arguably,

TABLE 7.5
Disbursed Tax Incentives, 2020–21

Incentives	*Amount (IDR)*	*US$ equivalent*	*Output*
CIT rate cut	18.47 trillion	1.29 billion	
'PPh 25'	47.45 trillion	3.31 billion	Around 67,000 taxpayers
'PPh 22 Import'	31.43 trillion	2.17 billion	Around 15,000 taxpayers
Accelerated VAT refund	13.7 trillion	956 million	Almost 3,000 taxpayers
Tax break for small-business	1.58 trillion	110 million	248,000 small businesses
VAT relaxation for outlet rent	180 billion	12 milion	900 retailers
Import levies relaxation	415 billion	25 million	162 taxpayers
Big-ticket items: Automobile	4.63 trillion	322 million	
Big-ticket item: Housing	0.8 trillion	56 million	
Payroll tax incentives	7.74 trillion	539 million	130,000 employers for around 2 million workers
Additional Tax Incentives to Support Pandemic Countermeasure	14.2 trillion	991 million	

Source: Ministry of Finance and authors' calculations.

part of the attempt to address the exclusion error as the government could include the previously "excluded" sectors in the following amendment. Another example of the government's attempt to address the exclusion error was during the moderation of incentives coverage in July 2021. The July 2021 amendment "excluded" the wholesale and retail sectors from the incentives eligibility. Consequently, the government reinstated the incentives eligibility for trading sectors in the subsequent regulation revision.

Aside from the exclusion error, the inclusion error was also prevalent during implementation. The "blanket" approach allows all the taxpayers operating within the eligible sector to qualify for incentives, although the performance and needs of businesses during a pandemic would vary. As a result, the incentives participation differs across the type of incentives, i.e., some incentives were more popular. One of the most distinct instances of inclusion error was in the tax break for small businesses. Even though the government relieved small businesses from paying turnover taxes in July 2020, the administrative data suggested that some thriving taxpayers were determined to pay the 0.5 per cent tax, notwithstanding the incentives (see Figure 7.8). Further inquiries suggested that the tax break might be insignificant for small businesses, especially those that experienced modest contraction during the pandemic.

7.6 SURVEYS AND OUTCOMES

The unprecedented nature of COVID-19 disruptions exacerbated the challenges for the government to formulate prompt policy responses. Therefore, as part of the policy monitoring and evaluation, the MoF initiated three surveys to capture the taxpayer's participation in the tax incentives programme, the pandemic impact on the businesses, and the taxpayers' expectations of future assistance. Coupled with administrative data (e.g., tax return), the survey result provided critical insights for the decision-maker, especially the MoF team, to keep up with the dynamic challenges of COVID-19.

7.6.1 Three Surveys: A Summary

The first survey was conducted online from 21 July to 7 August 2020, receiving almost 13,000 anonymous responses from strategic taxpayers.[29]

FIGURE 7.8
Small Business Turnover Tax Revenue Receipt, 2018–21

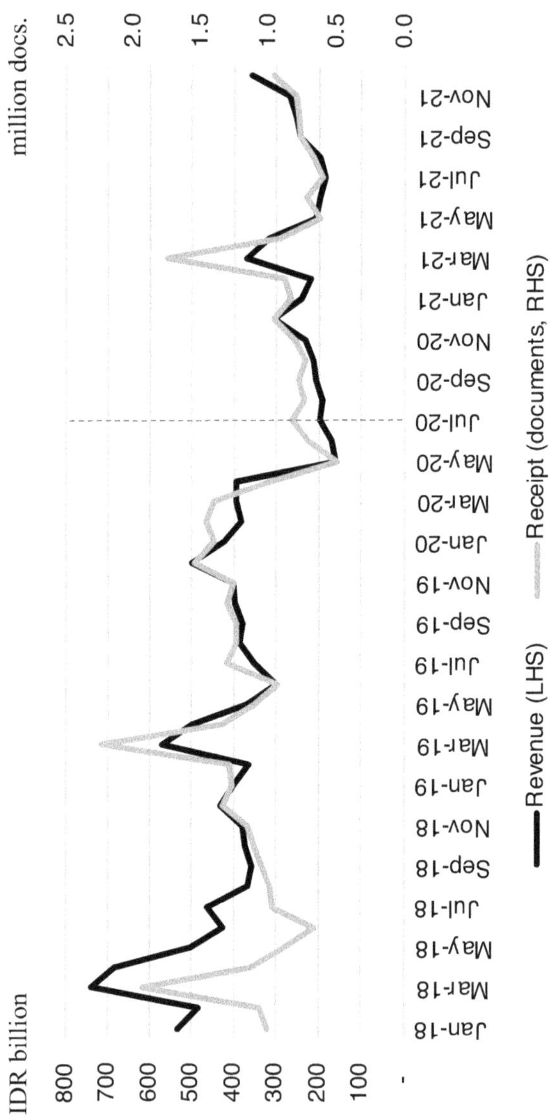

Source: Ministry of Finance and authors' calculations.

Through the first survey, the MoF focused on the pandemic's impact on taxpayers and the effectiveness of the initial COVID-19 tax incentives. For the pandemic impact, the survey respondents reported significant business disruptions, with 86 per cent of taxpayers experiencing lower business turnover—41 per cent had their sales slashed by more than half. The survey results echoed other COVID-19 surveys,[30] such as the World Bank[31] and Statistics Indonesia.[32] At the same time, around 88 per cent of the survey respondents reported a lower profit amidst moderate pressure on their business expenses (roughly 31 per cent of the taxpayers experienced higher costs during the pandemic, and 31 per cent reported no change in business expenses). Also, 73 per cent of taxpayers faced liquidity challenges stating that the cash-on-hand would suffice for a maximum of three months. Consequently, the respondents reported several strategies to support business continuity during the pandemic: lowered production or operation hours, reduced capacity, and employment-related strategy. The taxpayers implemented various temporary and permanent employment measures, such as temporary redundancy, furlough policy, lowered remuneration and rescheduled payroll.

On the COVID-19 tax incentives, the survey suggested that the incentives were generally favourably received, based on the participation rate and satisfaction rate. According to the survey, 65 per cent of the respondents enjoyed the COVID-19 tax incentives, and 70 per cent were "satisfied" (also "very satisfied") with the programme. Among the non-participants, 61 per cent claimed that the tax incentives were not the highest priority or were less informed about the programme. Also, only 28 per cent of the respondents claimed that the current tax incentives were sufficient. The respondents expected further assistance from the government, e.g., 24 per cent wanted more tax relaxation, 15 per cent asked for wage support programmes, and 14 per cent expected government financing support.

Subsequently, the MoF initiated the second online survey from 8 to 28 December 2020, reaching around 3,500 strategic taxpayers. The second survey focused on the incentives participation, benefits of the tax incentives, programme satisfaction, and further support needed. The survey further captured the COVID-19 impact: 92 per cent of the respondents struggled during the pandemic, and one-third of the taxpayers suffered a reduction of more than 30 per cent of their "normal" output.

For the tax incentives participation, around 58 per cent of the respondents were incentives participants, and both the participants and non-participants faced the information outreach challenges (30 per cent of the participants and 50 per cent of the non-participants). Based on the survey, the top-three incentive programmes were the payroll tax, PPh 25, and PPh 22 Imports, respectively. According to the second survey, the COVID-19 tax incentives fulfilled its primary objective: about two-thirds (66 per cent of the taxpayers) reported that the financial benefit (e.g., helping their cashflows) was the most significant impact. Nevertheless, the taxpayers wanted more non-fiscal stimulus from the government, such as wage support programmes, easing the business permit procedures, assisting electricity costs and credit support. Also, around 68 per cent of the survey respondents hoped the government could extend the COVID-19 fiscal incentives until December 2021. Lastly, the taxpayers expressed a positive outlook for the domestic economy over the next twelve months; around 62 per cent of the respondents reported either "positive" or "highly positive" expectations.

The MoF undertook the last round of the COVID-19 tax incentives survey between 12 and 30 July 2021, reaching around 7,500 anonymous strategic taxpayers. The third survey attempted to capture business conditions following one year of the pandemic and the impact of tax incentives on taxpayers. Also, the survey inquired about the challenges faced by the businesses and compared the participants and non-participants. Based on the survey, incentive participants were generally better off than those non-participants.

In short, aligned with previous surveys, 72 per cent of the respondents reported lower business activity, faced liquidity problems (30 per cent of the respondents), experienced reduced customer demand (47 per cent of the respondents), and maintained temporary employment measures as a business strategy to survive (30 per cent of the respondents). However, the uneven pressure hit small businesses significantly, especially those with less than IDR5 billion annual turnovers: They reported a cut of more than 30 per cent to output and insufficient cash flow. In contrast, respondents with a turnover of more than IDR100 billion (around USD7 million) reported expanded business activity and began to operate close to full capacity. Also, the survey suggested that taxpayers who received the COVID-19 tax stimulus reported relatively higher activity and sufficient cash flow.

Given the positive performance of tax incentive participants, the taxpayers' satisfaction level remained high, and almost two-thirds, 64 per cent, enjoyed the financial benefit of the COVID-19 tax incentives. Based on the survey, the highest incentive participation rate was the payroll tax incentives (75 per cent), followed by PPh 25 discounts and PPh 22 Imports—similar to the result from the second survey. However, compared to the previous surveys, only 51 per cent of the respondents enjoyed the incentives, suggesting that the recovered businesses became less dependent on the tax stimulus.

Lastly, in line with the previous two, the third survey indicated that the taxpayers expected a tax incentives extension until December 2021 (88 per cent of the respondents). The respondents also reported the need for non-fiscal support, such as wage support, easing of business licensing, electricity bill support, and credit assistance. In contrast to the previous surveys, the respondents reported a less confident outlook, with 36 per cent of the taxpayers having an optimistic expectation for the next six months—arguably, affected by the escalating COVID-19 cases (Delta wave), which peaked from mid-July to August.

7.6.2 Administrative Data to Complement the Surveys

Aside from the survey data analysis, the MoF team utilized tax administration data, such as tax returns, tax payment records and tax incentives administration, to assess the COVID-19 challenges and the impact of the tax stimulus on business survivability. Following the survey's approach, the administrative data analysis compared the incentives' participants and non-participants—where the non-participants served as counterfactuals for the participants' business performance.

The administrative data confirmed the COVID-19 disruption: business had had its business output slashed and redundancies were increasing. During the pandemic, 67 per cent of the taxpayers lost more than a quarter of their annual turnovers, while at the same time, 75 per cent of the taxpayers reported lower inputs. Also, echoing the survey result, small businesses suffered greatly due to the pandemic, especially those with less than IDR5 billion in annual sales. Accordingly, around 70 per cent of taxpayers, mainly small businesses, downsized both their full-time and part-time employment. The tax return data suggested that redundancy in full-time employment was relatively modest, less than 25 per cent of the "normal" capacity.

The downsizing happened more significantly in the part-time workforce—taxpayers reported a 25–75 per cent layoff rate. Fortunately, the administrative data suggested that the payroll tax incentives positively impacted the redundancy trend. The employers who participated in the payroll tax incentives programme reported a lower redundancy rate than those non-participants. Of the incentive participants, the smaller-sized business (up to IDR25 billion [around US$1.7 billion] annual turnover) reported a lower employment change during the pandemic.

The other tax incentives packages, i.e., PPh 25, PPh 25 Imports, and accelerated VAT refunds, helped business survivability or, at a minimum, alleviated the COVID-19 pressure on the taxpayers. For the PPh 25 stimulus, the participants reported a smaller contraction in domestic sales, annual turnover, and local purchases. At the same time, the PPh 22 Imports participants reported a more moderate impact on sales (including domestic sales), imports, and local purchases. Lastly, the accelerated VAT refund stimulus participants reported a smaller contraction in turnover and local purchases.

7.7 LESSON LEARNT

Fiscal support became the primary policy to protect the people and cushion the economy during the challenging time of the COVID-19 disruption. As part of the fiscal policy, the revenue side also played a significant role, especially in assisting affected businesses and bolstering economic recovery. Through the MoF, the government of Indonesia provided various revenue-related measures in the form of the existing tax expenditure and temporary COVID-19 tax incentives.

By implementing the COVID-19 tax incentives, the MoF experienced invaluable policy takeaways that could become robust building blocks in harnessing the potential of tax revenue policy as a critical fiscal instrument. One of the main takeaways is that prompt and targeted tax incentives can work in difficult times, e.g., helping impacted businesses during the pandemic. Following the three principles of fiscal stimulus, we expect the incentives (tax incentives) to be timely, targeted, and temporary. As a result, the government timed the COVID-19 tax incentives as one of the earliest policy responses in mid-March 2020, just after Indonesia's first confirmed COVID-19 case. Also, the government attempted to target the impacted businesses and taxpayers through regulation updates, aligning the incentives' coverage with the dynamic challenges of the pandemic. As for the accelerated VAT refunds, the "piloting" phase resulted in favourable outcomes, and the MoF implemented the incentives as part of the tax expenditures ("permanent" incentive measure).

Another lesson learnt during the COVID-19 tax incentives implementation is that collaboration with external stakeholders strengthens the government's analysis and assessment of the taxpayers' situation to allow the delivery of a targeted stimulus programme. Without such collaboration during the unprecedented crisis of COVID-19, the government could make an untimed and less efficient policy intervention. At the same time, comprehensive analysis through primary data collection (surveys) and administrative data is an essential process to provide compelling evidence for the policymaker. Besides, for the MoF, the COVID-19 tax incentives surveys were the first large-scale, multi-round polls for policy evaluation purposes.

Lastly, the challenging situation of COVID-19 required a fully digital tax incentives administration. For the first time, the taxpayers could apply for incentives, monitor the process, receive the results, and submit the required documentation electronically in an integrated web-based account. The technology-led tax incentives administration impact is twofold: significantly reducing the paperwork for the taxpayers and providing effective monitoring for the government. Altogether, the policy and administrative experience of the COVID-19 tax incentives set a new benchmark for policy formulation and evaluation of future tax policy instruments in Indonesia, e.g., tax expenditure.

7.8 WAY FORWARD

At the end of 2021, business activities and macroeconomic conditions remained robust, suggesting a continued recovery trend post-Delta wave in the third quarter. From a tax revenue perspective, expansive business indicators directly translated into an expansive revenue baseline and an opportunity to recover the slashed tax ratio due to the pandemic. In 2020, the revenue-to-GDP ratio reached an all-time low level from the automatic stabilizers and discretionary tax incentives (see Figure 7.9). However, even though the government expected to collect lower revenue due to COVID-19 disruption, tax revenue remains an integral part of the national budget. Therefore, while the government ensured the impacted businesses received comprehensive fiscal support during the pandemic, the tax authorities maintained the taxpayers' assessment to ensure they complied and paid their fair share, especially those who grasped new opportunities as a result of COVID-19. Also, in April 2020, PERPU 1/2020 enabled the DGT to collect VAT from cross-border digital services and intangibles.[33] In

FIGURE 7.9
Tax Revenue in 2020–21 (percentage of GDP)

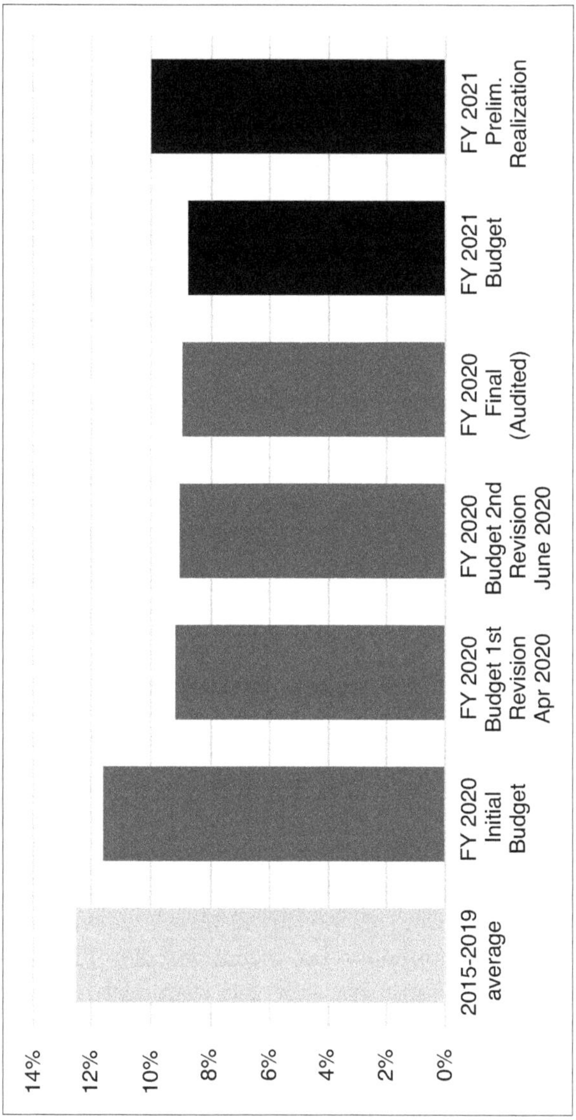

Source: Ministry of Finance.

hindsight, the preliminary ruling served as one of the legal frameworks for the upcoming implementation of Pillars 1 and 2.

Following on from the momentum of an expanding revenue trend and harnessing the experiences gained from the COVID-19 tax incentives, the government "resumed" the tax reform agenda in the latter months of 2021. For the government, the tax reform will serve as part of the exit policies to support the recovery phase, raising revenue to restore the budget.[34] Therefore, the government formulated the latest tax policy reform under the Harmonized Tax Law Bill (*Undang-Undang Harmonisasi Peraturan Perpajakan*, or HPP), ratified and implemented in 2022. Some of the policy highlights are an increased VAT rate (from 10 per cent to 11 per cent) and improved PIT progressivity for higher-income earners. Nevertheless, the HPP is not a panacea for improving the tax revenue in the long term but rather a critical stepping stone for comprehensive tax reform post-pandemic in Indonesia.

APPENDIX 7.1
Summary of COVID-19 Tax Incentives

No.	*Tax Incentives*	*"Normal" Condition*	*Incentives*
Tax Incentives to support household demand (purchasing power)			
1.	Payroll tax incentives for workers who earn less than IDR200 million a year (around US$17,000)	Subject to 5–10% progressive income tax (withholding tax)	No tax for workers from eligible sectors
Tax Incentives to support business			
2.	CIT Rate Cut	A 25% headline rate	Typically 22%, all taxpayers
3.	PPh 25 (monthly income tax payment) discount	Typically based on the total income tax due in the previous tax return, divided by 12	30% discount, then increased to 50% from August 2020, eligible sectors
4.	PPh 22 Import relaxation	Typically 2.5% on the import value	No tax for eligible sectors and export-oriented taxpayers
5.	Import duties relaxation	Single rate, based on the commodities and ranging from 5% to 30%	No tax for eligible sectors, export-oriented taxpayers, and qualified industries
6.	Accelerated VAT Refund	Maximum time to process VAT Refund: 12 months	A maximum of one month for eligible sectors
7.	Income tax break for taxpayers with an annual turnover of no more than IDR5 billion (around US$348 thousand).	0.5% final tax on turnover	No tax
8.	VAT exemption on property rental for retailers	10%	No tax

Tax incentives to support pandemic countermeasures			
9.	Import tax relaxation for pandemic-related importation, e.g., PPE, medication, vaccine, testing kits	Vary but typically includes VAT (10%), PPh 22 Import (2.5%), Import Duties (vary), and Excise (if applicable).	No tax
10.	Income tax exemption for healthcare workers' remuneration	Subject to withholding with progressive rate, ranging from 5% to 30%	No tax
11.	Deductible grants	Not deductible expenses	Deductible (if qualified as grants/gifts for pandemic countermeasure purposes)
12.	Additional income deduction for PPE manufacturers	—	30% additional deduction based on the PPE's direct production cost
Tax incentives for big-ticket items			
13.	LGST discount for new car purchases	Vary, typically ranging from 15% to 50%	Up to 100% discounts for qualified vehicles based on engine size and local content
14.	VAT discount for new house purchase (one per taxpayer)	10% VAT	100% discount (house price less than IDR2 billion [around US$139,000]), 50% discount (house price up to IDR5 billion [US$348,000])

Notes

1. For example, see the World Bank's *Indonesia Public Expenditure Review: Spending for Better Results*, "Indonesia's overall level of public spending is low relative to other emerging and developing market economies" (World Bank 2020, p. 24).
2. Ibid.
3. The two reform programmes signified the change of Indonesia's taxation landscape: the 1980s reform introduced "modern" taxes (e.g., income tax and value-added tax) and self-assessment system in Indonesia, while the 2000s reform revamped the tax authority organization and strengthen the computerized tax administration. Besides, there were several other smaller-scale reform programmes which create policy and/or administration changes but were less comparable (in terms of scale) to the previous two.
4. This is part of the Ease of Doing Business (EoDB) indicators, which has been discontinued in 2021 (see https://www.worldbank.org/en/programs/business-enabling-environment/doing-business-legacy). The Paying Taxes indicators measure several dimensions, such as number of payments, time to comply, tax rates, tax refund, and post-filing.
5. A more comprehensive discussion about the digitalization during the pandemic will be provided in Chapter 17: New Ways of Working: Bureaucracy Reforms.
6. The dilemma is largely aligned with OECD's comments on the tax measures during the pandemic: "these policies should be carefully targeted to provide the best balance of economic support and fiscal sustainability" (OECD 2020, p. 26).
7. The topic is discussed further in Chapter 2: Ensuring Indonesians Are Safe from COVID-19.
8. For example, see Auerbach and Feenberg (2000) on the role of federal taxes as automatic stabilizers.
9. Similar challenges and discussions are also provided in Chapter 6: Turning Bottlenecks into Breakthroughs.
10. For example, in the UK large corporations need to make quarterly payments based on estimated profits, and in Australia, corporate taxpayers are subject to corporate tax instalments on a monthly or quarterly basis.
11. In practice, the *pengurangan* and *pembebasan* mechanism would be equivalent with the payment deferral or the common tax policy practice to provide liquidity support during pandemic (OECD 2020, p. 15).
12. One of the primary concerns is the mandatory education spending (20 per cent of the budget). Because the "borne by the government" scheme will result in tax revenue recognition, it will also trigger the mandatory budget allocation for

education—even though the revenue is based on the government's spending for tax incentives. Therefore, the "borne by the government" is a double-whammy for the budget structure: no "real" revenue inflows (only accounting recognition) and will trigger additional spending on top of the tax incentives spending allocation.

13. Based on the revenue structure, "PPh 23/26" is also a significant withholding tax, but the payments were generally due for passive and/or contractual incomes, e.g., rent, interest, and royalty (rather than the transaction-based "PPh 22 Import"). Therefore, the "PPh 23/26" payments are, arguably, not based on projected incomes, but "real" income, compared to "PPh 22 Import" and "PPh 25 payments".
14. The topic of how the government provided support for the SMEs is further discussed in Chapter 14: Weathering and Recovering from the Pandemic: Lessons Learnt from MSMEs in Indonesia.
15. OECD (2020), p. 16.
16. In Indonesia, value-added taxes (VAT) and sales tax on luxury goods (LGST) contribute to around 40 per cent of total tax revenue. Thus, the relaxation for VAT would be significant in terms of forgone revenue, especially as the only possible channel of stimulus is through "borne by the government" scheme. However, the VAT facilities will be similar to "product-specific subsidies" which could trigger a consumption shift, making the incentives less targeted. Alternatively, the government could attempt for sector-specific products indirect taxes incentives to make the stimulus somewhat more "targeted".
17. Officially, the incentives were provided for Income Tax Article 21 or withholding tax for employment income. In general, this type of tax resembles the payroll tax or pay-as-you-earn mechanism for periodical income earners (typically monthly income). Therefore, for simplicity, we will use the payroll tax terminology in this chapter.
18. The topic of social protection during a pandemic will be extensively discussed in another chapter in this book, Chapter 8: Protecting the People.
19. This topic will be discussed in a dedicated chapter of this book, Chapter 9: *Kartu Prakerja*: A Breakthrough for Boosting Labour Market Productivity and Social Assistance Inclusiveness.
20. The annual personal income tax allowance of IDR54 million is just below the GDP per capita (2019, IDR59 million) and, in most of the regions, higher than the minimum wage level.
21. This topic is also discussed, in detail, in Chapter 6: Turning Bottlenecks into Breakthroughs.
22. PERPU 1/2020 enables various policy breakthroughs during the COVID-19 period, one of which is the relaxation of the budget deficit threshold, allowing expansionary fiscal policy without the 3 per cent-of-GDP deficit constraint.

Through the emergency legislation of PERPU 1/2020, it is possible for the MoF to provide more extensive discretionary COVID-19 tax incentives. The PERPU 1/2020 legislation and other policy breakthrough are discussed in Chapter 3: Maintaining Macroeconomic Stability during the Pandemic.

23. Prior to the CIT rate cut, Indonesia's CIT rate of 25 per cent is higher than the OECD and EU-22 average (22.9 per cent and 22 per cent, respectively), although relatively comparable to neighboring countries.
24. Several jurisdictions have imposed VAT collection on domestically consumed digital goods/services, such as the EU (2015), Australia (2017), Malaysia (2020), and Singapore (2020). The practice also adheres to the OECD's VAT/GST guidelines: "[f]or consumption tax purposes internationally traded services and intangibles should be taxed according to the rules of the jurisdiction of consumption." (OECD 2017, p. 38).
25. In Indonesia, the business/industrial classifications for tax purposes is a modified version of Statistics Indonesia's (National Bureau of Statistics) business classification which is adopted from the UN's International Standard Industrial Classification of All Economic Activities (ISIC). There are around 1,400 classes (codes) under the latest tax administration's business classifications.
26. Under "normal" conditions, the rental charge on a retail outlet is subject to 10 per cent VAT.
27. The incentives design, output, and outcomes will be discussed in detail in Chapter 15: Corporate Sector Performance during the COVID-19 Pandemic.
28. Based on the data from Indonesia Deposit Insurance Corporation (*Lembaga Penjamin Simpanan*, or LPS), saving accounts with a balance of more than IDR5 billion (approximately US$348,000) experienced robust growth during the pandemic—even higher than the pre-pandemic level. On a nominal basis, the high saving accounts recorded a double-digit growth since July 2020 while other saving groups dwindled. Thus, the higher income households were, arguably, better off or at least preserved their spending capacity during the pandemic.
29. For survey respondents, the MoF employed an email blast approach to all strategic taxpayers (typically the top 300–500 taxpayers in each tax office throughout Indonesia, 352 tax offices). Admittedly, the respondents and coverage would be biased towards those taxpayers who are administered within the tax system. However, we will argue that the survey approach is more relevant for the tax incentives context: incentives are provided for taxpayers who pay and remain compliant with the tax regulation during the pandemic. Also, we employed a representativeness test to compare the respondents and our target population in the tax administration. Based on the turnover size, industrial classification, and geographical distribution, the respondents' data well represent our target population. Equally important, around 73 per cent of

the respondents are from the managerial level (decision maker), which would improve the survey reliability.

30. For example, 73 per cent of the PEN respondents experience solvency problems (77 per cent based on the World Bank survey); 50 per cent of the PEN respondents experience lower demand (70–80 per cent based on the BPS survey).
31. High-Frequency Monitoring of COVID-19 Impacts, Rounds 1–6 2020–2021; Round 1 data collection from 1 to 17 May 2020, https://microdata.worldbank.org/index.php/catalog/3938
32. Survey on COVID-19 impact on businesses *(Survei Dampak COVID-19 Terhadap Pelaku Usaha)*, first survey period on 10–26 July 2020, https://www.bps.go.id/publication/2020/09/15/9efe2fbda7d674c09ffd0978/analisis-hasil-survei-dampak-COVID-19-terhadap-pelaku-usaha.html
33. The new regulation generally adheres to the OECD VAT standards on digitally traded services/intangibles which have been implemented by 76 countries as of 2021. The MoF, through the Directorate General of Taxes, periodically issued the list of appointed companies to collect the VAT. As of 31 December 2021, there were 87 mandated companies to withhold the VAT.
34. This is also aligned with the OECD (2020) commentary "[a]s countries look to restore their public finances, tax will have a key role to play, both in terms of revenue levels and of the tax structure, which may need to be adapted to a post-COVID era" (p. 42).

References

Auerbach, Alan J., and Daniel Feenberg. 2000. "The Significance of Federal Taxes as Automatic Stabilizers". NBER Working Paper Series. Working Paper 7662. https://www.nber.org/system/files/working_papers/w7662/w7662.pdf

de Mooij, Ruud, Suahasil Nazara, and Juan Toro. 2018. *Implementing a Medium-Term Revenue Strategy. In Realizing Indonesia's Economic Potential*, edited by Luis E. Breuer, Jaime Guajardo, and Tidiane Kinda, pp. 109–40. Washington, DC: International Monetary Fund.

Directorate General of Taxes. *Insentif Pajak Pandemi COVID-19 Tahun 2020: Fasilitas dan Dampaknya Terhadap Dunia Usaha* (in Indonesian). Jakarta: Directorate General of Taxes. 2021.

Elmendorf, Douglas W., and Jason Furman. 2008. *If, When, How: A Primer on Fiscal Stimulus*. Washington, DC: The Brooking Institution.

Ministry of Finance of the Republic of Indonesia (MoF). 2021. *Merekam Pandemi COVID-19 dan Memahami Kerja Keras Pengawal APBN* (in Indonesian). Jakarta: The MoF.

OECD. 2020. *Tax and Fiscal Policy in Response to the Coronavirus Crisis: Strengthening Confidence and Resilience*. OECD.

Summers, Lawrence. 2008. "Fiscal Stimulus Issue: Testimony before the Joint Economic Committee". http://larrysummers.com/wp-content/uploads/2012/10/1-16-08_Fiscal_Stimulus_Issues.pdf

Taylor, Jason E., and Andrea Castillo. 2015. "Timely, Targeted, and Temporary?". *An Analysis of Government Expansions over the Past Century*. Virginia: Mercatus Research, Mercatus Center at George Mason University.

World Bank. 2020. *Indonesia Public Expenditure Review: Spending for Better Result*. The World Bank.

PART IV

Expenditure Side (Human Capital)

8

Protecting the People

Wahyu Utomo, Sri Kusumastuti Rahayu,
Irma Marlina and Sudarno Sumarto

8.1 BACKGROUND

At the end of 2019, the world was stunned by the emergence of an alarming new virus. After numerous failed attempts to contain it, by March 2020 the World Health Organization finally recognized COVID-19 as a pandemic. The rapid spread of the virus gave little time for governments all over the world to brace for its impact. While some governments bought time by implementing travel restrictions, the Indonesian government, fearing an economic slowdown, initially played down the virus' threat by running a travel campaign in February 2020. However, as the COVID-19 death toll crept up, by March it was clear that the virus was a real threat. By April 2020 when the virus has spread to all of Indonesia's thirty-four provinces, the government finally implemented social restrictions in the Greater Jakarta area.

As people reduced their mobility, the economy slowed, and many breadwinners lost their income. Amidst such a condition, an increase in the poverty rate was expected. Although initially the poverty rate projections forecast that Indonesia's years of poverty alleviation efforts may be reversed as people fell into poverty, the country did better than expected. The poverty rate was projected to be as high as 13.38 per cent (World Bank 2020a). The actual outcome, however, defied many of these projections.

Considering that Indonesia experienced a significant economic contraction of up to –5.32 per cent in the second quarter of 2020, it was remarkable how Indonesia's poverty rate only climbed up to 9.78 per cent in March 2020 from its low of 9.22 per cent before the pandemic. This figure would then peak at 10.19 per cent in September 2020 (Statistics Indonesia 2020). By September 2021, Indonesia has returned to a single-digit poverty rate, which equated to 1.04 million people moving out of poverty (Statistics Indonesia 2022). International institutions, such as the World Bank, attributed the Indonesian government's success in keeping the country's poverty rate down to the many social assistance and social safety net programmes deployed throughout the pandemic.

When the pandemic struck, Indonesia was in a better position than in 1998 when the Asian Financial Crisis shook its economy. Before the COVID-19 pandemic, Indonesia already had a running social protection system. Despite its shortfalls, such as inaccurate beneficiary lists, this social protection system could be mobilized to dampen the pandemic's impact on the poor. While the 1998 crisis mainly impacted the poor, what was different this time is that the impact of the crisis had extended beyond the poor. As economic uncertainty and labour vulnerability were on the rise, citizens at every income level except the richest 5 per cent experienced negative income growth between September 2019 and September 2020 (Statistics Indonesia 2021). With the pandemic's widespread economic impact, the government saw the need to expand social assistance to the middle class by mobilizing its social protection system and expanding its coverage for crisis mitigation on a scale like never before.

This chapter lays out how the Indonesian government mobilized its social protection system to provide a social safety net to cushion the pandemic's socio-economic impact. This chapter will also evaluate the extent of the government's success in making its social protection system a key instrument in its crisis mitigation strategy. The chapter will conclude by reflecting upon the lessons learnt from the COVID-19 pandemic, particularly on how Indonesia could build a social protection system that is better at protecting its citizens from vulnerabilities.

8.2 INDONESIAN SOCIAL PROTECTION PROGRAMMES BEFORE COVID-19

Before the pandemic, Indonesia implemented social protection programmes which fell into two main groups: the non-contributory social assistance schemes to protect the poor and at-risk families, and the contributory social insurance schemes. These non-contributory programmes consist of assistance targeted towards families and individuals based on certain criteria, such as children, the elderly and people with disability. Meanwhile, the contributory scheme consists of social insurance for health and employment. Details of the programmes are provided in Table 8.1. This section will review key programmes that make up the Indonesian social protection system.

The Indonesian government's non-contributory social assistance programmes are transfers mainly aimed at the poor and vulnerable. These programmes are designed to reduce their spending burdens and lift them out of poverty. For programmes targeted at families, the Indonesian government runs the *Program Keluarga Harapan* (Family Hope Programme, or PKH) conditional cash transfer (CCT) and the *Program Sembako* food assistance. Meanwhile, a range of programmes targeted at individuals was rolled out to cover individuals throughout their life cycle as they pass through different life stages, among others *Program Indonesia Pintar* (Cash Transfer for the Poor Students), *Asistensi Sosial Lanjut Usia* (Social Assistance for the Elderly) and *Asistensi Sosial Penyandang Disabilitas* (Social Assistance for People with Disability).

Due to the means-tested nature of the non-contributory programmes in the Indonesian social protection system, some kind of targeting mechanism is needed. Since 2012, the government used the Unified Database (*Data Terpadu Kesejahteraan Sosial*, or DTKS) as a targeting instrument for many of its social assistance and fully subsidized social insurance for health (*Penerima Bantuan Iuran Jaminan Kesehatan Nasional*, or PBI-JKN) programmes. Under the management of the Ministry of Social Affairs, the DTKS lists the country's bottom 40 per cent households to determine eligibility for a range of government transfer programmes.[1]

PKH was launched in 2007 as the country's flagship conditional cash transfer programme for the country's poorest families. PKH beneficiary families would receive a certain amount of benefit that is given to the mother in families or the women in the household for a maximum of four

TABLE 8.1
Indonesian Social Protection Programmes in 2019

Key Non-contributory—Social Assistance Programmes

Programme	*Aim*	*Coverage*	*Benefit Level (per month*)*	*Government Budget**	*Implementing Ministry/ Institution*
Sembako/BPNT	Food assistance	15.6 million families (bottom 25% of the population)	IDR150,000	IDR28.1 trillion	Ministry of Social Affairs (MoSA)
Program Keluarga Harapan (PKH)	Conditional cash transfer (CCT) for health and education	10 million families (bottom 20% of the population)	Depends on the number of family members as component of PKH conditionality, currently is a maximum of 4 (either pregnant women, early childhood, school-aged children, elderly 70+, and/or people with disability: • See Table 8.2	IDR29.1 trillion	MoSA
Program Indonesia Pintar (PIP)	Support personal expenses of education	21.7 million students aged 6–21 years (bottom 25% of the population)	Depends on the education level • See Table 8.2	IDR11.1 trillion	Ministry of Education, Culture, Research, and Technology Ministry of Religious Affairs

Kartu Indonesia Pintar (KIP) *Kuliah*	Support personal expenses of tertiary education	819,000 students	2020: Average Tuition Fee IDR2.4 million per semester Living allowance: IDR700,000 per month 2021: Tuition fee: Max IDR2.4 million (Prodi C), IDR4 million (Prodi B) IDR12 million (Prodi A) Living Allowance: 5 cluster areas: IDR800,000 – IDR1.4 per month	IDR6.7 trillion	Ministry of Education, Culture, Research, and Technology
BANTU LU/ ASLU/ ASLUT *Bantuan Bertujuan Lanjut Usia*	Assistance for elderly	25,430 elderly	IDR200,000	IDR141 billion	MoSA
ASPDB (*Asistensi Sosial Penyandang Disabilitas Berat*)	Assistance for people with severe disability	28,383 people with severe disability (all ages)	IDR200,000	IDR317 billion	MoSA

continued on next page

TABLE 8.1 — *cont'd*

Contributory—Social Insurance programs					
Programme	*Aim*	*Coverage*	*Premium/Contribution Level*	*Government Budget*	*Implementing Ministry/ Institution*
Jaminan Kesehatan Nasional (National Health Insurance)	Social Insurance for Health	Total: 235,7 million people (2021) 32 million members are not active	Clause 34 Perpres No. 64/2020, the monthly contribution Class 3: IDR35,000 Class 2: IDR100,000 Class 1: IDR150,000	None	*BPJS Kesehatan*/ Social Security Agency for Health
		PBI JKN (fully subsidized): 96.8 million people – bottom 40% of the population	IDR42,000	IDR48.8 trillion	• *BPJS Kesehatan*/ Social Security Agency for Health • Ministry of Health
Jaminan Hari Tua (JHT)	Old age savings	50.7 million members Around 40.8% of members are inactive (TNP2K 2021)	PPU* 5.7% of the salary: 2% paid by the workers and 3.7% paid by the employers/company PBPU[b]: 2%	None	*BPJS Ketenagakerjaan*/ Social Security Agency for Employment
Jaminan Kecelakaan Kerja (JKK)	Work injury compensation		The lowest contribution for JKK-JKM is IDR16,800,		
Jaminan Kematian (JKM)	Survivor's benefits				

Jaminan Pensiun (JP)	Pension insurance		Only for PPU: 1% paid by the workers and 2% paid by employers/ companies).		
Jaminan Kehilangan Pekerjaan	Unemployment benefit	PPU[a] members who lost the jobs	Monthly salary for a maximum of 6 months. The first 3 months: 45% of salary and the next 3 months: 25% of the salary (with a limitation of the wage threshold ceiling at a maximum of IDR5 million) (PP No. 37/2021)	From other social insurance programme	*BPJS Ketenagakerjaan*/ Social Security Agendy for Employment

Notes:
* Average exchange rate 2019 US$1 = IDR14,510
a. PPU (*Peserta Penerima Upah)* = wage-earner members (It is mandatory for the PPU to participate in all programmes under the social insurance for employment programmes, excluding civil servants, military personnel and the police, while the participation of PBPU is voluntary.)
b. PBPU/*Peserta Bukan Penerima Upah* = non-wage earner members (For PBPU who wish to contribute to JHT, they must join JKK and JKM as preconditions. Currently, the JP programme is only for PPU not for PBPU.)
Source: TNP2K (2022).

family members with specific conditions, such as pregnant women, early childhood, and school-aged children.[2] Since 2017, both the elderly and people with disabilities have been included as programme recipients as part of four components to receive assistance. The programme's benefit schedule can be seen in Table 8.2. By 2018, PKH covered 10 million families, which was a massive increase in coverage from only 500,000 families when the programme was piloted in 2007 and the 3.2 million families when it was first scaled nationally in 2014. In 2022, the programme planned to provide transfers for around 50,697 pregnant women, 3 million early childhood, 5.1 million primary school children, as well as 3.4 million junior secondary and 2.9 million senior secondary students (Ministry of Social Affairs 2022). In 2022, the number of the elderly and people with disabilities who received PKH amounted to 1.5 million and approximately 113,883 beneficiaries respectively.

Another family-based transfer, *Program Sembako,* is an electronic food voucher programme previously known as the Non-Cash Food Assistance (*Bantuan Pangan Non Tunai, or* BPNT). This programme is the continued and revamped "in-kind" food assistance programme that was first launched as one of the social safety nets to support the poor and at-risk

TABLE 8.2
PKH and PIP Benefit Level in 2019

PKH			*PIP*	
Component/Family Member	*Benefit Value per year*			
	IDR	*US$*[a]	*IDR*	*US$*
Pregnant women	3,000,000	207		
Early childhood	3,000,000	207		
School-age children				
—Primary	900,000	62	450,000	31
—Junior secondary	1,500,000	103	750,000	51
—Senior secondary	2,000,000	138	1,000,000	69
Elderly 70 years and above	2,400,000	165		
Severe disability	2,400.000	165		

Note: a. Average exchange rate 2019 US$1 = IDR14,510.
Source: TNP2K, 2019.

households' nutritional intake during the 1997/98 Asian Financial Crisis.[3] The BPNT itself was launched in 2017 when the government provided an electronic food voucher that could be redeemed with rice and eggs in local shops. The transfer is given to the mother in families or the woman in the household. In 2019, the government transformed BPNT into *Program Sembako*. This transformation entails the addition of a range of food items, such as vegetables and protein sources. By 2019, *Program Sembako* covered 15.6 million beneficiary families, which was equal to the poorest 25 per cent of the population. This breadth of coverage means that this programme is the Indonesian government's largest income transfer that equates to 0.18 per cent of the country's GDP (TNP2K 2018). The programme's benefit schedule may be seen in Table 8.1.

Aside from transfers for families, the Indonesian government also rolled out non-contributory transfers for individuals. These transfers are mainly aimed at individuals pursuing an education. The Smart Indonesia Programme (*Program Indonesia Pintar*, or PIP) provides cash transfers to students from the poorest 25 per cent families in Indonesia. This programme is intended to cover their personal expenses, such as transportation costs, daily allowances and books. The programme was a transformation of a Cash Transfer for Poor Students scheme, initially called *Bantuan Siswa Miskin* (BSM) which was started in 2008. The PIP benefits vary depending on the beneficiaries' school grade level as shown in Table 8.2. Since it was launched in 2015, PIP has reached approximately 20 million students between 6 and 21 years old.

Meanwhile, *PIP Kuliah* extends PIP's benefits as it is intended to support university students from poor families with outstanding academic achievements. The programme covers tuition fees and monthly living allowances for its beneficiaries. By 2022, the programme that was launched in 2020 already provides assistance to around 200,000 new students. Finally, beyond transfers through PKH, assistance for the elderly and people with disability is also present. However, these programmes were limited in scale.

In terms of contributory programmes in the Indonesian social protection system, in 2004, the Indonesian government passed Law No. 40/2004 to consolidate all social insurance schemes under a unified national social security system. Two social security agencies were established through Law No. 24/2011, which were the Social Security Agency for Employment

(*BPJS Ketenagakerjaan*) and the Social Security Agency for Health (*BPJS Kesehatan*). Both institutions were established to implement and manage the country's social insurance for health and employment programmes. This entails awareness raising and education, expanding membership coverage, collecting contributions, administering benefits, and managing the investment funds (TNP2K 2022).

Based on Law No. 40/2004, the social insurance for employment consists of four schemes, which are the Work Injury Compensation (*Jaminan Kecelakaan Kerja*, or JKK), Survivor's Benefit (*Jaminan Kematian*, or JKm), Old Age Savings (*Jaminan Hari Tua*, or JHT), and Pension (*Jaminan Pensiun*, or JP) (see Table 8.1). In 2020, members of JKK, JKm, and JHT were around 50.7 million people, which was 39.4 per cent of the total Indonesian workforce (TNP2K 2022). However, around 40.8 per cent of the total members are inactive (TNP2K 2022). This practice is common though unfortunate since despite most members usually stopping payment of their contributions once they moved out of formal employment, they should be able to move and continue their membership through the non-wage earners (*Bukan Penerima Upah*, or BPU) scheme (portability principle within the social insurance scheme). This reflects the heightened vulnerability of informal sector workers. In 2022, the government included a new Unemployment Benefit (*Jaminan Kehilangan Pekerjaan*, or JKP) programme under *BPJS Ketenagakerjaan* as a mandate of Law No. 11/2020 on Work Creation.

In terms of social insurance for health, the Indonesian government established the National Health Insurance scheme (*Jaminan Kesehatan Nasional*, or JKN) in 2014. The government intended JKN to be a universal healthcare system that would allow every Indonesian citizen access to healthcare services and facilities. In 2021, the number of JKN members reached 235.7 million people or about 85 per cent of the population (DJSN 2021). Even though the number of JKN members increased, those who were inactive also increased to around 20 per cent of the total membership. Out of the total members, approximately 96.8 million people were fully subsidized by the government through the JKN's Non-Contributory Beneficiaries (*Penerima Bantuan Iuran*, or PBI) scheme. This fully subsidized insurance scheme covers poor and at-risk groups who are within the country's 40 per cent poorest families listed in the DTKS.

8.3 THE 2020 NATIONAL ECONOMIC RECOVERY (PEN 2020) BUDGET: SOCIAL PROTECTION EXPANSION

As a response to the COVID-19 pandemic, the government launched the PEN 2020 emergency budget. One of the main objectives of the PEN 2020 was to protect the people by maintaining their consumption level and purchasing power. During a crisis like the COVID-19 pandemic, providing social protection is a challenge. There is an urgent need to deliver the programmes on a timely basis and accurately. Therefore, the Government of Indonesia used a combination of two approaches. *First*, by adjusting the existing social protection programmes by increasing the amount of assistance or expanding the number of beneficiaries of the programme. *Second*, by creating new programmes that target new beneficiaries beyond those already covered by existing programmes. This was done to ensure that the new poor that resulted from the crisis are covered.

Out of the IDR575.85 trillion (USD40.0 billion) allocated for the PEN 2020, IDR216.59 trillion or about 38 per cent of it was budgeted to expand the existing social assistance schemes and launch additional social safety net programmes (Ministry of Finance 2021a). To retain the poor and vulnerable households' consumption level and cushion their fall, the Indonesian government rolled out a host of social safety net programmes in April 2020. Additionally, out of the funds allocated for health programmes, IDR4.1 trillion or 6.5 per cent of it was earmarked to subsidize the poor and vulnerable population's JKN contribution. This budget posture reflected the Indonesian government's commitment towards protecting the poor and vulnerable amidst the pandemic.

As a prompt response in the early stage of the pandemic, the government expanded the coverage of the existing *Program Sembako* social assistance programme to cover 20 million families from 15.6 million families before the pandemic (Ministry of Finance 2021b). At the same time, the government also decided to increase its benefits from IDR150,000 to IDR200,000 per month. Another existing programme that was adjusted during the pandemic, was the PKH. As in *Program Sembako*, the government increased the benefit's amount and adjusted its disbursement frequency from quarterly to monthly. The government chose to modify PKH and *Program Sembako* because it was the most practical plan due to the already existing regulatory framework, budgeting mechanism, delivery systems and institutional arrangements. Additionally, these two programmes would have provided benefits that are suitable to help people in meeting their basic needs during the pandemic.

The way the Indonesian social protection system could be adapted under PEN 2020 demonstrated its flexibility and responsiveness in responding to an emergency. Much of this adaptability was because Indonesia has increased its investment in building a social protection system since its last recession in the wake of the 1997/8 Asian Financial Crisis. Detailed information on all social protection programmes adopted in Indonesia throughout 2020 is presented in Table 8.3.

Beyond the existing programmes, the government also launched new ones to assist those who missed out on these programmes, the new poor, the near-poor, and the vulnerable population, such as people with disability and female-headed households. Although the government could benefit from the already existing social protection infrastructure, creating and running new programmes remains a challenge during a crisis like the COVID-19 pandemic as the benefits must be disbursed quickly to new beneficiaries. This means that the government cannot rely solely on the existing DTKS. Thus, aside from targeting families listed in the DTKS who have not yet received any assistance, the government mobilized social agency personnel; across Indonesia to enlist new programme beneficiaries and self-registration for several programmes. The rest of this section will discuss new programmes launched during the pandemic in 2020.

Kartu Prakerja

Kartu Prakerja is a new programme launched in April 2020, initially designed as an upskilling and reskilling programme. In light of the pandemic, the government adjusted it to become a hybrid between a training and social assistance programme. To do so, the government retained its training component, but offered all its courses online, and increased the value of its benefits. Instead of serving as an incentive to complete training as in its original design, the transfers were designed to maintain the beneficiary's household consumption levels.

Due to its social assistance component, *Kartu Prakerja* was intended for people in households who have not received any other assistance programmes. To reach new beneficiaries beyond the already existing benefit recipients, the government utilized self-targeting where people

TABLE 8.3
Indonesian Social Protection Programmes in 2020

		Existing Program			Addditional Program in Early Stage				Addditional Program in Second Semester 2020			
		Conditional Cash Transfer / PKH	Non-Cash Food Assistance	Pre-Employment Program	Eectricity Discount	Jabodetabek Food Assistance	Non-Jabodetabek Cash Transfer	Village Fund Cash Transfer	Rice Assistance	Expansion of Cash Transfer	Wage Subsidies	Internet Quota Assistance
Income Decile	6+			5,6 Million people							12,4 million workers and 2,6 million contract temporary teachers	51 Million recipients
	5				450VA: 24 million HHs 900VA: 7,2 million HHs	DKI: 1,3 Million Families Bodetabek: 600 K Families	9 Million Families	11 Million Families				Early Childhood (20 GB), students (35 GB), college Students (50 GB), and Teachers (42 GB), with the price of 1 GB for IDR 1,000
	4			Training: Rp 1 million/Mo Incentive: Rp600 K/Mo Survey (3x): Rp50 K								
	3		20 Million Families			Apr-Jun: Rp600 K/mo Jul-Dec: Rp300 K/mo	Apr-Jun: Rp600 K/mo Jul-Dec: Rp300 K/mo	Apr-Jun: Rp600 K/mo Jul-Dec: Rp300 K/mo		9 million people	Rp1,2 million / 2 Mo	
	2	10 Million Families							10 Million PKH Recipients	Rp500 K/Fam	salary < Rp5 million and registered on BPJS TK and contract temporary teachers	
	1	assistance index per component increases 25%	Rp200 K/month		450 VA Free 900VA 50% discount	outside recipients of PKH and Non-cash Food Assistance	outside recipients of PKH and Non-cash Food Assistance	outside PKH recipients, basic food cards, Non-cash Food Assistance, food assistance, cash assistance, and pre-employment cards	15 kg/Fam/Mo	Non-cash Food Assistance recipients who are not PKH Recipients		Student and Teacher
Duration		monthly for 12 months	monthly for 12 months	April - Nov Incentive for 4 months	9 months (April-Dec)	9 months (April-Dec)	9 months (April-Dec)	9 months (April-Dec)	3 months (August-October)	One shot disbursement	4 months (Sept-Dec)	4 months (Sept-Dec)
Realization (IDR T)		36,68	39,38	18,25	11,45	7,09	32,60	23,74	5,26	4,51	33,56	4,06

Source: Ministry of Finance (2021b).

could apply to become *Kartu Prakerja* beneficiaries. Chapter 9 discusses the *Kartu Prakerja* programme in greater detail.

Electricity Discount

While *Kartu Prakerja* needed to enlist new programme beneficiaries, the electricity subsidies/discounts programme for the COVID-19 pandemic affected households and individuals required no new data collection since the National Electricity Company (*Perusahaan Listrik Negara,* or PLN) already had a readily available list of electricity subscribers. The programme provided free electricity bills for 24 million households of 450VA electricity subscribers and a 50 per cent discount on electricity bills for 7 million households of 900VA electricity subscribers. Only those registered in the DTKS were considered eligible to receive this discount. This electricity discount was relatively well targeted since it had the privilege of a pre-existing beneficiary database and relatively simple delivery mechanisms that did not require logistical movement of goods or moneys. Initially planned only for 3 months from April to June 2020, this programme was later extended to 9 months until December 2020.

Village Fund Cash Transfer (*Bantuan Langsung Tunai-Desa*, or BLT-D)

An innovation in social protection design during the pandemic was a cash transfer for low-income families in rural areas known as the Village Fund Cash Transfer or *Bantuan Langsung Tunai-Desa* (BLT-D). The programme's novelty lies in its targeting mechanism. Unlike other social assistance programmes that usually used the DTKS for targeting purposes, BLT-D used a community targeting approach. The programme sought to reach low-income families in villages who were not yet covered by existing programmes or other DTKS-based social assistance programmes. Therefore, the first step in targeting BLT-D was getting a list of potential beneficiaries. Then, the community would verify and validate eligible potential beneficiaries from the initial list through a village council meeting. The final beneficiaries list was submitted to local government officers to be compiled with the list from other villages.

Another interesting feature of the BLT-D was its financing sources. Unlike the other programmes which were funded by the central government through line ministries budgets, BLT-D was funded by the Village Fund, which is the Indonesian government's transfer to villages across Indonesia aimed at fostering development. A study by the Fiscal Policy Agency (2021) found that BLT-D's bottom-up targeting mechanism complemented the DTKS-based top-down targeting mechanism in covering a broader set of eligible low-income families and helped to reduce the number of missed out people.

Cash and In-Kind Transfer

Early in the pandemic, the government provided cash or in-kind transfers based on the beneficiaries' location. For 1.9 million low-income households in the Greater Jakarta area, the government provided social assistance in the form of staple food known as *Bansos Sembako.* The decision to provide food assistance in the Greater Jakarta region was because this area was the most affected by the government's mobility restrictions policy to curb the spread of coronavirus. The assistance was provided to prevent the recipient families who lived in Greater Jakarta area from returning home to their villages and possibly spreading COVID-19.

Meanwhile, for families who lived in the urban area outside the Greater Jakarta area, a new cash transfer programme called *Bantuan Sosial Tunai* (BST) was targeted at 9 million low-income families being the poorest 40 per cent of families across Indonesia who were not already covered in the existing programmes. This targeting utilized the already existing data in the DTKS. The BST was delivered through a network of state-owned banks across Indonesia and the state-owned postal company (PT POS).

In the second semester of 2020, the Indonesian government extended some programmes and launched additional cash and in-kind transfer programmes. The duration of BST, BLT-D, *Bansos Sembako* and electricity discounts was extended from 3 months (April–June 2020) to 9 months (April–December 2020). Additionally, a one-time cash transfer of IDR500,000 was also given for a family who only received *Program Sembako* or equal to 9 million families. The PKH beneficiaries also receive 15 kg of rice per month for three months (August–October 2020).

Wage Subsidies (*Bantuan Subsidi Upah*, or BSU)

Beyond low-income families, the pandemic also affected middle-income families. Therefore, the government sought to reach families who were more likely to not be covered by existing social assistance programmes by launching social assistance for lower middle-income families through the wages support programme BSU. In targeting BSU beneficiaries, the government utilized the existing BPJS *Ketenagakerjaan* members database to target workers registered as active social insurance for employment scheme members. The targeted workers whose salary was below IDR5 million per month were deemed eligible to be BSU beneficiaries. By the end of 2020, the BSU covered 12.4 million workers and 2.6 million informal teachers.

Internet Quota Assistance

In the education sector, the COVID-19 pandemic caused school closures and forced schools to move teaching activities online. Since this distance learning needed an Internet-based digital platform, families needed to spend more on Internet expenses amidst already rising economic pressures from the COVID-19 pandemic. Hence, the government launched the Internet Quota Assistance not only for students from pre-school to university but also for teachers and university lecturers. Through this programme, free Internet credits were given to students. In 2020, this programme was enjoyed by 51 million beneficiaries between September and December 2020.

8.4 SOCIAL PROTECTION PROGRAMMES UNDER PEN 2021

As the pandemic extended beyond 2020, the Indonesian government continued a number of social protection programmes under PEN. This decision was in line with PEN 2021's focus on economic recovery efforts and a vaccine rollout with the hope of a swift return to normalcy. Thus, PEN 2021 saw a scaled-back budget for social assistance and social safety net and an increase in business stimulus, which also included micro, small, and medium enterprise and corporate support programmes that amounted to IDR186.64 trillion (US$12.9 billion) or 25.1 per cent of the PEN 2021 budget, as well as an almost-tripled health budget that reflected the government's vaccination drive. By the end of 2021, IDR167.72 trillion, or 89.9 per cent of the allocated funds had been used up to continue cushioning the impact of COVID-19 on welfare (Ministry of Finance 2022).

Table 8.4 shows detailed information on all social protection programmes in 2021.

Considering the moderately successful COVID-19 containment and the slowly improving economic condition by the end of 2020, the government was optimistic that there would be a recovery in 2021. In 2021, the government's primary strategy for accelerating socio-economic recovery focused on continuing intensified health measures, mobilizing the social protection system, ensuring business continuity, and fostering structural reform within the government. Through PEN 2021, increased benefits to regular programmes like PKH and *Program Sembako* continued. However, only four new programmes launched in 2020 were continued in 2021, which were BST, Electricity Discount, Internet Quota Assistance, and BLT-D.

To ensure a smooth recovery, the government continued to provide BST for four months and the Electricity Discount for nine months. Additionally, Internet Quota Assistance was still offered for the first semester of the school year in 2021 with the expectation of a transition towards face-to-face learning in the second semester. The BLT-D was also still provided with a smaller target of 11 million families. This target declined because several BLT-D beneficiaries in 2020 were already covered by BST in 2021.

Expansions to Mitigate New COVID-19 Waves

Despite expectations for a recovery in 2021, the pandemic has proven to be persistent. In July 2021, Indonesia experienced a severe second wave of COVID-19. As a response, the government implemented more social restrictions in July 2021, which came with an expectation of another welfare shock similar to the previous year's mobility restrictions. To mitigate this shock on the poor and vulnerable families, the government adjusted programmes under the PEN 2021 budget, focusing on health intervention, social protection, and medium and small enterprise (MSME) support activities. The government provided the 25 per cent poorest families in Indonesia with top-up benefits for the *Program Sembako* beneficiaries between July and August 2021. Additionally, the duration of the BST, Electricity Discount and Internet Quota Assistance were also extended. Moreover, *Kartu Prakerja*'s coverage was also expanded to cover an additional 336,000 people beyond the existing 5.6 million beneficiaries. Finally, to accelerate the BLT-D's disbursement, the government relaxed

TABLE 8.4
Indonesian Social Protection Programmes in 2021

	Initial Program						Addditional Program due to Delta Variant				
Income Decile	**Conditional Cash Transfer/PKH**	**Food Assistance/ Kartu Sembako**	**Electricity Discount**	**Cash Transfer/BST**	**Village Fund Cash Transfer/ BLT Desa**	**Pre-Employment Program**	**Rice Assistance Program**	**Additional PPKM Sembako Card**	**Wage Subsidy**	**Internet Quota Assistance**	**University Tuition Assistance**
6+						6.01 Million participants			7.39 million workers of non-critical sectors in PPKM level 3 and Level 4	73.28 Million Recipients	347,11 thousand university students
5			31.26 Million Households	10 Million Families	5.6 Million Families		28,8 Million Families (BST and Kartu Sembako)	6.01 million Families proposed by the local government			
4						Training: Rp 1 million Incentives: Rp600 K/mo Survey (3x): Rp50 K			registered on BPJS TK		
3		18.56 Million Families		Rp300 K/mo	Rp300 K/mo					Early Childhood (7GB/month), Elementary-High School (10GB/month), University (15GB/month), Teachers (12GB/month), and Lecturers (15GB/month), 1 GB for IDR 2,750	
2	10 Million Families	Rp200 K/month	450 VA, 100% discount on Jan-Mar, 50% on Apr-Dec					Rp200 K/month	Rp1 million/workers		up to IDR2,4 million per student
1	Per year: Pregnant and Early Childhood Rp3 mill , elementary Rp900 K, JHS Rp1,5 mill, SHS Rp2 mill, disabilities and elderly Rp2,4 mill	July and August are disbursed twice	900 VA, 50% discount on Jan-Mar, 25% on Apr-Dec	outside recipients of PKH and Food Assistance	outside resipientss of PKH, Food Assistance, Cash Transfer, and pre-employment cards	outside resipients of DTKS and BSU	10 kg/Families	outside resipientss of PKH, Basic Food Card, and BST Recipients	outside resipients of Pre-Employment Program	Teacher and Student	
Duration	quarterly for 12 months	monthly for 12 months + 2 months	12 months (Jan-Dec)	7 months (Jan-Jul)	monthly for 12 months	Incentive for 4 months	One-off disbursement	6 Months (Jul-Dec)	One-off disbursement	10 months (Jan-May + Agt-Dec)	1 Semester
Realization (IDR T)	27.93	47.56	8.78	16.76	20.24	18.26	-	6.84	7.50	5.22	0.74

Source: Ministry of Finance (2022).

the programme's targeting criteria and gave more authority to village governments to determine eligible benefit recipients.

Additionally, the government also expanded some social assistance programmes. For example, *Program Sembako's* coverage was expanded by adding 5.8 million families based on the local government's proposal. This expansion aimed to reach out to the poor and vulnerable who have not been covered by other programmes. Moreover, in-kind assistance of 10 kg of rice for two months was disbursed to 28.8 million families registered as *Program Sembako* and BST beneficiaries, which covered the poorest 40 per cent of families in Indonesia. This in-kind rice assistance was distributed by the Indonesian Bureau of Logistics (*Badan Urusan Logistik*, or BULOG) as a state-owned enterprise in charge of managing the supply, distribution, and price control of rice.

Beyond assistance to the poor, BSU was delivered to 7.39 million workers in areas with heightened mobility restrictions. However, the benefit was smaller compared to BSU's benefit in 2020. Moreover, in the education sector, the government covered tuition fees for up to IDR2.4 million per student to support university students. This programme was received by more than 347,000 university students across Indonesia.

8.5 LESSONS LEARNT FROM THE MOBILIZATION OF THE SOCIAL PROTECTION SYSTEM DURING PANDEMIC

Impact

Indonesia's poverty rate change as a result of the pandemic defied many projections. This was partly due to the extensive social protection programmes provided by the Indonesian government, which helped cushion the impact of the pandemic, especially for the poor and vulnerable. A joint survey conducted by UNICEF, UNDP, Prospera and the SMERU Research Institute (2021) shows that more than 85 per cent of surveyed households received at least one social protection programme. Another panel survey by the World Bank (2020b) showed that almost all households in the bottom 40 per cent received at least one form of social assistance. Social assistance coverage increased from 55 per cent in May 2020 to 73 per cent in November 2020.

Meanwhile, a study by Suryahadi, Al Izzati, and Yumna (2021) produced estimated growth incidence curves—defined as per capita household expenditure between September 2019 and September 2020 for each percentile of the expenditure distribution—and found that without the benefits from the government's social protection programmes, expenditure growth would be lower (Figure 8.1). This was especially true for households at the lower end of the expenditure levels. Wright et al.'s (2021) findings using a microsimulation method also corroborated Suryahadi, Al Izzati and Yumna's findings.

Overall, these reports found that social protection programmes were able to limit the increase in the poverty rate in Indonesia. In September 2020, the poverty rate rose to 10.19 per cent from 9.22 per cent in September 2019. Although this was a significant increase, it was still far lower than the estimate by the World Bank (2020c) of 11.8 per cent. In absolute terms, the number of new poor grew by 2.8 million people, which is significantly lower than the World Bank's estimate of 7.1 million people if there were no social protection programmes. By September 2021 the country's poverty rate had already fallen to 9.71 per cent. Although this figure is still higher than its pre-pandemic level, it is already on the right trajectory towards the government's goal of a 6–7 per cent poverty rate in 2024.

8.6 CHALLENGES

Data and Targeting Mechanism

Some challenges were faced during the planning and implementation of the social protection programmes during the pandemic. One of the biggest challenges is related to data. Even before the pandemic, the issue of data accuracy already existed. Inclusion and exclusion errors,[4] where people were wrongly included or excluded from programme beneficiary lists because the DTKS and its ranking system were not regularly updated. Moreover, there is also an issue of the database's limited coverage as it was designed to cover only the poorest 40 per cent of families, while during the crisis where many people were being pushed into poverty and it was very likely the coverage had to expand to lower-middle-income families or the poorest 50–60 per cent families. Moreover, the DTKS has not yet captured the new poor that were impacted by the crisis. Hence, setting target beneficiaries for the new social protection programmes became

FIGURE 8.1
Proportional Change (%) in Real Per Capita Household Expenditure from September 2019 to September 2020, by Percentile

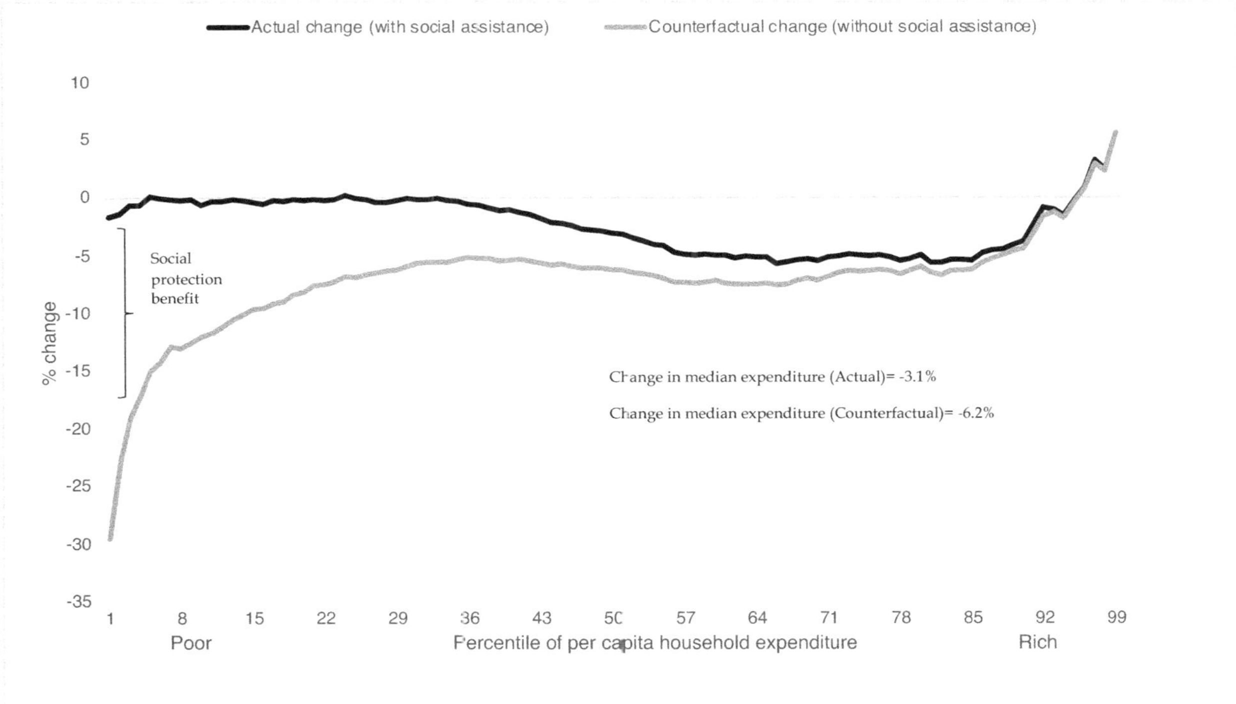

Source: Suryahadi, Al Izzati, and Yumna (2021).

extremely challenging. This affected the delivery of the programmes, particularly in the early stages of implementation. Meanwhile, in times of crisis, a quick response from social protection is needed. The pandemic has given a lesson on the importance of integrated and regularly updated data through active outreach from the government as well as on-demand registration from the public, to increase target accuracy.

Delivery Mechanism

Another challenge in social protection programmes during the pandemic is related to the delivery mechanism. During the pandemic when mobility was severely restricted, delivery of cash transfers using a banking system was constrained by the limited financial infrastructure mostly in remote areas and the financial literacy of the beneficiaries. Based on monitoring results conducted by Kemenko PMK together with the TNP2K Secretariat and other ministries in 2021, around 28.6 per cent of the respondents had to cash out their PKH benefit in other villages from where they lived and thus extra transportation costs were needed (Kemenko PMK 2021). The study also found almost half of respondents shared their card identification number with the merchants. For this reason, the government must ensure the most appropriate benefit delivery mechanism. However, under time pressures, this was proven to be hard to do.

Coverage

While the poorest 40 per cent across all age ranges were entitled to receive the government's non-contributory social assistance programmes, social protection coverage for the better-off groups was sparser. Although there were contributory social insurance programmes such as schemes under *BPJS Ketenagakerjaan*, they were mostly accessed by workers in the formal sector where 65 per cent of its members were male and only 35 per cent were female (TNP2K). With a high ratio of workers in the informal sector, despite being considered to be relatively more well-off than the poorest 40 per cent, there was a significant portion of the population that was considered to be vulnerable to falling into poverty. With their lack of social protection coverage and vulnerable economic condition, they are considered the "missing middle" (see Figure 8.2).

FIGURE 8.2
The Coverage of Indonesia's Social Protection

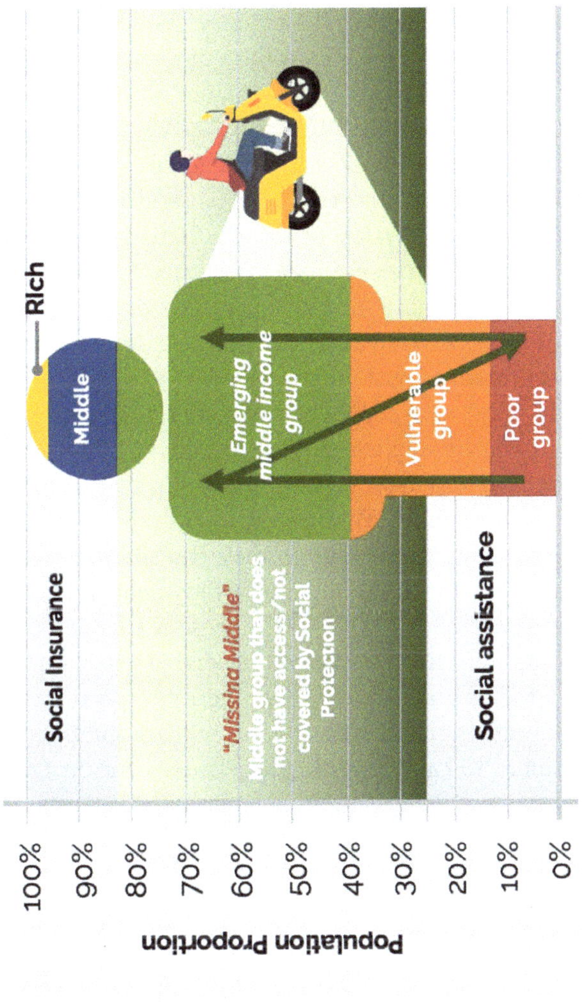

Source: TNP2K and MAHKOTA (2021).

Although through PEN 2020 and PEN 2021 the government expanded the coverage of the Indonesian social protection system to mitigate the pandemic's impact, this coverage for the missing middle population was intended to be temporary. Thus, beyond the comprehensive social protection that provides coverage across one's life cycle, the Indonesian government needs to also think of ways to expand coverage beyond the poorest 40 per cent families in the country. Aside from the much-needed coverage for the missing middle, some vulnerable populations were still overlooked in the design and implementation of the Indonesian social protection system, including the elderly (TNP2K 2018). The female elderly component is consistently higher than the male elderly component (52 per cent as compared to 48 per cent in 2021), and half of the elderly have disabilities or reduced physical functions (Statistics Indonesia 2018–2021). As a result, it is not surprising that the highest rate of poverty is among people over 60, and is more so among people over 80 (TNP2K 2018). Due to their higher tendency to fall into poverty, the elderly should be prioritized by the social protection system.

Similarly, the lives of people with disabilities are challenging given the high costs of care and medical services. Moreover, if their caregiver has to give up work or reduce their working hours, this may result in a diminished income for the household. Young people with disabilities are often in an even more challenging position as they transition from childhood into adulthood and face difficulties in both employment and independent living (Mitra, Posarac, and Vick 2013). Despite these challenges, most people with disabilities had very limited access to social assistance programmes and during the pandemic in 2020–21, they were not yet prioritized to receive benefits. Although the elderly and people with disabilities received benefits through regular PKH and *Sembako* programmes, the programmes' efficacy in cushioning their falls was limited. Chapter 12 in this volume discusses more details of social assistance for people with disabilities.

Benefit Level

Based on an analysis by TNP2K (2018), the transfer values of combined programmes are very small amounts and limit the potential impact of the programme. For example, the transfer of PIP does not cover the real costs, and parents spend extra annual out-of-pocket expenses of approximately

IDR1 million to IDR3 million for the different levels of education. For the *Sembako* programme, the transfer of IDR200,000 per month only covers around 10–17 per cent of a household's expenditure on food. Based on *Susenas* data of March 2019 analysed by TNP2K's Research Team in April 2020, the food expenditure per capita per month for Decile 1–4 was around IDR230,000–IDR420,000. With five members in a household on average, the household spent around IDR1,150,000–IDR2,100,000. Furthermore, the real value of the transfer has fallen significantly in recent years, reducing the programme's impact.

Levels of Investment

Before 2020–21, investment in social assistance schemes only amounted to 0.35 per cent of gross domestic product (GDP) and 0.20 per cent on fully subsidized national health insurance for the poor, equating to an investment of 0.55 per cent of GDP on non-contributory schemes (TNP2K 2018). This was less than expected for a middle-income country like Indonesia, resulting in major gaps in coverage. Other countries, have a much lower GDP than Indonesia but invest approximately 2 per cent of GDP on tax-financed social protection (TNP2K 2018). The PEN programmes have increased this investment to around 1.6 per cent of GDP (calculated by TNP2K 2021). The level of investment should also be combined with better programme setting policies, such as integrating various programmes with similar objectives and opting for targeted subsidies for more effective programme implementation.

Monitoring and Evaluation

During the pandemic, conducting, monitoring and evaluating of programme implementation is important but more challenging. Before the pandemic, various ministries overseeing different programmes oversaw the monitoring of each one of them. However, with restrictions on mobility, it was not possible to conduct field monitoring. Thus, most of the monitoring surveys were conducted through the telephone, which was more challenging than face-to-face interviews. As a result, programme evaluation was slower than usual and key decisions, such as programme expansion or extension, had to be made with more limited information.

8.7 DISCUSSION: THE FUTURE OF THE INDONESIAN SOCIAL PROTECTION SYSTEM

Aside from identifying issues within the Indonesian social protection system, this chapter also identifies areas for reform. This reform needs to be grounded on lessons learnt during the pandemic as well as a bigger vision of how the social protection system is going to look like in the future. This section discusses areas to focus on Indonesia's social protection reform. Indonesians face many risks throughout their lives, beginning in the womb and continuing through to their final days (TNP2K 2018). This is reflected in the high share of people who move in and out of poverty from one year to the next. These risks are exacerbated by the generally low incomes across the working population. Thus, they are less able to respond effectively to a crisis. Moreover, many are still facing barriers to accessing programmes in the social protection system. To respond to this condition, the government commits to expanding the national social protection system as stipulated in Indonesia's current long-term development plan (*Rencana Pembangunan Jangka Panjang Nasional*, or RPJPN 2005–25).

Despite the Indonesian social protection system's dramatic improvement throughout the years, significant challenges persist. Thus, Indonesia strives for an inclusive social protection system that could offer support to people as they move through their life cycle, from childhood to old age. Furthermore, in the future, Indonesia needs to move from a social protection system that only benefits the poor and a small percentage of the formal sector to a system that ensures access to social protection for everyone, including those in the missing middle who are also at risk of falling into poverty (TNP2K 2018). This system needs to be built gradually over time, ensuring the progressive realization of the right of all citizens to social protection while ensuring the fiscal space for the schemes.

Indonesia is on track to achieve these goals, which could be evident in how far the Indonesian protection system has developed in the past two decades. These developments were underpinned by clear plans and roadmaps towards a more inclusive and sustainable social protection system for all, which entails the establishment of a social registry system, the legislation of supporting regulations and laws, to the launch of complementary programmes that engage multiple ministries and agencies across the government. As Indonesia moves forward to attain its goals, there are several lessons to be learned from the pandemic.

Adaptive Social Protection

Between 2020 and 2021, Indonesia's social protection system went through significant changes in line with the government's response to the pandemic. This entailed efforts to adjust benefits and the coverage of existing programmes and swiftly launching ad hoc programmes to effectively protect the citizens' welfare. Beyond just protecting the poor and vulnerable, social protection system expansion during the pandemic also took into account how the crisis was also impacting middle-income groups who were not usually covered by any social assistance programmes before the pandemic. This lack of coverage before the pandemic meant that when they experienced a welfare shock the government could not immediately extend assistance to this group as they had done for the poor and near-poor.

Going forward, it is necessary to build an adaptive social protection system through the formalization of social safety nets and prepare a protocol for social assistance management during a disaster or crisis. Adaptive means that the social protection system infrastructure should be able to be mobilized in response to sudden changes in welfare levels, such as during a disaster or pandemic. This entails a range of programme options or programmes with some flexibility that could be mobilized to suit different circumstances, have a clear distribution mechanism and have a financing structure with legal bases to avoid conflicts of interest.

A lesson could be learnt from Brazil's effort to cover as many poor and vulnerable people as possible during the pandemic. Similar to Indonesia, Brazil was also able to mobilize its social welfare infrastructure to mitigate the pandemic's economic impact. The selection of beneficiaries targeted three groups, which were (i) people who lived in families who were already receiving cash transfers from the government's Bolsa Familia conditional cash transfer; (ii) citizens listed in the government's Single Registry who haven't yet received Bolsa Familia; and (iii) people who work in the informal sector who applied through a digital registration platform (Bilo et al. 2021). Although Brazil's strategy is quite similar to Indonesia's, in terms of ratio, its Single Registry's coverage is slightly larger than Indonesia's DTKS. Moreover, its self-registration system was able to better cover Brazil's missing middle than Indonesia did.

Establishing a Social Registry

A Social Registry includes the information systems that support outreach, intake, registration and determination of potential eligibility for one or more social programmes. They have both a social policy role, as inclusion systems, and an operational role, as information systems (World Bank 2017). Some social registries serve as a platform for dynamic inclusion when access to registration is open and continues. The data produced by Social Registries are also used by countries for other purposes, such as calculating benefit levels, validating information collected through other methods or sources, assessing potential demand for interventions, planning and costing interventions depending on projected coverage rates, monitoring and evaluating, or other analytics purposes (World Bank 2017).

The breadth of programmes offered in the Indonesian social protection system, coupled with the expectation that the system should be flexible in the face of a crisis means that there needs to be some form of reliable targeting mechanism. Social registries could serve that function by identifying and listing potential programme beneficiaries. The social registry could then be used as a beneficiary list for various government programmes. Although Indonesia's DTKS already serves as a promising basis for this social registry, it still lacks a dynamic updating system, which impacted its accuracy over time. Indonesia needs to think of a way to move towards a dynamic data updating approach, which combines top-down with bottom-up approaches and incorporates a robust data validation mechanism if it were to achieve the status of a reliable database that could support its social protection system.

What is important to note is that building a social registry is not simply a technical matter. If Indonesia is to create a social registry that could reliably be used across the government, a clear division between government bodies responsible for collecting data, hosting it, and maintaining it needs to be established. Indeed, the first hurdle in creating a social registry is political rather than technical. To bring many government bodies to the table, strong leadership and a clear roadmap need to be set.

On-Demand Application

The existing database used for targeting (DTKS) was developed using the top-down enumeration method. However, this method could not capture the poverty dynamics. Therefore, bottom-up self-registration using an on-demand application (ODA) is crucial to address this issue and exclusion errors. ODA should be built as an integral part of a social registry system that is used not only for collecting the data but also for regular updating and a grievance mechanism. This ODA would be the key feature of future social protection, utilizing the technology and big data and requiring active involvement from the people. Registration would be done through online applications that could be easily accessed by everyone. *Kartu Prakerja* already uses an on-demand registration method (see Chapter 9 in this volume).

Implementing Programme Integration

Poverty alleviation and welfare is a multidimensional issues. It is comprised of various factors, from social exclusion, lack of nutrition, poor employment conditions, and many more. This implies that if the Indonesian social protection system is to alleviate poverty and fully protect the citizens' welfare, it must take into account this multidimensionality by engaging multiple sectors of the government. Collaborative work across ministries and government agencies, as well as between the central and regional governments, is necessary for this effort, in particular, to integrate various programmes for better efficiency and efficacy in tackling poverty and welfare issues. The integration also means that programmes with similar objectives and target groups need to be integrated, for example between PIP and PKH for school-age children.

Protecting the Elderly and People with Disability

The population's age distribution shows that Indonesia is becoming an ageing society. Given the high rates of poverty among the elderly, the growing elderly population where a high percentage of them also have disabilities and more than 50 per cent are female will pose a challenge to future efforts to reduce poverty and tackle inequality unless effective social protection mechanisms are put in place for the elderly. To ensure that the Indonesian social protection system could fully protect all its citizens, social protection policy, programme design, implementation, and evaluation should be created with social inclusion issues in mind.

Expanding the Membership of Social Insurance for Employment Programmes

With 59.45 per cent of the country's workers in the informal sector (Statistics Indonesia 2021), over time, the government will need to offer incentives for people working in the informal sector to join the contributory social insurance schemes if they have the ability to pay (ATP) and the willingness to pay (WTP) the social insurance contribution and gradually reduce the percentage of the population receiving tax-financed (non-contributory scheme) insurance subsidies. Progressively, the government should ensure that every citizen (especially the elderly, people with disability, women, and children) is protected, either through the contributory or non-contributory tax-financed scheme. The national social protection system will ideally be funded through contributions from the Indonesian citizens as its main beneficiary, including through their taxes, and from insurance scheme premiums.

Increasing Levels of Investment

Moving forward, Indonesia needs to shift from broad-based and regressive subsidies, such as fuel subsidies, towards more targeted social programmes. Not only because targeted programmes are more efficient, but it is also in line with the principles of justice where only the deserving shall benefit from these programmes while the more well-off contribute more to the system. Finally, a shift towards more targeted programmes also means that the government could free up more fiscal space to invest in a more sustainable and equitable social protection system. This investment needs to combine with more effective and efficient programme implementations through better programme management, routine and rigorous monitoring and evaluation in addition to accurate targeting and coverage.

Regulation and Institutional Arrangement

While the contributory social insurance scheme is over-regulated in the form of law, presidential regulation, and ministerial regulation, there is a lack of regulation for the non-contributory social assistance scheme. This also includes COVID-19 crisis response programmes.

The relevant regulation is often stipulated to respond to the emerging situation rather than planned ahead. In order to improve the efficacy of Indonesia's social protection schemes, including those that serve as crisis response, a reform of the system's institutional structure is critical. This entails more streamlined regulation as a basis for cross-ministry or government agency collaboration and the clarification of funding structure for different programmes. It is time to consider the drafting and stipulation of Laws on Social Protection as a direction and basis for the future of Indonesia's social protection system to protect all Indonesian people. Similar to BPJS, both for employment and health, an independent institution is needed to manage all social assistance programmes based on the life-cycle approach. This institution can be under the supervision of a national council or relevant ministries.

8.8 CONCLUSION

The extensive breadth and coverage of the social protection programmes rolled out by the government in the 2020 and 2021 PEN played a key role in keeping Indonesia's poverty rate down. Despite this success, the Indonesian government cannot afford to be too complacent, particularly given that high spending on stimulus and aid combined with low tax revenue as in the 2020 PEN is untenable in the long run. With the pandemic still ongoing beyond 2020, the Indonesian government launched PEN 2021 to hasten economic recovery. However, with different rates of recovery between the haves and have-nots, Indonesia may face rising inequality. This raises the question of how Indonesia could rebuild the economy with a strong social protection system as its foundation—one that is prepared to take on future shocks like the current pandemic, and one that fosters inclusive economic growth to tackle inequality.

Prior to the pandemic, Indonesia already had a working social protection system that had been established over the years. Thus, when the pandemic hit the Indonesian government could swiftly mobilize this system to expand existing programmes and launch new programmes to mitigate the impact of the COVID-19 pandemic on people's welfare. However, Indonesia still has a long way to go. With shortfalls in the existing social protection system, such as benefit adequacy, coverage and targeting issues, there is still much to do to build a social protection system that could effectively protect its citizens from welfare shocks.

Social protection has been proven to play a critical role in protecting people and cushioning the impact of the COVID-19 pandemic. The COVID-19 pandemic amplified the need for a robust social protection system to protect people both in normal conditions and during a crisis. While its impact was devastating, the COVID-19 pandemic could also be used as momentum for Indonesia to enact reforms for a stronger social protection system.

Notes

1. In 2011, the Unified Database was developed by TNP2K (National Team for the Acceleration of Poverty Reduction) under the Vice President's Office, along with Statistics Indonesia. By 2020, it covered around the poorest 40 per cent of the population. Up until 2016, TNP2K managed the Unified Database and utilized it for central government and local governments' targeting purposes.
2. Previously all member who met the criteria of conditionality are included.
3. *Operasi Pasar Khusus* (OPK) was the first title of the programme, targeted for families to allow the beneficiary families to purchase rice at a subsidized price. Since then, this programme has been transforming into different title and mechanism, *Raskin* (2003) and *Rastra* (2015). Based on several evaluations results, the programme was recommended to be reformed into electronic food voucher programme.
4. Based on analysis using *Susenas*, almost all programmes consistently perform flat targeting, whereby all deciles, including the rich receive the programmes, which supposed to be only bottom 40 per cent at the maximum. Only less than half of the poorest decile including the extreme poor receive social assistance (calculated by TNP2K and BPS 2018–22).

References

Bilo, C., R. Brito, A. Peres, and Ma. Balboni. 2021. "What's Next for Social Protection in Light of COVID-19: Country Responses". *Policy in Focus*, No. 47. Brasilia: International Policy Centre for Inclusive Growth (IPC-IG).

Coordinating Ministry for Economic Affairs. 2021. *Kartu Prakerja Program Management Report 2020*. Jakarta: Coordinating Ministry for Economic Affairs.

Coordinating Ministry for Human Development and Culture (Kemenko PMK). 2021. "Hasil Pemantauan Program Sembako dan PKH". Presentation. Jakarta: Kemenko PMK.

Dewan Jaminan Sosial Nasional (DJSN)/National Social Security Council. 2021. *Sistem Monitoring dan Evaluation (Sismonev)*. Jakarta: BPJS Kesehatan.

Fiscal Policy Agency. 2021. "Internal FPA MOF Study". Unpublished. Jakarta: Fiscal Policy Agency.

Ministry of Finance. 2021a. "Pemulihan Ekonomi Nasional 2021". Presentation. Jakarta: Ministry of Finance.

———. 2021b. "Central Government Financial Report 2020". Jakarta: Ministry of Finance.

———. 2022. "Central Government Financial Report 2021" (unaudited). Jakarta: Ministry of Finance.

Ministry of Social Affairs. 2022. Presentation of Direktorat Jaminan Sosial Keluarga, Direktorat Jenderal Perlindungan dan Jaminan Sosial [Directorate General of Social Protection and Social Security]: *Penyaluran Bansos Program Keluarga Harapan Tahun 2022* [Distribution/Payment of Program Keluarga Harapan in 2022]. Jakarta: Ministry of Social Affairs.

Mitra, S., A. Posarac, and B. Vick. 2013. "Disability and Poverty in Developing Countries: A Multidimensional Study". *World Development* 41: 1–18. https://doi.org/10.1016/j.worlddev.2012.05.024

Statistics Indonesia. 2020. *Indikator Kesejahteraan Rakyat 2020* [Welfare Indicators]. Jakarta: Statistics Indonesia.

———. 2021. *Booklet Sakernas: Survei Angkatan Kerja Agustus 2021*. Jakarta: Statistics Indonesia.

———. 2022. *Profil Kemiskinan di Indonesia September 2021*. Berita Resmi Statistik, No. 07/01/Th. XXV. Jakarta: Statistics Indonesia.

Suryahadi, A., R. Al Izzati, and A. Yumna. 2021. "The Impact of and Social Protection Programs on Poverty in Indonesia". *Bulletin of Indonesian Economic Studies* 57, no. 3: 267–96.

TNP2K. 2018. "The Future of the Social Protection System in Indonesia: Social Protection for All". Jakarta: TNP2K.

———. 2022. "Rapid Assessment Report on Maintaining and Expanding Membership as an Effort to Ensure the Sustainability of the Social Insurance for Employment Program". Jakarta: TNP2K

———. 2022. "*Perluasan Kepesertaan Jaminan Sosial Ketenagakerjaan, terutama Jaminan Hari Tua (JHT) dan Jaminan Pensiun (JP) bagi Pekerja Rentan*". Presentation. Jakarta: TNP2K

———. 2022. "Social Insurance for Employment from a Gender Perspective". Presentation. Jakarta: TNP2K.

UNICEF, UNDP, Prospera, and the SMERU Research Institute. 2021. "Analysis of the Social and Economic Impacts of COVID-19 on Households and Strategic Policy Recommendations for Indonesia". Jakarta: UNICEF.

World Bank. 2017. "Social Registries for Social Assistance and Beyond: A Guidance Note and Assessment Tool". https://www.worldbank.org/en/topic/socialprotection/publication/social-registries-for-social-assistance-and-beyond-a-guidance-note-and-assessment-tool

———. 2020a. "Towards a Secure and Fast Recovery. Indonesia Economic Prospects". December 2020. Jakarta: World Bank.

———. 2020b. "Indonesia High-Frequency Monitoring of COVID-19 Impacts Round 4". Jakarta: World Bank.

———. 2020c. "Indonesia Economic Prospects July 2020: The Long Road to Recovery". Jakarta: World Bank.

Wright, G., M. Noble, H. Barnes, A. Moechtar, D. McLennan, A. Yusuf Anshory, K. Gasior, and R. Muyanto. 2021. "Estimating the Distributional Impacts of the COVID-19 Pandemic and the Remedial Tax and Benefit Policies in Indonesia". *International Journal of Microsimulation* 14, no. 2: 50–80.

9

Kartu Prakerja

A Breakthrough for Boosting Labour Market Productivity and Social Assistance Inclusiveness

Denni Puspa Purbasari, Elan Satriawan and Romora Edward Sitorus

9.1 BACKGROUND

The Vision of Indonesia 2045 sets out the goal for Indonesia to become a high-income country as it celebrates its centennial anniversary of independence. With strong economic growth and a substantial decrease in extreme poverty, Indonesia has already achieved middle-income country status. Nevertheless, Indonesia needs to further expand its middle-class population to unlock its development potential and transition to a high-income country status in 2045. Achieving the Vision of Indonesia 2045 will require an inclusive annual growth rate of 5.1 to 5.7 per cent, a GDP per capita of US$19,794–US$23,199 and a middle-income population of around 70 per cent of the total populace by 2045 (Bappenas 2019).

One of the main engines of Indonesia's economic growth is workforce productivity. According to the 2021 World Bank report *Pathways to Middle-Class Jobs in Indonesia*, the increase in workers' productivity could contribute as much as 88 per cent to the country's GDP per capita growth of 3.9 per cent between 2000 and 2017, equal to 3.5 percentage points annually. In other words, the pace of Indonesia's economic growth depends on how fast the productivity and skills of the workforce can be enhanced. Several studies have indicated that there is a skills mismatch issue in Indonesia, where the skill profile of the workforce has not kept up with the dynamic demands of the job market (World Bank 2018a; Yoong and Gil Sander 2020). The current economic growth momentum in Indonesia should be supported through innovative labour market policy measures to address this skill mismatch. The government can provide support through education and training scholarships, as well as on-the-job training, to upgrade the workforce.

The opportunity to become a high-income country in 2045 is also supported by Indonesia's ongoing demographic bonus where most of the population, or over 70 per cent, is in the prime working-age group. This demographic bonus, expected to last until 2030, has opened up an opportunity to accelerate Indonesia's economic development. However, Indonesia is also at risk of missing this opportunity without appropriate policies to equip the workforce with appropriate skills.

Three main issues have kept the impacts of the demographic bonus suboptimal. The *first* is the quality of the workforce, including the workforce's productivity, competitiveness and relevant skills. The labour productivity of Indonesian workers remains below the average of its ASEAN counterparts where Indonesia ranked 5th out of ten countries (Figure 9.1). Despite low productivity being a major hindrance, upskilling has not been a top priority for both workers and employers. According to the Labor Market Stakeholders' Perception Survey 2016 (World Bank 2018b), education and training are not the main priorities of companies (7th out of 10). Only 44 per cent of companies surveyed provide training for their workers. Similarly, workers place education and training as their last priority (10th out of 10).

The Indonesian workforce is dominated by low-skilled labourers with basic education. Statistics Indonesia (2019) indicates that 56 per cent of the Indonesian workforce are either elementary school dropouts or elementary school or junior high school graduates. Ninety per cent

FIGURE 9.1
Labour Productivity across ASEAN Member Countries—Output per Worker (GDP constant 2010 US$), 2019

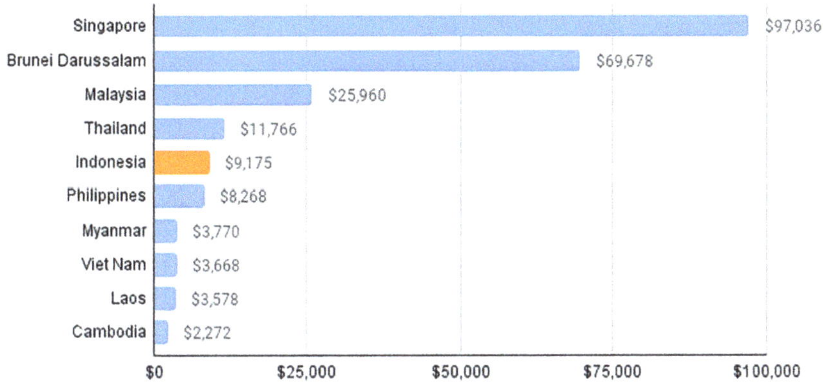

Source: International Labor Organization (2019).

or 120 million of them have never participated in any certified training. Moreover, the proportion of the younger population (15–24 years old) who are Not in Education, Employment, or Training (NEET) is at 22 per cent, one of the highest in ASEAN (Figure 9.2). Additionally, in 2019, the open unemployment rates (TPT) for youths aged 15–19 (26.12 per cent) and 20–24 (15.64 per cent) are far higher than the average unemployment rate of the total workforce at 5.23 per cent. Specifically, the unemployment rate based on the educational level was also the highest in high school (7.9 per cent) and vocational high school (11.18 per cent) graduates. This indicates that the younger workforce with formal education is not necessarily equipped for the job market.

The low quality of the Indonesian workforce is also reflected in its poor competitiveness in several human resources-related indicators. In the World Economic Forum's (WEF) 2019 Global Competitiveness Report index (Schwab 2019), Indonesia's competitiveness is ranked 50th out of 141 countries, below Singapore, Malaysia and Thailand. This ranking is in line with a 2018 Organization for Economic Cooperation and Development (OECD) report, which put Indonesia in the 72nd position out of 77 countries on its Programme for International Student Assessment (PISA),

FIGURE 9.2
Share of Young People Who Are Not in Employment, Education, or Training (NEET) and Share of Workforce with Basic Education

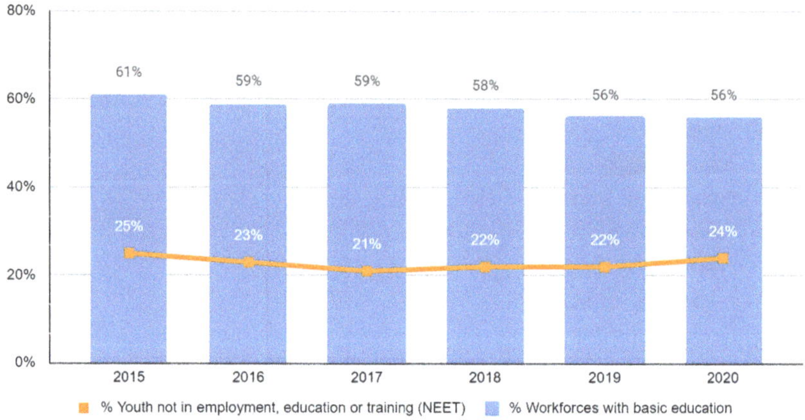

Source: Statistics Indonesia (2020).

which examined reading performance among school students. Related to this, at least 76.7 per cent of companies surveyed in a study (World Bank 2018a; Calì, Hidayat, and Hollweg 2019; Gomez-Mera dan Hollweg 2018) attributed their difficulty in finding people for managerial positions to the inadequate skills of people who applied.

Second, inadequate employment opportunities. On the demand side, job creation is restricted by employers' lack of growth and expansion. Statistics Indonesia (August 2020) showed that of the 128.45 million people in the workforce, 60.47 per cent or 77.68 million are working in the informal sector. Furthermore, Statistics Indonesia (August 2020) also recorded a 7.07 per cent unemployment rate, equal to 9.77 million people which was only 7.1 million in August 2019, meaning that an additional 2.67 million people had become unemployed since the COVID-19 pandemic. The highest unemployment rate was in the vocational and high school graduate category at 11.29 per cent. This indicates that many of those in the workforce with a secondary education have not been adequately absorbed by the job market.

Structural economic transformation, automation, and rampant technological advancements may also disrupt Indonesia's labour market.

Currently, most of the Indonesian workforce is employed in semi-skilled jobs, but jobs under this category have been decreasing due to automation, which may permanently replace manual labour. According to the World Bank's Indonesia's Critical Occupations List (2018), in 2017, 62 per cent of the Indonesian workforce worked in semi-skilled jobs, 21.5 per cent in low-skilled jobs, and 16.5 per cent in high-skilled jobs. Between 2016 and 2017, the proportion of semi-skilled jobs dwindled to 62 per cent from 66.2 per cent. The transition of Indonesia's economy from agriculture-based to manufacturing and services-based also played a role in this shift. The transition, combined with the high rate of technology adoption, can exacerbate skill imbalance and skill gaps throughout the period (Yoong and Gil Sander 2020).

The *third* is the absence of systematic job market information. This makes job seekers unaware of what the most-sought skills are. This can create mismatches between skills possessed by the workforce and skills required by the employers. For instance, nearly 90 per cent of job seekers still browse for job openings using conventional ways, such as word of mouth from friends and relatives. Less than 40 per cent use other methods, such as applying for jobs advertised in printed and electronic media, contacting employers directly to ask for job opportunities, or signing themselves up on job platforms (Wihardja and Cunningham 2021). This asymmetric job market information can lead to inefficient investment in education infrastructure and high costs for employers, especially when recruiting professional and high-skilled workers. This will result in job search inefficiency, low employment opportunities, as well as lower productivity and competitiveness.

To overcome the main labour issues and create a better job market that creates middle-income jobs, the Indonesian government needs to invest more in the workforce. Investments in the future workforce can be done in several ways, such as providing access to formal education, while the improvements in the current workforce can be facilitated by training access and assistance, including skilling, reskilling, and upskilling, to ensure that they remain productive and adaptive to new high-skilled jobs.

Today, a formal education diploma can no longer guarantee productivity. The workforce needs to invest in sought-out skills, while companies need to constantly train and retrain their employees as job descriptions change constantly and old jobs are getting replaced with new ones. In the current circumstances, the *Kartu Prakerja* programme has been implemented to provide training and help the workforce upgrade its skills and welfare. The Project Management Office (PMO) of *Kartu Prakerja* has been working together with private entities and training institutions in providing a wide variety of quality training for the Indonesian workforce.

The remainder of the chapter is as follows. Section 9.2 discusses the design of the *Kartu Prakerja* Programme. Section 9.3 describes *Kartu Prakerja's* innovations and breakthroughs. Section 9.4 lays out the implementation of *Kartu Prakerja*. Section 9.5 presents the scientific evidence of *Kartu Prakerja's* impacts. Section 9.6 explores *Kartu Prakerja's* transition back to the normal scheme, and lastly, Section 9.7 discusses the PMO *Kartu Prakerja's* long-term plans and concludes.

9.2 *KARTU PRAKERJA* PROGRAMME: REALIZING POLITICAL COMMITMENTS INTO POLICIES

9.2.1 Initial Design of *Kartu Prakerja* Programme

In response to the aforementioned labour market issues, President Joko Widodo has committed to creating labour market reforms, including the publicly funded provision of short-term vocational training for workers and potential workers, named the *Kartu Prakerja* (Pre-employment Card) programme. The programme was first mentioned by the President during the campaign for his second presidential term *"Optimis Indonesia Maju"* (With Optimism, Indonesia Progresses) on 24 February 2019, in Sentul, West Java. The programme is in line with his vision for his second presidential term from 2019 to 2024 of improving the quality of Indonesia's human resources. The President believed that the *Kartu Prakerja* programme will be able to reduce the skill gap and shortage, as well as skill and job mismatch.

Kartu Prakerja was designed following hundreds of focus group discussions since May 2019. Its initial concept was submitted by the National Team for the Acceleration of Poverty Reduction (TNP2K) and the Office of Presidential Staff (KSP). This concept was then discussed by TNP2K, KSP, the Ministry of Manpower, and the Coordinating Ministry for Economic Affairs, and involved other ministries and institutions, industry players, associations, academics, human resource development forums, digital platforms and training institutions. Throughout its journey, the concept of *Kartu Prakerja* had become quite dynamic and kept adjusting to the expected needs of its beneficiaries.

To follow up on the President's directives, a technical team comprised of concerned government institutions was then formed to oversee the formation of this new programme, ensuring its accountability. The technical team came up with various principles that were later incorporated into a Presidential Regulation. Finally, *Kartu Prakerja* was officially established by the President through Perpres No. 36/2020 on the Development of Work Competencies through the *Kartu Prakerja* Programme.

To fulfil the mandates dictated by Perpres No. 36/2020 and the Coordinating Ministry for Economic Affairs Regulation (Permenkoekon) No. 3/2020, in performing its duties, the Job Creation Committee (KCK) will be assisted by the PMO of *Kartu Prakerja*. The Coordinating Minister for Economic Affairs in his duty as head of KCK issued a decree on 17 March 2020, to appoint five PMO directors from the Coordinating Ministry for Economic Affairs, Ministry of Manpower, KSP, and private institutions. On 20 March 2020, a soft launching for *Kartu Prakerja* was held and its website was officially opened to the public. By then, the website was already accessible and had important information on *Kartu Prakerja*, such as the user's journey, registration steps, etc., even though registration had not been opened yet.

The main purpose of the *Kartu Prakerja* programme is to improve the competency, productivity, and competitiveness of the Indonesian workforce (Presidential Regulation [Perpres] No. 36/2020), and to develop entrepreneurship (Perpres No. 76/2020). The programme is open to all Indonesian citizens who are at least 18 years old, not enrolled in any formal education, and willing to apply for the programme. This programme is not only directed to benefit potential workers, but also workers who want to upskill themselves. This is to optimize workforce skill compatibility with market requirements.

Every beneficiary of *Kartu Prakerja* is entitled to assistance in two components. The first component is funding to participate in training that emphasizes skilling, reskilling and upskilling. The second component is cash incentives to cover the costs of job-seeking and to fulfil their daily needs. The aforementioned labour issues are complex and require thorough solutions, which *Kartu Prakerja* contributes to solving by complementing other formal education and government training programmes conducted by the government.

In the initial design stage, the components and distribution mechanism of the *Kartu Prakerja* incentives according to the regulation (Presidential

Regulation No. 36/2020 and Coordinating Minister for Economic Affairs Regulation No. 3/2020) that the fund consists of: (i) fees to purchase training which beneficiaries pay to the training providers via digital platforms, (ii) post-training incentives progressively disbursed over four months, and (iii) incentives for beneficiaries who are willing to fill out three evaluation surveys in three different periods. The distribution of the incentives would depend upon the purchase and completion of training by the beneficiary, which is proved by the beneficiary by providing reviews and ratings of the training, obtaining the training certificate; and filling out the evaluation surveys. The distribution of incentives is managed directly from the government's central account.

The ecosystem of *Kartu Prakerja* consists of several main elements, including training institutions, digital platforms, job platforms, payment system providers, and *Kartu Prakerja's* fund management partner (Figure 9.3). The training institutions are tasked to implement the training programmes, provide training certificates, and report the implementation to the PMO regularly. The digital platforms act as a digital marketplace and create training inventories and curate them, facilitate training institutions to register for the programme, as well as facilitate beneficiaries to browse and choose from various training offered on the platforms. In addition, the payment system providers, which consist of a state-owned bank and several e-wallet providers, are tasked with the distribution of incentives to the beneficiaries' accounts free of charge. Lastly, the fund management partner helps oversee the disbursement of the training funds and incentives by *Kartu Prakerja.*

9.2.2 COVID-19 and the Shift of *Kartu Prakerja* Programme Design

Initially, *Kartu Prakerja* was designed to focus only on improving competency, productivity and competitiveness of the workforce, especially among the unemployed young population. However, when Indonesia was struck by the COVID-19 pandemic and an immediate economic contraction took place in March 2020, the government thought social assistance for the poor and vulnerable citizens negatively affected by the pandemic must be expanded. For such an expansion, the government decided to increase the scope of beneficiaries from both the ongoing social assistance programmes and the newly rolled-out programmes. *Kartu Prakerja* was among the new

FIGURE 9.3
***Kartu Prakerja* Ecosystem**

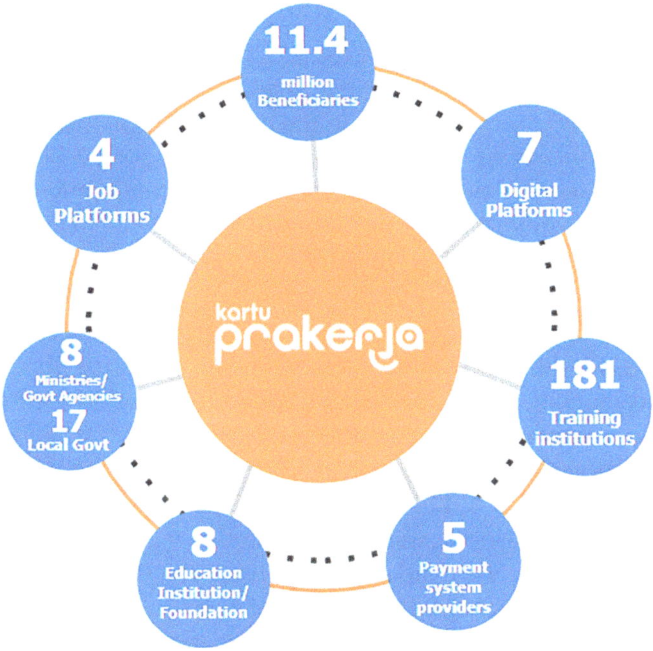

Source: Project Management Office (PMO) of *Kartu Prakerja.*

programmes that eventually became an instrument for social assistance, considering that the targeted beneficiaries were also likely to be among the most affected by the pandemic.

With this shift in its design, after its launch in April 2020, *Kartu Prakerja* adopted a "double mission", which was to improve competency and to secure and maintain purchasing power among workers and small business people who had fallen victim to the adverse economic impacts of the pandemic. In this revised programme design, beneficiaries of *Kartu Prakerja* will receive funding for online training of IDR1 million per person and a post-training incentive of IDR2.55 million per person, amounting to a total of IDR3.55 million benefits per beneficiary.

To make sure that as many people as possible can access the programme, *Kartu Prakerja* is aiming at the segment of the population which is vulnerable to falling below the poverty line due to COVID-19 but is not yet eligible for other social assistance programmes in the government's integrated social welfare database (Family Hope Programme [PKH], non-cash food assistance, [BPNT], Healthy Indonesia Card [KIS], Indonesia Smart Card [KIP]). As the decision to combine the social cash transfer to *Kartu Prakerja* was made suddenly, the government had to move quickly to establish regulation as the basis for the change, the Presidential Regulation (Perpres) No. 36/2020 on *Kartu Prakerja* Programme.

The pandemic also prompted other modifications of *Kartu Prakerja*. Before the pandemic, various focus group discussions (FGDs) organized by KSP and the Coordinating Ministry for Economic Affairs between 2019 and 2020 concluded that the effective amount of overall training incentives should be between IDR3 million to IDR7 million per person assuming that all training would be held offline and in person. However, the pandemic prompted mobility restrictions that made the plan to bring professional trainers to a training venue impossible. *Kartu Prakerja's* training courses shifted to fully online classes on digital platforms.

Throughout the COVID-19 pandemic, *Kartu Prakerja* has thus expanded its function as semi-social assistance to protect vulnerable groups from the adverse effects of the pandemic on welfare. The President, in his press conference on 31 March 2020, stated that the programme would serve as a social safety net instrument. Based on his directives and Presidential Instruction (Inpres) No. 4/2020, the Job Creation Committee (*Komite Cipta Kerja*, or KCK) made the necessary adjustments to the programme. Eventually, *Kartu Prakerja* became a social protection cluster in the national economic recovery (PEN) scheme.

In the first few months after its implementation, *Kartu Prakerja* immediately attracted public interest and positive responses. The number of applicants has been growing over time. This partly reflects an interest in accessing job training but also the intention to receive the "cash transfer"—something that is naturally needed when the pandemic and recession hit the country.

To target potential beneficiaries and select them, *Kartu Prakerja's* PMO uses population data and other relevant data managed by ministries, central government institutions, regional authorities, and/or other related bodies. The PMO synchronized all the obtained data and matched them with the existing database on social assistance recipients from the Ministry of Social Affairs. The data synchronization was done by filtering ID numbers of social assistance recipients and separating them into a negative list to avoid having one person as a beneficiary of multiple aid programmes.

Meanwhile, the quota for *Kartu Prakerja* beneficiaries must be maintained to meet the "needs" of the training across regions. Therefore, the quota was proportionally allocated to each province according to its unemployment rate, COVID-19 prevalence and the number of job opportunities available. The higher the unemployment figure and the COVID-19 prevalence rate, the higher the beneficiary quota. Ultimately, by its nature as a human capital investment seeking high returns, a greater beneficiary quota is allocated to provinces with higher job vacancies. The PMO then allocated the quota to provinces indicative of the total number of beneficiaries in each province. If the number of beneficiaries is smaller than its allocated provincial quota, the excess will be distributed proportionally to other provinces with an oversubscription of applicants.

All in all, *Kartu Prakerja* wants to prioritize applicants with certain characteristics. To achieve that principle, the selection is done through a randomization process with different scoring weights for participants with different characteristics. A higher score does not warrant an applicant's success, because the randomization process puts together people with low and high scoring standards. This process is proven effective as the actual beneficiaries are dominated by those who are in the younger working population but unemployed—those who need the *Kartu Prakerja* programme the most to boost their employment opportunities.

To benefit from the *Kartu Prakerja* programme, applicants must go through several processes (see Figure 9.4). *First,* applicants have to apply. Applicants must register through *Kartu Prakerja's* website. *Second,* applicants' personal information is verified by the PMO before they can take part in the selection process to become programme beneficiaries. *Third,* after the participant has passed the selection process, a decree will be established to recognize the selected applicant as a *Kartu Prakerja* beneficiary. *Fourth,* once the beneficiary is selected, a virtual account will be set up for each beneficiary. *Fifth,* the training vouchers and post-training incentives of IDR3.5 million will be transferred to the virtual account. *Sixth,* the beneficiary can select and pay for the training they choose on the digital platform by entering their *Kartu Prakerja* number. *Seventh,* after purchasing the training, the beneficiary must complete the training by taking a pre-test and a post-test to earn a certificate. After completing the training, the beneficiary must rate and review the training to be eligible

FIGURE 9.4
User's Journey of *Kartu Prakerja* Programme

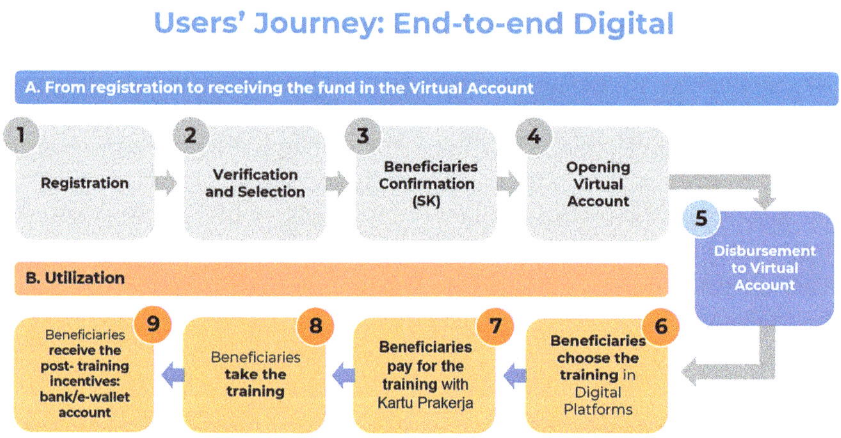

Source: PMO of *Kartu Prakerja*.

for post-training incentives. *Eighth*, the beneficiaries can select a bank or e-wallet, take the KYC (Know Your Customer) procedure conducted by payment partners, and then have the first post-training incentive transferred via a linked incentive channel account. *Ninth*, the beneficiaries can fill out Evaluation Surveys questionnaires after earning the first incentive.

9.3 *KARTU PRAKERJA* OFFERS INNOVATIONS AND BREAKTHROUGHS IN PUBLIC SERVICES

Kartu Prakerja has offered public service innovations and transformations in Indonesia. *First*, it is the first social assistance programme in Indonesia with a self-targeting, on-demand application that provides direct access for those who are interested in applying. The registration process is open and inclusive for anyone with any background, thus encouraging their initiative and independent mentality. *Kartu Prakerja* provides funding in the form of vouchers to purchase training so its beneficiaries are free to choose what they prefer, as well as to choose the e-wallet they will receive post-training incentives in. With its on-demand scheme, *Kartu Prakerja* can reach out to workers in the informal sector who were not protected by any social safety net, but whose purchasing power is affected by the pandemic. The programme also works to reach out to the vulnerable (people in the middle 40 per cent income group) and poor population affected by the pandemic who should have been eligible for social assistance but have yet to be registered in the social assistance database (DTKS) due to exclusion errors.

An on-demand-based social assistance programme such as *Kartu Prakerja* can serve as a reference for modernized social assistance programmes in the future, including complementing ongoing assistance programmes. This application of an on-demand scheme is a crucial element of the social safety net for the poor and vulnerable population, especially those affected by the economic shocks caused by a pandemic or natural disaster. This scheme allows for more dynamic beneficiary identification and a faster response to potential future shocks. In summary, an on-demand assistance programme can target people who suddenly fall below the poverty line and cannot be identified by a slow-paced, conventional social assistance system that relies on static data and looks into poverty snapshots that are only occasionally updated.

Based on the experience of *Kartu Prakerja's* PMO, an on-demand registration system for applicants to sign up independently will run well with certain support. First, there should be regulations and institutional support for backing the mechanism of the applicants' data collection. The PMO has been able to fulfil its mandate in the data collection of each applicant thanks to the legal support which provided clear and thorough instructions on the registration phase. Second, there should be adequate technology to verify the applicants' data. The PMO uses a multi-layered mechanism and thorough verification and identification of the personal data of each *Kartu Prakerja* applicant. Lastly, these processes should be digitalized to make sure that the registration process can be done easily, swiftly, simultaneously, and on a large scale. Further, a digitalized social assistance system with resilient information technology management can also ensure PMO's capability in collecting, managing and exchanging data with other management offices of social assistance programmes conveniently and accurately.

Second, Kartu Prakerja is an end-to-end digital ecosystem using advanced technology that enables every citizen to register themselves easily and efficiently, whenever they need to and wherever they are across the country. This digitalization allows people of various backgrounds and conditions to apply, such as the differently able, low-educated, and former migrant workers. The registration process can be done online and independently, without any intermediary, through the *Prakerja* website (www.prakerja.go.id). The incentives will also be transferred digitally using e-wallets or bank accounts. Beneficiaries are required to link their own e-wallet or bank accounts that have been verified using a KYC process, mitigating risks of fraud. *Kartu Prakerja* erases time and space limitations while also creating levelled access and training quality at a lower cost. Digitalization is inevitable, and therefore, *Kartu Prakerja* is not a physical card, but rather a 16-digit unique code that beneficiaries can use to access its services. This digitalized card saves a lot of budgets that otherwise would be used in card printing and distribution, eliminates the risk of losing cards, and encourages a digital-savvy society. Such processes and means encourage applicants and beneficiaries to improve their digital literacy as their user journey will be done independently. With this all-digital design, *Kartu Prakerja* has proven its inclusivity by serving citizens in all 34 provinces and 514 cities and regencies across Indonesia, including those living in the underdeveloped, outermost, and remote (3T) regions.

Third, the ecosystem of *Kartu Prakerja's* training is developed in an inclusive and competitive digital marketplace design. The programme bolsters collaboration between the government and private entities, devoid of the usual procurement steps. Every partner is given the freedom to compete in providing the best service and to enter and exit the ecosystem per the regulations. Training institutions and beneficiaries are also free to choose between the available digital platforms to sell and buy the training. This whole process is expected to encourage healthy competition within a perfectly competitive market that benefits all the actors. If a training institution is burdened by a high service fee in a platform, for example, they can opt for other platforms that offer cheaper or even no fee. Beneficiaries also have their own voice and choice to choose the training that suits them best. With rating and review features, beneficiaries can see for themselves which training offer the best quality and characteristics. Finally, this digital marketplace system advantages the ecosystem by bringing together training supply and demand in one place, reducing asymmetric information, browsing costs, and transaction costs, and supporting risk-sharing between the government and the private actors involved.

Fourth, *Kartu Prakerja* is a pioneer in Indonesia's Government-to-Person (G2P) programme, which puts together payment system providers like financial technology and conventional banks as partners of the programme. Post-training incentives are sent via these partners, allowing beneficiaries to minimize physical contact that is not encouraged during the pandemic. This method promotes a modern financial system and inclusion for beneficiaries who can get to know other features from the partners and use them for other private or business purposes. The incentives are transferred swiftly, accurately and accountably, ensuring zero corruption opportunities.

Fifth, *Kartu Prakerja* answers to the beneficiaries' needs using a customer-centric mindset. The PMO regularly evaluates the programme with inputs from the beneficiaries provided through reviews, ratings and periodical evaluation surveys, keeping the programme relevant to those who benefit from it. The PMO has administered various communication channels, both for the general public (Instagram, website, Facebook, YouTube), and the targeted beneficiaries (email, dashboard, text messages). The programme also provides multiple reliable contact centres to monitor all inquiries and complaints, such as a free hotline, live chat, and online forms. The monitoring is done through an integrated service dashboard.

9.4 IMPLEMENTATION OF *KARTU PRAKERJA*

9.4.1 The First Three Months

Since its launch on 11 April 2020, within the first three months, *Kartu Prakerja* has managed to reach 680,918 citizens in 34 provinces and 513 cities and regencies across Indonesia. As many as 168,111 applicants were selected for the first batch of the programme, followed by 288,154 and 224,657 people in the second and third batch. The applicants came from various locations. In these first three batches, applicants were recorded in every city except for one, which was in Deiyai Regent, Papua. In the early days of the programme, four provinces were undersubscribed, namely North Kalimantan, North Maluku, West Papua and Papua. Despite that, interest in this programme has generally kept improving, as seen in the registered applicants on the website, which amounted to an outstanding 11.3 million as of 15 July 2020.

To evaluate the programme, *Kartu Prakerja's* PMO partnered with TNP2K in conducting a rapid assessment survey from 19 May to 1 June 2020, on about 12,000 beneficiaries from the first to the third batch who have completed their training and received post-training incentives. The survey showed that most beneficiaries are vocational or high school graduates (58.93 per cent), undergraduates (25.27 per cent), and others. The survey also found that *Kartu Prakerja* beneficiaries were mostly male (66.5 per cent). The majority of beneficiaries were unemployed (80.5 per cent). From the perspective of age range, the most dominant range was 35 years old or younger (88 per cent).

Further results from the survey show that 95.8 per cent of beneficiaries believed that the programme was beneficial. Some 92.3 per cent agreed that the programme is an effective means of increasing competencies among workers/job seekers and entrepreneurs. Additionally, 96.3 per cent of beneficiaries stated that the supporting facilities and infrastructure for the training were satisfactory, and 79 per cent of them said they did not encounter any obstacles during the registration process.

Furthermore, the *Sakernas* survey in August 2020 on 300,000 Indonesian households spread proportionally to the city level also found that 88.92 per cent of the beneficiaries who completed their training considered the programme to have boosted their job skills. Moreover, 81.24 per cent of them used their post-training incentives to fulfil their daily needs, and 23.47 per cent used the incentives as capital for their businesses.

9.4.2 Two Years On

Between April 2020 and December 2021, *Kartu Prakerja* opened 22 batches that effectively reached 11.4 million beneficiaries in 34 provinces and 514 cities and regencies across Indonesia with 62 per cent of the beneficiaries living in rural areas, 3 per cent living in underdeveloped regions, 18 per cent are elementary school graduates or dropouts, 2 per cent are persons with disabilities, and 3 per cent are former migrant workers (see Figure 9.5). Within almost two years, a whopping 83 million applicants already registered on *Kartu Prakerja's* website. Interestingly, the programme is the only programme by the Indonesian government included in the ten most-searched topics on Google Indonesia in 2020 and 2021. *Kartu Prakerja* has been successful in extending its programmes to all layers of society and in achieving the double mission of providing empowerment through training and social assistance.

Within the ecosystem of *Kartu Prakerja*, there were a total of 1,987 training programmes provided by 181 institutions, costing an average of IDR383,000 per training programme. Meanwhile, the average funds

FIGURE 9.5
Map of Distribution of *Kartu Prakerja*'s Effective Beneficiaries, 2020–21 (in thousands)

(a) 2020

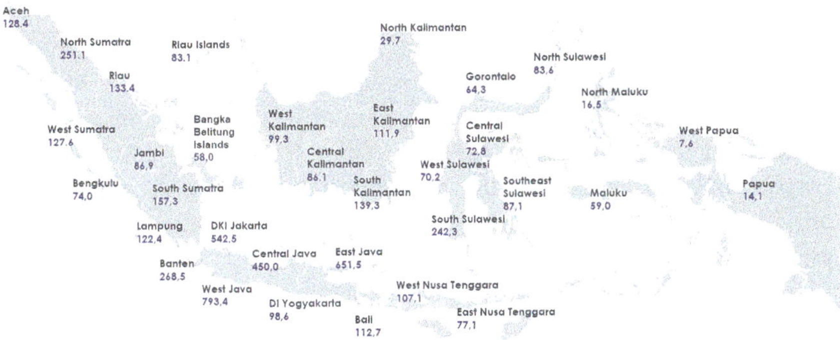

(b) 2021

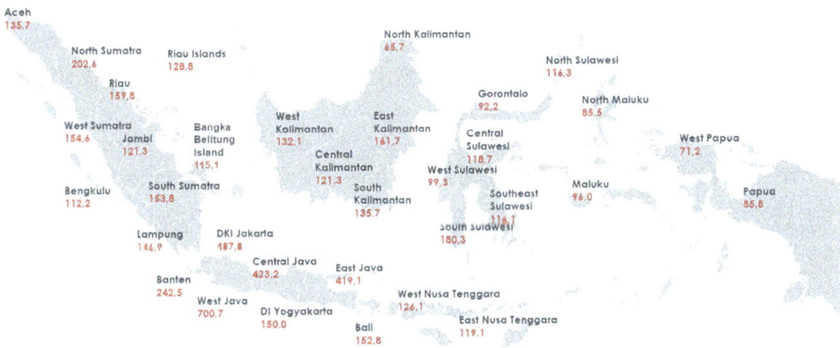

Note: Data as of 31 December 2021.
Source: PMO of *Kartu Prakerja*.

spent by each beneficiary to purchase training courses was IDR670,000. Most training (71 per cent) is self-paced (no fixed period is set for each beneficiary to complete the training), using the Learning Management System (LMS), in webinar format (15 per cent), and hybrid or combination between LMS and webinars (14 per cent). From the training aspect, the best-selling categories are (i) sales and marketing, (ii) food and beverages, (iii) lifestyle, (iv) management, (v) office work, (vi) information technology, and (vii) agriculture (see Table 9.1). The average rating of all training is 4.9 out of 5.

In improving the quality of the training and strengthening *Kartu Prakerja's* internal organization, the PMO has participated in a multi-stakeholder partnership with various colleges and other educational institutions. The PMO works together with the University of Indonesia, Gadjah Mada University, Airlangga University, Atma Jaya Catholic University and Indonesia Mengajar to evaluate the training. The PMO also collaborates with IPB University, Muhammadiyah Malang University and Nahdlatul Ulama Indonesia University in monitoring the ongoing training. Lastly, the PMO cooperates with the Office of the Attorney General, which provides legal handling in civil matters and state administration, as well as legal advice and/or considerations.

To evaluate *Kartu Prakerja's* achievements, the PMO has conducted several evaluation surveys. From 2020 to 2021, the periodical evaluation surveys have been responded to by 9.8 million beneficiaries. From 10 April to 10 December 2021, the surveys were responded to by 5,116,560 beneficiaries and showed that 90 per cent of them are unemployed, 56 per cent are aged 18 to 35, 64 per cent are high school graduates or higher, 52 per cent are male, and 87 per cent have never participated in any certified training/courses.

Further, *Kartu Prakerja* has successfully assisted and improved the knowledge/competencies of its beneficiaries. This improvement is seen in the significant increase in average post-test scores (68) compared to average

TABLE 9.1
***Kartu Prakerja*'s Training Categories**

Information Technology Microsoft Excel, data science, Phyton, MySQL, Agile, Scrum, Cisco, Trello	**Sales and Marketing** Online business, digital marketing, property marketing	**Lifestyle** Handcrafting, makeup, photography, hairstyling, barber skills
Office Work Secretary, administration customer service	**Technical Work** Audio mixing, computer maintenance, work health and safety	**Agriculture** Hydroponics, liquid fertilizer production, urban farming,
Food and Beverages Culinary art, barista, catering	**Management** Leadership, production strategy, starting a business	**Social Skills** Etiquette, effective marketing communication
Language English, Korean, Chinese, Japanese, Dutch, Spanish, German	**Finance** Venture capital, financial planning, accounting	**Others** Comic drawing, writing

Source: PMO of *Kartu Prakerja*.

pre-test scores (53) in all training. Moreover, 73 per cent of the recipients stated that they will attach their training certificates when applying for jobs. Over 84 per cent believed that their training had emphasized skilling, reskilling and upskilling. A majority (92 per cent) stated that they have been able to choose training according to their personal preferences. Twenty-seven of the surveyed beneficiaries who were unemployed when applying for the programme said that they are now employed or self-employed.

Additionally, *Kartu Prakerja* has been proven to support the purchasing power of its beneficiaries. The post-training incentives they received had been used to buy food (89 per cent), open/support their business (70 per cent) and pay for utilities (68 per cent). Beneficiaries have also been using their e-wallets and bank accounts within the *Kartu Prakerja* ecosystem for other personal necessities. In 2021, 28 per cent of surveyed beneficiaries said the programme made them open a bank account or e-wallet for the first time, and the majority (93 per cent) chose e-wallets (OVO, DANA, LinkAja and GoPay). Nearly all beneficiaries (99 per cent) stated they were satisfied with the services of the payment service providers partnering with *Kartu Prakerja*.

Kartu Prakerja's communication channels, such as live chats, call centres and online forms, have so far handled various complaints/inquiries. Seventy-eight per cent was through live chats, 15 per cent were through online forms, and 7 per cent were through the call centre. For live chat services, the satisfaction rate was recorded at 81 per cent, online forms at 86 per cent, and for overall contact centre services, the customer satisfaction rating (CSAT) has reached 94 per cent. Improvements in complaint handling are one of PMO's strategies in considering the people's needs, focusing on the complaint handling's infrastructure development, which had reached 220 per cent since *Kartu Prakerja* was established.

9.4.3 Continuous Improvements

Kartu Prakerja's PMO continues to improve the programme's services for beneficiaries and applicants. The PMO has been developing numerous features and details based on some of the most prevalent complaints, such as incentive distribution and certificate issuance, the PMO is also encouraging enhancement in all sectors to provide a better service, including through regulations in areas with limited infrastructure, i.e., through providing offline registration with Manpower Ministerial Regulation (Permenaker) No. 17/2020 as its basis.

At the same time, the government has been perfecting the governance of *Kartu Prakerja* by issuing Perpres No. 76/2020. This new regulation is part of the government's commitment to strengthen and improve the programme's quality, including its promise to ensure the programme can reach out to those who need it the most. Perpres No. 76/2020 also stipulates which parties are not eligible to apply for the programme, namely state officials, leaders and members of the Regional House of Representatives (DPRD), State Civil Apparatus (ASN), members of the Indonesian Military and the National Police, village heads and officials, and directors, commissioners, and members of the supervisory board of state or region-owned enterprises (BUMN/BUMD). The structure of the KCK is also strengthened through the addition of committee members comprising the State Secretary, Cabinet Secretary, Attorney General, Chief of the National Police, head of the Development Finance Comptroller (BPKP), and head of the National Public Procurement Agency (LKPP).

Since the first batch, many features have been added to *Kartu Prakerja's* website dashboard. The first is optical character recognition (OCR) technology to scan the photograph in the IDs uploaded by the applicants. The reading from OCR will be matched with the Population and Civil Registry Agency's (*Dukcapil*) database to confirm its credentials. Second, the newly designed *Kartu Prakerja* website is more attractive and user-friendly, making it easier for users to browse for information and thus improving the user's journey. Third, a training recommendation feature also assists beneficiaries in choosing between training by recommending courses based on preferences and previous training the beneficiaries have attended. Fourth, a job recommendation feature has been created to assist beneficiaries in getting job opportunities suitable to the skills they have obtained from the training. Fifth, a job search feature was also created to help beneficiaries look for jobs according to their needs and preferences, such as location, requirements, skills, and expected salary.

All in all, the PMO has committed to continue improving the standards set for the training over time. The PMO monitors the implementation of these standards using several indicators:

(1) Any training that will be included in *Kartu Prakerja* must have been offered to the general public before being proposed to the PMO, which can be proven by attaching links to other web portals that also offer the training.

(2) The proposed training should fulfil all interactive prerequisites as a fully online course.
(3) The training should be guided and taught by competent instructors with relevant experiences in their field, which can be proven by attaching certifications or a minimum of three years' worth of experience.

To make sure that the skills taught in the training are matched with the needs of the job market, *Kartu Prakerja* is made to be occupation-based, referring to Indonesia's Occupational Tasks and List (IndOTask), which was compiled and issued in early 2021 by the Ministry of Development Planning/National Development Planning Agency (*Bappenas*) and the World Bank. IndOTask lists fifty-one occupations identified to be in high demand and/or are strategic to the Indonesian economy, per the 2018 Indonesia's Critical Occupation List and in the 2020 Indonesia's Occupational Employment Outlook.

Kartu Prakerja, which was intended to be implemented as quickly as possible to mitigate the pandemic effects, has also faced several obstacles. At the beginning of the programme, there were challenges like high public expectations towards *Kartu Prakerja* being social assistance that did not require recipients to attend training. Many applicants were aware that the programme was just intended for furloughed or terminated workers, though in reality, unemployed people, business people, and workers were also allowed to sign up. Second, many believed that being a beneficiary will ensure that they get a job, though this is not plausible, because even more formal and established educational institutions cannot ensure such things, not to mention the enormous volume of applicants which made the idea impossible. Third, many adjustments needed to be made due to uneven digital infrastructure across the country.

9.5 SCIENTIFIC EVIDENCE OF *KARTU PRAKERJA*'S IMPACTS

9.5.1 Evaluation of the Impacts

Evaluation results from research by the Abdul Latif Jameel Poverty Action Lab Southeast Asia (J-PAL SEA), in collaboration with TNP2K and Prospera, which was conducted from June to October 2021 on 47,750 respondents, showed positive results of *Kartu Prakerja* as a programme. The evaluation used the randomized control trials (RCT) method that divided respondents into beneficiaries (treatment) and non-beneficiaries (control) randomized groups and compared the outcomes of interest between these two groups.

The study resulted in several positive pieces of evidence. First, *Kartu Prakerja* was found to have improved entrepreneurship among its beneficiaries by 30 per cent and increased their average monthly income by IDR122,500. Second, the programme has boosted several other indicators; the beneficiaries' food security increased by 6 per cent, and the probability of obtaining more personal assets increased by 21 per cent.

Further, *Kartu Prakerja* also improved the beneficiaries' competency and training, where they were found to be more likely to use their training certificates to apply for jobs (172 per cent), attend more training in recent months (119.4 per cent), and use the Internet for their job search (10 per cent). From the financial services aspect, beneficiaries of *Kartu Prakerja* are more likely to have e-wallet accounts than non-beneficiaries (53 per cent) and pay more by online purchases with their e-wallets (40 per cent).

Presisi Indonesia research agency also conducted research using the RCT method on 2,152 respondents from September to November 2021, finding similar positive results to J-PAL SEA's research. First, *Kartu Prakerja* was able to boost the work competencies of its beneficiaries by 74 percentage points (pp) or 2.2 per cent, productivity by 23 pp or 2.7 per cent, competitiveness by 67 pp or 3.8 per cent, and entrepreneurship skills by 177 pp (48.5 per cent). After participating in the training, not only were the beneficiaries able to improve competency, productivity and competitiveness, but they were also able to construct new ideas and strategies that could encourage them to start their own business. Second, *Kartu Prakerja* could improve the beneficiaries' average income by 17 to 21 per cent compared to non-beneficiaries. Third, 80 per cent of the beneficiaries confirmed that they opened a banking or e-wallet account for the first time when they were selected as *Kartu Prakerja's* beneficiaries. Fourth, female beneficiaries were able to improve their work competencies by 96 pp or 2.9 per cent higher than their non-beneficiary counterparts. Fifth, beneficiaries living outside Java Island have been enjoying more upskilling benefits than those living on Java Island (0.18 per cent). Finally, *Kartu Prakerja* was found to have been more effective for beneficiaries who are of productive age, live in urban areas, and hold a high school diploma or higher.

9.5.2 Findings from More Surveys Confirm *Kartu Prakerja*'s Positive Impacts

The results of several other independent surveys on *Kartu Prakerja* have confirmed positive findings by J-PAL SEA and Presisi Indonesia. The *Sakernas* August 2021 survey by Statistics Indonesia found that 87.22 per cent of beneficiaries who have completed their training considered that the programme has enhanced their work skills. Furthermore, 83.33 per cent were able to use their post-training incentive to fulfil their daily needs, and 34.15 per cent were able to use the incentive as capital for their businesses.

Ipsos, a France-based global research institute, also issued its independent survey on the impacts of *Kartu Prakerja*. Based on their survey of 500 respondents in 20 Indonesian cities from 16 to 24 June 2021, Ipsos found that *Kartu Prakerja* was the most widely received social assistance from the government throughout the pandemic (24 per cent) and also the most beneficial assistance programme (35 per cent).

Cyrus Network, an Indonesian survey body, revealed the positive impacts of *Kartu Prakerja* based on a survey it conducted on 2,000 respondents from 1 to 5 May 2021. Nearly all respondents agreed that training from *Kartu Prakerja* improved their knowledge (98.2 per cent), skills (96 per cent), and professional attitude (93.9 per cent). In general, 98.9 per cent of respondents stated that the programme is beneficial. They also agreed that other people around them could benefit from *Kartu Prakerja* (96.8 per cent) and that the programme should continue (98.4 per cent).

A CSIS Indonesia study is also in line with results from the other surveys, in that *Kartu Prakerja* could encourage improvements in competencies, productivity, competitiveness, and entrepreneurship. The study found improvements in employment and entrepreneurship among surveyed beneficiaries after the latter participated in *Kartu Prakerja*. Specifically, there was an increase in the number of beneficiaries who secured a job in the formal sector, opened a business, and became digital merchants on e-commerce platforms.

According to the study, beneficiaries also had their knowledge improved (95.1 per cent) and skills enhanced (93.4 per cent). Work competencies among beneficiaries have also developed, shown in their ability to complete an assignment better than before they attended *Kartu Prakerja* training (90.5 per cent), to be more innovative in problem-solving at work or in their business (90.2 per cent), to finish an assignment more effectively (90 per cent) and efficiently (89.8 per cent) than before. Nearly all beneficiaries were able to apply lessons they learned from training at work or in running a business (87.4 per cent) and to improve their competitiveness when applying for a job or starting a business (85.6 per cent).

9.6 TRANSITIONING BACK TO NORMAL

Taking into account the satisfactory output and results of *Kartu Prakerja's* implementation, that the Indonesian economy is still under the shadows of COVID-19, and the large number in the workforce who still have not participated in any training, the government has decided to continue the programme in 2022 as semi-social assistance. *Kartu Prakerja's* early adaptation into a semi-social assistance programme will be maintained but restoring it to its initial design is necessary as soon as the situation has become more normal—especially when the pandemic has become endemic. In its initial or normal scheme, the proportion of social assistance will be reduced, the funding for purchase training will be added, and finally, the training will be able to take place physically.

Based on these considerations, *Kartu Prakerja* has targeted to distribute assistance to 2.8 million beneficiaries under the semi-social assistance scheme, and 100,000 recipients under the initial/normal *Kartu Prakerja* scheme. The government is also preparing for more offline training starting in the second half of 2022, as the economy is recovering and the COVID-19's status is expected to be reduced to an endemic. Following its initial design, *Kartu Prakerja* will always be serving Indonesian citizens to improve their work competencies and the competitiveness of job seekers.

The promising vaccination rate is among the main factors that encouraged the government to set up in-person training under the normal scheme. To prepare for *Kartu Prakerja's* transition to normal, the PMO held a pilot project for the transition from 10 to 26 January 2022. This was done for several purposes. First, to analyse the difference in completion rates among training participants using different modes of training (online, offline and blended), and what factors affected them. Second, to measure and compare the effectiveness of offline (in-person) and blended training, which was measured by three outputs, namely reaction, knowledge and competence. Third, to do an inventory of offline/ blended training, identify its challenges and risks, and prepare the steps in implementing them. With this pilot project, the PMO aims for the implementation of *Kartu Prakerja's* initial/normal scheme by the second half of 2022, including the selection process, establishing standards for *Kartu Prakerja's* partners, drafting the necessary regulations, and most importantly, how Kartu Prakerja will respond to and communicate with these changes.

9.7 CONCLUSION

Kartu Prakerja has become a novel way in the government's attempts to address challenges in the labour market, which have become a major obstacle in Indonesia's aspirations to become a high-income country. This programme also applies several innovations, such as the programme "on-demand" assistance, whereby applicants can target themselves as fitting candidates, and then apply independently through the *Kartu Prakerja's* website. *Kartu Prakerja* also complements other existing training programmes as well as improves Indonesia's education outcome through innovative means to achieve significant and inclusive results within a short time.

Kartu Prakerja has also adopted information technology to provide customer-oriented services. This programme's presence has been online-based via digital marketplaces, encouraging easy convergence of supply and demand, overcoming asymmetric information, and reducing browsing and transaction costs; all to spur a faster market equilibrium. Reviews and ratings from training participants serve as a selection process that will help other beneficiaries discover the best training or courses. *Kartu Prakerja* is also a pioneer of social assistance programmes in Indonesia with 100 per cent digital implementation.

In the long term, various features of *Kartu Prakerja* can be adopted by other government initiatives. Specifically, the on-demand principle and adaptability can be advantageous to other social assistance programmes. *Kartu Prakerja* also shows how digitalization can optimize a large-scale programme, making implementation efficient, transparent, accountable and effective. *Kartu Prakerja* also demonstrates the importance of integrating data from different ministries and institutions.

Ultimately, *Kartu Prakerja* has become one of the government's strategic initiatives in overcoming challenges in the job market while also mitigating adverse economic effects from the COVID-19 pandemic through conditional cash transfers or post-training incentives. Not only has this programme become a means of distributing funding from the government to the people, but it also enables nationwide skill development that will become a foundation for achieving more job opportunities as the economy recovers. *Kartu Prakerja* is one of the campaign promises of President Joko Widodo that has been realized and proved successful, and one that should be sustained beyond the President's term. Therefore, the plan ahead is to maintain some of *Kartu Prakerja's* semi-social assistance features, refine and adapt its scheme as the economy normalizes, while further institutionalize the programme for its sustainability in the years to come.

Note

* From the beginning of the programme, to ensure that applicants are not recipients of other welfare assistance programmes and therefore eligible for *Kartu Prakerja's* incentives, the government has added an eligibility criterion, where an applicant must not be a primary account holder of any of the central government's other social assistance.

References

Cali, Massimiliano, Taufik Hidayat, and Claire H. Hollweg. 2019. *What is Behind Mobility Costs? Evidence from Indonesia.* Open Knowledge Repository, World Bank Group. https://openknowledge.worldbank.org/bitstream/handle/10986/32458/What-is-Behind-Labor-Mobility-Costs-Evidence-from-Indonesia.pdf?sequence=1&isAllowed=y (accessed 30 March 2022).

Gomez-Mera, Laura, and Claire H. Hollweg. 2018. *Firm Performance and Constraints in Indonesia.* Mimeo. The World Bank.

International Labor Organization. 2019. ILOSTAT database. Available from https://ilostat.ilo.org/data/

Kementerian Perencanaan Pembangunan Nasional/Badan Perencanaan Pembangunan Nasional. 2019. *Indonesia 2045: Berdaulat, Maju, Adil, dan Makmur* (in Indonesian). Jakarta: Bappenas. https://simantu.pu.go.id/content/?id=502 (accessed 1 April 2022).

OECD. 2019. *PISA 2018 Results (Volume I): What Students Know and Can Do.* Paris: OECD Publishing. https://doi.org/10.1787/5f07c754-en

Schwab, K. 2019. *The Global Competitiveness Report 2019.* Geneva: World Economic Forum. https://www3.weforum.org/docs/WEF_TheGlobalCompetitivenessReport2019.pdf (accessed 1 March 2022).

Statistics Indonesia. 2019. "Survei Angkatan Kerja Nasional" (National Labour Survey). Jakarta: BPS.

———. 2020. "Survei Angkatan Kerja Nasional" (National Labour Survey). Jakarta: BPS.

Wihardja, Maria Monica, and Wendy Cunningham. 2021. *Pathways to Middle-Class Jobs in Indonesia.* Washington, DC: World Bank Group. https://openknowledge.worldbank.org/bitstream/handle/10986/35848/Pathways-to-Middle-Class-Jobs-in-Indonesia.pdf?sequence=4&isAllowed=y (accessed 30 March 2022).

World Bank. 2018a. *Indonesia Economic Quarterly, December 2018: Strengthening Competitiveness.* Jakarta: World Bank. https://openknowledge.worldbank.org/bitstream/handle/10986/30969/IEQ2018Dec.pdf (accessed 1 February 2022).

———. 2018b. *Labor Market Stakeholders' Perception Survey 2016 (English).* Washington, DC: World Bank Group. http://documents.worldbank.org/curated/en/947781625046177722/Labor-Market-Stakeholders-Perception-Survey-2016 (accessed 1 March 2022).

Yoong, P.S., and Frederico Gil Sander. 2020. *Structural Transformation and Labor Productivity in Indonesia: Where are All the Good Jobs?.* Washington, DC: World Bank Group. https://openknowledge.worldbank.org/handle/10986/35951 (accessed 1 April 2022).

10

Mental Health during the COVID-19 Pandemic

An Issue Less Visited[1]

Chairina Hanum Siregar and Adiatma Y.M. Siregar

10.1 THE CURRENT TREND OF MENTAL ILLNESS

10.1.1 Global Trend

Globally, mental illness has been recognized as a less addressed disease while having a large economic impact (Chong et al. 2016; Steel et al. 2014; United Nations, Department of Economic and Social Affairs 2022). It is estimated that globally, in 2010, the productivity loss due to anxiety and depression amounted to US$1 trillion per year, while mental health in general resulted in losses as high as US$2.5 trillion per year due to poor health and productivity losses, and that number is projected to increase to US$6 trillion by 2030 (Lancet Global Health 2020).

As a type of mental illness, depressive disorders were among the leading causes of years lived in disability (YLD) counts in 2017, and mental disorders, in general, shared more than 14 per cent of age-standardized

YLDs during the last thirty years. The prevalence of mental disorders is higher than 10 per cent in all twenty-one Global Burden of Disease (GBD) regions (e.g., Southeast Asia, East Asia, and Oceania) (James et al. 2018; Moran et al. 2012).

Looking at figures taken from the Institute for Health Metrics and Evaluation (IHME) website (Institute for Health Metrics and Evaluation 2019), mental disorders have increased in rank in terms of Disability Adjusted Life Years (DALYs)[2] from number 13 in 1990 to number 7 in 2019 (Figure 10.1), potentially showing a substantial increase in severity and the number of diseases. However, in terms of Years Lived in Disability (YLD), mental disorders consistently sat at the 2nd rank in both 1990 and 2019, showing a potentially similar trend over the 29 years (Figure 10.2).

As an example of the burden of mental illness, studies have shown that psychotic disorders are associated with both health and non-healthcare costs. However, it is less known that the non-healthcare costs component such as productivity loss (Knapp and Wong 2020) has a large share (more than 50 per cent of the total cost). Such a trend is shown by various studies in different countries such as China, Australia, Japan, England, Ireland, Spain, Belgium, Korea, the United States of America and Canada (Sado et al. 2013; Mangalore and Knapp 2007; Phanthunane et al. 2012; Charrier, Chevreul, and Durand-Zaleski 2013; SANE Australia 2002; Fasseeh et al. 2018; Zhai et al. 2013). Non-healthcare costs also stem from, among others, the impact of the disease on the family members and/or caretakers. Taking care of people living with psychotic disorders requires efforts that cost time and may, subsequently, lead to productivity losses either within or outside of the household. In Indonesia, although the share of non-healthcare costs does not reach more than 50 per cent of the total social cost of treatment, the cost of seeking treatment per patient, for both inpatient and outpatient treatment, from the patient's perspective (e.g., transport costs, time/opportunity cost) far surpasses 10 per cent of the patient's monthly expenditure, making it a potentially catastrophic disease (Siregar et al. 2022; Russell 2004). It seems that cost has become a barrier to accessing mental health services a factor which persists in both developing and developed countries (Addo, Nonvignon, and Aikins 2013; Agboola et al. 2018; Hailemichael et al. 2019; Opoku-Boateng et al. 2017; Rowan, McAlpine, and Blewett 2013; Moroz, Moroz, and D'Angelo 2020).

FIGURE 10.1
Global Comparison of Disability Adjusted Life Years (DALYs) of Various Diseases in 1990 and 2019

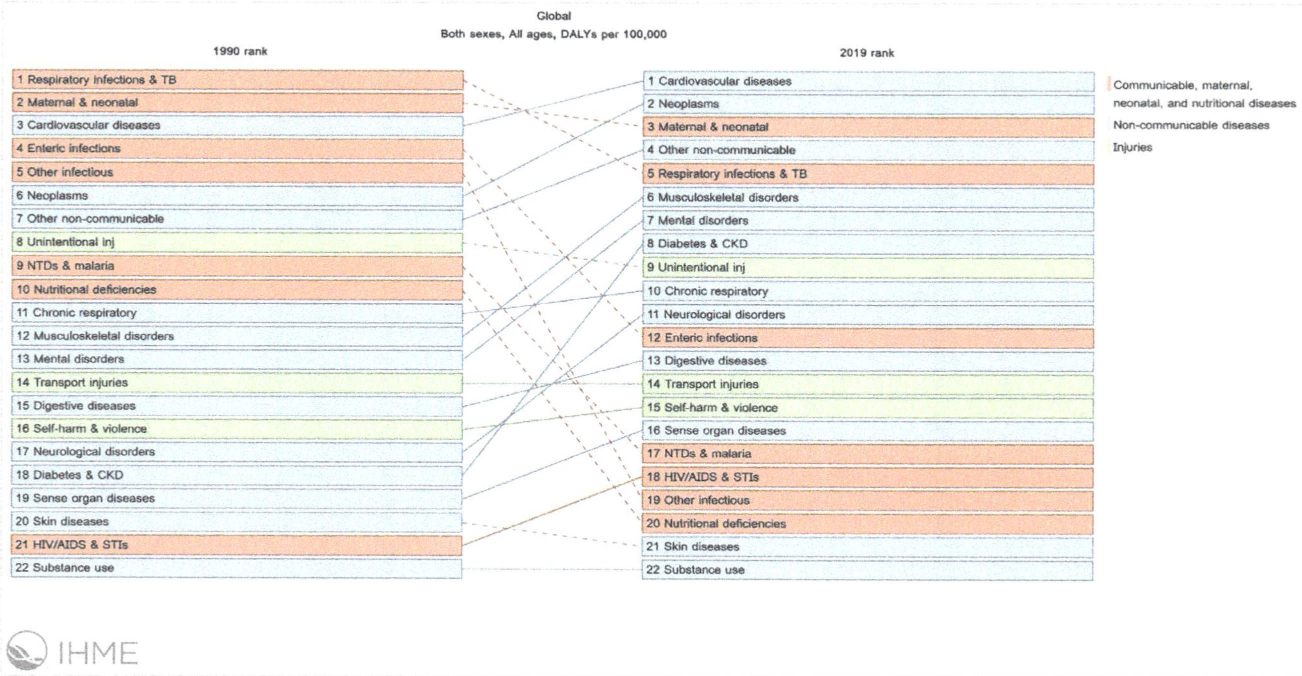

Source: Institute for Health Metrics and Evaluation (2019).

FIGURE 10.2
Global Comparison of Years Lived in Disability (YLD) of Various Diseases in 1990 and 2019

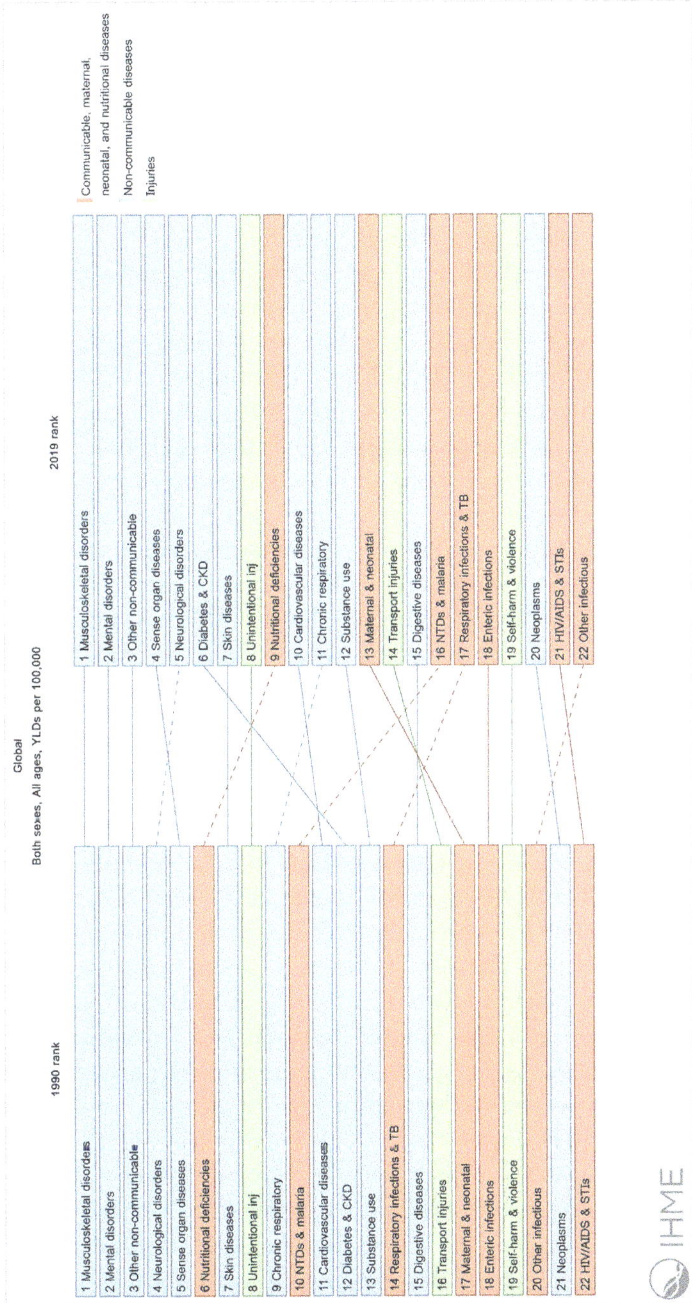

Source: Institute for Health Metrics and Evaluation (2019).

10.1.2 National Trend

The most common types of mental illness that occur in Indonesia are schizophrenia and depression (Ministry of Health of the Republic of Indonesia, Health Research and Development Agency 2019). The prevalence of psychosis and schizophrenia from 2013 to 2018 increased from 0.2 per cent to 0.7 per cent, respectively, and the prevalence of depression among the population aged more than 15 years old in 2018 was 6.1 per cent, amounting to 11.8 million people. Moreover, during the same period, the prevalence of the population aged more than 15 years old living with mental and emotional disorders in Indonesia increased from 6 per cent to 10 per cent (Ministry of Health of the Republic of Indonesia, Health Research and Development Agency 2013; 2019). In 2018, the percentage of females who live with depression is higher than their male counterparts (7.4 per cent vs. 4.7 per cent). Similarly, the percentage of females who live with mental and emotional disorders is higher than males (12.1 per cent vs. 7.6 per cent) (Ministry of Health of the Republic of Indonesia, Health Research and Development Agency 2019).

Still based on data from IHME (Institute for Health Metrics and Evaluation 2019), as with the global trend, the DALYs of mental disorders in Indonesia also experience an increase, from rank 16 in 1990 to rank 9 in 2019 (Figure 10.3). Similarly, in terms of YLD, mental disorders also sat at the second rank in 1990 and 2019 (Figure 10.4).

Properly treating the mentally ill is still a challenge in Indonesia. In 2018, only approximately 50 per cent of those living with schizophrenia were properly medicated (Ministry of Health of the Republic of Indonesia, Health Research and Development Agency 2019). Moreover, 14 per cent of households that had a member who lived with psychosis and schizophrenia still put physical restraint (e.g., confining a person in his/her own house) at least once in a lifetime between 2013 to 2018 (Ministry of Health of the Republic of Indonesia, Health Research and Development Agency 2019). This statistic demonstrates that there are still parts of society that still maintain a wrong perception of how to treat the disease properly (Laila et al. 2019; Hidayat et al. 2020; Ministry of Health of the Republic of Indonesia, Health Research and Development Agency 2013). At the same time, Indonesia has low health expenditure (Mahendradatha et al. 2017), which has potentially led to lower mental health expenditure, as mental health investment in developing countries typically ranges between 1.5 per cent and 2.4 per cent of their health expenditure (Chisholm and Saxena 2013).

FIGURE 10.3

Comparison of Disability Adjusted Life Years (DALYs) of Various Diseases in Indonesia in 1990 and 2019

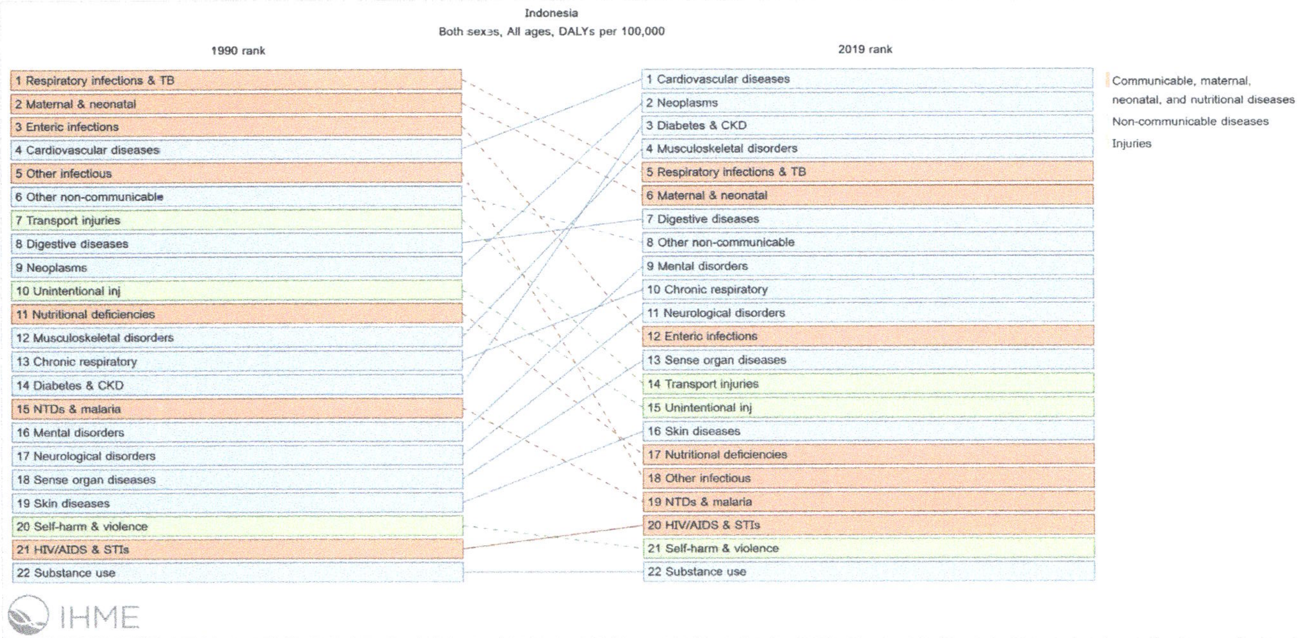

Source: Institute for Health Metrics and Evaluation (2019).

FIGURE 10.4
Comparison of Years Lived in Disability (YLD) of Various Diseases in 1990 and 2019 in Indonesia

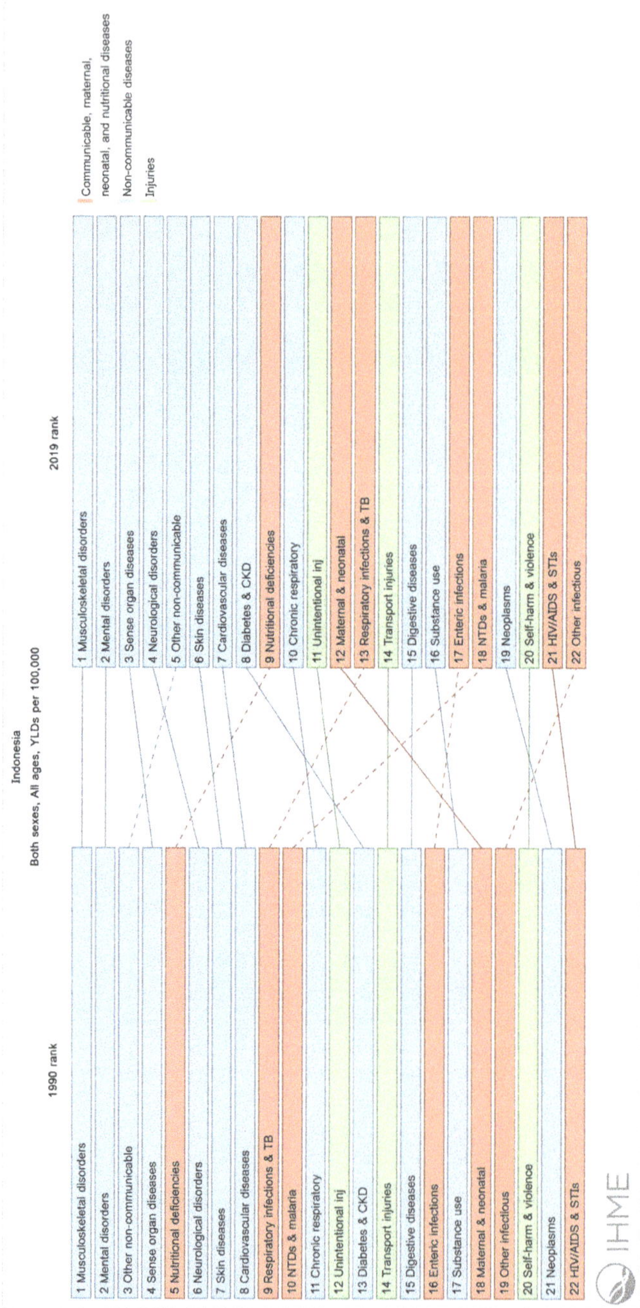

Source: Institute for Health Metrics and Evaluation (2019).

Table 10.1 shows the change of expenditures related to mental illness treatment based on BPJS Health (Social Health Insurance Administration Body) claim (sample) data in 2017 and 2018 in hospitals by province (Ariawan et al. 2020). Within one year, there was an increase of around 10,000 in the number of members of National Health Insurance (NHI) who were living with mental illness. Among the ten Indonesian provinces with the highest number of members living with mental illness, four of them are on Java Island. Interestingly, the total cost/claims within the same period decreased. The increase in the number of members living with mental illness and costs of treatment was mostly observed in provinces on Java Island (except for West Java and Yogyakarta Province).

While further analysing these findings is beyond the scope of the study, Table 10.2 has provided somewhat of a hint about the shift in the type of mental illness that occurred between or within the ICD10[3] categorization. For instance, within the group F20-F29 of schizophrenia, schizotypal, delusional and other non-mood psychotic disorders, although the number of cases increased from 2017 to 2018, the total cost decreased. In the future, recognizing the change in the pattern of the diseases can make for better policy development to target mental illness. Unfortunately, we did not have the detailed BPJS Health latest sample data at the time of writing this chapter, thus we cannot see the change in 2020 after the pandemic hit. Further studies should look into the changes in the pattern of mental illness from 2017 up to 2020 and beyond, preferably up to 2022 once the data is available. This will result in the better mapping of the change of type of mental illness before and after the pandemic and thus create a better basis for policymaking in this aspect.

10.2 MENTAL ILLNESS DURING THE COVID-19 PANDEMIC

10.2.1 Channels in Which the Pandemic Has Impact on Mental Illness

The COVID-19 pandemic has had a profound and different impact on mental illness. For instance, in Southeast Asia, the overall prevalence rates of anxiety and depression during the pandemic were estimated at 22 per cent and 16 per cent, respectively. Zooming in on separate groups within the population, the rate of anxiety and depression was estimated at:

TABLE 10.1
The Number of NHI Members Living with Any Mental Illness and the Number of Costs/Claims of All Type of Mental Illness Based on BPJS Health Sample Data in 2017 and 2018 in Hospitals by Province*

2017					2018				
Province	*Number of NHI Members Living with Mental Illness*	*Average of Visit Per Member*	*Total Cost/ Claim (IDR 000,000)*	*Cost/ Claim Per Member (IDR 000)*	*Province*	*Number of NHI Members Living with Mental Illness*	*Average of Visit Per Member*	*Total Cost/ Claim (IDR 000,000)*	*Cost/ Claim Per Member (IDR 000)*
Central Java	19,036	1.4	68,358	3,591	Central Java	22,191	1.6	81,578	3,676
West Java	18,092	1.5	32,456	1,794	West Java	17,284	1.5	24,388	1,411
Jakarta	11,672	1.9	22,519	1,929	East Java	14,469	1.6	36,532	2,525
East Java	8,541	1.7	32,263	3,777	Jakarta	13,737	1.6	46,145	3,359
South Celebes	6,955	1.6	20,973	3,015	West Sumatra	5,224	1.3	7,810	1,495
West Sumatra	4,548	1.5	12,686	2,789	South Celebes	4,642	1.4	6,690	1,441
Bali	4,490	1.6	15,108	3,365	South Sumatra	4,079	3.1	10,790	2,645
Banten	3,641	4.3	2,151	591	East Borneo	4,004	3.8	10,661	2,662
East Borneo	3,478	3.3	18,321	5,268	Aceh	3,312	1.4	13,195	3,984
Aceh	3,444	1.3	20,627	5,989	Bali	3,282	1.7	11,739	3,577
South Sumatra	3,337	3.1	8,772	2,629	West Nusa Tenggara	3,068	1.1	3,308	1,078
North Sumatra	2,990	1.2	9,713	3,249	South Borneo	2,889	1.6	5,397	1,868
Jambi	2,343	1.2	3,864	1,649	Riau	2,871	1.2	5,472	1,906
Yogyakarta	2,283	2.5	10,092	4,420	Banten	2,512	1.3	4,592	1,828
East Borneo	2,067	2.7	21,280	10,295	North Sumatra	1,909	1.3	2,259	1,183
West Nusa Tenggara	1,979	1.8	5,180	2,617	Central Celebes	1,899	1.2	3,825	2,014
Riau	1,665	1.6	6,674	4,009	Lampung	1,822	1.1	1,597	877
Central Celebes	1,493	2.1	2,569	1,721	Yogyakarta	1,772	3.1	3,795	2,142

Lampung	1,446	1.1	3,369	2,330	East Borneo	1,577	1.1	5,152	3,267
South Borneo	1,386	1.6	5,825	4,202	Central Borneo	1,375	1.5	2,854	2,076
Bengkulu	1,031	1.2	3,111	3,018	Riau Isle	1,343	4.2	1,057	787
North Celebes	961	3.4	8,516	8,862	North Celebes	1,266	2.3	5,945	4,696
Riau Isle	887	1.0	708	798	Bangka Belitung Isle	1,252	1.4	2,341	1,870
East Nusa Tenggara	885	1.0	242	274	Jambi	1,139	1.1	2,356	2,068
Southeast Celebes	774	1.4	6,388	8,253	Southeast Celebes	929	1.5	3,767	4,055
Central Borneo	574	2.3	1,086	1,892	Bengkulu	623	1.4	1,941	3,115
Bangka Belitung Isle	554	1.3	5,270	9,512	East Nusa Tenggara	606	1.4	1,561	2,576
Gorontalo	392	1.5	530	1,352	North Maluku	381	1.5	541	1,420
Maluku	306	2.0	728	2,378	West Papua	344	2.4	93	272
North Borneo	218	4.9	249	1,140	Maluku	299	1.2	706	2,362
Papua	200	1.0	620	3,098	West Celebes	237	1.0	639	2,697
North Maluku	189	2.0	1,145	6,060	Papua	146	1.5	231	1,581
West Papua	98	1.0	370	3,777	North Borneo	129	4.3	716	5,553
West Celebes	61	1.0	17	286	Gorontalo	32	1.3	208	6,495
Indonesia	112,016**	1.9***	351,780**	3,527***	Indonesia	122,644**	1.8***	309,880**	2,487***

Notes: *These include all mental illnesses categorized under ICD10 code F10 to F99, as stated in Table 10.2, **total, ***average.
Source: BPJS Health (Social Health Insurance Administration Body) sample data (Ariawan et al. 2020).

TABLE 10.2
The Total Cost/Claim of Mental Illness Treatment Based on BPJS Health Sample Data in Hospitals, 2017–18

Type of Mental Illness Based on ICD10	*Number of Members*		*Cost/Claim (in IDR 000,000)*	
	2017	*2018*	*2017*	*2018*
F10-F19 Mental and behavioural disorders due to psychoactive substance	8,628	11,669	29,617	31,057
F20-F29 Schizophrenia, schizotypal, delusional, and other non-mood psychotic disorders	48,672	57,396	270,945	216,226
F30-F39 Mood [affective] disorders	12,687	12,032	23,638	23,678
F40-F48 Anxiety, dissociative, stress-related, somatoform and other non-psychotic mental disorders	18,904	17,767	9,964	10,914
F50-F59 Behavioural syndromes associated with physiological disturbances and physical factors	2,115	2,451	1,671	8,113
F60-F69 Disorders of adult personality and behaviour	966	557	1,519	425
F70-F79 Intellectual disabilities	1,043	3,276	5,300	11,088
F80-F89 Pervasive and specific developmental disorders	14,763	15,459	7,538	7,129
F90-F98 Behavioural and emotional disorders with onset usually occurring in childhood and adolescence	3,231	2,880	1,458	1,242
F99-F99 Unspecified mental disorder	133	31	131	6
Total	111,142	123,518	351,781	309,879

Source: BPJS Health (Social Health Insurance Administration Body) sample data (Ariawan et al. 2020).

- 18 per cent of healthcare workers (HCWs);
- 17 per cent of general HCWs;
- 20 per cent of students; and
- 27 per cent of the general population.

These rates were lower than the prevalence rates in China, Spain, France, Italy and Greece (Pappa et al. 2022). In the Middle East and North Africa (MENA) regions, a survey on 6,142 adults in mid-2020 showed that 30.9 per cent of the respondents experienced a severe psychological impact. Between 45 and 62 per cent of the respondents reported feeling horrified, apprehensive, or helpless, while more than 40 per cent reported experiencing increased stress from work and financial matters. The study also shows that the state is more severe among females and those having lower education levels (Al Dhaheri et al. 2021).

The rise of mental illness cases triggered by viral outbreaks is termed a parallel epidemic (Yao, Chen, and Xu 2020; Vigo et al. 2020). However, the dynamic progression of mental illness during the COVID-19 pandemic was very much overshadowed by the pandemic itself (World Health Organization 2020). Most of the policies are aimed either at the economy or are health-related to control the pandemic. Lockdown-type policies[4] are a kind of bitter medicine that is needed to suppress the spread of COVID-19. We have all been in that situation: we loathe the taste of the medicine, but we need it to heal. Since the beginning of the pandemic, the policy to control the pandemic and the economy has mostly gone in opposite ways, with those controlling the pandemic mostly reducing economic activities, while those promoting the economy basically reducing the effectiveness of medical and public health intervention (Quah, Swee, and Park 2020). As adaptations are made, a delicate balance was somewhat achieved, and "stop and run" types of interventions became common with the timing and level of strictness of implementation being crucial (Shimul et al. 2021; Oraby et al. 2021; Besley and Stern 2020; Yazid and Palani 2022). When the pandemic is at a lower level, then economic activities run more loosely (although still under regulated health protocols), while when the pandemic is at a higher level the health protocols are applied strictly (depending on the level of the pandemic), meaning less economic activities. While these two different types of policies are discussed intensively, the mental state of the people who live within the scope of their implementation is less addressed (Ifdil et al. 2020).

The sudden appearance of the COVID-19 pandemic and its unclear finish line, as well as the severity and uncertainty of the disease in terms of symptoms, effects (health and social), and the nature of the spread, have challenged the (untrained) public to (quickly) cope and adapt with the new situation (Maison et al. 2021). In addition, while lockdown-type policies control the pandemic, they expose some potential health issues, and one of them is mental illness (Holmes et al. 2020; Brooks et al. 2020; Li et al. 2020). At the same time, relaxing lockdowns led to better freedom of activities, with the consequence of having a surge of COVID-19 cases in the near future (Shimul et al. 2021), which may result in feeling free and trapped at the same time. Either way, the whole situation creates stressful experiences that affect the mental state of the people (Pfefferbaum and North 2020). Within this context, the number of mental illness cases experienced an increasing trend.

At the same time, people and nations also adapt and find a way to cope with the pandemic. For example, in the MENA region, while the risk of mental illness increased, there was also a sign of increased solidarity, with almost half of the respondents (out of 6,142 adults) receiving increased support from family members (Al Dhaheri et al. 2021). One of the earlier initiatives in Indonesia, online mental health services such as the Mobile App Survey (AMMS) is being utilized (Ifdil et al. 2020; Sukmawati et al. 2019). Seventy per cent of nations have adopted telemedicine or teletherapy to cope with the mental illness effect due to the pandemic. This rate is higher in high-income countries (80 per cent) compared to low-income countries (less than 50 per cent) (World Health Organization 2020). The Organization for Economic Co-operation and Development (OECD) countries have responded by scaling up mental health services and implementing measures to protect jobs and incomes to reduce mental illness issues (OECD 2021).

On another note, working from home (WFH) in the context of lockdown brings another challenge. We are somewhat "lucky" that COVID-19 came during the era when technology and the Internet have been growing exponentially within the last decades (imagine if COVID-19 came twenty years ago!). The existence of online marketing and video conferencing have, to some extent, helped us survive through the current pandemic (Renu 2021). Video conferencing has effectively made WFH possible for those who can. Technology also provides medical care with the necessary apparatus and media to address the pandemic (Saher and Anjum 2021). At the same time, however, it seems that a lot of people are still adjusting to the relatively new phenomena and, in some ways, merely moving meetings that were commonly done offline to online, and/or redefining conventional working hours. While WFH brings convenience on the one hand, it also creates issues on the other hand as people are still adjusting. This leads to new challenges, and one of them is called "Zoom fatigue". Prolonged and inappropriate use of video conferencing may lead to stress, leading to video conference fatigue or Zoom fatigue (Riedl 2021). Although more studies are needed to isolate the true effect of WFH in terms of video conferencing, there are four potential reasons for Zoom fatigue: "excessive amounts of close-up eye gaze, cognitive load, increased self-evaluation from staring at video of oneself, and constraints on physical mobility" (Bailenson 2021). Zoom fatigue has the potential to lead to various medical symptoms, namely headache, back pain, visual disorders, and insomnia (Rump and Brandt 2020), where insomnia has a close relation with psychiatric disorders (Khurshid 2018).

The pandemic also affected the mental health of children and adolescents, especially those who are disadvantaged and marginalized (Fegert et al. 2020). Early evidence showed that the high prevalence of anxiety and depressive symptoms in children and adolescents was caused by the pandemic, social isolation and parents' stress. High-grade students, females and low-income families are at higher risk of developing psychiatric illness symptoms (Deolmi and Pisani 2020). They feared being infected by the virus, feared losing their close family and friends, and were anxious about the social and economic deprivation due to their parents' income loss and others. Moreover, as with the adults, the effect of lockdown policies along with home-schooling should be monitored as this may also have undesired effects on children's and adolescents' mental health and require supporting policies to mitigate the adverse effects (Alibudbud 2021; Fegert et al. 2020).

10.3 THE CASE OF INDONESIA: HAVE WE PAID ENOUGH ATTENTION TO MENTAL ILLNESS DURING THE PANDEMIC?

10.3.1 Mental Illness during the Pandemic: Different Group, Different Responses—Mental Health Among Groups at the Beginning of the Pandemic

The mental illness data in Indonesia during the pandemic was not largely studied, except for several studies that focused on certain aspects/groups and linked the studies with mental illness. These studies provide much-needed data on mental illness during the pandemic. A study from the Ministry of Health in 2020 shows that in May 2020, due to the large-scale social restriction, about 25 per cent of the respondents live with a sleeping disorder, 5.9 per cent of them experienced anxiety, and 7.2 per cent live with depression. About four months after the survey, around September 2020, this condition remained the same (interview with MoH).

The pandemic affected different groups differently. The study conducted by CEDS Universitas Padjadjaran (Sunjaya et al. 2020; Sunjaya, Herawati, and Siregar 2021) showed that healthcare workers are much more resilient and can cope much better with the pandemic compared with the general population. The survey was conducted on several distinct groups of the population, namely undergraduate students, newspaper reporters, and healthcare workers (HCWs). The description of the survey is presented in Table 10.1. A more detailed explanation of the methods and results is provided elsewhere (Sunjaya et al. 2020; Sunjaya, Herawati, and Siregar 2021). The purpose of the study was not to provide a survey that was representative at the population level, but more on providing a picture of mental health conditions at the beginning of the pandemic.

Table 10.3 shows that the undergraduate students and newspaper reporters shared a roughly similar rate of those having severe depression (around 50 per cent out of samples from respective groups) (Sunjaya et al. 2020). This rate was much lower compared to the rate experienced by

TABLE 10.3
A Survey of Mental Health State among Different Groups of Population at the Beginning of the COVID-19 Pandemic

Items/Type of Respondents	*University/College Students*	*Newspaper Reporters*	*HCWs*
Region of analysis	Indonesia, mostly West Java		
Number of respondents	1,465	98	563
% of those showing depression symptoms (n)	47%	45%	28%
% of those potentially living with depression (n)[a]	23%	22%	14%

Note: a. Based on the calculation performed by (Lim et al. 2018), in which the prevalence of depression seemed to be higher as measured by self-report instruments versus clinical interviews (17.3 per cent vs. 8.5 per cent) showing that, roughly, people actually living with depression was 49.1 per cent lower compared to those detected depressed through self-report instruments.
Source: Sunjaya et al. (2020); Sunjaya, Herawati, and Siregar (2021).

HCWs (around 20 per cent of the samples surveyed), and the rate also slightly differed given the different roles of the HCWs (Sunjaya, Herawati, and Siregar 2021). Although the rate shown by this study was higher than the systematic review at the global level (Pappa et al. 2022), the trend was similar, in that the HCWs have a lower rate of depression symptoms compared to the other groups. This is similar to another study in Indonesia (Anindyajati et al. 2021). Even so, given the constant pressure faced by HCWs in treating patients while struggling to keep themselves (and those living with them) safe, led to the question of how long this resiliency will hold. A study has shown that HCWs are indeed at risk of psychological distress due to the pandemic (De Kock et al. 2021). Although this question was not within the scope of this chapter, it warrants our attention in determining our course of action during the pandemic.

Perhaps the most striking finding was that, compared to the basic health research data, the rate of depression seemed to have the potential of substantially increasing in the population above 15 years of age (6.1 per cent) (Ministry of Health of the Republic of Indonesia, Health Research and Development Agency 2019). The study shows that around 50 per cent of the sampled general population (aside from HCWs) experienced depression symptoms. While this may not translate into experiencing depression itself, it does provide a warning that the prevalence of depression may increase. For instance, one study shows that 49.1 per cent of those detected having depression symptoms using self-report instruments (vs. clinical interviews) actually have the disease (Lim et al. 2018). Given the calculation by CEDS, we may (carefully) assume that, on average, 22.8 per cent of the general population respondents are potentially living with depression, four times higher than the rate found in basic health research in 2018. This provides an alarming insight into what might be happening at the beginning of the pandemic.

In addition, a simple logistic regression analysis performed in the study showed that, first, those who worried more and have pessimistic views towards the pandemic may have a higher probability of showing depression symptoms. On the other hand, having a better understanding of the disease may reduce the probability of showing depression symptoms. Another study involving respondents from thirty-three provinces in Indonesia also shows that a better understanding of how to treat the disease is associated with lower feelings of anxiety (Iskandarsyah et al. 2022). Understanding such factors may provide a better approach to applying lockdown policies, thus supporting policies that can be geared towards reducing the potential negative impact of lockdown, leading to a potentially more successful application of lockdown policies.

LPEM Faculty of Economics and Business Universitas Indonesia surveyed 4,000 respondents throughout Indonesia in July 2020. This survey captured several mental health indicators such as happiness, anxiety, sadness and anger. The results show that people were less happy and at the same time they also felt anxiety and sadness. It is a challenge since, on the other hand, they should also maintain their immunity due to the high infection rate of the virus. About 50 per cent of the respondents experienced deprivation of happiness (very slightly higher among the female respondents). They started to feel the deprivation of happiness in March 2020, the month when the Indonesian government announced the first case of COVID-19 in Indonesia and the lockdown or social restriction policy. Looking at the job sector, 60 per cent of the respondents who worked in the accommodation and restaurant sector experienced deprivation of happiness. This is most likely due to the condition where this economic sector became the most severely hit sector by the COVID-19 pandemic (LPEM FEB UI 2021).

The increase in anxiety disorders was experienced by 68 per cent of the respondents (73 per cent of female respondents and 62 per cent of male respondents). Most of them started to feel this in April 2020, when the impact of lockdown (or social restriction) and the COVID-19 pandemic started to hit the economy and business sectors. The increase in sadness was also experienced by 51 per cent of the respondents (56 per cent of female respondents and 45 per cent of male respondents), showing that females were impacted more severely in terms of mental health disorders. Interestingly, the rate of anger was rather stagnant at the beginning of the pandemic—only 32 per cent of respondents experienced increasing anger, while 39 per cent of the respondents did not feel any change in anger. This condition remained the same on the second wave survey. 45 per cent of the respondents did not feel any change of anger and only 26 per cent who do experience increasing anger (LPEM FEB UI 2021).

Moreover, the mental health of people between 15 and 34 years old was most affected by the pandemic. This was marked by the increasing rate of their anxiety, especially in those who experienced a job loss or a decrease in income. Four out of five young respondents who lost their jobs experienced an increase in anxiety. Meanwhile, seven out of ten who experienced a decrease in income also experienced an increase in anxiety. It was most likely due to the increased competition to acquire jobs amidst the crisis and uncertainty, which could reduce their opportunity to get a job or be re-employed as they needed a job to fulfil their needs.

The LPEM survey highlighted two main groups most affected by the pandemic in terms of mental illness, namely females and productive age workers. During the COVID-19 pandemic, females, especially married ones, had the extra task of not only doing household chores but also supporting their children during schooling from home periods and dealing with their family activities 24/7. Furthermore, the working ones also needed to balance doing household chores with their work assignments. Thus, these extra activities potentially affected their condition both physically and mentally. More severe conditions will be experienced by those who also underwent financial shocks.

On another note, mental illness experienced by productive aged workers will affect their working performance and productivity. They cannot focus on their jobs or may even have trouble working with other employees. This could affect the company's performance as a whole. In Europe, mental health problems are the leading cause of disability and the largest contributor to missed workdays. Employers should observe their employee's mental health, otherwise it will potentially increase the probability of the employee exiting the workforce, which increases the risk of unemployment (OECD 2021).

Social media also impacted the Indonesian mental health state during the pandemic. A study from MoH showed that 24.8 per cent of people who have social media has a sleeping disorder, while 6.8 per cent and 8.5 per cent of them experienced anxiety and depression, respectively. Whilst social media has become one of the more popular media to spread all kinds of news related to the COVID-19 pandemic, there is no filter that blocks news and information from being accessed by the general public, which could potentially affect some people's mental health (interview with MoH).

On the other hand, an internal survey of one of the ministries in Indonesia has shown a more positive result. The ministry has launched two wave surveys that captured the experiences of the leaders and staff undergoing WFH. Based on the second wave survey of 11,965 respondents (Ministry of Finance of Indonesia 2022), although there were respondents who stated that loneliness (3 per cent), lack of sleep (3 per cent), boredom (7 per cent), and more working hours (25 per cent) were among the challenges faced during WFH, most agreed that WFH is more effective (52 per cent) and have other benefits that are not otherwise experienced (e.g., more family time). Flexible working hours are seen as the way forward and adjustments in management, policies and business processes are in process. Interestingly, based on the first wave survey at the beginning of the pandemic (April 2020, completed by 18,254 staff), the ministry staff faced common challenges such as difficulty concentrating (39.5 per cent), lack of an appropriate workplace (25.3 per cent), boredom, no social activities, and high workload (12.1 per cent) (Ministry of Finance of Indonesia 2020).

In this particular case, it seems that the ministry staff has been able to cope well with the pandemic and the challenges that ensued, including the potential causes of mental illness. Although this internal survey cannot be generalized to other ministries and institutes, it highlights an understanding that in certain groups, coping with the pandemic and the changes in work arrangements can be dealt with relatively quickly that potentially reducing the pressure that the pandemic brought. More in-depth analysis should be done and the lessons learnt should be discussed with other parties and policymakers.

10.3.2 How Should We Position Mental Illness in View of Pandemic Control Policies in Indonesia?

Designing a proper lockdown and its supporting policies may go a long way in successfully encouraging people to stay at home and providing the necessary room for the pandemic to subside (Oraby et al. 2021; Besley and Stern 2020). During the two years course of the pandemic, we saw that it has created turbulence both in population health and the economy, e.g., lockdown policies vs. subsequent income/job loss (Witteveen and Velthorst 2020). The application of "stop and go" lockdown policies has been, to some extent, able to control the pandemic and promote economic activities. However, from global studies and national surveys, we have also observed that such an approach may also have negative implications, and one of them is mental illness.

The existence of mental illness in the middle of efforts to control the pandemic and the subsequent economic crisis hinders the effectiveness of such efforts. Putting aside the discussion on the economic impact of lockdown, mental illness may hamper the willingness and endurance of people to stay at home and let go of outdoor activities (Vigo et al. 2020).

Going outdoors to work is a necessity, and although this may increase the risk of getting infected, the reason underlining it is understandable. However, getting stressed by being forced to stay at home, especially for more outgoing people, may result in people starting to ignore the importance of lockdown and conduct outdoor activities that may not be as important as working. Recreational visits to relatives, eating in restaurants, and window shopping in malls are examples of activities that can be postponed if the pandemic is showing signs of growing. Experiencing mental illness during this period is challenging and may cause decisions to be made that conflict with safety measures, for instance, ignoring lockdown policy altogether (Vigo et al. 2020).

Given this context, mental illness is one of the factors that could determine the success of pandemic control and promoting economic activities. Hence, developing policies to promote mental health during the pandemic[5] is crucial to ensure the general public resilience in enduring the pandemic. Luckily, more institutions offer services to address mental illness (Sunjaya et al. 2020; Ifdil et al. 2020), and hopefully, this does bring benefits such as consistently obeying health protocols. This is not only limited to lockdown policies, but it is also relevant to other health protocols in general (e.g., wearing masks, physical distancing).

10.4 THREAT TO THE INDONESIAN ECONOMY DUE TO MENTAL HEALTH PROBLEMS DURING THE PANDEMIC

Mental health is affected by multiple pandemic-related stresses, including insecurity of income and employment, isolation, loss of social support, inability to access essential services such as health and education, as well as fear of contracting COVID-19 and becoming severely ill or dying (Mendez-Lopez et al. 2022). As previously mentioned, prolonged Work from Home without clear schemes and schedules can cause Zoom fatigue. Moreover, it also shows the tendencies towards a low quality of work life. It is associated with a higher level of work-related occupational stress, anxiety and burnout which may lead to lower job performance and induces significant costs for organizations (Leitão, Pereira, and Gonçalves 2021).

The mental health disorder experienced by workers may lead to a decrease in productivity. It will increase their absenteeism and presenteeism.

The workers tend to lose their concentration and ability to work. This condition will lead to monetary and non-monetary costs such as longer times needed to finish work or production errors. Employees' mental health problems could also affect how they socialize with other workers—if it becomes worse, it will create unpleasant working environments. Mental health problems can trigger workers to quit employment. Furthermore, it may also affect business productivity and increase unemployment, impacting the economy as a whole. On the other hand, the Government of Indonesia (GoI) is running *Pemulihan Ekonomi Nasional* (Economic Recovery Programme) to boost economic performance and needs support from the productive age groups as the drivers of economic activities.

Furthermore, the COVID-19 pandemic has also impacted children's and adolescents' mental health and as children and adolescents have a long journey ahead and can drive economic performance in the future, it is very important to keep their mental health in check. The role of school and teachers in supporting children and parents is important, especially as the condition of their parents could also be a trigger for the children's and adolescents' mental health. Moreover, since the long-term impact of the COVID-19 pandemic on mental health is crucial, this issue should be well addressed. LPEM FEB UI survey of 4,000 respondents in 2021 shows that 40.68 per cent of the respondents thought that mental health issues should be prioritized as well as poverty and inequality (78.15 per cent), health service provision (44.20 per cent), and decent job provision (42.38 per cent).

10.5 WHAT HAS THE INDONESIAN GOVERNMENT DONE IN TACKLING MENTAL HEALTH ISSUES?

10.5.1 Mental Health Programme and Policies, Before and During the Pandemic

Indonesia has enacted Act No. 18/2014 on Mental Health in 2014. This act does not only protect those living with mental problems or mental disorders, but is also a commitment by the Indonesian government to provide integrated, comprehensive and sustainable mental health services throughout the life cycle of people living with mental problems or mental disorders. The services consisted of promotive, preventive, curative, and rehabilitative actions, delivered by both the central and local governments.

The promotive action focuses on activities which can increase people's awareness regarding mental problems and disorders. Thus, it is expected to reduce stigma, discrimination, and human rights violation against people with a mental health disorder. The preventive action is aimed at preventing mental illness, relapses, and psychosocial problems and reducing risks due to mental health problems. Meanwhile, curative action consists of activities such as medication and diagnosis. As such, people living with mental illness can live well in society. Rehabilitative action focuses on the activities which can prepare people with mental disorders to be independent in society, such as psychiatric and psychosocial rehabilitation.

This act also guarantees the availability of mental health resources such as mental health professionals, mental health facilities, mental health service financing and also technology in mental health. Currently, there are 1,070 psychiatrists, 3,183 clinical psychologists and 14,752 mental health nurses in Indonesia (interview with MoH) Furthermore, the Ministry of Health through the Directorate of Mental Health and Drugs Problem Prevention and Control (Dit P2MKJN) has issued the action plan for 2020–24. This document becomes the reference for mental health-related activities and programmes that are delivered by the central and local governments.

Responding to the COVID-19 pandemic's impact on society, the GoI introduced the SEJIWA (Kesehatan Jiwa/Mental Health) counselling service in April 2020. This programme was initiated by the Association of Indonesian Psychology (HIMPSI) together with several ministries and institutions, including the Presidential Office, Ministry of Health, Ministry of Information and Communication, Ministry of Women Empowerment and Child Protection, National Disaster Prevention Agency, and Telkom Indonesia (a national communication company). This is a free fixed line programme that can be accessed by dialling 119 ext 8. Hundreds of psychologists and psychotherapists joined the team. According to HIMPSI, at the beginning of this programme, there were 162 voluntary psychologists and 522 referral psychologists in all provinces. In this programme, each person can receive counselling, consultation and education services for 30 minutes. Interestingly, one of the most common cases that happened during the COVID-19 pandemic was mental health disorders due to domestic violence.

Furthermore, as with the development of *Desa Siaga* (proactive village), the government also initiated *Desa Siaga Sehat Jiwa* (Mental Health Proactive Village). This is a community-based mental health service, which enabled the community to be aware and have proactive actions to increase the mental health quality of their community. Due to the pandemic, the GoI also initiated *Desa Siaga* COVID-19. This programme also included RT/RW (community group) *Siaga Jiwa*, which requires the community at the RT/RW level to take proactive action to address mental health issues. At the village level, the programme begins through socialization and cadres' selection. The selected cadres will be trained and visit the community.

In 2014, Indonesia implemented NHI. Following Presidential Decree No. 82/2018, NHI also finances mental health-related treatment such as medical rehabilitation and psychological counselling. All treatments must be based on diagnosis or medical indications that are given by doctors and performed in primary-level healthcare or hospitals that are registered as BPJS Health partners. In 2020, the highest claim for inpatient treatment for mental health is for schizophrenia, followed by bipolar disorder and depression. There were 51,000 schizophrenia cases in 2020 with a total cost amounted to IDR282 billion. Meanwhile, most of the outpatient treatments were for psychotherapy.[6]

Moreover, to achieve the target on mental health-related issues, according to the Action Plan of Dit P2MKJN, the ministry planned to allocate about IDR123,383 million in 2024 to finance all programmes related to mental health and drug disorder. This number will increase annually following the increase in the target. In 2024, it is planned that 50 per cent of people with depression as well as emotional and mental disorders can be well treated. Furthermore, the source of finance is planned to come from the national budget, loans or foreign loans or grants. The local government also play important role in managing mental health programmes. Thus, to support mental health-related activities, the Dit P2MKJN has allocated some funding through a special allocation fund or deconcentration fund.[7]

10.5.2 The Role of the Private Sector

The private sector also plays an important role in the Indonesian mental health programme. It supports the Indonesian government by funding the capacity-building of mental health workers, such as participating in training, workshops and other capacity-building programmes. They also support the MoH in developing guidance on mental health socialization programmes. According to our interview with MoH, institutions such as ALZI, Mother Hope, Into The Light and KPSI are several private sector institutions that actively engage with MoH in relation to mental health programmes.

For the past decade, many wellness centres were established in Indonesia, also managed by the community or private sector. They offer various programmes to preserve people's mental health and keep them in good condition, such as meditation, mindfulness programmes, wellness programmes and psychotherapy. All wellness centres offer various types of treatment programmes and methods, and people can choose based on their needs and convenience. Many of them also offer programmes for workers or children of school age. These places indirectly support the government's efforts to face mental health issues in Indonesia.

10.6 SOCIAL PROTECTION AND MENTAL HEALTH

10.6.1 What Is the Impact of Social Protection on Mental Health (Globally and Indonesia)

As the crises brought about by the COVID-19 pandemic led to mental health issues, the social protection programmes, hypothetically, might have helped to mitigate the impact of the pandemic. Several studies show that the impact depends on the type of social protection and the demography of the beneficiaries. Strengthening social protection systems might assist the mental health of the population to be more resilient in responding to the consequences of crises (OECD 2021). Stronger social support policies helped mitigate the mental health consequences of household income shocks during the COVID-19 pandemic (Donnelly and Farina 2021).

Several studies show that social protection that only provides monetary benefits can be perceived as a short-term remedy. In the US, men who were looking for work while receiving government benefits are more likely to report symptoms of depression than the employed. This could be due to the fact that government unemployment benefits are usually short-term subsidies, and depression could be higher during the initial period of unemployment (Rodriguez, Frongillo, and Chandra 2001). Meanwhile, social protection programmes that do not only give monetary benefits can have positive effects on mental health. In South Africa, the cash transfer programme called the Child Support Grant, not only gives monetary benefits, but also includes a programme with mental health promotion, prevention and treatment interventions that strengthen the resilience of young people and provide them with the necessary emotional, cognitive, and behavioural tools to escape from the consequences of the pandemic (Alvarez-iglesias et.al 2021). This phenomenon is also shown by the *Kartu Prakerja* programme in Indonesia.

10.6.2 Case of Indonesia: The Impact of *Kartu Prakerja* on Mental Health

The Indonesian business sector was hit severely by the pandemic. To survive, many businesses had to lay off their employees. The job losses and decreasing income experienced by many Indonesian workers due to the pandemic not only affected their social and economic conditions but also their mental health. This condition was also worsened by the implementation of social restrictions which made them feel disconnected from families, friends and relatives, and it may lead to mental health disorders such as anxiety, stress and depression.

The government of the Republic of Indonesia released the *Kartu Prakerja* programme in April 2020. This programme is aimed at addressing the increasing unemployment rate by accommodating the unemployed and or workers who want to increase their skills through online training. This programme is part of the National Economic Recovery Programme (PEN). Each beneficiary can join the training and receive financial incentives. A study conducted by LPEM FEB UI in 2020 showed that being accepted as a participant in the *Kartu Prakerja* programme reduced the probability of respondents becoming anxious, sad and angry during the pandemic.

Kartu Prakerja not only gives monetary benefits but also the opportunity to increase skills and get new jobs, essentially the things that are needed by the Indonesian workers who were impacted by the pandemic. Furthermore, this argument was strengthened by the regression result of this study, which showed that working during the pandemic reduced respondents' probability of becoming more anxious, sad and angry. In addition, fewer anxiety disorders were experienced by those who had higher education levels, most probably because of feeling more certain about better job opportunities compared to those with lower education levels. Income also has a significant effect on mental health conditions—receiving a steady or increasing income during the pandemic increased the probability of having a better mental health condition.

Amidst this extraordinary condition, which is full of uncertainty, the study from LPEM FEB UI shows that the social assistance programmes that significantly improve mental health conditions are the programmes that can give certainty on income and the opportunity to work. However, for the programme to be successfully implemented, several aspects should be considered by the government such as the certainty of the disbursement period.

10.7 CONCLUSION AND WAY FORWARD

The COVID-19 pandemic has had a severe impact on mental illness and causes or leads to worsening socio-economic consequences and hampers the implementation of policies to contain the pandemic. Thorough consideration of the timing and the form of implementing COVID-19 control policies should be conducted as even though such policies are greatly needed to control the pandemic, they may also have adverse effects including mental illness.

Strengthening mental health programmes should be considered a priority by the Indonesian government, following global trends and building on the current interventions that have been implemented by the government to face mental illness during the pandemic. Any socialization in community activities should be conducted. People living with mental illness should be treated well by their families and professionals, especially during the current pandemic. Engaging with private wellness centres can be an option, especially for the purpose of adding more mental health-related professionals. This can enhance the implementation of the *Desa Siaga Jiwa* programme through community assistantship from the professionals.

In terms of social protection, the programmes that only provide monetary benefits could be seen as short-term remedies for the beneficiaries' mental health as it only reduces the anxiety feeling of not being able to fulfil their needs. The *Kartu Prakerja* programme in Indonesia can be seen as an example as it provides beneficiaries with monetary benefits and can guarantee a better future through having more skills. However, a well-managed targeting and disbursement mechanism is important, unless it could lead to other tendencies of mental health disorders, such as anger and anxiety. In the future, the Government of Indonesia should pay attention to the benefits, targeting and disbursement mechanism so that the social protection programmes not only reduce economic problems but also improve the mental health of beneficiaries.

Mental health/illness should receive special attention within the context of the pandemic and beyond. The success of policies to control the pandemic as well as potential future and current productivity, to some extent, rely on how mental health issues are being addressed. As the COVID-19 pandemic has started to show signs of becoming endemic, we should not loosen mental illness control and be mindful that it requires never-ending and thorough attention.

Notes

1. The authors wish to acknowledge Donny Hardiawan from CEDS Universitas Padjadjaran for his assistance in analysing BPJS Health Sample Data.
2. Disability-adjusted life year (DALY) is a time-based measure that consists of a sum of years of life lost due to premature mortality (YLLs) and years of life lost due to time lived in states of less than full health or disability (YLDs). One DALY represents the loss of one year of full health. Using DALYs, a comparison between diseases is possible (Global Health Observatory 2022).
3. ICD stands for International Statistical Classification of Diseases and Related Health Problems. It serves as "critical knowledge on the extent, causes and consequences of human disease and death worldwide via data that is reported and coded with the ICD". ICD is used to estimate statistics on disease at the primary, secondary and tertiary level of care, and on cause of death certificates. Group F consists of diseases related to mental, behavioural, and neurodevelopmental disorders. While the BPJS Health data used ICD10 classification, the newer ICD11 has just been officially announced and may be used in future references. (Based on WHO webpage, https://www.who.int/standards/classifications/classification-of-diseases, accessed 24 May 2022.)
4. Or any variation of it, we use the term loosely and refer to any kind of policy that restrict the movement or social interaction of people to control the pandemic. For example, in Indonesia, it is currently termed PPKM, a short for *Pemberlakuan Pembatasan Kegiatan Masyarakat* or restrictions on community/social activities.
5. This should be done in any condition and not only during the COVID-19 pandemic. https://bpjs-kesehatan.go.id/bpjs/post/read/2022/2161/Gangguan-Kejiwaan-Dijamin-BPJS-Kesehatan
6. A more long-term treatment for mental health problems is by talking to a mental health professional such as a psychiatrist or psychologist. It focuses on a broader range of issues and helps people with mental health disorders to get better emotional and social functions.
7. Special Allocation Fund is a fund sourced from the national budget that allocated to particular province. This fund aims to finance special local activities in accordance with national priority. Deconcentration fund is a fund sourced from the national budget which managed by the governor in order to implement the deconcentration activities.

References

Addo, Rebecca, Justice Nonvignon, and Moses Aikins. 2013. "Household Costs of Mental Health Care in Ghana". *Journal of Mental Health Policy and Economics* 16 (December): 151–59.

Agboola, Afis A., Oluwaseun T. Esan, Oluwasegun T. Afolabi, Taiwo A. Soyinka, Adedunmola O. Oluwaranti, and Adeniji Adetayo. 2018. "Economic Burden of the Therapeutic Management of Mental Illnesses and Its Effect on Household Purchasing Power". Edited by Tomi F. Akinyemiju. *PLOS ONE* 13 (September): e0202396. https://doi.org/10.1371/journal.pone.0202396

Al Dhaheri, Ayesha S., Mo'Ath F. Bataineh, Maysm N. Mohamad, Abir Ajab, Amina Al Marzouqi, Amjad H. Jarrar, Carla Habib-Mourad, et al. 2021. "Impact of COVID-19 on Mental Health and Quality of Life: Is There Any Effect? A Cross-Sectional Study of the MENA Region". Edited by Bidhubhusan Mahapatra. *PLOS ONE* 16 (March): e0249107. https://doi.org/10.1371/journal.pone.0249107

Alibudbud, Rowalt. 2021. "On Online Learning and Mental Health during the COVID-19 Pandemic: Perspectives from the Philippines". *Asian Journal of Psychiatry* 66 (December). https://doi.org/10.1016/j.ajp.2021.102867

Álvarez-Iglesias, Alejandra, Emily Garman, and Crick Lund. 2021. "Effects of COVID-19 on the Economy and Mental Health of Young People in South Africa: Opportunities for Strengthening Social Protection Programmes by Integrating Mental Health". *South African Journal of Psychology* 51, no. 2: 199–204. https://doi.org/10.1177/ 00812463211015348

Anindyajati, Gina, Tjhin Wiguna, Belinda Julivia Murtani, Hans Christian, Ngurah Agung Wigantara, Anggi Aviandri Putra, Enjeline Hanafi, et al. 2021. "Anxiety and Its Associated Factors During the Initial Phase of the COVID-19 Pandemic in Indonesia". *Frontiers in Psychiatry* 12 (March): 1–10. https://doi.org/10.3389/fpsyt.2021.634585

Ariawan, Iwan, Bagus Sartono, Wiji Wahyuningsih, Syafrudin Imam Negara, Jusran Mawardi, Citra Jaya, Fatah Abdella Sutara, et al. 2020. *BPJS Kesehatan Sample Data Year 2015–2018*. Year 2020. Jakarta.

Bailenson, Jeremy N. 2021. "Nonverbal Overload: A Theoretical Argument for the Causes of Zoom Fatigue". *Technology, Mind, and Behavior*, no. 1 (February). https://doi.org/10.1037/tmb0000030

Besley, Timothy, and Nicholas Stern. 2020. "The Economics of Lockdown". *Fiscal Studies* 41 (September): 493–513. https://doi.org/10.1111/1475-5890.12246

Brooks, Samantha K., Rebecca K. Webster, Louise E. Smith, Lisa Woodland, Simon Wessely, Neil Greenberg, and Gideon James Rubin. 2020. "The Psychological Impact of Quarantine and How to Reduce It: Rapid Review of the Evidence". *The Lancet* 395: 912–20. https://doi.org/10.1016/S0140-6736(20)30460-8

Charrier, N., K. Chevreul, and I. Durand-Zaleski. 2013. "Le Coût de La

Schizophrénie: Revue de La Littérature Internationale". *Encephale* 39 (SUPPL. 1): S49-56. https://doi.org/10.1016/j.encep.2012.11.004

Chen, Patrick J., Yanna Pusica, Dorsa Sohaei, Ioannis Prassas, and Eleftherios P. Diamandis. 2021. "An Overview of Mental Health during the COVID-19 Pandemic". *Diagnosis* 8, no. 4: 403–12. https://doi.org/10.1515/dx-2021-0046

Chisholm, Dan, and Shekhar Saxena. 2013. "Investing in Mental Health: Evidence for Action". *World Health Organization*. Vol. 21.

Chong, Huey Yi, Siew Li Teoh, David Bin-Chia Wu, Surachai Kotirum, Chiun-Fang Chiou, and Nathorn Chaiyakunapruk. 2016. "Global Economic Burden of Schizophrenia: A Systematic Review". *Neuropsychiatric Disease and Treatment* 12 (February): 357–73. https://doi.org/10.2147/NDT.S96649

De Kock, Johannes H., Helen Ann Latham, Stephen J. Leslie, Mark Grindle, Sarah-Anne Munoz, Liz Ellis, Rob Polson, and Christopher M O'Malley. 2021. "A Rapid Review of the Impact of COVID-19 on the Mental Health of Healthcare Workers: Implications for Supporting Psychological Well-Being". *BMC Public Health* 21: 104. https://doi.org/10.1186/s12889-020-10070-3.

Deolmi, Michela, and Francesco Pisani. 2020. "Psychological and Psychiatric Impact of COVID-19 Pandemic among Children and Adolescents" 91: 10–14. https://doi.org/ 10.23750/abm.v91i4.10870

Donnelly, Rachel, and Mateo P. Farina. 2021. "How Do State Policies Shape Experiences of Household Income Shocks and Mental Health during the COVID-19 Pandemic?". *Social Science and Medicine* 269 (January). https://doi.org/10.1016/ j.socscimed.2020.113557

Fasseeh, A., B. Németh, A. Molnár, F-U Fricke, M. Horváth, K. Kóczián, Á Götze, and Z. Kaló. 2018. "A Systematic Review of the Indirect Costs of Schizophrenia in Europe". *European Journal of Public Health* 28 (6): 1043–49. https://doi.org/10.1093/eurpub/cky231

Fegert, Jörg M., Benedetto Vitiello, Paul L. Plener, and Vera Clemens. 2020. "Challenges and Burden of the Coronavirus 2019 (COVID-19) Pandemic for Child and Adolescent Mental Health: A Narrative Review to Highlight Clinical and Research Needs in the Acute Phase and the Long Return to Normality". *Child and Adolescent Psychiatry and Mental Health* 14: 20. https://doi.org/10.1186/s13034-020-00329-3

Global Health Observatory, The. 2022. "Disability-Adjusted Life Years (DALYs)". World Health Organization (WHO). 2022.

Hailemichael, Yohannes, Damen Hailemariam, Kebede Tirfessa, Sumaiyah Docrat, Atalay Alem, Girmay Medhin, Crick Lund, Dan Chisholm, Abebaw Fekadu, and Charlotte Hanlon. 2019. "Catastrophic Out-of-Pocket Payments for Households of People with Severe Mental Disorder: A Comparative Study in Rural Ethiopia". *International Journal of Mental Health Systems* 13 (December): 39. https://doi.org/10.1186/s13033-019-0294-7

Hidayat, Muhamad Taufik, Sharon Lawn, Eimear Muir-Cochrane, and Candice

Oster. 2020. "The Use of Pasung for People with Mental Illness: A Systematic Review and Narrative Synthesis". *International Journal of Mental Health Systems* 14, no. 1: 90. https://doi.org/10.1186/s13033-020-00424-0

Holmes, Emily A., Rory C. O'Connor, V. Hugh Perry, Irene Tracey, Simon Wessely, Louise Arseneault, Clive Ballard, et al. 2020. "Multidisciplinary Research Priorities for the COVID-19 Pandemic: A Call for Action for Mental Health Science". *The Lancet Psychiatry* 7 (June): 547–60. https://doi.org/10.1016/S2215-0366(20)30168-1

Ifdil, Rima Pratiwi Fadli, Kadek Suranata, Nilma Zola, and Zadrian Ardi. 2020. "Online Mental Health Services in Indonesia during the COVID-19 Outbreak". *Asian Journal of Psychiatry* 51 (June): 102153. https://doi.org/10.1016/j.ajp.2020.102153

Institute for Health Metrics and Evaluation. 2019. "Global Burden of Disease (GBD) Compare". University of Washington. 2019. https://vizhub.healthdata.org/gbd-compare/

Iskandarsyah, Aulia, Whisnu Yudiana, Arina Shabrina, and Jan Passchier. 2022. "Perception of Information about COVID-19 and Protective Behaviours in Relation to Feelings of Anxiety and Happiness". *International Journal of Public Health Science (IJPHS)* 11 (March): 8. https://doi.org/10.11591/ijphs.v11i1.21018

James, Spencer L., Degu Abate, Kalkidan Hassen Abate, Solomon M. Abay, Cristiana Abbafati, Nooshin Abbasi, Hedayat Abbastabar, et al. 2018. "Global, Regional, and National Incidence, Prevalence, and Years Lived with Disability for 354 Diseases and Injuries for 195 Countries and Territories, 1990–2017: A Systematic Analysis for the Global Burden of Disease Study 2017". *The Lancet* 392 (10159): 1789–1858. https://doi.org/10.1016/S0140-6736(18)32279-7

Khurshid, Khurshid A. 2018. "Comorbid Insomnia and Psychiatric Disorders: An Update". *Innovations in Clinical Neuroscience* 15 (April): 28–32.

Knapp, Martin, and Gloria Wong. 2020. "Economics and Mental Health: The Current Scenario". *World Psychiatry* 19 (February): 3–14. https://doi.org/10.1002/wps.20692

Laila, Nenden Hikmah, Renti Mahkota, Siddharudha Shivalli, Krisnawati Bantas, and Tri Krianto. 2019. "Factors Associated with Pasung (Physical Restraint and Confinement) of Schizophrenia Patients in Bogor Regency, West Java Province, Indonesia 2017". *BMC Psychiatry* 19 (December). https://doi.org/10.1186/s12888-019-2138-z

Lancet Global Health, The. 2020. "Mental Health Matters". *The Lancet Global Health* 8 (November): e1352. https://doi.org/10.1016/S2214-109X(20)30432-0

Leitão, João, Dina Pereira, and Ângela Gonçalves. 2021. "Quality of Work Life and Contribution to Productivity: Assessing the Moderator Effects of Burnout Syndrome". *International Journal of Environmental Research and Public Health* 18, no. 5: 1–20. https://doi.org/10.3390/ijerph18052425

Li, Hong Yan, Hui Cao, Doris Y.P. Leung, and Yim Wah Mak. 2020. "The

Psychological Impacts of a COVID-19 Outbreak on College Students in China: A Longitudinal Study". *International Journal of Environmental Research and Public Health* 17 (June): 3933. https://doi.org/10.3390/ijerph17113933

Lim, Grace Y., Wilson W. Tam, Yanxia Lu, Cyrus S Ho, Melvyn W. Zhang, and Roger C. Ho. 2018. "Prevalence of Depression in the Community from 30 Countries between 1994 and 2014". *Scientific Reports* 8: 2861. https://doi.org/10.1038/s41598-018-21243-x

LPEM FEB UI. 2021. "Buku Statistik Survei Dampak Pandemi COVID-19 2021". https://www.lpem.org/id/buku-statistik-survei-dampak-pandemi-COVID-19-2021/

Mahendradatha, Yodi, Laksono, Shita Trisnanto, Prastuti Listyadewi, Tiara Soewondo, Pandu Marthias, Harimurti, and John Prawira. 2017. *The Republic of Indonesia Health System Review. Health Systems in Transition*. Vol. 7. New Delhi: World Health Organization.

Maison, Dominika, Diana Jaworska, Dominika Adamczyk, and Daria Affeltowicz. 2021. "The Challenges Arising from the COVID-19 Pandemic and the Way People Deal with Them. A Qualitative Longitudinal Study". Edited by Shah Md Atiqul Haq. *PLOS ONE* 16 (October): e0258133. https://doi.org/10.1371/journal.pone.0258133

Mangalore, Roshni K., and Martin Knapp. 2007. "Cost of Schizophrenia in England". *Journal of Mental Health Policy and Economics* 10, no. 1: 23–41. http://www.icmpe.org/test1/journal/journal.htm

Mendez-Lopez, Ana, David Stuckler, Martin McKee, Jan C. Semenza, and Jeffrey v. Lazarus. 2022. "The Mental Health Crisis during the COVID-19 Pandemic in Older Adults and the Role of Physical Distancing Interventions and Social Protection Measures in 26 European Countries". *SSM – Population Health* 17 (March). https://doi.org/10.1016/j.ssmph.2021.101017

Ministry of Finance (MoF) of Indonesia. 2020. "WFH Evaluation During the Implementation of Social Distancing Policy Wave 1". Jakarta.

———. 2022. "WFH Evaluation During the Implementation of Social Distancing Policy Wave 2". Jakarta.

Ministry of Health of the Republic of Indonesia, Health Research and Development Agency. 2013. "Basic Health Research 2013". Jakarta.

———. 2019. "Basic Health Research 2018 – National Report". Jakarta: Health Research and Development Agency (LPB).

Moran, A.E., J.T. Oliver, M. Mirzaie, M.H. Forouzanfar, M. Chilov, L. Anderson, … G.A. Mensah. 2012. "Assessing the Global Burden of Ischemic Heart Disease: Part 1: Methods for a Systematic Review of the Global Epidemiology Of Ischemic Heart Disease in 1990 and 2010". *Global Heart* 7: 315–29. https://doi.org/10.1016/j.gheart.2012.10.004

Moroz, Nicholas, Isabella Moroz, and Monika Slovinec D'Angelo. 2020. "Mental Health Services in Canada: Barriers and Cost-Effective Solutions to Increase

Access". *Healthcare Management Forum* 33 (November): 282–87. https://doi.org/10.1177/0840470420933911

OECD. 2021. "Tackling the Mental Health Impact of the COVID-19 Crisis: An Integrated, Whole-of-Society Response". *OECD Policy Responses to Coronavirus (COVID-19).*

Opoku-Boateng, Yaw Nyarko, Irene A. Kretchy, Genevieve Cecilia Aryeetey, Duah Dwomoh, Sybil Decker, Samuel Agyei Agyemang, Yesim Tozan, Moses Aikins, and Justice Nonvignon. 2017. "Economic Cost and Quality of Life of Family Caregivers of Schizophrenic Patients Attending Psychiatric Hospitals in Ghana". *BMC Health Services Research* 17 (November): 697. https://doi.org/10.1186/s12913-017-2642-0

Oraby, Tamer, Michael G. Tyshenko, Jose Campo Maldonado, Kristina Vatcheva, Susie Elsaadany, Walid Q. Alali, Joseph C. Longenecker, and Mustafa Al-Zoughool. 2021. "Modeling the Effect of Lockdown Timing as a COVID-19 Control Measure in Countries with Differing Social Contacts". *Scientific Reports* 11 (December): 3354. https://doi.org/10.1038/s41598-021-82873-2

Pappa, Sofia, Jiyao Chen, Joshua Barnett, Anabel Chang, Rebecca Kechen Dong, Wen Xu, Allen Yin, et al. 2022. "A Systematic Review and Meta-Analysis of the Mental Health Symptoms during the COVID-19 Pandemic in Southeast Asia". *Psychiatry and Clinical Neurosciences* 76 (February): 41–50. https://doi.org/10.1111/pcn.13306

Pfefferbaum, Betty, and Carol S. North. 2020. "Mental Health and the COVID-19 Pandemic". *New England Journal of Medicine* 383 (August): 510–12. https://doi.org/10.1056/NEJMp2008017

Phanthunane, Pudtan, Harvey Whiteford, Theo Vos, and Melanie Bertram. 2012. "Economic Burden of Schizophrenia: Empirical Analyses from a Survey in Thailand". *Journal of Mental Health Policy and Economics* 15 (1): 25–32.

Quah, Euston, Eik Leong Swee, and Donghyun Park. 2020. "The COVID-19 Dilemma: Public Health Versus the Economy". Asian Development Blog. 2020. https://blogs.adb.org/blog/COVID-19-dilemma-public-health-versus-economy

Renu, Nishant. 2021. "Technological Advancement in the Era of COVID-19". *SAGE Open Medicine* 9 (January): 205031212110009. https://doi.org/10.1177/20503121211000912

Riedl, René. 2021. "On the Stress Potential of Videoconferencing: Definition and Root Causes of Zoom Fatigue". *Electronic Markets*, December. https://doi.org/10.1007/s12525 021 00501 3

Rodriguez, Eunice, Edward A Frongillo, and Pinky Chandra. 2001. "Do Social Programmes Contribute to Mental Well-Being? The Long-Term Impact of Unemployment on Depression in the United States". *International Journal of Epidemiology* 30.

Rowan, Kathleen, Donna D. McAlpine, and Lynn A. Blewett. 2013. "Access And

Cost Barriers to Mental Health Care, by Insurance Status, 1999–2010". *Health Affairs* 32 (October): 1723–30. https://doi.org/10.1377/hlthaff.2013.0133

Rump, Jutta, and Marc Brandt. 2020. "Zoom Fatigue. Report of Institute for Employment and Employability".

Russell, Steven. 2004. "The Economic Burden of Illness for Households in Developing Countries: A Review of Studies Focusing on Malaria, Tuberculosis, and Human Immunodeficiency Virus/Acquired Immunodeficiency Syndrome". *American Journal of Tropical Medicine and Hygiene* 71 (2 Suppl): 147–55. https://doi.org/71/2_suppl/147 [pii].

Sado, Mitsuhiro, Ataru Inagaki, Akihiro Koreki, Martin Knapp, Lee Andrew Kissane, Masaru Mimura, and Kimio Yoshimura. 2013. "The Cost of Schizophrenia in Japan". *Neuropsychiatric Disease and Treatment* 9: 787–98. https://doi.org/10.2147/ NDT.S41632

Saher, Raazia, and Madiha Anjum. 2021. "Role of Technology in COVID-19 Pandemic". In *Researches and Applications of Artificial Intelligence to Mitigate Pandemics*, pp. 109–38. Elsevier. https://doi.org/10.1016/B978-0-323-90959-4.00005-5

SANE Australia. 2002. "Schizophrenia: Costs. An Analysis of the Burden of Schizophrenia and Related Suicide in Australia". *Access Economics Report.*

Shimul, Shafiun Nahin, Angi Alradie-Mohamed, Russell Kabir, Abdulrahman Al-Mohaimeed, and Ilias Mahmud. 2021. "Effect of Easing Lockdown and Restriction Measures on COVID-19 Epidemic Projection: A Case Study of Saudi Arabia". Edited by Siew Ann Cheong. *PLOS ONE* 16 (September): e0256958. https://doi.org/10.1371/ journal.pone.0256958

Siregar, Adiatma Yudistira Manogar, Ibnu Habibie, Rykaard Baressi Sihotang, Rika Permatasari Allo, Rangga Kusumawardana, Deni Kurniadi Sunjaya, and Sutyastie Soemitro Remi. 2022. "Costs of Providing Hospital-Based Psychotic Disorder Treatment in Indonesia". *Journal of Mental Health*, January, 1–9. https://doi.org/10.1080/ 09638237.2021.2022609

Steel, Zachary, Claire Marnane, Changiz Iranpour, Tien Chey, John W Jackson, Vikram Patel, and Derrick Silove. 2014. "The Global Prevalence of Common Mental Disorders: A Systematic Review and Meta-Analysis 1980-2013". *International Journal of Epidemiology* 43, no. 2: 476–93. https://doi.org/10.1093/ije/dyu038

Sukmawati, I., Z. Ardi, I. Ifdil, and Z. Zikra. 2019. "Development and Validation of Acceptability of Mental-Health Mobile App Survey (AMMS) for Android-Based Online Counseling Service Assessment". *Journal of Physics: Conference Series* 1339 (December). https://doi.org/10.1088/1742-6596/1339/1/012124

Sunjaya, Deni Kurniadi, Dewi Marhaeni Diah Herawati, Aulia Iskandarsyah, Estro Dariatno Sihaloho, Riki Relaksana, Donny Hardiawan, Jorghi Vadra, Ghefiran Abdurrahimdzan, Teddy Hidayat, and Adiatma YM Siregar. 2020. "Monitoring the Effect of COVID-19 Pandemic: Trend of Depression Symptoms and Public Behavior".

Sunjaya, Deni Kurniadi, Dewi Marhaeni Diah Herawati, and Adiatma Y.M. Siregar. 2021. "Depressive, Anxiety, and Burnout Symptoms on Health Care Personnel at a Month after COVID-19 Outbreak in Indonesia". *BMC Public Health* 21 (December). https://doi.org/10.1186/s12889-021-10299-6

United Nations, Department of Economic and Social Affairs. 2022. "Mental Health and Development". 2022. https://www.un.org/development/desa/disabilities/issues/mental-health-and-development.html

Vigo, Daniel, Scott Patten, Kathleen Pajer, Michael Krausz, Steven Taylor, Brian Rush, Giuseppe Raviola, Shekhar Saxena, Graham Thornicroft, and Lakshmi N. Yatham. 2020. "Mental Health of Communities during the COVID-19 Pandemic". *Canadian Journal of Psychiatry* 65, no. 10: 681–87. https://doi.org/10.1177/0706743720926676

Witteveen, Dirk, and Eva Velthorst. 2020. "Economic Hardship and Mental Health Complaints during COVID-19". *Proceedings of the National Academy of Sciences* 117 (November). https://doi.org/10.1073/pnas.2009609117

World Health Organization. 2020. "COVID-19 Disrupting Mental Health Services in Most Countries, WHO Survey". 2020. https://www.who.int/news/item/05-10-2020-COVID-19-disrupting-mental-health-services-in-most-countries-who-survey

Yazid, E.K., and H. Palani. 2022. "Fight Against Death Tolls and Economic Slowdown: Striking a Balance Between Mobility and Vaccination". CSIS Indonesia Research Report.

Yao, Hao, Jian-Hua Chen, and Yi-Feng Xu. 2020. "Patients with Mental Health Disorders in the COVID-19 Epidemic". *The Lancet. Psychiatry* 7, no. 4: e21. https://doi.org/10.1016/S2215-0366(20)30090-0

Zhai, Jinguo, Xiaofeng Guo, Min Chen, Jingping Zhao, and Zhonghua Su. 2013. "An Investigation of Economic Costs of Schizophrenia in Two Areas of China". *International Journal of Mental Health Systems* 7, no. 1: 26. https://doi.org/10.1186/1752-4458-7-26

11

COVID-19 and Education in Indonesia

When School Reopening Is Not Enough to Avert Losing a Generation

Ririn Salwa Purnamasari, Putut Hari Satyaka, Suharti, Matthew Wai-Poi and Rythia Afkar[1]

11.1 INTRODUCTION

Indonesia has made remarkable development progress over the past twenty years, maintaining consistent annual economic growth of 5 per cent and attaining upper-middle-income country status by 2020.[2] The world's tenth-largest economy in terms of purchasing power parity and a member of the G20, Indonesia aspires to become the fifth-largest global economy by 2030. Access to essential services, including education and health, has improved steadily over the last decade. Nonetheless, progress has been uneven, resulting in significant disparities across geographic and income levels and undermining the ability of growth to be truly inclusive. In general, the poor and vulnerable continue to lag. Even though all income groups are achieving better educational achievement, less than one-third of the poorest ten per cent of the population completed basic education in 2018 (Holmemo et al. 2020).

At the same time, Indonesia is in a period of demographic transition which will affect its human capital accumulation and labour market dynamics for decades to come. The working-age population grew by about 24 million from 2013, reaching over 200 million in 2020 (Statistics Indonesia 2021). Currently, half of the population is under the age of 30. Ensuring this generation has a good education and the right skills for employment is critical for the country to increase the productivity of its remaining workforce when the population begins to age in 2025–30. Nevertheless, efforts to improve the quality of human capital are not without challenges. Even before COVID-19, there were problems with learning gaps and disparities in outcomes in the Indonesian education system, which have gotten worse in recent years, especially as an impact of the pandemic.

COVID-19 mitigation measures have resulted in nationwide school closures of at least three months.[3] While the government and educational community worked to maintain learning continuity, students and parents have had to use their own resources to continue learning while away from school, some through the Internet, TV, radio, or completing teacher assignments. At the same time, teachers had to adapt to new pedagogical concepts and teaching methods for which they did not receive any prior formal training. When it comes to the most disadvantaged students, those without access to digital tools or support to learn independently are particularly vulnerable to falling behind. This crisis has highlighted several inadequacies and inequities in the education system, ranging from access to broadband and the devices required for remote learning, to the supportive environment required for learning, to the misalignment of resources and needs.

Education is key to Indonesia's aspiration of becoming a high-income country. Many factors come into play. This chapter will present a comprehensive viewpoint on how Indonesia could better invest in quality education, taking into account linkages between macro- and micro-economic perspectives. The chapter is structured as follows: following this introduction, Section 11.2 unveils why quality education matters for Indonesian growth. Section 11.3 discusses how the COVID-19 pandemic exacerbates the pre-existing challenges in the Indonesian education system and showcases some of the findings from the World Bank's study on learning losses and High-Frequency (HiFy) monitoring of COVID-19 impacts on education. Section 11.4 examines the fiscal allocation and management for education, as well as enduring issues that pre-date COVID-19. Section 11.5 concludes with forward-looking policy implications for how Indonesia should address these growing challenges to help drive the country's transition to a high-income country.

11.2 WHY DOES EDUCATION MATTER FOR INDONESIA'S ASPIRATIONS?

A wealth of literature shows that, among key prerequisites, education—a critical component of human capital—plays a significant role in a country's economic development. However, recent studies reveal that the link between education and growth relates not only to access to education or years of schooling but the quality of education (World Bank 2018). In fact, across all countries, the relationship between annual growth and test scores is much stronger than that between annual growth and years of schooling. This holds for Indonesia, where the benefits in long-term economic growth from closing the education quality or learning gap are estimated to be around seven times higher than closing the education access gap.[4]

For Indonesia to become a high-income country, it needs high productivity and middle-class jobs. However, today's workforce is not equipped with the skills needed to hold middle-class jobs (World Bank 2021a). Indonesia's skills gap cannot be closed by only investing in additional years of schooling. While more educated people occupy most of the middle-class jobs, higher education does not guarantee a middle-class job. Currently, only 40 per cent of Indonesians with a post-secondary education hold a middle-class job. Meanwhile, the rapid increase in educational attainment does not necessarily lead to commensurate higher skills (World Bank 2020). Rather, it is critical to enhance the quality of learning in school, so young people can bring higher levels of knowledge and skill to the labour market.

Many consider education to be a fundamental human right, and investments in education have been shown to promote intergenerational socio-economic mobility. At the same time, a high degree of mobility underpins both fairness and economic growth (Narayan et al. 2018). Again, it is learning—not mere education enrolment or schooling—that fosters intergenerational mobility. While school quality referring to inputs such as school spending and class size have some predictive power for mobility, learning outcomes are particularly significant (Chetty et al. 2014). According to recent findings in the United States, the test scores of the community in which a child lives (adjusted for the income of that community) are among the strongest predictors of social mobility later in life (ibid.). Education has also been shown to be a key driver of the recent expansion in Indonesia's middle class and is understood as an important determinant of Indonesia's future economic growth (World Bank 2019).

Although education is potentially a powerful tool for individual and societal empowerment, education alone is not enough to solve development problems. There are several factors at play related to determining the returns to education, including economics, politics, and society. If an education system is poorly managed, it can actually promote social "ills" rather than "goods". Education has the potential to widen the gap between privileged and disadvantaged groups. Young people from low-income, rural, and otherwise disadvantaged families not only complete fewer years of education but also learn far less while in school (World Bank 2018). Furthermore, an investigation into the main drivers behind changes in mean earnings and earnings inequality in Indonesia shows the important role of education in increasing mean earnings and boosting middle-class job prospects, but also highlights that it brings with it increased risks of earnings inequality (World Bank 2021a).

In addition, a large body of literature shows that investments in early childhood education (ECE) will generate higher returns than those in later education. Besides bringing more children into education earlier, investments in ECE will also better prepare them to do well later (Heckman and Masterov 2007). However, although ECE is relatively inexpensive, it has not always been prioritized by many Indonesian households. Only half of children aged 5–6 years old in aspiring middle-class households are enrolled in school, and only 20 per cent of those aged 3–4 (World Bank 2019).

11.2.1 Challenges of the Indonesian Education System: Before and During the COVID-19 Pandemic

Even prior to the pandemic, the Indonesian education system faced issues related to learning gaps and disparities in outcomes. Before the pandemic, relative to global/regional standards, the Indonesian education system was delivering learning at low levels. According to the World Bank Human Capital Index 2020, although the expected years of schooling in Indonesia was 12.4 years, when adjusted for the quality of learning, they received only 7.8 learning-adjusted years of schooling (Human Capital Project 2020). Moreover, learning poverty, or the proportion of children who were unable to read and understand a short, age-appropriate text by age ten, was estimated at 53 per cent in 2021 (World Bank 2021b). This learning poverty rate is 18.9 percentage points higher than the average for the East Asia and Pacific region and 21.1 percentage points higher than the average for upper middle-income countries.

Even prior to the pandemic, Indonesia experienced a decline in learning outcomes despite major progress in school enrolment. According to the Indonesian Family Life Survey (IFLS), only 51 per cent of students in grade four in 2014 were able to answer a grade three question, which declined from 65 per cent in 2000. Meanwhile, only 65 per cent of students in grade three in 2014 were able to answer a grade one question, while no students in grade five were able to answer a grade four question. Moreover, the decline in learning over 14 years amounted to roughly one-fourth of a standard deviation which is the equivalent of nearly three grades of learning (Beatty et al. 2021).

Unequal access to education, particularly quality education, affects many children in Indonesia. According to the latest International Student PISA 2018, only about one-third of Indonesian students attained basic to intermediate levels of proficiency in reading (OECD 2019). This is particularly true among children from poor households and those in rural and lagging regions. Socio-economically disadvantaged students scored 57 points lower. Students in rural areas scored 35 points lower than peers in urban areas. Even within a district, the average gap in learning outcomes between students enrolled in a low-performing school and those enrolled in a high-performing school was the equivalent of six years of education (Dharmawan and Suryadarma 2021). Furthermore, most Indonesian students fail to meet the national learning targets. Results from the recent national assessment show that one out of two students have not reached the minimum competence in literacy and two out of three students have not reached minimum competence in numeracy.[5]

Indonesian teachers' knowledge is considered low. According to the Service Delivery Indicator (SDI) survey of more than 1,800 teachers across Indonesia in 2019, less than 8 per cent of all teachers surveyed obtained a score of 80 per cent in language. Teachers' mathematics scores are marginally better, with about one in three scoring 80 per cent or more. Gaps in teacher knowledge also exist between teachers in public and urban schools and their colleagues in the private[6] sector or rural schools. Meanwhile, the increase in the number of certified teachers has not been accompanied by an improvement in overall teacher quality (World Bank 2020).

Unequal teacher distribution is also a challenge to improving education quality in Indonesia. Teachers, particularly well-qualified ones, are unequally distributed and while developed regions tend to have sufficient numbers, this is not the case in underdeveloped and/or remote regions. This is partly the result of the policy of decentralized teacher management whereby teacher recruitment is under the authority of subnational governments since 2001. Meanwhile, a moratorium on civil service teacher appointments in 2011 led to a lack of teachers in many schools. To meet the needs, schools had to recruit contract teachers. Following the end of the moratorium in 2013, teacher appointments were often made based on social connection, instead of merit (Rosser and Fahmi 2016), further lowering education quality. As part of an effort to improve teachers' quality, in 2021 the government established a new entry system for hiring civil service teachers by ensuring only candidates who achieved a minimum score in the selection exam were included in the hiring pool.[7]

Limited access to basic learning materials is also observed. Nearly one-third of grade four classes included in the SDI survey did not have minimum instructional materials such as textbooks and exercise books.[8] Over 40 per cent of schools do not have working toilets for students or sufficient light in the classroom. A recent study on water, sanitation and hygiene facilities at schools and *madrasahs* found that nearly half of both MoECRT (Ministry of Education, Culture, Research, and Technology) schools and MoRA (Ministry of Religious Affairs) *madrasahs* in the sample had no soap or running water. Similar conditions were found in primary MoRA schools, inhibiting students and teachers from practising basic hygiene.

11.3 TO WHAT EXTENT HAS THE PANDEMIC EXACERBATED PRE-EXISTING INEQUALITIES IN THE INDONESIAN EDUCATION SYSTEM?

The COVID-19 pandemic has exacerbated pre-existing learning gaps and inequality. A recent study estimates[9] that COVID-driven school closures lowered education attainment by 0.9 to 1.2 learning adjusted years and PISA reading scores by 25 to 35 points, even after taking into account government mitigating measures (Figure 11.1) (Afkar and Yarrow 2021). Further, such learning losses translate into annual earning losses equivalent to 7–10 per cent per annum per student. This will widen pre-existing inequalities in the short and longer term, where the gap between the richest and poorest quintiles in Indonesia is predicted to increase from 57 PISA reading points (1.4 years of schooling) to 64 PISA points (1.6 years of schooling) as a result of COVID-19 (Yarrow, Masood, and Afkar 2020).

These estimates are saddening but not surprising. Since March 2020, most of Indonesia's 68 million primary and secondary students have been away from their classrooms; instead participating in distance learning. According to the World Bank's High-Frequency (HiFy) phone survey (Box 11.1), most schools remained closed as of November 2020, with 93 per cent of students engaged in distance learning (Purnamasari and Ali 2021). One in four accessed hybrid learning—a mix of face-to-face and distance learning—and the rest accessed fully online or distance learning. Around 6 per cent of students attended face-to-face instruction, only available in a small number of schools, mostly in rural areas and outside of DKI Jakarta. In those schools that remained open, most students only went to school a few days a week. Amidst COVID-19, a small minority of students dropped out. About 2 per cent of children aged 5–18 years who attended school before the pandemic were no longer enrolled in November 2020. About

FIGURE 11.1
Estimated Learning Loss Based on the Observed Period of School Closure, January 2020 – June 2021

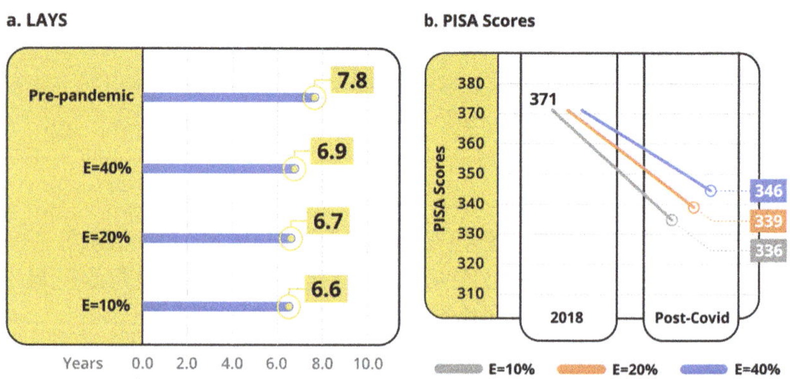

Source: Afkar and Yarrow (2021).

BOX 11.1
The High-Frequency Monitoring of COVID-19 Impacts on Households in Indonesia

The World Bank is administering a series of High-Frequency (HiFy) Monitoring phone surveys to track the impacts of the COVID-19 pandemic on households in over 100 countries. Indonesia's HiFy was among the first to launch globally in May 2020, two months after the first few COVID-19 cases were identified in the country. The HiFy is representative at the national level, administered as a 25- to 30-minute phone-based interview to roughly 4,000 households. It covers 40 districts and 35 cities in 27 provinces.

The HiFy sampling strategy is drawn from three World Bank key surveys, namely the Urban Perception Survey (2018), the Rural Poverty Survey (2019), and the Digital Economy Survey (2020). Nationally representative, Indonesia's HiFy has a balanced household distribution across five major regions in Indonesia, namely, DKI Jakarta, Rural Java (outside DKI Jakarta), Urban Java (outside DKI Jakarta), off Java Rural and off Java Urban. The sampling strategy also takes into account the gender and education levels of household heads.

Seven survey rounds have been completed, spanning from May 2020 to April 2022, implemented at different stages of the pandemic, collecting information on household socio-economic conditions, such as breadwinner employment and income, food security, access to health, education, social assistance and household coping mechanisms. The education modules were implemented in Round 2 (May–June 2020), Round 4 (November 2020), and Round 7 (April 2022).

The Indonesia COVID-19 Observatory

The HiFy survey is a key component of the Indonesia COVID-19 Observatory, which monitors social media platforms and the impacts of the pandemic on firms. More detailed information on the Observatory and HiFy microdata is available from World Bank (2021c).

the same dropout rate was also observed in April 2022. Over 25 per cent of students who dropped out as a result of the pandemic said they were delaying their education temporarily.

The need to learn from home during the pandemic has presented education challenges in terms of both access to and quality of learning. Although the vast majority of students continued to participate in distance learning, the amount of time spent on learning varied significantly across regions and socio-economic status (Figure 11.2). By November 2020, on average, students in the bottom 40th percentile of household income spent 2.2 hours daily on distance learning, while those in the top 20th percentile spent 2.7 hours, indicating that wealthier students tend to have greater options to participate in distance learning. Similarly, when compared to their peers outside DKI Jakarta, students in DKI Jakarta spend more time on distance learning, with an average of 3.5 hours daily. In April 2022, the number of hours that students were engaged in online learning remained relatively unchanged across regions and socio-economic status compared to November 2020—except across education levels, particularly among senior secondary students, which showed a reduction of about 40 minutes per day. The reduction in time spent on distance learning could partly be explained by the resumption of in-person activities at school.

FIGURE 11.2
Average Time Spent for Distance Learning Lower among Children in the Poorer Households

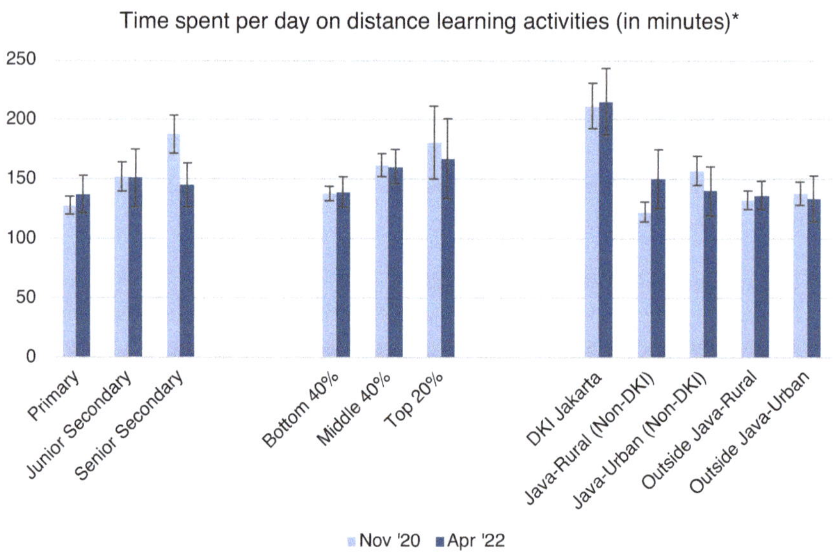

Notes: *Out of students who engaged in distance learning activities at home, which is 93 per cent and 35 per cent of students who enrolled in school in November 2020 (Round 4) and April 2022 (Round 7), respectively.
Source: HiFy Round 4 and Round 7.

The type of distance learning and the degree of difficulty faced by students are among the drivers of different educational outcomes. In the HiFy survey in November 2020, only 40 per cent of students reported using mobile learning apps and/or online schooling. This increased slightly to above 50 per cent in April 2022. Online learning was also significantly more prevalent in DKI Jakarta, with 74 per cent of students participating in online learning in November 2020—almost double the rate in other regions, either inside or outside Java (Figure 11.3). Likewise, students in the richest 20 per cent of households were also more likely to use online learning. In April 2022, online learning adoption rates increased, particularly among students in the bottom and middle 40 per cent of household consumption distribution and those who live in Java—although those in DKI Jakarta and the richest 20 per cent still maintained the highest usage rate. In regions outside Java, either urban or rural, the rate of online learning usage never reached 40 per cent.

During distance learning activities, three in four students expressed encountering at least one constraint. Although the most common learning modality was completing teacher assignments, the most frequently mentioned difficulties throughout the pandemic were limited Internet

FIGURE 11.3
The Rate of Online/Mobile Learning Mode for Remote Learning Varied Widely across Regions and Socio-economic Status

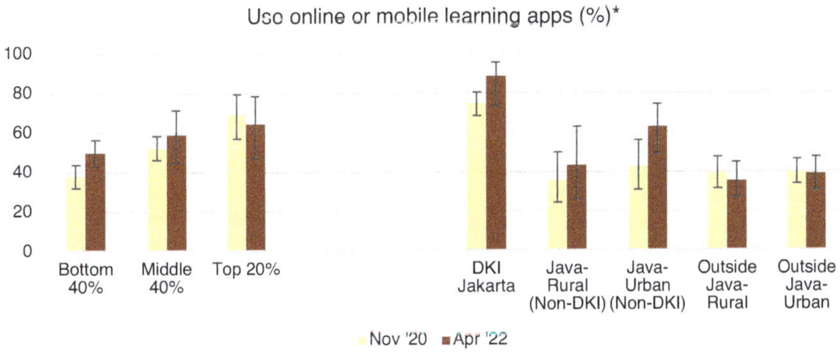

Notes: *Out of students who engaged in distance learning activities at home, which is 93 per cent and 35 per cent of students who enrolled in school in November 2020 (Round 4) and April 2022 (Round 7), respectively.
Source: HiFy Round 4 and Round 7.

access, problems with focusing and concentrating, and lack of an Internet-connected device. Students also reported other household constraints, including no or limited guidance from parents or other adult household members and no or limited space for studying at home.

The Government of Indonesia has made major efforts to mitigate the impacts of the pandemic on education, introducing an emergency curriculum and different modes of distance learning as well as providing free Internet credit to students since August 2020. Surprisingly, while there was no reduction in the target allocated Internet quota over time, the HiFy surveys found that the share of students who received the quota dropped from 51 per cent in November 2020 to 43 per cent by the end of 2021 (Figure 11.4). One possible reason for this decline could be that by end of 2021 most schools had started reopening for face-to-face learning, hence the reduction in online participation and the need to obtain the Internet quota. The share of students who successfully used the credit to engage in online learning was also stagnant. Among students who obtained Internet credit, approximately 50 per cent used it for online study in April 2022, which is the same as observed in November 2020. Meanwhile, student access and uptake vary widely. Potentially due to significant challenges in the way the credits were distributed and requested, students from the bottom 40 per cent of households, and those residing in rural areas and outside Java were less likely to receive an Internet quota. Sadly, these

FIGURE 11.4
The Share of Students Who Received Internet Quota Decreased

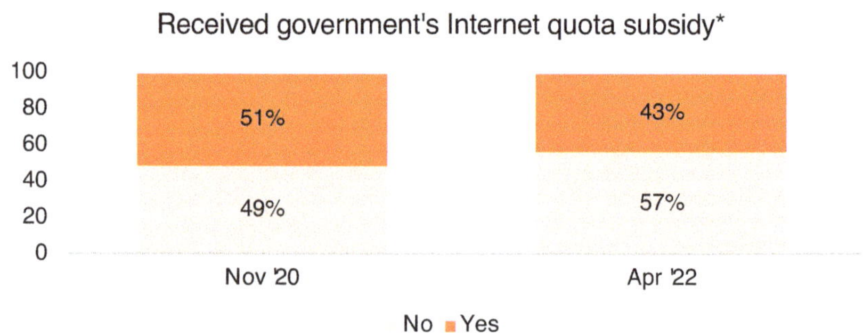

Note: *Out of students currently enrolled in school.
Source: HiFy Round 4 and Round 7.

groups of students were the ones who tended to be already disadvantaged even before the pandemic.

As one may expect, in the early onset of the pandemic, engaging in online learning was a challenge for students and teachers alike, both due to the fact that it was a new mode of learning and also due to the lack of supporting equipment and Internet credit for many. However, even within six months of the outbreak and with the provision of free Internet credit, student participation in online/mobile learning (conditional on engagement in distance learning) hovered only at 40 per cent. Slowly picking up, after almost two years of programme implementation, this only rose to around 50 per cent in April 2022—with continuing wide variation across regions and socio-economic status (Figure 11.3). By early 2022, however, participation in distance learning seemed to be more a matter of choice for some students who had the capacity and/or preference to do so. Nonetheless, the number of hours spent on distance learning for those who received Internet credit fell from, on average, 30 minutes to 20 minutes more than those who did not. The decline in time spent on distance learning may be explained partly by the greater implementation of hybrid modes by those who were still involved in distance learning.

As social distancing measures eased by the end of 2021, *Pembelajaran Tatap Muka Terbatas* (PTM *terbatas,* or Limited Face-to-Face Learning) has been gradually resumed in schools across Indonesia, following health protocols. The implementation of PTM *terbatas* is governed by local governments based on the Joint Ministerial Decree (*Surat Keputusan Bersama,* or SKB) of the Ministers of Education and Culture, Religious Affairs, Health and Home Affairs. To ensure the safety of all students and school personnel, PTM *terbatas* with 100 per cent attendance can only be implemented if at least 80 per cent of teachers and school personnel are fully vaccinated, otherwise, schools are only allowed to hold a limited PTM *terbatas* at 50 per cent classroom capacity. As of January 2022, out of 4.5 million teachers and education personnel, 72 per cent had received two doses of the vaccine.[10] Numerous other efforts have also been made, including putting social distancing markings on school facilities, ensuring teacher instructions to students on social distancing and safety and health precautions, and surveillance by the COVID-19 Task Force. In practice, however, only 76 per cent of provincial governments follow SKB. Moreover, according to the community health centre (*Puskesmas*) random behaviour monitoring of 4,609 education units implementing PTM *terbatas,* 22 per cent were still not adhering to good health measures—mainly within early childhood education.

By April 2022, most schools across all levels of education had reopened and resumed face-to-face activities: over 90 per cent of students could go to school for face-to-face activities, and 98 per cent of them went to school physically. Among students whose schools open for in-person activities, on average nearly three quarters had been fully vaccinated, but with quite a variation in shares across regions[11] and less than 3 per cent had received the booster dose. Moreover, more than half of students physically went to school 5–7 days per week. About a third of students who were currently in school continued to learn from home, with 86 per cent following hybrid learning. Less than 5 per cent of students currently in school were still engaged in "full" distance learning because their schools were still closed. Despite the reopening of schools across all regions in Indonesia, in-person learning was slightly lower in DKI Jakarta compared to other areas in Java or outside Java. Similarly, the share of students who physically went to school for 5–7 days a week was higher in rural areas which were about 70 per cent, and only around 50 per cent in urban areas, in and outside of Java.

Findings from the HiFy highlight a persistent disparity in access and learning quality across regions and socio-economic status. Disadvantaged students and those in lagging areas continue to be left behind. The school closures that forced students to study remotely have disproportionately affected these groups and exacerbated existing inequality in education. Even after accounting for government mitigating measures, many who benefited from the programme were from wealthier households and those who live in DKI Jakarta. Without urgent and appropriate policies, this situation will widen pre-existing inequalities and have an impact on the trajectory of educational attainment and the quality of human resources in the future, hampering Indonesia's attempt to reap its demographic dividend and aspiration to become the fifth-largest global economy by 2030.

11.4 FISCAL ALLOCATION AND MANAGEMENT FOR EDUCATION

Education spending in Indonesia significantly increased in the past two decades, driven by the constitutional amendment mandating a minimum of 20 per cent of the national budget for education. Since then, financial resources for education have increased more than threefold in real terms since 2001, reaching IDR550 trillion in 2021. There was, however, a slight decline both in real and nominal terms in 2022 due to fiscal policy changes. In 2019, the education budget was IDR493 trillion, increasing to IDR550 trillion in 2021 as a consequence of the 20 per cent rule when the national budget increased to cover COVID-19 response programmes. Part of the education budget increase was for Internet quotas for students and teachers.

The education budget in Indonesia is managed by both national and subnational governments, with the largest proportion spent subnationally (53–63 per cent of the total education budget), following the decentralized structure of the education sector in Indonesia. Central education spending is mostly managed by the two main ministries responsible for education service delivery: the Ministry of Education, Culture, Research and Technology (14 per cent of total education budget) and the Ministry of Religious Affairs (10 per cent of total education budget). In 2019, the central government managed 35 per cent of total education spending, with the remaining 65 per cent managed by subnational governments through transfers, more than half of which were in the form of block grants. In 2022, however, the allocation of the subnational transfers declined to 54 per cent as a consequence of fund reallocation for COVID-19 response measures and to maintain the mandated budget for education.

Subnational government transfers include earmarked and non-earmarked transfers. Earmarked transfers, or DAK (*Dana Alokasi Khusus*, or Special Allocation Fund) consists of DAK *fisik*, include grants for school infrastructure and DAK *non-fisik*, which includes BOS (*Bantuan Operasional Sekolah*, or School Operational Grants), TPG (*Tunjangan Profesi Guru*, or Teacher Professional Allowance), and BOP-PAUD (*Bantuan Operasional Penyelenggaraan* PAUD). Meanwhile, non-earmarked transfers, or DAU (*Dana Alokasi Umum*, or General Allocation Fund) are for general budgetary needs, mostly for the salaries of district civil servants, including civil service (PNS) teachers.

However, fiscal allocation issues for education existed even before COVID-19. *First, there is not enough spending on education.* Indonesia's spending on education as a share of the total government budget (20 per cent) is one of the highest in the world, about double that of advanced East Asian countries such as Japan (9.3 per cent) and the Republic of Korea (12.8 per cent), and on a par with Malaysia (21 per cent) and Singapore

(17.7 per cent). However, if measured as a share of GDP, Indonesia's education expenditure—at 3.0 per cent of GDP in 2018—is lower than the East Asia and Pacific regional average of 4.7 per cent and the averages of both lower-middle-income (4.5 per cent) and upper-middle-income countries (4.7 per cent) (World Bank 2020). That is, while education spending makes up a high level of total public spending, total public spending is low (due to low public revenues), making it low in absolute terms.

Second, what is spent is not optimally allocated across levels. The allocation for ECE is much lower than for other levels. In 2018, the Directorate General of Early Childhood Education only received 4.5 per cent of the MoECRT's budget, or about IDR1.8 trillion. A recent Education Public Expenditure Review also found that sampled districts/cities spent very little on ECE, averaging only 2.6 per cent of their education budget (Afkar et al. 2020). This is not aligned with international evidence that strongly indicates that expanding access to quality ECE services gives the highest return on investment in education, as these are the most important years of a child's cognitive development that influences future health and productivity (Carneiro Cunha, and Heckman 2003; World Bank 2018).

Nor are allocations equitable across the country. There is significant variation in terms of the allocation of resources per student across provinces and districts. Part of the problem is due to DAU transfers not being allocated on a per capita basis, but mostly in the form of a block grant allocating the same to all districts regardless of population. For example, the province of West Java receives about IDR29 trillion, or IDR4.4 million per student, while West Papua receives IDR3 trillion, or IDR19 million per student. While these differences may account for differences in the cost of providing education services across regions, the more than sixfold variation suggests that the allocation of these transfers is not aligned with educational needs. Per-student education transfers are not targeted to poorer districts either. There is no clear positive or negative correlation between the per-student transfer and poverty rate, indicating that the current budget allocation at subnational levels does not promote equity within the system. Nonetheless, in 2021 MoECRT introduced calibrated school assistance fund (*BOS Majemuk*), a price-calibrated allocation budgeting for DAK *non-fisik* of which districts with relatively higher price index, particularly remote areas, will receive larger amount of assistance per student.

Moreover, funding is not always spent in line with the intended purpose. DAK *fisik*, earmarked grants to subnational governments, aims to address

FIGURE 11.5
Allocation of DAK *Fisik* Transfer Is Only Weakly Related to Infrastructure Needs, Comparing Damage Classrooms in 2016 with DAK Fisik Allocation in 2017

Note: Afkar and Yarrow (2021).
Source: World Bank (2020).

school infrastructure gaps such as school rehabilitation and additional classroom construction. However, DAK *fisik* allocation in 2017 had a weak relationship with the number of damaged classrooms, especially for primary and junior secondary levels (Figure 11.5) (World Bank 2020). During the pandemic, DAK *fisik* has been prioritized for communication and information technology for distance learning. Furthermore, the fund is also strategically allocated to improve access to learning resources.

The minimum allocation of 20 per cent of the budget to education has not always been met at the local level. In 2019, 22 per cent of district governments did not meet the mandate to allocate at least 20 per cent of the regional income and expenditure budget (APBD) to education.[12] Similarly, at the provincial level, 12 out of 34 provinces did not comply with this mandate (Afkar et al. 2020). Sanctions have been issued[13] and several areas have been reported to have received them.[14] However, given that many subnational governments did not fulfil the mandate, enforcement of these sanctions should be tightened.

Furthermore, not all local governments have the capacity to fully execute their budgets. Of the districts that allocated 20 per cent of their budgets to education in 2019, only 270 (70 per cent) achieved more than 95 per cent realization. The remainder of these districts/cities had low realization rates and low capacity. Most were located in Sulawesi and Sumatra, with a few in the Java/Bali region. In 2021, only 62 per cent of the allocated budget was executed.

Increases in education spending have financed an increase in the number of certified teachers. However, this has not contributed to significant improvements in teacher quality. The number of teachers increased by 30 per cent between 2003 and 2015. With the enactment of the Teacher Law in 2005, many teachers met certification and became entitled to professional allowances (*Tunjangan Profesi Guru*, or TPG) on top of their salary. In 2020, the budget for TPG, as part of the transfer to local governments through DAK *non fisik*, was nearly IDR54 trillion and accounted for 11 per cent of the total education budget. However, there is little difference in teacher competencies between certified and non-certified teachers. An impact evaluation considered TPG's effects on teacher quality and student learning, measured by test scores. De Ree et al. (2017) found that TPG had an impact on teacher welfare but not on student learning outcomes.

Meanwhile, with the onset of the pandemic in 2020, the government allocated IDR3.8 trillion to provide internet credits for students. In 2021, the budget for this programme increased to IDR4.7 trillion, distributed in two periods: IDR2.3 trillion for 30 million students from March to May, and another IDR2.4 trillion for 28.9 million students from September to December. Moreover, IDR745 billion was allocated through a single tuition fee subsidy (*Uang Kuliah Tunggal*, or UKT) to support college students facing difficulties. The programme targeted 310,000 college students, allocating IDR2.4 million per student. The government also introduced *Kartu Indonesia Pintar (KIP) Kuliah* as a reformed version of *Bidik Misi*. Starting from the second semester of 2021, the programme has been adjusted in which the amount of support is differentiated by the programme taken and the cost-of-living to encourage students from low socio-economic status family to enter higher-quality programmes. In regard to subnational transfer funds, the government implemented a calibrated BOS (*BOS Majemuk*) for additional allocation to districts with higher price index, particularly those in remote areas. In addition, the government introduced *BOS Kinerja*, an additional funding package to schools with outstanding performance.

There were also some changes in the policy related to the use of BOS, i.e., to allow BOS spending on COVID-19-related equipment such as hand sanitizer, masks and media for online study (MoECRT Ministerial Regulation No. 19/2020). Another policy change related to DAK *fisik*, as a response to declining purchasing power, enables the inclusion of labour-intensive projects involving local workers and local supplies (Ministry of Finance Ministerial Regulation No. 17/2021).

11.5 LOOKING FORWARD

11.5.1 Lessons Learnt

While the impacts of the pandemic on education were widespread, its adverse consequences were more severe among students from poor and vulnerable households thus widening existing learning gaps. The disproportionate impact of the pandemic on learning losses could result in children's future earning losses, risking further exacerbating socio-economic inequalities.

The Government of Indonesia has worked to mitigate the impacts of the pandemic on education, introducing an emergency curriculum, different modes of distance learning, and hybrid learning. However, significant variation remains in terms of access across students and variation in school readiness to deliver quality education.

On the fiscal side, the government increased the budget allocation for education, and this was partly used for pandemic response programmes. There have also been changes in the guidelines regarding the utilization of DAK funding to accommodate different urgent needs at the subnational level during the pandemic. However, challenges remain regarding the ability to execute allocated funds, centrally and subnationally, potentially aggravating pre-existing concerns regarding the effectiveness of education spending.

To ensure Indonesia achieves its high-income aspirations and fulfils its growth potential in the years to come, this is a critical and opportune time to address the education problems which existed before the crisis and were emphasized and exacerbated during it. This has policy implications for both the education sector and the fiscal system. Below are several policy recommendations relating to both the focus of the education sector as well as its funding that could be considered to promote student outcomes and increase the resilience of the Indonesian education system.

11.5.2 Education Sector Policy

1. *Revitalize the national education system to focus on student learning*. Instead of simply reopening the former education system, which delivered low levels of student learning on average, the government could support the opening of a renewed and revitalized system that focuses on student learning and not just attendance. The focus on student learning should be prioritized at all levels of education. Implementing diagnostic assessments to identify what the students have and have not learnt during school closures is crucial to understand where they are in terms of their level of knowledge/skills. A personalized approach to the catch-up strategy and teaching at the right level for each child needs to be developed to accelerate their learning recovery. If no urgent action is taken for learning recovery, the current education system may produce graduates with even lower productivity than currently. Greater attention needs to be given to those in rural and remote areas and from low-income households to ensure they engage in learning recovery.
2. *Ensuring that teachers have the right knowledge, support and tools to ensure their students are learning.* Teachers are the fundamental ingredient for student learning. They need to have access to training using differentiated teaching methods including the use of educational technologies, variation in teaching techniques, conducting diagnostic assessments, as well as developing strategies for catch-up and teaching at the right level. This is essential not only for helping teachers to cope more effectively as schools reopen to face-to-face instruction but also in the longer term for improving the quality of teaching. Teachers are also encouraged to learn and improve their capacity through government-funded training and a platform for teachers to share and learn with their peers.
3. *Improving the school-based management with stronger inter-school collaboration from early childhood education through senior secondary education.* Schools need more autonomy and authority, from curriculum development to resource management. The government has supported this by providing schools with a report that captures diagnostic information on performance based on the national assessment. The government has started to provide facilitation and a more relevant accountability system to ensure budgets prioritize student learning.

4. *Supporting parental engagement to ensure children are learning.* During the school closures, many parents felt overwhelmed by their new roles in their children's education. When the schools have started to reopen, parents should still be supported to prepare their children to be ready for transitioning back to face-to-face learning. The government can provide materials which can help parents in guiding and tracking student learning. Schools and teachers can support parents by providing information on student learning recovery plans and targets to achieve together with guidance on their respective roles in supporting students to catch up.
5. *Enhancing collaboration with local governments in ensuring equitable distribution of quality education services.* Considering its vast geographical size, the Indonesian central government needs to collaborate with local governments and local actors. The education development in some provinces—e.g., Jakarta and Yogyakarta—has been very rapid while in the outer provinces have been very slow. For example, while 83 per cent of schools in Jakarta and Yogyakarta have access to soap and flowing water, only 32 per cent of schools in Maluku and Papua have soap and flowing water. This is another urgent gap that needs to be addressed especially during the pandemic. The central government has started to produce education reports at district and provincial levels which can be used by subnational governments to understand their problems and identify priority areas and schools where support is needed the most. MoF and MoECRT could further identify districts/province governments with low capacity in planning and budgeting and provide capacity-building and assistance to improve areas where they are lagging.
6. *Increasing the resilience of education service delivery to pandemics, climate change and other threats.* The government can improve the accuracy of the national education data system to track school conditions in real-time. This information is crucial for the government to identify areas and schools with the greatest need for support and to develop a more effective education plan. An accurate, reliable, timely data system is needed not only for the current COVID-19 pandemic but also for future crises. A technology-based national education platform can be built to promote student-centred, interdisciplinary, project-based, and collaborative learning. This strategy is born through the pandemic, utilized as one of the modalities for recovery, and can also be

employed to ensure future improvement of the education system. The government has started to develop a massive education platform that is versatile, user-friendly, light, and engaging to better accommodate student needs.

7. *Involving the private sector, community and parents to improve quality education.* Apart from local government's involvement, private sectors and communities including non-government organizations have a large role in improving education access and quality. The government started to promote various incentives to encourage broader private sector participation, including a matching fund for private sector investment that provides opportunities to students to be involved. At the same time, the key to successful implementation is regular monitoring and evaluation to ensure the delivery of quality education over time, including through greater involvement of parents and local communities.

11.5.3 Education Funding Policy

The forthcoming 2022 Poverty and Shared Prosperity Report (World Bank forthcoming) highlights some of the international lessons from middle-income countries which manage to sustain significant investments in human capital accumulation while also reducing poverty and inequality. The study discusses the importance of spending decisions, with space for important spending on health, education and social protection often being squeezed out by expensive and regressive subsidy spending. However, fiscal reform in Indonesia over the past decade has already reduced subsidy spending significantly.[15] While it is important that subsidy spending does not re-emerge as a major budget item, the main constraint on higher education spending in Indonesia is its relatively low revenue levels. As discussed, education spending is (by law) high relative to total spending but low relative to GDP and in international comparison; this reflects low total public spending driven by low revenues. Indonesia's revenues as a percentage of GDP are not only low for the region (Figure 11.6), but they are also considerably lower than both upper-middle- and lower-middle-income averages (Figure 11.7).[16]

Richer countries, particularly in the OECD, have high revenue and spending levels but also use fiscal policy to significantly reduce inequality. This is achieved not only through well-targeted social assistance but also

FIGURE 11.6
Tax Revenues, East Asia and the Pacific

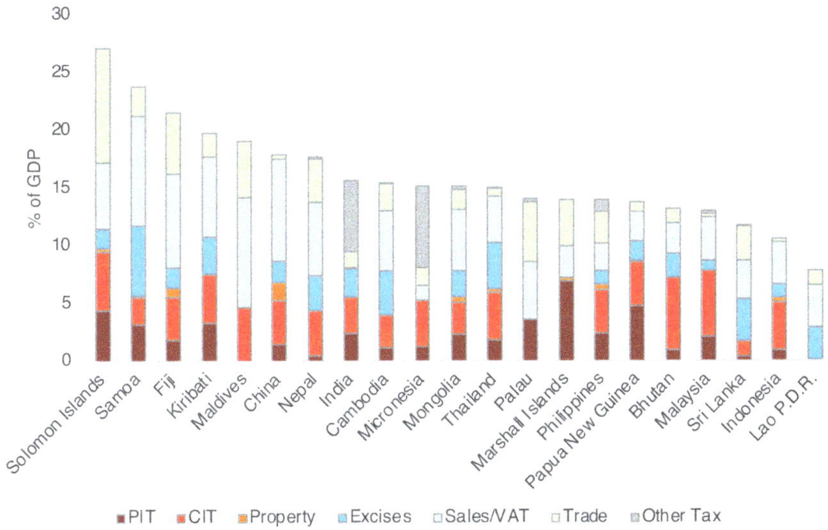

Source: IMF WoRLD.

FIGURE 11.7
Tax Revenues by Income Category

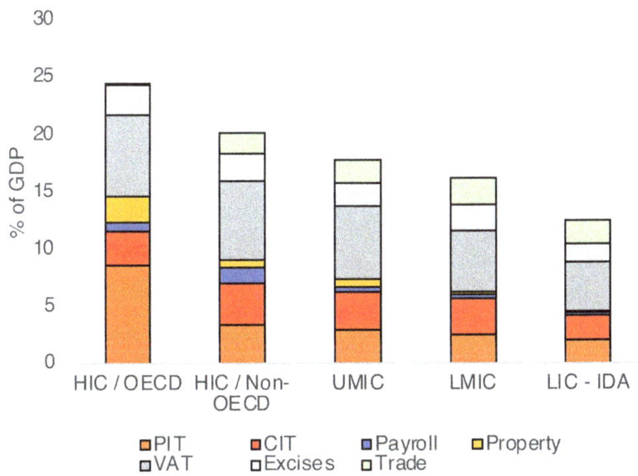

Source: IMF WoRLD and World Bank calculations in 2022 Poverty and Shared Prosperity Report (forthcoming)

by relying upon progressive direct taxation (such as personal income tax) for most income (as Figure 11.7 shows). Indonesia has made considerable progress since the Asian Financial Crisis and over the last ten years in establishing a modern social protection system with a broad and targeted safety net.[17] It now needs greater revenues to finance the investments needed to become a high-income country, including in education. However, while action has been taken to broaden the personal income tax base this is a longer-term agenda.[18]

In the meantime, Indonesia can follow the path highlighted in the report by the World Bank (forthcoming) of those middle-income countries which enjoy higher revenues than Indonesia without placing an undue burden on the poor. This has begun with the 2021 Harmonization of Tax Regulations Law and the increase of the VAT standard rate from 10 to 11 per cent, and some of the expensive and regressive VAT exemptions and preferential rates have been eliminated. While these were often on items more important to the poor such as food, rich households also consume such items and spend much more on them, meaning that such exemptions led to considerable foregone revenue while providing relatively little support for the poor. However, while the new 11 per cent rate (increasing to 12 per cent in 2025) and the removal of some exemptions will increase revenues (and indirectly the education budget), higher prices will affect poorer households. A part of the extra revenues raised from eliminating exemptions can be reinvested in Indonesia's well-developed social protection programmes to offset any poverty and inequality impacts while leaving significant new revenues for other important investments including education.

In addition to sufficiency of spending on education, effectiveness is important. Improving the quality of education means revising how education budgets are allocated and used, centrally and locally. The budget allocation formulation, mainly governing transfers to the regions, has been amended through Law Number 1 of 2022 concerning Central and Regional Financial Relations (UU HKPD). Although it does not specifically regulate the allocation of the education budget, the allocation of regional transfers could be strengthened through closer ties to performance, both in allocation and distribution. This will be relevant to the problem of too large a budget for education through transfers to regions using block grants. With the HKPD Law, the government can provide instructions to the regions for the implementation of the budget sourced from the DAU and include performance indicators. For example, in the DAU allocation method in the HKPD Law, a previous assessment on the achievement of regional minimum service standards (one of which is education) found that if the achievement of the education standard is poor, a portion of the DAU allocation will be used to improve the quality of education using Central Government guidelines (the worse the achievement, the larger the portion of the DAU). This will require work and adequate data.

In addition, there are efforts to improve the allocation of central education expenditure (through the Ministry of Education and Culture and several other ministries/agencies, through the planned amendment of PP 48/2008 on education funding).

Notes

1. The authors thank Dyah Pritadrajati for her outstanding research assistance for the chapter.
2. The economic shock resulting from COVID-19 led Indonesia to fall back to lower-middle-income status in 2021, likely on a temporary basis.
3. In March 2020, the GoI policy was to close all schools, but it changed to a more flexible one that allows for some decentralized decision-making by launching a Regulation on Learning Activities during the Pandemic that allows districts in "green zones" to reopen schools and conduct face-to-face learning after receiving permission from local governments through provincial or district/city education offices following approval from the local COVID-19 task force.
4. OECD (2015) analysed two different scenarios: bringing all current students to basic skills by 2030 (closing the quality gap) and full participation in secondary school at current quality levels (closing the access gap). For Indonesia, they estimated the benefits in terms of economic growth to be around seven times higher for closing the quality gap compared with closing the access gap. Closing the quality gap: Bringing all current students to basic skills by 2030 (level 2,420 points) would mean a 62 per cent higher GDP in 2095, 0.92 percentage point higher long-run growth and 14.5 per cent higher discounted future GDP. Closing the access gap: Full participation in secondary school at current quality would mean a 7 per cent higher 2095 GDP, 0.13 percentage point higher long-run growth and 1.8 per cent higher discounted future GDP. Closing both gaps: An 84 per cent higher 2095 GDP, 1.16 point higher long-run growth and 19 per cent higher discounted future GDP (see Hanushek and Woessmann, 2015).
5. MoEC's "Merdeka Belajar Episode: 19" on "Indonesian Education Report", https://www.youtube.com/watch?v=NbD96YWKh84

6. Most "private" schools in Indonesia are *madrasah* under MoRA, which are more accurately described as community-based schools and are non-profit. *Madrasahs* are generally inexpensive and not necessarily better quality than public schools. *Madrasahs* often fill the gap in rural areas where public schools are not nearby.
7. Peraturan Menteri Pendayagunaan Aparatur Negara dan Reformasi Birokrasi Republik Indonesia No. 28/2021 (MoSAUBR Regulation No. 28/2021).
8. The School Operational Assistance (BOS) dedicates a particular proportion of the funds for books and learning resources procurement for each student. Previously, the governmental had also allocated BOS *Buku*, a specific funding to procure books for all students. Considering the amount of funding is not strategically allocated, the funding is merged with the BOS and a certain proportion is allocated for book procurements.
9. Estimates are based on the retrospective learning loss calculation in accordance with the observed school closure from January 2020 to June 2021 by varying the alternative teaching and learning modalities to be 10 to 40 per cent as effective as face-to-face instruction.
10. https://www.kemdikbud.go.id/main/blog/2022/01/syarat-ptm-100-persen-ppkm-level-12-dan-capaian-vaksinasi-guru
11. Significant variations across regions on fully vaccinated rate among students whose school had already opened for face-to-face learning: 83 per cent in DKI Jakarta and rural areas in Java (outside DKI Jakarta), 87 per cent in urban areas in Java (outside DKI Jakarta), 60 per cent in rural areas outside Java, and 56 per cent in urban areas outside Java.
12. Quote from Article 31, paragraph 4, 1945 Constitution of the Republic of Indonesia: The state shall prioritize the education budget by at least 20 per cent of the state income and expenditure budget as well as from the regional income and expenditure budget to fulfil the needs of the administration of national education.
13. Peraturan Menteri Keuangan No. 139/PMK.07/2019 (MoF Regulation No. 139/PMK.07/2019), https://jdih.kemenkeu.go.id/fullText/2019/139~PMK.07~2019Per.pdf
14. https://money.kompas.com/read/2020/07/07/174710726/6-daerah-kena-sanksi-dari-sri-mulyani-karena-apbd-tak-seusai-ketentuan
15. For example, see Ministry of Finance and World Bank (2020).
16. Data for Indonesia are from 2018.
17. See World Bank (2012) for the evolution of social protection in the decade since *krismon* and Holmemo et al. (2020) for the last decade.
18. For example, the recently passed Tax Harmonization Law in 2021 brings in a new top rate of 35 per cent for those earning over IDR5 billion.

References

Afkar, Rythia, and Noah Yarrow, 2021. *Rewrite the Future: How Indonesia's Education System Can Overcome the Losses from the Covid-19 Pandemic and Raise Learning Outcomes for All*. Washington, DC: World Bank. https://openknowledge.worldbank.org/handle/10986/36327

———, Joppe de Ree, and Noviandri Khairin. 2018. *Who Learns What in Basic Education? Evidence from Indonesia*. Washington, DC: World Bank. https://openknowledge.worldbank.org/handle/10986/32396

———, Noah Yarrow, Soedarti Surbakti, and Rachel Cooper. 2021. *Inclusion in Indonesia's Education Sector: A Subnational Review of Gender Gaps and Children with Disabilities*. Washington, DC: World Bank. https://openknowledge.worldbank.org/handle/10986/33943

———, Javier Luque, Shinsaku Nomura, and Jeffery Marshall. 2020. *Revealing How Indonesia's Subnational Governments Spend Their Money on Education*. World Bank.

Agol, Dorice, and Peter Harvey. 2018. "Gender Differences Related to WASH in Schools and Educational Efficiency". *Water Alternatives* 11, no. 2: 284.

Beatty, Amanda, Emilie Berkhout, Luhur Bima, Menno Pradhan, and Daniel Suryadarma. 2021. "Schooling Progress, Learning Reversal: Indonesia's Learning Profiles between 2000 and 2014". *International Journal of Educational Development* 85.

Carneiro, Pedro, Flavio Cunha, and James J. Heckman. 2003. "Interpreting the Evidence of Family Influence on Child Development". *Economics of Early Childhood Development: Lessons for Economic Policy*.

Chetty, Raj, Nathaniel Hendren, Patrick Kline, and Emmanuel Saez. 2014. "Where Is the Land of Opportunity? The Geography of Intergenerational Mobility in the United States". *Quarterly Journal of Economics* 129, no. 4: 1553–623.

De Ree, Joppe Jaitze, Karthik Muralidharan, Menno Prasad Pradhan, and F. Halsey Rogers. 2017. "Double for Nothing? Experimental Evidence on an Unconditional Teacher Salary Increase in Indonesia". World Bank Policy Research Working Paper 8264 (2017).

Dharmawan, G., and D. Suryadarma. 2021. "Education Quality Across Indonesia's Districts: Estimations from a Policy Experiment". *Journal of Southeast Asian Economies* 38, no. 3: 401–25.

Durán-Narucki, Valkiria, 2008. "School Building Condition, School Attendance, and Academic Achievement in New York City Public Schools: A Mediation Model". *Journal of Environmental Psychology* 28, no. 3: 278–86.

Hanushek, E.A., and L. Woessmann. 2015. *Universal Basic Skills: What Countries Stand to Gain*. Paris: Organization for Economic Co-operation and Development.

Heckman, James J., and Dimitriy V. Masterov. 2007. "The Productivity Argument for Investing in Young Children". *NBER Working Paper 13016*. National Bureau of Economic Research.

Holmemo, Camilla, Pablo Acosta, Tina George, Robert J. Palacios, Juul Pinxten, Shonali Sen, and Sailesh Tiwari. 2020. *Investing in People: Social Protection for Indonesia's 2045 Vision*. Washington, DC: World Bank. https://openknowledge.worldbank.org/handle/10986/33767

Human Capital Project. 2020. *Indonesia Human Capital Index 2020*. Washington, DC: World Bank. https://databank.worldbank.org/data/download/hci/HCI_2pager_IDN.pdf

International Monetary Fund. 2022. IMF World Revenue Longitudinal Data (WoRLD). https://data.imf.org/?sk=77413f1d-1525-450a-a23a-47aeed40fe78

McMichael, Celia, 2019. "Water, Sanitation and Hygiene (WASH) in Schools in Low-Income Countries: A Review of Evidence of Impact". *International Journal of Environmental Research and Public Health* 16, no. 3: 359.

Narayan, Ambar, Roy Van der Weide, Alexandru Cojocaru, Christoph Lakner, Silvia Redaelli, Daniel Gerszon Mahler, Rakesh Gupta N. Ramasubbaiah, and Stefan Thewissen. 2018. *Fair Progress?: Economic Mobility across Generations Around the World*. Washington, DC: World Bank. https://openknowledge.worldbank.org/handle/10986/28428

OECD. 2015. *Universal Basic Skills: What Countries Stand to Gain*. OECD Publishing. https://www.oecd-ilibrary.org/education/universal-basic-skills_9789264234833-en

———. 2019. *Indonesia Country Note: Programme for International Student Assessment (PISA) Results for PISA 2018*. OECD Publishing. https://www.oecd.org/pisa/publications/PISA2018_CN_IDN.pdf

Purnamasari, R., and R. Ali. 2021. *Indonesia COVID-19 Observatory: Education Services during the COVID-19 Pandemic—November to December 2020*. Washington, DC: World Bank. https://openknowledge.worldbank.org/bitstream/handle/10986/35125/Indonesia-COVID-19-Observatory-Education-Services-During-the-COVID-19-Pandemic-November-to-December-2020.pdf?sequence=1&isAllowed=y

Rosser, Andrew J., and Mohamad Fahmi. 2016. "The Political Economy of Teacher Management in Decentralized Indonesia". *World Bank Policy Research Working Paper 7913*. Washington, DC: World Bank. https://openknowledge.worldbank.org/handle/10986/25812

Statistic Indonesia. 2021. *Indonesia's Employment Status August 2021*. Statistic Indonesia. https://www.bps.go.id/pressrelease/2021/11/05/1816/agustus-2021--tingkat-pengangguran-terbuka--tpt--sebesar-6-49-persen.html

World Bank. 2012. *History and Evolution of Social Assistance in Indonesia*. Washington, DC: World Bank. https://openknowledge.worldbank.org/handle/10986/12259

———. 2018. *World Development Report 2018: Learning to Realize Education's Promise*. Washington, DC: World Bank. https://www.worldbank.org/en/publication/wdr2018

———. 2019. *Aspiring Indonesia: Expanding the Middle Class*. Washington, DC: World Bank. https://www.worldbank.org/en/country/indonesia/publication/aspiring-indonesia-expanding-the-middle-class

———. 2020. *Indonesia Public Expenditure Review: Spending for Better Results*. Washington, DC: World Bank. https://www.worldbank.org/en/country/indonesia/publication/indonesia-public-expenditure-review

———. 2021a. *Pathways to Middle-Class Jobs in Indonesia*. Washington, DC: World Bank. https://openknowledge.worldbank.org/handle/10986/35848

———. 2021b. *Indonesia Learning Poverty Brief*. Washington, DC: World Bank. https://documents1.worldbank.org/curated/en/579771624553117186/pdf/Indonesia-Learning-Poverty-Brief-2021.pdf

———. 2021c. "Indonesia COVID-19 Observatory". 19 October 2021. https://www.worldbank.org/en/country/indonesia/brief/indonesia-covid-19-observatory

———. Forthcoming. *2022 Poverty and Shared Prosperity Report*. Washington, DC: World Bank.

Yarrow, Noah, Eema Masood, and Rythia Afkar, 2020. *Estimates of Covid-19 Impacts on Learning and Earning in Indonesia: How to Turn Tide*. Washington, DC: World Bank. https://openknowledge.worldbank.org/handle/10986/34378

12

Towards an Inclusive Response to Combat COVID-19 Impacts on Women and People with Disabilities

Lessons from Indonesia for Peer Countries[1]

Bimbika Sijapati Basnett, Usha Adelina Riyanto, Aktiva Primananda Hadiarta and R. Wiwin Istanti

12.1 INTRODUCTION

The first year of the COVID-19 pandemic and the subsequent measures to contain its spread have magnified existing burdens on women and people living with disabilities in G20 countries and around the world.

This period has been referred to as a "Shecession" or "Momcession" because larger employment penalties were borne by women across advanced and emerging countries, particularly when schools and childcare facilities shut down (Bluedorn et al. 2021; OECD 2021). McKinsey (2020)

estimated that women made up 39 per cent of global employment before the pandemic hit but took 54 per cent of the job losses. Women gave up paid work faster than men due to increased family responsibilities during the pandemic.

Beyond impacts on employment and unpaid work, women and girls also endured more domestic violence as the poor economic and social conditions coupled with lockdown measures exacerbated existing abuse and control (Gavrilovic et al. 2022). Besides being devastating to individual well-being, such violence takes a heavy economic toll (Oedraogo and Stenzel 2021; UN Women 2020a). With the pandemic and its impact on women, the World Economic Forum estimates that it will take an additional generation to close the large gender gap that prevailed even prior to the pandemic.[2]

Concurrently, in regular circumstances, people with disabilities—which comprise 15 per cent of the world's population—are more exposed to economic insecurity and shocks because they are more likely to be poor and have higher health costs, and have lower levels of education and economic participation (UNPRPD, UNICEF, IDA, and ILO 2020). People with disabilities also have more healthcare needs than others and are therefore vulnerable to the impact of low-quality or inaccessible healthcare services (WHO 2020).

A consensus is building that social protection is a key policy response to address pandemic-related social and economic crises, and that timely action can counter the trends. McKinsey (2020) suggests taking timely action to advance gender equality could add US$13 trillion to the global gross domestic product (GDP) in 2030 compared with a situation where no action is taken.[3]

However, by July 2021, out of 3,099 social protection and labour market measures worldwide, only 19.6 per cent took gender into account because existing systems were inadequate for considering gender within shock-response planning. Gavrilovic et al (2022) reported that among those that did, their approaches were designed or adapted to mitigate gendered risks across three domains: (i) supporting women in informal employment; (ii) tackling the risk of violence against women, and (iii) confronting the unequal distribution of care work and strengthening care systems.

The overarching purpose of this chapter is to respond to three questions: Does Indonesia mirror the global findings on the gender and disability differentiated effects of the pandemic? How effective have government responses been to mitigate these effects? And what learnings can Indonesia pass on to other countries for inclusively tackling future economic crises? The empirical evidence presented in this chapter draws on primary research and original analyses of available national datasets (such as the national labour force survey and socio-economic survey), and a desktop review. Its focus is on the first year of the pandemic.

12.2 A SNAPSHOT OF THE SITUATION BEFORE THE PANDEMIC

12.2.1 Women's Economic Participation in Indonesia before COVID-19

Indonesia has the fourth-largest population in the world, almost half of which are women. Despite considerable changes to the Indonesian economy, rising average incomes and declining poverty rates, women's economic participation had stalled in the two decades before the pandemic with female participation at only 52 per cent, as opposed to 83 per cent for males.

Women's marital status, educational attainment and number of children aged 0–2 years in the household, combined with greater urbanization and agricultural decline, were the main factors driving female labour force participation. Single and highly educated women participated in the labour market the most, while married women with low education levels and children participated the least (Schaner and Das 2016; Cameron, Suarez, and Rowell 2019).

Despite these persistent challenges, Indonesia's performance against global gender and development indicators had begun to show signs of improvement. According to the Global Gender Gap Index (GGGI), up until 2019, Indonesia had closed 70 per cent of its gender gap with overwhelmingly positive trends in the economic, health and education dimensions (World Economic Forum 2019).[4] Furthermore, 55 per cent of Indonesia's senior and leadership roles were held by women in 2020. Indonesia was among six countries where most of such roles were held by women. Both the educational and health gender gaps were closing.

12.2.2 Disability Inclusion in Indonesia before COVID-19

In Indonesia, as many as 1 in 10 people have some form of disability, and 1 in 50 (or 2.1 per cent) have a moderate to severe disability. In general, there is a higher prevalence of women with a disability than men, across all types of disabilities (Gunawan and Rezki 2022).

Even before the pandemic, people with disabilities faced higher barriers to participation in the economy and society. In 2019, the school completion rate for young adults with severe disabilities was 30 per cent less than for those without disabilities. Such low educational attainment, along with the discrimination and stigma that many people with disabilities experience, pose additional barriers to entry into the labour market.

During the same year, less than half (44 per cent) of people with disabilities were in the labour force compared with 69.8 per cent of those with no disability. When they did work, people with disabilities earned 20 per cent less than the national average. This is because those who did find employment worked predominantly in the informal sector, notable for poor and irregular work.

And yet people with disabilities had 20 per cent higher costs of living than those without disabilities due to extra spending on regular items (e.g., higher needs in healthcare, higher transportation costs) and disability-specific spending (e.g., assistive products, rehabilitation, personal care). These extra costs are too high for households that earn the minimum wage. Figure 12.1 depicts the median disability-related cost of living in 2019.

Poverty lines are set at an expenditure level considered sufficient for a minimum standard of living. Figure 12.2 shows that people with severe disabilities are more likely to be poor than those without. However, the minimum standards are much higher for people with disabilities due to

FIGURE 12.1
Median Disability-Related Cost of Living, Compared with Yogyakarta Expenditure Percentile

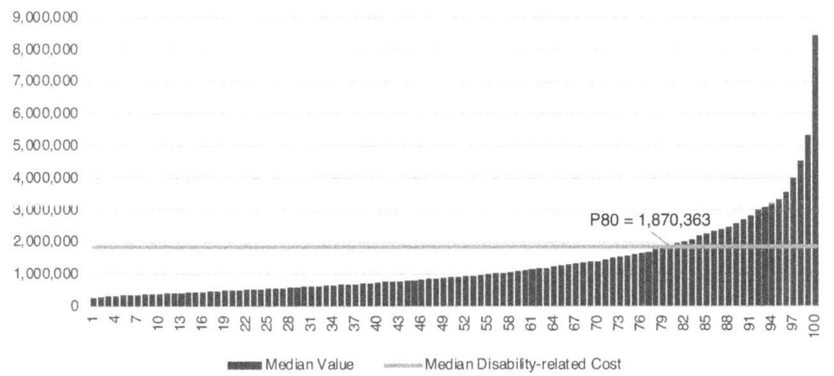

Source: National Socioeconomic Survey 2019, BKF and PROSPERA (forthcoming).

FIGURE 12.2
Poverty Rate by Disability Status, Using Official and Adjusted Poverty Line (PL)

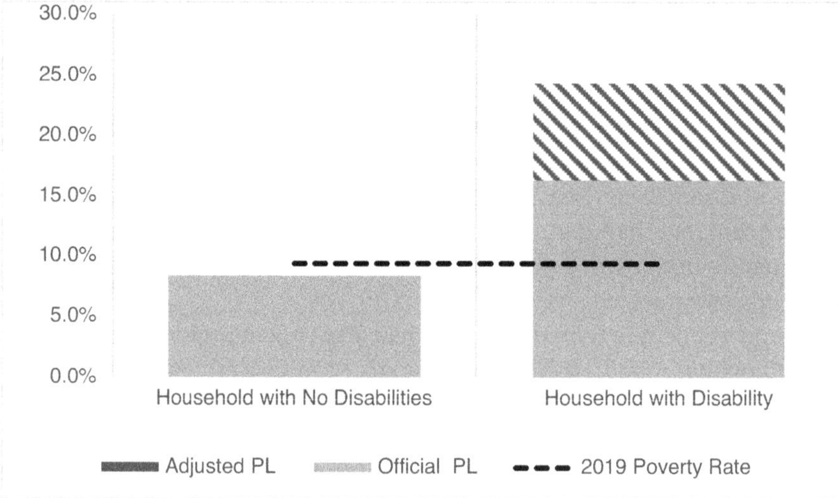

Source: National Socioeconomic Survey 2019.

the extra costs they incur to attain the same standard of living as those without.

After adjusting the poverty rate to better reflect the extra costs that people with disabilities face, it was revealed that 1 in 4 households with a family member with a severe disability is poor. That is three times more than households with no disabilities (1 in 12).

Indonesia, along with most other G20 countries, stands at the lower part of the 45-degree line indicating the low labour force participation of people with disabilities is a common challenge (see Figure 12.3).

12.3 PART I: GENDERED IMPACTS OF COVID-19 IN INDONESIA

To avoid further virus transmission, the Indonesian government introduced large-scale social restrictions on 31 March 2020. Offices, schools and other economic centres had to close. Many Indonesians experienced adverse impacts, with women being disproportionately affected.

The GGGI (see Table 12.1) shows Indonesia's progress towards gender equality then went backwards. This decline was driven by wider gaps in

FIGURE 12.3
Labour Force Participation Rate among G20 Countries

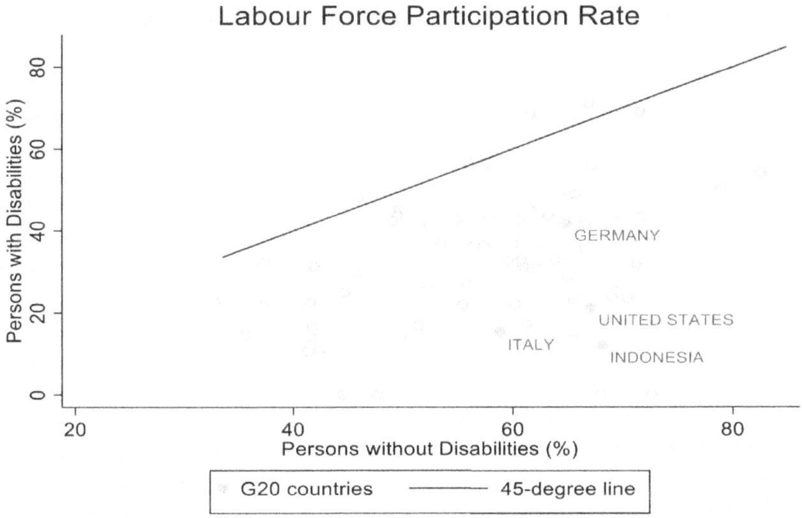

Source: ILOSTAT data.

TABLE 12.1
Indonesia's Global Gender Gap Index and Subindices

	2020 (Before the Pandemic)	*2021 (After the Pandemic)*
Global Gender Gap Index	0.700 (85)	0.688 (101)
Economic participation and opportunity	0.685 (68)	0.647 (99)
Educational attainment	0.970 (105)	0.970 (107)
Health and survival	0.974 (79)	0.971 (76)
Political empowerment	0.172 (82)	0.164 (92)

Note: Indonesia's rank in parentheses.
Source: World Economic Forum (2020, 2021).

economic participation and opportunity—women's participation in the labour market remains significantly less than men's (55.9 per cent versus 84 per cent) and wage and income gaps stay large (69.7 per cent and 51.7 per cent respectively). The setback has put Indonesia in the ten G20 countries with the lowest GGGI (Figure 12.4).

FIGURE 12.4
Global Gender Gap Index: 19 G20 Member Countries (2020 and 2021)

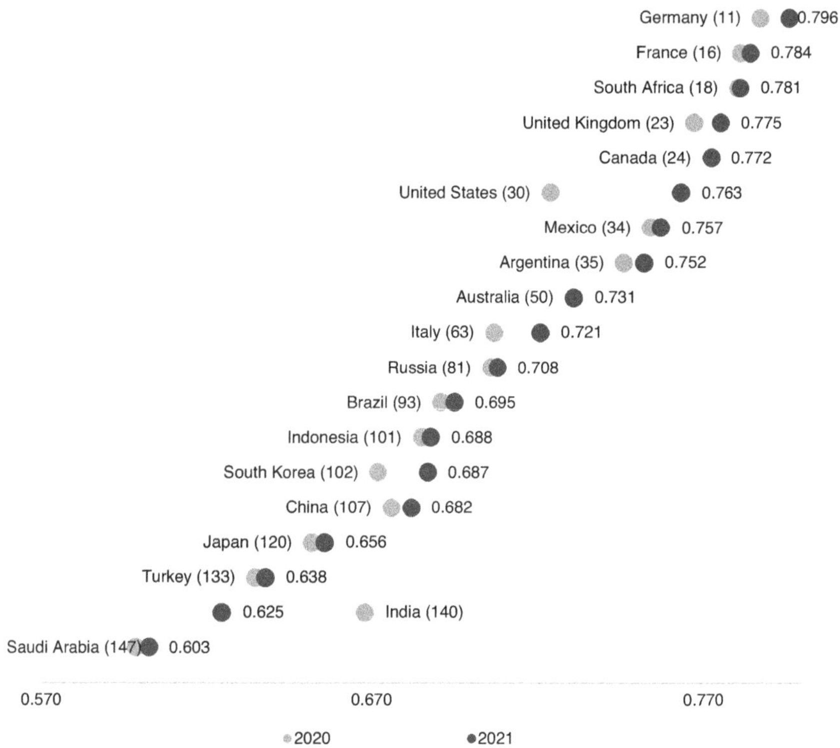

Source: GGGI Index from 19 G20 countries, 2021 rank in parenthesis. Global Gender Gap Report, World Economic Forum.

Drawing from a framework proposed by the World Bank (2020b), this section explores the main channels through which the gendered impacts of COVID-19 may transpire, including the endowment, agency and economic dimensions (see Box 12.1).

12.3.1 Gender-Differentiated Impacts of COVID-19: Jobs

Finding 1: Women Are Over-Represented in Economic Sectors Most Affected by COVID-19

Women made up 40 per cent of Indonesian workers in August 2020 but were over-represented in the human health and social work sector

BOX 12.1
Framework to Examine the Pandemic's Gender-Differentiated Effects (see Figure 12.5)

In the area of economic conditions, our examination considers the composition of female workers at the sectoral level. Within the scope of endowment, we delve into how men and women face different risks of virus transmission due to the demographic structure of the health and social service sector. Finally, we assess the agency of women in Indonesia throughout the pandemic along the dimensions of care work, the prevalence of gender-based violence, and women's mental health.

FIGURE 12.5
Transmission Channel of Gendered Impacts of COVID-19

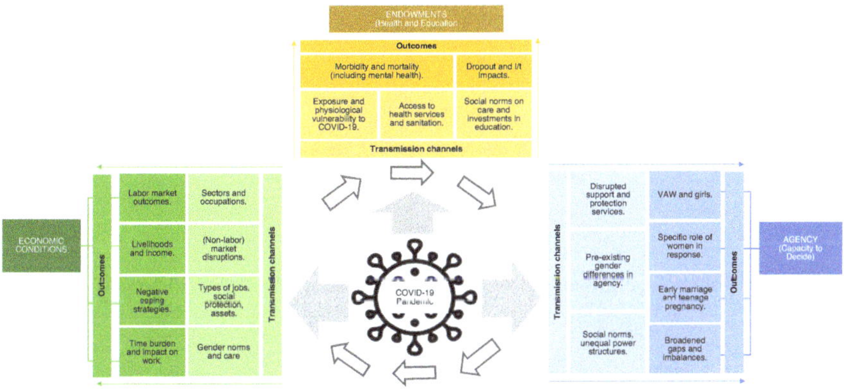

Source: World Bank (2020b).

(67.7 per cent), education (62.1 per cent) and hospitality (59.3 per cent). The sectors absorbing the most female workers in August 2020 were among the hardest hit by the COVID-19 downturn, such as wholesale and retail trade, manufacturing, and hospitality (see Figure 12.6). When combined, these three sectors employed half of Indonesia's female workers in 2020.

Female workers who remained in the workforce also faced precarity as wage levels shrank in sectors where most women were employed (see Figure 12.7). Between February 2020 and February 2021, each of the top

FIGURE 12.6
Year-to-Year GDP Growth in 2020, by Sector

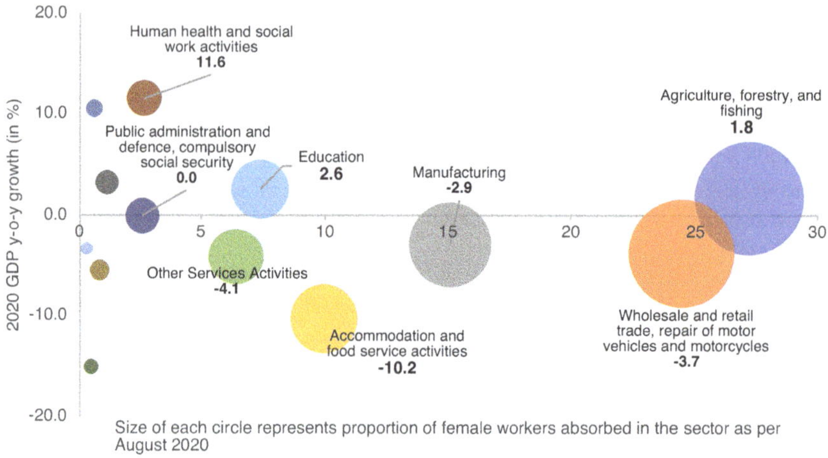

Source: Indonesia Labour Force Survey (August 2020), Statistics Indonesia (2021).

FIGURE 12.7
Change in Sectoral Median Wages between February 2020 and February 2021 (Adjusted to Inflation), by Sector

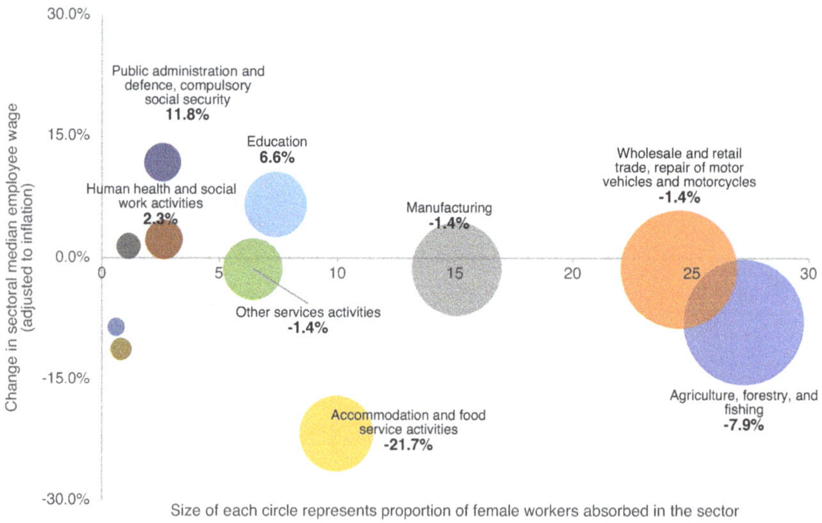

Source: Indonesia Labour Force Survey (February 2020, August 2020, and February 2021).

four sectors with the most women workers saw a median wage dip of 1.4 per cent to 21.7 per cent. Workers in agriculture, forestry and fisheries went through a median wage decrease of almost 8 per cent, despite its positive output growth. Additionally, as international travel restrictions remained in place throughout the year, the hospitality sector experienced the largest median wage drop of 21.7 per cent.

A World Bank study (forthcoming) echoes these findings. Women who were employed as formal and informal workers were found to face larger impacts from the pandemic than men. Formally employed women worked 1.5 hours less than their male counterparts. Meanwhile, women employed in the informal sector worked 1.5 hours more than their male counterparts. Women's earnings also went down 22.6 per cent per month from the start of the pandemic, a much larger reduction than their male counterparts.

Finding 2: Paradoxically, women's labour force participation rates increased during the pandemic but less-optimistic results prevail upon closer examination
From August 2019 to August 2020, women's participation rates increased slightly by 1.2 percentage points (see Figure 12.8). This finding comes as a surprise for two reasons. First, most countries have witnessed a historic decline in women's labour force participation. Second, even before COVID-19, Indonesia's female labour force participation rates had been stagnant for two decades.

FIGURE 12.8
Labour Force Participation Trend

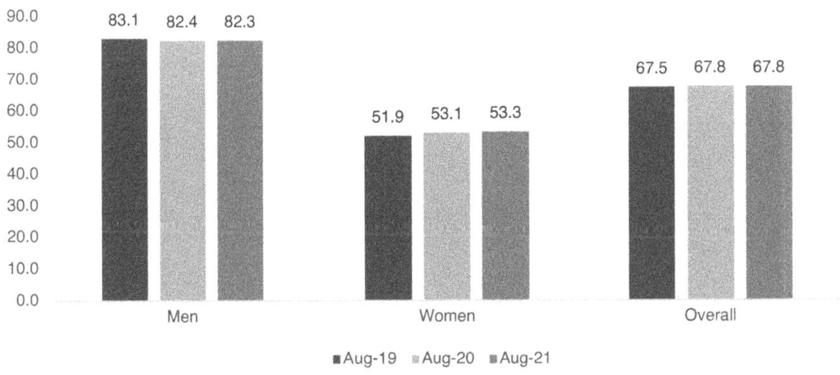

Source: Indonesia Labour Force Survey (August 2019, August 2020, and August 2021).

However, a closer examination reveals the increase is made up of younger women (aged 15–19) who were otherwise in education, and older women (60+) entering the labour force to compensate for falls in family income (see Figure 12.9). Meanwhile, the labour force participation of women of childbearing age, particularly for the age group of 20–25 and 25–29, declined. This finding resonates with those of the World Bank (forthcoming), showing that many women needed to join the labour force for the first time as an added worker—more than 20 per cent of whom had no prior work experience. However, women of childbearing age (19–29) were pushed out, likely due to increased care responsibilities.

In general, both men and women workers had to find informal employment during the pandemic. However, a higher proportion of women were pushed into informal employment between August 2019 and 2020 (see Figure 12.10). As the economy started to pick up again in 2021, the share increased but not to its pre-pandemic levels. Therefore, the increase in women's labour force participation during the pandemic was not uniform and signalled distressed participation.

By August 2020, 45.4 per cent of people who were temporarily not working cited reasons related to the pandemic (see Figure 12.11). One year later, temporary work suspension had become less prevalent. However, the proportion of women temporarily not working with a guarantee to return to work remained similar, whereas it expanded for men.

In a rapid survey by PROSPERA (forthcoming), 24.6 per cent of 549 female homemaker respondents had stopped work within the previous

FIGURE 12.9
Female Labour Force Participation Trend, by Age

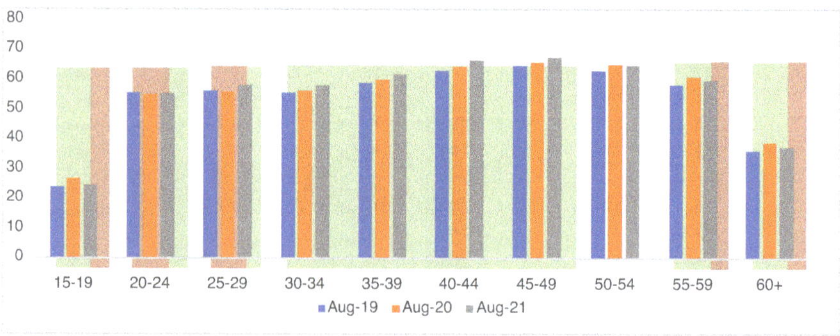

Source: Indonesia Labour Force Survey (August 2019, August 2020, and August 2021).

FIGURE 12.10
Proportion of Formally Employed Workers, by Gender (in %)

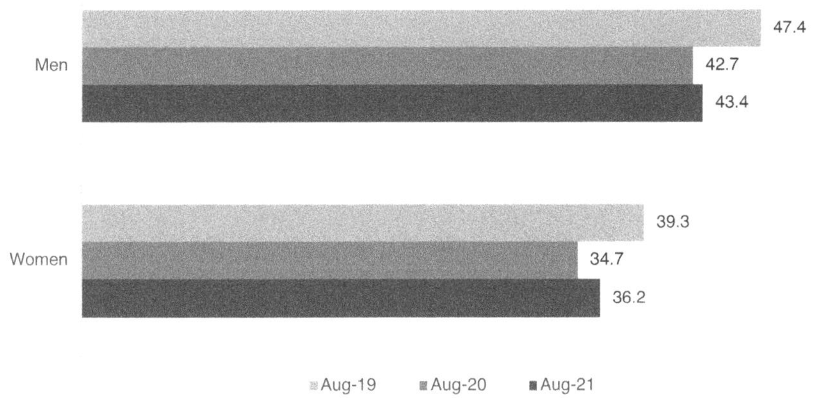

Source: Indonesia Labour Force Survey (August 2019, August 2020, and August 2021).

FIGURE 12.11
Proportion of Workers Citing COVID-Related Reasons for Not Working, by Gender (in %)

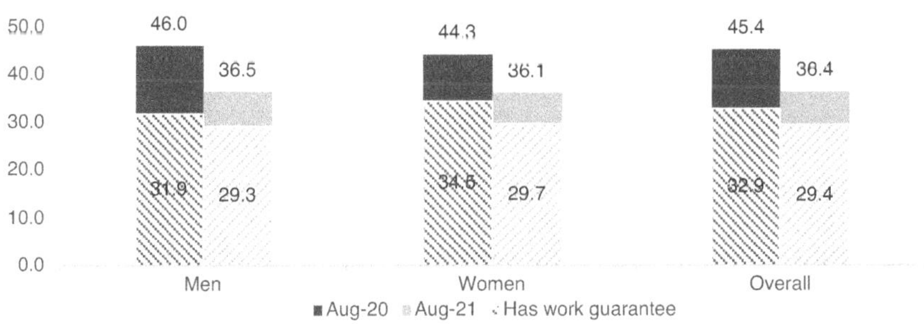

Source: Indonesia Labour Force Survey (August 2019, August 2020, and August 2021).

year. As suggested in Figure 12.12, among those who had to stop working, 62.6 per cent cited care responsibilities or managing their household. Yet 95 per cent of full-time female homemakers aspired to either have a business or have full/part-time employment. For 71.8 per cent of respondents, the

FIGURE 12.12
Work Status of Female Homemakers and Reason for Not Continuing Work (in %)

Source: PROSPERA (forthcoming) 2022 Rapid Mass-Scale Household and Economic Inclusion Survey.

BOX 12.2
Women at Risk of COVID-19 Infection Due to Clustering in the Health Sector and Commuting Patterns

In 2020, 67 per cent of health and social workers were women. Among doctors and nurses, the proportion of women was even greater at 74 per cent. Such over-representation exposes more women health and social workers to a higher risk of virus transmission. Soebandrio et al. (2021) found that in Greater Jakarta, COVID-19 cases among healthcare workers were mostly among females (62.1 per cent).

More than a year after the pandemic began, more workers in the health and social work sector had health protection in August 2021 (see Figure 12.13). However, the proportion of male and female workers who were fully insured (i.e., having access to health, disability and death protection in the workplace) was 50.9 per cent and 48.1 per cent respectively. For female workers, the proportion dropped by 4.0 percentage points from its pre-pandemic level (see Figure 12.14). The commuting patterns of women workers in Indonesia also put them at higher risk of exposure to COVID-19. More women had to commute than men (see Figure 12.15). Furthermore, a larger proportion of women workers took public transport to commute, which exposed them to a higher risk of transmission (Figure 12.16).

FIGURE 12.13
Overall Insurance Coverage of Health and Social Workers (in %)

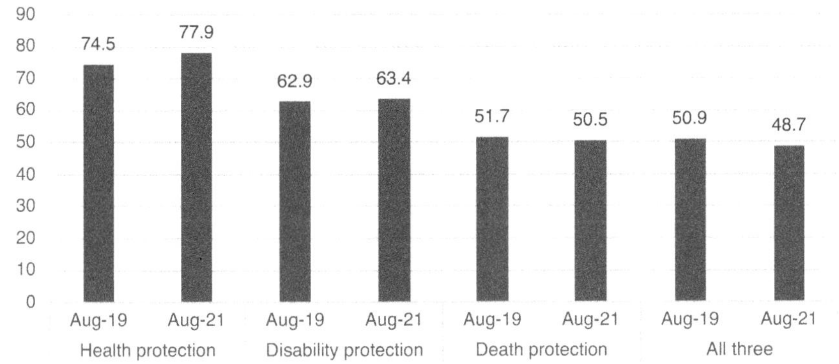

Source: Indonesia Labour Force Survey (August 2019 and August 2021).

FIGURE 12.14
Insurance Coverage of Health and Social Workers, by Gender

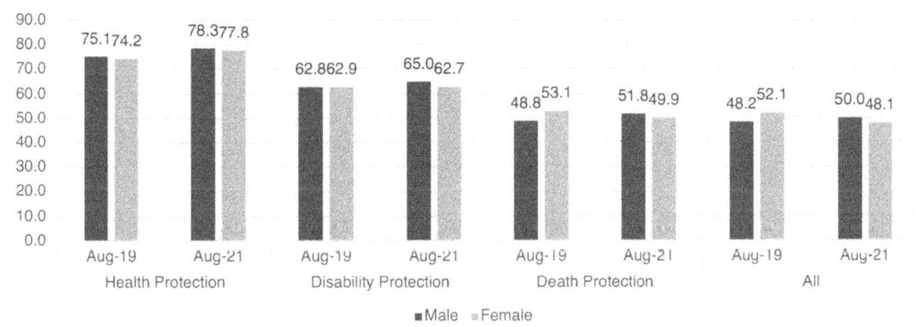

Source: Indonesia Labour Force Survey (August 2019 and August 2021).

FIGURE 12.15
Proportion of Workers Commuting Every Day, by Gender (in %)

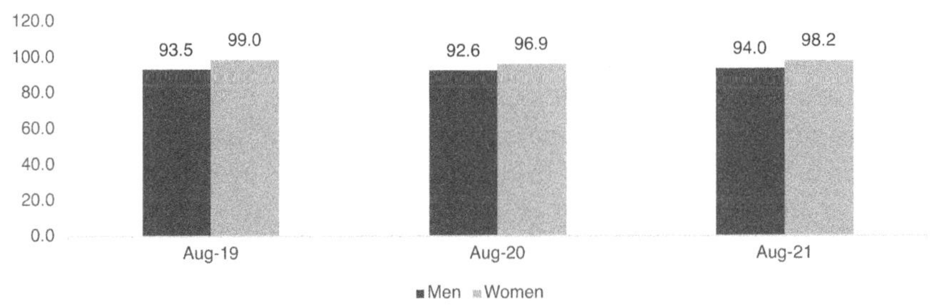

Source: Indonesia Labour Force Survey (August 2019, August 2020, and August 2021).

FIGURE 12.16
Proportion of Workers Commuting by Public Transport, by Gender (in %)

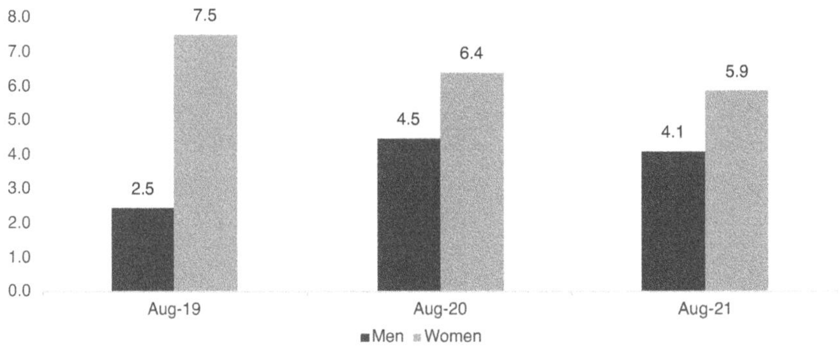

Source: Indonesia Labour Force Survey (August 2019, August 2020, and August 2021).

aspiration arose from the need to support their household income during the pandemic.

12.3.2 Gender-Differentiated Effects of COVID-19: Businesses

Finding 3: COVID-19 downturn has been hitting small businesses hard and women-owned micro-businesses operating out of necessity have been the worst affected

With curbed mobility and low purchasing power, demand for products from micro, small and medium enterprises (MSMEs) took a huge hit. About 87.5 per cent of households with businesses across Indonesia were impacted by the pandemic (UNICEF, UNDP, PROSPERA, the SMERU Research Institute 2021). The same study found that 70.2 per cent of female-owned household businesses saw fewer buyers, compared with 61.0 per cent of male-owned businesses.

The study also found that the proportion of women-owned family businesses that had to close down was twice that of male-owned businesses. The concentration of such businesses in the hardest-hit sectors during the pandemic, such as retail trade and restaurant and accommodation services, may explain the result. Concurrently, nearly 60 per cent of the women in this sector had school-age children, which also had a bearing on how much time they could allocate for business during mass school closures.

Eventually, the supply side mirrored the disruption in the demand side as travel restrictions and manufacturing plant closures disrupted the distribution chain. Forty-five per cent of MSMEs in Indonesia had problems in obtaining raw materials, with the issue being more prevalent among female-owned businesses (50 per cent) compared to male-owned businesses (44 per cent) (UNDP and LPEM FEB UI 2021). The twin disruption exerted shocks to small businesses' balance sheets and cash flow. Even before the pandemic, PROSPERA's study showed that 70 per cent of all women-owned businesses generated monthly profits of less than IDR1.4 million (US$100), an amount that barely keeps a family above the poverty line. UN Women (2020b) also noted the limited options for women-owned businesses in coping with financial adversity—compared to men-owned businesses, they are less likely to ask for a loan from a legitimate financial institution or even their close networks.

Paradoxically, the MSME sector also expanded during the pandemic with an unprecedented surge in online sales. A World Bank (2021) survey—in collaboration with Shopee, a digital marketplace—found that 25 per cent of respondents were new merchants. They were mostly young people, female students and female part-time employees who had started a business. Furthermore, existing micro-entrepreneurs who could shift to online business were more likely to sustain their operations and thrive than those who could not (World Bank 2021). Furthermore, digital solutions were also enabling women-owned businesses to better balance increased home and work responsibilities during the pandemic (UN Women 2020b).

Yet many existing businesses could not automatically shift to online selling, thereby exposing them to future uncertainties. According to a representative survey of micro-entrepreneurs registered with the Jakarta government, 51 per cent of the respondents (2,578 women) only used social media to market their products and had not fully digitalized. Additionally, only 5.4 per cent of the respondents shifted to online selling during the pandemic (PROSPERA and Jakpreneur programme, forthcoming).

While a plethora of training modules and business development support emerged to support micro-entrepreneurs during the pandemic, most (60 per cent) had not accessed any because they were either unaware of it and/or could not find anything to suit their needs. Available training focused too much on production techniques and not enough on expanding women's digital skills and capabilities, sales and marketing—among the top skills merchants needed during the pandemic. Much of the training was targeted at women who had enrolled in online marketing, making it harder for older and less digitally savvy business owners to grasp (PROSPERA and Jakpreneur programme, forthcoming). Such mismatches between available supply and the needs of micro-entrepreneurs are echoed by other research findings (World Bank 2021; UN Women 2020b).

12.3.3 Gender-Differentiated Effects of COVID-19: Care Burden

Finding 4: Prolonged school closures have had a disproportionate impact on women

To curb transmission, schools first closed in March 2020. Since all learning had to take place remotely, 3.3 million teachers had to confront the sudden shift to online learning. With 6 out of 10 teachers in Indonesia being women, the highly feminized Indonesian education sector meant that more female teachers had to quickly adjust to the new arrangement (see Figure 12.17).

FIGURE 12.17
Registered Teachers in Indonesia, by Gender (in %)

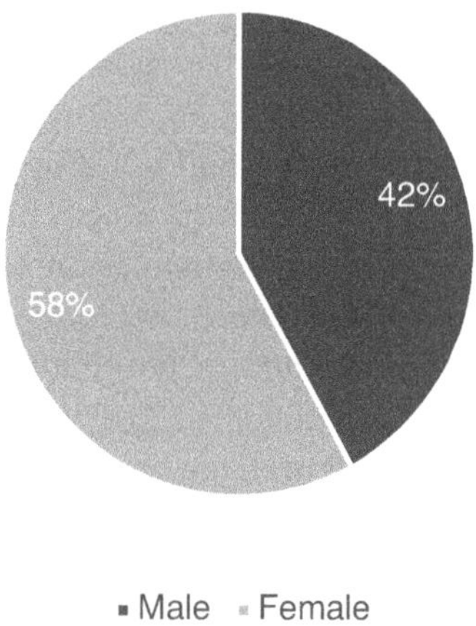

Source: Ministry of Education, Culture, Technology and Research (2021).

Among all teachers, those in the early childhood education and care (ECEC) sector faced more obstacles and precarity. The ECEC sector is highly feminized, with 94.6 per cent of its teachers being female (see Figure 12.18). Unfortunately, 43.9 per cent of ECEC teachers work in non-formal ECEC settings such as playgroups, and lack the earnings and job security of those working in formal settings such as kindergartens.

In the meantime, the unpaid care burden for both stay-at-home and working mothers increased due to the need to look after children who would have otherwise been in school. UNDP, UNICEF, PROSPERA and the SMERU Research Institute (2021) found that mothers were three times more likely than fathers to help their children study at home (see Figure 12.19). Additionally, half of them were still engaged in paid work.

A UN Women and ADB (forthcoming) survey of 2,364 respondents in September 2021 found that the proportion of women who spent more time on domestic work was larger than that of men across different types

FIGURE 12.18
Gender Distribution of Early Childhood Education and Care Teachers in Indonesia

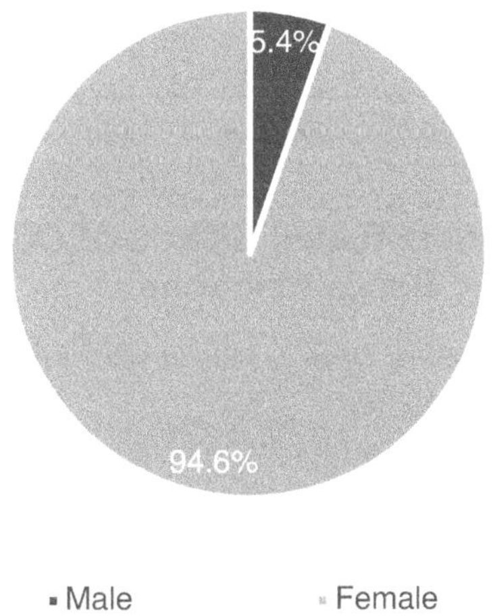

Note: Excludes data on Islamic kindergartens under Ministry of Religious Affairs (RA) and informal ECEC institutions.
Source: 2020–2021 ECEC statistics, Ministry of Education (2021).

FIGURE 12.19
Main Carer Supporting Children with Remote Learning

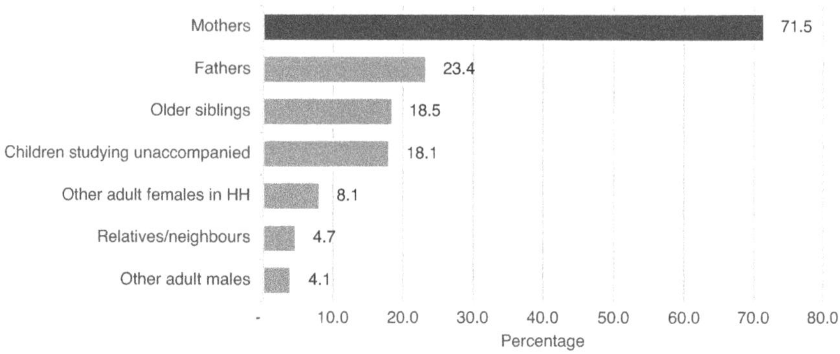

Source: UNICEF, UNDP, PROSPERA and the SMERU Research Institute (2021).

of chores. The difference was most pronounced when it came to child-rearing, as 18.8 per cent of female respondents cited increased time spent tending to children, while the proportion was 11.4 per cent among men.

Accordingly, in a 2022 rapid survey carried out by PROSPERA (forthcoming) with a sample size of 510 respondents, more than half (55.3 per cent) of female homemakers said having affordable and quality childcare would help them become employed. One in 10 reported a dire need for childcare whereas 4 in 10 said childcare would be of great assistance if available.

12.3.4 Gender-Differentiated Effects of COVID-19: Mental Health and Social Relations

Finding 6: Pandemic-related stress led to a decline in women's mental health and strained their familial relations[5]

Much higher rates of mental health problems have been reported among female rather than male heads of the household. One in five of these women were unhappy, stressed and/or depressed (UNICEF, UNDP, PROSPERA, the SMERU Research Institute 2021). They worried about virus transmission, financial predicaments and their children's education and development. In a follow-up survey of the same 2,400 households two months later, they reported a higher prevalence of mental health disruptions in their family, from 29.5 per cent in the full-scale survey to

50 per cent (see Figure 12.20) (UNICEF, UNDP, PROSPERA, the SMERU Research Institute 2022).

The pandemic also took a toll on women's social relations with other household members. At least 36.1 per cent of female heads of the household reported heightened conflict with their children during the pandemic (UNICEF, UNDP, PROSPERA, the SMERU Research Institute 2021). Meanwhile, 4 in 10 male household heads reported escalated conflicts with their spouses.

Findings from an online survey by the National Commission on Violence Against Women/Komnas Perempuan (2020) on 2,285 respondents also corroborated the conflict trend—10.3 per cent cited more arguments taking place with their partners during the pandemic. In this group, respondents earning less than IDR5 million per month had twice the number of arguments as those earning more. At the same time, Komnas Perempuan (2021) saw a 60 per cent increase in the number of reports of violence against women in 2020.

While estimates on the economic costs of violence against women in Indonesia are not yet available, the World Bank estimates such costs can add up to 3.7 per cent of GDP in some countries. The main channels include fewer hours worked (absenteeism) and reduced productivity per hour (presenteeism) among others (Ouedraogo and Stenzel 2021).

FIGURE 12.20
Proportion of Households with Unhappiness/Depression, by Gender of Household Head

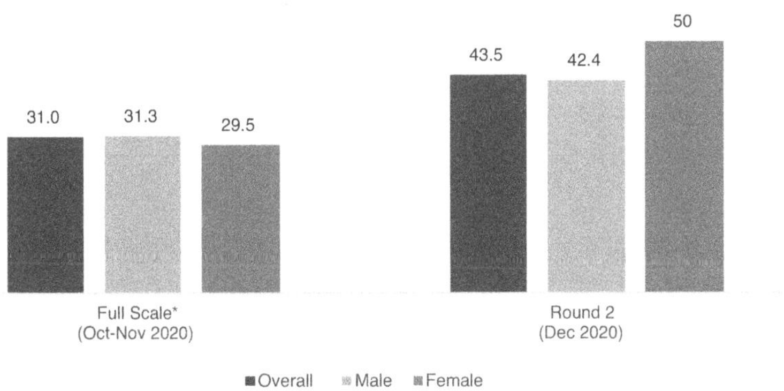

Source: UNICEF, UNDP, PROSPERA and the SMERU Research Institute (2022).

BOX 12.3
Pandemic Impacts on Women in the Public Sector and Employer Response: A Case Study from the Ministry of Finance (MoF)

In the early days of the pandemic, many women working remotely had to take on more unpaid care work at home. In August 2020, MoF conducted an online survey of 171 employees to understand the impacts of office and school closures and to elicit the kind of support they needed most.

The survey found that among respondents:

- 93 per cent of women and 84 per cent of men viewed the pandemic as disproportionately impacting female staff;
- 74 per cent of women reported an increased workload in terms of the number and variety of office tasks, demands from superiors, and frequency of online meetings;
- 89 per cent of women had more household chores, in contrast to 68 per cent of men;
- 56 per cent of women found it difficult to handle children learning from home;
- 50 per cent of women and 45 per cent of men felt the pandemic had impacted their careers;
- both genders expressed the need for adequate work facilities at home such as laptops and internet packages; and
- 91 per cent of women and 82 per cent of men suggested a counselling service would help to counter a deterioration in their well-being.

In response to these findings, the MoF held two mental health support activities under the themes "Married Life in the Pandemic" and "Parenthood in the Pandemic". MoF also stipulated additional "flexible time" that its employees might use, from the previous 30 minutes to 90 minutes. Finally, MoF established a counselling service for its employees.

12.4 PART II: IMPACT OF COVID-19 ON PEOPLE WITH DISABILITIES

While the pandemic's economic impacts have brought hardships across the population, people with disabilities have been worse off due to the multiple layers of vulnerability they already faced.

Finding 1: School closures were a major stumbling block for students with disabilities

Due to their specific needs, students with disabilities often require specially designed materials and/or more intensive one-to-one and often in-person support. The pandemic limited their opportunities to obtain adequate learning support according to needs (World Bank 2020c). Teachers also found it challenging to accommodate the learning needs of students with disabilities in a remote learning environment (Save the Children 2020).

Students with disabilities in Indonesia have not been exempt from such challenges. According to the 2020 National Socioeconomic Survey, 31 per cent of children with disabilities between the ages of 13 to 15 dropped out of school. The number was substantially higher than the 7 per cent dropout rate of children without a disability. Other surveys also corroborated such findings. Based on a survey of 82,000 poor families from September to December 2020 (conducted by UNICEF and the Ministry of Villages, Development of Disadvantaged Regions and Transmigration), the school dropout rate was three times higher among children and young people with disabilities, in comparison to those without.

Teachers of students with disabilities also voiced their struggles with the remote learning arrangements. Australia-Indonesia Disability Research and Network (AIDRAN) and the Centre for Studies on Disability Services (PSLD) at Universitas Brawijaya (2020) conducted an online survey of teachers in East Java. Held only three weeks after the remote learning policy was announced, 34 per cent of teachers said their students' learning capacity had declined. Almost all of them (99.2 per cent) noted difficulties in providing remote learning, and 26.2 per cent said the difficulties stemmed from a lack of infrastructure and equipment.

Finding 2: Compromised access to health services for people with disabilities may result in long-term negative outcomes

Aside from the direct effects of COVID-19, the pandemic also had indirect effects on people's health due to disruptions to essential services, limited social and care networks, and increased mental health problems. People with disabilities are more susceptible to these challenges because many have underlying health conditions and have higher healthcare needs.

For instance, during the early days of the pandemic, many rehabilitation services had to close or significantly reduce their onsite services to limit the risks of exposure. This is because such therapies either require contact between clients and therapists and/or were provided in a residential setting (MAHKOTA & KOMPAK 2020).

Finding 3: The pandemic jeopardized the livelihood of households and people with disabilities

During the early days of the pandemic in 2020, Indonesia's economy went through a shock from the sudden halt in economic activities. Labour force participation took a sharply negative turn—see Figure 12.21. However, the trend picked up slightly in 2021 for the overall level and people without disabilities. Meanwhile, labour force participation for people with disabilities has a continuous declining trend, even after a short period of recovery in 2021. The trend is expounded by the consistent downturn of participation among people with disabilities in the productive age (15–60)—see Figure 12.22.

The most alarming trend appears to be lower job absorption among productive-age people with disabilities (Figure 12.23). When asked about why they were unemployed, the number of people with disabilities who said "to establish a new business" had reduced to half compared with 2019, while the proportion answering "future job arranged" had doubled. The latter suggests they were being sent home during the pandemic.

FIGURE 12.21
Labour Force Participation Trend by Disability Status

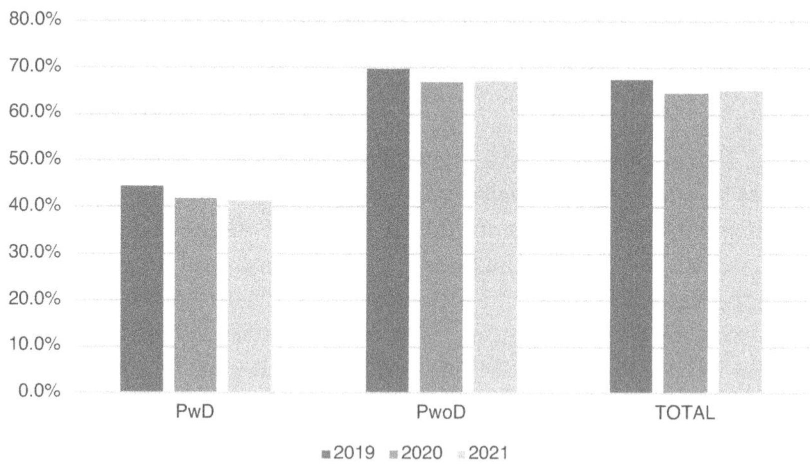

Source: Indonesia Labour Force Survey (August 2019, August 2020 and August 2021).

FIGURE 12.22
Labour Force Participation of People with Disabilities by Age

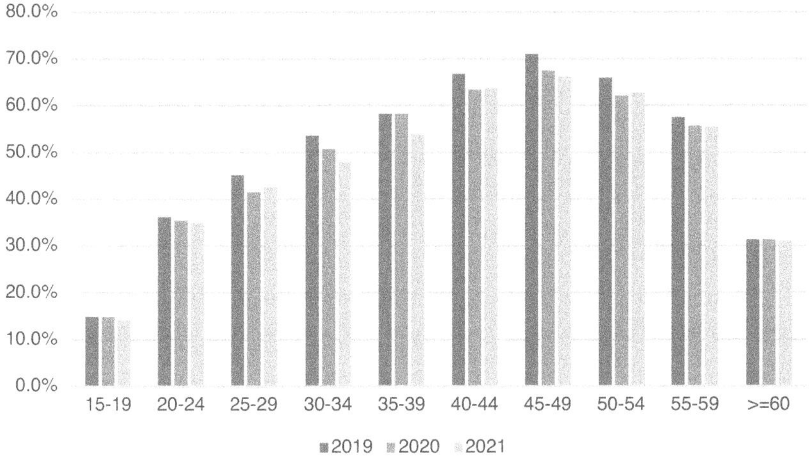

Source: Indonesia Labour Force Survey (August 2019, August 2020 and August 2021).

FIGURE 12.23
Participation Status in Labour Force of People with Disabilities

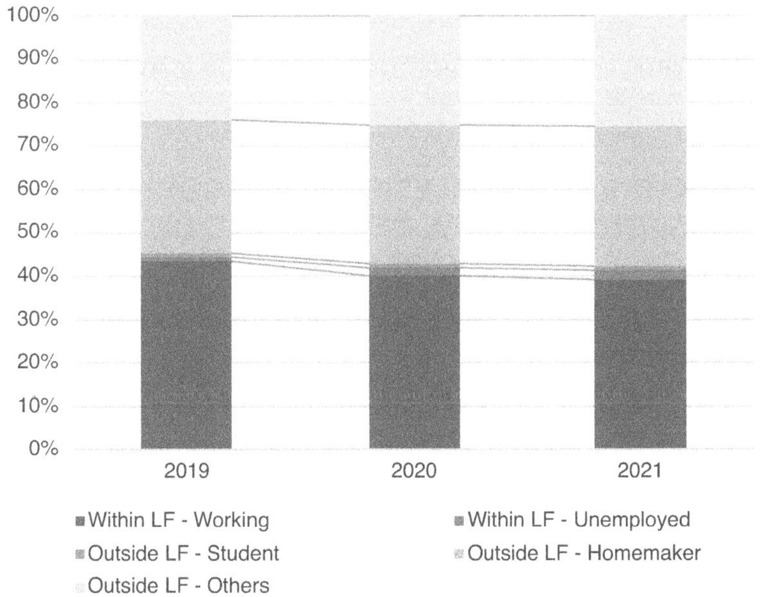

Surveys carried out among people with disabilities during the pandemic described the condition of those who did remain in employment. By April 2020, 81 per cent of people with disabilities who participated in the MAHKOTA and KOMPAK (2020) joint survey had lost 50 to 80 per cent of their income. There was also a higher proportion of those working informally (97 per cent) who lost income relative to those in formal employment (67 per cent) (Satriana 2020). A J-PAL South East Asia (2020) survey undertaken in the same period also found a higher percentage of respondents with a disability (68 per cent) had stopped working after the COVID-19 crisis, compared with respondents in the general category (55 per cent).

Given most were already starting at a lower base, such income shortfalls left households and individuals with disabilities in even more precarious situations. The survey undertaken by MAHKOTA and KOMPAK (2020) found that 68 per cent of the respondents with disabilities had become poor or fallen deeper into poverty compared with the pre-pandemic period.

To cope with precarity, households with a person with a disability often reduce the quality and quantity of food consumption. Other ways to cope include reducing expenditure on therapy or food supplements, borrowing money, and selling or pawning assets. The UN-PROSPERA-SMERU survey found that 15 per cent of such households reported experiencing "moderate or severe" food insecurity, based on FAO's Food Insecurity Experience Scale (FIES) estimates, which was higher than the national average of 11.7 per cent.

12.5 PART III: AN ANALYSIS OF THE GOVERNMENT'S RESPONSE FROM A GENDER AND DISABILITY PERSPECTIVE

12.5.1 Analysis of the Government's Response from a Gender Perspective

Well-designed social protection programmes and competent delivery of these during economic crises may be cogent in narrowing gender gaps in poverty rates, cushioning the negative impacts on poor women (especially single mothers) and safeguarding women's economic security (Gavrilovic et al. 2022).

Throughout the pandemic, the Indonesian government has been proactive in recognizing the severity of the crisis and devising several complementing strategies to safeguard the economic well-being of households, businesses and individuals. In lieu of Law No. 1 of 2020, the government put in place an extraordinary measure through the National Economic Recovery programme (PEN), which focuses on the health sector, social assistance and support for businesses.

Some pre-pandemic government measures such as the conditional cash transfer from the Family Hope Programme (*Program Keluarga Harapan*, or PKH) and MSME financing through the Fostering the Economy of the Prosperous Family Programme (*Program Permodalan Nasional Madani Membina Ekonomi Keluarga Sejahtera*, or PNM Mekaar), and Ultra-Micro Financing Programme (*Pembiayaan Ultra Mikro*, or UMi), by design, seek to benefit women. These programmes were either adjusted or expanded to cushion the adverse impacts of the pandemic on families and women-owned businesses. Meanwhile, most other measures were not designed with gender and disability considerations in mind. However, women and people living with a disability have nevertheless been covered through these programmes as they comprised some or most of the beneficiaries. This chapter discusses government responses that have benefited women and people with disabilities by design and in practice (see Chapter 8 in this volume for a thorough walkthrough of the social assistance programmes during the pandemic).

12.5.2 Government Response Throughout the Pandemic Which Benefited Women in Practice

In the health cluster, the PEN was directed to the treatment of COVID-19 patients and protecting health workers through vaccine prioritization in late 2020 and boosters in mid-2021. The government topped up the salary for health workers dealing with COVID-19 cases through the *Insentif Tenaga Kesehatan* (Health Workers Incentives) initiative, the allocated budget of which reached as high as IDR18.4 trillion in 2021 (US$1.2 billion). As women make up almost 70 per cent of health workers in Indonesia, these measures stood to benefit women more.

To swiftly protect the well-being of households, the government introduced new adaptive measures. The village fund cash assistance (*Bantuan Langsung Tunai Desa*, or BLT *Desa*) programme promoted inclusivity. The BLT *Desa* programme gave villages a higher agency over how to target the assistance. By 2021, the Ministry of Villages data suggested that 38 per cent of the 5.62 million BLT *Desa* recipients were female family heads.

The wage subsidy programme (*Bantuan Subsidi Upah*) protected and improved the economic capacity of workers during the pandemic, with those in the manufacturing, trade, services and transport sectors being prioritized. These sectors were hardest hit by the pandemic, with nearly 60 per cent of workers being women.

For online learning support during the pandemic, Internet quotas were given to teachers and caregivers. Such measures also benefited women because the majority of teachers in Indonesia are women.

To support those who had lost jobs or needed training support, Indonesia devised the Pre-employment Card Programme (*Kartu Prakerja*). From 2020 to 2021, almost half (49 per cent) of the recipients were women. With the skills accrued from the training, 23 per cent of female beneficiaries who were unemployed before the training were eventually able to secure a job (10 per cent) or start a business (13 per cent). See also Chapter 9 in this volume for more information about the programme.

12.5.3 Specific Social Protection Measures to Safeguard Women and Their Livelihood Throughout the Pandemic

A few programmes specifically targeted women in their design and implementation. Notably, increasing the amount of aid distributed through Indonesia's flagship social assistance programme—the Family Hope Programme (PKH)—was one of the first measures the government took to cushion the poorest families from the economic downturn. Existing beneficiaries were entitled to a 25 per cent top-up on their regular transfers and could receive monthly instead of quarterly transfers. PKH beneficiaries include pregnant women (health assistance), early childhood and elementary to high school students (basic education), the elderly, and people with disabilities. The joint nationally representative survey by UNICEF, UNDP, PROSPERA, the SMERU Research Institute (2021) found that 33 per cent of the poorest households (quintile 1) had benefited from the programme by November 2020.

As previously mentioned, the government also implemented policies that specifically favour women entrepreneurs, such as the MSMEs financing scheme through the PNM *Mekaar* and *Mekaar Shariah* programme. Another pathway included the Ultra Micro Credit programme (or UMi), which targets micro-businesses whose access to banks are still compromised. As many as 95 per cent of UMi programme debtors are women, the majority of whom dominate the retail trade business sector (95 per cent). Meanwhile, 100 per cent of the PNM *Mekaar* programme recipient are women (TNP2K 2021).

While both programmes existed before the pandemic, the government established several concessions to its debtors to allow them to cope with the pandemic. The concessions included loan relaxation such as extensions of loan grace periods, loan rescheduling and restructuring, as well as interest payment subsidies. In March 2021, the interest payment subsidy had been given to at least 5.06 million PNM *Mekaar* debtors (TNP2K 2021). The same study by TNP2K also found that 4.06 million *Mekaar* debtors passed the 2020 screening of the self-registered cash assistance for the micro-businesses programme (BPUM), of which 1.8 million became beneficiaries.

As digitalization was seen as crucial for MSMEs to stay afloat during the pandemic (UNICEF, UNDP, PROSPERA, the SMERU Research Institute 2021; UNDP and LPEM FEB UI 2021). The Ministry of Finance developed a digital payment marketplace to facilitate procurement between the government and registered MSMEs. For MSMEs, this platform ensures timely payment, open and free marketing, as well as an opportunity to raise working capital through bank lending facilities. Women-owned businesses are well positioned to benefit from such a platform as they comprise a majority (64.5 per cent) of all such businesses. Efforts are also underway to ensure that public procurement systems are gender responsive (Ministry of Women Empowerment and Child Protection 2022).

12.5.4 Indonesia Relative to Global Endeavours to Create Gender-Responsive Policy Measures

The World Bank and partners have been tracking social protection (contributory and non-contributory) and labour market measures (reduced work time, wage subsidies, training programmes) introduced around the world since the onset of the pandemic. UNDP and UN Women have contributed to this effort by assessing whether these measures work for women and girls through a Global Gender Response Tracker, which tracks the proportion of "gender-sensitive measures" out of the total social protection and labour market response.[7]

BOX 12.4
Gender-Responsive Capital Grant and Wrap-Around Business Support for Women

Small informal businesses, including those run by women, proved to be harder to reach through the policy measures that were first introduced to ease pressures on business during the pandemic, such as tax deferrals, interest subsidies and loan structuring. High informality, low Internet access, poor digital literacy and weak identification systems further compounded the challenges of identifying and reaching the most vulnerable (PROSPERA forthcoming).

In recognition of these challenges, Indonesia introduced a direct cash transfer of IDR2,400,000 (US$167) per year to a target of 12 million informal micro-businesses through the *Bantuan Produktif Usaha Mikro* (BPUM) scheme in 2020. This was to ensure small informal businesses had enough funds to meet their financial obligations and continue their operations. The need to reach women-owned businesses underpinned the scheme's design, as articulated by the Indonesian Finance Minister:

> When we had a financial crisis, it was the banks or big companies which were devastated by those crises. This time, the pandemic is attacking the grassroots people, the informal sector, the small medium enterprises, the poor and especially women. And this is why, when designing for "rebirthing the economy", we really have to pay attention to the poor who were excluded from government policy; apply a gender point of view and consider women.
> *Sri Mulyani Indrawati, Indonesia's Minister of Finance*[6]

The joint UN-PROSPERA-SMERU nationally representative survey found that 7 per cent of households with a family business reported receiving BPUM in late 2020. Eighty per cent of recipients put it towards additional capital, as intended by the programme. Interestingly, men were more likely to put assistance towards new capital, whereas women used it as additional capital and for family essentials, indicating the wider benefits of reaching women (Figure 12.24).

Some local governments also topped up central government support for micro-businesses. For instance, the Jakarta government's flagship development programme for entrepreneurs (Jakpreneur) supported women to digitalize their businesses during the pandemic. The programme designed and delivered a three-week virtual exposition bringing together women Jakpreneurs and 25 different collaborators from government agencies, e-commerce platforms and women's organizations.

An evaluation showed women participants benefited from increased business knowledge (59 per cent), obtained useful business strategies (34 per cent) and gained business confidence (29 per cent). Many managed to secure the necessary business permits and successfully registered their businesses on the online platform of their choice.

FIGURE 12.24
Use of BPUM Benefits, Disaggregated by Gender of Beneficiaries

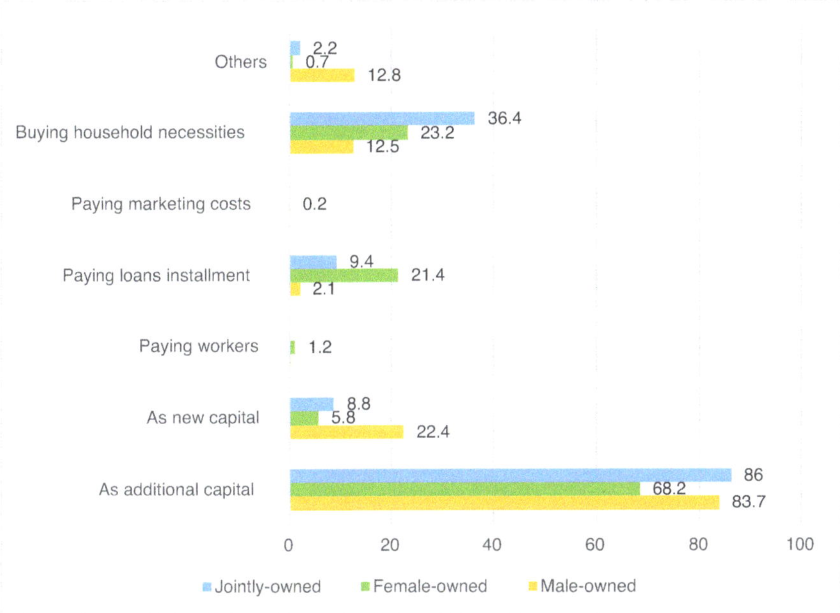

Source: UN-PROSPERA-SMERU (2021).

When compared with other G20 countries, Indonesia has fared just as well as others when it comes to the gender sensitivity of its response. Based on the November 2021 Global Gender Response Tracker data, 33 per cent of the forty recorded policy measures Indonesia has put in place were found to be gender sensitive. The tracker also showed Indonesia had given substantial attention to preventing violence against women from increasing during the pandemic, with 1 in 5 of its recorded policy measures addressing the issue (see Figure 12.25).

Before the pandemic, people with disabilities were eligible for three disability-specific social protection programmes. However, both the coverage and the benefit amount were relatively low.

In 2019, 227,500 people with disabilities (or 0.42 per cent of the population with severe disabilities) received IDR2,000,000 (or approximately US$140) per year through the Social Assistance for Persons with Disability (*Asistensi Sosial Penyandang Disabilitas)* programme. While children and pregnant women were the main beneficiaries of the PKH programme, since 2016 households that were existing beneficiaries were eligible for a top-up

FIGURE 12.25
Profile of COVID-19 Policy Measures in Indonesia and 18 G20 Countries

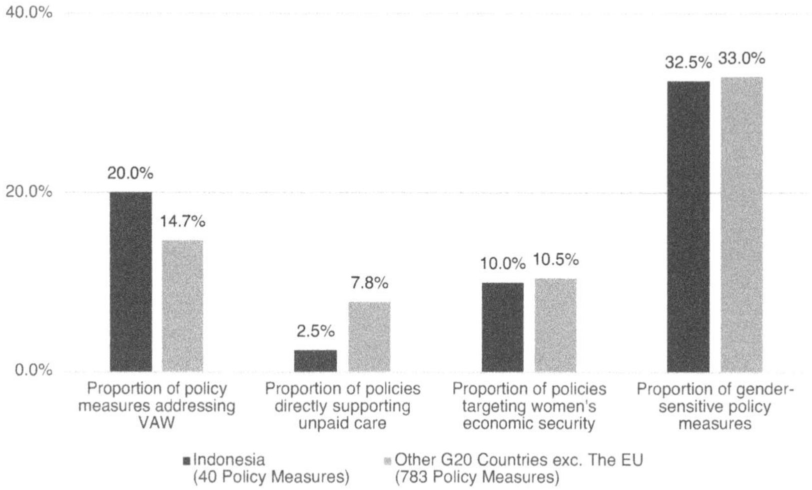

Source: UNDP-UNW COVID-19 Global Gender Response Tracker.

if they had a member with a severe disability. By 2019, households with 108,863 members with disabilities (2.03 per cent of the total population) received a top-up of IDR2,400,000 (or US$167) per year.

It is noteworthy that during the pandemic, social assistance through PKH was continued, and its coverage expanded to 10 million family beneficiaries from the previous 9.2 million. Other new programmes also reached people with disabilities—see Box 12.5 for an example.

It is important to note that the Global Gender Response Tracker has not been without problems—due to lack of information, under-reporting and over-reporting.[8] Additionally, Indonesia has implemented gender-responsive budgeting, under the *Anggaran Responsif Gender* approach. Central or subnational government agencies are encouraged and allowed to tag gender-responsive budget items.[9] However, this effort has not yet tagged funds exclusively prepared to empower women or mitigate the gendered impacts of COVID-19 on women, making it challenging to assess the quality of spending on national economic recovery from a gender perspective. Meanwhile, social protection spending has helped reach a large proportion of households containing a member with a disability. Questions

BOX 12.5
Significant Improvement in Coverage of People Living with Disabilities during the Pandemic

Social assistance coverage for people living with disabilities increased from only 5 per cent in 2019 (KemenPPN, KOMPAK & MAHKOTA 2021) to 87 per cent during the first year of the pandemic (UN-PROSPERA-SMERU 2021). Households containing a member with a disability were covered through one-off food assistance to the more substantial periodic cash transfers.

A higher proportion of households with disability were covered through large programmes such as the electricity subsidy, unconditional cash transfer in Greater Jakarta (BST), unconditional cash transfer funded from village funds (BLT *Desa*) and an expanded food assistance programme (*Program Sembako*). Other innovations were also introduced at the national, local and village levels to improve social protection access to people with disabilities.

The Ministry of Social Affairs specifically allocated a portion of the BST programme for people with disabilities and decided to use a disability-specific database (rather than the national social registry), which proved to reach people with disabilities quickly and efficiently. Equally importantly, newly established programmes such as BLT *Desa* allowed communities to cover residents who were otherwise missed by other programmes.

about the adequacy of the programmes, whether they effectively cushioned people with disabilities and their families during the time of crisis, and what would have happened to their socio-economic well-being in their absence are currently being evaluated (UNICEF, UNDP, PROSPERA, the SMERU Research Institute forthcoming).

12.6 PART IV: CONCLUSIONS AND MAIN LESSONS FROM INDONESIA'S EXPERIENCE TO SHARE WITH PEERS IN G20

The crisis has revealed deeply rooted challenges for achieving gender equality, which has been complicated by interlocking inequalities along income, life cycle process and education lines. The pandemic has also amplified multiple layers of vulnerability that people with disabilities already faced before the pandemic.

The government of Indonesia has addressed these challenges head-on through effective policy measures. Several lessons can be drawn from Indonesia's experience in responding to the crisis.

- First, during a crisis of such unprecedented proportions, vulnerable women and people with disabilities can be protected quickly and inclusively through multiple programmes designed for broader outreach and specific support tailored for them.
- Second, a combination of approaches is useful to provide effective and timely relief in an emergency, including through reliance on existing national registries, by enabling potential beneficiaries to self-register and empowering sectoral ministries, local communities and the private sector to play a role in prioritizing women and people with disabilities who are most in need of support.
- Third, continuously monitoring the pulse of the country while assessing the reach and effectiveness of social assistance programmes is critical, as is reflected in the government's decision to introduce capital grants (BPUM) for micro businesses.

The pandemic response serves as an opportunity to begin long-term and sustainable reform. This begins with building a consensus that gender equality and disability inclusion are moral imperatives and critical for the economic well-being of both women and men, and societies as a whole. Addressing gender gaps in the labour market can deliver gains to national income, while narrowing gender gaps in economic opportunities and wages also lowers income inequality (IMF, UN Women and UNDP 2021).

As Indonesia grapples with the challenge of addressing the long-term scarring of COVID-19, demographic transition and the effects of climate change, tapping into the huge potential of women while supporting people with disabilities who are able to work, will be critical for goals of equality as well as of inclusive economic growth. Measures such as investments in better education and skills training, higher spending on childcare and aged care, flexible working arrangements, and well-designed workplace regulations are proven examples of concrete measures to level the playing field for women.

Equally importantly, investments in universal basic coverage and adaptive social protection reform also require the systems to address the needs of different segments of the population. Indonesia's social protection systems for people with disabilities can be significantly improved by adopting a multi-tiered system, including *disability top-up* in mainstream social protection programmes (such as cash transfer programmes) for poor households containing a person with a disability (Tier 1); *disability allowance* for all children and adults with severe disabilities and non-social protection beneficiaries (Tier 2); contributory health insurance (BPJS employment schemes) for formal sector workers (Tier 3); and *disability-specific* discounts, including transport, health and assistive devices, education, and utilities for all people with disabilities (Tier 4) (Laraswati et al. 2019).[10]

Learning from experiences during the pandemic, disruptions to the delivery of healthcare services can be reduced by implementing alternative modes of care delivery, such as home visit programmes. Integrating existing digital mental health services into the national health insurance scheme (*BPJS-Kesehatan*) will improve access to affordable mental healthcare.

Meanwhile, children with special needs can be supported to continue learning by assisting schools to remain open and by rolling out a "skills boost programme", with adequate funding to help students recover from remote learning. Ensuring mainstream schools are inclusive of students with different needs will be integral to narrowing the educational attainment gap. Monitoring and oversight over the quality of spending also contribute to the effectiveness of the resources allocated to achieve these objectives.

12.6.1 Opportunities during Indonesia's G20 Presidency

Both disability inclusion and gender equality are global challenges, even though these may manifest differently in Indonesia. Indonesia's G20 presidency serves as an opportunity to elevate these challenges, deliberate on collective solutions, and gain country-specific momentum to address them.

Indonesia's commitment to developing a *G20 Action plan for the participation of persons with disabilities in the workplace*, as a part of the G20 Employment Working Group (Sherpa Track), could be a unique opportunity to advance disability employment in Indonesia and across the G20 countries. This can be done by committing to progress on a suite of proven policies, including employment quotas, entrepreneurship opportunities, inclusive skills development, vocational rehabilitation and job placement services, among others.

Similarly, Indonesia's commitment to ensure that the post-pandemic economic recovery process responds to gender issues, as experienced by Indonesian women and women from G20 countries, may help advance four priority areas: women's economic participation, support for women-owned MSMEs, reducing the vulnerabilities of women with disabilities and rural women, and adopting gender-responsive health measures. G20 peers could share and learn from one another on measures to support women workers to transition from education to work, through the implementation of family-friendly policies (such as maternity leave benefits and flexible working arrangements); improved access to job information and matching skills with jobs available (World Bank forthcoming); and effective campaigns to shift restrictive norms that view women as natural "homemakers" and men as "breadwinners".

"Unpaid care" is a key public policy issue that intersects with both disability and gender equality goals. This can be addressed through investments in care-related social and physical infrastructure, care-related social transfers, care services, and employment-related care policies such as creches linked to workplaces, flexible work policies, paid sick leave and health insurance (UNESCAP 2021). Such investments in unpaid care work can in turn contribute to addressing G20 gender-specific priorities, including barriers to women's economic participation and reducing vulnerabilities faced by women with disabilities.

As countries emerge from the pandemic, investment in a resilient and inclusive future will be more critical than ever. The investments outlined in this chapter require learning by doing, building the evidence, and fostering global alliances and cooperation for change. Indonesia can lead the way through its motto of "recovering together, recovering stronger".

Notes

1. This chapter is co-authored by Bimbika Sijapati Basnett (PROSPERA), Usha Adelina Riyanto (PROSPERA), R. Wiwin Istani (Sekretariat Jenderal, Kementerian Keuangan RI/General Secretariat, Ministry of Finance), and Aktiva Primananda Hadiarta (PKN STAN/Polytechnic of State Finance, Ministry of Finance) with inputs and support from Sekretariat Tim Penggerak Implementasi PUG, Kementerian Keuangan RI/Secretariat of Gender Mainstreaming Implementation Team, Ministry of Finance and Mercoledi Nasiir (PROSPERA).
2. Based on how much of the gap has been reduced each year since the index was first reported in 2006, the World Economic Forum has been able to project

the number of years needed to close the gender gap. The index is concerned with gender gaps across four dimensions: employment, education, health and politics.

3. The number is the result of McKinsey's estimate under the "Take action now" scenario, which assumes immediate action to address the higher negative impact of COVID-19 on women.
4. The Global Gender Gap Index measures the extent to which gender-based gaps exist across four dimensions (subindex), including economic participation and opportunity, educational attainment, health and survival, and political empowerment. Various indicators are factored in the calculation of the subindex, with each subindex having the lowest-possible score of 0 (imparity) to 1 (gender parity). The overall Global Gender Gap Index is measured by taking an average of all the subindex scores, with the scoring and interpretation similar to that of the subindex.
5. See Chapter 10 in this volume for a more comprehensive assessment of the COVID-19 impacts on mental health.
6. Sri Mulyani Indrawati, Minister of Finance, Government of Indonesia, "Rebirthing the Global Economy to Deliver Sustainable Development", A United Nations Roundtable Series of Renowned Economists, convened by the UN Secretary-General, 1 July 2020.
7. Gender-sensitive measures are those that aim to address the gendered risks and challenges imposed by the COVID-19 crisis. These risks include violence against women and girls, women's economic security, and unpaid care work. Government measures to address violence against women and girls are by default gender sensitive. Meanwhile, gender-sensitive measures that support women's economic security and unpaid care may include social protection measures, labour market measures, and fiscal interventions.
8. They must be complemented with additional efforts to monitor coverage, benefits received, and actual impacts on women's lives. Nevertheless, the tracker is guided by long-standing calls to address gendered poverty and risks through a systematic intervention of gender in all stages of intervention—from design and implementation to monitoring and evaluation. Data elicited serves as a useful benchmark against which to compare responses across countries in planning and prioritizing the needs of women, girls and people with disabilities (Gavrilovic et al. 2022).
9. Budget items are considered gender responsive if the budget in its preparation uses standardized gender analysis to identify gender inequality issues, and thus is designed to tackle those issues. In 2020 roughly 6.14 per cent (IDR51.3 trillion or US$3.53 million) of the 2020 central government budget was tagged as gender-responsive, while the 2021 figure reached IDR55.4 trillion (equal to US$3.82 million) or around 5.37 per cent. Indonesia's gender-responsive

budgeting is a tool which focuses on integrating gender perspectives into the general government budgeting process.

10. Over sixty countries, including many low and emerging economies such as Nepal, Vietnam, South Africa and Mauritius, have implemented such comprehensive disability-inclusive social protection systems (Laraswati et al. 2019).

References

AIDRAN & PSLD Universitas Brawijaya. 2020. "Can the COVID-19 Pandemic Boost Inclusive Education?". *Knowledge Sector Initiatives.* https://www.ksi-indonesia.org/id/ wawasan/detail/2008-can-the-COVID-19-pandemic-boost-inclusive-education

AIPEG and Monash University. 2017. "Women's Economic Participation in Indonesia: A Study of Gender Inequality in Employment, Entrepreneurship, and Key Enablers for Change". https://www.monash.edu/business/cdes/assets/documents/publications2/Womens-economic-participation-in-Indonesia-June-2017.pdf

Asian Development Bank. 2021. "ADB COVID-19 Policy Database". https://covid19policy. adb.org/

Badan Pusat Statistik. 2019. "Survei Angkatan Kerja Nasional".

———. 2019. "Survei Sosial dan Ekonomi Nasional".

———. 2020. "Survei Angkatan Kerja Nasional".

———. 2021. "Survei Angkatan Kerja Nasional".

———. 2022. "PDB Seri 2010, 2010–2021". https://bps.go.id/indicator/ 11/65/1/-seri-2010-pdb-seri-2010.html

———. 2022. "Statistik Indonesia". https://www.bps.go.id/publication/2022/02/25/0a2afea4fab72a5d052cb315/statistik-indonesia-2022.html

Bluedorn, John, Francesca Caselli, Niels-Jakob Hansen, Ippei Shibata, and Marina M. Tavares. 2021. "Gender and Employment in the COVID-19 Recession: Evidence on "She-cessions"". *IMF Working Papers* 95.

Cameron, Lisa, Diana C. Suarez, and Diana Rowell. 2019. "Female Labour Force Participation in Indonesia: Why Has it Stalled?". *Bulletin of Indonesian Economic Studies* 157–92.

Gavrilovic, Maja, Monica Rubio, Francesca Bastagli, Roopa Hinton, Silke Staab, Ruth Graham Goulder, Charlotte Bilo, Ruby Khan, Amber Peterman, and Bobo Diallo. 2022. "Gender-Responsive Social Protection Post–COVID-19". *Science* 375 (6585): 1111–13.

Gunawan, Tendy, and Jahen F. Rezki. 2022. *Mapping Workers with Disabilities in Indonesia - Policy Suggestions and Recommendations.* ILO. https://www.ilo.org/wcmsp5/groups/ public/---asia/---ro-bangkok/---ilo-jakarta/documents/publication/wcms_836028.pdf

———, and Jahen F. Rezki. 2022. *Mapping Workers with Disabilities in Indonesia.* Jakarta: International Labor Organization. https://www.ilo.org/jakarta/whatwedo/ publications/WCMS_836028/lang--en/index.htm

Hanna, R., and B. Olken. 2020. *Current Results of Online Survey on Economic Impact of COVID-19 in Indonesia, Findings from Week 2.* J-PAL Southeast Asia (J-PAL SEA).

IMF, UN Women and UNDP. 2021. *Gender Equality and COVID-19: Policies and Institutions for Mitigating the Crisis.* Special Series on COVID-19, Washington, DC.: IMF Fiscal Affairs. file:///C:/Users/Bimbika/Downloads/en-special-series-on-COVID-19-gender-equality-and-COVID-19%20(1).pdf

J-PAL South East Asia. 2020. "Online Survey on Economic Impact of COVID-19 in Indonesia: Results for People with Disablities (PPT)".

KemenPPN, KOMPAK & MAHKOTA. 2021. "COVID-19 Impacts on People with Disabilities in Indonesia: An In-Depth Look". https://kompak.or.id/id/download/519/2021_COVID-19%20Impacts%20on%20People%20With%20Disabilities%20in%20Indonesia_Bappenas_MAHKOTA-KOMPAK.pdf

Komnas Perempuan. 2020. "Dinamika Perubahan Rumah Tangga Selama Masa COVID-19". https://komnasperempuan.go.id/uploadedFiles/webOld/file/pdf_file/2020/Hasil%20Survei%20COVID%2019-KP-2020_17.06.pdf

———. 2021. "CATAHU 2020 Komnas Perempuan: Lembar Fakta dan Poin Kunci (5 Maret 2021)". https://komnasperempuan.go.id/siaran-pers-detail/catahu-2020-komnas-perempuan-lembar-fakta-dan-poin-kunci-5-maret-2021

Laraswati, Dyah, Karishma Huda, Alexandre Cote, Sri Kusumastuti Rahayu, and Martin Siyaranamual. 2019. *Policy Brief: Inclusive Social Protection for Persons with Disablity in Indonesia.* Jakarta: The National Team for Acceleration of Poverty Reduction and Australian Government. http://www.tnp2k.go.id/download/65217190113-PB%20DisabilitiesEng-web.pdf

MAHKOTA & KOMPAK. 2020. "Economic Impacts and Access to Social Protection during the COVID-19 Crisis: The Experiences of People with Disabilities in Indonesia". https://www.ksi-indonesia.org/assets/uploads/original/2020/09/ksi-1600400214.pdf

McKinsey & Company. 2020. "COVID-19 and Gender Equality: Countering the Regressive Effects". https://www.mckinsey.com/featured-insights/future-of-work/COVID-19-and-gender-equality-countering-the-regressive-effects

Ministry of Women Empowerment and Child Protection. 2022. "Pengadaan Barang/Jasa yang Inklusif dan Responsif Gender". ADB Workshop on Gender-Responsive Procurement.

OECD. 2021. "Caregiving in Crisis: Gender Inequality in Paid and Unpaid Work during COVID-19". https://www.oecd.org/coronavirus/policy-responses/caregiving-in-crisis-gender-inequality-in-paid-and-unpaid-work-during-COVID-19-3555d164/

Oedraogo, Rasmani, and David Stenzel. 2021. "The Heavy Economic Toll of Gender-based Violence: Evidence from Sub-Saharan AfricaIMF Working Papers".

IMF Working Papers 2021 (277). https://doi.org/10.5089/9781557754073.001.A001

PMO Prakerja. 2021. "Hasil Survei Evaluasi Kartu Prakerja". https://www.instagram.com/ p/CXxfK_BPr_2/?utm_medium=copy_link

PROSPERA. Forthcoming. "COVID-19 Impact on Women-Owned Micro Businesses in Jakarta: Results Related with Financial Inclusion and the Reach of PEN 2020".

———. Forthcoming. "Rapid Mass-Scale Survey on Household and Economic Inclusion".

Satriana, Sinta. 2020. *Economic Impacts and Access to Social Protection during the COVID-19 Crisis: The Experiences of People with Disabilities in Indonesia.* Policy Brief 1, August 2020, Jakarta: MAHKOTA. https://www.ksi-indonesia.org/assets/uploads/original/ 2020/09/ksi-1600223534.pdf

Satuan Tugas Penanganan COVID-19. 2021. "Program Kartu Prakerja Diakui Bank Dunia sebagai Program Perlindungan Sosial Yang Ideal". *Laman COVID-19 Indonesia.* https://covid19.go.id/p/masyarakat-umum/program-kartu-prakerja-diakui-bank-dunia-sebagai-program-perlindungan-sosial-yang-ideal

Save the Children. 2020. "The Hidden Impact of COVID-19 on Children and Families with Disabilities".https://resource-centre-uploads.s3.amazonaws.com/uploads/the_hidden_impact_of_COVID-19_on_children_and_families_with_disabilities.pdf

Schaner, Simone, and Smita Das. 2016. *Female Labor Force Participation in Asia: Indonesia Country Study.* Asian Development Bank. https://ecommons.cornell.edu/ handle/1813/87170

Soebandrio, Amin, Tina Kusumaningrum, Frilasita A. Yudhaputri, Sukma Oktavianthi, Dodi Safari, Safarina G. Malik, and Khin Saw Aye Myint. 2021. "COVID-19 Prevalence among Healthcare Workers in Jakarta and Neighbouring Areas in Indonesia during Early 2020 Pandemic". *Annals of Medicine* 53, no. 1: 1896–904. https://doi.org/ 10.1080/07853890.2021.1975309

TNP2K. 2021. "Kertas Kerja TNP2K No. 61-2021: Pemantauan Pelaksanaan Program Pemulihan Ekonomi Nasional (PEN) untuk UMKM di PNM Mekaar". http://www.tnp2k.go.id/download/80805Working_Paper_No_61.pdf

UN Women and the Asian Development Bank. Forthcoming. "Two Years on: The Lingering Gendered Effects of the COVID-19 Pandemic in Asia and the Pacific".

UN Women. 2017. "Making Social Protection Gender-Responsive: Lessons from UN Women's Work in the Eastern Caribbean". https://www.unwomen.org/en/digital-library/publications/2017/2/making-social-protection-gender-responsive#view

———. 2020a. "COVID-19 and Ending Violence Against Women and Crisis". https://www.unwomen.org/sites/default/files/Headquarters/Attachments/Sections/Library/Publications/2020/Issue-brief-COVID-19-and-ending-violence-against-women-and-girls-en.pdf

———. 2020b. "Leveraging Digitalization to Cope with COVID-19: An Indonesia Case Study on Women-Owned Micro and Small Businesses". https://www.unglobalpulse.org/wp-content/uploads/2020/12/Indonesia-Digitalization-Women-MSBs-COVID19-EN.pdf

UNDP and LPEM FEB UI. 2021. "Impact of COVID-19 Pandemic on MSMEs in Indonesia". https://www.id.undp.org/content/indonesia/en/home/library/ImpactofCOVID19MSMEs.html

UNDP. 2020. "Human Development Report 2020: The Next Frontier: Human Development and the Anthropocene". https://hdr.undp.org/en/content/human-development-report-2020

UNESCAP and ASEAN. 2021. "Addressing Unpaid Care Work in ASEAN". https://www.unescap.org/sites/default/d8files/knowledge-products/SDD-ASEAN-21022-Unpaid-Care-report_2.pdf

UNESCAP. 2021. *COVID-19 and the Unpaid Care Economy in Asia and the Pacific.* Bangkok: United Nations Economic and Social Commission for Asia and the Pacific. https://www.unescap.org/sites/default/d8files/knowledge-products/2021_Regional_Report_COVID19-Care-Economy.pdf

UNICEF, UNDP, PROSPERA, the SMERU Research Institute. 2021. "Analysis of the Social and Economic Impacts of COVID-19 on Households and Strategic Policy Recommendations for Indonesia". https://www.unicef.org/indonesia/media/9501/file/Analysis%20of%20the%20Social%20and%20Economic%20Impacts%20of%20COVID-19%20on%20Household%20and%20Strategic%20Policy%20Recommendations%20for%20Indonesia.pdf

———, UNDP, PROSPERA, the SMERU Research Institute. 2022. "Socio-Economic Impact of COVID-19 on Households in Indonesia: Three Rounds of Monitoring Surveys". https://www.unicef.org/indonesia/reports/socio-economic-impact-COVID-19-households-indonesia-three-rounds-monitoring-surveys.

———, UNDP, PROSPERA, the SMERU Research Institute. Forthcoming. "Second Round of the Assessment of COVID-19 Impacts on Households".

United Nations Department of Economic and Social Affairs. 2019. "Disability and Development Report 2018: Realizing the Sustainable Development Goals by, for and with Persons with Disabilities". https://www.un-ilibrary.org/content/books/9789210479035

UNPRPD, UNICEF, IDA, and ILO. 2020. "Disability Inclusive Social Protection Response to COVID-19 Crisis". https://www.social-protection.org/gimi/RessourcePDF.action?id=56029

WHO. 2020. *Disability Considerations during the COVID-19 Outbreak.* https://www.who.int/docs/default-source/documents/disability/eng-COVID-19-disability-briefing-who.pdf?sfvrsn=963e22fe_1 (accessed 22 May 2022).

World Bank. 2020a. "Indonesia Country Gender Assessment: Investing in Opportunities for Women". https://documents1.worldbank.org/curated/

en/732951615961029941/pdf/Indonesia-Country-Gender-Assessment-Investing-in-Opportunities-for-Women.pdf

———. 2020b. "Gender Dimensions of the COVID-19 pandemic". https://openknowledge.worldbank.org/bitstream/handle/10986/33622/Gender-Dimensions-of-the-COVID-19-Pandemic.pdf

———. 2020c. *Estimates of COVID-19 Impacts on Learning and Earning in Indonesia*. The World Bank. https://documents1.worldbank.org/curated/en/184651597383628008/pdf /Main-Report.pdf

———. 2021. "World Bank Indonesia Survey on Digital Merchant Shopee". https://thedocs.worldbank.org/en/doc/e975e535c0a25907216079e138c56307-0070012021/world-bank-indonesia-survey-on-digital-merchant-shopee

———. Forthcoming. "The Initial Gendered Impacts of the COVID-19 Pandemic on Indonesia's Labor Market: How Does It Shape the Future of Women's Work?".

World Economic Forum. 2019. "2020 Global Gender Gap Report". https://www.weforum.org/reports/gender-gap-2020-report-100-years-pay-equality

———. 2021. "2021 Global Gender Gap Report". https://www.weforum.org/reports/global-gender-gap-report-2021

PART V

Expenditure Side (MSMEs and Corporate Sector)

13

Weathering and Recovering from the Pandemic

Lesson Learnt from MSMEs in Indonesia

Mohamad Dian Revindo, Jahen Fachrul Rezki, Devina Anindita and Calista Endrina Dewi

13.1 PROLOGUE

Micro, Small and Medium Enterprises (MSMEs) have been critical to the Indonesian economy, not only for their contribution to GDP and job creation but also for their resilience throughout prior economic crises, thanks to their agility, flexibility and less dependency on external resources.[1] However, the COVID-19 pandemic has hit the MSMEs severely, as it unprecedentedly disrupted supply, distribution and demand simultaneously. UNDP and LPEM FEB UI (2020) revealed that nine out of ten MSMEs suffered a drop in demand for their products during the pandemic, while around 53 per cent recorded a decrease in asset value.

The survival of MSMEs in the current pandemic is contingent on both internal and external factors. Internally, MSMEs have to adjust their financial, production and marketing strategies to cope with the changing business landscape. Externally, given the scale of the pandemic, assistance from both government and non-government agencies is crucial.

Three major challenges, however, stand in the way of implementing these programmes. The Government of Indonesia (GoI) needed to design assistance programmes that can mitigate various types of hardships encountered by MSMEs due to the pandemic. The GOI then launched the largest economic recovery programmes for MSMEs in the country's history including, but not limited to, deferred principal and interest loan payments, loan interest subsidies, tax incentives and working capital loan guarantees. Second, the GOI needed to ensure all MSMEs had the same access to the programmes. This was not a simple matter, given the unavailability of a single updated MSMEs database in Indonesia. Third, the assistance should be designed not only to ease the impact of the pandemic but also to help MSMEs jumpstart and transform their businesses in the recovery period.

This chapter provides an analysis of the impact of the pandemic on MSMEs, the GOI's response to mitigate the impact on MSMEs, the effectiveness of government support, and MSMEs' internal strategy and business transformation to weather and recover from the pandemic.

13.2 MSMEs IN INDONESIA PRIOR TO THE PANDEMIC

13.2.1 Characteristics of MSMEs

MSMEs in many countries across the globe, including Indonesia, have shown their resilience in previous crises, especially the 1998 Asian Financial Crisis (AFC) and the 2007–8 Global Financial Crisis (GFC) (Gunadi et al. 2021; Iborra, Safón, and Dolz 2020). The resilience was primarily due to their small-scale production assets and manual production techniques. SMEs were also less dependent on third-party (mainly foreign) investments and were less affected by the currency and exchange rate crises.

In 2019 there were around 65.5 million MSMEs in Indonesia, constituting 99.99 per cent of business establishments, contributing 96.92 per cent of employment providers, 60.61 per cent of GDP, 60.03 per cent of total investment, and 15.65 per cent of the total export (Ministry of Cooperatives and SMEs 2020). The low value-added contribution relative to the number of establishments is due to the persistent dominance of micro-sized enterprises (MiEs), which constitute 98.68 per cent of all firms in the country.

According to the 2016 Economic Census (BPS-Statistics Indonesia 2018), MSMEs' contribution mainly came from the wholesale and retail trade sector (46.19 per cent), followed by accommodation and food service (16.74 per cent), manufacturing (16.51 per cent), transportation and storage (5.00 per cent), and other service activities (4.36 per cent). In terms of sparsity, MSMEs are mostly concentrated on Java Island (57.15 per cent), in line with the population concentration in Indonesia.

13.2.2 Challenges for Scaling up MSMEs' Business

MSMEs are often plagued with productivity and efficiency problems caused by factors such as limited access to finance (Tambunan 2015; Harvie, Narjoko, and Oum 2013; Revindo and Gan 2017), limited access to the market (Rogerson 2013; Revindo, 2017), limited technical and management knowledge (ADB 2015), capacity to compete (OECD 2008), limited access to raw materials, administrative and regulatory issues (World Bank 2012), technological gap (ADB 2015), difficulties in transportation and distribution, inadequate infrastructure facilities, as well as a lack of general guidance or support (ADB 2015).

Table 13.1 further specifies various specific challenges that are generally encountered by MSMEs. These wide-ranging factors have caused many SMEs to lag in their development and upscaling attempts even before the pandemic. Moreover, despite MSMEs' resilience during the previous crises, they are generally also sensitive to the changing business environment conditions and suffer from economic downturns (Latham 2009).

13.3 THE CONSEQUENCES OF THE COVID-19 PANDEMIC ON MSMEs' BUSINESS PERFORMANCE

Whilst facing the pandemic, MSMEs had to solve extra multifaceted economic challenges and not only the traditional challenges which continued to exist. Demand- and supply-side problems became more apparent—including falling demand, liquidity problems, and disruptions in supply chains and logistics—making MSMEs even more vulnerable. This vulnerability was heightened as many governments adopted periods of closure and movement prevention policies which brought MSMEs'

TABLE 13.1
Various Challenges for MSMEs Business Scaling-up

	Pre-Pandemic Challenges
Financial Challenges	• Limited access to finance • Little or no formal history of credit • Reluctancy in participating in equity financing • Lack of financial knowledge to plan and assess financial strategies and risks
Distribution/ Marketing Challenges	• Limited access to the market. • Lack of market information • Poor access to physical markets • Lack of networks and channels to market their products • Poor linkages with export markets • Poor quality products and service with restricted entry to some markets • Limited market research and analysis • Narrow product diversity • Weak capacity for e-commerce • High cost of doing business • Regulatory inefficiencies and imperfect market
Production Process Challenges	• Lack of up-to-date information, awareness and knowledge of the latest technological development • Lag in using information and communication technology (ICT)-based platforms such as e-commerce • Lack of quality control and quality improvement • Lack of clear division of labour and procedures • Inadequate infrastructure facilities • Lack of general guidance or support
Employment Challenges	• Low productivity and technical skills • Poor working conditions due to informality, low wages • Low entrepreneurial, organizational and management skills with no business plans • Risk aversion for investing in more capital • Easily discourage with complex processes

Source: Compiled by authors.

operations to a halt, weakening their financial positions, and exposing them to financial risks (Omar, Ishak, and Jusoh 2020; Oyewale, Adebayo, and Kehinde 2020). The pandemic which creates a socio-economic crisis related to the health of people can have a dire impact on MSMEs as they require strong connections with both their customers and suppliers (Nugent and Yhee 2002).

13.3.1 Demand-Side Shock

Decreased demand was caused by two major factors, those being large-scale social restrictions (*Pembatasan Sosial Berskala Besar*, or PSBB) by GOI and health precautionary measures in society. PSBB led to a drastic decrease in economic activities, as restrictions were implemented for travelling across countries and regions, attending schools, working in offices, and organizing major social activities. In addition, people also tended to reduce their consumption due to economic uncertainty. They were more prone to build their savings and emergency funds to survive the pandemic period.

UNDP and LPEM FEB UI (2020) reported that almost nine out of ten MSMEs faced lower demand for their products during the pandemic. This figure is consistent when the data is broken down by firm size and owner's gender. In terms of the extent of the decrease, around one-third of MSMEs reported a 40 to 60 per cent drop in demand for their products. The figure is consistent by owner's gender but varies when broken down by firm size, with medium-sized enterprises (MEs) reporting 45 per cent, small-sized enterprises (SEs) 28 per cent, and MiEs 29 per cent.

Further, UNDP and LPEM FEB UI (2020) also reported that the decreasing demand was further exacerbated by the difficulty in product pricing, experienced by more than 70 per cent of both genders in the MSMEs. However, in terms of firm size, this problem was reported more by MEs (79 per cent) as compared to SEs (70 per cent) and MiEs (69 per cent).

13.3.2 Supply-Side Shock

The pandemic also hit the MSMEs hard from the supply side, particularly in terms of input access and pricing. UNDP and LPEM FEB UI (2020) reported that around 47 per cent of MSMEs encountered difficulties accessing raw materials during the pandemic. The difficulty was particularly noticeable in MiEs and SEs as compared to their ME counterparts. Further, the difficulty was more prevalent in female-owned businesses than in their male-owned counterparts.

In terms of input price, UNDP and LPEM FEB UI (2020) revealed that around three-quarters of MSMEs experienced an increase in the price of raw materials during the pandemic. This problem was more common in MEs than in their smaller counterparts. In terms of the magnitude of change, more than one-third of MSMEs experienced up to 20 per cent higher costs of raw materials, almost one-fourth had to pay 20 to 40 per cent higher, and around one-fourth had to pay 40 to 60 per cent higher.

The problem of input access was due to logistical issues which arose from the implementation of social restrictions by the GOI. Many MSMEs could not obtain material from their regular suppliers. Hence, they were forced to switch to other suppliers who could deliver material, which may have cost more although they were geographically closer.

13.3.3 Other Problems Faced Due to the Pandemic

Financial Problems

MSMEs have been especially hit hard by the pandemic, particularly in the financial aspects of their business. Starting with a dramatic and sudden loss of demand a few weeks after the COVID-19 pandemic was officially declared in Indonesia, the declining spending and consumption of consumers due to the fear of contagion, loss of income, and heightened uncertainty pushed the MSMEs into severe liquidity shortfalls. Additionally, the shortage of workers and input materials prevented firms from operating at full production capacity, further driving down the MSMEs' revenue.

Many MSMEs are also the suppliers for larger firms; thus, their cash flows are highly dependent on the larger firms and the payments from these firms, which might be delayed during the pandemic. Liquidity is required for the day-to-day operations of any business including payments for their payroll, utilities and rent, in addition to business taxes, purchase of supplies and equipment and other expenses. In normal times, liquidity has been a problem for many struggling SMEs but it has been worsened with the pandemic liquidity crunch. The longer the pandemic crisis lasts, the greater the risk of business closure (Bartik et al. 2020) and each MSME has different expectations regarding the potential length of disruptions caused by COVID-19.

The simultaneous demand- and supply-side shocks inevitably reduced MSMEs' profit margins, including MSMEs in Indonesia. Gunadi et al. (2021) reported that medium-sized firms in Indonesia suffered from a greater profit margin decline with 60 to 80 per cent lower profit margins than in the pre-pandemic period. The pandemic had a greater adverse impact on MSMEs in transportation and warehousing as well as the manufacturing sector compared to other sectors. A comparison between regions highlighted that MSMEs in Sumatra suffered the worst drop in profit margins with an average of 60 to 80 per cent lower profit margins compared to pre-pandemic.

With the shortage of funds, many MSMEs required additional financing to ease the cost of doing business. However, even in normal conditions, access to financing continues to be a significant challenge for many MSMEs, especially financing from financial institutions. They are considered to be a higher risk sector for non-performing loans compared to larger firms. Therefore, many MSMEs depend greatly on alternative ways to finance their business such as selling their existing assets as well as taking loans from close relatives. It has been observed that the crisis has affected the MSMEs' asset values. UNDP and LPEM FEB UI (2020) revealed that more than half of MSMEs recorded a decrease in asset value due to the pandemic. The decrease in asset value was less severe in MiEs and male-owned businesses than in their respective counterparts. The extent of the drop in asset value ranged mostly between 20 per cent to 40 per cent and across form size and owner gender by 40 per cent to 60 per cent.

Non-Financial Problems

The pandemic also exposed MSMEs to other non-financial problems. Strict restrictions regarding business operational hours and protocols during the pandemic led to many MSMEs suffering as they used to depend heavily on physical workplaces and marketplaces. There were also changing trends in consumer behaviour, a lack of supporting infrastructure to access online platforms and online marketing, and a lack of information whilst navigating the online platform. MSMEs that still relied on physical places were obligated to follow the government regulations and follow health protocols and wear health protection equipment (facemasks, hand sanitizer, gloves, etc.) which was not easily obtained, especially at the beginning of the pandemic.

MSMEs also encountered difficulties in distributing their products (logistics problems). The logistical problems stemmed from the government's enactment of PSBB, which put high uncertainty on many logistics companies. This was evident in most MSMEs operating in the agriculture sector, processing industries, and trading, as well as those in Java-Bali and Sumatra regions (Gunadi et al. 2021). This problem was evident in most MSMEs regardless of firm size and owner gender (UNDP and LPEM FEB UI 2020).

The decline in demand and orders led to massive layoffs of employees nationwide, salary cuts and salary payment postponement. In turn, this led to MSMEs being unable to fulfil their orders due to labour shortages. UNDP and LPEM FEB UI (2020) reported that more than half of MSMEs had to adjust the number of staff. The larger the firm size, the larger number of workers laid off. In general, 43 per cent of MEs had to reduce 40 to 60 per cent of their workforce while 30 per cent SEs and 24 per cent MiEs had to lay off 20 to 40 per cent of their workers.

The reduction in employment had an asymmetric impact from a gender perspective. Overall, 38 per cent of MSMEs said that between 1 and 9 female employees could not be physically present at work and could not work adequately from home (UNDP and LPEM FEB UI 2020). This problem was less evident in smaller firms and male-owned firms. For medium and large enterprises, around 12 per cent answered that 10 to 19 of their female employees could not come to work.

13.3.4 Time Perspective of the Impact

The time from which the pandemic began to affect the MSMEs was also critical from a policy-making point of view. Figure 13.1 shows that MSMEs had generally already begun to experience a decline in revenue in March or April (Figure 13.1a). Interestingly, a number of the MEs only began to exhibit revenue decline during April–June as they were more likely to have had medium- or long-term production contracts with their customers to fulfil. If viewed by the business sector, MSMEs generally began to experience revenue declines in March, except those in the trade sector, which reported that the decline began in March and April (Figure 13.1b). This is because from a demand perspective, during the first month of the pandemic, consumers still purchased groceries for consumption or as a precaution. From the supply side, the MSMEs still had stocks to be sold in their shops. By region, generally, MSMEs began to exhibit a revenue decline in March, except for those in NTT, Maluku and Papua Region, which reported a decline in March and April (Figure 13.1c). This is possibly due to the low capacity for COVID-19 rapid tests in these areas, which led to low reported infection cases and late imposition of social distancing.

FIGURE 13.1
Beginning of MSMEs' Revenue Decline

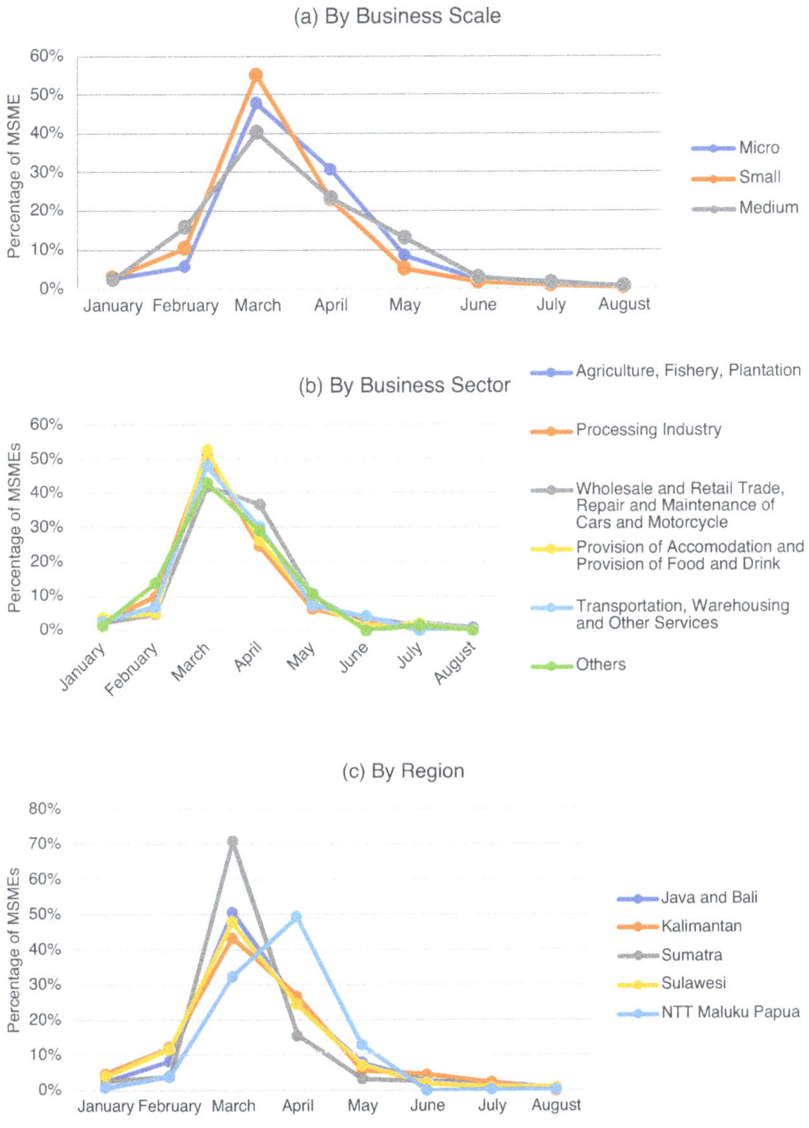

Source: Gunadi et al. (2021).

MSMEs' revenue then continued to decline in the months that followed until they reached the lowest levels of monthly revenue before reaching the turnaround point, as shown in Figure 13.2. MiEs and SEs generally reported the lowest revenue in April, but MEs experienced it in May (Figure 13.2a). MEs are more likely to have internal and external resources to mitigate the impact of the pandemic than their smaller counterparts.

By business sector, MSMEs generally recorded the largest revenue fall in April (Figure 13.2b), including those in the trading sector. By April, household incomes and savings began to decrease while there were also delays in the delivery of raw materials from other regions and imports. Likewise, in terms of region, MSMEs generally recorded the largest revenue fall in April, including those in NTT, Maluku and Papua (Figure 13.2c). Interestingly, a considerable share of MSMEs in Java and Bali only recorded the lowest revenue in May, June and July. One possible explanation for this is their ability to use online marketing, coupled with good Internet access and the ability of consumers to switch to online purchasing.

13.4 GOVERNMENT RESPONSE TO SUPPORT MSMEs

13.4.1 Constraints Faced by the Governments

While it is clear that the GoI had to respond in order to assist MSMEs during the crisis, there were several constraints faced by the policymaker when formulating the policy. First, it was unclear what would be the best response to help MSMEs—due to the type of crisis. Whether subsidizing the enterprises would be beneficial, or on the other hand just providing aid to those working in MSMEs. Second, because the government had limited information about the exact number of MSMEs, there may be exclusion or inclusion issues. It is relatively difficult for the government to decide whether they need to help only some MSMEs based on several criteria, or they can just broadly allocate funds regardless of the size and sector. Finally, there was the same issue that has been encountered implementing other government policies during the pandemic namely its execution. The government had to decide quickly on the policy but also the correct manner to implement it. Thus, implementation would be pivotal because the policy needed to be both well implemented and well targeted. Given the constraints faced by the government including limited knowledge about what should be done in this unprecedented time, the government

FIGURE 13.2
Lowest MSMEs' Revenue Period

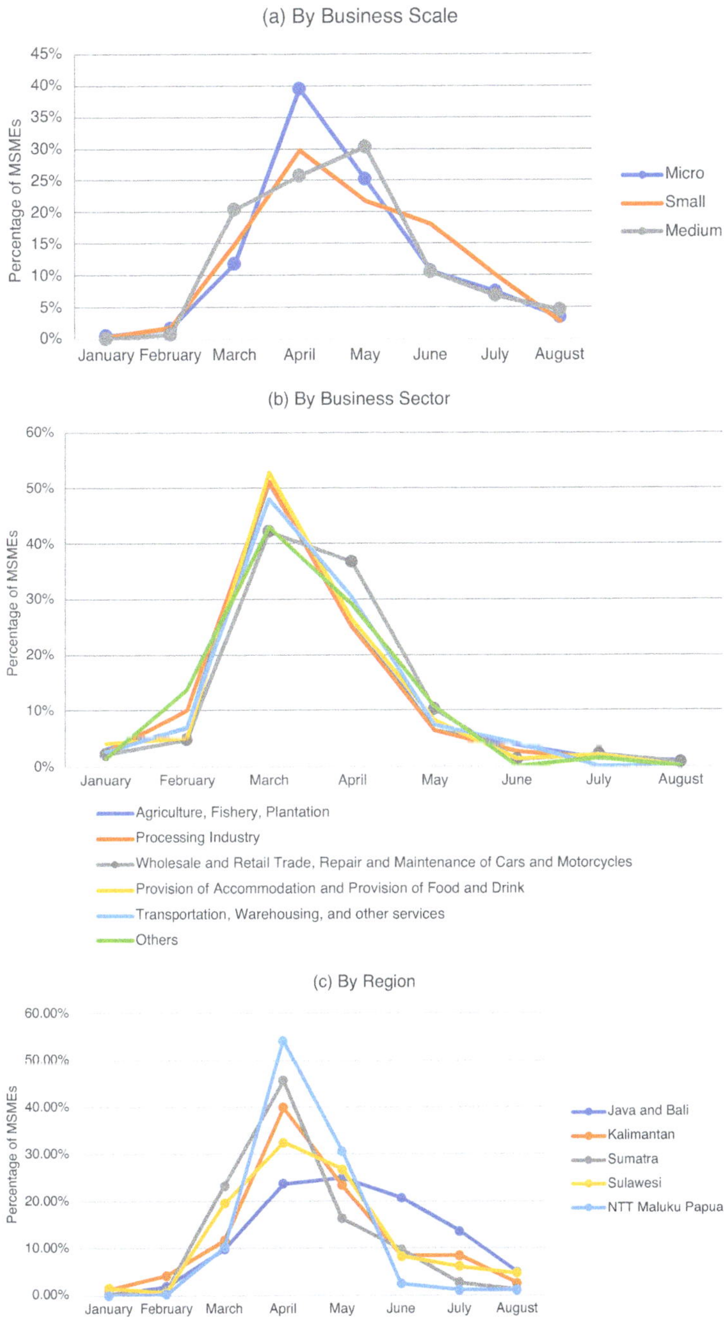

Source: Gunadi et al. (2021).

decided to implement the policies that would potentially help MSMEs to curb the negative impact of the pandemic.

13.4.2 National Economic Recovery (PEN) Programme for MSMEs

Government Supports for MSMEs in Mitigating the Pandemic's Impact[2]

To help MSMEs mitigate the pandemic's impact, in 2020, the government implemented social assistance policies and economic stimulus targeted at MSMEs nationwide. The government designed a national economic recovery programme through the modalities regulated in Government Regulation Number 23 of 2020 (PP 23/2020) regarding the implementation of the PEN programme, aimed at MSMEs, ultra-micro businesses, strategic business sectors in the economy and the state-owned enterprises (SOEs), as illustrated in Table 13.2. Specifically, for MSMEs, up to IDR116.3 trillion of the 2020 PEN programme funds (16.7 per cent) were allocated to mitigating the pandemic impact and MSMEs' business recovery (Ministry of Finance 2021). Table 13.3 specifies each of the PEN programmes for MSMEs in 2020.

Furthermore, in 2021, the GoI continued the PEN programme by increasing the budget allocation to IDR744.77 trillion.[3] The benefits of the PEN funds allocation for MSMEs in 2021 include (Ministry of Finance 2022):

1. Productive Presidential Assistance for Micro Business Actors (BPUM) for 12.8 million businesses and Cash Assistance for PKL Business Actors and Stall Owners (BPTKLW) for 1 million businesses;
2. guarantee fee for 2.45 million MSMEs and 69 cooperatives;
3. fund placement in banks for 5.49 million debtors;
4. interest subsidy for 14.53 debtors; and
5. State Equity Participation (PMN) for seven SOEs.

13.4.3 The Effectiveness of the PEN Programme

SMEs' Awareness of the PEN Programme

Even though the government has designed policy actions to cushion the pandemic's impact on MSMEs, there are still issues at the implementation

TABLE 13.2
National Economic Recovery Design in 2020

<table>
<tr><th></th><th></th><th colspan="2">Q2</th><th colspan="2">Q3</th><th>Q4</th></tr>
<tr><td rowspan="3">Economic Impact Scenario</td><td>Production Impact Baseline</td><td colspan="4">• Tourism halted (Transportation, Accommodation, Restaurants)
• Trade & commerce plunged sharply
• Manufacturing disrupted</td><td>• Tourism activities recovers
• Trade & commerce pick up
• Manufacturing activities resume</td></tr>
<tr><td rowspan="2">Consumption Impact Baseline</td><td colspan="2">• Social distancing significantly reduced public consumption, in formal and informal sectors</td><td colspan="3">Consumption activities gradually recovered (electronics, clothing, restaurants, hotels, tourism, transportation, etc.)</td></tr>
<tr><td colspan="4">• Poverty and unemployment rose sharply (especially in informal sectors)</td><td>Unemployment & poverty</td></tr>
<tr><td rowspan="3">Policy Response Design</td><td>Consumer Stimulus</td><td colspan="2">Acceleration of subsidies & social assistance for the poor and vulnerable households (basic necessities, pre-employment cards, electricity tariff exemption, etc.)</td><td colspan="3">Stimulus for expansion of consumption with a focus on middle class income (tourism, restaurants, transportation, etc.)</td></tr>
<tr><td rowspan="2">Business Stimulus</td><td colspan="4">Ultra Micro Businesses and MSMEs
• Deferred principal and interest loan repayment
• Loan interest subsidies
• Tax incentives
• Working capital loans guarantee
• Regional incentive funds</td><td rowspan="2">Jumpstarting the Business
• MSME working capital loan guarantee
• Distribution of SoEs working capital loans
• Government fund placement in banks affected by credit restructuring
• Government fund placement in SOEs
• Regional incentive funds
• Support fund for Biodiesel Program</td></tr>
<tr><td colspan="4">Industry and State-owned Enterprises (SoEs)
• Tax incentives
• Bailout funds
• Distribution of SoEs working capital loans
• Government fund placement in banks affected by credit restructuring
• Support fund for Biodiesel Program</td></tr>
</table>

Source: Ministry of Finance (2020).

TABLE 13.3
PEN Programmes for MSMEs in 2020

No.	*Programmes*	*Realization*	*Objective*	*Beneficiaries*
1.	State fund placement in banks	IDR66.75 trillion	Credit restructuring and channelling additional new working capital credit to the bank	4.7 million debtors
2.	Tax incentives for MSMEs	IDR0.67 trillion	MSMEs' taxpayers who have a certain gross turnover and are subject to final income tax	245.65 thousand taxpayers
3.	Working capital credit guarantee for MSMEs	IDR2.09 trillion	Working capital credit guarantee through IJP subsidies and loss limit support	890.2 thousand debtors
4.	Investment financing for Revolving Fund Management Agency (LPDB)	IDR1.29 trillion	Absorb MSME products and increase agricultural production capacity	63 cooperatives and 101,011 MSMEs
5.	Interest subsidy for MSMEs' loans	IDR12.83 trillion	Interest subsidies for MSMEs customers, finance companies, UMi, Mekaar, Procurement, and LPDB	25.4 million debtors
6.	Productive presidential aid for micro business actors (BPUM)	IDR28.80 trillion	Capital aid for micro or ultra-micro businesses	12 million businesses

Source: Ministry of Finance (2021).

level. Some evidence indicates that the effectiveness of the programmes for the beneficiaries needs to be evaluated.[4]

Table 13.4 shows surveyed MSMEs' perception of eight programmes aimed at MSMEs. In general, only a small share of MiEs was aware of the programmes, except for the postponement of principal and interest instalments. However, the MiEs' participation level for such programs was low because most of them did not use banking services. The most attractive programs were mostly cash-based, such as working capital credit guarantees, loan interest subsidies, tax reduction incentives, and emergency working capital stimulus.

SEs were aware of all the programmes, except for the government's procurement of MSME products, SOEs' cooperation with e-commerce for the digitalization of MSMEs', and online training/capacity-building. This is mainly because these programmes may not be relevant to SEs. Moreover, SEs' highest participation was recorded in tax reduction incentives and emergency working capital stimulus. This finding suggests that the policy to lower tax payments and granting working capital stimulus may help most SEs. As for the MEs, most of them were aware of all the programmes, and the highest participation was recorded in the government's procurement of MSMEs products, the cooperation by SOEs with e-commerce for digitalization of MSMEs', online training/capacity-building and tax reduction incentives.

There are information gaps between MSMEs operating in Java-Bali and other areas when viewed by region which suggests there were heterogeneity issues in terms of the effectiveness and other information related to the program. This result indicates unequal access to information, especially for those MSMEs located further from Java and the capital. Looking at the heterogeneity based on gender, male-owned MSMEs were generally more informed about the PEN programme.

SMEs' Application of the PEN Programme

MSMEs' awareness of a programme does not necessarily lead to programme registration/access. Studies revealed that several factors might affect MSMEs' decision to access the programme: (i) perception of eligibility for the programme, (ii) unable to meet the requirements documents/paperwork, (iii) unsure about the registration requirements and procedures, (iv) informally declined or discouraged by the local officials, or (v) unsure about the location of the registration offices location.

TABLE 13.4
MSMEs Awareness of the PEN Programme (%)

No.	*Programmes*	*By Scale*			*By Region*		*By Gender*	
		Micro	*Small*	*Medium*	*Java-Bali*	*Rest of Indonesia*	*Male*	*Female*
1.	Postponement of principal and interest loan repayment for MSMEs	69.40	74.10	79.80	73.41	69.80	76.05	67.47
2.	Tax incentives for MSMEs	34.20	51.40	67.50	50.61	37.48	50.42	37.90
3.	Working capital credit guarantee for MSMEs	37.88	50.48	55.84	50.10	39.37	48.13	41.09
4.	Loan interest subsidy for micro-enterprises and MSMEs	35.91	57.59	62.34	51.94	42.49	53.14	41.17
5.	Emergency working capital for ultra-micro businesses and MSMEs	49.61	63.13	62.34	62.03	50.76	60.88	51.88
6.	Government procurement prioritization for MSMEs products	28.05	30.84	50.65	31.96	30.12	29.92	31.83
7.	SOEs cooperation with e-commerce for MSMEs digitalization	25.19	34.70	48.05	27.82	32.84	29.92	31.70
8.	Online trainings	38.76	45.65	58.44	43.82	42.56	39.96	45.94

Notes: Values above represent the percentage of respondents who were aware of the PEN programme. Green boxes indicate higher than 75 per cent while red boxes indicate lower than 50 per cent awareness.
Source: Survey data and Gunadi et al. (2021).

Table 13.5 shows a large share of MSMEs that are aware of the PEN programme would likely apply, except for the postponement of principal and interest loan repayment. A lower take-up in such a policy could be because this programme was channelled through banks and targeted MSMEs holding bank accounts. A considerable share of MSMEs in Indonesia, especially the MiEs, still does not use bank services yet. When viewed by gender, there was some heterogeneity. While by region, MSMEs in Java-Bali showed a higher registration rate in almost all programmes.

SMEs' Main Sources of Information Regarding the PEN Programme

The issue of where to find and source information about the PEN programme has become an obstacle in accelerating the programme's disbursement. Thus, it is worth seeing where MSMEs will receive the information about the PEN programme. Table 13.6 shows MSMEs' sources of information regarding each of the PEN programmes. There are several sources of information that were asked in the survey. It includes local government agencies, central government agencies, newspapers and online sources, television, business associations, business associates, family and relatives, non-government organizations and business mentors. The list of the source of information mentioned in each table cell is the primary source of information for the respective programme and respondent category. Dark grey indicates that the source of information was very dominant and used as a reference by more than 60 per cent of respondents, light grey indicates it was used as a reference by 40 to 60 per cent of respondents, while the white cells indicate that it was used only by 20 to 40 per cent of the respondents.

Business associations were the most reliable source of information for MiEs and SEs, while MEs can afford other sources, mainly newspapers or other online sources. Hence, the socialization of future programmes should closely involve business associations, especially those targeting MiEs and SEs. When viewed by gender, business communities and associations were also the most reliable source of information in general, although male-owned MSMEs tended to have more varied sources of information. Interestingly, when viewed by region, business communities and associations were also the most reliable source of information in general. However, MSMEs outside Java-Bali region tend to have more varied sources of information.

TABLE 13.5
MSMEs' Application of the PEN Programme (%)

No.	*Programme*	*By Scale*			*By Region*		*By Gender*	
		Micro	*Small*	*Medium*	*Java-Bali*	*Rest of Indonesia*	*Male*	*Female*
1.	Postponement of principal and interest loan repayment for MSMEs	34.90	61.80	70.30	51.88	39.28	48.83	43.02
2.	Tax incentives for MSMEs	82.90	78.10	84.60	87.29	73.13	81.17	80.30
3.	Working capital credit guarantee for MSMEs	75.26	74.29	67.44	80.60	66.82	75.44	72.56
4.	Loan interest subsidy for micro-enterprises and MSMEs	83.43	74.89	62.50	80.33	73.33	76.98	76.89
5.	Emergency working capital for ultra-micro businesses and MSMEs	84.46	80.46	70.83	84.98	77.53	78.40	84.62
6.	Government procurement prioritization for MSMEs products	71.74	67.72	79.49	73.02	69.66	67.63	73.94
7.	SOEs cooperation with e-commerce for MSMEs digitalization	69.84	64.79	77.14	60.36	72.92	64.08	72.05
8.	Online trainings	68.75	74.59	81.82	71.86	73.23	75.27	70.64

Notes: Values above represent the percentage of respondents informed about the PEN programme who would likely to apply. Green boxes indicate higher than 75 per cent while red boxes indicate lower than 50 per cent awareness.
Source: Survey data and Gunadi et al. (2021).

TABLE 13.6
MSMEs' Main Source of Information Regarding the PEN Programme

No.	Programme	By Scale			By Gender		By Region	
		Micro	*Small*	*Medium*	*Male*	*Female*	*Java-Bali*	*Rest of Indonesia*
1.	Postponement of principal and interest loan repayment for MSMEs	NOS	BCA	NOS	NOS	BCA	BCA	NOS
2.	Tax incentives for MSMEs	BCA	BCA	BCA	BCA	BCA	BCA	NOS
3.	Working capital credit guarantee for MSMEs	BCA	BCA	BCA	BCA	BCA	BCA	BCA
4.	Loan interest subsidy for ultra micro businesses and MSMEs	BCA	BCA	NOS	BCA	BCA	BCA	NOS
5.	Emergency working capital support for MSMEs	BCA	BCA	NOS	BCA	BCA	BCA	NOS
6.	Government procurement prioritization for MSMEs products	BCA	BCA	NOS	BCA	BCA	BCA	BCA
7.	SoEs cooperation with e-commerce for MSMEs digitalization	BCA	BCA	NOS	BCA	BCA	BCA	BCA
8.	Online trainings	BCA	BCA	NOS	BCA	BCA	BCA	BCA

Notes: NOS stands for Newspaper and Online Sources; BCA stands for Business Community and Association. Dark grey indicates >60 per cent, light grey indicates 40–60 per cent and white indicates 20–40 per cent.
Source: Survey data and Gunadi et al. (2021).

13.5 HOW THE PEN PROGRAMME PROTECTS AND SUPPORTS MSMEs IN WEATHERING THE PANDEMIC

13.5.1 Accession of the Programmes

To understand how the PEN programme helps and supports SMEs during the pandemic, it is crucial to understand the type of government assistance that the enterprises have received. We use the result from a study by UNDP and LPEM FEB UI (2020) to answer this question. This study observes that government assistance is the most common source of aid obtained across all scales of MSME, with a percentage of 70 per cent. Regarding the type of assistance, distribution of goods was the most common type received by large enterprises (LEs), MEs, and SEs. Assistance related to distribution was the second most common type of assistance for MiEs, slightly less than other forms of assistance.

As for assistance related to credit (e.g., interest subsidy and financing through the Revolving Fund Management Agency, or LPDB), credit-based assistance was mainly received by LEs and was less common as the size of the enterprise becomes smaller. This result is in concordance with qualitative information obtained in the in-depth interview and focus group discussions (FGDs), where most MiEs owners are not concerned with access to loans since their main problem is a significant decrease in demand. Thus, getting access to a financing scheme will not solve their problem.

Further, smaller enterprises are less likely to pay government-borne income tax. This may be due to MSMEs that often do not have a legal business permit. Thus, they are not eligible for this type of assistance because their revenue is too low and does not exceed the taxable income threshold. Among all SEs respondents who have a business permit, only 13.3 per cent receive government-borne income tax. This suggests that other factors limit SEs from receiving income tax borne by the government, such as limited information or administrative requirements that are considered too complicated for smaller enterprises.

13.5.2 Approval Rate of the PEN Programme

When MSMEs decided to apply for the programme, the application was not approved automatically. Table 13.7 shows a relatively low success rate for applications for the postponement of the principal and interest loan repayment programme. The lower success rate could be because this

TABLE 13.7
Approval Rate and Helpfulness of PEN Programme Application

No.	*Programmes*	*Approval (% of Respondents Who Applied for the Programme)*	*Helpfulness (% of Respondents Whose Applications Were Granted)*
1.	Postponement of principal and interest loan repayment for MSMEs	45.45%	99.4%
2.	Tax incentives for MSMEs	78.72%	99.1%
3.	Working capital credit guarantee for MSMEs	73.36%	99.0%
4.	Loan interest subsidy for micro-enterprises and MSMEs	76.08%	99.1%
5.	Emergency working capital for ultra-micro businesses and MSMEs	80.36%	99.2%
6.	Government procurement prioritization for MSMEs products	69.74%	98.5%
7.	SOEs cooperation with e-commerce for MSMEs digitalization	67.66%	98.4%
8.	Online trainings	71.97%	98.9%

Source: Gunadi et al. (2021).

programme's decision-makers are the banks of the respective MSMEs' and each bank may have its own risk assessment of the individual customer. Other factors that may result in the rejection of the MSMEs' application include incomplete documents/paperwork or poor credit histories.

13.5.3 The Impact of the PEN Programme

Table 13.7 also shows that most MSMEs who successfully became programme beneficiaries perceived that each programme was helpful for their businesses. A small share of respondents who perceived that the programmes were not too helpful argued that the programme package was too small, had too short a duration or did not cater to their needs (did not match the assistance they needed most).

Another finding from LPEM FEB UI and LD UI (2020) suggests that the majority of the utilization of the existing assistance programmes was to purchase raw materials and capital goods. In the case of its perceived benefit, 49 per cent of respondents found the current assistance programme useful.

Nonetheless, it is also worth noting that the information about the causal impact of PEN on firms' recovery, unfortunately, remains limited. One of the key problems is that most surveys are not conducted in a longitudinal setting. Thus, it is not easy to estimate the actual impact. Many studies have investigated the impact of the pandemic on firms' performance. However, it remains a challenge to see how significant the contribution from PEN was to a firm's recovery. Another study by LPEM FEB UI (2021) suggests that the loan restructuring programme introduced by the banking sector has helped most MSMEs reallocate their capital and assets and allowed them to focus on them as an input for production.[5]

Finally, it is also important to know how the PEN programme would help MSMEs recover faster and to be more robust. Figure 13.3 plots the period of the decline of MSMEs' revenue (beginning and the lowest points) in general (all scales, sectors, and regions) along with the disbursements from the government's PEN programme. At least two types of gaps can be observed: (1) the time gap between the time the MSMEs need external assistance and the acceleration of PEN distribution, and (2) the gap between the magnitude of the impact of the pandemic on MSMEs' revenue and the level of PEN realization.

13.5.4 Evaluation of the PEN Programme

It is also interesting to see what needs to be improved in the PEN programme. Most MSMEs generally perceived the need for improvement in the programme distribution to ensure that it reached the targeted beneficiaries, more widespread and massive socialization, broadening the targeted beneficiaries, and increasing the number of assistance packages (Gunadi et al. 2021).

The understanding of government assistance programmes by business owners is still relatively low. A survey conducted by LPEM FEB UI and LD UI (2020) showed that most MSMEs only know about the Deferment of Principal and Interest Instalments for MSMEs and House Ownership Loan (*Kredit Kepemilikan Rumah*, or KPR), and the Working Capital Stimulus Programme and Emergency Working Capital Assistance for Affected MSMEs. There is still much room for the government to be able

FIGURE 13.3
Timeline of MSMEs Revenue Decline and PEN Disbursement

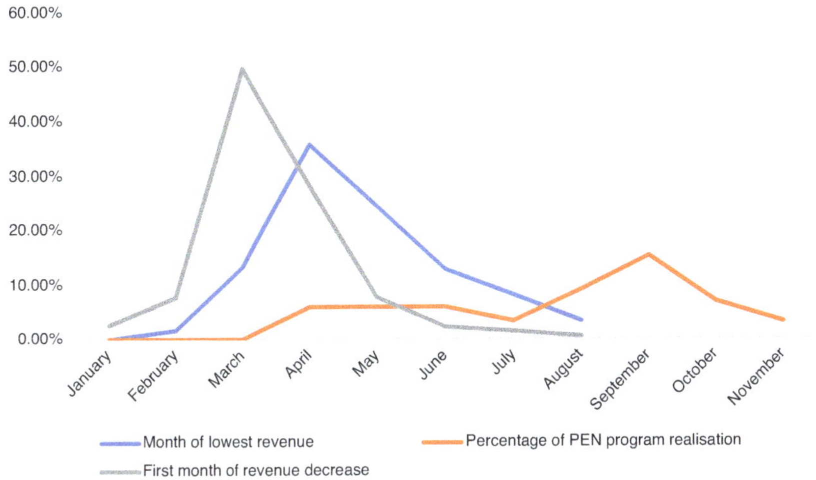

Source: Gunadi et al. (2021).

to carry out socialization related to government assistance programmes for MSMEs. It is reflected in the limited knowledge of respondents about government assistance programmes. To encourage the expansion of the assistance programmes, several things can be done by banks and the government, including:

(a) simplifying the registration process,
(b) simplifying the required requirements while still adhering to the precautionary principle, and
(c) expanding the programme's scope so that more MSMEs are compatible with the programme.

Of the several known programmes, most respondents only know about the Deferment of Principal and Interest Instalments Programme for MSMEs and KPR; and the Working Capital Stimulus Programme and Emergency Working Capital Assistance for Affected MSMEs. On the other hand, respondents' awareness of programmes related to assistance and collaboration with e-commerce is still relatively low. It is also relevant to the lower use of technology in respondents' business activities, where marketing activities using digital platforms and social media are still relatively low. Most respondents have never done marketing using these media. Moreover, during the pandemic, most respondents did not try to adapt by starting to digitize their business activities.

As for the respondents who can access government assistance programmes, the programmes that were most suited to the respondent's needs were the loan interest subsidy programme for MSMEs and the postponement of principal and interest instalments. It indicates that reducing liabilities are the two most important aspects of the respondents' business continuity in the short term.

13.6 SMEs' BUSINESS TRANSFORMATION AND FURTHER SUPPORT TO RECOVER

13.6.1 Period of Time Businesses Expected to Survive during the COVID-19 Pandemic

MSMEs' survival during the pandemic differed across sectors and by firm size (UNDP and LPEM 2020). In general, the larger the firm, the longer the period of survival. This is due to better cash flows, availability of inventories, the use of ICT to adapt to mobility restrictions, and the use of contract-based transactions both with suppliers and buyers. However, this does not apply to MSMEs in the processing industry, which reported longer survival for MiEs and SEs compared to their larger counterparts. This is because the medium and large processing industries generally employ a large number of workers and therefore have to bear a larger labour cost.

13.6.2 Short-Term Strategy

To cope with the impact of the pandemic, MSMEs pursue four main production and cost reduction strategies (UNDP and LPEM FEB UI 2020). The most common strategy was product modification, for example offering smaller units and therefore cheaper products as an adaption to lower consumer purchasing power. This strategy was more dominantly chosen by female entrepreneurs. Other notable strategies included temporary closure of their businesses (more dominantly pursued by male entrepreneurs) or changing their business focus, for example shifting to or adding new business offerings which were in high demand during the pandemic, such as food, personal care and healthcare equipment. A number of MSMEs also adapted by changing their production techniques and/or raw material composition to lower production costs. Other actions MSMEs have taken include conducting new research related to production, rotating staff and maximizing current production capacity

With declining sales and mounting costs, MSMEs have to manage labour costs which are often one of the main cost components. UNDP and LPEM (2020) reported that the most common strategy was furloughing the workers with a reduced salary, followed by a reduction in bonuses, incentives and religious holiday allowances and workers' salaries payment rescheduling.

Gunadi et al. (2022) reported that the employment-related strategies did not vary greatly by MSMEs owners' gender and location (Java-Bali and the rest of Indonesia). However, the larger the enterprise scale, the greater the tendency to implement specific employment policies. A large share of MiEs reported that they did not carry out any measure related to employment and only around 17 per cent laid off some workers. By contrast, small and medium-sized enterprises implemented several strategies including laying off workers, reducing salaries, salary payment rescheduling and reducing bonuses. In terms of the business sector, laying off workers was the most dominant strategy in general, with a notable additional strategy of sending home workers with reduced salaries which were reported by those operating in the agriculture, fisheries and plantation sectors, in contrast with the trading sector which mostly did not impose any specific measure.

With cashflow problems, MSMEs needed other specific financial strategies. UNDP and LPEM (2020) reported that the most common strategy was reducing utility costs, such as electricity, water, gas, and communications, followed by reductions in transportation costs, and reducing rental costs. Other actions taken by MSMEs have been laying off employees, postponing outgoing payments, reducing operational hours, and asking for debt restructuring. This pattern of strategies was applied across business sectors and locations, regardless of the owner's gender and firm size.

The restriction in social mobility and the changing consumer shopping behaviour has also forced MSMEs to adjust their marketing strategies. The most common action taken by MSMEs has been selling their products using different strategies, particularly through the online marketplace, followed by discounting or gifts for their customers and/or using special product packaging (i.e., Eid edition) (more common for SEs and MEs) and repackaging the products into smaller packages (more common for MiEs and food-beverages producers) (UNDP and LPEM 2020; Gunadi et al. 2022). There were similar patterns across all locations and business sectors regardless of owner gender.

13.6.3 Recovery Strategy

With the perception that the pandemic would flatten at one point, in the third quarter of 2020, MSMEs had already considered and prepared their recovery strategy. Most MSMEs devised marketing or promotional plans, being aware that some changes in consumer shopping behaviour would be sustained beyond the pandemic (UNDP and LPEM FEB UI 2020). The core of an effective marketing strategy is the choice of the most appropriate marketing channels. The marketing channel most commonly chosen by MSMEs is free advertising on social media, followed by paid advertising on social media, and print-based media (more common for medium and large businesses). It is worth noting, however, that there was still a considerable share of MSMEs in all business sectors regardless of their size that still had no plan to innovate their marketing strategy (Gunadi et al. 2022). This can be one focal point to address in order to accelerate the economic recovery.

To get back on track with various planning and adaptation strategies, MSMEs need funding (UNDP and LPEM FEB UI 2020; Gunadi et al. 2022). The common choice for a potential source of funding for recovery was banks, except by MiEs. The second most common source of funding was from families/relatives, more commonly reported by micro-enterprises and female entrepreneurs. This suggests that female entrepreneurs have a better reputation and stronger social bonds that allow them to access funds through their family ties but at the same time they are less bankable compared to their male counterparts. This reaffirms that female-headed households are less likely to access formal financing (Ghosh and Vinod 2017) and there are significant gender gaps in account ownership as well as savings and credit product usage (Demirguc-Kunt, Klapper, and Singer 2013). Other reported sources of funding for recovery include cooperatives, fellow entrepreneurs and private assets.

Despite the difficulties and challenges that have arisen during this pandemic and the many aspects of their businesses that needed adjustment, more than 90 per cent of MSMEs did not have plans to shut down their businesses (UNDP and LPEM FEB UI 2020). This observation was made across different firm sizes regardless of the owners' gender. Further, Gunadi (2022) reported that most MSMEs, regardless of size, sector, location and owners' gender, stated that they planned to set up new business lines/products/services but also to maintain their current business to bear the risk of new business failure.

13.6.4 Medium and Long-Term Strategy

The pandemic has forced MSMEs not only to adapt in the short run but also to rethink their medium- and long-term plans. UNDP and LPEM FEB UI (2020) reported that more than 80 per cent of MiEs, regardless of the owner's gender, plan to formalize their businesses. The said formalization was mostly limited to business establishments and business operations. From the government side, this can be useful for database and taxation purposes, and can also be useful for the next step of formalization covering social security.[6] Interestingly, less than a third of MiEs have plans to switch to other business/sectors in the future, indicating their risk-averse nature in doing business, owing to their limited resources and savings.

As for the SEs, the pandemic has changed their long-term investment plan (UNDP and LPEM FEB UI 2020). About 57 per cent of SEs reported that they have cancelled or delayed investment or expansion plans. This is due to either an internal financial shock or credit restraints or both. SEs avoid investing in risky projects and investment will recover only gradually as uncertainty dissipates.

Changing investment plans was also reported by MEs (UNDP and LPEM FEB UI 2020). In addition, around a fourth of MEs said that in the long run they will change their target market orientation to fully concentrate on the domestic market. The pandemic has been perceived as creating more uncertainty in international markets. This is especially prevalent in female entrepreneurs. Only around 5 per cent of MEs perceived that the pandemic created new international market opportunities, on which they can focus in the future.

In the long term, MSMEs also perceived that there will be some post-pandemic potential challenges that persist (UNDP and LPEM

FEB UI 2020). The most challenging aspect was perceived as increasing costs that will not return to pre-pandemic levels, followed by changing promotion strategies which will require an additional cost and labour and fiercer competition, especially against survivors of the pandemic and new businesses bringing innovative concepts, while they are less concerned about challenges in production and human resources. The concerns about those future challenges are generally more prevalent in female entrepreneurs and MEs.

Interestingly, the pandemic also caused many MSMEs to plan for mitigating the impact of similar crises should they take place in the future. UNDP and LPEM FEB UI (2020) reported that 29 per cent of MiEs, 29.3 per cent of SEs and 33 per cent of MEs plan to allocate part of their operating profit for reserve funding purposes. Further, 4.7 per cent of MiEs, 6.5 per cent of SEs and 9.1 per cent of MEs plan to have their business insured.

13.6.5 Additional Supports Needed

Gunadi et al. (2021) reported MSMEs' suggestions and expectations for future or follow-up programmes. Should the pandemic experience another wave of mass infection, the MSMEs mostly need additional working capital, business coaching mainly related to digital marketing and financial management, production equipment, business regulation simplification, and lower cost of transportation to obtain cheaper inputs as well as lower cost of delivering their product to the market.

When the pandemic is under control and the businesses recover, those six programmes are mostly still the most demanded by MSMEs. There was a minor difference with business regulation simplification being selected as the third most expected. However, when viewed by sector, the order of importance of the expected future programmes varied across sectors and some more specific programmes appeared among the most expected. The support programmes demanded included business insurance, production techniques and standardization, transportation infrastructure improvement, transportation cost subsidies, better internet access, and digital marketing skills.

In addition, MSMEs also expected further financial and non-financial assistance. Most MSMEs across business types expect the government to enhance the targeting process of those recipients potentially eligible for the programmes. Another widely voiced expectation is that the government should do a better job at publicizing such programmes. As for the non-financial assistance, access to the market and the distribution process is the type of assistance that is expected the most across MSMEs, strengthening the previous result that the most damaging blow of this pandemic to the MSME is a significant drop in sales.

13.7 EPILOGUE

The COVID-19 pandemic has disrupted Indonesian MSMEs in unprecedented ways and on a large scale. MSMEs' internal coping strategy and external assistance are keys to weathering and recovering from the pandemic. This chapter puts together findings from various studies to analyse the impact of the pandemic on MSMEs and how MSMEs, even with persistent problems hampering their development before the pandemic, adapted through internal strategies and business transformation. This chapter also analysed the GoI's responses to support MSMEs, how the devised programmes helped mitigate the impact of the pandemic, and how such programmes can be improved should a similar disruption occur in the future.

The findings show that MSMEs have to adjust their financial, production, employment and marketing strategies to cope with a rapidly changing business environment. However, given the multidimensional shocks caused by the pandemic which affected MSMEs' supply, distribution and demand, external assistance is crucial for MSMEs' survival.

The GoI's PEN programme for MSMEs was the largest in terms of monetary value and beneficiary coverage in the country's history. These policies have helped many SMEs to keep their business afloat. However, various studies also showed that there is still room for improvement. Simplification of the types of programmes, simplification of application procedure and increased socialization involving the private sector and business societies/associations is crucial. The development of a single and up-to-date MSMEs database is imperative for the future. A participatory database could be considered. Further, government support should not only focus on mitigating the impact of the crisis but also to enable MSMEs to recover and transform their business. This is crucial not only to accelerate the recovery of the overall economy but also to facilitate the most resilient and adaptive MSMEs to jumpstart their businesses.

Notes

1. In this chapter, we use the terms SME and MSME interchangeably.
2. For further information about government support for MSMEs during the pandemic, see Gunadi et al. (2021).
3. Source: Ministry of Finance (2022). See https://pen.kemenkeu.go.id/api/Medias/58973996-0bfd-4e57-b14b-def1e90107b9 (accessed 18 March 2022).
4. A point that needs to be highlighted is that this analysis is based on a survey that was conducted in the second half of 2020 (Gunadi et al. 2021). Thus, this finding may only reflect the condition during the survey implementation.
5. Another study by PT PNM and TNP2K in 2021 suggests that programmes for MSMEs are well targeted and well benefited the majority of beneficiaries.
6. According to Rothenberg et al. (2016) based on the 2015 Doing Business Report for Indonesia, one of the obstacles faced by enterprises in formalizing their business is completing the required procedures. To officially register a business in Indonesia, there are at least ten different procedures that firms are required to comply with, depending on the industry and the location of the business operation. The entire process takes about 53 days to complete on average and costs 21.1 per cent of annual per capita income. Although many of these processes are officially free of charge, some firms partially complete the registration process, taking some steps but not others, while other firms avoid registration entirely.

References

Asian Development Bank (ADB). 2015. *Integrating SMEs Into Global Value Chains: Challenges and Policy Actions in Asia*. Mandaluyong City: Asian Development Bank.

BPS-Statistics Indonesia. 2018. "The 2016 Economic Census". https://se2016.bps.go.id/umkumb/

Bartik, Alexander W., Marianne Bertrand, Zoe Cullen, Edward L. Glaeser, Michael Luca, and Christopher Stanton. 2020. "The Impact of COVID-19 on Small Business Outcomes and Expectations". *Proceedings of the National Academy of Sciences* 117, no. 30: 17656–66. https://doi.org/10.1073/pnas.2006991117

Demirgüç-Kunt, A., L.F. Klapper, and D. Singer. 2013. "Financial Inclusion and Legal Discrimination against Women: Evidence from Developing Countries". World Bank Policy Research Working Paper, (6416). https://openknowledge.worldbank.org/handle/10986/15553

Ghosh, S., and D. Vinod. 2017. "What Constrains Financial Inclusion for Women? Evidence from Indian Micro Data". *World Development* 92: 60–81. https://doi.org/10.1016/j.worlddev.2016.11.011

Gunadi, Ahmad Dading, Harry Lesmana, Hilda Fachrizah, Mohamad Dian Revindo, and Rama Vandika Daniswara. 2021. "COVID-19 Pandemic and MSMEs in Indonesia: Impact and Policy Responses". *Jurnal Ekonomi Indonesia* 10, no. 2: 143–71.

———, Harry Lesmana, Hilda Fachrizah, Mohamad Dian Revindo, and Rama Vandika Daniswara. 2022. "Dealing with the COVID-19 Pandemic in Indonesia: MSMEs' Coping Strategy, Recovery Path and Business Transformation". *Jurnal Ekonomi Indonesia* 11, no. 1: 25–62.

Harvie, Charles, Dionisius Narjoko, and Sothea Oum. 2013. "Small and Medium Enterprises' Access to Finance: Evidence from Selected Asian Economies". *ERIA Discussion Paper Series* 23.

Iborra, María, Vicente Safón, and Consuelo Dolz. 2020. "What Explains the Resilience of SMEs? Ambidexterity Capability and Strategic Consistency". *Long Range Planning* 53, no. 6: 101947.

Latham, S. 2009. "Contrasting Strategic Response to Economic Recession in Start-Up Versus Established Software Firms". *Journal of Small Business Management* 47, no. 2: 180–201.

LPEM FEB UI. 2021. *Ketahanan UMKM di Segmen Mikro terhadap Pandemi COVID-19*.

LPEM FEB and UI-LD. 2020. "Survei Dampak Programme PEN terhadap UMKM".

Ministry of Cooperatives and SMEs. 2020. "Data UMKM". https://kemenkopukm.go.id/data-umkm

Ministry of Finance. 2020. "Laporan Mingguan Tahun 2020". https://pen.kemenkeu.go.id/ in/page/laporan-mingguan-2020

———. 2021. "Perkembangan Pelaksanaan Program Penanganan COVID-19 dan Pemulihan Ekonomi Nasional (PC&PEN)". https://pen.kemenkeu.go.id/ api/Medias/23a61caf-2596-4229-ad56-97a6ba733578

———. 2022. "Laporan Monitoring dan Evaluasi Penanganan COVID-19 dan Pemulihan Ekonomi Nasional 2021". https://pen.kemenkeu.go.id/ api/Medias/58973996-0bfd-4e57-b14b-def1e90107b9

Nugent, J.B., and S.-J. Yhee. 2002. "Small and Medium Enterprises in Korea: Achievements, Constraints and Policy Issues". *Small Business Economics* 18: 85–119.

Omar, A.R.C., S. Ishak, and M.A. Jusoh. 2020. "The Impact of COVID-19 Movement Control Order on SMEs' Businesses and Survival Strategies". *Geografia-Malaysian Journal of Society and Space* 16, no. 2: 90–103.

Organization for Economic Cooperation and Development (OECD). 2008. *Enhancing the Role of SMEs in Global Value Chains*. Paris: Organization for Economic Cooperation and Development.

———. 2019. "Fostering Greater SME Participation in a Globally Integrated Economy". In *Strengthening SMEs and Entrepreneurship for Productivity and*

Inclusive Growth: OECD 2018 Ministerial Conference on SMEs. Paris: Organization for Economic Cooperation and Development Publishing. https://doi.org/10.1787/400c491d-en

Oyewale, A., O. Adebayo, and O. Kehinde. 2020. "Estimating the Impact of COVID-19 on Small and Medium Scale Enterprise: Evidence from Nigeria", pp. 1–19.

Ozili, P. 2020. "COVID-19 in Africa: Socio-Economic Impact, Policy Response and Opportunities". *International Journal of Sociology and Social Policy*. https://doi.org/ 10.1108/IJSSP-05-2020-0171

Revindo, M.D. 2017. "Internationalisation of Indonesian SMEs: A Thesis Submitted in Partial Fulfilment of the Requirements for the degree of Doctor of Philosophy at Lincoln University". PhD dissertation, Lincoln University.

———, and Christopher Gan. 2017. "Rural Microfinance Banking Viability and Outreach: A Case of Bank Rakyat Indonesia". *Microfinance in Asia*: 337–56.

Rogerson, C.M. 2013. "Improving Marker Access Opportunities for Urban Small, Medium and Micro-Enterprises in South Africa". *Urbani Izziv* 24, no. 2: 133–43.

Rothenberg, Alexander D., Arya Gaduh, Nicholas E. Burger, Charina Chazali, Indrasari Tjandraningsih, Rini Radikun, Cole Sutera, and Sarah Weilant. 2016. "Rethinking Indonesia's Informal Sector". *World Development* 80: 96–113. https://doi.org/10.1016/ j.worlddev.2015.11.005

Tambunan, Tulus. 2015. "Financial Inclusion, Financial Education, and Financial Regulation: A Story from Indonesia". *ADBI Working Paper 535*. Tokyo: Asian Development Bank Institute.

UNDP and LPEM FEB UI. 2020. "Impact of COVID-19 Pandemic on MSMEs in Indonesia" https://www.id.undp.org/content/indonesia/en/home/library/ImpactofCOVID19MSMEs.html

14

Financial Inclusion and Economic Recovery Programme

From Limiting Factor to Opportunity

Raden Muhamad Purnagunawan,
Della Temenggung, Latif Adam and
Florischa Ayu Tresnatri

14.1 INTRODUCTION

Financial inclusion is a key enabler to reducing poverty and boosting prosperity as financial access facilitates day-to-day living, and helps families and small business owners generate income, invest in opportunities and work their way out of poverty. Financial inclusion can empower communities to meet their basic needs and has an important role in the efforts to help people prepare for, respond to, and recover from health and economic crises, such as COVID-19. Financial inclusion has been among the important development policy instruments with more than fifty-five countries launching the National Financial Inclusion Strategy (NFIS) as of early 2020, and a further thirty-four countries are currently in the process of doing so (World Bank 2021).

In Indonesia, the initiative to implement financial inclusion strategy has been officially started in 2016 in line with the introduction of Presidential Regulation/*Perpres* No. 82/2016 on NFIS (*Strategi National Keuangan Inklusif*, or SNKI). The NFIS is a legal framework to promote financial inclusion by opening access for more Indonesian to banking and other financial services. The state of financial inclusion in Indonesia saw a marked improvement over the last decades, but compared to peer countries, Indonesian financial inclusiveness is still lagging. Moreover, the inclusiveness gap between the poorest and the richest population is still considerable.

The COVID-19 pandemic has brought both challenges and opportunities for Indonesia's financial inclusion. On the one hand, the implementation of mobility restriction measures to control the spread of the virus resulted in the closure of bank branches and halted operations of mobile money agents in compliance with restrictions. On the other hand, government officials and health practitioners encouraged the use of cashless and contactless modes of payment to reduce the risk of viruses spread through the handling of cash. This will create new opportunities for the potential adoption of Digital Financial Services (DFS). Small businesses and low-income households can directly benefit from digital solutions such as mobile money services, online banking and other financial technology innovations.

Financial inclusion plays an important role in delivering government support to those whose income was negatively affected by the pandemic. The pandemic provided a lesson that massive delivery of government support during mobility restrictions can be done quickly if people have access to the financial system. In turn, the delivery of government support can also create opportunities to bring more people into financial services as they have to create new accounts to access the support.

This chapter will focus on examining how government policy response to the COVID-19 pandemic is influenced by the state of the country's financial inclusion and in turn, how the pandemic and government economic recovery/PEN programme may contribute to a more inclusive financial sector going forward. Lack of financial inclusion became one of the limiting factors for the massive delivery of government support at the onset of the crisis. Thus, the PEN programme that was initially delivered through the banking system was expanded to include other channels to allow the support to reach more people and micro and small businesses.

It may be too early to show the full impact of the pandemic and the PEN programme on Indonesia's financial inclusion, but initial findings show a positive sign that the programme can increase inclusion as more people are brought into the financial system. The chapter is organized as follows. Section 14.2 provides an overview of the Indonesian NFIS, while the state of financial inclusion in Indonesia is discussed in section 14.3. Section 14.4 summarizes the government social safety net and other PEN programmes and support to Micro, Small and Medium Enterprises (MSMEs) during the COVID-19 pandemic and their delivery channel. Section 14.5 assesses the potential impact of several PEN programmes on financial inclusion. Section 14.6 discusses challenges that may limit the potential impact of the PEN programme in improving financial inclusion. Section 14.7 concludes and summarizes the key recommendations of the chapter.

14.2 BRIEF OVERVIEW OF THE NATIONAL FINANCIAL INCLUSION STRATEGY

The Indonesian government adopted the financial inclusion policy to encourage economic growth, create financial system stability, support poverty alleviation programmes, and reduce disparities between both individuals and regions. Financial inclusion is expected to increase economic growth as low socio-economic groups of people would have access to formal financial institutions (World Bank 2021; Sirtaine 2022). Such access would ease their daily financial transactions (e.g., sending and receiving money) and allow them to save and apply for credit, thus accumulating financial capital and investment. Access to formal financial institutions would also avoid them from going to informal financial institutions that pose many high risks, such as high collateral costs or excessive lending rates.

Despite playing a crucial role, the effort to accelerate financial inclusion is not an easy task. In the early 2000s, most Indonesians are socio-economically excluded from the financial system. Efforts to accelerate financial inclusion become complicated because of the overlapping functions of the multiple stakeholders. Thus, as lessons learnt from other countries suggested, efforts to accelerate financial inclusion will require an NFIS to provide an effective instrument to map a clear and coordinated pathway towards improving financial inclusion. The NFIS will also enable stakeholders to work collaboratively and supported by governance arrangements and a monitoring and evaluation (M&E) system to ensure continued collaboration during NFIS implementation and the implementation progress is tracked and assessed (World Bank 2018, 2021).

The initiative to roll out the NFIS in Indonesia started in June 2012 (OJK 2020). However, the government formally introduced NFIS in 2016 by issuing Presidential Regulation (*Perpres)* No. 82/2016 on NFIS. The introduction of *Perpres* No. 82/2016 indeed accelerated and strengthened collaboration among government stakeholders involved in the improvement of financial inclusion. This is indicated in the transformation of several Government-to-Person (G2P) programme deliveries from in-kind to cash and transferred to them through the banking system (TNP2K 2020).

Perpres No. 82/2016 has been recently replaced by *Perpres* No. 114/2020. In the new *Perpres*, financial inclusion is defined as the condition where the Indonesian community have access to a full range of quality formal financial products and services in a timely, streamlined and safe manner and at an affordable cost according to their needs and abilities to improve their socio-economic prosperity. The provision of financial services is intended to cover all segments of society. However, particular attention is devoted to the low-income poor, MSEs, and cross-cutting categories, including migrant workers, women, people with specific social assistance needs (such as disabilities, neglected children, elderly), people living in remote areas, and youth and students.

The *Perpres* further defines three dimensions of financial inclusion, namely: access, usage, and quality. *Access* refers to the ability to utilize affordable formal financial services physically and cost-wise. Specific access indicators include the amount of formal financial services per 100,000 adults, the amount of ATM/EDC machines per 1,000 adults, and the number of financial service agents per 100,000 adults. *Usage* refers to the actual use of financial products and services, measured by indicators, such as, the amount of savings account in formal financial institutions per 1,000 adults, amount of credit account in formal financial institutions per 1,000 adults, amount of registered electronic money account in DFS, percentage of credit/financing for MSMEs to total credit/financing in formal financial institutions, and amount of social assistance disbursed by non-cash. *Quality* is defined as the fulfilment level of financial products and services that can meet society's needs. This is measured by indicators such as the financial literacy index, number of financial service complaints and percentage of financial complaints settlement.

NFIS achievement can be measured by the financial inclusion index. The index is referred to at least the proportion of adults who have access to formal financial products and services. On 28 January 2020, the President as the head of the National Council for Financial Inclusion or *Dewan Nasional Keuangan Inklusif* (DNKI) targeted the index to reach 90 per cent by 2024. To achieve improvement in the financial inclusion index of 90 per cent, NFIS will take various crucial agendas as follows:[1] *First*, improving access to formal financial services. *Second*, improving public literacy and consumer protection. *Third*, expanding outreach of the financial services. *Fourth*, strengthening MSEs' access to financial and other empowerment support facilities. *Fifth*, improving digital financial products and services. *Sixth*, strengthening integration between economic activities and financial inclusion.

To provide a solid foundation for the implementation of the agendas, NFIS has been developed based on five pillars: financial education, property right, intermediation facilities and financial distribution channels, financial services in the government sector, and consumer protection. It also refers to three foundations, namely, conducive policies and regulations; supportive infrastructure and financial information technology; as well as the effective organization and implementation mechanism.

NFIS's working scope and its priority action are adaptive to the market entry of new technology-driven providers. Regarding the payment system, for example, the 2016 NFIS only involved conventional payment service providers, banks and non-banks, operating under Bank Indonesia System, including Real Time Gross Settlement, National Clearing System, ATM card/debit card network, credit card network operator, electronic money issuers, and money transfer/remittance service providers. To expand public access to financial services, the 2020 NFIS has accommodated the updated PAFI 2020 (Payment Aspect of Financial Inclusion), including fintech (financial technology) and DFS which can issue electronic money. For archipelago countries like Indonesia where financial inclusion has been a persistent challenge, Fintech and DFS can become a solution for people that are not eligible for financing offered by traditional financial institutions.

14.3 THE CURRENT STATE OF FINANCIAL INCLUSION

Various surveys, including the OJK's (Financial Services Authority) National Financial Literacy and Inclusion Survey (SNLIK), the World Bank's Global

FIGURE 14.1
Financial Inclusion and Literacy Indexes

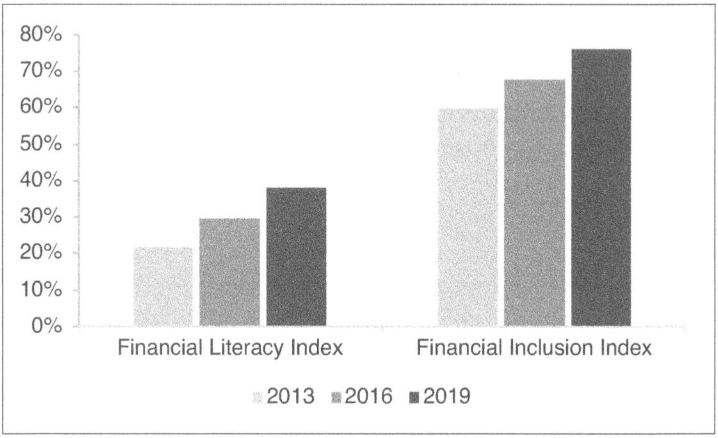

Source: OJK (2019).

Findex Survey, and the collaborative Kantar[2]-DNKI's Financial Inclusion Insights Survey (FII), were conducted to measure Indonesia's financial inclusion development. All these surveys recorded significant financial inclusion improvements in Indonesia over the last few years. The SNLIK surveys reported that in 2013, 2016 and 2019, Indonesia's financial inclusion index was 59.7 per cent, 67.8 per cent and 76.2 per cent, respectively (Figure 14.1). The 2019's index even surpassed its target of 75 per cent as explicitly stated in the *Perpres* No. 82/2016. This achievement motivated the government to improve its target to 90 per cent by 2024.

Improvement in Indonesia's financial inclusion can be represented by three indicators, namely, access, usage and quality.

14.3.1 Current State of Financial Service Access

Indonesia's ability to provide its people access to formal financial services improved in terms of physical proximity and cost affordability. Between 2014 and 2020 there has been a general increase in the numbers of financial service offices, ATMs, and financial service agents from both Digital Financial Services or LKD (*Layanan Keuangan Digita*) and Branchless Banking or *Laku Pandai*.[3] However, since 2019 there has been a slight

FIGURE 14.2
Access to Financial Services Indicators per 100,000 Indonesian Adults

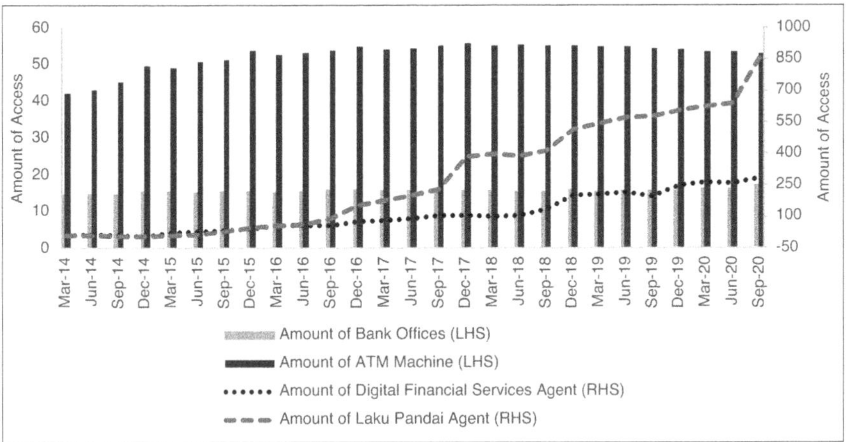

Source: DNKI Secretariat, December 2020.

decrease in the number of financial service offices and ATMs. The decrease in these two access indicators has been compensated by the considerable increase in the number of financial service agents (Figure 14.2). Have financial service agents taken over the role of financial service offices and ATMs in providing access for people to financial services? Unfortunately, there has been no strong evidence yet to answer such a question.

It was found that the geographical distribution of financial service offices and ATMs has been very uneven and heavily concentrated in Java and urban areas (Shrestha and Nursamsu 2020; OJK 2020). The higher the number of financial institutions in a region, the greater the probability of its residents accessing financial institutions. This explains why the SNLIK survey shows that the financial inclusion index in Java and urban areas is higher than those in outside Java and rural areas. The financial inclusion index in urban areas has reached 84 per cent, much higher than that in rural areas which only achieved 65 per cent.

The adoption of DFS could be a solution to compensate for less availability of financial institutions outside Java dan rural areas. However, challenges remain when the adoption of DFS tries to reach rural remote areas and distant islands. By surveying *Laku Pandai*, Nuryakin et al. (2018) concluded that the majority of *Laku Pandai* users are those who have already owned bank accounts and are actively using financial services provided by banks. They are mostly not categorized as poor people. This suggests that branchless banking agents have a limited inclusion function and only deliver complimentary service for those who already have bank accounts. This might be because the *Laku Pandai* programme heavily relies on the availability of communication services, which are still poorly available to many outside Java and rural areas.

To enhance financial inclusion, the recruited agents should provide financial services to people who live in remote areas which are not yet reached by banks. Unfortunately, Nuryakin et al. (2018) also found that most of *Laku Pandai* agents are located near bank offices and ATMs. Half of them is even located less than 1 kilometre from the nearest bank. It indicates that the bank fails to hire agents who live nearby remote areas or far away from the bank's location. As a result, the role of agents would not be maximized and in turn, could restrain the penetration rate.

This situation can be explained by the fact that remote areas usually do not have adequate information and communication technology (ICT) infrastructures. Therefore, banks tend to recruit agents in urban areas where financial access is not a problem. In dealing with such a situation, the *Laku Pandai* programme needs government support. The government should provide and develop much more ICT infrastructure in distant outside Java and rural remote areas.

14.3.2 Current State of Financial Service Usage

From the financial services usage dimension, Indonesia's financial inclusion exhibits marked improvement. This can be seen by the significant increase in the percentage of adults who own accounts at financial institutions reported by the Findex database in Figure 14.3. It increases from 19.6 per cent in 2011 to 48.9 per cent in 2017. However, Indonesia's account ownership is lower compared to Singapore, Thailand and Malaysia, and only slightly higher than Vietnam and the Philippines. Moreover, the inclusiveness gap is still considerable, and lagging compared to peer countries. The gap in bank account ownership between the poorest 40 per cent and richest 60 per cent reached 21 pp in 2017, only slightly better than in the Philippines. This gap in account ownership across different income levels can be attributed to the insufficiency of funds that inhibits poor people from having a formal financial account (FII 2020).

FIGURE 14.3
Accounts at Financial Institution (Age 15+ Years)

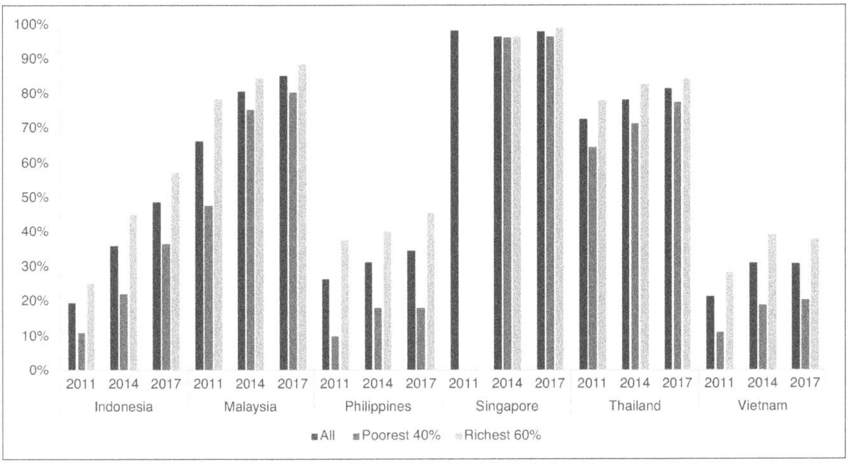

Source: World Bank, The Global Findex Database 2011–17.

Similar to the Findex survey, the 2020 FII survey pointed to an increase in Indonesian adults who own formal financial accounts. Between 2018 and 2020, the percentage of account ownership rose from 55.7 per cent to 61.7 per cent. During this period, the proportion of formal financial account owners in urban areas (61.2 per cent in 2018 and 66.2 per cent in 2020) has been consistently higher than those in rural areas (48.9 per cent in 2018 and 55.7 per cent in 2020). However, its growth has been faster in rural areas than that in urban areas. Account ownership in rural areas rose by almost 25 per cent as compared to 6.4 per cent in urban areas. Bank agents are one of the reasons behind this rapid account ownership growth in rural areas.

During 2014–20, other financial services usage indicators have also nicely progressed. The number of bank account ownership (third-party fund/saving and credit accounts), registered electronic money, and MSME credit accounts have increased over the last seven years (Figure 14.4). The most significant growth is electronic money, rising by around 9 times over the last seven years due to intensifying usage of electronic money in urban areas, such as OVO Cash, GoPay and e-money Mandiri.

Despite the increase in bank account ownership, the number of inactive accounts doubled to reach 30 per cent in 2017 (World Bank 2017).

FIGURE 14.4
Financial Services Usage Indicators per 100,000 Indonesian Adults

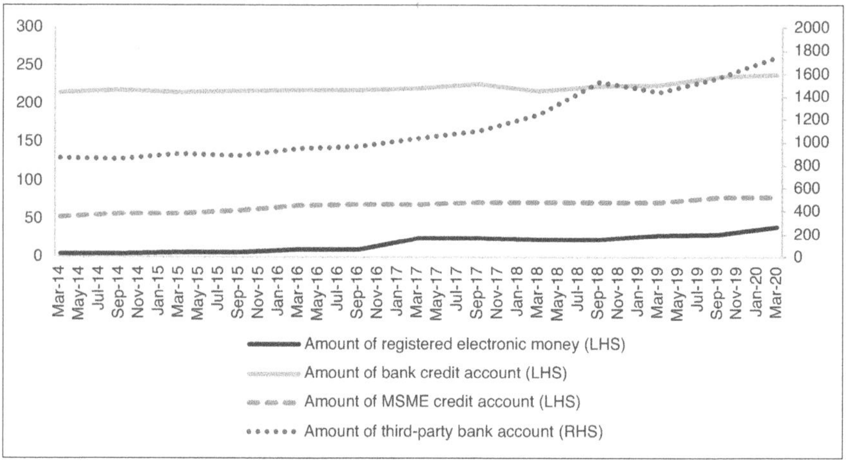

Source: Statistik Sistem Pembayaran dan Infrastruktur Pasar Keuangan Indonesia, April 2022.

One explanation for this phenomenon is people who have more than one account prefer to use their main bank account, especially if the other bank account is issued by other parties such as school, office or the government. Another explanation is the shift in the preferences of Indonesian people, particularly adults who reside in urban areas, to use digital payments instead of bank payments.

In Indonesia, most account owners have both a financial institution account and an electronic (mobile) money account. This is reflected in how people make electronic payments. Some might use only an electronic money account to make such payments, while others might rely on two methods using an electronic money account and using a mobile phone or the Internet to access their financial institution account. The rest might make mobile payments only by using a mobile phone or the Internet to access their financial institution account (World Bank 2021). Thus, intensifying the usage of electronic money could be leveraged to further increase account use.

The government's strategy to convert some of its social assistance deliveries since 2016, from in-kind to cash and transfer to the recipients through the bank system also contributed to the improvement in the usage of the financial services. By transferring its social assistance payments directly to recipients' bank accounts, the government "forced" the recipients to have bank accounts by collectively opening bank accounts for all beneficiaries. Between 2016 and 2017, the proportion of adults receiving government transfers into a financial institution account almost doubled to 41 per cent. Government strategy seems to work well as half of them were having a bank account for the first time as a requirement to receive government transfers (Shrestha and Nursamsu 2020). However, their complexity, particularly in relation to its business processes, the database used, and interoperability issue, makes this method currently not feasible to be adopted by all programmes. This suggests that in addition to providing infrastructure, simplifying the complexity of social assistance programmes is an urgent challenge that the government should handle to improve financial inclusion usage.

Improvement in Indonesia's financial services usage is also due to the government's efforts to pay special attention to the underserved group of MSMEs. The important role they played in the Indonesian economy, particularly in creating job opportunities and income for the poor, encouraged the government to implement various strategies to improve the financial access of MSMEs. These included introducing no-frills MSMEs owner bank accounts, creating financial identity programmes, supporting various interest rate subsidized micro credit programmes, simplifying borrowing procedures, and mandating banks to lend for at least 20 per cent of their total credit to MSMEs (Shrestha and Nursamsu 2020; Adam, Soekarni, and Inayah 2021).

These government efforts make the number of MSMEs included in the financial system and its credit amount continue to increase steadily over the last six years (Figure 14.4). However, these figures have not reached the desired level. Most Indonesian firms are still small and informal with the majority being unbanked and having no access to commercial credit from financial institutions (Figure 14.5). Much more effort should be devoted to encouraging small and informal firms to access and harness financial services. In addition to reforming and simplifying supply-side financial service arrangement, the government need to intensify its efforts to address the demand side of small and informal firms. These include providing adequate financial education and improving their production, managerial and entrepreneurial capacities. Without intervening in their demand side, small and informal firms will be unable to access and utilize financial services properly.

FIGURE 14.5
Percentage of Non-Agriculture Firms Having Access to Commercial Loan

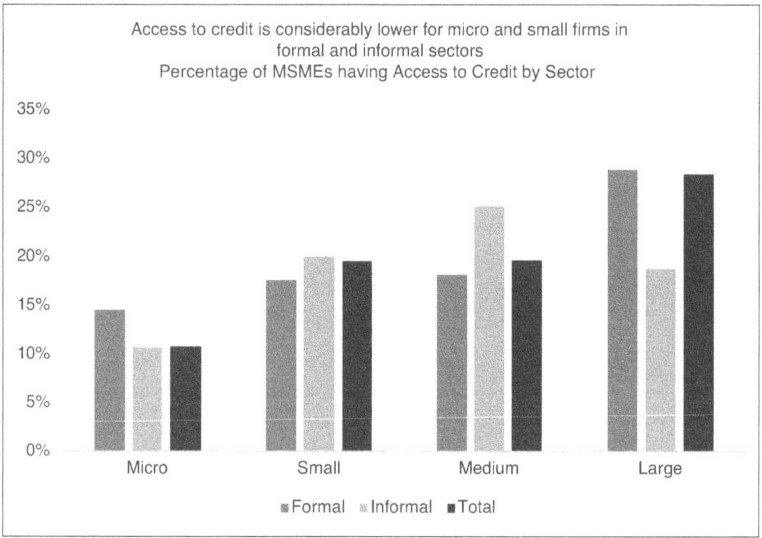

Source: Badan Pusat Statistik, 2016, Sensus Ekonomi 2016.

14.3.3 Current State of Financial Service Quality

During 2015–19, Indonesia's financial service quality dimension indicators also advanced. Complaints about financial services and the resolved cases have increased by about 50 per cent over the last five years (Figure 14.6). This indicates that the Indonesian people have enhanced their awareness to obtain better-quality financial services. This is consistent with an improvement in the Indonesian financial literacy index (Figure 14.1).

Although improved, financial literacy is one of the main challenges which could impede Indonesia from achieving its financial inclusion objectives. By referring to financial literacy data, the OECD concluded that financial literacy in Indonesia and the other twenty-five sampled countries are still low.[4] The average score across all participating countries is just 12.7 out of a possible 21 and 13.0 for OECD member countries only. The highest score achieved by any country was 14.8 by Hong Kong or 71 per cent of the maximum, and a minimum of 11.1 was scored by Italy (53 per cent of the maximum). Most countries, including Indonesia, scored between 12 and 14 (Figure 14.7).

FIGURE 14.6
Achievements in the Indonesia Financial Services Quality Indicators

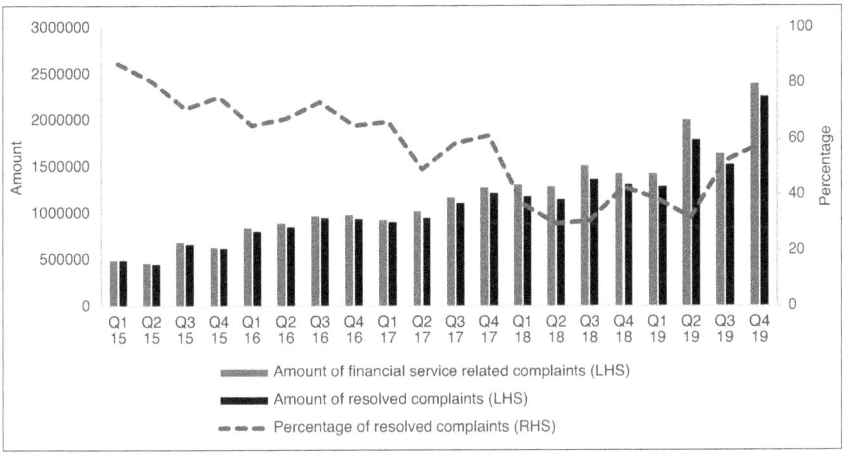

Source: DNKI Secretariat, December 2020.

FIGURE 14.7
Financial Literacy Score in the 26 OECD Participated Countries Survey

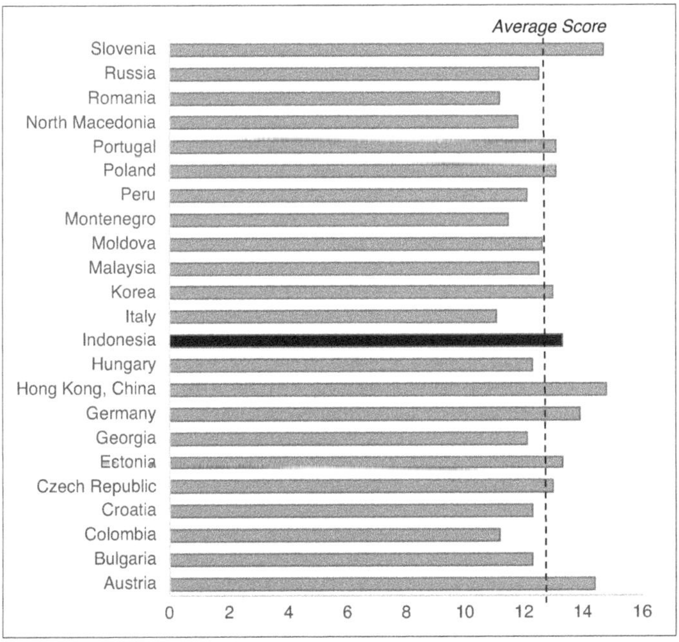

Source: OECD (2020), OECD/INFE International Survey of Adult Financial Literacy.

Indonesia's financial literacy score was 13.3 or 63.3 per cent of the maximum. In comparison with other Asian participating countries, the Indonesian score was lower than Hong Kong but slightly higher than Korea (13.0) and Malaysia (12.5). The fact that Indonesian financial literacy is still low is also indicated by the SNLIK survey (Figure 14.1). During 2013–19, the financial literacy index is consistently lower than its inclusion index. This suggests that financial inclusion has not yet resulted in financial quality. People who have been included in financial services do not completely understand how to use financial products/services for their own benefit.

14.4 SOCIAL SAFETY NET STRATEGIC ACTIONS AND OTHER PEN PROGRAMMES DURING COVID-19

The COVID-19 pandemic negatively impacted Indonesian economic growth which further adversely affected economic prosperity. To countermeasure the COVID-19 pandemic's negative effect, the government has introduced various policy initiatives under PEN (*Pemulihan Ekonomi Nasional* or National Economic Recovery) programme. A significant amount of spending has been allocated to support its PEN programme over the last three years. The PEN programme features a package of social protection assistance, labour market initiatives, and economic (fiscal and financial) stimulus which have evolved over the three years to address a range of risks across different vulnerable socio-economic conditions.

Initiatives under the PEN programme can be divided into two categories. *First*, existing initiatives that have been designed and implemented before the COVID-19 pandemic. These initiatives are mostly social protection assistance, including PKH (Family Hope Programme) and *Program Sembako* (Basic Food Assistance programme, and previously known as Non-Cash Food Assistance/BPNT). Depending on their existing business process, each initiative has its delivery system which varies from one another (Table 14.1). These existing initiatives have also been utilized to address the negative impact of the pandemic by expanding their beneficiaries to the economically vulnerable population and topping up their budgets. *Second*, new initiatives that are launched by the government as rapid responses to mitigate the negative impact of COVID-19. These include social protection assistance, such as unconditional cash transfer (UCT) as Cash Social Assistance (BST) and Village Fund Cash Transfer (BLTDD),

TABLE 14.1
Overview of PEN Programmes and Delivery Methods

Programmes	*Brief Description*	*Coverage*	*Benefits*	*Delivery Method*
		Social Safety Net for Households		
PKH	Existing family conditional cash transfer, targeting the poorest 20% in the DTKS.	Expansion from 9.2 to 10 million families identified among those already in DTKS per April 2020.	Increased annual benefits by 25% (equal to additional 3 months) and the increase was distributed in April–June 2020. The benefit was distributed monthly for April–September 2020, then reverted to quarterly per October 2020.	Transfer to the bank account in the KKS (Prosperous Family Card). The bank is assigned for each district/city, using the same bank as *Program Sembako* (BNI, BRI, BTN, Mandiri, BSI).
Program Sembako (Food Assistance Program/BPNT)	Existing food assistance programme, targeting the poorest 30% included in the DTKS. The benefit is used to purchase eligible food items in *Program Sembako's* e-Warung.	Expansion from 15.2 to 20 million households, identified among those already in the DTKS (April–December 2020).	Increased benefits of IDR200,000 per month from IDR150,000 per month (March/April 2020 – December 2020): • For existing beneficiaries, the additional benefit starts from March 2020 • For new beneficiaries, the additional benefit starts from April 2020.	Transfer to the e-Wallet in the KKS (Prosperous Family Card). The bank is assigned to each district/city (BNI, BRI, BTN, Mandiri, BSI).

continued on next page

TABLE 14.1 — *cont'd*

Programmes	*Brief Description*	*Coverage*	*Benefits*	*Delivery Method*
Prakerja	A pivot from skill development programme to include social assistance component targeting jobseekers, aged 18 or above who are not in formal education and not receiving PKH, *Sembako*, or BST. Launched in April 2020 and rolling out progressively.	Targeted 5.6 million individuals in 2020.	The benefits in 2020 are: training with value of IDR1 million (one time), post-training benefit of IDR600,000 per month (4 months), post-programme survey incentives of IDR50,000 per survey (3 surveys).	• The training benefit is transferred via BNI virtual account • The post-training benefit is transferred to the payment method selected by the beneficiaries (BNI, LinkAja, OVO, GoPay, or DANA).
Wage Subsidy (BSU)	Newly launched unconditional cash transfer managed by MoM. In 2020, the programme covers workers with a salary < IDR5,000,000 and registered on BPJS TK. In 2021, the coverage was changed to only cover workers with salary <IDR3.500.000, registered on BPJS TK and located in the area where restriction of mobility was high (PPKM levels 3 and 4).	Targeted 15.7 million workers in 2020.	In 2020: IDR1,200,000 per two-month for 2 times. In 2021: IDR1,000,000 per two-month for 1 time.	2020: Transfer to the existing bank accounts listed in the BPJS TK's enrolment, otherwise opened a new bank account in Himbara (SOE) Banks 2021: Transfer to the existing SOE bank accounts listed in the BPJS TK's enrolment, if not available, will be opened a new bank account in BRI, BNI, Bank Syariah Indonesia, or BTN.

BST (Cash Transfer Assistance)	Newly launched unconditional cash transfer targeted at families who are listed in DTKS, but not currently covered in any of the existing programmes (*Program Sembako*, PKH). In April–December 2020, BST is targeted at families outside Jabodetabek area. However, since January 2021, BST also included Greater Jakarta areas as a replacement for *Bantuan Sosial Sembako*. Initially BST targets households in DTKS, however, the programme also receives names from regional governments and ministries.	Targeted 9 million families (April–December 2020)	April–June 2020: IDR600,000 per month July–December 2020: IDR300,000 per month	Mostly cash based delivered via the post office, only 2 first batches via transfer to the bank account (for those who have accounts in BNI, BRI, BTN, or Mandiri)

continued on next page

TABLE 14.1 — *cont'd*

Programmes	*Brief Description*	*Coverage*	*Benefits*	*Delivery Method*
BLTD	Newly launched unconditional cash transfer using Indonesia's Village Fund (Dana Desa), targeting rural households, uncovered by Sembako, PKH, BST, and *Prakerja* programs, and affected by COVID-19. The village government has full discretion for the household selection	Target 11 million households.	April–June 2020: IDR600,000/month July–December 2020: IDR300,000 per month	Distributed in cash by the village government.
Assistance for Firms to Address Debt or Insolvency Issues				
Credit Restructuring	Government fund placement in banks to restructure credit for MSMEs. The placement of funds in banks is aimed at giving liquidity support to banks that undertake credit restructuring. Thus, maintaining banks' intermediary function, financial system stability, and improving economic growth with attention to prudentialism.	A total of IDR35 trillion was aimed to target MSMEs that are directly or indirectly affected by the pandemic and had good performance before the pandemic.	Reduction of credit interest rate, extension of credit tenor, reduction of principal credit arrears, addition of credit facility or financing, and credit or financing conversion into Temporary Equity Participation.	Through banks' credit payments.

Interest Subsidy	Interest subsidy aimed to ease the burden of businesses affected by the COVID-19 pandemic through the postponement of payment instalments.	A total of IDR34.15 trillion was aimed to target 60.66 million bank accounts.	BPR, Banking, and Financing Corporation disbursed IDR27.26 trillion. The benefits included postponement of instalment payment and interest subsidy of 6% in the first 3 months and 3% in the next 3 months for Micro and Small Enterprises, while for Medium Enterprises, an interest subsidy of 3% in the first 3 months and 2% in the next 3 months. KUR (subsidized credit for MSMEs), UMi, Mekaar, and Pegadaian disbursed IDR6.4 trillion. The benefits included the postponement of principal instalment and interest subsidy for KUR, UMi, Mekaar, and Pegadaian for 6 months. Online, Farmers, LPDB, LPMUKP, and Local Government MSMEs disbursed IDR0.49 trillion. The benefit included an interest subsidy of 6% in 6 months.	Through banks' and Public Service Agency's (i.e., *Badan Layanan Umum*) credit payment.

continued on next page

TABLE 14.1 — *cont'd*

Programmes	*Brief Description*	*Coverage*	*Benefits*	*Delivery Method*
		Financing Assistance for Firm		
BPUM	Newly launched grant for micro/ultra-micro enterprises affected by COVID-19 and not receiving credit programme. The application process involves endorsement from the Local Cooperative and MSMEs Agency (*Dinas Koperasi dan UMKM*), hence potentially covering MSMEs that previously had been unbanked.	Delivered to 12 million micro/ultra-micro enterprises in 2020, and 12.8 million beneficiaries in 2021.	August–December 2020: IDR2,400,000 per firm. June–December 2021: IDR1,200,000 per firm.	Transfer to the enterprise's bank account or, if not available, will be opened a new bank account in BRI, BNI, Bank Syariah Mandiri, or BPD Aceh.

and economic (fiscal/financial) stimulus namely, credit restructuring and interest subsidy.

The new initiatives and expansion of the existing PEN programmes were introduced to dampen the negative impacts of the pandemic on households and MSMEs. Earlier chapters mentioned that the pandemic caused a tightening of household balance sheets as household income dropped due to job loss or reduction in business revenue. From the perspective of MSMEs, the pandemic caused a spike in defaults on consumer debt, insolvency and credit tightening due to worsening access to financial loans during the period of high uncertainty. This chapter will focus on the PEN programmes that are aimed to address the resulting issues encountered by households and firms due to the pandemic.

14.4.1 PEN Programmes for Households/Individuals

Social safety net programmes were mainly used to address the tightening of household balance sheets or the drop in households' income due to the pandemic.[5] These programmes are distributed through two distinct channels, namely, bank accounts (including electronic money) and non-bank accounts (cash or in-kind). The PKH, *Program Sembako*, *Prakerja* and Wage Subsidy (BSU) are the programmes disbursed through bank accounts. However, because of time constraints, lack of bank account ownership, lack of digital identifier, lack of financial literacy, and lack of supporting financial infrastructure, BST and BLTDD are delivered through cash-based channels.

Examining each household social safety net programme, the existing PKH and *Program Sembako* assistance programmes were expanded to cover the economically vulnerable people due to the pandemic. Earlier PEN support for households struggled with inflexible targeting mechanisms which left the new-poor vulnerable since they were not previously eligible for existing support such as PKH and *Sembako* assistances. Hence, in May 2020, the PKH and *Program Sembako* were expanded to target the vulnerable new-poor population to receive conditional cash transfers and food as assistance (see Table 14.1 for details of the programmes). It should be noted that although *Program Sembako* is disbursed through an e-wallet in a banking account, the account cannot be used as a savings account. As *Sembako* assistance is disbursed specifically for buying food products, this delivery mechanism was one of the reasons for the selection.

Nevertheless, the account can be easily transformed into a basic savings account if the government would like to change it. PKH recipients, on the other hand, receive basic savings accounts that can be used like any ordinary savings account.

To cover those affected families that were not covered by existing programmes (PKH or *Program Sembako*) and not listed in the unified database for social welfare (DTKS), the government launched three new social assistance programmes, namely, BST (*Bantuan Sosial Tunai*, Social Cash Assistance), BLT-D (*Bantuan Langsung Tunai Desa*, Village Cash Transfer) and BSU (*Bantuan Subsidi Upah*, Wage Subsidy Assistance). Both BST and BLT-D are disbursed through the non-banking mechanism, which is through the post office for BST recipients and directly given to BLT-D recipients in each village. Time constraints, limited information on the prospected recipient and their bank account ownership, and infrastructure constraints have forced the government to use a non-bank mechanism to disburse BST and BLT-D.

For the BSU programme (which target low and lower-middle-income families who are likely to be affected by the pandemic) the government disburses the assistance using recipients' bank account. Recipients of the BSU programme are mostly formal sector workers who are registered as BPJS *Ketenagakerjaan* (a National Employment Insurance programme) and have salaries below IDR5 million per month. Although the BPJS *Ketenagakerjaan* database can be used to select the recipients, information on bank accounts still must be collected by coordinating with recipients' firms. Some problems arise when firms did not use bank transfers for the monthly salary, the nominated bank account is different from the recipient's name, or even an invalid or inactive bank account. For those cases, the BPJS *Ketenagakerjaan* collaborate with state-owned banks to open a bank account for the recipients at the firms. Another problem is the diversity of recipient banks which incur quite significant money transfer costs. In 2021, the coverage of BSU was changed to only focus on regions where mobility restrictions were heavily applied due to the high incidence of COVID-19 (PPKM levels 3 & 4) and for BPJS *Ketenagakerjaan* members who earn less than IDR3.5 million per month. To reduce the money transfer cost and administrative burden, the 2021 BSU only uses bank accounts from selected state and regional-owned banks.

Another new programme that aims to reduce the negative impact of the pandemic is the *Prakerja* programme. The *Prakerja* programme was initially designated for labour skills development through the provision of job training. However, the programme was pivoted to include social assistance component during the pandemic as the government needed to mobilize various channels to deliver financial support to the poor and vulnerable groups at the onset of the crisis. The *Prakerja* especially targeted support for those who were laid off or unemployed due to the pandemic (see Chapter 9 on *Kartu Prakerja* in this volume).

The special feature of the *Prakerja* programme which is highly related to financial inclusion is the freedom to choose the benefit disbursement channel. The beneficiaries of *Prakerja* can choose either one of four registered e-wallets or a bank account for receiving the post-training incentives. This flexibility is expected to increase the possibility of continuous usage of the account because beneficiaries have the option to select payment channels according to their needs.

14.4.2 PEN Programmes for MSMEs

During the pandemic, MSMEs struggled to fulfil their obligations, especially paying their credit (see Chapter 13 on MSMEs). The amount of MSMEs outstanding stagnates since April 2020. As expected, the number of MSMEs' credit accounts dropped (Figure 14.8). This leads to declining MSMEs credit growth both for working capital and investment credit (Figure 14.9). Against this backdrop, MSME support had been one of the government's concerns in the earlier iteration of PEN. The spike in defaults on consumer debt and insolvency triggered the issuance of credit restructuring and interest subsidy programmes through credit accounts (Table 14.1).

With regard to the credit restructuring programme, government fund placement in banks is aimed to restructure credit for MSMEs. The placement of fund gives liquidity support for banks that undertake credit restructuring and provide a stimulus for MSMEs' growth amidst the pandemic. A total of IDR35 trillion was aimed to target MSMEs that are directly or indirectly affected by the pandemic and had good performance before the pandemic.

Additionally, an interest subsidy programme was introduced to ease the burden of businesses affected by the COVID-19 pandemic through the postponement of payment instalments through banks' and Public Service Agency's (i.e., *Badan Layanan Umum*) credit payments, and the reduction of credit tariffs through government subsidy intervention. A

FIGURE 14.8
Number of MSMEs Credit Accounts

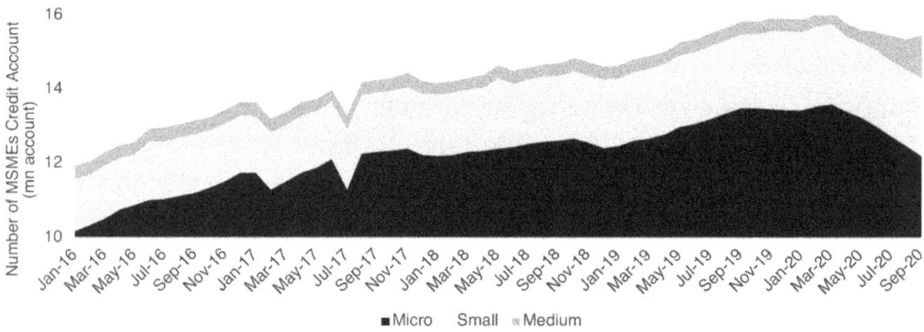

Source: Bank Indonesia, Indonesia Financial System Statistics 2016–20.

FIGURE 14.9
MSMEs Credit Growth

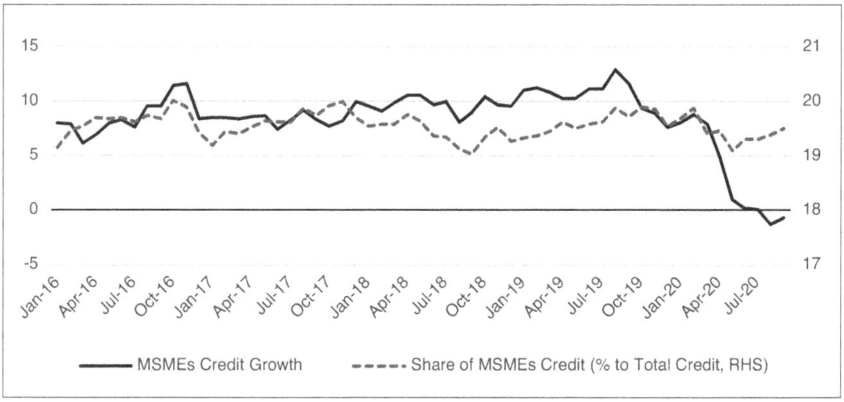

Source: Bank Indonesia, Indonesia Financial System Statistics 2016–20.

total of IDR34.15 trillion was aimed to target 60.66 million accounts of *Bank Perkreditan Rakyat* (BPR), banking and financing corporations, as well as government programmes (such as KUR, UMi, and local government MSMEs programme). Interest subsidy is particularly channelled through the KUR programme which is aimed at expanding financing access to productive MSMEs but previously unbanked, especially those with insufficient additional collaterals. Figure 14.10 shows that during the

FIGURE 14.10
Annual Target and Realization of KUR

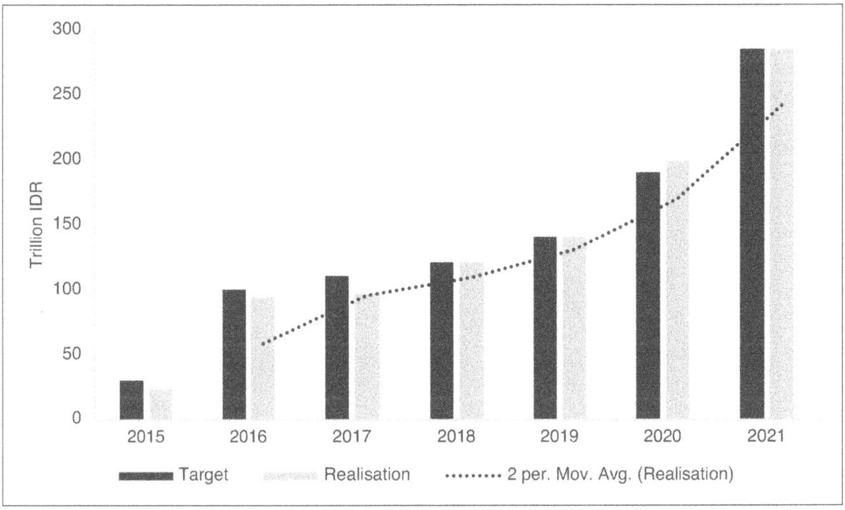

Source: Ministry of Finance, 2021.

pandemic, KUR budget realization significantly increased due to the national economic recovery programme.

However, there is a serious challenge for the coverage of fiscal and financial packages such as the aforementioned credit restructuring and interest subsidy programmes. Most Indonesian, including MSME owners, are still unbanked, while the packages are delivered through the banking system for those who already owned banking accounts. Therefore, these initiatives may have a limited outreach and exclude a large portion of unbanked people and MSMEs. This is important as the gap in bank account ownership is still considerable for the low-income population. Only 19 per cent of people in decile 1 has a bank account and 26 per cent of that in decile 4, noting that the bottom 40 per cent are the main target of social assistance (Figure 14.11).

To overcome this problem, the government introduced more direct support such as BPUM (Productive Presidential Assistance for Micro Businesses). BPUM was primarily aimed at encouraging businesses to adapt to and maintain their businesses during the COVID-19 pandemic, particularly addressing the issue of worsening access to financing and

FIGURE 14.11
Percentage of Population Owning a Bank Account by Decile

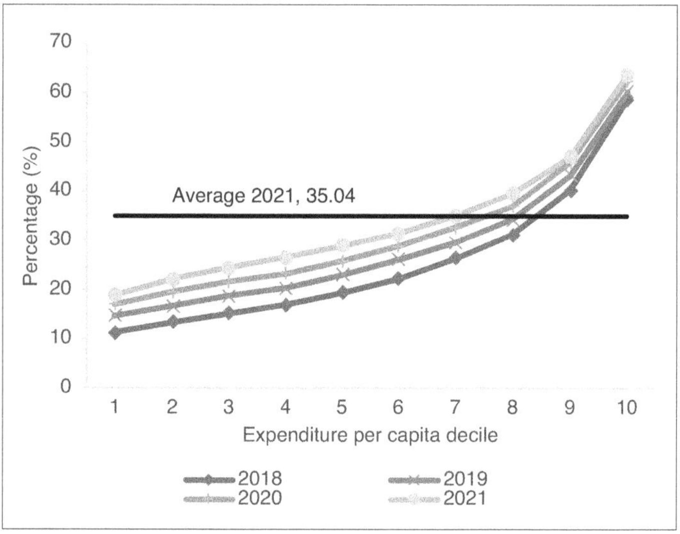

Source: Badan Pusat Statistik, Survei Sosial Ekonomi Nasional 2018–21.

credit tightening. The application process involves endorsement from the Local Cooperative and MSMEs Agency (*Dinas Koperasi dan UMKM*) and opening a new bank account for owners who did not have a bank account, hence potentially covering MSMEs that previously had been unbanked. It is expected that the new delivery strategy can reach a larger population. BPUM initiative is regulated by *Permenkop UKM*/ Ministry of Cooperative and SME Regulation No. 6/2020. According to this *Permenkop*, BPUM is the government grant for unbanked micro businesses that run businesses in which each micro business will be granted IDR2.4 million in 2020.

In the initial stage, BPUM would be disbursed gradually to reach 12 million unbanked micro businesses. However, its disbursement can only reach around 9.1 million micro businesses during the hardest-hit period of August–October 2020. The target of 12 million was able to be delivered in the second round (October–December 2020). In 2021, BPUM was delivered to 12.8 million beneficiaries to mitigate the severe impact of activity and mobility restrictions due to the Delta variant. Although this improved outreach and coverage of the programme, the benefit was halved from IDR2.4 million to only IDR1.2 million in 2021. See Table 14.1 for further details about the existing and new initiatives of the PEN programme.

By referring to their delivery methods, Table 14.1 indicated that several initiatives adopted a delivery system which could contribute to financial inclusion improvement. These initiatives are delivered through the financial system, specifically banks, which require their participants to open and have banking accounts. The next section (section 14.5) will investigate the impact of the PEN programmes on financial inclusion, specifically from the dimensions of access and usage.

14.5 PEN PROGRAMME AND FINANCIAL INCLUSION

The PEN programmes have the potential to improve financial inclusion due to their ability to accommodate the previously marginalized population segment from financial service, into accessing and using financial services. One channel that this may occur is through the opening of a bank account or e-wallet as a means to receive the benefits from the PEN programmes. To test such a hypothesis, this section examines the impact of PEN programmes on households and firms' financial inclusion, specifically on the access and usage dimensions.[6]

14.5.1 Impact of PEN Programmes for Households on Financial Inclusion

Most of the new beneficiaries of the PKH and *Program Sembako*/BPNT expansions are the poor and vulnerable population who had no bank account before the expansion. From SUSENAS 2020, we calculated that around 70 per cent of each of the PKH and *Program Sembako*/BPNT recipients who had not previously possessed a bank account (49,875 and 1,534,163 recipients, respectively), have a new bank account upon receiving the benefit up until August 2020.[7] During 2020–21 approximately 5 million new beneficiaries of PKH and/or *Program Sembako* have been given access to banking accounts due to the expansion of these programmes.

It also appears that the PKH is more financially inclusive compared to the *Program Sembako*/BPNT. This is due to the higher number of disadvantaged population groups (i.e., women, living in rural areas, low educational attainment, living outside of Java, poor household, and lack

TABLE 14.2
Characteristics of Financially Included People due to the PKH and *Program Sembako*/BPNT Expansions

Variable	*Percentage of Financially Included People Due to PKH Expansion*	*Percentage of Financially Included People Due to Program Sembako/BPNT Expansion*
Male	48.53	49.00
Live in rural areas	70.16	45.27
Has university degree (bachelor/master/doctoral)	0.60	0.75
Highest education attainment: senior high school	11.04	14.56
Highest education attainment: junior high school	16.84	17.55
Highest education attainment: elementary school	23.65	32.17
No schooling at all	13.52	7.92
Elderly (60 years old and beyond)	10.88	16.38
Disabled	6.02	4.03
Java Island	43.10	70.18
Poor (expenditure per capita below poverty line)	17.19	8.84
Poorest 40% based on expenditure per capita	72.76	51.89
Possess/has a good grip on using mobile phone in the past 3 months	34.25	48.22
Has used laptop/PC/tablet in the past 3 months	2.15	5.53
Has used the Internet in the past 3 months	34.66	41.37

Source: Badan Pusat Statistik, 2020, Survei Sosial Ekonomi Nasional 2020.

access to digital infrastructure) who shifted to possess savings accounts due to the PKH expansion programme in 2020, as shown in the Table 14.2.

Through the Wage Subsidy/BSU programme, BPJS *Ketenagakerjaan* and the state-owned banks (Himbara) collectively open almost 4 million new bank accounts for those who did not have an account in Himbara or those who did not have any bank accounts in 2021. Unfortunately, there is no information on how many recipients have bank accounts due to the programme. Nevertheless, the bank accounts will likely be used again as the government is planning to continue with the programme in 2023.[8]

Another form of social protection programme for households amidst the pandemic is the *Prakerja* skills development programme, which has been proven to improve financial inclusion through the usage of e-wallets. Based on an endline survey conducted by J-PAL (2021), *Prakerja* recipients

FIGURE 14.12
Impact of *Prakerja* on Financial Inclusion

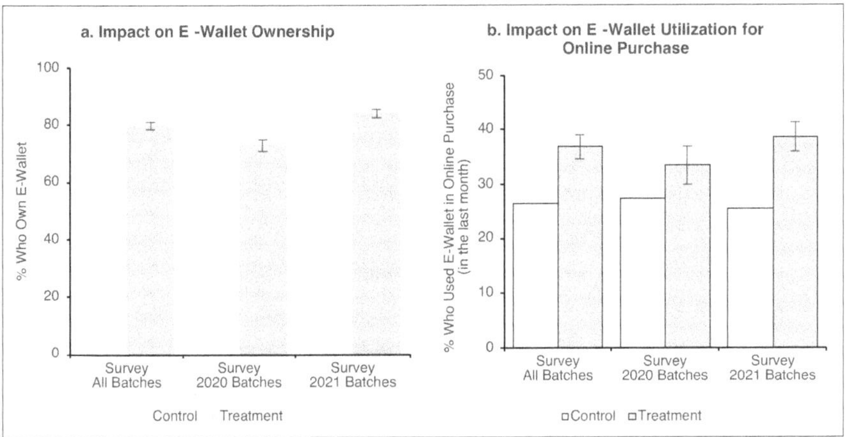

Source: J-PAL (2021).

are 27.8 percentage points more likely to own an e-wallet account. This is equivalent to a 53 per cent increase in e-wallet ownership (Figure 14.12a). Additionally, *Prakerja* recipients are 10.5 percentage points more likely to have made an online purchase with an e-wallet in the last month. This is equivalent to a 40 per cent increase in the likelihood of an online purchase with an e-wallet occurring in the last month (Figure 14.12b).

In addition, from Figure 14.13, it can be inferred that *Prakerja* recipients use e-wallets for several areas of financial and digital services, from transfers to cash withdrawals, and various types of payments. It is also shown that bank transfer contributes most to e-wallet usage, whereas credit undertaken through e-wallet is still low.

14.5.2 Impact of PEN Programmes for MSMEs on Financial Inclusion

The PEN programmes that are designated to assist firms through credit restructuring and interest subsidy may be considered as having the lowest impact on financial inclusion. This is due to the nature of such firm assistance that can be utilized and received only by firms that are already registered in the banking system. Nevertheless, these types of assistance help firms, especially small firms through the KUR (subsidized credit for

FIGURE 14.13
E-Wallet Utilization

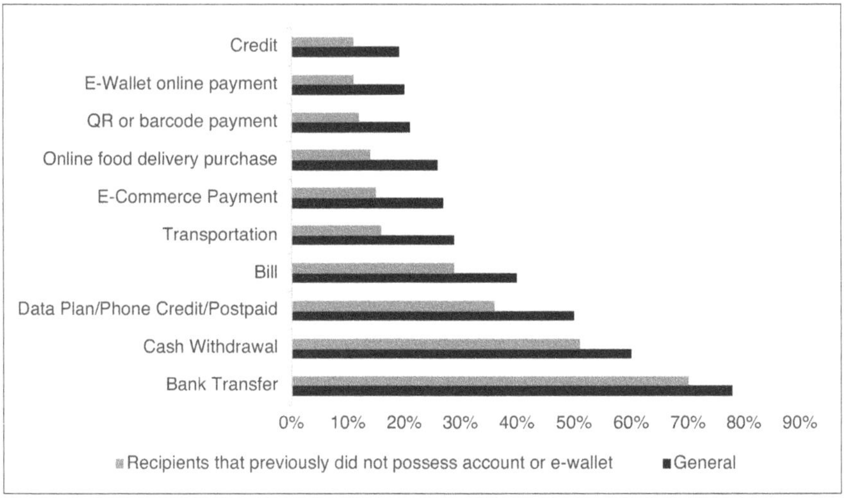

Source: Coordinating Ministry of Economic Affairs, 2021, Survey Insight of *Kartu Prakerja* Evaluation: Financial Inclusion.

MSMEs), in maintaining their credit from the risk of default during the pandemic.

Examining the change in loan disbursement before and after the pandemic, the PEN programmes through credit restructuring and interest subsidy programmes are proven to expand the government support to small firms. Specifically, while commercial financial institutions are reluctant to disburse credit due to increasing uncertainty during the pandemic (Figure 14.14a), the government's subsidized programmes such as KUR saw increases in credit uptake by MSMEs (Figure 14.14b). In addition, loans to MSMEs increased in the government-owned bank as the support is channelled through these banks, thus making government-owned banks the frontline for support delivery (Figure 14.15). These resulted from the need for business expansion in the effort for economic recovery during the pandemic.

In addition, during the pandemic, KUR added around 3 million new debtors in 2020 and 4 million in 2021. Figure 14.16 exhibits that the increase in the percentage of new debtors is followed by the decrease in the percentage of recurring debtors during the last two years of the

FIGURE 14.14
Share of Population (Self-Employed) with Access to Loan by Decile

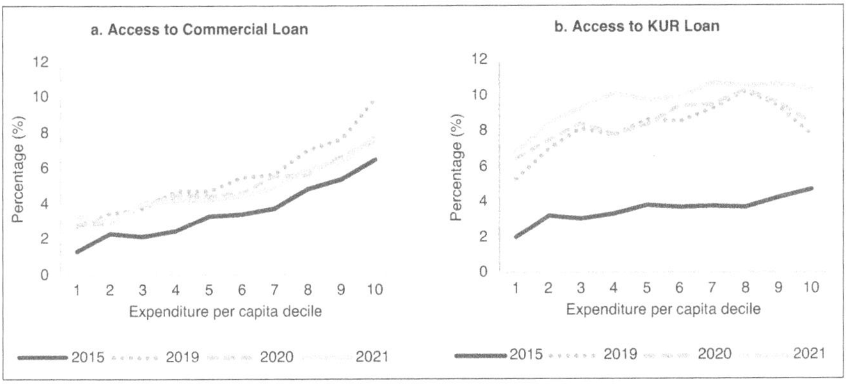

Source: Indonesia Statistics, Survei Sosial Ekonomi Nasional 2015–21.

FIGURE 14.15
Loan to MSMEs by Type of Bank

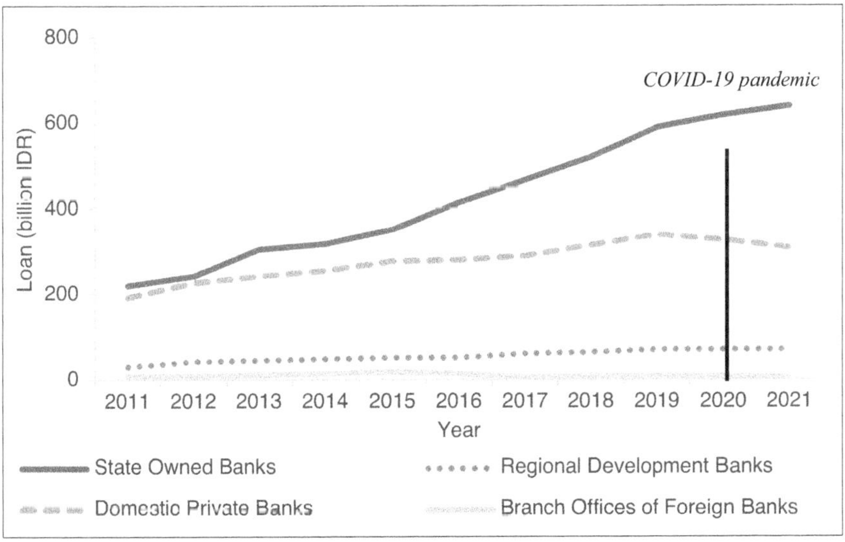

Source: FSA, Micro Medium and Small Enterprises Loan 2011–21.

FIGURE 14.16
Ratio of the New and Recurring KUR Debtors

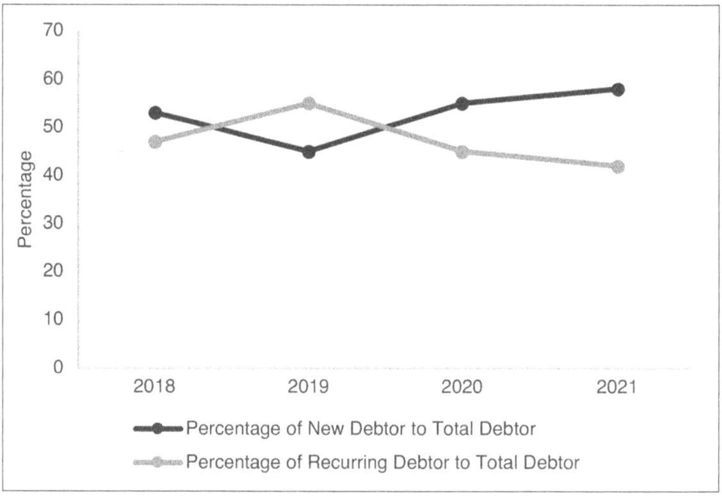

Source: Ministry of Finance, 2021.

pandemic. This implies that the KUR programme has better targeted and covered the previously unbanked MSMEs due to limited access to bank credit for financing. Additionally, this achievement also shows that more MSMEs are graduating and developing to become independent and can access other commercial non-subsidized credits.

Nevertheless, acknowledging the limitation of credit restructuring and interest subsidy to be financially inclusive, BPUM was introduced to address such issues and include firms that had been unbanked previously. The endorsements of small firms from proposers such as the Local Cooperative and MSMEs Agency and other financial institutions, facilitate the firms through all the registration processes in the financial institutions and eventually create a new bank account.

From a financial usage perspective, Figure 14.17 shows that BPUM increases the likelihood of owning a savings account by 16 percentage points (i.e., 30.83 per cent) and utilizing the Internet for e-commerce by 1.74 percentage points (i.e., 13.89 per cent). Nevertheless, BPUM only results in a small positive yet insignificant impact on e-banking utilization.[9]

FIGURE 14.17
Impact of BPUM on Financial Inclusion

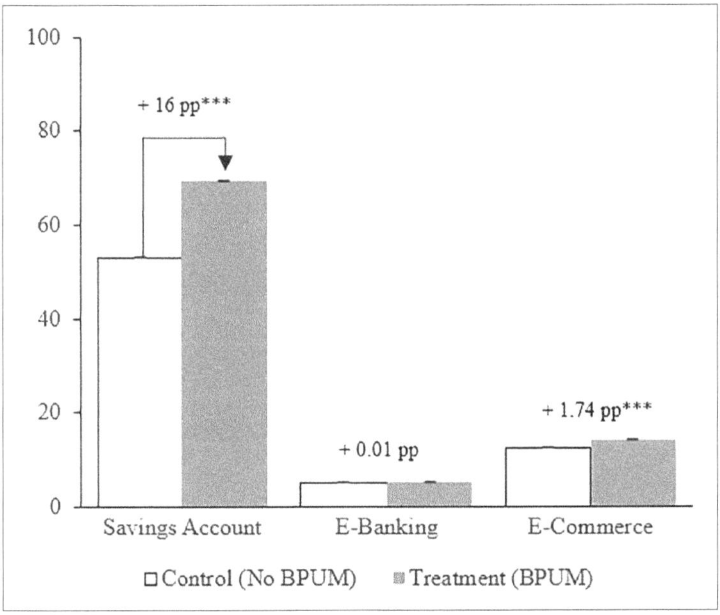

Source: Indonesia Statistics, 2021, Survei Sosial Ekonomi Nasional 2021.

However, from a financial access point of view, BPUM encountered several issues. In November 2020, it was found that the majority of BPUM beneficiaries (75.6 per cent) had successfully activated the accounts while there was still 8.3 per cent of the beneficiaries who failed to activate their accounts (TNP2K and Ministry of Cooperatives and SMEs 2021). As Figure 14.18 shows, the most common reason for beneficiaries failing to activate their accounts was a blocked account (61.9 per cent). A blocked account might be due to a blocking request from the Ministry of Cooperatives and SMEs to the channelling bank as the business field was not consistent with eligible criteria (i.e., civil servants, members of military/police, an employee of a state-owned or regional-owned enterprise), or the business field did not match with the format or was left blank in the application. The next most common reason was that the beneficiaries did not have the time to go to the bank (5.7 per cent). Additionally, 2.9 per cent reported that they were unable to complete the documents required

FIGURE 14.18
Reasons for Unsuccessful Accounts Activation by Beneficiaries

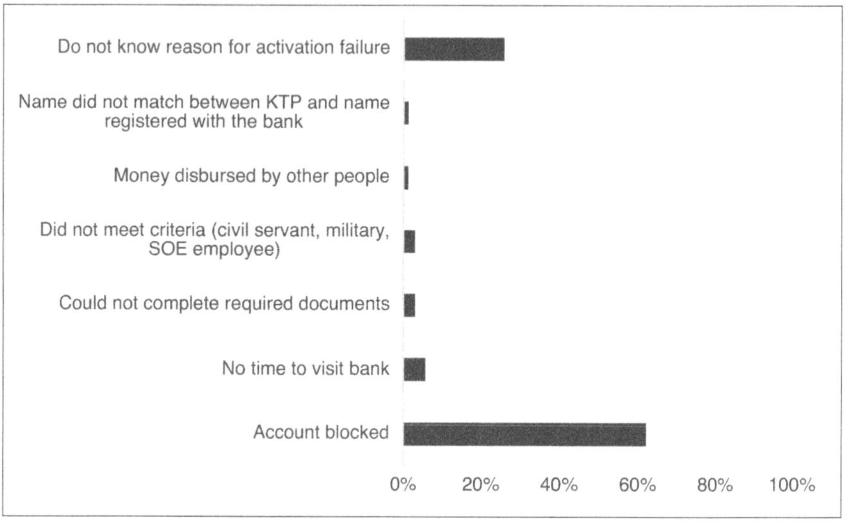

Source: TNP2K and Ministry of Cooperatives and SMEs, 2021, Sustaining Micro Enterprises During the COVID-19 Pandemic.

by the bank, while 25.7 per cent did not know the reason why they were unable to activate their accounts (ibid.).

In addition, although the disbursement of BPUM from the government's bank account to the beneficiaries' bank accounts had reached 100 per cent in 2020, 31 per cent of the beneficiaries had not withdrawn the BPUM funds. Those who had not withdrawn reported not receiving notification, not having time to withdraw the funds, and/or were still in the activation process by the distributing bank.

14.6 CHALLENGES

The essence of effective policy responses is to be designed properly, and they are subsequently placed into practice as rapidly as possible (OECD 2020). The focus of the PEN programme is to ensure the poor and vulnerable receive support immediately. The initial implementation of the PEN programme has limited outreach and potentially excludes a large portion of the population that has no account or outstanding loans, particularly at commercial banks. In the beginning, the lack of financial inclusion became a limiting factor for the massive delivery of the PEN programme. To address this limitation, the government expanded the existing programmes and delivered cash distribution via the post office and head of villages. The use of e-wallets was introduced by the *Prakerja* programme to allow alternative distribution of incentives. This is a good initiative as an e-wallet is easier to access and utilize compared to a bank account. These efforts in turn can provide opportunities to maintain and increase financial inclusion through the PEN programme. However, some challenges reduced the potential contribution of the PEN programme in improving financial inclusion, as discussed in the following subsections.

14.6.1 Poor Quality Data and Lack of On-Demand Application

The unavailability of reliable data to target programme recipients, particularly those who are currently excluded from the financial system, may impede the PEN programme from contributing to financial inclusion. As a unified database for the poor and vulnerable people need to be improved (see Chapter 8 on the improvement of BDT-DTKS), the Indonesian MSMEs unified database is not yet available. The poor quality of data might lead to various problems, including the exclusion of unbanked people and businesses. For example, in the first stage, more than 61 per cent of BPUM recipients came from financial institutions, including BRI, BNI, BPDs, BPRs, Cooperatives, and PT PNM proposals. Of this 61 per cent, the majority might have been included in the financial system, pushing other unbanked micro businesses untouched by the programmes. Therefore, the government should intensify its innovative efforts to improve the quality of data to ensure the targeted people and micro-small businesses including the unbankable can be reached.[10]

Another way to increase the effectiveness of the programme and potentially increase financial inclusion is to allow on-demand applications (ODA). Target people and businesses can apply directly to receive the benefit even though they do not have any access to the current system and financial services. The programme that has an on-demand application can facilitate the creation of new accounts to transfer the benefit. For the PEN programme, only *Prakerja* managed to provide this service to its potential recipients and received massive interest (see Chapter 9). Expansion of other programs to have ODA will increase the opportunity for unbankable recipients to access the programme and improve financial inclusion.

14.6.2 Limited Use of Digital Technology and Lack of Infrastructure

The use of digital technology to provide better public services including government support delivery was still very limited. Innovative programmes such as *Prakerja* introduced e-wallets to transfer the incentives to recipients, eliminating the requirement to have a bank account. This approach allows recipients to further utilize the money and contribute to the improvement of quality financial inclusion. Moreover, the utilization of digital technology will need acceleration of digital infrastructure development in remote areas to ensure equity. Poor information and communication technology (ICT) infrastructure is an important problem that Indonesia faces to improve its financial inclusion.[11] Developing ICT infrastructure to support the utilization of financial technology will therefore have a critical impact on supporting financial inclusion improvement. In the future, government support programmes should rely more on a fintech delivery channel.

14.6.3 Weak Financial Literacy

Although the Indonesian financial literacy index is improving, it was still considered low. The OJK's SNLIK (2019) showed that the Indonesian financial literacy index was around 38 per cent in 2019. The majority of people have insufficient knowledge regarding various financial products and services offered by formal financial institutions. Low financial literacy is even more severe among poor people which leads to low usage and higher risk of their bank accounts. World Bank (2020) found that nearly half of PKH beneficiaries still rely on others (agents, security guards) to operate the ATM. They also found that some beneficiaries withdraw the fund immediately for fear of losing the money. With the rapid advancement of DFS, people with a low level of financial literacy might face steep gaps and challenges. To this end, the government should focus on two critical actions. *First*, improving public financial literacy capacity in utilizing DFS through intensifying education of digital financial products and services. *Second*, strengthening institutions and regulations related to consumer protection. In addition, the government should focus on providing technical guidance on how to use DFS wisely and issuing regulations including personal data protection and consumer protection.

14.7 CONCLUSION

Considering that a significant number of households and small businesses are still excluded from the financial system, the government will not be able to reach the poor and vulnerable population if they rely on the existing social assistance delivery mechanism. Hence, the government expanded existing programmes and introduced new initiatives to allow the delivery of massive support to protect households and micro and small businesses from the severe impact of the pandemic-induced economic crisis. In this case, the government managed to address the limited financial inclusion state of the country, and arguably use the economic recovery programme to maintain and add more people to access financial services. Although it is a bit early to assess the full impact of the PEN programme on financial inclusion, this chapter found that the programme increases financial inclusion in Indonesia. Most of the new beneficiaries of the PKH and *Program Sembako*/BPNT expansions are the poor and vulnerable population that had no bank account prior to the expansion. The wage subsidy/BSU programme also facilitated the opening of new accounts for its recipients. The *Prakerja* programme shows a positive impact on financial inclusion through the use of e-wallets. Moreover, a government-subsidized programme such as KUR saw increases in credit uptake by MSMEs during 2020–21. We also found that although BPUM increases the likelihood of owning a savings account and utilizing the Internet for e-commerce, many recipients still encountered issues in account activation and fund withdrawals.

However, the impact on financial inclusion is limited due to various challenges laid out in section 14.6. Further initiatives to accelerate and improve financial inclusion through a government support programme can be achieved by improving the quality of data and introducing more on demand applications in government support programmes, using innovative digital technology to deliver the support as well as improving ICT infrastructure to allow more use of DFS and non-bank channels to reach more recipients, as well as improving financial literacy to increase usage and quality of financial inclusion. Adoption of biometric technology and other innovative ideas can also help overcome the problem of literacy and improve financial inclusion through a government support programme.

Notes

1. Detailed elaboration of each step can be found in *Permenko Bidang Ekonomi No. 4/2021*.
2. Kantar is the world's leading data and evidence-based consulting company providing insights and actionable recommendations to clients.
3. *Laku Pandai* is abbreviated from *Layanan Keuangan Tanpa Kantor dalam Rangka Keuangan Inklusif* (Officeless Financial Services to Support Financial Inclusion), the OJK programme for the provision of banking and other financial services through collaboration with other parties (bank agents) and supported by the use of information technology facilities.
4. The financial literacy score is a derived value that ranges between 1 and 21. It is calculated following the methodology described in the OECD/INFE Toolkit for Measuring Financial Literacy and Financial Inclusion and consists of the sum of three elements: (1) financial knowledge score (takes the range 0 to 7); (2) financial behaviour score (takes the range 0 to 9); (3) financial attitude score (takes the range 1 to 5).
5. Detailed explanation of the social assistance programme is explained in Chapter 8 of this book.
6. Due to data availability limitations, the "quality" dimension of financial inclusion is not included in the examination of the impact of the PEN programme.
7. The respective beneficiaries did not have a savings account in March 2020 and did not receive the PKH or BPNT in March 2020, yet in August 2020 they received the PKH or BPNT programmes. As the programmes' disbursement is transferred to bank accounts, thus we can say that receiving either PKH or BPNT in August 2020 implied the ownership of a bank savings account.
8. An important point to note is that the BSU programme creates a positive externality for the compliance and membership of BPJS *Ketenagakerjaan*. There were reported cases of firms that under-reported wages paid to the employee and ended up revising the reported wage that will be used to calculate the insurance premium. There were also cases of firms that under-reported the number of employees, compensate eligible workers who has not been registered to BPJS *Ketenagakerjaan* and finally registered all of their employees. In both cases, compliance to correctly report wages and employees seems to increase. The BSU programme also increases awareness of mandatory employment insurance benefits for those who have yet to register as BPJS *Ketenagakerjaan*

members, which is in line with government efforts at increasing social protection for workers.

9. We examine the impact of BPUM on several dimensions of financial inclusion, namely, savings account ownership, e-banking transaction and e-commerce utilization. We utilized propensity score matching on SUSENAS 2021 data by matching the BPUM beneficiaries with the non-BPUM beneficiaries by covariates: gender, age, lives in rural or urban areas, whether highest educational attainment is senior high school degree, lives in Java, own MSME, poor (expenditure per capita below district poverty line), possession of a mobile phone, laptop/PC/tablet, Internet use, has received PKH/BPNT, and whether has obtained credit from banks. The matching process resulted in 933,653 BPUM beneficiaries (Treatment Group) and 949,394 non-BPUM beneficiaries (Control Group).
10. It is worth noting that efforts to develop MSME unified database will take time. Alternatively, the government could utilize mobile phones (phone numbers synchronized with ID numbers) and e-commerce data (partnership with marketplace) to develop an MSME data directory. As a good start, a unified database on poor families (BDT-DTKS) already stored by name, by address information can be used for data supplement. BDT-DTKS recorded the occupation or type of business of poor families. It is estimated there are around 10.5 million poor families recorded as having a self-employed business.
11. Indonesia's electricity and telephony infrastructure is ranked 77th of 137 countries (World Economic Forum 2020). Estimates of its Internet usage vary considerably but, according to the WEF, only 25 per cent of the adult population uses the Internet, leaving Indonesia as the 109th ranked country in the survey on that criterion. Internet bandwidth is low, at an average of around 24 kbs per second, and the number of fixed broadband Internet subscriptions is equivalent to only 1.9 per cent of the population.

References

Adam, Latif, M. Soekarni, and Ika Inayah. 2021. "Indonesia's Ultra Microcredit Programme Financing Micro Businesses, Empowering the Poor". *Journal of Southeast Asian Economies* 38, no. 2: 263–80.

DNKI-Kantar. 2020. *Financial Inclusion Insight 2020*. Jakarta: DNKI.

J-PAL. 2021. *Kartu Prakerja Impact Evaluation: Preliminary Findings*. Jakarta: J-PAL.

Nuryakin, Chaikal, Prani Sastiono, Faradina Alifia Maizar, Pyan Amin, Nanda Puspita, Wahyu Pramono, and Christine Tjen. 2018. "Toward Higher Financial Inclusion Rate: Service Quality, Cost of Access, and Awareness". *LPEM-FEB UI Working Paper.*

OECD. 2020. *Coronavirus (COVID-19): SME Policy Responses*. Paris: OECD.

OJK. 2019. *Survei Nasional Literasi dan Inklusi Keuangan 2019*. Jakarta: OJK.

———. 2020. *Supporting Financial Inclusion for MSMEs through Fintech*. Jakarta: OJK.

Shrestha, Rashesh, and Samuel Nursamsu. 2020. "Financial Inclusion and Savings in Indonesia". *ERIA Discussion Paper Series*, no. 344.

Sirtaine, Sophie. 2022. *Financial Inclusion for an Inclusive, Greener, More Resilient World*. Washington: CGAP.

TNP2K. 2020. *Modernisasi Government to Person (G2P) Melalui Solusi Financial Technology (Fintech) di Indonesia*. Jakarta: TNP2K.

———, and Ministry of Cooperatives and SMEs. 2021. *Sustaining Micro Enterprises During the COVID-19 Pandemic*. Jakarta: TNP2K

World Bank. 2017. *The Global Findex Database: Measuring Financial Inclusion and the Fintech Revolution*. Washington, DC: World Bank.

———. 2018. *Developing and Operationalizing a National Financial Inclusion Strategy*. Washington, DC: World Bank.

———. 2021. *Lessons from Implementing a National Financial Inclusion Strategy: Financial Inclusion Support Framework*. Washington, DC: World Bank.

World Economic Forum. 2020. *The Global Competitiveness Report 2020*. Geneva: World Economic Forum.

15

Corporate Sector Performance during the COVID-19 Pandemic

Suminto Sastrosuwito, Abdurohman,
Anton Gunawan and Yusuf A. M. Sujono

15.1 INTRODUCTION

The private sector accounts for more than 90 per cent of the total Indonesian GDP and plays an important role in the Indonesian economy and employment. This chapter focuses on non-financial large and medium businesses which are the main economic drivers of the private sector. Non-financial large and medium businesses account for approximately half of the total private sector contribution to real GDP. Following this introductory section, section 15.2 describes Indonesian corporate performance prior to COVID-19. Subsequently, section 15.3 discusses the economic impacts of COVID-19 that appeared in multiple non-financial sectors during 2020–21. Next, section 15.4 zooms in on the impact by looking at how financial pressure on corporates evolved within the 18-plus months from the beginning of the COVID-19 pandemic, which was subsequently followed by changes in government objectives and support. It is then followed by section 15.5 covering how the Government of Indonesia (GoI) has applied an adaptive policy approach with a better understanding of the COVID-19 pandemic and its impact on both the global and domestic economy. The last section summarizes the discussion as well as gives a reflective discussion on past policies and potential future interventions. Additionally, two case studies on Value Added Tax (*Pajak Pertambahan Nilai,* or VAT) are presented to provide evidence at a micro level to support the discussions at a macro level in the previous sections.

The COVID-19 pandemic hit the corporate sector hard, especially in 2020, as public authorities across the globe implemented unprecedented measures to contain the spread of the virus. Restrictions on mobility and social contact, school and business shutdowns, quarantine and border closures brought the economy to almost a standstill. Sales across many sectors were plummeting as demand fell sharply. While financial commitments with respect to workers, suppliers and lenders remained, firms had to face abrupt and sharp reversals in earnings. This situation has depleted the liquidity buffer of firms across many sectors. The risk caused by liquidity shortages in the corporate sector rose and potentially affected the stability of the financial system.

The impact of the pandemic was, nonetheless, heterogeneous across sectors, depending on each sector's reliance on social contact and mobility. Stringent social restrictions imposed by the government to contain the spread of the virus dramatically affected services involving direct contact between buyers and sellers, activities in which people gathered in public places, travelling as well as non-essential sectors involving physical contact among employees. Meanwhile, business activities that could be undertaken remotely and those related to medical and pharmaceutical industries are benefiting from the pandemic.

The COVID-19 pandemic appeared to start to weigh on economic growth in the first quarter of 2020. The country's economy expanded at a slower pace of 3 per cent year-on-year (YoY) compared to the average of 5 per cent growth in the previous years. Since February 2020, high-frequency readings started to point to a slowdown. For instance, the number of holidaymakers originating from neighbouring ASEAN member states and other parts of Asia—which normally account for 70 per cent of the total number of incoming foreigners—halved from a year earlier. The picture deteriorated rapidly from March 2020 when the Ministry of Health confirmed the country's first infection.

15.2 CORPORATES PERFORMANCE BEFORE COVID-19 PANDEMIC

The private sector in Indonesia is classified into four categories pursuant to Law No. 20 Year 2009 regarding Micro, Small, and Medium Enterprises ("MSMEs") measured by annual revenue and net assets. The four categories are (a) micro, (b) small, (c) medium, and (d) large. Micro businesses are defined as those with annual revenue of less than IDR300 million or net assets of less than IDR50 million. Small businesses are defined as those businesses with annual revenue ranging from IDR300 million to IDR2.5 billion or net assets ranging from IDR50 million to IDR500 million. Medium businesses are defined as those businesses with annual revenue ranging from IDR2.5 billion to IDR50 billion and nets assets ranging from IDR500 million to IDR10 billion. Large businesses are defined as anything greater than IDR50 billion or IDR10 billion in annual revenue and net assets, respectively.

Despite most regulations consider medium businesses as an integral part of MSMEs, the complexity and nature of their operations make medium businesses more similar to large businesses when considering economic assistance. Therefore, the reference to corporates in this chapter refers to both non-financial medium and large businesses including state-owned enterprises (SOEs). SOEs play an important role in defining corporates in Indonesia. Mega corporates, those with net assets greater than IDR10 trillion, consist primarily of conglomerates and SOEs. Instances of mega SOEs include PLN and Pertamina which are the national electricity company and national oil company, respectively.

Corporates grew at a relatively slower compound annual growth rate (CAGR) during 2014–19 at 11.3 per cent in comparison to the overall economy at 11.7 per cent at current prices. Corporates contribute approximately 50 per cent of Indonesia's GDP or more than IDR8,000 trillion in 2019, primarily driven by large businesses. The GDP contribution of corporates was higher at circa 53 per cent of total GDP. Additionally, corporates are responsible for more than 7 million direct employment or 6 per cent of total employment in Indonesia.[1] Corporates predominantly accommodate higher-skill workers in comparison to micro and small counterparts.

Corporates' performance in Indonesia was considered to be healthy prior to the COVID-19 pandemic. Insolvent corporates in 2019 accounted for 8 per cent of the sampling which is significantly below the global trend of 15 per cent (Banerjee and Hofmann 2020). Nonetheless, the debt suspension case showed an increasing trend starting from 2015–19 which implies the increase in insolvency issues. New debt suspension registration was more than doubled in late 2019 in comparison to early 2015.

15.3 COVID-19 PANDEMIC AND ITS EFFECT ON THE REAL SECTOR

The detrimental effect of COVID-19 on corporates can be grouped into two primary observable phases: supply shock and demand shock in Phase I and Phase II, respectively. The shock to aggregate supply can be observed primarily in Phase I which occurred from January to June 2020. This supply shock appeared because business operations slowed down as a result of voluntarily or compulsory restrictions on activities. Subsequently, the shock to aggregate demand can be observed in Phase II, starting from June 2020 and ongoing as a result of changing consumer behaviour in response to the COVID-19 pandemic.

Indonesia officially fell into recession in the third quarter of 2020 as its GDP shrank by 3.5 per cent YoY following a drop in 2Q20 by 5.3 per cent. As the government started to impose mobility measures to slow the spread of the virus and people limited their activities to prevent infection, the transportation sector crashed. Amidst cancelled flights and grounded aircraft fleets, the air transportation subsector saw the sharpest contraction, at 80.3 per cent YoY in 2020. The accommodation service sector also experienced a 28.1 per cent YoY contraction following a nosedive in hotel room occupancy. Thereafter, albeit with a softening trend, Indonesia continued to record economic contractions for a full year (see Figure 15.1).

Early 2021 produced a grim perception of the job market and dragged down consumer confidence, in line with the plummeting retail sales and vehicle purchases. While the manufacturing industry saw a sharp contraction, the transportation and leisure-related industry were the hardest hit.

Driven mainly by the effect of a low base, GDP rebounded sharply in the second quarter of 2021, but the Delta variant outbreak dampened the recovering economy in the next quarter, before gaining pace in the last quarter. Theoretically, Indonesia has escaped the deep crisis, as its economy shrank by 2.1 per cent YoY in 2020 and then grew by 3.7 per cent

FIGURE 15.1
GDP Growth and Performance of Various Industries during the Pandemic

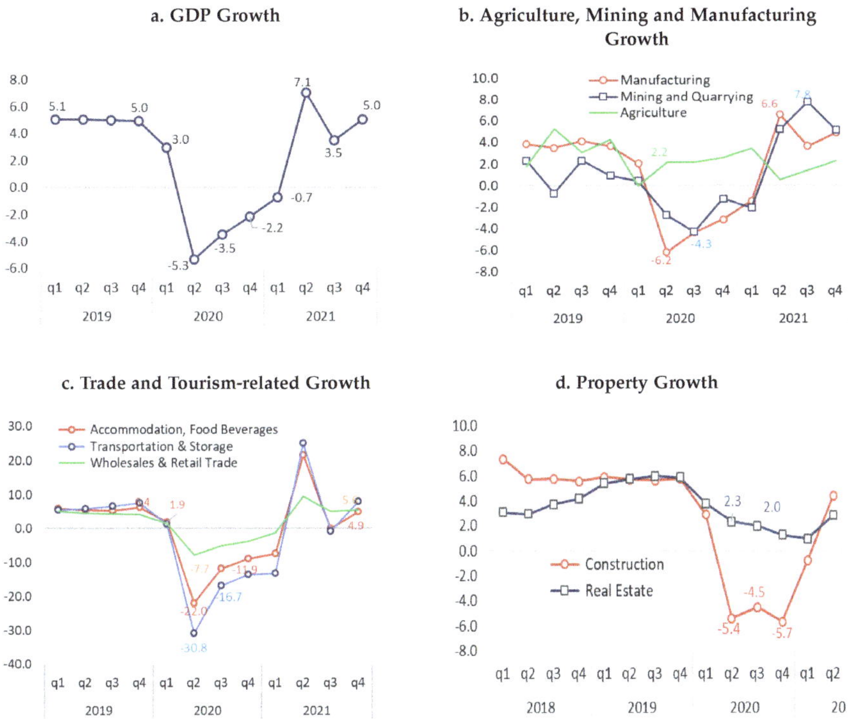

Source: Indonesia's Statistic.

YoY in 2021. Overall output already exceeded its pre-pandemic level by 1.6 per cent, which is relatively better than its peers including Malaysia, the Philippines, and Thailand, whose outputs remained lower than their respective levels in 2019.

However, the path to recovery was not uniform across sectors. There are sectors whose expansion accelerated and seemingly were not touched by the downturn at all. Some sectors only started to grow rapidly quite recently, either because of favourable global conditions or because of the role of government support. On the extreme opposite, output in several sectors remained low, a far cry from the period before the pandemic.

The sector involving human health and social work activities outpaced every other major sector in the economy since the start of the pandemic. The pandemic not only boosted demand for healthcare and screening services but also benefited the pharmaceutical industry. Compared to the 2019 level, the output of healthcare and screening services increased by more than 20 per cent by the end of 2021, while pharmaceuticals was just slightly lower. The pandemic also put the information and communication industry under the spotlight. But unlike the healthcare and pharmaceutical industries, the information and communication industries were already growing rapidly before the pandemic, expanding by around 9 per cent each year. Limited mobility forces consumers and businesses to accelerate their digital adoption, through the increasing usage of telecommunication networks and digital products ranging from schooling, health, entertainment, work-related tasks, and many others.

The mining industry is a mixed bag in comparison. The mineral fuel extraction industry dragged down the sector's overall performance because lower mobility translated into lower demand for energy. Its largest subsectors, covering petroleum, natural gas and geothermal, partly continued their pre-pandemic deceleration, in line with declining oil extraction. In fact, the last time its output grew was in 2016. Meanwhile, the coal mining industry went back to positive growth in the second quarter of 2021, aided by the trade diversion of China and the broader global energy crunch. In the second half of 2021, coal price had doubled from its 2019 average, incentivizing miners to ramp up production. A rather similar narration was seen in the mining of metal ores, particularly those related to basic metal industries. The sector's value-added soared to 47.7 per cent from the pre-pandemic level, a trend not seen elsewhere. Its downstream manufacturing subsector as well as the manufacturing of machinery and equipment also witnessed a similar pattern. In turn, metal-rich provinces such as North Maluku, West Papua and Central Sulawesi outpaced other regions throughout the past two years.

During the early period of the pandemic, the agricultural sector became the cushion for the newly laid-off workforce. As the job shedding intensified in certain services sectors in the cities, some opted to move back to their rural hometowns and worked as farmworkers. Yet during almost the whole of 2021 farm food crops declined, likely linked to the re-urbanization pattern as the economy of the urban areas started to recover.

Contrary to the agriculture sector story, the automotive industry and the vehicle trade only started to catch up in the second quarter of 2021. Fiscal incentives played a significant role in this development. Annexes 15.1 and 15.2 elaborate further on this issue.

The manufacturers of textile and wearing apparel as well as leather products and footwear—both employing a significant share of workers—did not fare as well as the automakers. In line with slugging domestic purchases of clothing, those industries lagged relative to others. However, the footwear sector has recently gained pace, thanks to the rising global demand.

Unsurprisingly, the transportation, accommodation, and food and beverages sectors ranked at the bottom of the recovery path. While the number of cargoes has helped the transportation sector, it has not been strong enough to offset the crashing passenger ridership. Similarly, the close-contact nature of the services of hoteliers and restauranteurs has spared them from full recovery even two years after the pandemic started.

One interesting observation in the diverging path of recovery is the inability of the supply side to catch up rapidly with demand. In general, it is easier for corporates to slash production when demand is falling than scale it back up when demand recovers. Even in the absence of new orders, corporates may still have to fund some of their commitments, including rent, debt, wages of core workers, and more. Those with shallow pockets or limited access to government assistance faced greater pressures to close their business entirely or even sell their assets, thus hindering the prospect to restart their businesses.

A series of surveys run by the Government of Indonesia, the World Bank, and PROSPERA[2] shows that after a year from the start of the pandemic in Indonesia, at least 8.2 per cent of all corporates in the country have stopped operating permanently. When the Delta variant outbreak hit the country, more than half of medium and large corporates said that their revenue remained below the pre-pandemic level. PT Matahari Department Store Tbk (IDX:LPPF), a national retail department store company, reported annual revenues of IDR5.5 trillion for 2021, only half of the IDR10.3 trillion revenue for 2019. PT AirAsia Indonesia Tbk (IDX:CMPP), an airline company, reported revenue of IDR0.7 trillion in 2021 which was only one-tenth of the IDR6.7 trillion revenue in 2019. PT Pakuwon Jati Tbk (IDX:PWON), a real estate developer notably managing several prime shopping malls in Jakarta and Surabaya, reported revenue of IDR5.7 trillion in 2021, 20.7 per cent lower than the IDR7.2 trillion for 2019.

In addition, the number of staff employed was also highly affected thus hindering the overall economic recovery. The Indonesian Stock Exchange (IDX) performed monthly surveys in 2020 with all its listed companies to explore the impact of COVID-19. The survey includes employment figures. Overall, large corporates lost more than 48,000 employees throughout 2020, a 5.1 per cent decline in employment level in 2019. Retail, automotive, and household goods sectors saw the biggest drop. The remaining employees were having adverse adjustments such as furloughing, hours reduction, and wage cuts. These measures were mostly prevalent in the travel and leisure, real estate, and chemical sectors. PT Astra Otoparts Tbk (IDX: AUTO), the largest Indonesian auto spare part company, admitted to reducing 4,829 employees or 13.7 per cent of its workforce. PT Tirta Mahakam Resources Tbk (IDX:TIRT), a wood processing company, reduced 92.5 per cent or 1,434 employees. PT Sarimelati Kencana Tbk (IDX:PZZA), the licence holder of Pizza Hut in Indonesia, saw a reduction of 831 employees or 9.6 per cent.

Data from Statistics Indonesia shows that the unemployment rate by the end of 2021 (6.5 per cent) remained higher than the pre-pandemic level (5.0 per cent), albeit improving from the second half of 2020 (7.1 per cent). The share of those working in formal jobs also followed a similar trend: 44 per cent in August 2019 versus 41 per cent in August 2021.

The permanent damage left by the crisis in the economy, dubbed the scarring phenomenon, spills beyond the business environment. In the real term, household consumption and gross fixed capital formation by the end of last year have not returned to the pre-pandemic level. In 2021, the average real GDP per capita stood at IDR40.7 million, slightly below the 2019 level of IDR41.0 million (0.6 per cent). Similarly, capital expenditure of large public companies included in the LQ45 index fell by nearly 13 per cent from 2019 to 2020, adjusted by inflation. By 2021, it remained lower than the pandemic level, widening to 30.2 per cent.

Like most countries globally, the COVID-19 pandemic has disrupted the overall economic growth of Indonesia and caused a deviation from projected long-term goals. The impact of the COVID-19 shock was tangibly felt and realized by most sectors especially those that require close human interaction. The mobility restriction resulted in a supply shock which was subsequently prolonged by a demand shock making it harder for the economy to recover. Twenty-one months after the pandemic began, economic recovery had not occurred equally across sectors. While commodity-based sectors prevailed due to high global commodity prices, the transportation and hospitality sectors continued to suffer. History shows that recession is useful to eliminate less-efficient operations and therefore, allow better resource allocation but the process is always a painful experience.

15.4 MONITORING FINANCIAL PERFORMANCE OF CORPORATES DURING THE PANDEMIC

Solvency and liquidity have been the two main financial performance areas of corporates observed during this crisis. Solvency refers to the ability of a company to meet debt obligations while liquidity refers to the ability of a company to meet the day-to-day financial needs of its operations. Understanding the latest solvency status is critical in anticipating the potential systemic effect on the banking and financial industry which may result in economic failure when large-scale problems occur. Further, understanding liquidity is critical to allow the measurement of financial pressure on corporates to ensure continuous payment to their employees and suppliers who are an essential part of the economy.

There are many financial indicators used to measure both solvency and liquidity such as quick ratio, current ratio, and interest coverage ratio. Unfortunately, these indicators only measure from a particular financial angle and do not necessarily explain the complete picture of a corporates' health status. Combining these indicators whilst minimizing financial bias appears to be challenging especially when comparing them across sectors as each sector has its own characteristic. The Ministry of Finance was assisted by PROSPERA in developing a six-point scoring model for determining and monitoring corporates' vulnerability quarterly by taking a sample of 395 Indonesian corporates. These samples are obtained by accessing publicly published financial statements. These 395 samples included total debt of approximately IDR2,500 trillion or 26.9 per cent of total domestic credit in Indonesia as of December 2021.[3]

The six-points scoring assigns scores 0 to 5 to determine the vulnerability of such companies. A score of 0 (zero) implies that such a company is in a healthy financial condition and can sustain its operations and debt obligation for the next 12 months without external intervention. Scores 1–5, in ordinal order, imply vulnerability with 1 and 5 being the lowest and the highest, respectively. This score is further classified according to the likelihood of default in the next 12 months. Scores 1 and 2 are labelled stressed corporates which are underperforming corporates that could be in serious financial distress within 9 to 18 months without external intervention. Scores 3 and 4 are labelled distressed corporates which are troubled corporates that will be in serious financial distress in less than 9 months without external intervention. Score 5 is labelled insolvent corporates which are damaged corporates whose business operations barely have sustainable going concerns in the next 24 months or more.

The scoring is determined by evaluating the latest financial performance of a company based on multiple dimensions. Evaluated financial dimensions include profitability, liquidity, and solvency. First, profitability is measured by reviewing revenue and Net Operating Profit After Tax (NOPAT). Second, liquidity is measured by reviewing cash from operations and working capital ratios. Last, solvency is measured by reviewing Debt-to-Equity Ratio (DER) and Debt Service Coverage Ratio (DSCR).

In addition to historical performance evaluation, stress testing financial projection for the next 12 months of performance is performed. Revenue and exchange rate shocks are performed to understand the ability of such a company to sustain amid these shocks.

Figure 15.2 depicts the movement in the number of vulnerable corporates and the respective Debt at Risk (DaR) of 395 corporate sampled from their December 2019 position to December 2021 position. DaR refers to aggregated interest bearing-debt possessed by vulnerable corporates. The following paragraphs elaborate more on key observations.

First of all, it is observed that many Indonesian corporates had already been under financial pressure as of December 2019 (or prior to the COVID-19 pandemic). Stable, stressed, distressed, and insolvent corporates were 203, 110, 51, and 31, respectively. 192 vulnerable corporates (or 49 per cent of total samples) accounted for IDR603 trillion debt or 28 per cent of the total debt of the samples. This number was rising when compared to a year earlier.

Next, financial pressure built gradually over the next 9 months following voluntarily and compulsory mobility restrictions arising from COVID-19 which harmed productivity and significantly lowered revenue. 57 per cent of those sampled or 224 corporates fell into vulnerable categories as of September 2020. DaR jumped to IDR988 trillion or 40 per cent of the total debt of the samples. DaR was built rapidly from hospitality, transportation, and real estate corporates that were hit hardest by mobility restrictions. 2020 also saw a series of defaults of delayed payments from notable corporates including SOEs. Instances are (a) Garuda Indonesia

FIGURE 15.2
Quarterly Movement of Vulnerable Corporates and Debt at Risk from December 2019 to December 2021

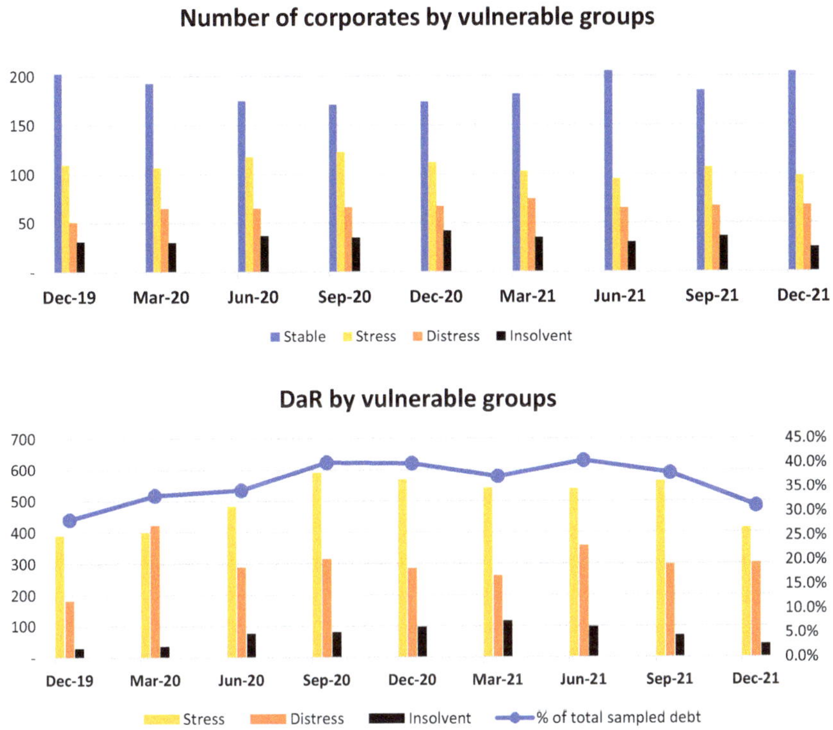

(IDX:GIAA) underwent a hard restructuring of a US$500 million global bond in July 2020, (b) Perum Perumnas delayed IDR200 billion bonds payment in April 2020, and (c) PT Modernland Realty Tbk (IDX:MDLN) defaulted on IDR150 billion bonds in July 2020.

Recovery returned in the fourth quarter of 2020 but progress was slow. Despite a number of vulnerable companies returning to the pre-pandemic level in June 2021, it rapidly increased in September 2021 due to mobility restrictions before decreasing again in December 2021. Furthermore, DaR is still high at IDR757 billion or 31 per cent of the total debt of the samples. Economic recovery in the fourth quarter of 2020 and the first semester of 2021 were wiped out by mobility restrictions in July 2021 due to a new wave of Delta variant of COVID-19. 2021 saw more corporates defaulting including (a) PT Sri Rejeki Isman Tbk (IDX:SRIL) defaulting on a IDR12.1 billion interest payment on a US$350 million syndicated loan in April 2021, (b) PT Tridomain Performance Materials Tbk (IDX:TDPM) defaulting IDR410 billion in May 2021, and (c) PT Indah Karya (Persero) defaulting on the interest due on an IDR150 billion bond.

Recovery did not occur equally across sectors. Twenty-one months after the appearance of COVID-19 in Indonesia, aggregate revenue levels of (a) travel and leisure, (b) transportation, and (c) construction significantly remain below the pre-pandemic level. The aggregate annual revenue of travel and leisure samples as of December 2021 is greater than 90 per cent below 2019 performance. On the other hand, (a) palm oil, (b) healthcare, and (c) chemicals were thriving. Our samples in these sectors reported increases in aggregate revenue of 21–56 per cent during the same period.

Despite DaR jumping significantly in the aftermath of COVID-19, overall pressure on local banks is mild since (a) significant amounts are in offshore loans, (b) onshore loans are predominantly local currency denominated, and (c) DaR exposure in each bank can be covered by the capital of the respective bank. First, 30–40 per cent of the DaR is offshore reducing pressure on local banks and financial institutions. Next, more than 80 per cent of DaR is denominated in Indonesian rupiah implying low foreign exchange pressure. Finally, most banks have sufficient capital adequacy ratio (CAR) levels as required by the government implying banking stability in manoeuvring for the DaR shock.

Supply shock and demand shock arising from the COVID-19 pandemic have exacerbated corporate vulnerability. Prior to the COVID-19 pandemic, insolvent corporates accounted for 8 per cent of the samples which is significantly below the global trend of 15 per cent, and therefore, is considered at healthy levels (Banerjee and Hofmann 2020). Nonetheless, corporate vulnerability is not a clear black-and-white state. Grey areas exist between stable and insolvent corporates. Stressed and distressed corporates, which represent the grey areas, were in constant need of external financing to support their operations. These corporates were very prone to economic shock particularly when financing is tight. These segments were also amongst the hardest to recover as they would require significant cash support to rebuild capacity and sustain operations. Despite many of them being profitable companies, they experienced negative cash flow. These segments should be monitored regularly even in the aftermath of this crisis in order to understand private sector vulnerability and employment security. Profit is important but at the end of the day, cash is king.

15.5 POLICY EFFECTIVENESS (FISCAL AND COORDINATED POLICIES) AND EXIT STRATEGIES

Overall, government support for corporates can be grouped into two main measures, namely (a) expenses relief (*dukungan usaha*) and (b) corporate financing. Expenses relief refers to various fiscal waivers provided for corporates to reduce expenses whilst corporate financing refers to various financing support and guarantees provided to tackle corporate solvency. Throughout the process, the GoI also had to maintain an appropriate balance between spending and fiscal capacity as well as between solvency support and potential systemic risk.

Given the dynamics of the COVID-19 pandemic, the government support to corporates went through some changes, both in terms of the scheme and sectoral coverage. Government supports towards corporates during the COVID-19 pandemic was designed according to the targeted economic objectives. In the early period of the pandemic, the government objectives were to save lives and sustain jobs. The GoI provided expenses relief support such as (a) individual income tax (PPh 21), (b) corporate income tax (PPh 25), (c) accelerated VAT restitution, (d) import income tax (PPh 22 for imports), (e) loan restructuring, (f) pension subsidies, (g) wage subsidies (see also Chapter 7 for more detailed discussion on tax incentives).

In terms of sectoral coverage, the manufacturing industry was considered the most affected sector and had received tax incentives from the government through PMK 23/PMK.03/2020 by 21 March 2020 in the early stage of the pandemic. Along the way, more sectors were included in the scheme prompting the government to amend the regulation on 27 April 2020. As the pandemic evolved with more severe cases triggered by the Delta variant, the government expanded the sectors included in the scheme as well as extended the eligibility period while also simplifying the delivery procedures to speed up the execution of the support programmes to corporates. This incentive cost IDR55.4 trillion and IDR67.6 trillion in 2020 and 2021, respectively. On top of those incentives, the government support for MSMEs and corporates cost around IDR173.0 trillion in 2020 and IDR116.2 trillion in 2021, which among others is a credit guarantee to SMEs and corporates.

The Longitudinal Business Survey found that around two-thirds of all corporates had received at least one type of government support since the crisis began (Table 15.1). If we look at the distribution across sectors, the gap is not apparent. However, there is a stark difference if we zoom in on the size of the enterprise. The share of medium and large corporates that received assistance outnumbered those smaller entities. We also note that this finding is consistent with the figures from the previous rounds of the survey.

One main reason is that medium and large corporates—which tend to have a greater share of formal businesses amongst them—are offered a greater variety of government support. For example, workers registered by their companies in the mandatory pension programme can access wage subsidies. As smaller corporates are likely to be informal, they could not enjoy this assistance. Similarly, only formal business entities can tap into the various tax incentive schemes.

Several months into the pandemic, the government's objective shifted to minimizing the hysteresis effect to allow speedy recovery post-pandemic.

TABLE 15.1
Percentage of Corporates That Have Received Government Support

	Share (August 2021 Survey)
Total	66%
Based on Size	
Micro	65%
Small	59%
Medium and Large	80%
Based on Sector	
Mining	63%
Manufacturing	68%
Trade	66%
Tourism	64%
Services	67%

Notes: Supports include BPUM, electricity fee waiver, loan restructuring, interest rate subsidy, tax incentives, wage subsidy, BPJS-*Tenagakerja* subsidy, and household support.
Source: Ministry of Finance.

The Financial System Stability Committee (FSSC, or *Komite Stabilitas Sistem Keuangan*), which consists of (a) the Ministry of Finance, (b) Bank of Indonesia (BI or the central bank), and (c) the Financial Service Authority (FSA, or *Otoritas Jasa Keuangan*), coordinated and concerted financing policies to tackle solvency issues in corporates. FSSC formulated Law No. 2 Year 2020 regarding Fiscal and Financial System Stability Policies in Tackling the COVID-19 Pandemic. While the fiscal policy was focused on tackling the COVID-19 pandemic and cushioning its impact on society, the monetary and financial sector policies were provided to help easing financial distress in corporate sectors. BI lowered policy rates and reserve requirement ratio to give easier and cheaper access to fund while also providing support to government financing through the burden sharing scheme. On the other side, FSA relaxed several regulations on assessment of credit quality as well as credit restructuring. Deposit guarantee rates were also lowered by Indonesia Deposit Insurance Corporation (IDIC, or *Lembaga Penjamin Simpanan*) to ease the cost of funds further. A credit guarantee scheme was also initiated by the government in 2020 and directed at both large corporates and SMEs to increase the willingness of banks to channelling loans to both large corporates and SMEs to sustain their business. These measures cost the GoI IDR60.7 trillion in 2020 primarily for capital injection and loans to SOEs amounting to IDR58.7 trillion or 96.7 per cent of total corporate financing.

Additionally, the Minister of Finance issued Regulation No. 98/PMK.08/2020 dated 28 July 2020 which was later amended through Regulation No. 32/PMK.08/2021 dated 1 April 2021 regarding government guarantee for corporates. These guarantees had a greater impact in 2021 when the GoI provided IDR5.2 trillion and IDR8.2 trillion of working capital guarantees for 68 corporates and 1 SOE, respectively. These corporates employed more than 153,000 people in 2021.

The corporate financing measures appeared to be more meaningful in helping corporates avoid bankruptcies and therefore, minimize the scarring effect. As depicted in Figure 15.3, bankruptcy registrations in Indonesia increased in early 2021 but overall remained relatively stable compared to historical performance. On the other hand, debt suspension cases rose significantly commencing in June 2020 and subsequently declined in the second quarter of 2021.

Coordinated policies in 2021 were formulated based on the sectoral mapping classified into three different sectors: (a) resilient, (b) growth driver

FIGURE 15.3
Movement of New Registration of (a) Bankruptcy and (b) Debt Suspension Cases from March 2015 to December 2021

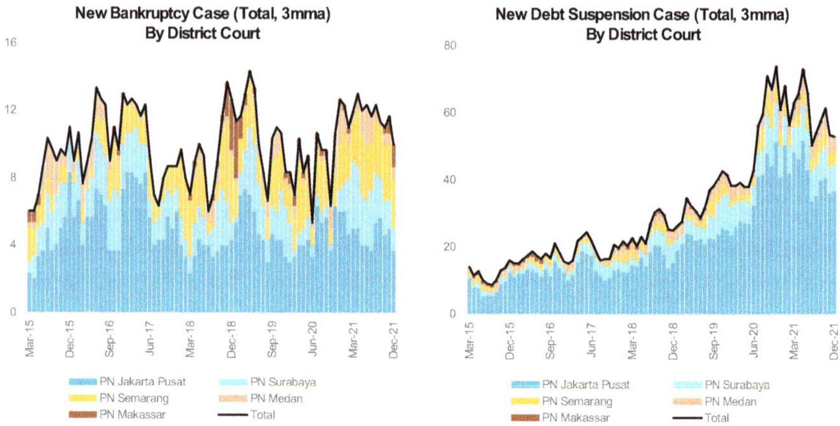

Source: KSSK.

and (c) slow starter.[4] Support measures under the coordinated policy mix can be categorized into two broad policies: (i) cross-cutting policies aimed at helping specific sectors, and (ii) a stand-alone policy by each member institution applied to all sectors. Supports to the property and automotive industry are the two most prominent cross-cutting policies initiated under the coordinated policy mix. The property sector is considered an important sector with a high multiplier effect and job creation. Thus, providing comprehensive and integrated support to the property sector is crucial. Under the coordinated policy mix, fiscal support is given through the VAT exemption, while on the macroprudential policy, BI relaxes the loan to value (LTV) ratio. Lastly, FSA provided relaxation on (a) risk-weighted assets, (b) insurance premium rate, and (c) down payment on financing institutions. Similar incentives were also provided to the automotive industry which was the exemption of VAT on luxury goods.

Additionally, loan/financing restructuring data of both banking and financing companies as of 2021 demonstrates that many corporates were still desperately in need of cash. Overall restructured loan/financing declined in 2021 as banks applied tighter loan policies. Overall restructured loan/financing in 2021 decreased by 9.7 per cent and by 17.4 per cent in terms of the number of debtors when compared to 2020. Nonetheless, loan/financing restructuring remained high in 2021 primarily contributed by increases in financing companies. Restructured loan/financing by financing companies increased by 47.3 per cent and 5.4 per cent in terms of value and number of debtors, respectively. Average loan value/debtor increased sharply in all categories in 2021. This fact demonstrates that many debtors, especially those who have limited access to financing from banks, have been shifting away to less stringent institutions to obtain financing solutions at even higher cost such as financing companies. Corporates are no exception. A detailed breakdown is presented in Table 15.2. Given that vulnerability of corporates remains higher than at its pre-pandemic level, the Ministry of Finance continues to monitor corporate performance regularly before deciding to revoke any government support. In contrast, recent increases in debt suspension cases and restructured loan/financing demonstrate additional room for the government to help.

From 2022 onward, FSSC is formulating coordinated policy support to further accelerate economic recovery, in particular, to tackle the various long-term binding constraints on the corporate sectors. FSSC has been identifying structural constraints through a series of discussions with corporate sectors, represented by various business associations, and line ministries in charge of relevant regulations. The coordinated policy measures to debottleneck structural constraints are currently being prepared.

TABLE 15.2
Restructured Loan/Financing for 2020 and 2021

	2020			*2021*		
Category	*Value (IDR trillion)*	*# Debtor (million)*	*Average loan/ debtor (IDR million)*	*Value (IDR trillion)*	*# Debtor (million)*	*Average loan/ debtor (IDR million)*
MSMEs	335.04	4.57	73.31	256.73	3.11	82.55
Non-MSMEs	494.68	1.68	294.45	406.76	0.93	437.38
Banking	829.72	6.26	132.54	663.49	4.04	164.23
Financing companies	149.60	4.96	30.16	220.38	5.23	42.14
Total banking and financing companies	979.32	11.22	87.28	883.87	9.27	95.35

Source: Ministry of Finance.

While the expense relief and corporate financing support are considered as direct support, the government also provided indirect support to businesses through the demand side. Various forms of social assistance, both cash and in-kind transfers, as well as electricity bills and wage subsidies, helped cushion domestic demand from further fall-out due to the COVID-19 pandemic. The government is expected to continue applying a prudent approach to ensure smooth recovery to pre-pandemic long-term trajectory growth beyond 2023 whilst maintaining its fiscal capacity.

15.6 CONCLUSION AND CLOSING

The economic crisis arising from the COVID-19 pandemic has resulted in many important lessons being learnt by policymakers including in Indonesia. Policymakers have learned how a health crisis can evolve into an economic crisis and can further develop into a prolonged crisis. Thanks to technology advancements, policymakers can have a better and faster understanding of issues faced by the people not only at an aggregate macro level but also on the ground. Additionally, the technology advancements have allowed Indonesian policymakers to learn from international evidence and to adapt both the policy objectives and measures taken accordingly in a rapid manner. Data, which used to be available within months, can become available within weeks or even days by applying appropriate proxies.

Similar to MSMEs, corporates appear to have been badly hurt by this crisis but not to the same extent across all sectors. This situation complicated the issues for policymakers who needed to formulate appropriate support measures that could help certain sectors without jeopardizing the other sectors. What made matters worse was that many vulnerable corporates were walking on thin ice prior to the pandemic. These corporates were operating with the constant support of external financing, making them struggle to stay afloat when financing was halted or limited. Policymakers were challenged to filter good corporates, which were to be prioritized, over less-efficient ones given limited fiscal resources.

The Ministry of Finance has learnt that the two measures commonly used: (a) expense relief, and (b) corporate financing resulted in different outcomes for corporates. Support in the form of wages-related expense relief, such as (i) wage subsidies and (ii) pension subsidies, is useful to maintain employment. On the other hand, corporate financing, such as loan restructuring, is more useful than expense relief in sustaining corporate operations and hence, avoiding the hysteresis effect. Furthermore, as presented in two case studies in this chapter, an appropriate expense relief policy can be useful for stimulating demand which has led to faster recovery in some sectors.

Periodic monitoring of corporates' financial performance demonstrates that many corporates were still struggling in late 2021 which allowed room for more government intervention to expedite economic and employment recovery. A recent analysis showed that stimulating consumption is more effective to jumpstart economic recovery than stimulating investment (Ing, Basri, and Fitrania 2022). Consumption drives investment in the Indonesian economic environment. It implies that the government may add similar support as was given to the auto and real estate sectors which stimulated the demand within those sectors. On the other hand, the government should also ensure that capacity on the producer side is maintained or at a minimum, does not deteriorate further amplifying the hysteresis effect. After all, it takes two to tango. The government may consider continuing to expand corporate financing support to achieve this objective. Expedited economic recovery will allow a smooth government support exit. A decade from now, history will record that the COVID-19 crisis was among the greatest crisis ever known to Indonesia. How Indonesia has endured and survived is history in the making, and we are yet to complete the process.

ANNEXE 15.1
Case Study of Luxury Goods VAT to Stimulate Recovery in the Automotive Sector

The automotive sector was amongst the worst hit sectors in 2020. The Association of Indonesia Automotive Industries reported auto sales in 2020 dropped by 48 per cent to 532,027 units from circa 1 million units in 2019. The drop in auto sales in 2020 was also observed globally. Worldwide car sales were down by 15 per cent from 74.9 million in 2019 to 63.8 million in 2020.[5]

The auto sector was hit by both supply and demand shocks. Supply disruption in the auto sector commenced relatively early in the first quarter of 2020 when COVID-19 struck China and delayed supplies to Indonesia. The Indonesian auto industry is highly dependent on imports as circa 34 per cent of inputs are imported. Further supply chain disruptions were caused by the closure of factories in Japan and Thailand which are two major exporting countries for spare parts. The sector ceased operations due to tight inventories arising from just-in-time delivery practices. The supply disruption continued till mid-2020 when many factories in the auto manufacturing areas in Bekasi, West Java had to close because of the large concentration of COVID-19 cases.

On the other hand, industry players predict that the demand shock will be severe and last longer. To begin with, mobility restrictions lower the demand for transportation including cars. Second, economic downturns mean lower demand for consumer durables as consumers prioritize basic needs. Demand was expected to recover to pre-pandemic levels after 2022.[6]

The auto sector is considered a strategic sector since it is among a few complex industries in Indonesia with extensive forward and backward linkages. The sector itself employs approximately half a million skilled workers and accounts for 22 per cent of high-tech exports. The inability to recover the sector will be likely to contribute to deindustrialization.

The GoI saw an opening opportunity to stimulate demand for cars considering that (a) retail sales had gradually rebounded in the second semester of 2020 and (b) the middle class possessed high savings due to constrained spending. Despite monthly sales being below the average of 80,000 units in 2019, retail sales in December 2020 sat at 68,600 units but increased by 130 per cent or 29,900 units in June 2020. An HSBC survey in the third quarter of 2020 showed that 90 per cent of respondents preferred to travel by personal vehicle to minimize the chance of COVID-19 infection. 23 per cent of the respondents planned to purchase 4-wheelers.[7]

On 25 February 2021, the Ministry of Finance issued Regulation No. 20/PMK.010/2021 regarding introduced incentives on Luxury-Goods Sales

Tax (LST) and Value Added Tax (VAT) for certain purchases of cars. This regulation stipulates that the sales tax on sedans or station wagons with a cylinder capacity of up to 1,500 cc will be eligible for government incentives. The government incentive was designed to commence in March 2020 and end in December 2021 with gradual exposure from 100 per cent in the earlier stage and 25 per cent at the end. This policy appeared to be successful in enticing consumers to spend money on motor cars. Monthly retail sales in March and April 2020 jumped to 77,500 and 79,500, respectively.

In the light of favourable performance shown by strong retail sales in March 2020, the Ministry of Finance expanded the coverage of sales tax for luxury goods to include 2,500 cc sedans by issuing Regulation of Minister of Finance No. 31/PMK.010/2021 on 1 April 2020. All in all, retail car sales in 2021 were reported to have reached 887,200 units or an increase of 66.7 per cent compared to 2020. Overall, the government forewent sales tax on luxury goods amounting to IDR4.63 trillion but gained the economic contribution of car sales increases by 49.2 per cent from 578,300 units in 2020 to 863,300 units in 2021. By comparison, average annual retail car sales during 2016–19 were 1,085,000 units.[8]

This incentive was extended in 2022 through Regulation of Minister of Finance No. 5/PMK.010/2022 dated 2 February 2022. The incentive extension was issued as the GoI is expecting car sales in 2022 to recover to the pre-pandemic level of 1 million units and therefore, reverse the scarring effect in the automotive industry. The incentive is valid until September 2022. The GoI is unlikely to extend this incentive considering that the main objective has been achieved whilst monitoring the auto sales performance regularly.

ANNEXE 15.2
Case Study of Government-Borne VAT to Stimulate Recovery in the Real Estate Sector

The real estate sector was among the worst-hit sectors similar to the automotive sector. Interestingly, the real estate sector's performance was polarized in this crisis. Medium-low housing segments recorded average revenue increases of 71.9 per cent in 2020 and a further 46.7 per cent in 2021. In contrast, medium-high housing segments suffered and recorded an average revenue drop of 31.8 per cent in 2020 before bouncing back by 25.7 per cent in 2021.[9] This performance occurred because the medium-low segments are primarily driven by real home buyers who expedited purchases when property prices were discounted. On the other hand, medium-high segments are primarily driven by home investors who purchase property for speculative capital gain. These investors ceased purchases in anticipation of further property price drops.

The real estate sector is critical to the Indonesian economy because of its supply chain multiplier effect. Real estate demand stimulates demand for construction, manufacturing, logistics, electronics and retail. These sectors support >10 million jobs[10] altogether. Real estate and construction contributed 13.6 per cent to GDP in 2020.[11] The real estate sector is primarily supplied by private players, unlike the infrastructure sector which is primarily driven by government projects.

The government provided a VAT incentive in 2021 to the real estate sector to stimulate demand in medium-high segments after considering the abovementioned issues. The VAT incentive for the real estate sector is called Government-borne VAT (GB VAT). Property sales from developers at that time were subject to 10 per cent VAT on the selling value. The Minister of Finance issued Regulation No. 21/PMK.010/2021 on 1 March 2021 stipulating that the government would absorb the VAT obligation to the level of 100 per cent and 50 per cent for both house and land sales and apartment sales below and above IDR2 billion, respectively. Whilst the incentive was initially scheduled until August 2021, this regulation was extended to December 2021 through Regulation No. 103/PMK.010/2021.

Realization of GB VAT for the real estate sector reached IDR790 billion and was applicable to 941 sales nationwide in 2021. BI reported increases in loan disbursements to the property sector in 2021 of 9.7 per cent more than in 2020.[12] 2021 saw housing and apartment loan disbursements of IDR572.4 trillion accessed by 2.67 million borrowers.

Despite favourable results in 2021, the Ministry of Finance considers that there is more room to push upscale property demand as the realization of GB VAT in 2021 was only 23.8 per cent of budgeted spending. The Ministry of Finance extended this facility in 2022 to 30 September 2022 through Regulation of Minister of Finance No. 6/PMK.010/2022 dated 2 February 2022. This extension is expected to be the last but the government will continue to monitor the performance of the real estate and construction sectors before deciding to exit completely.

Notes

1. Statistics Indonesia, *National Labour Force Survey*.
2. Longitudinal Business Survey, ran on June 2020, November 2020, March 2021, and August 2021. Respondents included 1,515 enterprises across various scales and sectors in Indonesia, excluding agriculture.
3. CEIC (accessed 20 March 2022).
4. The resilient sector refers to sectors in which they are not affected significantly by the pandemic and has performed well in term of output and export growth. The growth driver consists mainly of manufacturing sectors with higher value-added sectors and large contributions to export, affected by the pandemic, and is in the recovering phase. The slow starter, mostly those who were affected badly by the pandemic, mostly tourism-related sectors, such as transportation and accommodation.
5. https://www.statista.com/statistics/200002/international-car-sales-since-1990
6. A. Aszhari, "Penjualan Mobil Diprediksi Normal Pada 2023", *Liputan6.com*, 16 October 2020, https://www.liputan6.com/otomotif/read/4384274/penjualan-mobil-diprediksi-normal-pada-2023
7. HSBC Global Research, "Indonesian Autos: Personal Mobility to Support Auto Sales in 2021". Survey was performed on 2,000 respondents throughout Indonesia, 26 November 2020.
8. The Association of Indonesia Automotive Industries.
9. PROSPERA Quarterly Corporate Outlook; data for 2021 is taken from the trailing twelve months for the financial period ended on 30 September 2021.
10. Sakernas (2018).
11. BPS (Indonesia's Statistic).
12. Bank of Indonesia (2022), Indonesian Economic and Financial Statistics.

References

Association of Indonesia Automotive Industries. https://www.statista.com/statistics/200002/international-car-sales-since-1990

Aszhari, A. 2020. "Penjualan Mobil Diprediksi Normal Pada 2023". *Liputan6.com*, 16 October 2020. https://www.liputan6.com/otomotif/read/4384274/penjualan-mobil-diprediksi-normal-pada-2023

Banerjee, Ryan Niladri, and Boris Hofmann. 2020. *Corporate Zombies: Anatomy and Life Cycle*. Bank for International Settlements Working Paper No. 882, 2020.

Bank of Indonesia. 2022. Indonesian Economic and Financial Statistics International Settlements Working Paper No. 882.

CEIC. 2021. "Indonesia Domestic Credit: Industrial (Non-Banking & Financial Institutions)" (accessed 20 March 2022).

HSBC Global Research. 2020. "Indonesian Autos: Personal Mobility to Support Auto Sales in 2021". Survey, 26 November 2020.

Ing, L.Y., C. Basri, and N. Fitrania. 2022. *COVID-19 in Indonesia: Impacts on the Economy and Ways to Recovery*. Routledge-ERIA Studies in Development Economics.

Statistics Indonesia. 2018. "Population Aged 15 Years Old and Over Who Worked During the Past Week by Main Employment (17 Sectors) and Highest Education Graduated (Person), 2021–2022". National Labour Survey or Survei Angkatan Kerja Nasional (Sakernas) August 2018.

PART VI

Regional Dynamics

16

Regional Dynamics during the COVID-19 Pandemic in Indonesia

I Kadek D.S. Artha, Dewinta Illinia Sumartono and Yadi Hadian

16.1 INTRODUCTION

The impact of COVID-19 on the economy is more severe than the 2008 global economic crisis that was felt by many countries in the world because the global economic crisis was mainly related to the global financial crisis and mostly felt by developed countries, while the economic crisis due to the COVID-19 pandemic is a health crisis that crippled the economy and felt by all countries, and not a single country was free from the COVID-19 pandemic. The crisis caused by the pandemic is also the first experience in the modern era and it needs extraordinary policies that had never been implemented before. The rapid spread of the COVID-19 virus globally in 2020 negatively impacted the world's economy, including Indonesia. Implementation of government policies to restrict mobility and direct interaction among the population has a significant impact on the decline of economic and social activities. In 2020, the world economy contracted by 3.1 per cent, in which the economies of developed countries recorded a larger contraction of 4.5 per cent than the emerging market and developing economies which experienced a decline of 2.1 per cent (IMF 2021). Meanwhile, the Indonesian economy also contracted by 2.1 per cent lower than the rate at which the global economy declines (BPS 2021). When looking at economic growth on quarterly bases, economic growth in the first quarter of 2020 was only 3.0 per cent, lower than an average year-on-year (YoY) growth of 5.0 per cent. This was followed by consecutive contractions of –5.3 per cent in Q2 2020, –3.5 per cent in Q3 2020 and –2.2 per cent in Q4 2020. Those declines indicated that the Indonesian economy fell into recession.

The COVID-19 pandemic had a detrimental effect on Indonesia's economy, not only at the national level but also at the regional level. This was shown by slowing economic growth, increasing unemployment and poverty in almost all provinces. However, the diverse characteristics of regions in Indonesia create regional dynamics where the impact of the pandemic on the regional economy is not symmetrical. For instance, Bali, which is highly dependent on the tourism sector, was most significantly affected by the COVID-19 pandemic. On the other hand, regions that are dominant in the mining sector experienced high growth during the pandemic. Likewise, regions with higher sector diversification are less affected by the pandemic. The COVID-19 pandemic also impacted regional government budgets, the magnitude of which varies between regions. It is interesting to see the different impacts the COVID-19 pandemic has on each regional economy. In this chapter, the topic of regional dynamics will be investigated further.

In an attempt to save the economy from the pandemic, the Government of Indonesia has taken extraordinary policies through relaxation in the implementation of the State Revenue and Expenditure Budget (*Anggaran Pendapatan dan Belanja Negara,* or APBN). This was done through the issuance of PERPU No. 1 of 2020 which allows the APBN deficit to reach more than 3 per cent of GDP. The widening of the APBN deficit provides more fiscal space for the government to provide a stimulus to the economy in which spending will be focused on health, social safety nets and regional economic recovery. Refocusing spending from regional transfer funds to spending for the handling of COVID-19 as well as social protection is also part of the central government's policy in overcoming the pandemic and restoring the economy. The regional dynamics that come with the new refocusing approach implemented during the pandemic will be different in terms of the integration of central and regional programmes as well as the harmonization of fiscal and regional policies.

Given the variety of regional dynamics during the COVID-19 pandemic, this chapter will discuss more deeply the impact of the COVID-19 pandemic on the regional economy. Furthermore, this chapter will discuss the policies taken both by the central and regional governments in reducing the impact of the pandemic and restoring the regional economy. Finally, this chapter will analyse the impact of government policies on regional economic recovery as well as the policies needed for sustainable regional economic recovery in the future after the pandemic.

16.2 IMPACT OF THE COVID-19 PANDEMIC ON THE REGIONAL ECONOMY

The COVID-19 pandemic affected not only the national economy but also on regional levels. The rippling effect of mobility restrictions by the government to suppress the spread of the COVID-19 virus was apparent as economic and social activities decline significantly. As a result, the Indonesian economy contracted by 2.07 per cent in 2020. The ramification of negative economic growth was apparent through higher levels of poverty, inequality of income distribution, and unemployment. Most regions in Indonesia experience economic contractions due to the COVID-19 pandemic.

As briefly mentioned before, the impact of the COVID-19 pandemic on regional economies is not symmetrical. While almost all provinces in Indonesia experienced a contraction in 2020, three provinces reported positive growth despite the pandemic. The three provinces are Central Sulawesi, North Maluku and Papua, which grew by 4.86 per cent, 4.92 per cent and 2.23 per cent, respectively. The two main contributors to positive economic growth in the three provinces are the mining and quarrying sector as well as the manufacturing sector, particularly the downstream nickel (smelter) industry. The positive performance of the mining and quarrying sector was driven by rising commodity prices which were partly due to China's economic recovery that has pushed the demand for mining commodities.

Sectors related to tourism such as transportation, accommodation, food and beverage were highly affected during the pandemic due to mobility restrictions in place in many countries including Indonesia. Bali's economy, which is largely dependent on the tourism sector, experienced the deepest economic contraction compared to other regions, posting negative growth of 12.2 per cent in 2020. The magnitude of the COVID-19 impact in Bali was caused by the sharp decline in the number of tourist visits, both domestic and foreign. Furthermore, Bali has no other source of growth that can withstand the negative impact of the pandemic as its economy is highly concentrated on the tourism sector.

To see whether the regions with a higher share of tourism sectors were more affected by the COVID-19 pandemic, a correlation between the magnitude of the share of the tourism sector and economic growth in 2020 in each province is measured. Here the tourism sector is made up of the transportation and warehousing sector as well as the accommodation, food and beverage sector. As can be seen from Figure 16.1, there seems to be a negative correlation between the two variables. It indicates that provinces with a relatively larger share of the tourism sector are more likely to feel

FIGURE 16.1
A Correlation between Economic Growth in 2020 (percentage YoY) and Share of Tourism Sector of Each Province

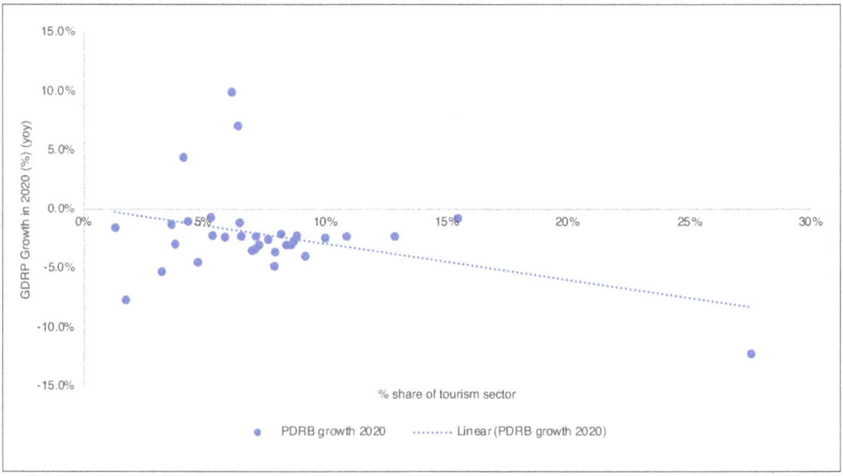

Source: Authors' calculation.

more impacted by the pandemic. As previously mentioned, Bali recorded the lowest economic growth in 2020 and it can be seen from the above figure that Bali's share of the tourism sector is the biggest among other provinces, at around 27 per cent. Interestingly, DI Yogyakarta with a tourism share sector of 15 per cent (the second highest among other provinces) fared much better compared to Bali whereby its economy contracted only at –0.7 per cent YoY in 2020. This could be due to a relatively larger share of other sectors such as the information and technology sector that DI Yogyakarta has (11.4 per cent) compared to Bali (7.2 per cent). During the pandemic, the information and technology sector was among the highest growing sector given that many activities are being carried out through online platforms, such as office and school activities. Therefore, in addition to the share of the tourism sector, it is also very interesting to look at the relationship between sector concentration or sector specialization in each region and the magnitude of the impact of the COVID-19 pandemic on regional economies.

Based on the theory presented by Ezcurra (2010), there is a positive relationship between volatility and the level of specialization of a region, in other words, regions with a diversified economy are likely to experience lower fluctuations. However, Baldwin and Brown (2004) found that although economic stability is considered a desirable characteristic, regions that are too diversified in their economy will lose their comparative advantage. Every local government certainly wants to encourage its economy to grow. As trade between regions increases, the government of each region may choose to focus their economy on a few sectors in which they have an advantage. However, a higher level of specialization will likely lead to fluctuations in the economy in times of external shocks (Baldwin and Brown 2004).

A study conducted by Athanassiou (2020) regarding the impact of the COVID-19 pandemic on regions in Greece supports this theory where it was found that areas that have a high concentration in sectors such as tourism, food and drink, and transportation are affected the most by the COVID-19 pandemic. These sectors are greatly affected by COVID-19 because these sectors are closely related to population mobility and require direct interaction. The study conducted by Ezcurra (2010) came to a similar conclusion in which it aims to see whether or not the volatility of the unemployment level is related to the level of sector specialization in the European Union countries. That is, it was found that countries with a low level of specialization experienced lower fluctuations in the unemployment rate which indicates a more stable economy.

When viewed from the perspective of sectors concentration at the district level (measured by the Herfindahl Index or HI), it can be seen that districts that have a high sector concentration (high level of HI) in the tourism sector, such as Badung Regency and Maros Regency, are significantly affected by the pandemic in 2020. Badung Regency, which has HI of 23.7 per cent, recorded the lowest economic growth at –16.5 per cent. Likewise, Maros Regency with HI of 23.7 per cent posted a very low growth of –10.9 per cent. Moreover, Cilacap Regency has HI of 36.02 per cent in the manufacturing industry sector and was also heavily affected by the pandemic, shown by its economic growth which contracted by –10.4 per cent in 2020. However, other areas with high sector concentration such as Morowali Regency (52.7 per cent), West Sumbawa Regency (58.9 per cent), and Mimika Regency (54.5 per cent) have benefited from the pandemic, whereby they experienced high growth of 28.9 per cent, 28.8 per cent, and 11.5 per cent, respectively, in 2020 (Figure 16.2). This was mainly due to their dependence on the mining sector and the processing industry related to mining.

FIGURE 16.2
Region Specialization (Herfindahl Index) and Economic Growth Performance

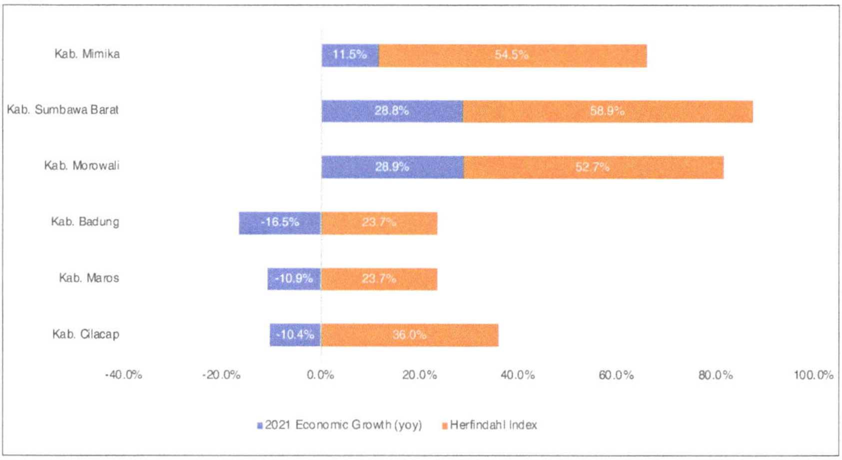

Notes: Kab. = District.
Source: Authors' calculation (2022).

The above findings are in accordance with several existing studies where areas that are concentrated in vulnerable sectors will be greatly affected if external shocks occur. On the other hand, regions whose sectors are more diversified are less affected by the pandemic because these regions have other sources of growth despite the occurrence of an external shock, such as the COVID-19 pandemic. However, looking at the observations above, it can also be concluded that the type of external shock that occurs also plays a role in the magnitude of impact felt by the regional economy. For instance, even though both West Sumbawa and Mimika Regencies have high sector concentration (indicated by high HI), they managed to post positive growth during the pandemic since the external shock does not have a direct impact on their sector specialization.

Besides giving a negative impact on economic growth, the COVID-19 pandemic also increased the unemployment rate. However, the impact was asymmetric across regions. The unemployment level in Bali was hit the hardest whereby the pandemic has paralysed the tourism industry in Bali causing many people to lose their job. The unemployment rate surged more than four times, from 1.21 per cent in February 2020 to 5.63 per cent in August 2020 (Figure 16.3). It was a significant increase for Bali since it had the lowest unemployment rate in the country before the pandemic, with an unemployment rate of less than 2 per cent, far below the national level at around 6 per cent yearly. DKI Jakarta and West Java, the epicentre of COVID-19 in 2020, held the highest unemployment rate that exceed 10 per cent. Restriction of some economic activities contributed to the increasing unemployment rate in both provinces. Meanwhile, the pandemic has had no serious impact on the unemployment rate in East Kalimantan, Banten, and North Kalimantan. The mining industry in East Kalimantan and North Kalimantan was relatively stable during the pandemic hence unemployment rate did not increase significantly.

The COVID-19 pandemic did not only negatively affect regional economic growth and unemployment, but it also impacted the poverty rate. In line with the increase in the unemployment rate, higher poverty levels were also reported in some regions during the COVID-19 pandemic. The national poverty rate increased from 9.22 per cent in September 2019 to 10.19 per cent in September 2020. The poverty rate in rural areas increased from 12.6 per cent in September 2019 to 13.2 per cent in September 2020. Meanwhile, the poverty rate in urban areas increased from 6.56 per cent in September 2019 to 7.88 per cent in September 2020 (Figure 16.4). Provinces

FIGURE 16.3
Unemployment Rate (TPT) 2020 by Province

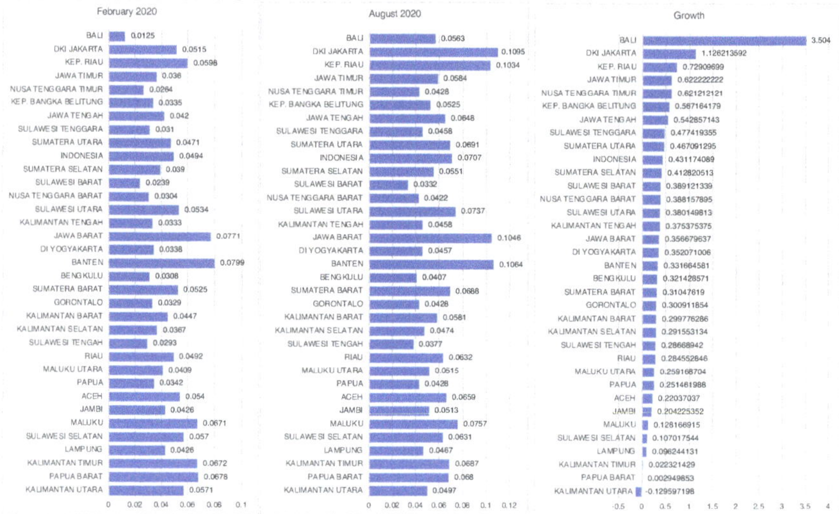

Source: Indonesia's Statistics.

FIGURE 16.4
Poverty Rate in Rural and Urban Areas, 2015–21 (in percentage)

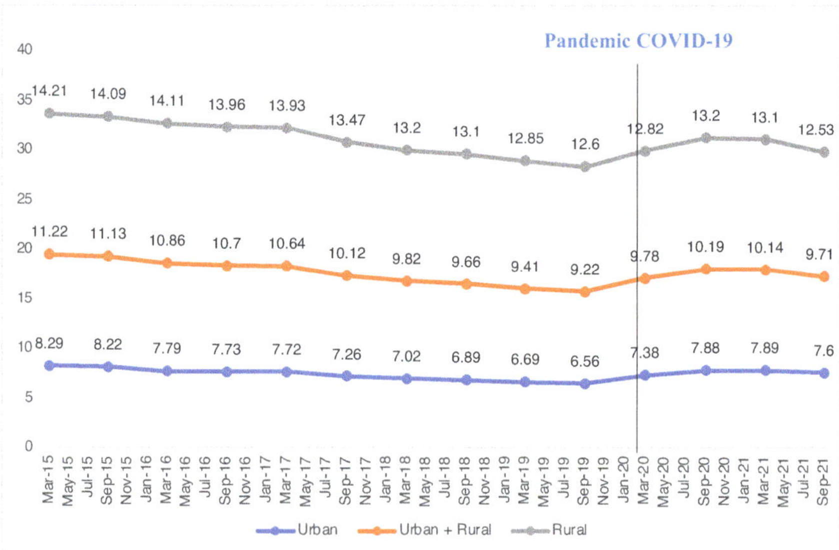

Source: Indonesia's Statistics.

that experienced a high increase in poverty rates in 2020 included Banten, West Java, DI Yogyakarta, and DKI Jakarta. Bali is included in the top ten provinces with the highest increase in poverty in 2020.

16.3 THE DYNAMIC OF REGIONAL BUDGET AND INTERGOVERNMENTAL TRANSFER (TKDD) DURING THE COVID-19 PANDEMIC

16.3.1 The Framework of Regional Dynamic during the Pandemic

The COVID-19 pandemic has caused population mobility to decline and has had a negative impact on various economic actors, be it consumers, producers, and the government, both nationally and at the regional level. The impact on economic actors is illustrated in Figure 16.5. The limited mobility of the population during the pandemic has reduced household consumption, company revenues and government revenues. Economic actors most affected by the pandemic are low-income households, micro, small and medium-sized enterprises (MSMEs), as well as economic sectors related to population mobility such as the transportation, accommodation and also food and beverage sectors.

FIGURE 16.5
Framework of Regional Dynamic during the COVID-19 Pandemic

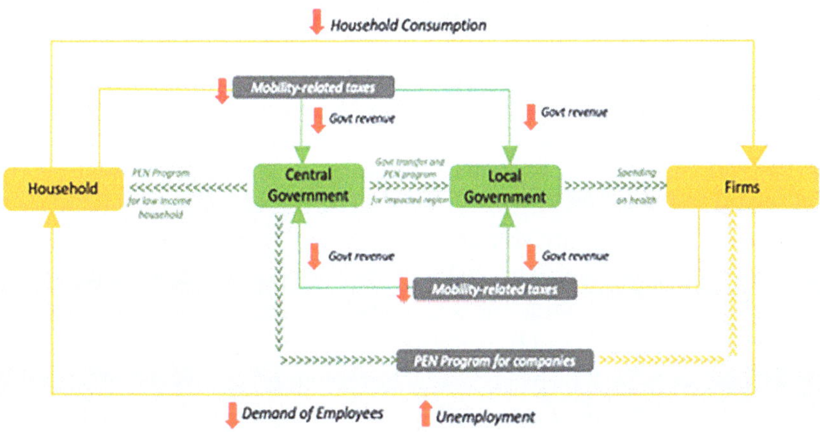

Source: Authors' illustration.

The decline in company revenues will affect the company's ability to pay employee salaries and pay taxes, among other things, which in turn may reduce the number of workers employed thus increasing the level of unemployment during the pandemic. The decline in corporate revenues also reduces the amount of taxes paid to the government, both at the central and regional levels, which ultimately affects the financial condition of the central and local governments. Local governments, especially those whose local own-source revenues (*Pendapatan Asli Daerah*, or PAD) are highly dependent on taxes that are related to mobility, such as motor vehicle taxes as well as hotel and restaurant taxes, will be greatly affected by the pandemic. Local government budgets that are dominantly dependent on the tourism sector will be affected more than other regions. The decline in central government revenue also affects the number of intergovernmental transfers (*Transfer ke Daerah dan Dana Desa*, or TKDD) provided by the central government to regions where TKDD is the dominant source of revenue for regional governments.

In conditions of weakening regional economies during the pandemic, the central government must remain a source of growth by implementing a countercyclical policy through the National Economic Recovery (PEN) programme. The PEN programme is focused on handling COVID-19 and stimulating demand through the provision of social protection for the poor, assistance to affected businesses, and assistance to regions, especially in areas that are severely affected by COVID-19. In addition, the central government also requires local governments to redirect the use of TKDD for handling COVID-19.

16.3.2 Provincial and District/City Government Revenue

As the pandemic has given a negative impact on the regional economies, it has also reduced government revenues at the central and regional government levels. As shown in Table 16.1, central government revenue declined at a higher rate compared to revenue decrease at the provincial and district/city levels. In 2020, central government revenue fell by 16.53 per cent (YoY), while the provincial government revenue decreased by 6.56 per cent (YoY) and the district/city government revenue decreased by 7.07 per cent (YoY). The central government revenue was hit harder by the pandemic since tax revenue dropped by 16.99 per cent (YoY) due to the decline in income tax and value-added tax as a result of activity restrictions

TABLE 16.1
The Central Government, Provincial and District/City Revenue, 2019–20 (IDR trillion)

year	The Central Government	Growth	Provincial Governments	Growth	District/City Governments	Growth
Total Revenue						
2019	1,957.20	1.51%	356.60	6.22%	841.81	8.58%
2020	1,628.95	-16.77%	333.22	-6.56%	782.27	-7.07%
Tax Revenue						
2019	1,546.14	1.80%	143.98	5.76%	64.96	11.89%
2020	1,285.14	-16.88%	124.90	-13.25%	54.27	-16.46%
Ratio Tax to total Revenue						
2019	79.00%	1.08%	40.37%	-0.43%	7.72%	3.04%
2020	78.89%	-0.10%	37.48%	-7.16%	6.94%	-10.11%

Source: Authors' calculation.

after the pandemic. Revenue from taxes makes up the majority of central government revenue, at almost 80 per cent. Thus, lower tax revenue caused the central government revenue to decrease at almost the same rate. It is interesting to note that the shortfall of tax revenue was lower at the provincial and district/city levels compared to the central government. Tax revenue decreased by 13.25 per cent (YoY) at the provincial government level, while at the district/city level it fell by 16.46 per cent (YoY). This indicates that the pandemic has more impact on central and district/city tax revenue compared to the provincial level. The impact caused by the fall of taxes revenues of the province and district/city government on their total revenues was much lower compared to the impact felt by the central government since the share of tax revenues of province and district/city government is only around 37.5 per cent and 7 per cent, respectively.

Both provincial and district/city government revenue is mainly made up of two sources of income, namely TKDD and PAD. It is then unsurprising that local government revenues were not only affected by tax revenues, as part of own-source revenue, but also affected by the intergovernmental transfer. In 2020, total revenues declined by 7.1 per cent (YoY) at the district/city level and 6.6 per cent (YoY) at the provincial level. Meanwhile, in 2021, district/city total revenues fell by 1.0 per cent (YoY) and total revenue at the provincial level fell by 3.1 per cent (YoY). The COVID-19 pandemic

FIGURE 16.6
Budget Revenue at Provincial and District/City Level 2019–21 (IDR trillion)

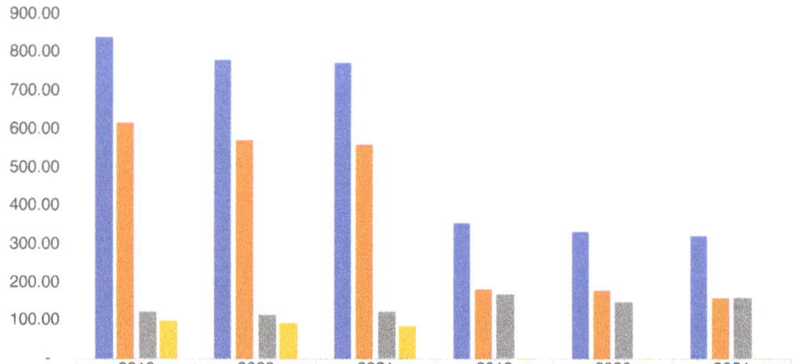

	District/City 2019	District/City 2020	District/City 2021	Province 2019	Province 2020	Province 2021
Total Revenues	841.81	782.27	774.60	356.60	333.22	322.77
Intergovernmental Transfer	615.79	572.04	562.19	183.22	180.36	159.64
Own-Source Revenue	124.63	115.35	125.02	169.03	148.72	160.25
Other Revenues	101.38	94.88	87.39	4.36	4.14	2.89

Total Revenues · Intergovernmental Transfer · Own-Source Revenue · Other Revenues

Source: Authors' calculation.

has more impact on district/city revenues in 2020, while revenues at the provincial level were more badly hit in 2021. Although intergovernmental transfers decreased at both the provincial and district/city level in 2020, the rate at which own-source income decreased was higher at the district/city level than at the provincial level which caused a deeper contraction in total revenues at the district/city level in 2020. Meanwhile, intergovernmental transfer declined at a larger rate at both district/city and provincial levels in 2021 which caused total revenue to decrease despite positive growth reported in own-source income at both the district/city and provincial levels at 7.7 per cent (YoY) and 8.4 per cent (YoY), respectively.

When comparing tax revenues at the provincial and district/city levels, those at the provincial level are more vulnerable to mobility restrictions due to the pandemic. Almost all provinces rely on vehicle-type related tax, such as motor vehicle tax, tax on the transfer of motor vehicles, and tax on motor vehicle fuel, as a major revenue source for their local tax revenue. For instance, in seven provinces that are most reliant on vehicle-type related tax (which makes up the top 10 per cent), vehicle-type related tax collections in 2020 constituted more than 85 per cent of total local taxes. Consequently, mobility restrictions which caused a decline

TABLE 16.2
Taxes Revenue at Provincial Level (IDR billion)

Provincial Taxes	2017	growth	2018	growth	2019	growth	2020	growth
Motor vehicle tax	29,336.9	6.2%	32,702.6	11.5%	30,732.3	-6.0%	22,886.9	-26%
Tax on transfer of motor vehicle	21,744.6	51.5%	19,549.5	-10.1%	21,983.7	12.5%	19,407.8	-12%
Tax on motor vehicle fuel	17,673.8	17.0%	20,701.0	17.1%	21,167.9	2.3%	18,152.7	-14%
Surface water tax	427.9	-13.2%	396.1	-7.4%	1,101.5	178.1%	697.5	-37%
Tobacco tax	15,195.6	18.7%	14,441.9	-5.0%	13,935.8	-3.5%	17,992.3	29%
	84,378.9	19.9%	87,791.0	4.0%	88,921.1	1.3%	79,137.2	-11%

Source: Authors' calculation.

in vehicle-type related taxes during the pandemic will affect the tax revenues of the provinces. As mentioned in a study by Qibthiyyah (2021), all provinces experienced a decline in vehicle-type related tax revenues in 2020 due to the low mobility of the population. Hence, provinces that rely more heavily on vehicle-type related tax revenues such as Bali and East Kalimantan have seen larger revenue declines than those that rely on other tax revenues.

While the COVID-19 pandemic detrimentally affected all provinces, there were some variations in terms of tax revenues recorded by provinces whereby some provinces recorded a slight increase in tax revenue in 2020 (Figure 16.7). On average, provincial tax revenues declined by 11 per cent (YoY) in 2020, mostly due to lower motor vehicle tax which fell by 25.5 per cent (YoY). Provinces like Papua, Bali, East Kalimantan, South Kalimantan, Bangka Belitung and DKI Jakarta recorded the largest percentage decline in tax revenue which was mostly from the decline in vehicles-type related taxes. Some provinces, such as Banten, West Java, East Java, DI Yogyakarta, Bali, Bengkulu, Lampung and Sulawesi Selatan, implemented policies which eliminate penalties of prior taxes delinquencies of motor vehicle tax to maintain tax revenue.

On the other hand, Maluku, Aceh, Central Sulawesi and East Nusa Tenggara recorded a slight increase in tax revenue which was caused by a significant increase in tobacco tax revenues. Interestingly, tobacco tax revenue grew by 29.1 per cent in 2020 which indicates that consumption of tobacco was not affected by the pandemic. Even though all provinces

FIGURE 16.7
The Growth of Provincial Government Taxes Revenue in 2020 (YoY)

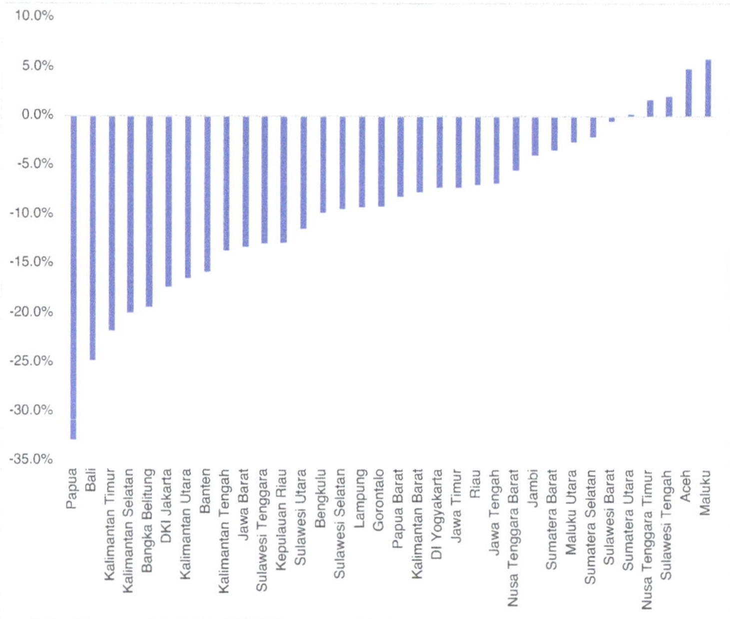

Source: Ministry of Finance.

recorded lower vehicle-type related tax revenue, the revenue recorded from tobacco tax, particularly in Maluku, Aceh, Sulawesi Tengah and East Nusa Tenggara, manage to offset the decline of vehicle-type related tax revenue. For instance, in Maluku, while vehicle-type related tax revenue fell by 7.28 per cent in 2020, tobacco tax revenue increased by 44.1 per cent. The same is also true in Central Sulawesi, whereby tobacco tax revenue increased by 60.0 per cent in 2020, the highest among other provinces, while vehicle-type related tax revenue fell 7.28 per cent. This shows that the variation of tax revenue losses across provinces during the COVID-19 pandemic was driven by a combination of factors including a variation of level in mobility restriction, the structure of the industry, and regional characteristics.

The impact of the pandemic on tax revenues also varied across districts and cities depending on the composition of tax revenues. There were larger declines in tax revenues in regions that have substantial tourism sectors. Lower tax revenues were recorded in those regions as a result of lower revenues from taxes on hotels, restaurants and entertainment, which plummeted because of low population mobility thus consumption level has fallen sharply. In contrast, some districts/cities like North Konawe, Deiyai, Taliabu Island, Musi Rawas, Konawe, Paniai, Puncak Jaya, West Sumbawa and Morotai Island have shown significant growth in tax revenues during the pandemic. Tax revenue on hotels, restaurants and entertainment in those districts/cities is considerably small and instead, they receive more revenues from taxes on land and building, transfer of land and C category mining taxes. At the district/city government level, land-type related taxes, such as the tax on land and building and tax on the transfer of land, make up most of district/city revenues followed by street lighting tax, at 57 per cent and 20 per cent of total tax revenue, respectively. Heavy reliance on land-type related tax protected district/city governments from extreme tax revenue shortfall during the COVID-19 pandemic since tax revenue from the land-type related tax is considerably more stable compared to other taxes, such as the tax on hotels, restaurants and entertainment.

16.3.3 Provincial and District/City Government Expenditure

In addition to the detrimental effect on government revenue, the COVID-19 pandemic also affected the government in terms of its fiscal capacity. The provincial and district/city governments had little fiscal space to deal with the pandemic which led to budget cuts and reallocations. As shown in Table 16.3, government expenditure at the provincial and district/city level both declined almost at the same rate at 5.7 per cent (YoY) in 2020, while the rate of decline was lower in 2021 at both levels. Despite the significant drop in tax revenue, the central government still managed to maintain its expenditure level by widening its budget deficit allowance to increase expenditure. During the pandemic, the central government played a more significant role in handling the pandemic and carrying out economic recovery efforts. In 2020, the central government budget rose 12.11 per cent (YoY) to IDR2,589.9 trillion, almost 8 times larger than provincial governments' budget and more than 3 times larger than district/city governments' budget. Furthermore, health-related expenditure by the central government increased by 51.61 per cent (YoY) while social protection expenditure increased by 13.94 per cent. This shows that the central government is at the forefront in dealing with the COVID-19 pandemic.

TABLE 16.3
Expenditure at Various Government Levels, 2019–20 (IDR trillion)

Year	The Central Government	Growth	Provincial Governments	Growth	% of Total Govt. Expd.	District/City Governments	Growth	% of Total Govt. Expd.	Total Govt. Expenditure
2019	2,310.20	4.39%	355.92	9.0%	10.2%	831.76	8.42%	23.8%	3,497.88
2020	2,589.90	12.11%	335.63	-5.7%	9.0%	784.11	-5.73%	21.1%	3,709.64
2021	2,786.80	7.60%	328.51	-2.1%	8.5%	751.21	-4.20%	19.4%	3,866.52

Source: Authors' calculation.

After decentralization, provincial and district/city governments had more authority and responsibility for public functions, including the health sector. However, during the pandemic, their ability to deliver public service and manage the health crises was lower compared to the central government as provincial and district/city governments had less capacity due to limited budgets. To put it in perspective, the government expenditure at the provincial level made up only 9 per cent of total government expenditure in 2020, down from 10.2 per cent in 2019, and its share continue to decrease in 2021 to only 8.5 per cent. Meanwhile, the share of expenditure at the district/city governments level constituted 23.8 per cent of total government expenditure in 2019. After the pandemic, the share of district/city governments expenditure decreased to 21.1 per cent in 2020 and 19.4 per cent in 2021. In total, if all the provincial and district/city government expenditures were combined, it only amounted to 21.1 per cent and 19.4 per cent of total government expenditure in 2020 and 2021, respectively. Therefore, the pandemic lowered the degree of fiscal decentralization on the expenditure side.

Due to limited fiscal space during the pandemic, the provincial and district/city governments had to reallocate and, to some extent, cut their budgets. The central government had issued a guideline on budget refocusing for provincial and district/city governments. Minister of Home Affairs Regulation No. 20 of 2020 Concerning the Acceleration of Handling of COVID-19 within the Local Government Environment was a legal basis for the provincial and district/city governments to allocate higher proportions in their expenditure to mitigate health crises caused by the pandemic. Consequently, provincial and district/city governments revised their budget to focus on health expenditure. By the function of expenditure, as shown in Table 16.4, in 2020 the district/city governments had reduced their expenditure budget on housing and public facility, economy, social protection, and education, and increased their budget on health by 5.97 per cent (YoY) and public service expenditure by 2.00 per cent (YoY). In 2021, more money was spent on the economy and health sectors though, surprisingly, social protection expenditure decreased by 57.59 per cent. Public service and health expenditure by the provincial government increased in 2020, while expenditures on the economy, housing and public facility, and social protection declined. However, the economy, social protection and health expenditure increased in 2021. Health expenditure was consistently the major priority for both the provincial and district/city governments. The district/city governments have tendencies to cut housing and public facility expenditures to make room for higher health expenditures, while provincial governments were making cuts on the economy, housing, and public facility expenditures. Changes in the level of spending on health at the provincial and district/city government level can be seen in Table 16.4.

When looking at other types of expenditure such as capital expenditure, good and service expenditure, personnel expenditure, and other expenditures, there seems to be a similar pattern. As housing and public facility expenditure decreased, capital expenditure at the provincial and district/city level also decreased. Almost all types of expenditure at the provincial and district/city level declined in 2020 and 2021. However,

TABLE 16.4
The Growth of Provincial and District/City Expenditure, 2019–21

Expenditure	District/City					Province				
	2019	2020	Growth	2021	Growth	2019	2020	Growth	2021	Growth
Total Expenditures	831.76	784.11	-5.73%	751.21	-9.69%	355.92	335.63	-5.70%	328.51	-7.70%
Public Service	266.20	271.52	2.00%	262.92	-1.23%	125.88	131.07	4.13%	121.03	-3.85%
Education	220.89	210.00	-4.93%	206.07	-6.71%	115.44	113.51	-1.67%	106.72	-7.56%
Social Protection	11.59	10.48	-9.60%	4.92	-57.59%	4.14	3.28	-20.73%	5.59	34.96%
Housing and Public Facility	113.55	79.75	-29.77%	32.11	-71.72%	34.74	24.03	-30.82%	18.83	-45.79%
Health	133.98	141.99	5.97%	146.16	9.09%	33.19	34.51	3.97%	37.29	12.34%
Economy	50.60	40.73	-19.52%	73.77	45.80%	23.27	14.99	-35.56%	29.47	26.66%

Source: Authors' calculation.

capital expenditure fell at a larger rate compared to other expenditures. Personnel expenditure was the only expenditure that did not decline during the pandemic since personnel salaries could not be reduced.

To see the overall dynamic impact of COVID-19 on regional fiscal at the district/city level, a mapping was conducted by comparing data on the realization of regional revenues and expenditures between 2020 and 2019. The mapping uses 66 sample regions, out of 514 cities and districts, consisting of the capital city (except for the capital DKI Jakarta) and one district in each province. The mapping is carried out by grouping regions into another four quadrants:

- 1st Quadrant: areas that experienced an increase in both regional income and regional expenditure (minimally affected).
- 2nd Quadrant: areas that experienced a decrease in revenue but relatively stable or increased expenditure during the pandemic.
- 3rd Quadrant: areas that experienced a decrease in both income and expenditure during the pandemic (most affected).
- 4th Quadrant: areas that experienced an increase in income but decrease in expenditures.

As can be seen from Figure 16.8, Quadrant III have the largest number of regions (29 regions), namely areas where both spending and income have decreased during the pandemic. Furthermore, Quadrant II have the second highest number of regions (20 regions), whereby these regions experienced a decrease in income, but expenditures increase during the pandemic. Meanwhile, the lowest number of regions is in Quadrant IV, where income increases while spending decreases during the pandemic. The decline in district/city revenue in the regions in Quadrants II and III was largely due to a decrease in regional taxes. Above all, the regional mapping into these four quadrants shows that the impact of the COVID-19 pandemic on local government budgets at the district/city level is very diverse.

16.3.4 Intergovernmental Transfer from the Central Government

As discussed in the previous section, the structure of local government revenue in Indonesia is dominated by revenue from the central government (intergovernmental transfer). At the district/city level, revenue from the

FIGURE 16.8
Regional Mapping of COVID-19 Pandemic Impact at District/City Level

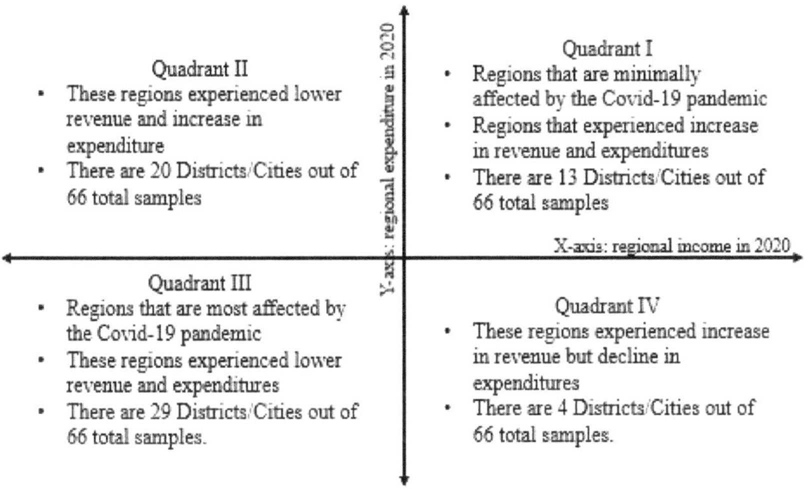

Source: PT SMI (2020).

central government contributes almost three-quarters of total revenue. The pandemic led to lower levels of central government revenue as well as provincial and district/city government revenue. However, there is no significant change in the ratio of the intergovernmental transfer to total revenue at the district/city level from 2019 to 2021 (Figure 16.9). The ratio remains high at around 73 per cent, with a slight decrease in 2021 to 72.6 per cent. It means that districts/cities have a high dependence on intergovernmental transfers from the central government. Meanwhile, at the provincial level, the ratio of intergovernmental transfer to total revenue is much lower compared to district/city at half of the total revenue. The intergovernmental transfer to provincial governments decreased from 2019 to 2021 while the share of own-source revenue increased during the same period. In 2020, the ratio slightly increased from 51.4 per cent in 2019 to 54.1 per cent in 2020 due to the pandemic that hit the province's own-source revenues.

Intergovernmental fiscal transfer in Indonesia consists of a general allocation fund (DAU) for horizontal fiscal imbalance, a specific allocation fund (DAK) for matching grants, a revenue sharing fund (DBH) for vertical

FIGURE 16.9
The Proportion of the Provincial and District/City Government Revenue 2019–21

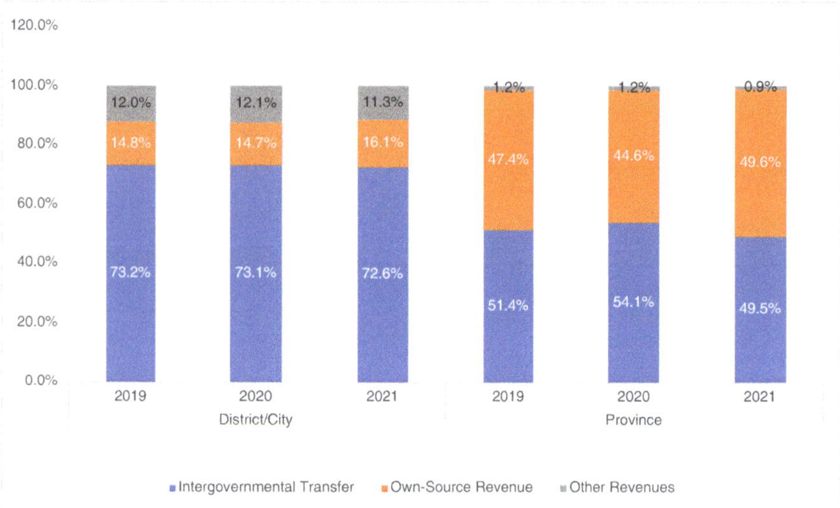

Source: Authors' calculation.

fiscal imbalance and a regional incentive fund (DID) for local government incentives. In addition, a Special Autonomy Fund is allocated for special autonomous regions such as Papua and Aceh. In 2020, most of the intergovernmental transfers had been cut due to the COVID-19 pandemic which lowered the central government revenue. As the pandemic worsens following the outbreak on March 2020, the central government issued Presidential Regulation 72 of 2020 to revise the national budget for handling the COVID-19 pandemic and economic recovery. As a result, transfer to the provincial and district/city government was cut by 11.75 per cent from IDR784.9 trillion to IDR692.7 trillion. DAU, the primary source of the provincial and district/city government revenue, was cut by 13.57 per cent from IDR544.7 trillion to IDR470.8 trillion. Other intergovernmental transfers were also cut, except for DID which increased 23.33 per cent from IDR15 trillion to IDR18.5 trillion.

By issuing the Presidential Regulation 72 of 2020, the central government has implemented a countercyclical fiscal policy as a response to the pandemic. The regulation was essential as it provides a legal basis for increasing spending due to the pandemic that was getting more severe and deteriorating economic activities. The budget deficit for 2020 was revised from 5.07 per cent of GDP in Presidential Decree 54/2020 to 6.34 per cent in Presidential Regulation 72 of 2020 because state revenues were projected to be lower than expected, by IDR60.9 trillion. As part of countercyclical fiscal policy, the central government expanded state expenditure from IDR2,540 trillion to IDR2,739 trillion to accommodate additional spending for handling the COVID-19 pandemic which amounted to IDR358,88 trillion and for economic recovery programmes. As a consequence, the budget deficit has widened to 6.34 per cent of GDP. Budget financing increased by IDR1,039.21 trillion which consists of debt financing, investment financing, lending, guarantee obligations, and other financings. Moreover, the Minister of Finance also allowed changes to be made to the details of state spending and budget financing related to the PEN programme.

Presidential Regulation 72/2020 also stimulated mandatory spending in the APBN by allocating a certain percentage of spending that must be allotted every year. The purpose of mandatory spending is to reduce the problem of regional social and economic inequality. The types of mandatory spending in the APBN are divided into five categories, as follows:

1. The education budget allocation is 20 per cent of the APBN or APBD. This budget allocation is budgeted at IDR547.8 trillion.
2. The budget allocation for DAU is at least 26 per cent of net domestic revenues or equivalent to IDR384.4 trillion.
3. The allocation of DBH for the calculation of this budget allocation in the APBN is IDR86.4 trillion.
4. The health budget allocation is 5 per cent of the APBN or equivalent to IDR212.3 trillion.
5. The budget allocation for special autonomy is 2 per cent each for the provinces of Aceh and Papua from the DAU or equivalent to IDR20 trillion.

A quick response had been taken by the central government to overcome the impact of the COVID-19 pandemic by issuing two extraordinary steps to protect the people and the economy. The first step was to issue a policy on the distribution and use of intergovernmental transfers (TKDD). Before the pandemic, the TKDD budget during 2016–19 tended to increase every year with an average growth of 4.6 per cent per year, from IDR710,26 trillion in 2016 to IDR812,9 trillion in 2019. By 2020, with the impact of the COVID-19 pandemic, the APBN underwent very significant changes, including the TKDD budget. The TKDD budget fell by 6.2 per cent to IDR762,718.9 billion. The TKDD policies in 2020 focused more on handling health and economic impacts arising from the COVID-19 pandemic. The government's quick response through the TKDD policy was realized through budget reallocation and simplification of requirements for the distribution and use of DBH, DAU, and DID which had been carried out since the beginning of the outbreak of COVID-19 in Indonesia.

The second step taken by the Indonesian government to handle the impact of the COVID-19 pandemic was conducting the National Economic Recovery (PEN) programme. The government has allocated Physical DAK Reserves of IDR8.7 trillion to support the PEN programme, which was obtained from the reallocation and refocusing of the state treasury. As the pandemic has brought a significant negative impact on regional economies, especially in tourism regions and on poor people, especially in the villages, therefore the PEN was directed for social protection and regional economic recovery. The Physical DAK Reserve is intended to fund activities that have a high carrying capacity for regional economic recovery, support food security, and support the development of national tourism strategic areas. In addition, to maintain the economic resilience of rural communities, the government provides Village Cash Assistance (BLT *Desa*) whose funds come from the Village Fund. BLT *Desa*, as a part of social protection in the rural community, was given in the amount of IDR600,000 per month per family in the second quarter and IDR300,000 per month per family in the third and fourth quarters as a result of the higher poverty rate due to the pandemic. In 2021, the BLT *Desa* continued to be given in the amount of IDR300,000 per month per family for 12 months. The criteria of beneficiary families for the BLT *Desa* are villagers who are unable or have lost their livelihoods and have not received other social assistance from the central government. Moreover, additional DID was also provided by the government to accelerate recovery in the regions. The additional DID is allocated to local governments that perform well in preventing and managing the spread of COVID-19 in their regions and create the best innovations in the preparation and implementation of a new normal order that is productive and safe from COVID-19.

As part of the PEN programme, in order to help local governments impacted by the pandemic, the central government provided a new scheme, namely Regional PEN loans to accelerate economic recovery through infrastructure development. The Regional PEN loans are managed by the Directorate General of Fiscal Balance and implemented through PT Sarana Multi Infrastruktur (Persero) (PT SMI) as a Special Mission Vehicle under the Ministry of Finance. Regional PEN loans are given to regions that are interested and meet the requirements and criteria, by submitting a letter of application to the Minister of Finance *c.q.* Director General of Fiscal Balance in accordance with the provisions of PMK Number 105/PMK.07/2020 as amended by PMK Number 179/PMK.07/2020, which if approved will be stated in the Loan Agreement between PT SMI and the regional government.

As of 31 December 2021, 92 local governments have signed loan agreements under the PEN programme (a total of 107 loan facilities) with a total of IDR37.23 trillion. In terms of regions, majority of the 92 regional governments are located in Java (45 per cent), followed by Sulawesi (24 per cent), Bali and Nusa Tenggara (14 per cent), Sumatra (11 per cent), Maluku and Papua (4 per cent), and Kalimantan (2 per cent). Moreover, the number of activities financed with regional PEN loans is 7,579 activities (as of 31 December 2021). The dominant sector being financed is the road and bridge sector with 4,366 activities, followed by the water resources sector with 961 activities and the health sector with 470 activities. In terms of value, the value of activities being financed in the road and bridge sector is IDR14.27 trillion, while the value of activities in the water resources sector and the health sector is IDR6.29 trillion and IDR3.89 trillion, respectively.

16.4 THE RECOVERY PATH OF REGIONAL ECONOMIES

By taking several policies mentioned above both at national and regional levels, Indonesia's economy has shown moderate recovery with positive growth of 3.69 per cent (YoY) in 2021 after experiencing a contraction of 2.07 per cent (YoY) in 2020. Looking at the economic growth of each province, most provinces have shown positive growth in 2021 except for Bali and West Papua with growth of –2.5 per cent and –0.5 per cent, respectively (Figure 16.11). Meanwhile, other regions such as North Maluku, Papua and Central Sulawesi are regions that have the highest economic growth in 2021 with economic growth of 16.4 per cent, 15.1 per cent, and 11.7 per cent respectively. The provinces in Java grew at an average of

FIGURE 16.10
A Correlation between Economic Growth in 2021 (percentage YoY) and Share of Tourism Sector in Each Province

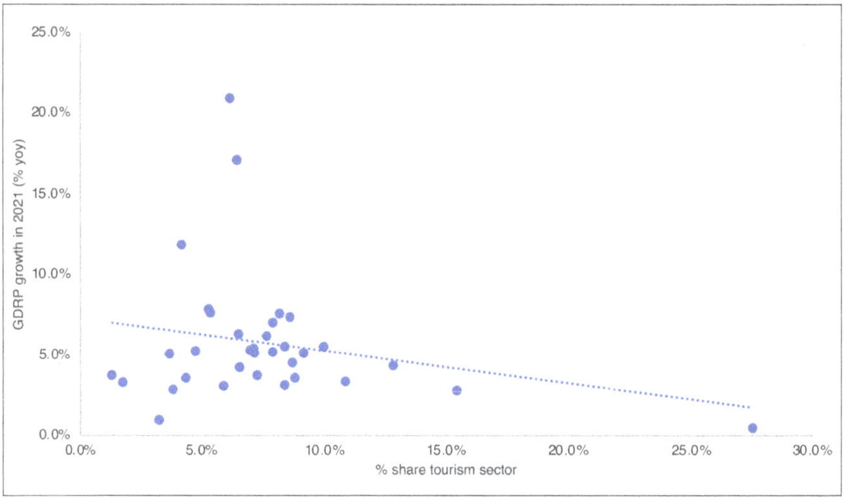

Source: Authors' calculation.

FIGURE 16.11
Provincial Recovery Rate in Indonesia (GRDP 2021 vs GRDP 2019)

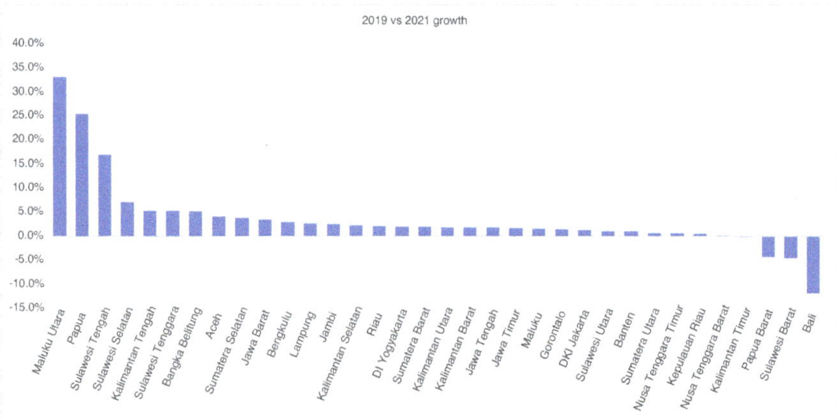

Source: Authors' calculation (2022).

4 per cent in 2021, making them the largest contributors to the national economic growth as they account for 57.9 per cent of Indonesia's economy.

Furthermore, relating the share of the tourism sector and economic growth of each region in 2021, as can be seen from Figure 16.11 that those provinces with a relatively higher share of the tourism sector posted lower economic growth in 2021. Bali with a share of 27 per cent in the tourism sector still posted the lowest economic growth in 2021 at 0.5 per cent (YoY). This may partly be due to the mobility restriction that was still implemented in mid-2021 as a result of the spike in the number of cases due to the Delta variant. On the other hand, provinces which have dominant sectors in mining and agriculture and have relatively higher people mobility were less affected by the pandemic and also recover faster than the other regions.

16.5 LESSON LEARNT FROM COVID-19 PANDEMIC AND THE FUTURE OF CENTRAL-REGIONAL GOVERNMENT RELATIONS

The recovery of national and regional economies in 2021 has shown that Indonesia has been performing very well in limiting the spread of the virus, managing community health, giving social protection as well as promoting economic recovery. The central government at the forefront of dealing with the coronavirus pandemic has more capability and capacity to cope with the pandemic compared to the provincial and district/city government since the central government has bigger capacity in terms of budget, facilities and human resources. A low realization of spending on COVID-19 in some regions during the pandemic showed that local governments face several obstacles in dealing with COVID-19 including the limitations in COVID-19 spending budgeting, difficulties in communication and coordination with related parties, and limited time for tender implementation for programmes and activities. Therefore, a lesson learnt from the COVID-19 pandemic is that the significant role of the central government at the forefront of handling the COVID-19 pandemic has been proven as an effective way to deal with the pandemic given the limited and heterogeneity of local government's capacity and characteristic. However, coordination between central and local governments and alignment of central and local government objectives should be strengthened in the future, especially to overcome the common shock like COVID-19.

FIGURE 16.12
Revenue and Expenditure Growth at District/City Level (percentage, YoY)

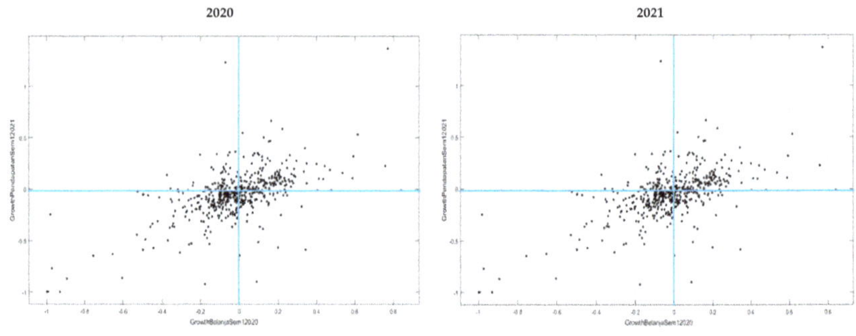

Source: Ministry of Finance, Indonesia (2021).

Based on the findings of this chapter, the regions that are concentrated in vulnerable sectors like the tourism region are greatly affected during the pandemic. On the other hand, the regions with a high concentration in agriculture and mining sectors receive benefits from the pandemic. In addition, the regions whose sectors are more diversified are less affected by the pandemic because those regions have other sources of growth. Therefore, learning from the pandemic, regions with a high concentration in a particular sector should start diversifying their economies so that there are other sources of growth to minimize fluctuation in the economy when external shocks occur. However, based on existing studies, a certain degree of sector specialization is still needed to maintain the regional comparative advantage and foster economic growth.

In addition, the fiscal condition of the provincial and district/city governments had been affected by the pandemic severely. Their government revenue, as well as expenditure, dropped significantly for the first time after regional autonomy two decades ago. It needs time to recover from the previous fiscal condition. Changes in people's behaviour, as well as changes in the growth structure of each sector during the pandemic, are important factors to be considered by the governments to ensure sustainable economic growth both at the national and regional levels and, thus, are more resilient in the event of shocks, such as the COVID-19 pandemic. The high growth of the information and technology sector and the health sector during the pandemic become another source of growth for the regional economy after the pandemic. Therefore, local governments should consider the structural change in the economy after the pandemic and need to be more creative to increase their revenues and be more efficient and effective in their spending. Increasing resilience and sustainability of local government budget after the pandemic needs better governance, more solid coordination with the other local government and ministries, more productive spending, and improvement of government officials' capability to adapt to the new normal.

Learning from regional dynamics during the COVID-19 pandemic above, the Indonesian government needs to improve the quality of the central-regional financial relation and the quality of fiscal decentralization. Therefore, the Indonesian government has enacted Law No. 1 of 2022 as a revision of Law No. 33 of 2004 regarding central and regional financial relations or fiscal decentralization law (HKPD Law). The law aims to encourage quality decentralization for the benefit of the people through improving regional performance. This is a form of accountability to all Indonesian people, that every rupiah in the national budget (APBN) and local government budget (APBD) is for the greatest prosperity of the Indonesian people. Transfers to regions as the main instrument of the HKPD Law are comprehensively prepared so as not only to focus on reducing inequality but also to encourage regional performance.

The various improvements made in the HKPD Law are motivated by the evaluation results of the implementation of fiscal decentralization which has not been optimal for the past two decades, such as:

1. The increase in the allocation of TKDD has not been used optimally. This can be seen from the use of DAU which is still dominated by personnel expenditure (30–65 per cent) and DAK which is one of the main sources of capital expenditure in the regions.
2. The regional capacity is still minimal in optimizing own-source revenue (PAD) where for the last three years, the portion of PAD to APBD is still in the range of 24.7 per cent.
3. Regional spending has not been focused and efficient due to a large number of programmes and activities, as well as the pattern of execution of the APBD which is still business as usual, mostly disbursed in the fourth quarter to encourage idle cash in the regions.
4. Limited utilization of regional financing, thus limiting the acceleration of development in the regions.
5. Synergy of APBN and APBD policies has not run optimally.

These things have had an impact on the achievement of development outputs and outcomes that are not optimal and unequal in the regions, so new policies are needed that are oriented towards regional performance and capacity through synergy and collaboration to support national development. For this reason, the HKPD Law was designed with comprehensive reform efforts, not only in terms of fiscal resource allocation but also in strengthening regional spending to be more efficient, focused and synergistic with the central government. It is important to achieve equitable distribution of public services and community welfare in the regions. Intergovernmental transfers as the main instrument of the HKPD Law are comprehensively structured in the new law so as not only to focus on reducing inequality but also to encourage regional performance.

References

Athanassiou, Ersi. 2020. "The Regional Specialisation and Geographic Concentration of Economic Activities in the Light of the COVID-19 Pandemic". *ResearchGate*. June 2020. https://www.researchgate.net/publication/343431527_The_regional_specialisation_and_geographic_concentration_of_economic_activities_in_the_light_of_the_COVID-19_pandemic (accessed 3 March 2022).

Baldwin, J.T., and W.M. Brown. 2004. "Regional Manufacturing Employment Volatility in Canada: The Effects of Specialisation and Trade". *Papers in Regional Science* 83: 519–41.

Ezcurra, R. 2010. "Unemployment Volatility and Regional Specialization in the European Union". *Regional Studies* 45, no. 8: 1121–37.

International Monetary Fund (IMF). 2021. *World Economic Outlook*. Washington, DC: International Monetary Fund.

PT Sarana Multi Infrastruktur (SMI). 2020. "Pemetaan Fiskal Daerah pada Masa Pandemi". *Monthly Economic Update*. October 2020.

———. 2021. "Pemetaan Kondisi Perekonomian dan Keuangan Pemerintah Provinsi di Indonesia pada Masa Pandemi". *Monthly Economic Update*. April 2021.

Qibthiyyah, R. 2021. "Province and Local Finances in Indonesia during COVID-19 Pandemic". LPEM-FEB UI Working Paper 059. April 2021.

Statistics Indonesia. 2021. "Indonesian Economy 2020 Decreases by 2,07 percent (c-to-c)". Press Release. February 2021.

Suparman, N. 2021. "Dampak Pandemi COVID-19 terhadap Pengelolaan Keuangan Negara". *Indonesian Treasury Review: Jurnal Perbendaharaan, Keuangan Negara Dan Kebijakan Publik* 6, no. 1: 31–42.

PART VII

New Ways of Working

17

New Ways of Working

Bureaucracy Reforms[1]

Bobby A.A. Nazief and Prasetya Dwicahya

17.1 INTRODUCTION

Indonesia announced its first COVID-19 case in the second week of March 2020 and then, to prevent COVID-19 from further spreading, the Government of Indonesia eventually enforced a social restriction called PSBB (Large-Scale Social Restriction) which later became PPKM (Community Activities Restriction Enforcement),[2] with various levels of implementation, even until today. This restriction has forced most people to work from home, regardless of their readiness.

The COVID-19 pandemic has changed the way the government works in a very significant way. Suddenly, without any preparation, government employees were forced to work in a very intensive information technology environment and to work from home. The Indonesian Ministry of Finance (MoF) is no exception to this situation. Compared to other government ministries and agencies in Indonesia, the MoF was in a relatively better position, thanks to its long track record of adopting digital transformation.

Given the urgency of the government to adopt flexible working arrangements, this chapter was written to elaborate on how bureaucracy is adapting to the new ways of working (NWOW) due to the COVID-19 pandemic with the support of digital technology and how this NWOW can then be adopted and be a norm in the future. We analyse how civil servants adapted to this NWOW by utilizing available digital tools to conduct their administration tasks and deliver services to the public. Specifically, we would like to know the answers to the following questions:

1. How well do civil servants accept the NWOW?
2. What are the requirements for having an effective NWOW?
3. What are the side effects of the adoption of the NWOW?
4. What are the civil servants' expectations for the future NWOW?
5. How does the NWOW affect civil servants' performance?

We conducted our analysis based on the results of internal surveys administered by the MoF (*Program Reformasi Birokrasi dan Transformasi Kelembagaan* 2020a, 2020b). The surveys were conducted online and participation was by respondents representing the MoF employees belonging to different organizational units. We understand that these surveys are not representative of the Government of Indonesia as a whole. However, we believe that the results provide valid findings regarding the adoption of the NWOW as they are commensurate with findings from other similar surveys done by other prominent institutions. The results show that civil servants can adapt to the NWOW without affecting their performance. However, the supporting soft and hard infrastructure needs to be improved. Furthermore, care must also be taken to cater to their mental health needs.

This chapter will start with a brief description of how the MoF had developed its digital transformation initiatives long before the COVID-19 pandemic started to spread, to consider what helped the organization adapt to the NWOW during the pandemic and beyond. This is then followed by an elaboration on the NWOW implementation by the government, starting with the challenges imposed by the pandemic and then followed by the government's response in the form of flexible working arrangements. We also describe briefly how the Ministry of Education and Culture, and Research and Technology (MoECRT) implemented their flexible working arrangement and used digital technology to ensure education services remain available to citizens to illustrate how other government ministries/ agencies adapted to the NWOW. We then analyse the effectiveness of those arrangements and how they have affected civil servants (Ministry of Finance 2020). Finally, we provide suggestions for future ways of working based on the lessons learnt.

17.2 MoF DIGITAL TRANSFORMATION

The COVID-19 pandemic highlighted the need for a digital government and increased the urgency to undertake a truly digital government transformation. Challenges that were long known became urgent including the need to improve access and service delivery, covering offline and online service delivery. Like many governments around the world, the pandemic forced Indonesia to attempt transformation overnight, moving their operations and transactions online, affecting everything from government offices and schools to national ID and civil registration services.

The pandemic also had the right momentum to accelerate the implementation of digital government transformation in Indonesia. During a cabinet meeting on 3 August 2020, the President acknowledged the importance of government digital transformation, especially to address the pandemic situation and stressed the importance of developing the infrastructure for digital transformation.[3]

The MoF as the key public financial management institution in Indonesia has a long history of Bureaucratic Reform programmes initiated since 2007 (*Program Reformasi Birokrasi dan Transformasi Kelembagaan* 2021, 2022). The ministry has consistently demonstrated its extraordinary levels of breakthrough, tackling and solving problems swiftly and deploying resources including teams and technologies at speed to address fast-moving challenges both internally and externally. The scale, speed and nature of the COVID-19 pandemic have further triggered and brought the MoF to a level of creativity and agility rarely seen in many government institutions in Indonesia.

The COVID-19 pandemic was not only a wake-up call for the world, but COVID-19 also proved to be the best CIO (Chief Information Officer) for many corporations and government agencies around the world, including the MoF. The digital transformation programme launched in 2018[4] has helped the MoF implement and accelerate its NWOW initiatives in a manner that is effective, innovative and efficient. Some of these initiatives were implemented much sooner than planned by the arrival of COVID-19.

Given the ministry's mandate, the digital transformation of the MoF was reoriented within the four major themes of transformation, namely Revenue, Budget, Treasury and Cross-Cutting (Corporate). As a foundation, the digital transformation within the ministry is trying to address the following three major important initiatives to enhance the abovementioned transformation themes, namely:

1. Ease of integration between multiple ICT systems and applications internally and externally to improve MoF service delivery effectiveness. For example, the use and deployment of e-Kemenkeu (an office automation app), and KLC2 (an e-learning app), which later turned out to be critical in supporting Flexible Working Arrangement (FWA) (see Box 17.1);
2. Increase data exchange and integration to result in increased data quality in the ministry that is accurate, complete, and timely to inform decision making; and
3. Enhanced experience of citizens, businesses, public officers, and other key stakeholders when interacting and engaging with MoF through the "One Stop Shop" Digital Services portal. For example, the ministry's services like DJP Online and CEISA help citizens and businesses fulfil their tax and customs and excise obligations (see Box 17.2). Also, SPAN and SAKTI systems that serve other ministries and agencies to manage their budgets (see Box 17.3).

Building capacity and capability to effectively respond to the COVID-19 pandemic was not an overnight journey. Long before the COVID-19 pandemic took place, the MoF had built up and accumulated massive experience from the State Financial Management Reform and Tax Office Modernization conducted in 2002–6. To maintain the momentum of the reform and respond to the national bureaucratic reform agenda, the ministry subsequently continued with its bureaucratic reform programme from 2007 until 2012 focusing on three pillars of reform, namely Organization, Business Processes and Human Resources Management, and later integrated with eight areas of change per MENPAN-RB's regulation.[5]

Having been the best national institution for the reform,[6] the ministry continued its reform journey again by embarking on MoF institutional transformation from 2013 to 2016 focusing on eighty-seven Strategic Initiatives with the four major reform themes mandated in the MoF

BOX 17.1
Office Automation and Learning Management System

e-Kemenkeu

e-Kemenkeu is an application internally developed by MoF to provide end-to-end basic functions of office automation (powered by NADINE) covering personnel/HR-related matters such as HR information, attendance (leave, absence, and permission) and overtime, and general office administration such as email, file management (*tata naskah*), meeting arrangement and scheduling. During the pandemic, new features were added such as online attendance with geotagging (mobile version) and reporting. The application also provides staff with collaboration/communication tools such as chatting, file sharing and video conference which are critical during the COVID-19 pandemic. Further, the application provides specific modules personalized to each staff such as MyTask and TeamTask to monitor and manage their own routine work/activities, projects being handled, and teamwork.

KLC2

March 2017 saw the first introduction of KLC (MoF Learning Centre) to support the needs of MoF staff to upgrade their knowledge and competencies through a modern e-learning system. KLC has adopted the following basic principles, such as flexibility and convenience for the reform, accommodating people's needs, interactivity and gamification, and digital record keeping and administration. KLC 1.0 came with the following features, such as online courses (e-learning), community practice (forum), knowledge centre (articles), gamification/badges, ability to differentiate between MoF users and non-users, standard search engine and mobile-friendly access. The second generation of KLC or KLC2.0 added the following features: "advanced search" based on a prediction feature, webinar facility using Zoom and mobile friendly, separation of access rights to participants, organizers and lecturers, and addition of business processes on training evaluation for levels 1 and 3.

Institutional Transformation Blueprint prepared in 2013.[7] From 2016 to 2018, the ministry embarked on another comprehensive reform called the Bureaucracy Reform and Institutional Transformation (RBTK) Programme with twenty Strategic Initiatives, and finally, Digital Transformation was coming its way in 2018 as part of the RBTK programme[8] with Enterprise Architecture (EA) as a primary diagnostic tool to analyse and digitalize MoF services (G2B, G2C, G2E and G2G).

BOX 17.2
Revenue Systems

DJP Online

DJP Online is designed to help MoF to scale its tax collection services to both individual and corporate taxpayers and it consists of features such as e-Filing and e-Form, enabling taxpayers to file their tax reports online, without the need to visit tax offices. At its peak, this translated to more than 10 million tax reports being submitted annually through the system. The amount of paperwork has been significantly reduced and taxpayers can save time doing their taxes. It aids both citizens and MoF officials to do their obligations without taxing their time. Since its inception in 2014, DJP Online has been applauded as one of the best innovations in digital public services. The service was awarded in 2019 as one of the top public service innovation awards organized by the Ministry of Administrative and Bureaucratic Reform and the institution itself was recognized as the Top Digital Implementation 2020 on Institution Level Stars 5 by Top Digital Award 2020.

CEISA

CEISA (Customs and Excise Information System and Automation) could be described as a one-stop service for custom and excise services that include document collection, administration, and supervision. The primary purpose of this application is to help C&E officers and customers conduct their business effectively and enable them to have proper document trails which are essential for C&E monitoring purposes. CEISA allows C&E officers to conduct inspections more effectively and without face-to-face interaction, a beneficial feature, especially during the pandemic where social distancing is the norm. As the primary facilitator of custom and excise, most revenues from export and activities are collected through this application and it contributes significantly to Indonesia's revenue collection. CEISA was initiated in 2011 as part of C&E modernization. It was developed under these principles: centralized, integrated, interconnected, and automated.

This accumulated first-hand experience for almost twenty years has built up and reshaped the capacity and capability of the individuals within the ministry and the ministry itself to respond to a rapidly changing environment, including COVID-19.

BOX 17.3
Budget and Treasury Systems

SPAN and SAKTI

In 2015, when Indonesia launched and implemented SPAN (State Budget and Treasury System), government officials experienced new ways of working with advanced information and communications technology. Before SPAN, many public financial management (PFM) processes were carried out on paper, on spreadsheets, or in fragmented computer systems, which required a great deal of manual work. SPAN is designed to improve transparency, efficiency, and accountability of the government's financial expenditure transactions through business process enhancement and integrated use of ICT. SPAN has also enhanced the quality and efficiency of the budget and would translate into faster expenditure payment, reduce errors in payments, and better accuracy and reliability of financial reports. Thus, SPAN has substantially transformed the management of public finances, as it automated many processes and centralized and integrated certain key PFM functions. SPAN is used by more than 200 MoF treasury offices around the country. Following SPAN, MoF developed SAKTI, a counterpart application intended to be used by the spending units of line ministries and agencies. SPAN and SAKTI radically improved the efficiency of the government's financial transactions by implementing an integrated PFM system to replace the myriad of different stand-alone application systems formerly used by the government.

The organization of the MoF has been exposed to a significant number and many levels of disruption, changes, and turbulence for more than two decades which has resulted in organizational innovation and agility to better respond and anticipate similar events in the future. FWA as part of the NWOW is one of the good examples of how the ministry anticipated and reacted to the COVID-19 pandemic that has significantly weakened the foundations and pillars of the economy, health, education, and social sectors, and at the same time taken many lives from families and put the remaining lives deeply into poverty that require immediate help.

17.3 IMPLEMENTATION OF NWOW

In this section we will describe the implementation of the NWOW in the MoF in some detail and then give a short description of its implementation in the MoECRT. We start by highlighting the challenges imposed by the pandemic and then follow by describing the specific arrangement of the NWOW at MoF (Ministry of Finance 2021) which consisted of Flexible Working Space (FWS) and Flexible Working Hours (FWH). In addition, we also describe how the MoF delivered its online public services during the pandemic. We will then close this section by describing the experience of the MoECRT for comparison.

17.3.1 Challenges Imposed by the Pandemic

When the pandemic hit Indonesia in March 2020, just like other government ministries and agencies, MoF was not fully ready to implement the NWOW. While public service delivery such as tax services (payment, filing return), import/export services, and budget disbursement have already been done online, support for online office administration was still limited. In addition, government bureaucracy also still required manual processes (e.g., "wet" signature) that made online working difficult.

Just like most other government employees, MoF employees were not yet accustomed to working from home (WFH). Before the pandemic, most of them used their desktop computers at the office to access e-Kemenkeu, working on official memos with NADINE (see Box 17.1) or exchanging emails with their counterparts. A few of them started to use the mobile app versions of those applications on their smartphones. Therefore, when they suddenly had to work remotely, they had many challenges to deal with even before doing the work itself.

These challenges started with getting a computer for WFH because, as explained earlier, most of them had previously worked with desktop computers at the office. Next was getting Internet access with sufficient bandwidth capacity to support various online activities associated with WFH, ranging from online document editing to video conferencing. Finally, the challenge was the computer applications to work with because MoF did not yet have a standard set of applications to facilitate WFH.

On the other hand, from the organization's perspective, the MoF had to prepare the necessary soft infrastructure ranging from standard operating procedures to regulations that would serve as a legal basis for this NWOW.

Meetings would be done virtually using a video conferencing application instead of being physically present in a meeting room. Exchanging official notes as part of the decision-making process would be conducted using electronic documents signed electronically instead of physical documents with a "wet" signature.

17.3.2 Response of the Government

> We need to take up the momentum and learn from the current COVID-19 pandemic experience to push *a radical change* within our organization. *Reduce the number of meeting rooms* and *use technology* like we do when implementing Work from Home (WFH). Think about the *required numbers of staff, types of jobs and skills* needed to run the Ministry. *Build the infrastructures* that support a *new culture* for the MoF
>
> *A directive from the Minister of Finance, 24 April 2020*

Responding to the challenges caused by the COVID-19 pandemic, the MoF with the full support and endorsement from the Minister has initiated and secured the new agility of its employees by formalizing agile working practices, particularly FWA. The MoF developed several standard operating procedures (SOPs) or operational guidelines to support the implementation of FWA on the ground and ensured the continued smooth and seamless functioning of the core operations, thanks to the rapid advancement of the digital transformation the institution embarked on in 2018.

The shift to WFH can be seen in the increased number of NADINE transactions. As mentioned in the previous section, NADINE is one of the backbones of e-Kemenkeu which provides the basic functions of office work and automation covering mainly official memos supported by e-signature. Figure 17.1 shows that the number of NADINE transactions has increased significantly during the COVID-19 pandemic, and it reached its peak in March 2021 to a level of more than seven million transactions (particularly dispositions). The continued use of NADINE cannot be underestimated since it will significantly improve efficiency, preventing the massive use of papers for circulation of letters and dispositions within the Ministry.

A similar phenomenon was also observed in the use of KLC2. WFH does not mean employees can neglect training to improve their knowledge and skills. KLC2 provided a modern platform for employees to join learning and development programmes from anywhere and at any time. It was reported that by the end of 2020 when the COVID-19 pandemic hit hard,

FIGURE 17.1
Trend in Using NADINE during the COVID-19 Pandemic

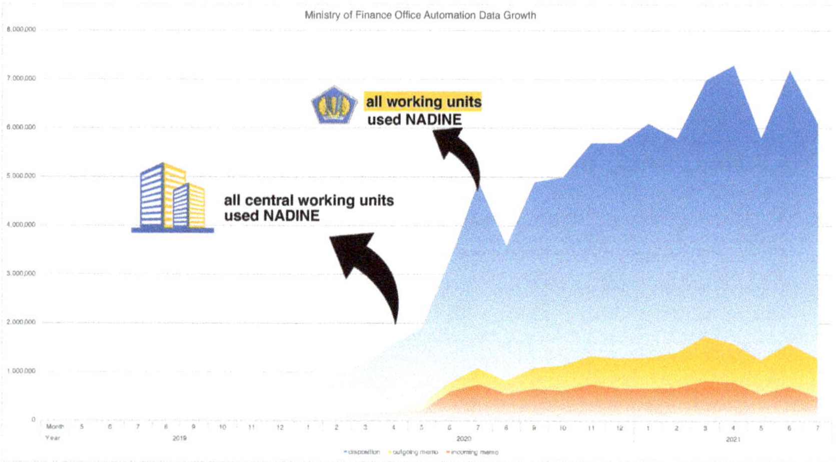

the realization of full e-learning reached 74.99 per cent (478 programmes and 352,581 participants). Throughout 2021 when the COVID-19 pandemic hit even harder, the number of participants increased and by the end of the year, the figure topped 360,190 participants compared to the lowest ever number of 176 participants that had attended classical training.

17.3.3 Flexible Working Space

FWS is considered the first response from the MoF in addressing the challenges that the COVID-19 pandemic brought about which reflects the agility and innovation of the MoF as an institution. The FWS has four major mechanisms in its implementation since its first introduction in 2020 as follows:

1. *Work From Home,* a mechanism that allows MoF staff to work from home, temporarily and at home-base. To be effective, this mechanism requires not only supporting facilities like computers/ laptops and Internet connections for the staff to perform their work but also a self-disciplined mentality to always be accountable when performing the work independently without being physically supervised.

2. *Co-Working Space*, a mechanism that allows MoF staff to work in MoF offices that provide co-working space facilities as part of the Activity Based Workplace (ABW). In this co-working space setting, staff do not have a dedicated table or workstation to perform the work rather they can freely choose the facilities that are available for their use or what activities they want to perform in that shared facility (see Figure 17.2.).
3. *Satellite Office*, a mechanism that allows MoF staff to work in an appointed MoF satellite office which is closer to where the staff live. (Figure 17.3 shows a Treasury Office located in Bogor that also functions as a Satellite Office.) These offices are deemed effective when staff are trapped in traffic jams for long hours. They can reroute their destination to the closest satellite office to work.
4. *Other locations*, a mechanism that allows MoF staff to work in a location other than those stated previously, taking ethics, security, safety, dignity, proprietary and health into account. In this mechanism, security will be the top priority that staff should be concerned about and aware of.

FIGURE 17.2
Co-Working Space in One of the MoF Offices

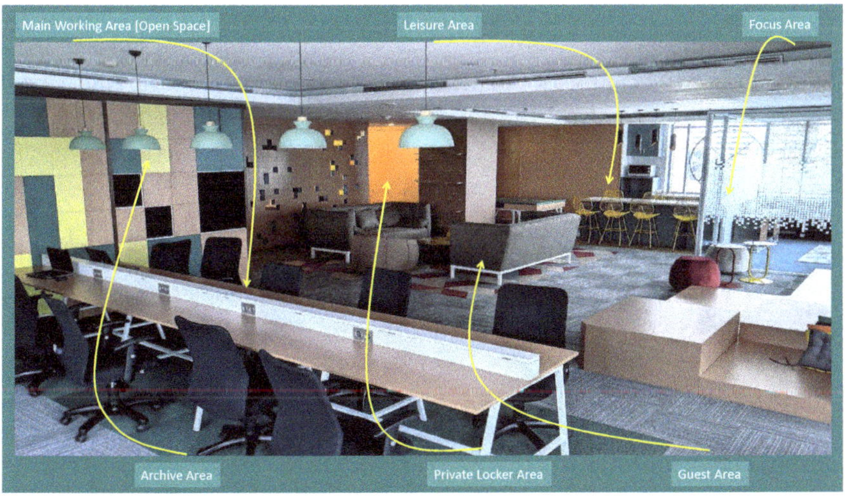

FIGURE 17.3
Satellite Office in KPPN Bogor

FWS performed by the MoF has become a benchmark for many government institutions in Indonesia since the institution has managed to combine two critical aspects of flexible work during the implementation: (1) availability and reliability of digital platforms to support individuals working independently and accountably; and (2) digital mindset and change behaviour to adopt and embrace the NWOW. e-Kemenkeu, which is the G2E Super App of the MoF, has been playing a critical role in supporting the implementation of FWS.

17.3.4 Flexible Working Hours

In addition to FWS, to support the NWOW and improve organizational agility, the MoF has also introduced FWH which also can be differentiated between the following:

1. *Flexi Time*, a mechanism that allows MoF staff to start and finish work in the office 90 minutes earlier than the usual working hours.[9]
2. *Flexibility in Work Rosters*, a mechanism that allows MoF DG Customs and Excise Staff (DJBC) to work for three consecutive weeks and to have one full week off resulting from accumulated hours of working for four weeks.
3. *Compressed Work Schedule* which is applied to all MoF staff in any echelon I unit.
4. *Working in Shifts*, a mechanism which allows MoF DG Custom and Excise Staff, DG Treasury and PUSINTEK to work in shifts.[10] This

mechanism had been in place well before the COVID-19 pandemic and before technology disrupted the way people and organizations think and work in the public sector in Indonesia.

Combining and putting FWS and FWH into action during the COVID-19 pandemic, MoF staff feel that they could do their work more effectively, independently, and accountably with minimum supervision. This has been reflected in the results from the two online surveys the MoF administered in 2020.

17.3.5 Online Public Service Delivery

The COVID-19 pandemic had a more significant impact on the adoption of online services by Indonesian citizens. Research has shown that with social restrictions, businesses move to online platforms and utilized them to remain relevant in the market.[11] At the same time, the MoF also provided online delivery services to the public using applications it had developed before the pandemic (see Boxes 17.2 and 17.33).

Providing Seamless Tax Experience to Citizens

COVID-19 has posed challenges to many aspects of financial administration, and tax administration has been hit the hardest. Related to this, DJP Online has played a critical role to enable tax officers to perform their duties during the pandemic in situations where face-to-face interaction is limited. Taxpayers can still be served without being physically present in the tax offices. The DJP Online with its features enables effective monitoring of tax collection and administration.

During the pandemic, an extra service was added to DJP Online: e-Reporting for COVID-19 Incentive. The feature helps taxpayers to claim their COVID-19 tax benefits. This feature was launched as part of a government programme to revitalize income through COVID-19 relief policy packages.

To see how the pandemic affected government tax services, people should look at the annual Customer Satisfaction Index for the three consecutive years, 2019, 2020, and 2021 where the results were 4.45, 4.10, and 4.10 respectively. Clearly, there was a decrease in 2020, the first year of the pandemic. Given that not all taxpayer services can be done online, this decrease in the Customer Satisfaction Index is understandable. It could have been much worse had MoF not developed the online service.

Managing Export and Import

Customs transactions were reduced when the COVID-19 pandemic hit the country as import and export activities were also affected by the restrictions imposed by the government. However, imports of certain goods such as COVID-19-related medication, HAZMAT suits and face masks needed to be processed expeditiously. With CEISA (see Box 17.2), customs-related documents were already processed online, without the need for importers to come to the customs office. CEISA with its capabilities to automate and produce the required documents efficiently has helped MoF officers to handle business even with the constraints resulting from the pandemic situations.

Just like in tax services, to see how the COVID-19 pandemic affected customs services people may refer to the annual Customer Satisfaction Index for the three consecutive years—2019, 2020, and 2021—where the results were 4.61, 4.62, and 4.49 respectively. Different from tax services, customs services did not experience a performance drop during the first year of the COVID-19 pandemic, but they did so for the second year. However, this may be due to a computer system incident that took place in July 2021 which caused disruption for several days. Other than that, CEISA continued to provide online customs services that minimize face-to-face interaction.

Managing the State Budget

As mentioned previously, the MoF has developed SPAN and SAKTI to manage the state budget. One of the intended functions of SAKTI is to allow the spending units of line ministries and agencies to submit their payment requests online in a timely, reliable and efficient manner. With SAKTI, officials from the spending units will no longer have to come to treasury payment offices (KPPNs) to submit their payment requests. However, prior to the pandemic, SAKTI was not yet fully operational and, as a result, spending units still had to come to MoF's KPPNs to process their budget disbursement. When the COVID-19 pandemic hit, the aforementioned SAKTI's functionality was expedited to comply with the social distancing restrictions imposed by the government. This confirms that the COVID-19 pandemic has acted as a catalyst that expedited the implementation of online disbursements.

The implementation of SAKTI is just one of a series of public financial management reforms in Indonesia. It widened the benefits of Indonesia's new financial management information system and reduced the need for in-person visits to submit payment requests. Hence, the use of SAKTI has reduced the need for physical movement and human interactions which are very relevant during the pandemic and supports the NWOW within the government of the Republic of Indonesia.

17.3.6 MoECRT

The MoF was not the only ministry that was forced to adapt to the new environment by the COVID-19 pandemic. Other ministries had similar experiences as well. Here we share the experience of the Ministry of Education, Culture, Research and Technology (MoECRT), one of the big portfolio ministries, that has undergone a massive change in delivering its services during the pandemic.

Since the beginning of the pandemic, the MoECRT has had to rethink how education services must be delivered. At the height of the pandemic when social distancing was enforced, school activities around the country had to be suspended and students were instructed to study from home. This caused a twofold major disruption: (i) the learning activities needed to be redesigned; and (ii) digital technology became the centrepiece of learning activity.

The challenge was how to minimize the resulting learning loss[12] caused by those disruptions. The phenomenon is not unique to Indonesia and can be attributed to the lack of an enabling environment to allow digital technology to facilitate learning effectively. One major reason why digital technology cannot effectively facilitate learning is due to the structural inequality of internet access in Indonesia. Some parts of Indonesia, especially in the remote regions still suffer from inadequate internet infrastructure.

The MoECRT introduced several initiatives to mitigate the inadequacy of access and accelerate the adoption of digital technologies. Those initiatives were: (i) Internet quota distribution to all students and teachers so learning can still happen in the digital space; (ii) provision of *Akun*

Pembelajaran or Learning Account that helps teachers and students to conduct classes through Google Classroom that is considered to be the largest Google Classroom platform in the world; and (iii) Platform *Merdeka Mengajar*—a super app for teachers to teach and improve their skills (Ministry of Education, Culture, Research, and Technology 2022a, 2022b).

The digital transformation did not only take place on the student- or teacher-facing side of the MoECRT, but the institution has also pushed massive digital transformation internally. The pandemic has forced the MoECRT to rethink how government programmes should be run and scaled effectively. When the pandemic started, the digitalization of correspondence and the use of video conference technology were prevalent, a similar trend that happened in most Indonesian public sector organizations. However, one thing that might be unique to the MoECRT is that the pandemic also shifted the way the MoECRT conducted training for teachers and headmasters especially when in-country travel and physical meetings were restricted.

The current flagship programme of the MoECRT, *Guru Penggerak* (Teacher Activator), is a comprehensive training programme for teachers across Indonesia to become agents of change. It is a massive programme that targeted up to 400,000 teachers by 2024.[13] Since the programme commenced during the pandemic, training could not be done using traditional means such as in-person workshops or seminars. Therefore, the MoECRT transformed the training programme to be fully online, whereby the MoECRT could still conduct the training effectively and at scale. By going online, more people were able to join the training. This could not be achieved if all training were still conducted in a physical space where the venue and costs are the largest constraints to achieving scale.

One thing that must be noted, all these digital transformation initiatives that occurred in the MoECRT cannot be separated from the policy transformations that were introduced by the ministry. Policies such as the flexible use of school operational funds, emergency curriculums, and other forms of flexibility that help teachers and students to continue learning are important aspects of the education transformation. The use of digital technology has made all these transformations faster, more cost-efficient and more scalable.

The digital transformation that occurred in the MoECRT is a glimpse of how public sector organizations and bureaucracy other than the MoF are trying to thrive and remain current amid the pandemic. The lesson from the MoECRT shows that even with the inequality of access and digital literacy skills, the introduction of digital technology at the right time and in the right way can push public sector organizations to soar to a greater height in serving citizens.

17.4 LESSONS LEARNT

During the implementation of the NWOW, the MoF conducted internal online surveys to better understand the perception of the MOF staff on WFH as part of the FWA. The surveys were conducted twice; the first one was conducted on 12–14 April 2020, with 18,254 respondents and the second one on 2–4 June 2020, with 12,174 respondents. The first survey was to identify and understand the following: (i) the overall acceptance of FWA by the employees; (ii) the availability, readiness, and performance of the supporting ICT infrastructures to support FWA implementation; (iii) the experience of MOF employees when undertaking FWA; (iv) the challenges when working under FWA mechanism; and (v) the benefits of doing FWA. While the second survey was made to better comprehend (i) the acceptance of the FWS after the previous survey; (ii) the cost implication of doing FWA; (iii) the experience of doing FWS after the first survey; and (iv) the further challenges when performing FWA.

The results of the surveys can be valuable inputs for the MOF to improve its FWA implementation going forward and can be a reliable reference for other government agencies that intend to apply the same. The results of the surveys are also commensurate with findings from other similar surveys done by other institutions which highlight the unintended impacts of the FWA that could undermine the sustainability of WFH.

The results of the surveys which focus on four important elements of the implementation of WFH in the MoF and the result of the official performance evaluation are discussed in the following subsections.

17.4.1 Acceptance

On the question of how well civil servants accept FWA, the first survey reveals that WFH can be a new norm after the pandemic. Specifically, 89 per cent of the respondents mentioned that they could do their work accountably and independently under the WFH mechanism (see

Figure 17.4). However, 11 per cent stated that their work could not be done away from the office and that physical presence was required to accomplish their tasks. Regarding the WFH frequency, 61 per cent of the respondents mentioned two days in a week as their most preferred WFH frequency. This acceptance of WFH was also complemented by its effectiveness, of which 73 per cent of the respondents mentioned that WFH was as effective as or more effective than before the pandemic.

The second survey revealed even more interesting findings with 90 per cent of the respondents mentioning that they could do the work online which confirms the findings of the first survey, and 64 per cent mentioned that they could do the work independently. Figure 17.5 shows that the level of effectiveness was increased as well, with 87 per cent of the respondents mentioning that WFH was as effective as or more effective than before (14 per cent increase from the first survey). Regarding the WFH frequency, the second survey reveals that two days in a week was no longer the more predominant preference with 27 per cent of the respondents preferring to have three days in a week and 17 per cent preferring to have it as needed, while only 31 per cent chose to stay with two days in a week.

One interesting finding is that respondents spent their time in a meaningful way, like attending e-learnings (18 per cent) and webinars (13 per cent) to improve their skills and knowledge. This fact is very

FIGURE 17.4
WFH Acceptance

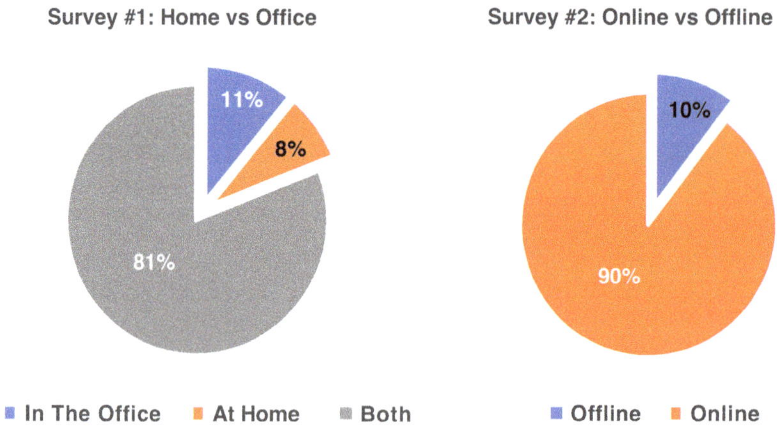

FIGURE 17.5
WFH Effectiveness

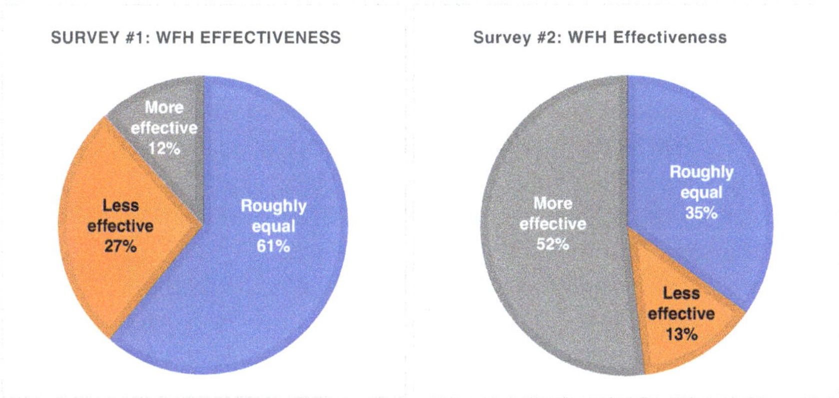

encouraging since digital technology facilitates employees to manage their time better for self-learning without being constrained by space or time.

These two surveys give a clear message that the adoption of FWA as part of the NWOW is more than promising and should become a new norm post-COVID-19 pandemic. The reason is that 90 per cent of the respondents could complete their task accountably and 87 per cent of respondents said working under WFH was proving to be very effective.

17.4.2 Required Infrastructure

The first survey reveals that the majority of the respondents (88 per cent) mentioned that they had used e-Kemenkeu since the beginning of WFH and 75 per cent felt that the quality of e-Kemenkeu was improving. However, most of the respondents still used commercial applications like WhatsApp, Line, Zoom, etc., for coordination among team members (92 per cent), video conferencing (77 per cent), exchanging emails (55 per cent), sharing files/documents (89 per cent), and arranging meetings and travels (91 per cent). This shows how MoF should put an effort into improving e-Kemenkeu to make it the first choice of applications.

Regarding the required infrastructure, most of the respondents (75 per cent) used their personal laptop/computer for work, while only 18 per cent used equipment provided by the office when performing WFH. Moreover, almost 40 per cent used tethering from their mobile phone for Internet access (see Figure 17.6).

The second survey shows that during WFH, almost 48 per cent and 31 per cent of the respondents had to bear an additional cost of IDR100,000–IDR250,000 and IDR250,000–IDR500,000 respectively for their Internet cost. Further, 45 per cent and almost 25.5 per cent had to pay extra costs of IDR100,000–IDR250,000 and IDR250,000–IDR500,000 respectively for their electricity. On the other hand, their transportation expenses were reduced. The potential reductions were IDR500,000–IDR1 million for 46 per cent and 33 per cent of the respondents, respectively.

More work needs to be done to make MOF staff fully utilize e-Kemenkeu alongside NADINE since their features have been improved. Also, the ministry needs to find the optimum solution to compensate for the additional costs that have been and will be incurred during WFH implementation. Neglecting these issues might potentially jeopardize the real benefits of WFH and make the pendulum swing back to its initial position.

17.4.3 Experience

Major challenges, such as insufficient infrastructure to support WFH (39 per cent), difficulty in concentrating (35 per cent) and communications

FIGURE 17.6
Required Infrastructure

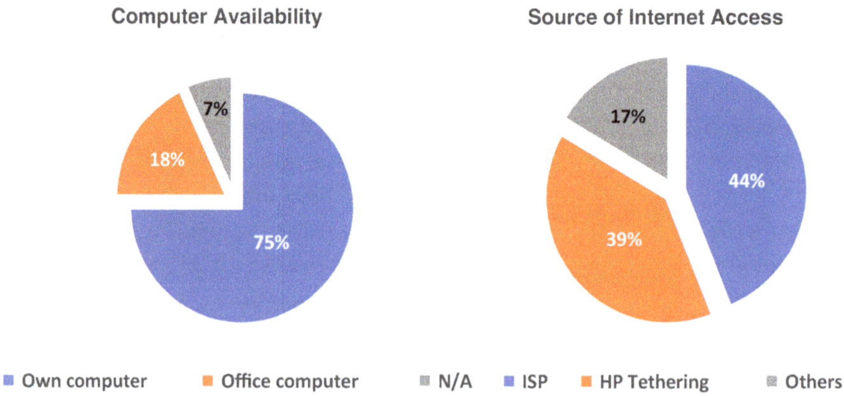

(33 per cent), and inconvenient working space (25 per cent) were mentioned in the first month of the WFH, while other challenges like collaborating with other teams (50 per cent), communicating with stakeholders (35 per cent) and supervisors (24 per cent) also need to be dealt by the respondents at the same time. One thing to note is that 25 per cent of respondents experienced longer work hours and 20 per cent felt they had an increased workload compared to that of the WFO (see Figure 17.7). Also, 54 per cent mentioned that the challenges when performing WFH were increasing.

The same survey also indicated that less commuting (79 per cent), more time with family (62 per cent), more time to do personal things (58.6 per cent) and more convenience (43 per cent) were the major factors that the respondents liked from WFH. However, WFH also prevented them from having social interaction with colleagues (88 per cent), doing sports together (38 per cent) and having lunch together (28 per cent).

Further, communication and coordination (16 per cent), business processes which cannot fully accommodate the WFH mechanism (13 per cent), self-discipline/time management (11 per cent) and inadequate infrastructure to support WFH (10 per cent) were mentioned to be the top four challenges resulting from changes in work patterns. While for the supervisors, the results were, most notably: (i) business processes that cannot

FIGURE 17.7
WFH Working Hours and Workload

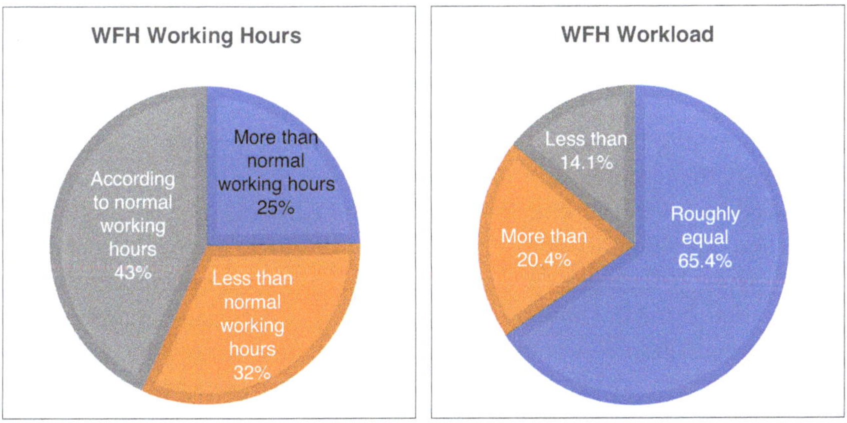

fully accommodate the WFH mechanism (62 per cent); (ii) communication and coordination with staff (46 per cent); and (iii) coordination with stakeholders and external parties (40 per cent).

WFH arrangements are proving to bring many benefits for employees ranging from less commuting and more time with family to more time to do their own thing; therefore, employees are confident that WFH should be a new norm when the pandemic is diminishing. Despite the many benefits of WFH, unfortunately, it also brings some unintended implications like lack of social interactions and a reduction in other social activities with colleagues, which can potentially lead to excessive stress or worse, a mental health problem for the staff. Some employees felt WFH made them work extra hours and have a heavier workload. Although this may be caused by their own poor work management, it may also be a sign of other serious factors that need attention. Further, both supervisors and staff also felt that communication and coordination, business processes that cannot fully accommodate WFH and lack of infrastructures were the major problems that need to be properly tackled and solved to ensure effective WFH.

17.4.4 Expectation

The respondents expected to receive cost compensation mostly for computers/laptops (23 per cent), Internet (23 per cent) and electricity (14 per cent) with the following priority for the compensation: computer/laptop (63 per cent), Internet (37 per cent) and electricity (7 per cent).

On the expected guidance, more than 87 per cent of respondents stated that the guidance for productivity and for a Business Continuity Plan (BCP) was effective or very effective. Likewise, more than 90 per cent stated that information about e-Kemenkeu was effective or very effective.

Concerning the types of flexibility that suited the respondents most, the respondents stated that FWS and FWH are the top ones (61 per cent), followed by WFO (Working from Office) and ABW (53 per cent), WFO and cubicle room (46 per cent) and FWS and WFO/cafe/library (34 per cent).

As described earlier, the institution should find the optimum solutions or a trade-off for the cost compensation issues, especially compensating for the acquisition of a computer/laptop that could be costly. Also, staff expressed their preference for a hybrid work arrangement. However, according to a TINYpulse survey report (Voyles and Niu 2021) more than 80 per cent of HR executives say that hybrid work is proving to be exhausting for employees. Therefore, companies should help ease the stress by not dictating a hybrid schedule, but rather letting employees and managers work it out together.

17.4.5 Performance Evaluation

Following the two internal surveys, a performance evaluation of staff was carried out from 6 to 17 July 2022.[14] In this evaluation, supervisors (echelons III and IV) filled in a questionnaire online to evaluate their direct subordinates' performance during WFH implementation.[15]

The results of the evaluation showed interesting findings that on average, the overall performance of the staff at the ministerial level is 87.95/100, which was considered acceptable. The most intriguing part is that compared to the staff performance before the pandemic, most high-performers retain their performance, while for 44 per cent of less performing and 43 per cent of average performing staff, their performance significantly increased when they worked under WFH. This is certainly very encouraging, even though further assessment needs to be done to analyse what has caused staff performance to increase for those groups.

Additionally, there was a trend that the performance of staff was decreasing with the length of service. For example, for those with less than five years of service, their performance was 88.08/100 (the best) and for those with more than 35 years of service, their performance was 83.39/100 (the worst). Moreover, the ability of staff with longer length of service to accomplish the work tended to be decreasing. For example, those with five years of service or less could fully accomplish the work (71 per cent) compared to those with more than 35 years of service, which was only 59 per cent. The same trend also applied to the ability of staff to use applications to support WFH in which staff with five years of service or less were much more capable (3.84/5.00) compared with those with more than 35 years of service (2.61/5.00). What we learnt here is that age seriously matters when (i) working with applications; and (ii) the ability to work under the WFH mechanism.

17.4.6 Summary

Both surveys and performance evaluations demonstrated solid evidence that FWA has worked well thanks to the effective organizational response of the MoF to the COVID-19 pandemic. The WFH mechanism has proven to sustain the effectiveness and productivity of the employees and gives many benefits to both employees and the organization. Besides these benefits, as indicated in the surveys, WFH also brings about some challenges that the ministry must mitigate and solve.

Reliability of the ICT infrastructure and supporting applications to assist the staff in accomplishing their tasks, collaboration with team members, sharing, and reviewing files/documents, and delivery of important outputs are proving to be critical during WFH. Accountability is also another important element since it is related to self-discipline, focus and commitment of individuals to deliver the expected results. Supervision is not an easy task during WFH and is important to be effectively done to ensure everyone is held accountable for what they must deliver and ensure that the outputs are delivered in good quality.

The success of the WFH implementation in the MoF is also partly supported by the demographic profile of the employees of which Gen Z (digital native) and Gen Y/Millennial (digital savvy)[16] account for around 29 per cent and 41 per cent, respectively, of the total MoF employees. Also, the readiness for change by MOF employees is high, which is indicated by a score of 3.51/4.00 in 2019, as compared to 3.27/4.00 in 2017. These two important elements have proven to have helped the institution adopt and experience WFH effectively.

FWA is proving to be the most preferred alternative for work and is deemed effective, and this will give the MoF extra motivation and drive to make WFH a new norm post the COVID-19 pandemic. However, experience from the MoF suggests that building the capacity and capability to effectively respond to the pandemic is not an overnight exercise and it takes a full commitment and strong sponsorship from the top. Further, digital talent is key in building up digital capabilities; nevertheless, acquiring, developing, and maintaining digital talent is also another challenge.

The survey reveals that effective supervision and monitoring is a prerequisite for the effective implementation of a flexible working system. Effective supervision requires good and reliable tools to supervise, interact, and monitor staff that are working under FWA. On the other hand, supervisors also require managerial competencies to not merely supervise, but also to manage and motivate staff and evaluate their performance. Effective coordination and communication with staff and team members and the quality of the deliverables are among the major concerns for supervisors.

Despite the success story, the WFH implementation also brings some challenges both for individuals and for the organization. Even though these challenges would not prevent the organization from completely moving to FWA mode, effective solutions to the challenges are required.

The surveys indicate that not all jobs can fully adopt the WFH mechanism since a few jobs require the physical presence of staff to accomplish the tasks even though the percentage is relatively small (around 11 per cent). Business processes also need to be improved to fully accommodate the staff and managers working from home effectively. For example, a "wet" signature is still required to get the administrative matters done and some processes still require documents to be physically presented.

Inadequate ICT infrastructures and supporting equipment also pose challenges to employees working under WFH since many staff must buy or use their own equipment to complete the tasks and pay the additional cost for Internet and electricity from their own pocket even though the cost incurred may be offset by a reduction in transportation cost.

Another challenge is that only several features in e-Kemenkeu or NADINE are utilized because the staff still use commercial applications to accomplish their work. The assessment also reveals that older staff are struggling to utilize the applications to get the job done. Likewise, it was also found that staff with a longer length of service tend towards not being able to accomplish the tasks on time.

17.5 WHAT NEXT?

The results of the internal surveys and performance evaluation have built a solid foundation for the MoF to move to a more advanced level of NWOW implementation:

1. *Sharing the ministry's NWOW first-hand experiences (PROSPERA 2022) to remaining government institutions so that they can learn, follow the path, and not make the same mistakes:* (i) building an organizational culture that is innovative, agile and responsive to any types of disruption; (ii) equipping staff with necessary digital skills to effectively complete the tasks; (iii) availability and reliability of ICT infrastructures and business processes to effectively support and accommodate FWA implementation; (iv) availability of a reliable monitoring system to monitor staff

and ensure that they are accountable; and (v) strong and solid sponsorship and commitment from top leaders, are key for successful NWOW implementation.

2. *In the spirit of the implementation of Presidential Regulation No. 95 Year 2018 on e-Government (SPBE), interoperability between government platforms is very important to provide standardization, efficiency and productivity.* Government agencies will not be able to fully reap the benefits if they keep developing their own applications. Even though surveys indicate that e-Kemenkeu and NADINE still need improvements, the opportunity for the system to be used by the remaining government agencies which do not have such a system is very high. Interoperability would be the first step for it but the next step, using NADINE as a standard for office automation, needs to be encouraged.
3. *Investing in people, especially digital talent, in addition to improving digital literacy within the institution, is very critical and urgent.* Acquiring and maintaining the right digital talent during the COVID-19 pandemic is even more challenging since the talent war has been intensifying. Consistently upskilling the existing digital talents through a proper combination of 70-20-10 learning principles[17] is very essential. Acquiring more digital talent with the required technical skills is also key to realizing and expediting government services which are better, easier, and faster.
4. *Ensuring that flexible work is the new norm for the post-COVID-19 pandemic and the impediments need to be resolved.* Hybrid work[18] that the MoF staff wanted to pursue based on the surveys, is proving to be exhausting for employees and is more emotionally draining since it requires frequent changes to the daily habits of employees.[19] To solve this, effective communication between supervisors and their direct staff to work this out together is required. Also, the institution needs to have a policy that can give certainty to employees to make them properly schedule their hybrid work. Other burning issues like excessive working hours and increasing workload that can seriously affect the mental health of employees should be immediately mitigated and solved without further ado (Microsoft 2021).

Notes

1. The authors wish to acknowledge Erwin Ariadharma and Hari Purnomo for their valuable input and for sharing their observations on MoF's digital transformation journey from the perspective of external observers.
2. The first social restriction was introduced in April 2020 with the name of PSBB (Large Scale Social Restriction) and after a while, PSBB was changed to PPKM (Community Activities Restrictions Enforcement) starting from February 2021 with some variations until now.
3. The directives are as follows: (i) accelerating and improving Internet access penetration and digital infrastructure as well as Internet service provision; (ii) preparing and developing a digital transformation roadmap for strategic sectors, like government, public service, social assistance, education, health, trade, industry and broadcasting; (iii) accelerating integration of national data centres; (iv) developing digital talents; and (v) developing and finalizing all required regulations and financing modalities.
4. 2018 is the year when the Enterprise Architecture (EA) governance structure was first set up and the engagement on EA as part of the MoF Bureaucratic Reform and Institutional Transformation (RBTK) programme was first started.
5. MENPAN-RB Ministerial Regulation No. 20 Year 2010 on 2010–14 Bureaucratic Reform Roadmap.
6. Based on MENPAN-RB's evaluation of the progress and achievement of the BR programme during the period of 2014–20. The score of BR for MoF was 77.31, 82.19, 82.72, 84.4, 85.68, 87.70 and 87.63 in 2014, 2015, 2016, 2017, 2018, 2019 and 2020, respectively. There was a small decrease after 2019 due to the COVID-19 pandemic situation.
7. MOF Ministerial Decree KMK No. 36/KMK.01/2014 on MOF Institutional Transformation Blueprint.
8. MOF Ministerial Decree KMK No. 88/KMK.01/2022 on the implementation of RBTK.
9. The Flexi Time mechanism is supported by MoF Ministerial Regulation (PMK) No. 221/PMK.01/2021.
10. This time-related mechanism implementation is supported by Ministerial Regulation No. 509/PMK.04/2009 (DJBC) and Ministerial Decree No. 40/KMK.01/2014.
11. The research was focused on Gojek, one of the super apps for Indonesians. It covers services from ride-hailing to online food delivery services. Source: https://www.thejakartapost.com/ms/gojek-2019/2021/10/27/gojek-drivesindonesias-economic-recovery-post-COVID-19-slump.html

12. See Chapter 11: "COVID-19 and Education in Indonesia: When School Reopening Is Not Enough to Avert Losing a Generation" for more detail.
13. Source: https://www.kemdikbud.go.id/main/blog/2021/09/animo-tinggi-program-guru-penggerak-targetkan-405-ribu-guru-hingga-2024#:~:text=Ditargetkan%2C%20jumlah%20Guru%20Penggerak%20hingga,ada%202.800%20orang%20per%20angkatan
14. There were 64,587 staff (82.12 per cent of the total MoF employees) that were evaluated of whom 32 per cent are male staff. The range of staff's age is from 20 years old or less until more than 55 years old and the range of length of service is from less than five years up to more than 35 years.
15. Echelon I and II officials, officials on leave for study, officials who are on unpaid leave and officials who are assigned to other government agencies are excluded from this evaluation.
16. In its publication, MoF used Gen Z as people who were born between 1995 and 2010 while Gen Y (Millennial) as those that were born between 1981 and 1994.
17. The 70-20-10 learning model suggests that people obtain 70 per cent of their knowledge from job-related experiences, 20 per cent from interactions with others, like co-workers and managers, and 10 per cent from formal learning events.
18. A hybrid work arrangement blends pre-pandemic patterns of office-based work with remote in a way that enables in-person collaboration and the flexibility and greater focus of working from home, or anywhere (source: https://www.cnbc.com/amp/2022/02/08/workers-say-hybrid-is-exhausting-them-heres-how-companies-fixthat.html).
19. A hybrid work, if not managed well, could create uncertainty and lack of control. For example, an employee may work in the office on one day, and then work from home on the next day. There is no consistency and rhythm to the employee's week. When a company tells its employees which days to work from the office, all the back and forth can be exhausting for them (source: https://www.cnbc.com/amp/2022/02/08/workers-say-hybrid-is-exhausting-themheres-how-companies-fix-that.html).

References

Microsoft. 2021. *Work Trend Index: 2021 Annual Report*. Microsoft.

Ministry of Education, Culture, Research, and Technology. 2022a. "Merdeka Belajar—Episode Ketujuh: Program Sekolah Penggerak". February. https://merdekabelajar.kemdikbud.go.id/upload/file/ 107_1638183646.pdf (accessed April 2022).

———. 2022b. "Merdeka Belajar—Episode Kelima Belas: Kurikulum Merdeka dan Platform Merdeka Mengajar". February. https://merdekabelajar.kemdikbud.go.id/upload/file/170_1645510611.pdf (accessed April 2022).

Ministry of Finance. 2020. *Laporan Tentang Hasil Evaluasi Kinerja Pegawai Selama Pelaksanaan Work From Home (WFH)*. Ministry of Finance.

———. 2021. *Penguatan Budaya Organisasi: The New Ways of Working*. Ministry of Finance.

Program Reformasi Birokrasi dan Transformasi Kelembagaan. 2020a. *Evaluasi FWH Selama Penerapan Kebijakan Social Distancing*. Ministry of Finance.

———. 2020b. *Survei WFH Tahap II*. Ministry of Finance.

———. 2021. *Laporan Tahunan Program Reformasi Birokrasi dan Transformasi Kelembagaan 2020*. Ministry of Finance.

———. 2022. *Laporan Tahunan Program Reformasi Birokrasi dan Transformasi Kelembagaan 2021*. Ministry of Finance.

PROSPERA. 2022. *New Ways of Working & Absorbing the Lessons of COVID-19*. PROSPERA.

Voyles, Elora, and David Niu. 2021. *State of Employee Engagement Q3 2021*. TINYpulse.

INDEX

www.ingramcontent.com/pod-product-compliance
Ingram Content Group UK Ltd.
Pitfield, Milton Keynes, MK11 3LW, UK
UKHW021933100826
474166UK00001B/53

9 789815 011609